Dog Owner's Home

VETERINARY

Handbook

Dog Owner's Home
VETERINARY
Handbook

Third Edition

James M. Giffin, M.D.
and
Liisa Carlson, D.V.M.

**HOWELL
BOOK
HOUSE**
New York

HUNGRY MINDS, INC.
New York, NY ◆ Cleveland, OH ◆ Indianapolis, IN
Chicago, IL ◆ Foster City, CA ◆ San Francisco, CA

Howell Book House
Hungry Minds, Inc.
909 Third Avenue
New York, NY 10022

Howell Book House is a registered trademark under exclusive license to Hungry Minds, Inc.

The Hungry Minds logo is a registered trademark under exclusive license to Hungry Minds, Inc.

For general information on Hungry Minds' books in the U.S., please call our Consumer Customer Care department at 800-762-2974. For reseller infor-mation, including discounts and premium sales, please call our Reseller Customer Care department at 800-434-3422.

ISBN: 0-87605-201-4
Library of Congress Catalog Number: 99-62755

Manufactured in the United States of America

10 9 8 7 6 5

FINDING IT QUICK

A special **Index of Signs and Symptoms** is on the inside of the front cover for fast referral. Consult this if your dog exhibits any unexplained behavior. It will help you locate the problem.

The detailed **Contents** outlines the organs and the systems that are the usual sites of disease. If you can locate the problem anatomically, consult here first.

The **General Index** begins on page 541 and gives you a comprehensive guide to the book's medical information. Where a page number is in boldface, it indicates more detailed coverage of the subject.

Cross-References note pertinent supplementary information. When the reference is in italics, it refers to a specific subject heading elsewhere in the book, or to a word that can be found in the Glossary or General Index. Italics may also be used for emphasis.

A **Glossary** on page 521 defines medical terms used preferentially to best explain the subject or condition. Many of these words are now being used commonly among veterinarians and their clients. Glossary words will usually be found in italics.

CONTENTS

CHAPTER 3—**INFECTIOUS DISEASES**—57

CHAPTER 4—**THE SKIN AND COAT**—89

CHAPTER 5—**THE EYES**—149

CHAPTER 8—THE MOUTH AND THROAT—209

CHAPTER 9—THE DIGESTIVE SYSTEM—233

CHAPTER 14—THE URINARY SYSTEM—369

CHAPTER 15—SEX AND REPRODUCTION—381

CHAPTER 19—**GERIATRICS**—491

CHAPTER 20—**DRUGS AND MEDICATIONS**—503

APPENDIX A—**NORMAL PHYSIOLOGICAL DATA**—515

APPENDIX B— **COMPARATIVE AGE OF DOGS TO HUMANS**—517

APPENDIX C—**ORGANIZATIONS AND ADDRESSES**—519

GLOSSARY—521

BIBLIOGRAPHY—537

THE AUTHORS—539

GENERAL INDEX—541

LIST OF CHARTS AND TABLES

TRIBUTE TO A DOG

The one absolutely unselfish friend that man can have in this selfish world, the one that never deserts him, the one that never proves ungrateful or treacherous, is his dog. A man's dog stands by him in prosperity and in poverty, in health and in sickness. He will sleep on the cold ground, where the wintry winds blow and the snow drives fiercely, if only he may be near his master's side. He will kiss the hand that has no food to offer; he will lick the wounds and sores that come in encounter with the roughness of the world. He guards the sleep of his pauper master as if he were a prince. When all other friends desert, he remains. When riches take wings and reputation falls to pieces, he is as constant in his love as the sun in its journey through the heavens.

—Senator George Vest, 1870

INTRODUCTION

Veterinary medicine has progressed so rapidly that much of what was new at the beginning of the 1990s is now out of date. The time has come to update and expand the *Dog Owner's Home Veterinary Handbook,* so that you, our readers, can have the latest and best information to care for their pets.

The greatest changes have occurred in veterinarian technology—making diagnosis more specific and treatment more accurate. New drugs are available for treating everything from fleas to old-age depression. Vaccines recommended for decades have been replaced with new and more effective products and protocols. We now know that some immunizations should be given more frequently and others less frequently than formerly recommended. New and safer dewormers have replaced many of the old standards. More is known about the diagnosis and treatment of hereditary diseases. An aging geriatric population has focused attention on how we can better meet the physical and behavioral needs of the elderly dog. Diagnostic procedures in the field of human medicine are now available to veterinarians. This has made it possible to diagnose cancer and other diseases at an earlier stage.

In this Third Edition, as in prior editions, we have attempted to describe the signs and symptoms that will help you arrive at a preliminary diagnosis, so you can weigh the severity of the problem. Some health problems are not serious and can be treated at home. Others can be potentially life threatening. Knowing when to call your veterinarian is of great importance. Delays can be costly.

At the same time, we have sought to provide guidance for the acute or emergency situations that common sense dictates you should handle on your own. Lifesaving procedures such as artificial respiration and heart massage, the emergency treatment of accidents, poisonings, choking and electrocution, and the management of obstetrical complications, seizures, heatstroke and the like are illustrated and explained, step by step.

In this edition you will find the basics of health care and disease prevention for the young and the old. A well-cared-for dog suffers fewer illnesses and infirmities in the aging process.

Breeders will find the latest medical information on genetics, selecting stock, managing the mating process, diagnosing and treating infertility, delivering puppies and saving puppies that might otherwise die. Other important subjects that have been extensively updated in the Third Edition include flea control, heartworm prevention, allergic skin diseases, bloat, canine hip dysplasia, tick-borne diseases, hypothyroidism, cardiopulmonary resuscitation, pancreatic diseases, canine cancer, behavioral disorders and the treatment of arthritis.

Medical terminology has been avoided whenever possible, but at times we have chosen to use medical words when they best explain the concept; furthermore, these terms will be used by your veterinarian in discussing your dog's diagnosis and treatment. To make it easier to understand unfamiliar words, we have added a Glossary to the Third Edition. Many of the words that are defined in the Glossary will be found in italics in the text.

This book is not intended to be a substitute for professional care. Book advice can never be as helpful or as safe as actual medical assistance. No text can replace the interview and physical examination, during which the veterinarian elicits the sort of information that leads to a speedy and accurate diagnosis. But the knowledge provided in this book will enable you to work in better understanding and more effective cooperation with your veterinarian. You'll be more alert to the symptoms of disease and be better able to describe them.

The combined efforts of many people made this book possible. We are especially indebted to Susan Stamilio (SKS Designs) for the fine anatomical drawings. Unless attributed to another artist, all drawings were done by Susan. Dr. James Clawson, Krist Carlson and James A. Giffin contributed photographs to the First Edition, many of which have been retained in the Third Edition. Diane Giffin was of tremendous help in preparing the manuscript.

Recognition would not be complete without mentioning the many researchers, clinicians and educators whose works have served as a source for our information. A bibliography of the books and articles used to reference the Third Edition can be found on page 537.

Dr. Del Carlson, the co-author of the first edition, continues to inspire us both. Dr. Carlson, now deceased, will be long remembered with affection by the many clients and friends who brought their dogs and cats to the Carlson Pet Hospital and always found professional excellence and compassion.

To Howell Book House and Dominique DeVito, who gave us the opportunity to produce this work, and to Beth Adelman and Nikki Moustaki, who did such a great job of editing, we are indeed grateful.

James M. Giffin
Liisa D. Carlson

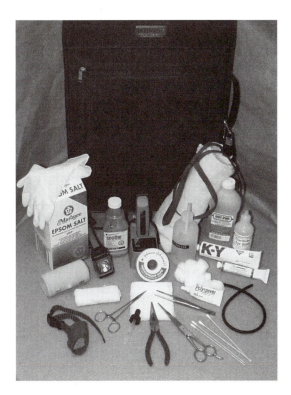

Home Emergency Medical Kit

1. Container for equipment
2. Penlight
3. Blanket
4. Nylon leash
5. Muzzle (nylon or leather)
6. Rectal thermometer
7. Surgical gloves (latex or plastic)
8. Cotton balls
9. Gauze pads (3" × 3")
10. Gauze roll (3")
11. Ace bandage (3")
12. Tourniquet (rubber tubing)
13. Adhesive tape (1" roll)
14. Eyedropper (plastic)
15. Compressed activated charcoal (5 grams, #30)
16. Cotton-tip applicators
17. Tweezers
18. Scissors
19. Grooming clippers
20. Needle-nose pliers
21. K-Y or petroleum jelly
22. Rubbing alcohol
23. Sterile saline eye wash
24. Topical antibiotic ointment
25. Stomach tube (optional)
26. List of emergency phone numbers:

    Your veterinarian's office

    After-hours emergency clinic

    National Animal Poison Control Center: (800) 548-2423 or (900) 680-0000

EMERGENCIES

Any dog, no matter how docile he may be, has the potential to bite when he is severely injured, frightened or in pain. It is important to recognize this and take proper precautions to keep from being bitten.

Handling and Restraint

An injured dog that growls, snarls or raises his hackles is sending a clear message. Do not approach or attempt to restrain this dog. Call your local animal shelter or animal care and control agency for help.

MUZZLES

All dogs should be muzzled for any handling or treatment that may be frightening or painful. Cloth muzzles take up little space and can be slipped on easily. Soft muzzles with Velcro closures in the back can be ordered through your veterinarian or a pet supply store. An open cage muzzle is preferred for an injured or sick dog. It allows the dog to breathe easily, and if the dog vomits he will not aspirate the vomitus. Keep the muzzle with your *Home Emergency Medical Kit*.

If you don't have a commercial muzzle, you can make an acceptable substitute using adhesive tape, a piece of cloth or a leash. Wind the tape around the dog's muzzle. Or tie a scarf or leash around the dog's muzzle, then bring the two ends under the dog's ears and tie the ends behind his head.

There are circumstances in which a dog should not be muzzled. It can be dangerous to muzzle a dog that is vomiting, coughing, having difficulty breathing or aggressively resisting the muzzle. Never muzzle an unconscious dog.

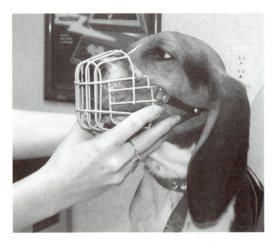

A cage muzzle should be used if the dog is vomiting or breathing rapidly.

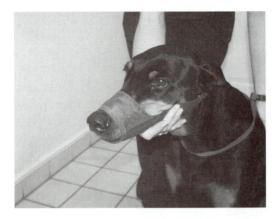

A cloth muzzle is convenient and can be slipped on easily.

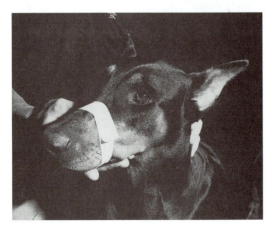

A strip of adhesive tape makes an expedient temporary muzzle.

RESTRAINING FOR EXAMINATION AND TREATMENT

For the cooperative dog, routine procedures such as grooming, bathing and even medicating seldom require restraint. Gentle handling and a soothing voice will coax most dogs to accept such handling. Approach the task with quiet confidence. Dogs are quick to sense anxiety in their masters and copy it.

For examinations and treatments that may excite or hurt the dog, it is important to restrain the dog *before* attempting the treatment. Once a dog is restrained, he usually settles down and accepts the procedure with little complaint.

The headlock is a excellent restraint for a large dog. First muzzle the dog. Then hold the dog securely against your chest with one arm around his neck and the other around his waist. This is the most commonly used restraint for a quick procedure such as giving an injection. To restrain a small dog, support the abdomen with one arm and grasp the outside front leg. Immobilize the head with the other arm. Hold the dog close to your body.

The headlock is an excellent restraint for a large dog. For treatment, the dog should be muzzled.

Restraining and carrying a small dog.

An *Elizabethan collar*, named for the high neck ruff popular during the reign of Queen Elizabeth I of England, is also an excellent way of restraining dogs that are prone to bite. The collar is also used to keep a dog from scratching at his ears and biting at wounds and skin sores. These collars can be purchased from some veterinarians and pet supply stores. The size of the collar must be tailored to the dog. For the dog to be able to eat and drink, the outer edge of the collar should not extend more than one to two inches beyond the dog's nose. Most dogs adjust well to an Elizabethan collar. If the dog refuses to eat or drink with the collar on, temporarily remove it.

A newer option is the *bite-not collar*. This high-necked collar prevents a dog from turning his head to bite. As with an Elizabethan collar, good fit is important. The collar must be just as long as the dog's neck.

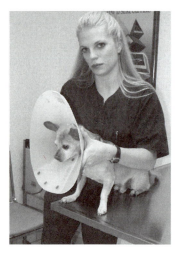

An Elizabethan collar is an excellent restraint for dogs that are prone to snap.

A bite-not collar is a humane restraint frequently used by veterinarians.

Another way to restrain the dog is to lay him on his side by grasping the inside front and back legs and then sliding the dog down your knees to the floor. Hold his legs out straight and keep pressure with your forearms on his chest and pelvis to prevent him from getting up.

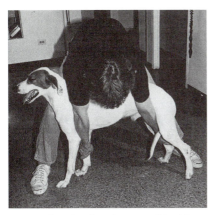 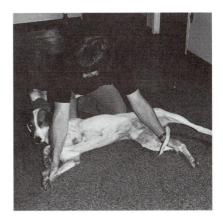

How to lay the dog down on his side.

CARRYING A DOG

Incorrectly picking up or carrying a dog can make injuries much worse. Never pick up a dog by his front legs, as this can result in a dislocated elbow or shoulder.

Carry a small dog cuddled in your arms with the injured side away from your body. For a large dog, place one arm around his chest or between his front legs. Place the other arm around his rump—or between his back legs if you suspect a hind-limb injury. Hold the dog close to your chest so you can't drop him if he squirms.

Carry an injured dog with one arm around his chest and the other around his back legs.

TRANSPORTING AN INJURED DOG

A dog in shock should be transported lying down on a flat surface or in a hammock stretcher to facilitate breathing and to prevent a sudden drop in blood pressure.

Suspect a broken back or spinal cord injury in all dogs that are unconscious or unable to stand after a fall from a height or being struck by a car. These dogs require special handling. See *Treating Head Injuries* and *Spinal Cord Injuries* in Chapter 12 for more on what to do in these cases.

Acute Painful Abdomen

The acute painful abdomen is an emergency that may lead to death of the dog unless treatment is started at once. The signs of an acute abdomen are the *sudden onset* of pain, along with whining and crying, retching and vomiting, extreme restlessness and inability to find a comfortable position, grunting and labored breathing. The abdomen is extremely painful when pressed. Characteristically, the dog may assume a prayer position with his chest to the floor and his rump in the air. As the condition worsens, the dog's pulse becomes weak and thready, the mucous membranes become pale, and the dog goes into shock.

If you see any of these symptoms, call your veterinarian at once! Early surgical intervention is life-saving.

One of the following conditions may be the cause of acute abdomen:

- Bloat
- Urinary stones obstructing the bladder
- Trauma to the abdomen with internal injury
- Rupture of the bladder
- Poisoning
- Rupture of the pregnant uterus
- Peritonitis
- Acute pancreatitis
- Intestinal obstruction

Artificial Respiration and Heart Massage

Artificial respiration, or *rescue breathing*, is the emergency procedure used to assist air exchange in an unconscious dog. *Heart massage* (chest compression) is used when no heartbeat can be felt or heard. When chest compression is combined with artificial respiration, it is called *cardiopulmonary resuscitation* (CPR). Because cessation of breathing is soon followed by heart stoppage and vice versa, CPR is required in most life-threatening situations.

While CPR can be performed by one person, it is easier and more often successful when done by two. One person does the rescue breathing while the other does the chest compression.

The following emergencies may require artificial respiration or CPR:

- Shock
- Poisoning
- Prolonged seizure
- Coma
- Head injury
- Electric shock
- Obstructed airway (choking)
- Sudden cessation of heart activity and breathing

STEPS IN CPR

First, determine which basic life-support technique will be required in an unconscious dog:

Is the dog breathing? Observe the rise and fall of the chest. Feel for air against your cheek.

If **YES**, pull out the tongue and clear the airway. Observe.

If **NO**, feel for a pulse.

Does the dog have a pulse? Feel for the femoral artery located in the midthigh.

If **YES**, start *rescue breathing*.

If **NO**, start CPR.

RESCUE BREATHING (MOUTH-TO-NOSE RESPIRATIONS)

Lay the dog on a flat surface with his right side down. Open his mouth and pull his tongue forward as far as you can. Clear any secretions with a cloth or handkerchief. Check for a foreign body. If present, remove it if possible. If impossible to dislodge, perform the Heimlich Maneuver, described on page 288.

For puppies and small dogs under 30 pounds:

1. Pull the tongue forward so it is even with the canine teeth. Close the mouth.
2. Place your mouth over the dog's nose. Blow gently into the dog's nostrils. The chest will expand.

3. Release your mouth to let the air return. Excess air will escape through the dog's lips, preventing over-inflation of the lungs and over-distension of the stomach.

4. If the chest does not rise and fall, blow more forcefully or seal the lips.

5. Continue at a rate of 20 to 30 breaths per minute (one breath every two to three seconds).

6. Continue until the dog breathes on his own, or as long as the heart beats.

For medium and large dogs:

1. Proceed as for small dogs, but seal the lips by placing a hand around the muzzle to prevent the escape of air.

2. If the chest does not rise and fall, blow more forcefully.

3. The breathing rate is 20 breaths per minute (one every three seconds).

4. Continue until the dog breathes on his own, or as long as the heart beats.

CPR (ARTIFICIAL BREATHING AND HEART MASSAGE)

To begin CPR, open the mouth and pull the tongue foreword as far as you can. Check for a foreign body.

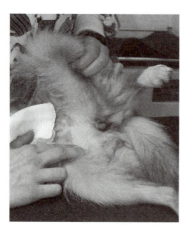

Feel for the femoral pulse in the mid-thigh to determine if the dog has a heartbeat.

Rescue breathing for dogs with a heartbeat. Blow gently into the nose every two to three seconds.

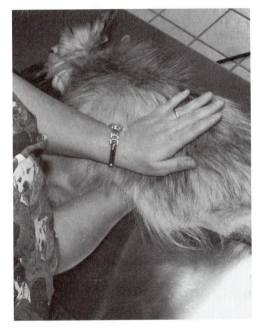

Chest compression on a *small* dog. Note the placement of hands on either side of the chest. Compression rate is 100 per minute.

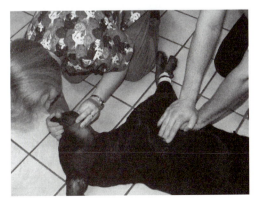

Two-person CPR on a *large* dog. Note the placement of hands for chest compression. Compression rate is 80 per minute.

For puppies and small dogs under 30 pounds:

1. Place the dog on a flat surface, right side down.
2. Place your cupped hands on either side of the rib cage *over the heart*, immediately behind the point of the elbow. (For puppies, use the thumb on one side of the chest and the rest of the fingers on the other.)
3. Compress the chest 1" to 1 1/2" (1/4 to 1/3 the width of the chest). Squeeze for a count of 1, then release for a count of 1. Continue at a rate of 100 compressions per minute.
4. With one-person CPR, administer a breath after every 5 compressions. With two-person CPR, administer a breath after every 2 to 3 compressions.

For medium and large dogs:

1. Place the dog on a flat surface, right side down. Position yourself behind the dog's back.
2. Place the heel of one hand *over the widest portion of the rib cage*, not over the heart. Place the heel of the second hand on top of the first.
3. Keep both elbows straight and push down firmly on the rib cage. Compress the chest 1/4 to 1/3 of its width. Compress for a count of 1, then release for a count of 1. Continue at a rate of 80 compressions per minute.
4. With one-person CPR, administer a breath after every 5 compressions. With two-person CPR, administer a breath after every 2 to 3 compressions.

Continue CPR until the dog breathes on his own and has a steady pulse. If vital signs do not return after 10 minutes of CPR, the likelihood of success is remote. Consider stopping CPR.

Note that CPR is associated with potential complications, including broken ribs and pneumothorax. Also, *never* practice rescue breathing or heart massage on a healthy dog; you can seriously injure the dog.

Burns

Burns are caused by heat, chemicals, electric shocks and radiation. A dog may be scalded by hot liquids. Sunburn is an example of a radiation burn. It occurs on the noses of dogs with insufficient pigment, and on the skin of white-coated dogs clipped short in summer.

The extent of skin damage depends upon the length of exposure. With a *first degree* burn the skin is red, slightly swollen and painful. Healing usually occurs in about five days. A *second degree* burn is deeper and is associated with blistering.

These burns are extremely painful. If there is no infection, healing is usually complete in 21 days. A *third degree* burn involves the full thickness of skin and extends into the subcutaneous fat. These burns appear charred, dry and leathery. The hair comes out easily when pulled. Deep burns, because they destroy nerve endings, usually are not as painful as second degree burns.

If more than 50 percent of the dog's body surface is involved with second degree burns, or if more than 30 percent is involved with third degree burns, survival is unlikely.

Treatment: All but minor burns require professional attention. Protect the area from further injury by wrapping it with a loose-fitting damp gauze dressing and proceed at once to the veterinary clinic. Extensive burns require intensive care to treat shock, fluid and electrolyte losses, and to prevent secondary infection.

Small superficial burns that involve less than 5 percent of the body surface can be treated at home. Apply cool compresses (*not ice packs*) for 20 minutes to relieve pain and lessen the depth of injury. Clip the coat over the burn and wash the skin gently with a surgical antiseptic such as dilute chlorhexidine solution (see *Wounds*). Apply a topical antibiotic ointment such as *triple antibiotic*, and bandage. The bandage should be removed daily and the wound medicated and redressed.

When acid, alkali, gasoline, kerosene or other chemicals have caused the burn, or even come in contact with the skin, immediately flush the area with large amounts of water for 10 minutes. Wear rubber or plastic gloves and bathe the dog with mild soap and water. Blot dry. If there are any signs of burning (such as redness or blistering), call your veterinarian for further instructions.

Cold Exposure

HYPOTHERMIA (LOW BODY TEMPERATURE)

Prolonged exposure to cold results in a drop in body temperature. Because a wet coat loses its insulating properties, hypothermia is a potential complication in all dogs submerged in cold water. Toy breeds, breeds with short coats, puppies and very old dogs are most susceptible to hypothermia. Hypothermia also occurs along with shock, after a long anesthetic and in newborn puppies that get chilled because of inadequately heated whelping quarters. Prolonged cold exposure burns up stored energy and results in a low blood sugar.

Signs of hypothermia are violent shivering followed by listlessness, a rectal temperature below 95°F, weak pulse, lethargy and coma. Note that hypothermic dogs can withstand prolonged periods of cardiac arrest, owing to the effects of low body temperature and lowered metabolic rate. CPR may be successful in such individuals.

Treatment: Wrap the dog in a blanket or coat and carry him into a warm building. If the dog is wet (having fallen into icy water), dry him vigorously with towels. Wrap the dog in a warm blanket and take his rectal temperature. If the temperature is *above* 95°, continue the warm blankets and encourage the dog to take a sugar solution such as honey, or four teaspoons of sugar dissolved in a pint of water.

If the dog's rectal temperature is below 95°, notify your veterinarian. While awaiting instructions, begin rapid warming by applying warm water bottles *wrapped in towels* to the dog's armpits and chest, then wrap the dog in a blanket. The temperature of the packs should be about that of a baby bottle (warm to the wrist). Take the rectal temperature every 10 minutes. Change the warming packs until the rectal temperature reaches 100°F. Do not apply heat directly to the dog, as this may cause burns. For the same reason, avoid the use of hair dryers.

How to warm a chilled puppy is discussed in Chapter 17, *Reviving a Weak Puppy.*

FROSTBITE

Frostbite occurs when a part of the body freezes. It often accompanies hypothermia. Frostbite tends to involve the tail, ear tips, pads of the feet and scrotum. These parts are the most exposed and least protected by fur. Frostbite of the ears is discussed in Chapter 6, page 188.

Frostbitten skin is pale white or blue. As circulation returns, it becomes red and swollen and may begin to peel. Eventually it looks black with a line of demarcation between live and dead tissue. Dead skin separates in one to three weeks.

Treatment: Apply warm (not hot) water soaks to the frostbitten part for 20 minutes, or until the tissue becomes flushed. Never use snow or ice; tissue damage is made much more severe if thawing is followed by refreezing. Do not rub or massage the affected parts. Handle them carefully. Take your dog to a veterinarian for further evaluation and treatment.

Note that as sensation returns, frostbitten parts can be painful. Prevent the dog from biting at the skin and inflicting further injury using the restraint techniques described at the beginning of this chapter (*Handling and Restraint*).

Dehydration

Dehydration occurs when a dog loses body fluids faster than he can replace them. Dehydration usually involves the loss of both water and *electrolytes*. In dogs, the most common causes of dehydration are severe vomiting and diarrhea. Dehydration can also be caused by inadequate fluid intake, often associated with fever and severe illness. A rapid loss of fluids also occurs with heat stroke.

A prominent sign of dehydration is loss of skin elasticity. When the skin along the back is pulled up, it should spring back into place. In a dehydrated animal, the skin stays up in a ridge.

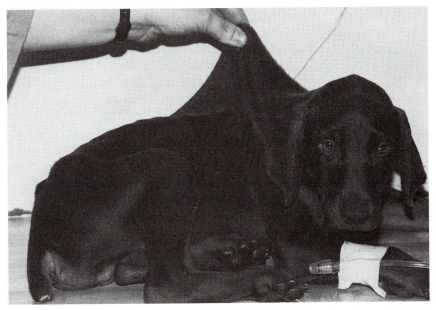

Loss of skin elasticity in severe dehydration. Note the dog is getting intravenous fluids, which are of extreme importance.

Another sign of dehydration is dryness of the mouth. The gums, which should be wet and glistening, become dry and tacky. The saliva is thick and tenacious. In advanced dehydration the eyes are sunken and the dog exhibits signs of shock, including collapse.

Treatment: A dog that is visibly dehydrated should receive immediate veterinary attention, including intravenous fluids, to replace fluids and prevent further loss.

For mild dehydration, if the dog is not vomiting you can give an electrolyte solution by bottle or syringe into the cheek pouch (see Chapter 20, *How to Give Medications*). Balanced electrolyte solutions for treating dehydration in children, such as Ringer's lactate with 5 percent dextrose in water and Pedialyte solution, are available at drugstores and are also suitable for dogs. Administer the solution at a rate of 2 to 4 mL per pound of body weight per hour, depending on the severity of the dehydration (or as directed by your veterinarian).

Treatment of dehydration in infant puppies is discussed in Chapter 17, *Dehydration*.

Drowning and Suffocation

Any condition that prevents oxygen from getting to the tissues causes suffocation. The most common emergencies in this category are drowning, smothering in an airtight space, being overcome by toxic fumes (smoke, gasoline, propane, refriger-ants, solvents), choking from a foreign body in the throat, being poisoned by car-bon monoxide and suffering a penetrating wound of the chest.

Signs of oxygen deprivation (called *hypoxia*) are extreme anxiety, straining to breathe and gasping for air (often with the head and neck extended), followed by loss of consciousness as the dog succumbs. The tongue and mucous membranes turn blue, a condition called *cyanosis*.

One exception to the blue color of hypoxia is *carbon monoxide poisoning*. Car-bon monoxide turns the blood and mucous membranes bright red. Carbon monox-ide poisoning is seen in dogs trapped in burning buildings, transported in the trunk of a car or left in an unventilated enclosure such as a garage with an operating gasoline engine.

Although dogs are good swimmers, drowning can occur if a dog swims too far out and becomes fatigued, falls through ice, is caught in a flood, or is unable to climb out of a swimming pool.

The sudden onset of gasping and struggling to breathe in a healthy dog suggests a foreign object lodged in the throat. See *Choking* in Chapter 10, page 287.

Treatment: The immediate need is to reestablish breathing with fresh air. If breathing is shallow or absent, begin artificial respiration (see *Rescue Breathing*, page 7). As soon as possible, transport your pet to the nearest veterinary facility for ventilation support.

Carbon monoxide poisoning is frequently associated with smoke injury and burns of the mouth and throat. Carbon monoxide binds with hemoglobin and blocks the delivery of oxygen to the tissues. Even though the dog is breathing deeply, oxygen transport will be compromised for several hours. Breathing a high concentration of oxygen helps to overcome these effects. A veterinarian will be able to provide this therapy.

If the dog has an open wound in the chest (*pneumothorax*) with air sucking in and out, pinch the skin together over the wound to seal the chest. Maintain the seal and transport the dog to the nearest veterinary facility.

The first step in treating drowning is to remove water from the dog's lungs. Hold the unconscious dog upside down by his middle, or in the case of a small dog by his rear legs, and allow as much water as possible to run out his nose and mouth. Then quickly position the dog on his right side with his head lower than his chest (accom-plish this by placing a blanket or coat beneath his hindquarters) and begin mouth-to-nose breathing. Check for a pulse. If absent, begin CPR (see page 7). Continue to resuscitate the dog until he breathes on his own or until no pulse is felt for 10 minutes. Dogs that drown in cold water are often hypothermic and can sometimes be resuscitated even though they have been under water for a considerable time.

Following resuscitation, the dog should be seen and treated by a veterinarian. Inhalation pneumonia is a frequent complication.

Electric Shock

Electric shock (*electrocution*) can occur when dogs bite electric cords or come into contact with downed wires. A lightening strike is a rare cause of electrocution, but a dog does not have to be struck to be seriously injured or killed. A tall tree with deep roots and spreading branches can act as a conduit for a bolt of lightening, conducting electricity through the ground to any animal in the immediate vicinity. Most lightening strikes are fatal. The singed hair and skin give evidence of the cause of death.

Dogs that receive electric shocks may be burned. The electric shock may cause an irregular heartbeat with circulatory collapse, followed by cardiac arrest. Electric current also damages the capillaries of the lungs and leads to the accumulation of fluid in the air sacs, a condition called *pulmonary edema*.

A characteristic sign of electric-shock injury is finding the unconscious dog on the floor near an electrical outlet. Electric shocks cause involuntary muscle contractions of the dog's jaw that may prevent him from releasing his hold on a live wire. Dogs that survive electric shocks may cough, have difficulty breathing, drool, have an offensive mouth odor and burns in the mouth.

Treatment: If your dog is found in contact with an electric cord or appliance, DO NOT TOUCH THE DOG. First shut off the main power and pull the plug. If the dog is unconscious and not breathing, administer CPR (see page 7). Dogs that recover from electric shocks should be seen and examined by a veterinarian at once.

The treatment of mouth burns is discussed in Chapter 8, page 212.

Prevention: Electric cord injuries can be prevented by placing cords in inaccessible locations, covering cords with plastic sleeves, unplugging cords when not in use and providing appropriate chewing toys for puppies.

Heat Stroke

Heat stroke is an emergency that requires immediate treatment. Because dogs do not sweat, they do not tolerate high environmental temperatures as well as humans do. Dogs depend upon panting to exchange warm air for cool air. When air temperature is close to body temperature, cooling by panting is not an efficient process.

Common situations that can set the stage for heat stroke in dogs include:

- Being left in a car in hot weather
- Exercising strenuously in hot, humid weather
- Being of a *brachycephalic* breed, especially a Bulldog, Pug or Pekingese

- Suffering from a heart or lung disease that interferes with efficient breathing
- Being muzzled while put under a hair dryer
- Suffering from a high fever or seizures
- Being confined to concrete or asphalt surfaces
- Being confined without shade in hot weather
- Having a history of heat stroke

Heat stroke begins with heavy panting and difficulty breathing. The tongue and mucous membranes appear bright red. The saliva is thick and tenacious, and the dog often vomits. The rectal temperature rises to 104° to 110°F. The dog becomes progressively unsteady and passes bloody diarrhea. With shock, the lips and mucous membranes turn gray. Collapse, seizures, coma and death ensue rapidly.

Treatment: Emergency measures to cool the dog must begin at once. Move the dog out of the source of heat, preferably into an air-conditioned building. Take the rectal temperature every 10 minutes. Mild cases respond by moving the dog into a cool environment.

If the rectal temperature is above 104°F, begin rapid cooling by spraying the dog with a garden hose or immersing him in a tub of cold water for up to two minutes. Alternatively, place the wet dog in front of an electric fan. Monitor his rectal temperature and continue the cooling process until the rectal temperature falls below 103°F. At this point, stop the cooling process and dry the dog. Further cooling may produce hypothermia and shock.

Following an episode of heat stroke, take your dog to a veterinarian as soon as possible. Heat stroke can be associated with *Laryngeal Edema* (see Chapter 10). This seriously worsens the breathing problem and may require an emergency tracheostomy. An injection of cortisone before the onset of respiratory distress may prevent this from happening. Other consequences of hyperthermia including kidney failure, spontaneous bleeding, cardiac arrhythmias and seizures. These complications can occur hours or days later.

Prevention:

- Dogs with airway disease and breathing problems should be kept indoors during periods of high heat and humidity.
- Never leave your dog in a car with the windows closed, even though the car may be parked in the shade.
- When traveling by car, crate the dog in a well-ventilated dog carrier, or better yet, an open wire cage.
- Restrict exercise in hot weather.
- Always provide shade and plenty of cool water to dogs outdoors, particularly those kenneled on cement or asphalt surfaces.

Poisoning

A poison is any substance harmful to the body. Dogs, being curious by nature, tend to explore out-of-the-way places such as wood piles, weed thickets and storage areas. These environs put them into contact with insects, dead animals, toxic plants and poison baits. It also means the exact cause of poisoning will not be known in many cases.

Intentional, malicious poisoning is a factor to consider whenever a dog is found dead without apparent cause. However, several studies have shown that most cases of sudden death are caused by accidents and natural events. Malicious poisoning does occur, but it is far less common than accidental poisoning.

General recommendations for the treatment of poisoning are discussed in the next section. In the sections that follow, specific poisons are discussed in the order in which they are most frequently seen by veterinarians.

GENERAL TREATMENT OF POISONING

If your dog ingests an unknown substance, it is important to determine whether that substance is a poison. Most products containing chemicals are labeled, but if the label doesn't tell you the composition and toxicity of the product, call the *National Animal Poison Control Center* at (800) 548-2423 or (900) 680-0000 for specific information. In some cases you can call the emergency room at your local hospital. Specific antidotes are available for some poisons, but they cannot be administered unless the poison is known, or at least suspected by the circumstances.

When signs of poisoning develop, the most important consideration is to get your dog to the nearest emergency veterinary facility at once. If possible, find the source of the poison and bring the container with you. This provides the emergency personnel with an immediate diagnosis and expedites treatment.

With recent ingestion, residual poison is often present in the dog's stomach. An initial and most important step is to rid the dog's stomach of any remaining poison. The most effective way to empty the stomach is to pass a stomach tube, remove as much of the stomach contents as possible, and then wash the stomach out with large volumes of water. This must be done by your veterinarian.

In many cases it is preferable to induce vomiting at the scene of the accident rather than proceed directly to the veterinary hospital. For example, if you see the dog swallow the poisonous substance, it is obviously best to make the dog vomit it right back up. Similarly, if the poison was ingested within two hours but it will take 30 minutes or longer to get to a veterinary facility, it is frequently advisable to induce vomiting at home. However, *do not* induce vomiting if the poison is a household or petroleum product; if the dog is in a stupor, breathing with difficulty or shows any sign of neurologic involvement; or if the label on the product says *not to induce vomiting*. In summary:

DO NOT *induce vomiting:*

- If the dog has already vomited.
- If the dog is unconscious, convulsing or having difficulty breathing.
- If the dog has swallowed an acid, alkali, cleaning solution, household chemical or petroleum product.
- If the dog has swallowed a sharp object that could lodge in the esophagus or perforate the stomach.
- If the label on the product says: *Do not induce vomiting.*

How to Induce Vomiting and Prevent Poison Absorption

Induce vomiting by giving the dog hydrogen peroxide. A 3 percent solution is most effective. Give one teaspoon per 10 pounds body weight of the dog. Repeat every 15 to 20 minutes, up to three times, until the dog vomits.

Syrup of ipecac has been recommended in the past, but hydrogen peroxide is a better choice for dogs. Syrup of ipecac (*not* ipecac fluid extract, which is 14 times stronger) is only 50 percent effective and can be dangerous to dogs. *It should not be used to induce vomiting unless specifically advised by your veterinarian.* The dose is .5 to 1 mL per pound of body weight with a maximum dose of 15 mL (one tablespoon). Repeat in 20 minutes (once only) if the dog does not vomit.

Once the poison has been cleared from the dog's stomach, activated charcoal should be given to bind any remaining poison and prevent further absorption. The most effective and easily administered home oral charcoal product is *compressed activated charcoal*, which comes in 5-gram tablets (recommended for the *Home Emergency Medical Kit*). The dose is one tablet per 10 pounds of body weight. Products that come in a liquid base or as a powder made into a slurry are extremely difficult to administer at home with a syringe or medicine bottle. The slurry is dense and gooey, and few dogs will swallow it voluntarily. These products are best administered by stomach tube. This is routinely done by your veterinarian after flushing out the stomach.

If charcoal is not available, coat the intestines with milk and egg white using 1/4 cup egg white and 1/4 cup milk per 10 pounds of body weight. Administer into the cheek pouch using a plastic syringe (see *How to Give Medications* in Chapter 20).

Intensive care in a veterinary hospital improves the survival rate for dogs that have been poisoned. Intravenous fluids support the circulation, treat shock and protect the kidneys. A large urine output assists in eliminating the poison. Corticosteroids are given for their anti-inflammatory effects. A dog in a coma may benefit from tracheal intubation and artificial ventilation during the acute phase of respiratory depression.

Seizures

Seizures caused by poisons are associated with prolonged periods of *hypoxia* and the potential for brain damage. Continuous or recurrent seizures are controlled with intravenous diazepam (Valium) or barbiturates.

Note that seizures caused by strychnine and other central nervous system poisons may be mistaken for epilepsy. This could be a problem, because immediate veterinary attention is needed in cases of poisoning, but not for most epileptic seizures. Seizures caused by poisoning usually are continuous or recur within minutes. Between seizures the dog may exhibit tremors, lack of coordination, weakness, abdominal pain and diarrhea. In contrast, most epileptic seizures are brief, seldom lasting more than two minutes, and are followed by a quiet period in which the dog appears dazed but otherwise normal.

CONTACT POISONS

If your dog's coat or skin comes in contact with a poisonous substance or toxic chemical, flush the site with copious amounts of water for 30 minutes. Wear rubber or plastic gloves and give the dog a complete bath in *lukewarm* water. Even if the substance is not irritating to the skin, it must be removed. Otherwise the dog may lick it off and swallow it.

DRUG POISONING

Unintentional overdose with veterinary medications and accidental ingestion of both human and veterinary pills are the most common causes of poisoning in pets. Veterinary products in particular are often flavored to encourage acceptance and will be eagerly consumed if they are discovered.

Many over-the-counter medications are given to dogs for a variety of symptoms without veterinary approval on the belief that what works in people works in dogs. Unfortunately, this assumption is not correct. Drugs given to dogs in human dosages are often toxic.

Common pain relievers such as aspirin, ibuprofen (Advil) and acetaminophen (Tylenol) are a particular problem. Dogs and cats do not have the necessary enzymes to detoxify and eliminate these drugs. This can lead to the accumulation of dangerous breakdown products in the animal. As few as two regular-strength aspirin or Tylenol tablets can produce severe organ damage in a medium-size dog. Symptoms develop quickly and include abdominal pain, salivation, vomiting and weakness.

Other human drugs producing a variety of toxic effects and commonly involved in accidental poisonings include antihistamines, sleeping pills, diet pills, heart and blood pressure pills and vitamins.

Treatment: If you suspect your pet has swallowed a drug, immediately induce vomiting. Call your veterinarian for further instructions. A specific antidote may well be available for the drug in question.

Prevention: Accidental poisoning can be prevented by always consulting your veterinarian before administering any medication. Follow instructions exactly for frequency and dosage. Store all drugs in a secure place to prevent inadvertent consumption by pets and children. *Never assume that a human drug is safe for pets!*

RODENT POISONS

Common rat and mouse poisons include anticoagulants and hypercalcemic agents.

Anticoagulants

Anticoagulant rat and mouse poisons are the most commonly used household poisons. These products account for a large number of accidental poisonings in dogs and cats. Anticoagulants exert their effect by blocking the synthesis of vitamin K, essential for normal clotting. Vitamin K deficiency results in spontaneous bleeding.

Observable signs of poisoning do not occur until several days after exposure. The dog may become weak and pale from blood loss, have nose bleeds, vomit blood, experience rectal bleeding, develop hematomas and bruises beneath the skin or have hemorrhages beneath the gums. The dog may be found dead from bleeding into the chest or abdomen.

There are two generations of anticoagulants, both in current use. The first generation are cumulative poisons that require multiple feedings over several days to kill the rodent. These poisons contain the anticoagulants warfarin and hydroxycoumadin. Examples are D-Con, Ward 42, Rax, Rodex, Tox hid, Ratifin, Rat-A-Way, Lurat, Krunkill and Fumisol.

Second-generation anticoagulants contain bromadiolone and brodifacoum, poisons that are 50 to 200 times more toxic than warfarin and hydroxycoumadin. These products are more dangerous to pets and are capable of killing rodents after a single feeding. It is even possible for a small dog to be poisoned by eating a dead rodent with residual poison in his stomach. Examples are Mouse Prufe II, Havoc, Talon, Weather Block, Super Caid, Ratimus and Contrac.

Closely related to the second-generation anticoagulants are the long-acting anticoagulants of the indanedione class, (pindone, diphacinone, diphenadione and chlorphacinone) including the products Valone, Promar, Ramik, Diphacin, Ciad Drat, Rozol, Pival and PMP.

Treatment: If at all possible, bring in the container for product identification. This is important because treatment depends on whether the poison was a first- or second-generation anticoagulant. With observed or suspected recent ingestion, induce vomiting (see page 18). Seek veterinary help.

Treatment of spontaneous bleeding caused by all anticoagulants involves the administration of fresh whole blood or frozen plasma in amounts determined by the rate and volume of blood loss. Vitamin K_1 is a specific antidote. It is given by subcutaneous injection and repeated subcutaneously or orally as necessary until the clotting time returns to normal. With first-generation anticoagulants, this often occurs within a week. With long-acting anticoagulants, treatment takes up to a month because of the length of time the poison remains in the dog's system.

Hypercalcemic Agents

Hypercalcemic agents—that is, rat poisons containing vitamin D (cholecalciferol) as their effective agent—are becoming increasingly popular because rodents do not develop resistance and, with the rare exception of a puppy or small dog, dogs who eat poisoned rodents will not develop toxicity. Examples are Rampage, Quintox, Rat-B-Gone and Mouse-B-Gone. Cholecalciferol poisons work by raising the calcium content in blood serum to toxic levels, eventually producing cardiac arrhythmias and death.

In dogs, signs of hypercalcemia appear 18 to 36 hours after ingestion of the poison. They include thirst and frequent urination, vomiting, generalized weakness, muscle twitching, seizures and death. Among survivors the effects of an elevated serum calcium may persist for weeks.

Treatment: If you suspect your dog has ingested one of these poisons within the past four hours, induce vomiting (see page 18) and notify your veterinarian. Veterinary treatment involves correcting the fluid and electrolyte imbalances and lowering calcium levels using diuretics, prednisone, oral phosphorus binders and feeding a low-calcium prescription diet. Calcitonin is a specific antidote, but is difficult to obtain and has only short-term effects.

ANTIFREEZE POISONING (ETHYLENE GLYCOL)

Poisoning by antifreeze containing ethylene glycol is one of the most common small animal toxicities. Antifreeze has a sweet taste and appeals to dogs and cats. Exposure typically occurs when antifreeze is drained from the car radiator and is lapped up by the pet. Less than three ounces is enough to poison a 40-pound dog. The poison primarily affects the brain and the kidneys.

Signs of toxicity are dose-related, and occur within 30 minutes to 12 hours after ingestion. They include depression, vomiting, an uncoordinated "drunken" gait and seizures. Coma and death can occur in a matter of hours. Dogs that recover from acute intoxication frequently develop kidney failure one to three days later. Death is common.

Treatment: If you see or suspect that your pet has ingested even a small amount of antifreeze, immediately induce vomiting (see page 18) and take your dog to the veterinarian. If treatment will be delayed, administer activated charcoal (see page 18) to prevent further absorption of ethylene glycol. A specific antidote (4-Methylpyrazole) is available to treat poisoning. It is most effective when given shortly after ingestion and early in the course of treatment. Intensive care in an animal hospital may prevent kidney failure.

Prevention: This common cause of pet and child poisoning can be prevented by keeping all containers tightly closed and properly stored, preventing antifreeze spills and properly disposing of used antifreeze. A new antifreeze product (trade name *Sierra*) contains propylene glycol instead of ethylene glycol. Poisoning causes incoordination and possibly seizures, but is alleged not to cause fatal kidney damage.

POISON BAITS

Animal baits containing strychnine, sodium fluoroacetate, phosphorus, zinc phosphide and metaldehyde are used in rural areas to control gophers, coyotes and other predators. They are also used in stables and barns to eliminate rodents. These baits are highly palatable and are thus good candidates for accidental ingestion. Many are extremely toxic and kill in a matter of minutes. Fortunately, they are being used less frequently because of livestock losses, concerns about persistence in the environment and the potential to poison pets and children.

Strychnine

Strychnine is used as a rat, gopher, mole and coyote poison. In concentrations greater than 0.5 percent it is restricted to certified exterminators. It is available to the public in concentrations of 0.3 percent or less. With better regulation and the use of lower concentrations, strychnine is becoming a less common cause of accidental poisoning.

Signs of strychnine poisoning appear within two hours of ingestion. They include agitation, excitability and apprehension, followed rather quickly by intensely painful convulsions with rigid extension of all four limbs. Seizures last about 60 seconds, during which time the dog throws his head back, stops breathing and turns blue. The slightest stimulation, even touching the dog or clapping the hands, can trigger a seizure. This type of seizure response is typical only of strychnine. Other signs of poisoning include tremors, champing, drooling, uncoordinated muscle spasms, collapse and paddling of the legs.

Treatment: Induce vomiting immediately after ingestion (see page 18). But do not induce vomiting if the dog is unresponsive, convulsing or having difficulty breathing. Cover the dog with a coat or blanket and proceed as quickly as possible to the nearest veterinary clinic. Further treatment involves the administration of intravenous diazepam (*Valium*) or barbiturates to control seizures. The dog is placed in a dark, quiet room and disturbed as little as possible.

Sodium Fluoroacetate

Sodium fluoroacetate (compound 1080/1081), a very potent rat and gopher poison, is restricted to licensed pest control operators and is used infrequently in the United States. Dogs and cats have been poisoned by eating a dead rodent that has ingested the poison. The onset is sudden and begins with vomiting, followed by agitation, staggering, convulsions and collapse.

Treatment: It is like that described for *strychnine poisoning*.

Metaldehyde

This poison, often combined with arsenic, is found in rat, snail and slug baits. It is also used as a solid fuel for camp stoves. The dry form looks and tastes like dog food. Signs of toxicity, which appear immediately or up to three hours after ingestion, include excitation, drooling and slobbering, uncoordinated gait, muscle tremors, inability to stand and continuous seizures that lead to death by respiratory paralysis. Dogs that survive the acute poisoning may die of secondary liver failure.

Treatment: It is like that described for *strychnine poisoning*.

Phosphorus

This extremely toxic chemical is used in rat and roach poisons and is also found in fireworks, matches and matchboxes. A poisoned dog may have a garlic odor to his breath. The first signs of intoxication are vomiting and diarrhea. This is followed by a normal interval, then by further vomiting, cramps, pain in the abdomen, convulsions and coma.

Treatment: Induce vomiting (see page 18) when you suspect ingestion of a product or poison containing phosphorus. Do not coat the bowel with milk or egg white, as this can actually promote absorption. Take your dog to the nearest veterinary facility. There is no specific antidote.

Zinc Phosphide

This substance is found in rat poisons and is used by pest control professionals as a grain fumigant. Zinc phosphide in the stomach releases gas that has the odor of garlic or rotten fish. Intoxication causes depression, rapid labored breathing, vomiting (often of blood), weakness, convulsions and death.

Treatment: It is like that described for *strychnine poisoning.* There is no specific antidote. The stomach should be lavaged with 5 percent sodium bicarbonate, which raises the gastric pH and delays the formation of gas.

INSECTICIDES

There are dozens of products sold at hardware, home repair and agricultural stores to kill ants, termites, wasps, garden pests and other insects. Most of them contain organophosphates and carbamates as their active ingredients. At one time these compounds were incorporated into most sprays, powders and dips used to control fleas and ticks on dogs. With the development of pyrethrin insecticides that are equally effective but much less toxic, organophosphates and carbamates are being used less frequently in topical preparations. For information on using insecticides, see Chapter 4, *Topical Insecticides for Flea Control.*

Organophosphates and Carbamates

The organophosphates include *chlorpyrifos, diazinon, phosmet, fenthion, cythioate* and *tetrachlorvinphos.* The common carbamates are carbyl and propexur. Most cases of organophosphate or carbamate poisoning are due to ingestion of a poison bait. Exposure to high concentrations of chemicals in sprays and dusts also occurs.

Signs of toxicity are hyperexcitability, excessive salivation and drooling, frequent urination, diarrhea, muscle twitching, weakness, staggering, collapse and coma. Death is by respiratory failure.

Treatment: If you suspect that your dog has ingested an insecticide poison, immediately induce vomiting (see page 18) and notify your veterinarian. With any sign of toxicity, the first priority is to get your dog to the veterinarian as quickly as possible. The specific antidote for organophosphate poisoning (not carbamate poisoning) is 2-PAM (protopam chloride). Atropine is given for both organophosphate and carbamate poisoning to control excessive salivation, vomiting, frequent urination and defecation, and to reverse a slow heart rate. Seizures are controlled with diazepam (*Valium*) or barbiturates.

Following skin exposure, give the dog a bath with soapy water and rinse thoroughly to remove residual insecticide.

Chlorinated Hydrocarbons

These compounds, of which the prototype is DDT, are added to sprays and dusts to control plant pests. Their use has been curtailed because of persistent toxicity in the environment. Only *lindane, methoxychlor* and *Toxaphene* are approved for use around livestock. Chlorinated hydrocarbons are readily inhaled and easily absorbed through the skin. Toxicity can occur from repeated or excessive exposure.

Signs of toxicity occur rapidly. They include hyperexcitability with twitching of the face, followed by muscle tremors that begin at the head and progress back to involve the neck, shoulder, trunk and rear legs. Seizures and convulsions are followed by respiratory paralysis and death.

Treatment: This includes supporting life functions, removing ingested poison from the stomach and controlling seizures. There is no specific antidote.

Pyrethrin/Pyrethroids

These compounds are incorporated into many insecitcidal shampoos, sprays, dusts, dips, foggers and sprays. Pyrethrins and the synthetic pyrethroids are much safer to use on dogs than are other insecticides, and they are being used more widely. Common chemicals in this class include *permethrin, allethrin, fenvalerate, resmethrin* and *sumethrin*.

Signs of toxicity include drooling, depression, muscle tremors, staggering, vomiting and rapid labored breathing. Toxicity occurs primarily in small dogs. Death is rare. Simultaneous exposure to organophosphates increases the toxicity of pyrethroids.

Treatment: Induce vomiting (see page 18) within two hours of ingestion. Call your veterinarian for further instructions. Do not induce vomiting if the product contains a petroleum distillate. With signs of toxicity, proceed immediately to the veterinary clinic.

For topical exposure, remove residual insecticide by bathing the dog in *lukewarm* water and rinse thoroughly. Bathing in hot or cold water may actually increase the rate of absorption or cause hypothermia, which increases toxicity. After bathing, *keep the dog warm*.

Prevention: Most cases of poisoning occur because of improper application of flea control products. That may be because the product is being used more often than the instructions call for, or is being combined with another flea control product. Follow all instructions carefully.

Arsenic

This heavy metal is used in herbicides, insecticides and wood preservatives. Sodium and potassium arsenate are used in ant poisons. Arsenic has a very rapid action and therefore poses a major risk for accidental poisoning. Death can occur quickly, even before symptoms are observed. Fortunately, the use of arsenic has been greatly curtailed.

Signs of poisoning are thirst, drooling, vomiting, staggering, intense abdominal pain, cramps, diarrhea, paralysis and death. The breath of the dog has a strong garlic odor.

Treatment: Proceed at once to the nearest emergency veterinary facility. BAL is a specific antidote and should be given as soon as the diagnosis is suspected.

GARBAGE (FOOD) POISONING

Dogs that scavenge come into contact with garbage, decomposing food and carrion, some of which contain endotoxins produced by bacteria. Once ingested, the endotoxins are absorbed and poison the dog.

Signs appear within two to six hours. They include an acute painful abdomen accompanied by vomiting and diarrhea (often bloody). The dog may have noticeably bad breath. Shock and death can occur in severe cases.

Treatment: If you see your dog eating garbage or a dead animal, immediately induce vomiting (see page 18). Follow with liquid Pepto-Bismol; give a dose every 12 hours for two days. Administer by plastic syringe (see Chapter 20, *Drugs and Medications*). If the dog begins to vomit or develops other signs of poisoning, notify your veterinarian. Mild cases recover in one to two days.

CHOCOLATE POISONING

Most dogs like chocolate, but ingestion can be dangerous. Chocolate contains methylxanthines (caffeine and the alkaloid theobromine). Methylxanthines are not toxic to people in the concentrations found in candy and baked goods, but when ingested by dogs the effects can be lethal. Although some dogs tolerate chocolate far better than others, note that a dog weighing five to 10 pounds could die after eating as little as four ounces of *baking chocolate* (not candy); a dog weighing 20 to 40 pounds after eating as little as 16 ounces; and a larger dog after eating two pounds. Dogs have been poisoned by eating an entire pan of brownies or a chocolate cake.

Signs of chocolate toxicity occur within hours after the dog ingests the chocolate. They include hyperexcitability, vomiting, frequent urination, diarrhea, rapid breathing, weakness, seizures and coma. Death, which is rare, occurs by cardiac arrest.

Treatment: If you know your dog has eaten chocolate within the past six hours, and he has not already vomited, induce vomiting (see page 18). Record the type and amount of chocolate ingested. (Sweet and semi-sweet chocolate in candy bars is not nearly as toxic as baking chocolate.) Then call your veterinarian for further instructions.

Prevention: Use commercial dog products as treats. Keep chocolates stored securely to prevent accidental ingestion.

CORROSIVE HOUSEHOLD PRODUCTS

Corrosives and caustics (acid and alkali) are found in household cleaners, toilet bowl cleaners, dishwasher detergents, anti-rust compounds, alkaline batteries, drain decloggers and commercial solvents. When ingested, they cause burns of the mouth, esophagus and stomach. Severe cases cause perforations of the stomach and late strictures of the esophagus.

Treatment: Do not induce vomiting. Vomiting can result in rupture of the stomach and burns of the esophagus. Rinse the dog's mouth immediately after contact and take him as quickly as possible to the nearest veterinary clinic. If you can't get to the vet very quickly, give the dog water or milk (30 mL per six pounds of body weight) by plastic syringe to dilute the acid or alkali in the stomach.

The practice of giving an acid to neutralize an alkali and vice versa is no longer recommended, because it causes heat injury to the tissues.

With topical exposure, flush the area with water for 30 minutes. If the substance is in the eye, see *Burns of the Eyes* in Chapter 5.

PETROLEUM PRODUCTS (GASOLINE, KEROSENE, TURPENTINE)

Gasoline, kerosene and turpentine can cause pneumonia if aspirated or inhaled. Signs of toxicity are vomiting, rapid labored breathing, tremors, convulsions and coma. Death is by respiratory failure.

Treatment: Do not induce vomiting. Treat as described above for *corrosives*. Flush the mouth with water to remove petroleum residue. Petroleum products are extremely irritating to the skin and must be removed as quickly as possible. Bathe the skin using warm soapy water. For tar in the coat, see *Special Bath Problems* in Chapter 4.

POISONOUS PLANTS, TREES AND SHRUBS

Eating plants and vegetation is an infrequent cause of poisoning in dogs. Note that with some plants, only certain parts are toxic. With others, the whole plant is poisonous.

The variety of potentially poisonous plants and shrubs allows for a wide range of symptoms. Signs include mouth irritation, drooling, vomiting, diarrhea, hallucinations, rapid labored breathing, staggering, muscle tremors, seizures, coma and death. Some plants cause sudden death without premonitory signs. Other plants contain chemicals that are extremely irritating to the skin.

Plants of the *rhododendron* family (milkweeds, lily-of-the-valley, laurel, azalea, foxglove) all contain cardiac glycosides of the *digitalis* class. Even though these plants have a bitter taste, pets do sometimes eat enough to cause death. Ornamental plants of the *nightshade* family, including Chinese lantern, Christmas cherry and ornamental pepper, contain solanines that are toxic to the gastrointestinal system and brain. They, too, are a rare cause of death. Below is a list of common toxic plants, shrubs and trees, but this list does not include all potentially poisonous plants. If you're not sure about a plant, ask your veterinarian or the local plant nursery.

Puppies going through the chewing stage are more likely to ingest indoor and outdoor plants. In adult dogs, chewing on plants may be an indication of boredom or frustration associated with separation anxiety or a recent change in the household routine. To prevent houseplant poisoning, determine which plants are toxic and either dispose of them or keep them in a place the dog is unable to reach.

Treatment: Upon suspicion of ingestion, induce vomiting (see page 18) and call your veterinarian for further instructions.

Indoor Plants with Toxic Effects

Houseplants that cause a skin reaction after contact with the skin or mouth:

Chrysanthemum	Poinsettia
Creeping fig	Weeping fig

Irritating plants, some of which contain oxalic acid, which causes mouth swelling, difficulty swallowing, respiratory problems and gastrointestinal upsets:

Arrowhead vine	Malanga
Boston ivy	Marble queen
Caladium	Mother-in-law plant
Calla or arum lily	Neththyis
Dumbcane (diffenbachia)	Parlor ivy
Elephant's ear	Pothos or devil's lily
Emerald duke	Peace lily
Heart leaf (philodendron)	Red princess
Jack-in-the-pulpit	Saddle leaf (philodendron)
Majesty	Split leaf (philodendron)
Tuberous begonia	

Plants that contain a wide variety of poisons. Most cause vomiting, an acutely painful abdomen and cramps; some cause tremors, heart and respiratory and/or kidney problems, which are difficult for owners to interpret:

Amaryllis	Jerusalem cherry
Asparagus fern	Nightshade
Azalea	Pot mum
Bird-of-paradise	Ripple ivy
Creeping Charlie	Spider mum
Crown of thorns	Sprangeri fern
Elephant's ear	Umbrella plant
Ivies	

Outdoor Plants with Toxic Effects

Outdoor plants that can produce vomiting and diarrhea:

Bittersweet woody	Indian turnip
Castor bean	Larkspur woody
Daffodil	Poke weed
Delphinium	Skunk cabbage
Foxglove	Soapberry
Ground cherry	Wisteria
Indian tobacco	

Trees and shrubs that may produce vomiting, painful abdomen and diarrhea:

American yew	English yew
Apricot	Horse chestnut
Almond	Japanese plum
Azalea (rhododendron)	Mock orange
Balsam pear	Monkey pod
Bird-of-paradise bush	Peach
Buckeye	Privet
Cherry	Rain tree
English holly	Western black locust yew
Wild cherry	

Outdoor plants with varied toxic effects:

Angel's trumpet	Mescal bean
Buttercup	Moonseed
Dologeton	Mushrooms
Rhubarb	Nightshades
Dutchman's breeches	Pigweed
Jasmine	Poison hemlock
Jimsonweed	Spinach
Locoweed	Sunburned potatoes
Lupine	Tomato vine
May apple	Water hemlock
Matrimony vine	

Hallucinogens:

Locoweed	Nutmeg
Marijuana	Periwinkle
Morning glory	Peyote
Poppies	

Outdoor plants that produce convulsions:

Chinaberry	Nux vomica
Coriaria	Water hemlock
Moonweed	

LEAD

Lead is found in fishing weights and is a base for some artist's paints. Other sources of lead are linoleum, dry walls, batteries, plumbing materials, putty, lead foil, solder, golf balls and tar paper. The use of commercial lead-free paints has significantly reduced the frequency of lead intoxication. Poisoning occurs primarily in puppies and dogs that chew and swallow objects that contain lead. Toxicity usually requires repeated exposure.

Acute lead intoxication is characterized by vomiting and a very painful abdomen. With chronic exposure, a variety of central nervous system signs can develop. They include seizures, uncoordinated gait, excitation, continuous barking, attacks of hysteria, weakness, stupor and blindness. Chewing and champing fits may be mistaken for the encephalitis of distemper.

Treatment: **If you suspect your dog has ingested lead,** induce vomiting. Seek veterinary attention. Specific antidotes to bind and remove lead from the dog's system are available from your veterinarian.

Insect and Amphibian Bites

INSECT STINGS

The stings of bees, wasps, yellow jackets and ants all cause painful swelling and redness at the site of the sting, usually on a hairless area such as the nose or feet. The swelling may include the face and neck. If the dog is stung many times, he could go into shock as a result of absorbed toxins. Occasionally, *anaphylactic shock* develops in a dog that has been stung in the past.

The bites of black widow and brown recluse spiders are toxic to animals. Signs are sharp pain at the site of the sting. Later the dog develops intense excitability, fever, weakness, and muscle and joint pains. Seizures, shock and death can occur, especially with the bite of the black widow spider. An antivenin is available to treat these bites.

The stings of centipedes and scorpions cause a local reaction and at times severe illness. These bites heal slowly.

The bite of a female wood tick can cause *tick paralysis* (see Chapter 12). The bites of other common insect parasites are discussed in Chapter 4.

Treatment:

1. Identify the insect.
2. If the stinger is found (a small black sac), remove it by scraping it out with your fingernail or a credit card. Do not squeeze or use tweezers, as this can inject more venom. (Only bees leave their stingers behind.)
3. Make a paste of baking soda and apply it directly to the sting.
4. Apply an ice pack to relieve pain and swelling.
5. Apply calamine lotion to relieve itching.
6. Your veterinarian may prescrive an antihistamine such as Benadryl.

If the dog exhibits signs of hypersensitivity to the venom (agitation, face scratching, drooling, vomiting, diarrhea, difficulty breathing, collapse or seizures), take him at once to the nearest veterinary facility for treatment of *anaphylactic shock* (see *Shock*, page 33).

TOAD AND SALAMANDER POISONING

There are two species of poisonous toads in the United States: the Colorado River toad, found in the Southwest and Hawaii; and the marine toad, found in

Florida. There is one species of poisonous salamander: the California newt, found in California.

All toads have a bad taste. Dogs that mouth them slobber, spit and drool. The marine toad is highly poisonous, causing death in as quickly as 15 minutes.

Toxicity depends upon the virulence of the toad or salamander, the size of the dog and the amount of poison absorbed. Symptoms can vary from slobbering to convulsions, blindness and death. Puppies and small dogs are more likely to develop toxicity.

Treatment: Repeatedly flush the dog's mouth using a garden hose, if necessary, and induce vomiting (see page 18). Be prepared to administer CPR (see page 7). Dogs with salamander poisoning generally recover quickly.

Snake Bites

Poisonous and non-poisonous snakes are widely distributed throughout the United States. In general, bites of non-poisonous snakes do not cause swelling or pain. They show teeth marks in the shape of a horseshoe, but no fang marks.

In the United States there are four poisonous snakes: cottonmouths (also called water moccasins), rattlesnakes, copperheads and coral snakes. The diagnosis of poisonous snake bite is made by the appearance of the bite, behavior of the animal and identification of the species of snake. Ninety percent of snake bites in dogs involve the head and legs.

PIT VIPERS (RATTLESNAKES, COTTONMOUTHS AND COPPERHEADS)

You can identify these species by their large size (four to eight feet long), triangular heads, pits below and between the eyes, elliptical pupils, rough scales and the presence of retractable fangs in the upper jaw.

The bite: You may see one or two bleeding puncture wounds in the skin, which are fang marks. These marks may not be visible because of the dog's coat. The pain is immediate and severe. The tissues are swollen and discolored due to bleeding at the site of the bite.

Note that 25 percent of poisonous snake bites lack venom and thus do not produce a local reaction. While absence of local swelling and pain is a good sign, it does not guarantee the dog won't become sick. Severe venom poisoning has been known to occur without a local reaction.

Behavior of the animal: Signs of envenomation may take several hours to appear because of variables such as the time of the year, species of the snake, toxicity of the venom, amount injected, location of the bite, and size and health of the dog. The amount of venom injected bears no relationship to the size of the snake. Signs of venom poisoning include extreme restlessness, panting, drooling, vomiting, diarrhea, uncoordinated gait, respiratory depression, shock and sometimes death.

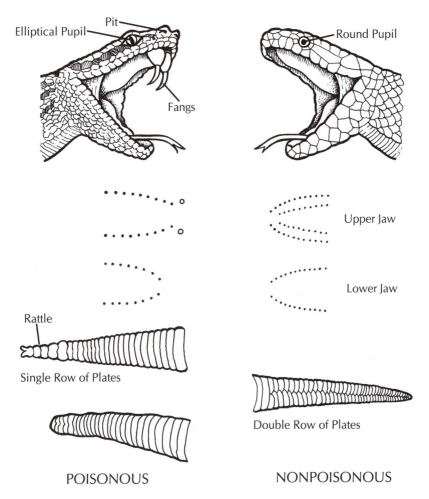

Elliptical Pupil — Pit

Fangs

Round Pupil

Upper Jaw

Lower Jaw

Rattle

Single Row of Plates

Double Row of Plates

POISONOUS   NONPOISONOUS

Characteristics of pit vipers and nonpoisonous snakes. Note the elliptical pupil, pit below the eye, large fangs, characteristic bite and single row of subcaudal plates on the belly of the pit viper.

CORAL SNAKES

Identify this snake by its rather small size (less than three feet long), small head with black nose, and brightly colored alternating bands (red, yellow and black) fully encircling the body. The fangs in the upper jaw are not retractable.

The bite: The puncture wounds from a bite are small and the pain is mild. There is little local reaction.

Behavior of the animal: Coral snake venom is neurotoxic, meaning it affects the nerves and causes weakness and paralysis. Signs may be delayed for several hours. They include muscle twitching, pinpoint pupils, weakness, difficulty swallowing, shock and collapse. Death is by respiratory paralysis.

TREATMENT OF SNAKE BITES

First identify the snake and look at the bite. If the snake is not poisonous, clean and dress the wound as described in the section on *Wounds* (page 36). If it appears the dog has been bitten by a poisonous snake, *proceed at once to the veterinary hospital*. (If the snake has been killed, take it with you for identification.) Some specific precautions:

- *Keep the dog quiet.* Venom spreads rapidly. Excitement, exercise and struggling increase the rate of absorption. If possible, carry the dog.
- Do not wash the wound, as this increases venom absorption.
- Do not apply ice, as this does not slow absorption and can damage tissue.
- Do not make cuts over the wound and/or attempt to suck out venom. This is never successful and you could absorb venom.
- Be aware that the snake's fangs may be venomous for up to two hours after it dies, even if you have cut off the head.

Veterinary treatment involves respiratory and circulatory support, antihistamines, intravenous fluids and species-specific antivenin. The earlier the antivenin is given, the better the results. Because signs of envenomation are often delayed, all dogs bitten by a poisonous snake (even those that don't show signs) should be hospitalized and observed for 24 hours.

Shock

Shock is caused by insufficient blood flow and oxygen to meet the body's needs. Adequate blood flow requires effective heart pumping, open, intact blood vessels and sufficient blood volume to maintain flow and pressure. Adequate oxygenation requires an open respiratory tract and enough energy to breathe. Any condition that adversely affects the circulatory or respiratory systems can cause shock.

The cardiovascular system of an animal in shock will try to compensate for inadequate oxygen and blood flow by increasing the heart and respiratory rates, constricting the skin's blood vessels and maintaining fluid in the circulation by reducing urinary output. This requires additional energy at a time when the vital organs aren't getting enough oxygen to carry out normal activities. After a time, shock becomes self-perpetuating. Untreated, it results in death.

Common causes of shock are hemorrhage, heart failure, anaphylactic (allergic) reactions, dehydration (heat stroke, vomiting, diarrhea), poisoning and toxic shock associated with sepsis and peritonitis.

Signs of early shock include panting, rapid heart rate, bounding pulses, and a bright red color to the mucous membranes of the lips, gums and tongue. Signs of late shock (the ones seen most often) are pale skin and mucous membranes, a drop in body temperature, cold feet and legs, a slow respiratory rate, apathy and depression, unconsciousness, and a weak or absent pulse.

Treatment: First, evaluate. Is the dog breathing? Is there a heartbeat? What is the extent of the injuries? Is the dog in shock?

If so, proceed as follows:

1. If the dog is not breathing, proceed with *artificial respiration* (see page 6).

2. If there is no heartbeat or pulse, administer *CPR* (see page 7).

3. If the dog is unconscious, check to be sure the airway is open. Clear secretions from the mouth with your fingers and a piece of cloth. Pull the tip of the tongue foreword beyond the front teeth to make it easier for the dog to breathe. Keep the dog's head lower than his body by placing a blanket beneath his hindquarters.

4. Control bleeding as described under *Wounds* (page 36).

5. Wrap the dog in a coat or blanket to provide warmth and protect injured extremities.

6. *Transport to a veterinary hospital.*

To avoid aggravating the shock:

- Calm the dog and speak soothingly.

- Allow the dog to assume the most comfortable position in which breathing is easiest. An animal will naturally adopt the position of least pain.

- When possible, splint or support broken bones before moving the dog (see *Broken Bones* in Chapter 13).

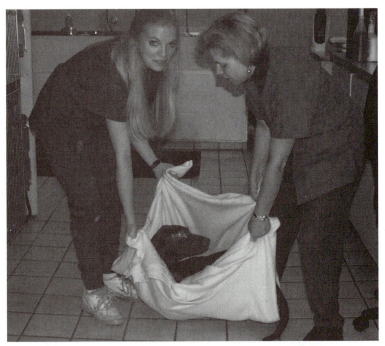

Transporting a dog in shock.

- All dogs that are unconscious or found lying down after an accident must be considered to have spinal cord injuries and should be handled accordingly (see *Spinal Cord Injuries* in Chapter 12).

- Transport large dogs on a flat surface or in a hammock stretcher. Carry small dogs in a blanket with injured parts protected.

- Avoid using a muzzle except for short periods, such as when moving the dog from the scene of the accident into a car, or from a car into the veterinary clinic. Muzzling can interfere with breathing.

ANAPHYLACTIC SHOCK

Anaphylactic shock is an immediate, serious allergic reaction. It occurs when a dog is exposed to an *allergen* to which he has been sensitized. Sensitivity occurs through prior contact.

The most common agent producing anaphylactic shock is penicillin. The venom in the stings of bees and wasps can also occasionally produce anaphylactic shock. Some dogs have been known to experience shock after a vaccination, but this is quite rare.

Anaphylactic shock causes signs and symptoms different from those previously described for shock. Initially there may be local signs at the point of contact, including pain, itching, swelling and redness of the skin. With *acute anaphylaxis*, the allergic response becomes generalized, either immediately or over the course of several hours. Signs are agitation, diarrhea, vomiting, difficulty breathing, *stridor* (harsh breathing sounds) from a swollen voice box, weakness and circulatory collapse. In untreated cases, coma and death follow.

A dog in anaphylactic shock, in this case following a routine vaccination. The dog responded well to emergency treatment, and 30 minutes later was fine.

Emergency treatment of anaphylactic shock involves administering intravenous or subcutaneous adrenaline, oxygen, Benadryl, IV fluids and hydrocortisone—drugs not available in the home. This is why it is best to have your veterinarian give vaccines—he or she has the drugs and equipment to treat allergic reactions in time.

A dog that has had an allergic reaction to a drug in the past should not be given that drug again.

Wounds

The two most important goals in treating wounds are to stop the bleeding and to prevent infection. Wounds are painful, so be prepared to restrain and muzzle the dog before treating the wound.

CONTROLLING BLEEDING

Bleeding may be arterial (bright red blood will spurt out) or venous (dark red blood will ooze out), or sometimes both. Do not wipe a wound that has stopped bleeding, as this will dislodge the clot. Similarly, don't pour hydrogen peroxide on a fresh wound. Peroxide dissolves clots and starts a fresh round of bleeding.

The two methods used to control bleeding in an emergency situation are a pressure dressing and a tourniquet.

The Pressure Dressing

The most effective and safest method for controlling bleeding is to apply pressure directly to the wound. Take several sterile gauze squares (or in an emergency use any clean cloth such as a thickly folded pad of clothing) and place it over the wound. Apply direct pressure for 5 to 10 minutes. Leave the dressing in place and bandage snugly. If material for bandaging is not available, hold the pack in place until help arrives. Watch for signs of swelling of the limb below the pressure pack (see *Foot and Leg Bandages*, page 41). This indicates impaired circulation. If present, the bandage must be loosened or removed.

Consider using a tourniquet or add more bulk to the pack and apply a second bandage over the first. Transport the dog to a veterinary hospital.

The Tourniquet

Tourniquets can be used on the extremities and tail to control arterial bleeding that can't be controlled with a pressure pack. *Tourniquets should never be used if bleeding can be controlled by direct pressure.* Always place the tourniquet *above* the wound (between the wound and the heart).

A suitable tourniquet can be made from a piece of cloth, belt, tire, or gauze. Loop the tourniquet around the limb as shown below. Then tighten it by hand or with a stick inserted beneath the loop. Twist the loop until the bleeding stops.

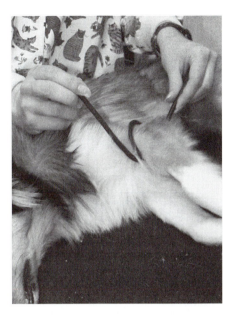

A tourniquet should be used only if bleeding cannot be controlled with a pressure dressing.

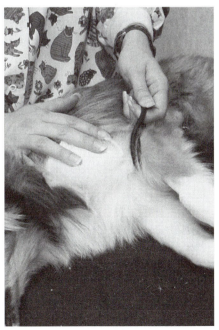

The tourniquet is looped twice around the leg and tightened by twisting.

A tourniquet should be loosened every 10 minutes to prevent tissue *hypoxia* and to check for persistent bleeding. If bleeding has stopped, apply a pressure bandage as described previously. If bleeding continues, let the blood flow for a few seconds and then re-tighten the tourniquet for another 10 minutes.

TREATING THE WOUND

Nearly all animal wounds are contaminated with dirt and bacteria. Proper care and handling will reduce the risk of tetanus and prevent many infections.

The five steps in wound care are:

- Skin preparation
- Wound irrigation
- Debridement
- Wound closure
- Bandaging

Skin Preparation

Remove the original pressure dressing and cleanse the area around the wound with a surgical scrub solution. The most commonly used solutions are Betadine (povidone-iodine) and Nolvasan (chlorhexidine diacetate). Both products are extremely irritating to exposed tissue in the concentrations provided in the stock solutions (Betadine 10 percent; chlorhexidine 2 percent). Be sure the solution does not get in the wound while scrubbing the skin around it. Three percent hydrogen peroxide, often recommended as a wound cleanser, has little value as an antiseptic and is extremely toxic to tissues. Do not use it on a fresh wound.

After the scrub, start at the edges of the wound and clip the dog's coat back far enough to prevent any long hairs from getting into the wound.

Wound Irrigation

The purpose of irrigation is to remove dirt and bacteria. The gentlest and most effective method of wound cleansing is by *lavage*, which involves irrigating the wound with large amounts of fluid until the tissues are clean and glistening. Do not vigorously cleanse the wound using a brush or gauze pad because it causes bleeding and traumatizes the exposed tissue.

Tap water is an acceptable and convenient irrigating solution. Tap water has a negligible bacterial count and is known to cause less tissue reaction than sterile or distilled water. If possible, add chlorhexidine solution or Betadine solution to the tap water for antibacterial activity. Chlorhexidine has the greater residual antiseptic effect, but either antiseptic solution (not the soap solutions) is satisfactory when correctly diluted.

To dilute chlorhexidine, add 25 mL of the 2 percent stock solution to two quarts of water, making a 0.05 percent irrigating solution. To dilute Betadine, add 10 mL of the 10 percent stock solution to two quarts of water to make a 0.2 percent irrigating solution.

The effectiveness of the irrigation is related to the volume and pressure of the fluid used. A bulb syringe is a low-pressure system. It is least effective and requires more fluid to achieve satisfactory irrigation. A large plastic syringe removes a moderate amount of dirt and bacteria. A home Water Pik unit (used by people to clean their teeth) or a commercial lavage unit that provides a high-pressure stream of fluid is the most effective. A garden hose with a pressure nozzle for the initial lavage, followed by one of the methods just described to deliver the antiseptic, is a good alternative.

Debridement

Debridement, which follows wound lavage, means removing dying tissue and any remaining foreign matter using tissue forceps (tweezers) and scissors or a scalpel. Debridement requires experience to determine the difference between normal and devitalized tissue, and instruments to control hemorrhage and close the wound. Accordingly, wounds that require debridement and closure should be treated by a professional.

Closure

Fresh lacerations on the lips, face, eyelids and ears are best sutured to prevent infection, minimize scarring and speed recovery. Lacerations longer than half an inch on the body and extremities probably should be sutured, but small lacerations may not need to be sutured.

Wounds contaminated by dirt and debris are quite likely to become infected if closed at the time of injury. These wounds should be left open or sutured around a drain that can be used for through and through irrigation. Similarly, wounds older than 12 hours should not be closed without drainage. Suturing should be avoided if the wound appears to be infected (is red, swollen, or has a surface discharge).

Your veterinarian may decide to close a wound that has been left open for several days and has developed a bed of clean tissue. Wounds that are clean after several days are resistant to infection and usually can be closed with impunity. Suturing such a wound is called *delayed primary closure*.

The length of time sutures should remain in place depends on the wound's location and other characteristics. Most sutures can be removed after 10 to 14 days.

Small open wounds can be treated at home without sutures. Medicate twice a day with a topical antibiotic ointment such as triple antibiotic. The wound can be left open or covered with a dressing.

Infected wounds draining pus require the application of moist sterile compresses. A number of topical antiseptics are effective in treating superficial wound infections. They include chlorhexidine and Betadine (diluted as described in *Skin Preparation*), Furacin (both the topical cream and 0.2 percent solution), 1 percent Silvadene cream, and topical antibiotics containing bacitracin, neomycin and polymyxin B (triple antibiotic). Apply the topical antibiotic directly to the wound or place it first on a gauze pad. Change the dressing once or twice a day to facilitate pus drainage.

Antibiotics are frequently used for bite wounds and wounds that are heavily contaminated, such as puncture wounds.

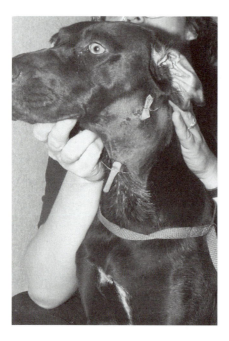

A wound sutured around a drain allows for through and through flushing.

Puncture wounds are caused by bites and pointed objects. Animal bites, in particular, are heavily contaminated with bacteria. Bleeding may occur. There may also be bruising, particularly if the dog was picked up in the teeth of a bigger dog and shaken. Puncture wounds are often concealed by the dog's coat and easily overlooked until an abscess develops a few days later.

Treatment of a puncture wound involves surgically enlarging the skin opening to provide drainage, after which the area is irrigated with a dilute antiseptic surgical solution. These wounds should not be sutured. With all animal bites, keep in mind the possibility of rabies.

BANDAGING

Wounds can be left open or bandaged, depending on their location and other factors. Wounds about the head and neck are often left open to facilitate treatment. Many wounds of the upper body are difficult to bandage and do not benefit greatly from being covered.

Bandaging has the advantage of protecting the wound from dirt and contaminants. It also restricts movement, compresses skin flaps, eliminates pockets of serum, keeps the edges of the wound from pulling apart, and prevents the dog from biting and licking at the wound. Bandaging is most effective for wounds to the extremities. In fact, nearly all leg and foot wounds can benefit from a bandage.

Dressings over draining or infected wounds must be changed once or twice a day. The bandage should be bulky enough to absorb the drainage without soaking through.

Foot and Leg Bandages

To bandage the foot, place several sterile gauze pads over the wound and secure with adhesive tape. Be careful not to make the tape too tight. To secure a foot dressing, you will need to continue the bandage up the leg.

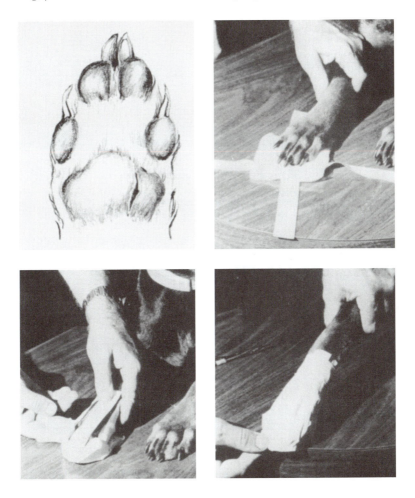

Applying a foot bandage for a lacerated pad. Finish with a leg bandage to hold the foot bandage in place.

For leg wounds, cover the wound with sterile gauze pads. On top, pad the entire leg with plenty of cotton so the dressing won't become too tight and interfere with the circulation. Wrap the leg with elastic tape or bandage, as shown in the photographs. Flex the knee and foot several times to be sure the bandage is not too tight and that there is good movement at the joints.

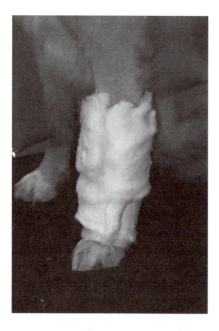

To make a leg bandage, apply a gauze square over the wound and pad the leg well.

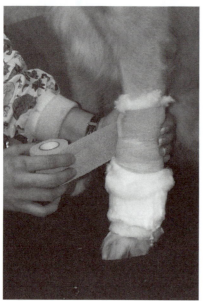

Wrap the leg with an elastic tape or bandage. Do not stretch the elastic wrap as you apply it, or the dressing will be too tight.

Over the next few hours, check the toes for coolness and observe the feet for swelling. Swelling of the leg below a bandage will be seen in the toes. When the toes are swollen, the nails are spread apart instead of being side-by-side. If this swelling is not treated by removing the bandage, the foot becomes cold and loses feeling. If there is any question about the circulation, remove the dressing.

Bandages over clean, healing wounds can be changed every two days, but should be inspected twice daily for signs of constriction, limb swelling, slippage, drainage or soiling. If there are signs of any of these problems, replace the bandage.

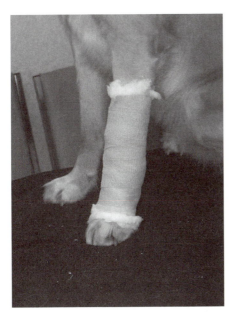

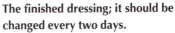

The finished dressing; it should be changed every two days.

Many-Tailed Bandage

This type of bandage is used to hold dressings in place and to protect the covered skin from the dog's scratching and biting. It is made by taking a rectangular piece of linen and cutting the sides to make tails. Tie the tails together over the dog's back to hold the bandage in place.

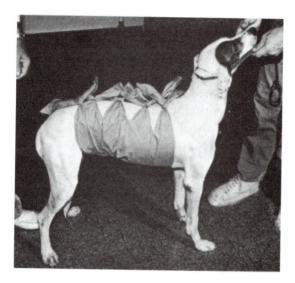

A many-tailed bandage.
(J. Clawson)

Eye Bandage

Your veterinarian may prescribe an eye bandage to help treat an eye ailment. Place a sterile gauze square over the affected eye and hold it in place by taping it around the head with one-inch-wide adhesive. Be careful not to get the tape too tight. Apply the dressing so that the ears are free. You may be required to change the dressing from time to time to apply medication to the eye.

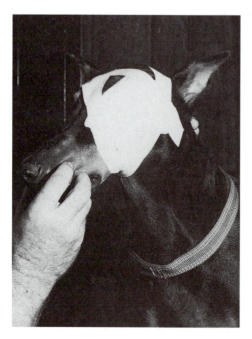

An eye bandage, properly applied.
(J. Clawson)

INTESTINAL PARASITES

Most dog owners believe that if a dog has eggs or parasites in his stools, he must be suffering from an intestinal infestation. This is not necessarily the case. Although nearly all dogs are infested with parasites at one time or another, most develop an immunity that keeps the worms in check. This immunity can break down, however, under conditions of stress or ill health. When that happens, the worms increase in number and eventually produce signs of intestinal infection, including diarrhea, weight loss, anemia and blood in the feces.

Dogs develop the highest level of immunity to worms that have a larval phase that migrates in tissue. These are the ascarids, hookworms and threadworms. Whipworms and tapeworms, however, do not have a migratory phase and thus produce little immunity.

Immunosuppressive drugs such as cortisone have been shown to activate large numbers of encysted hookworm larvae. Stressful events such as pregnancy, surgery, severe illness, trauma and emotional upsets (such as shipping or going to a new home) can also activate dormant larvae.

Dewormers for Puppies and Adult Dogs

Although some deworming preparations are effective against more than one species of worm, no preparation is effective against them all. A specific diagnosis is required to choose the safest and most effective drug. This requires an examination of stools and identification of the egg, larval or adult stage of the parasite. It is not advisable to deworm a dog suffering from an unexplained illness assumed to be caused by "worms."

All *anthelmintics* (medications that act to expel or destroy parasitic intestinal worms) are poisons—meant to poison the worm but not the dog. Dogs debilitated by heartworms or some other infection may be too weak to resist the toxicity of the dewormer. If there is any doubt, be sure to check with your veterinarian before using any dewormer. It is also important to give the medication exactly as prescribed.

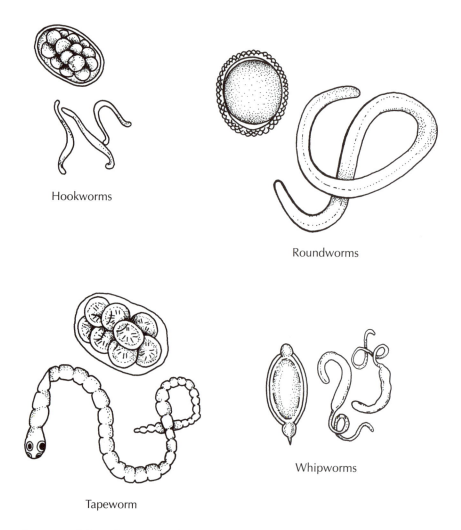

Hookworms

Roundworms

Tapeworm

Whipworms

Common adult canine worms, showing the relative size and appearance of adult worms and eggs. The eggs are magnified 500x.

Deworming agents that are effective against various species of worm are listed in the table on page 48.

Deworming Puppies

Most young puppies are infested with roundworms. Other worm parasites may also be present, but they're not as common. It is advisable to have your veterinarian check your puppy's stool before deworming for roundworms, because if other worms are present, a broad-spectrum deworming agent may be recommended.

Puppies should be dewormed at two weeks of age (before roundworm eggs are passed in the stool) and again at four, six and eight weeks of age. This schedule kills all roundworms, whether acquired *in utero*, through infected milk or by ingesting the eggs. Pyrantel pamoate (Nemex) is an excellent choice for roundworms and can be safely given to two-week-old puppies. It is available as a liquid suspension or tablet (see *How to Give Medications* in Chapter 20).

Worm medications can be harmful to puppies that are ill from a respiratory infection, chilled, crowded in unsanitary surroundings or abruptly weaned from their mothers. Stressful conditions such as these should be corrected before administering the dewormer. Do not deworm a puppy that has diarrhea unless your veterinarian has determined that the diarrhea is caused by the parasite.

Deworming Adult Dogs

Most veterinarians recommend that adult dogs be dewormed only when there is specific reason to do so, such as when eggs or parasites are found during a fecal examination.

Most dogs carry ascarids as encysted larvae, but intestinal infestation by the adult worm is rare in the healthy dog. Hookworms are likely to be a problem in adults only during periods of stress. Routine deworming may catch an intestinal phase, but only milbemycin (Interceptor) is effective against encysted larvae.

Whipworms are a frequent cause of acute and chronic diarrhea in adult dogs. They are difficult to diagnose on routine fecal examination. Eradication requires the use of specific agents not commonly used for other worms.

Tapeworms are common in dogs but, fortunately, cause few symptoms. The worm segments are easy to detect in the stool. Threadworms are not common. Very few agents are effective against this parasite.

A brood bitch should have her stool checked prior to breeding. If parasites are found, she should be dewormed. Deworming during pregnancy should be done only as determined by your veterinarian. Note that some dewormers are contraindicated during pregnancy. See accompanying table.

How to Control Worms

The life cycle of most worms is such that the possibility of reinfestation is great. To keep worms under control, one must destroy the eggs and larvae *before* they reinfest the dog. This means good sanitation and maintaining clean, dry quarters.

Dogs should not be kenneled on dirt runs, which provide ideal conditions for seeding eggs and larvae. A watertight surface, such as cement, is the easiest to keep clean. Gravel is a good substitute. It provides effective drainage and allows for easy removal of stools. Hose down each kennel or run daily and allow it to dry in the sun.

Deworming Agents

Type of Worm Involved

Drug	Hook	Ascarid	Whip	Tape	Comments
CANOPAR (Thenium Closylate)	**	—	—	—	Do not use in nursing puppies or lactating females. Dose is weight related. Avoid in Airedales. May induce vomiting.
CESTEX (Espisprantel)	—	—	—	***	Do not use in puppies younger than 7 weeks old.
DICHLORVOS (Many trade names)	***	***	**	—	Do not use if dog is debilitated or has heartworms, liver or kidney disease. May increase the effects of insecticides in coat preparations and flea collars.
DRONTAL PLUS (Praziquantel, Pyrantel Pamoate, Febantel)	***	***	***	***	Available in 2 tablet sizes, depending on the weight of the dog. Broad-spectrum. Do not use in pregnant bitches and puppies less than 3 weeks old or weighing less than 2 pounds.
DRONCIT (Praziquantel)	—	—	—	***	Single dose. Available as a pill or injection.
FILARBITS PLUS (Oxibendazole, Diethylcarbamizine)	**	**	*	—	Used primarily for heartworm prevention, but is contraindicated if microfilariae are present in the blood. Can be used in puppies 8 weeks and older as a daily tablet. Can cause liver dysfunction.
INTERCEPTOR (Milbemycin Oxime)	**	**	**	—	One tablet a month prevents heartworms and controls hookworms, ascarids and whipworms. Can be used in puppies 8 weeks and older. Wide margin of safety. Does not cause a problem in Collies. Contraindicated if microfilaria are present in the blood.
IVOMEC (Ivermectin)	**	**	**	—	Approved only for heartworm prevention. Non-heartworm doses may cause death in herding breeds and their mixes.
NEMEX (Pyrantel Pamoate)	***	***	—	—	Safe. Can be given to nursing puppies. Available as liquid suspension or tablets.
PANACUR (Fenbendazole)	***	***	***	**	Granular formulation. No contraindications.
PIPERAZINE (Many trade names)	—	**	—	—	Inexpensive. Safe. Do not overdose.
TELMINTIC (Mebendazole)	***	***	***	**	Wide range of safety. Give for 3 days.
VERCOM PASTE (Febantel, Praziquantel)	***	***	***	***	Administer to adults by mouth or in food without regard to feeding schedule. Administer to puppies less than 6 months of age only by mouth on a full stomach.

***Excellent **Good *Fair —No effect

Remove stools daily from runs and pens. Lawns should be cut short and watered only when necessary. Stools in the yard should also be removed every day.

Concrete and gravel surfaces can be disinfected with lime or salt. Lime is an alkaline corrosive, so hose down all pens after disinfecting with lime to prevent injury to dogs. Borax (one ounce per 10 square feet) is another good disinfectant.

Kennels that have persistent problems with worms usually have other problems as well, including chronic skin diseases and recurrent respiratory infections. Steps must be taken to improve the management of the kennel, especially in the area of sanitation.

Fleas, lice, cockroaches, beetles, waterbugs and rodents are intermediate hosts of tapeworms and roundworms. To control reinfestation, it is necessary to get rid of these pests (see *Disinfecting the Premises*, Chapter 4).

Many intestinal parasites spend their larval stages in other animals and develop into adults only when the dog eats one of these animals. Preventing dogs from roaming and hunting will reduce exposure to parasites, as well as toxic substances and poisons. Be sure to thoroughly cook all fresh meat before feeding it to your dog.

Heartworm preventives, such as Filaribits Plus and Interceptor, also prevent and control roundworms, hookworms and whipworms. Heartgard Plus controls roundworms and hookworms but not whipworms. These agents are given in low dosages. The beneficial effect lasts only as long as you give the medication.

Ascarids (Roundworms)

Ascarids (roundworms) are the most frequent worm parasite in dogs and cats. There are two species that commonly infect dogs: *Toxocara canis* and *Toxascaris leonina*. Adult roundworms live in the stomach and intestine and can grow to seven inches long. A female may lay 200,000 eggs in a day. The eggs are protected by a hard shell. They are extremely hardy and can live for months or years in the soil.

There are four ways dogs can become infected with roundworms. Prenatal infection occurs when the larvae migrate through the placenta *in utero*. Virtually all puppies are infected in this manner before birth. Milk-borne transmission also occurs. In addition, puppies and adults can become infected by ingesting eggs in the soil. And finally, dogs can acquire the eggs by ingesting a transport or intermediate host.

The life cycle of *T. canis* in young puppies is as follows: Eggs entering through the mouth hatch in the stomach. The larvae are carried to the lungs by the circulatory system. Here they break through the capillaries into the air-sacs, sometimes giving rise to bouts of coughing and gagging. Once in the lungs, the larvae crawl up the windpipe and are swallowed. Back in the intestine the larvae develop into adult worms. The adults pass eggs that become infective in soil in three to four weeks.

Dogs older than six months develop an acquired resistance to roundworms. Few, if any, larvae complete the life cycle. Most come to rest in various body tissues, where they encyst. While encysted, they are protected against the dog's antibodies and also the effects of most dewormers. (Interceptor is an exception. This dewormer has some effect on encysted larvae). During pregnancy, however, encysted larvae are activated and migrate to the placenta and mammary glands. Deworming the dam before pregnancy reduces the burden of migrating larvae but does not eliminate all puppy infestation because there are still encysted larvae in her body.

Roundworms rarely cause symptoms in adult dogs; in puppies older than two months, they usually produce only mild intermittent vomiting and diarrhea. Worms may be found in the vomitus or passed in the stool. Typically, they look like white earthworms or strands of spaghetti that may be moving.

In very young puppies, a heavy infestation can result in severe illness or even death. These puppies often fail to thrive, have a dull coat and a pot-bellied appearance, and are anemic and stunted in growth. Such puppies may experience abdominal pain with whimpering and groaning. Rarely, a tangled mass of worms in the small intestine can cause death from intestinal obstruction.

Treatment: Nemex (pyrantel pamoate suspension) is an excellent dewormer for nursing pups, because it is safe and active against both roundworms and hookworms. This makes it the agent of choice for these youngsters. Pyrantel pamoate dewormers can be obtained from your veterinarian. You do not have to fast your pup before using this agent. Be sure to follow the directions of the manufacturer in regard to dosage.

Puppies should be dewormed by two weeks of age—before they begin to pass roundworm eggs and contaminate the environment. Repeat the treatment at four, six and eight weeks of age. The purpose of retreating is to kill worms that were in the larval stage during the first dewormings. Subsequent treatments are indicated if eggs or worms are found in the stools.

Drontal Plus, Vercom Paste and Panacur have a broad spectrum of activity and are all highly effective against roundworms, hookworms and whipworms. Drontal and Vercom are also highly effective against tapeworms. Panacur is only partially effective against tapeworms. Deworming the brood bitch with Panacur during the last two weeks of gestation and during lactation reduces environmental exposure and helps to control puppy infection.

Drontal Plus comes in two tablet sizes: one for small dogs and another for medium and large dogs. The prescribed number of tablets (based on the dog's weight) is given as a single dose. The dose should be repeated in two to four weeks. Drontal Plus cannot be used in dogs that weigh less than two pounds or in puppies less than three weeks old. A stool sample should be checked following the second course of treatment.

Vercom and Panacur are given daily for three consecutive days. The entire course should be repeated in two to four weeks, followed by a stool check to make sure that the worms have been eliminated.

Prevention: Heartworm preventives such as Interceptor and Filaribits Plus prevent and control roundworms as well as hookworms and whipworms. Heartgard Plus controls roundworms and hookworms but not whipworms.

Public Health Considerations: Roundworms can cause a serious disease in humans called *visceral larva migrans*. The infection is acquired when the eggs of *T. canis* are ingested by a human. Children one to four years old are most frequently affected, and often have a history of dirt-eating. The frequent use of city parks by pets has resulted in heavy contamination of soil and sandboxes in these areas. One study of parks in a large U.S. city revealed that one of three soil samples contained *T. canis* eggs.

When a human eats a roundworm egg, larvae develop as in the dog. However, because humans are not a definitive host, the larvae do not progress to adult roundworms. Instead, they burrow into the intestinal wall and migrate to the liver, lungs and skin. Symptoms, which develop only when the infestation is heavy, include abdominal pain, cough, wheezing, itching and a papular skin rash. In a very heavy infestation larvae may reach the heart, kidneys, spleen, brain, eyes and other tissues.

Prevention of human infection is based on recognizing that the vast majority of eggs excreted in the environment are produced by nursing puppies and lactating bitches. This is one reason why it is so important to deworm puppies before eggs appear in the stools.

Older children should be instructed not to put soil and sand in their mouths. Infants and toddlers require parental supervision to prevent this from happening. Infants and young children should not be allowed to play with and handle nursing pups until they have mastered the discipline of hand-washing after petting an animal. Better enforcement of leash laws and pooper-scooper ordinances would reduce environmental contamination.

Hookworms (Ancylostoma)

There are three species of hookworms that afflict dogs. These parasites are most prevalent in areas of high temperature and humidity (such as the southern United States), where conditions are favorable for the rapid development and spread of larvae.

Hookworms are small, thin worms about one-quarter to one-half inch long. They fasten their mouth parts onto the mucosa of the small intestine and suck blood and tissue fluids from the host. This can result in severe blood loss and malnutrition.

There are five routes by which puppies (and adults) can acquire the infection: migration through the placenta in utero; ingesting larvae in mother's milk; ingesting larvae in the soil; direct penetration of the skin (usually through the pads of the feet); and ingesting an intermediate host.

The majority of serious hookworm infestations in puppies occur during the first two months of life and are acquired through the milk-borne route. Signs of illness are bloody, wine-dark or tar-black diarrhea. Progressive blood loss may cause these puppies to rapidly sicken and die. Intensive veterinary management is required.

In adult dogs, the most common routes of infection are ingesting larvae and larvae migrating through the skin. Some larvae encyst in tissues, while others migrate through the lungs to the intestine where they mature into adults. In two to three weeks the dog begins to pass eggs in the feces. These eggs incubate in the soil. Under proper conditions, the eggs hatch in 48 hours and release larvae that are infective in five to seven days.

Dogs with chronic hookworm often have no symptoms. When symptoms do occur they include tarry or bloody diarrhea, pale mucous membranes caused by anemia, weight loss and emaciation, and progressive weakness. Symptoms can appear as early as 10 days after exposure. The diagnosis is made by finding eggs in the feces. Because eggs do not appear in the feces for two to three weeks, however, there may be an interval during which stool examination is negative, and the diagnosis must be made on the basis of clinical signs.

Most dogs that recover from hookworms become carriers via larvae encysted in tissues. During periods of stress or concurrent illness, these larvae are released and a new outbreak of bloody diarrhea occurs as worms appear in the intestine.

A itchy disease in humans called *cutaneous larvae migrans* (creeping eruption) is caused by the hookworm *A. brasiliense*. Larvae present in soil penetrate the skin, causing lumps and streaks beneath the skin. The condition usually clears up on its own.

Treatment: A number of dewormers are highly effective in treating hookworms. They include Nemex, Panacur, Drontal Plus and Vercom Paste. Treatment should be repeated in one to two weeks, because the initial deworming activates encysted larvae and causes a new crop of adult worms to appear in 10 to 12 days.

Prevention: Good sanitation and periodic stool checks with appropriate deworming will prevent the serious consequences of hookworms. In addition, heartworm preventives such as Interceptor and Filaribits Plus are also effective against hookworms, roundworms and whipworms. Heartgard Plus controls hookworms and roundworms but not whipworms.

Tapeworms

Tapeworms live in the small intestine and vary from less than an inch to several feet in length. The head (*scolex*) of the worm fastens to the wall of the gut by hooks and suckers. The body is composed of segments that contain the egg packets. To cure tapeworm infection, the head must be destroyed. If it is not, the worm will regenerate.

The body segments containing the eggs are passed in the feces. Fresh, moist segments are about a quarter-inch long and are capable of moving. Occasionally you may see them crawling through the fur near your dog's anus. When dry, they resemble kernels of rice. Some individual dogs experience anal itching from the segments. Aside from this symptom, tapeworms cause no apparent harm to the dog.

The common tapeworm of dogs is *Diphylidium caninum*. Fleas and lice serve as intermediate hosts when they ingest the eggs. A dog must bite or swallow an infected flea or louse to acquire the parasite. A human could also acquire *D. caninum* if they accidentally swallow an infected flea.

Several species of *Taenia*, another type of tapeworm, parasitize dogs. Taenia are acquired by eating infected rodents, rabbits and sheep. *Diphyllobothrium* species are found encysted in the organs of fish. These tapeworms are found in the northern United States and Canada.

Echinococcus tapeworms are uncommon in dogs. Intermediate hosts are deer, elk, goats, sheep, cattle, swine, horses and some rodents.

Treatment: Droncit, Cestex, Drontal Plus and Vercom Paste are highly effective against all the common dog tapeworms. Use them under veterinary guidance.

Prevention: The common dog tapeworm can be controlled by eliminating fleas and lice from the environment, as described in Chapter 4, *Disinfecting the Premises*. Dogs should be confined to prevent them from roaming and eating dead animals. Avoid feeding your dog uncooked meat and raw game.

Public Health Considerations: *Echinococcus granulosa* is a significant public health problem. Dogs and humans can acquire the infection from eating

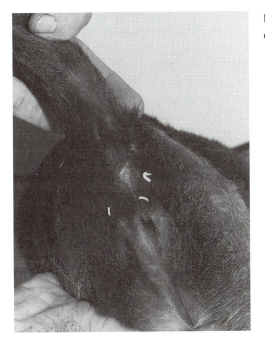

Fresh tapeworm segments about one-quarter inch long.

contaminated uncooked meat, and, in the case of dogs, by feeding on the carcass of an infected animal. Humans can also acquire the disease by ingesting eggs passed in the feces of dogs. Since humans are not the definitive host, adult worms do not develop. Instead, the larvae produce large cysts in the liver, lungs and brain. These cysts are called hydatids, and they can cause serious illness and even death.

Echinococcus granulosus is found in the southern, western and southwestern United States—areas where sheep and cattle are common. Although dog-to-human transmission is rare, a number of human cases (presumably from eating uncooked meat) are reported each year. If your dog runs free in a rural area where this tapeworm could be a problem, ask your veterinarian to check the stools for tapeworms twice a year. This species of tapeworm can be identified only after the head has been recovered by effective deworming. Until a definite diagnosis is made, a dog with a tapeworm that could be *Echinococcus* must be handled with extreme care to avoid fecal contamination of hands and food.

Whipworms

The adult whipworm is two to three inches long. It is threadlike for the most part, but is thicker at one end, which gives it the appearance of a whip.

The adult worm lives in the last part of the small intestine and the first part of the large intestine, where it fastens to the wall of the gut. The female lays fewer eggs than other worms, and there are long periods during which eggs are not shed. Accordingly, identifying eggs in the feces is difficult, even with repeated stool examinations.

Whipworms can cause acute, chronic and intermittent diarrhea in dogs. Typically the stool is mucoid and bloody. The diarrhea is often accompanied by urgency and straining (see *Colitis*, Chapter 9). Dogs with a heavy infestation may lose weight, fail to thrive and develop anemia.

Treatment: A number of preparations are effective against whipworms. They include Panacur, Drontal Plus and Vercom Paste. However, it is difficult to attain high drug concentrations in the colon, where the whipworms reside, and this makes them difficult to eradicate. To maximize success, follow up the initial deworming with a second deworming three weeks later, and a third deworming in three months.

Prevention: Eggs remain infective in the environment for up to five years. In areas such as public parks and back yards where the ground has been heavily contaminated with whipworm eggs, frequent reinfection is a common problem. It is important to observe pooper-scooper ordinances and remove stools in the yard daily. Dirt runs should be relocated and paved with concrete or new gravel. Use household bleach in a 1:32 dilution to disinfect concrete and gravel runs.

The drugs Interceptor and Filaribits Plus, given to prevent heartworms, also controlling and prevent whipworms.

Threadworms (Strongyloides)

Threadworms are round worms just 2 millimeters long that live in the small intestine and infect both dogs and humans. The parasite is found in humid, subtropical regions such as the southeastern United States and Gulf Coast areas.

The life cycle of the threadworm is complex. Eggs and larvae are passed in the feces. Larvae become infective and are either ingested or gain entrance by directly penetrating the skin.

Threadworms are mainly a problem in puppies. Infected pups suffer from a profuse watery or bloody diarrhea that can be fatal. Pneumonia may occur as the larvae migrate through the lungs.

Treatment: The diagnosis is made by finding eggs or larvae on microscopic examination of stool, both fresh and after incubation. A five-day course of Panacur is the treatment of choice. Retreatment in 30 days is recommended. Ivermectin has also been used effectively, although it is not labeled for this purpose.

Public Health Considerations: Dogs can readily infect humans, and vice versa. *Strongyloides* infection in humans is a debilitating disease accompanied by chronic diarrhea. Accordingly, infected pups must be isolated until treated and cured. Extreme care must be taken to avoid human contact with the feces of threadworm-infected dogs.

Other Worm Parasites

PINWORMS

Pinworms are sometimes a concern to families with pets and children. However, dogs and cats are not a source of human pinworm infection as they do not acquire or spread this disease.

TRICHINOSIS

This is a disease acquired by ingesting uncooked pork containing the encysted larvae of *Trichina spiralis*. In humans, only a few cases are reported each year. The incidence is probably somewhat higher in dogs. Prevent trichinosis by keeping your dog from roaming, especially if you live in a rural area. Cook all fresh meat for consumption by you *and* your dog.

LUNGWORMS

Lungworms are slender hairlike parasites about one centimeter long. There are several species of lungworm that affect dogs. *Capillaria aerophila* is acquired by ingesting eggs or a transport host. These parasites reside in the nasal cavity and upper air passages, producing a mild cough. *Filaroides* species produce a tracheal and bronchial infection that tends to be a kennel-related problem, especially in Greyhounds.

Most dogs with lungworms have mild infections and do not show clinical signs. Heavily infested dogs (usually under two years of age) may have a persistent dry cough, weight loss and exercise intolerance.

Diagnosis is based on clinical signs, a chest X-ray (not always positive), and identification of the eggs or larvae in stools or respiratory secretions. *Bronchoscopy* in a *Filaroides* infection may reveal small nodules in the wall of the trachea. Larvae may be seen peeking out of these growths.

LUNG FLUKES

The lung fluke *Paragonimus kellicotti* infects dogs living around the Great Lakes, in the Midwest and in the southern United States. Flukes are flatworms ranging in size from a few millimeters up to one or two inches in length. The disease is acquired by eating aquatic snails and crayfish. Cysts develop in the lungs. Rarely, a cyst ruptures and causes a collapsed lung (*pneumothorax*).

The safest and most effective agent for treating all species of lungworm and lung flukes is Panacur. The drug must be given daily for 10 days. Prevent lungworms by cooking fish and restricting your dog's hunting forays.

HEARTWORMS

Heartworms are common in dogs. They are discussed in Chapter 11.

C h a p t e r **3**

INFECTIOUS DISEASES

Infectious diseases are caused by bacteria, viruses, protozoa, fungi and rickettsia that invade the body of a susceptible host and cause an illness. They are transmitted from one animal to another by contact with infected urine, feces and other bodily secretions, or by inhaling germ-laden droplets. They may also be acquired by contact with spores in the soil that enter the body through the respiratory tract or a break in the skin. A few are sexually transmitted. Although germs exist throughout the environment, only a few cause infection. Fewer still are contagious.

Bacteria are single-celled germs. *Viruses*, the tiniest germs known, are even more basic than cells—they are simply packages of molecules. *Protozoa* are also single-celled organisms that are usually carried in water. *Fungi* are a large family that includes mushrooms. Many types of fungi spread via airborne spores. *Rickettsia* are various disease-causing bacteria that are carried as parasites by fleas, ticks and lice.

Many infectious agents are able to survive for long periods outside of the host animal. This knowledge is important in determining how to contain the spread of infection.

Antibodies and Immunity

An animal that is immune to a specific germ has chemical substances in his system called antibodies that attack and destroy that germ before it can cause disease.

Natural immunity can be species related. For example, a dog cannot catch a disease that is specific to a horse, and vice versa. But many infectious diseases are not specific; they are capable of causing disease in many animals, including humans.

When a dog becomes ill with an infectious disease, his immune system makes antibodies against that particular germ. These antibodies protect the dog against reinfection. The dog has acquired active immunity. Active immunity is self-perpetuating, in that the dog continues to make antibodies long after the disease

57

has gone away. The duration of active immunity varies, depending on the germ and the dog. Following natural exposure, active immunity often persists for life.

Active immunity also can be induced by vaccination. The dog is exposed to heat-killed germs, live or attenuated germs rendered incapable of disease, or toxins and germ products. As with natural exposure, vaccination stimulates the production of antibodies that are specific for the particular germ in the vaccine. However, unlike natural exposure, the duration of protection is limited. Accordingly, to maintain high levels of protection, booster vaccines will be needed.

Vaccinations may not be successful in all dogs. Run-down, malnourished, debilitated dogs may not be capable of responding to a disease challenge by developing antibodies or building immunity. Such dogs can be vaccinated, but should be revaccinated when they're in better health. Immunosuppressive drugs, such as cortisone and chemotherapy agents, depress the immune system and also prevent the body from making antibodies.

Another type of immunity is called passive. Passive immunity is passed from one animal to another. The classic example is the antibodies newborn pups absorb from the first milk (*colostrum*) of their mother. Puppies are best able to absorb antibodies from mother's milk during the first 24 hours of life. The immunity persists only as long as the antibodies remain in the puppies' circulation. The duration of immunity depends on the concentration of antibodies in maternal milk when the pups were born. Dams vaccinated just before they were bred have the highest antibody levels, capable of protecting puppies for up to 16 weeks.

Puppies less than three weeks old may be incapable of developing antibodies in response to vaccination because of physical immaturity or interference by passive maternally acquired antibodies. Maternal antibodies can bind the antigen in the vaccine and keep it from stimulating the immune system. As noted, these passive antibodies disappear at between six and 16 weeks of age. When vaccinating very young puppies, the vaccine must be given repeatedly (every two weeks) to ensure that the vaccine will stimulate immunity as soon as maternal antibody levels decline to levels that no longer interfere with the vaccine.

Vaccinations

TYPES OF VACCINES

There are three types of vaccines currently available for use in dogs: *modified live virus* (MLV), *inactivated* or *killed virus*, and *recombinant* vaccines. Modified live vaccines are more effective and produce longer-lasting immunity than do killed vaccines. Recombinant vaccines are too new to establish the duration of immunity for each product, but preliminary results indicate that immunity can last as long as MLVs. With all types of vaccine, booster shots are necessary to maintain an adequate level of protection.

Recombinant vaccines are among the newest products in the rapidly emerging biotechnology market. The technology relies on the ability to splice gene-sized fragments of DNA from one organism (a virus or bacteria) and to deliver these fragments to another organism (the dog), where they stimulate the production of antibodies. Thus, recombinant vaccines deliver specific antigen material on a cellular level without the risk of vaccination reactions associated with giving the entire disease-causing organism. This represents a truly new development. It is expected that recombinant vaccines will soon replace MLVs and whole killed vaccines for many, if not most, canine infectious disease vaccinations.

THE REVACCINATION DEBATE

A subject of much debate in the field of immunology is the timing of booster injections. Based on a growing body of evidence, recommendations for booster vaccinations may soon be changing. It is now believed that the protective response to vaccines for distemper, parvovirus and rabies probably persists for several years following a vaccination series, and that booster shots can be given every three years instead of every year (as is the current practice).

On the other hand, evidence also suggests that vaccines for parainfluenza, bordetella bronchiseptica and leptospirosis fail to protect for the full 12 months. These vaccines probably should be given twice a year, rather than annually (as is the current practice), especially to dogs at increased risk.

WHY VACCINES FAIL

Vaccines are highly effective in preventing certain infectious diseases in dogs, but failures do occur. Failures can be due to improper vaccine handling and storage, incorrect administration, inability of the dog to respond because of a depressed immune system, or the presence of neutralizing maternal antibodies.

Stretching out the vaccine by dividing a single dose between two dogs is another reason why a vaccine may not be effective. And if the dog is already infected, vaccinating it will not alter the course of the disease.

Because proper handling and administration of vaccines is so essential, vaccinations should be given by those familiar with the technique. In addition, when you go to your veterinarian for a booster shot, your dog will get a physical checkup and a fecal exam. The veterinarian may detect worm parasites or some other condition of which you were not aware.

Diseases and Their Vaccines

Young puppies are highly susceptible to certain infectious diseases and should be vaccinated against them as soon as they are old enough to build immunity. These diseases are distemper, infectious hepatitis, parvovirus, parainfluenza and rabies. Leptospirosis, coronavirus, bordetella bronchiseptica and Lyme disease vaccinations are optional, depending on the occurrence of these diseases in your area.

CANINE DISTEMPER VACCINE

The first distemper shot should be given shortly after weaning and before a puppy is placed in his new home and exposed to other dogs. Most veterinarians recommend vaccinating puppies at five to six weeks of age using a combination canine distemper-measles-parainfluenza vaccine.

The rationale for combining distemper and measles vaccines is that a high percentage of six-week-old puppies do not get a satisfactory response from the distemper vaccine alone because of maternal antibodies that neutralize the distemper antigen. The measles virus, which is quite similar to the distemper virus, can overcome maternal antibody interference and induce partial distemper protection. Alternatively, if maternal antibodies have actually disappeared in the six-week-old puppy, the distemper portion of the vaccine will induce complete protection. The distemper-measles vaccine should be used only once, for the first vaccination.

Postvaccination encephalitis has occasionally occurred when an MLV distemper vaccine has been used along with a parvovirus vaccine in pups younger than six to eight weeks of age. Therefore, parvovirus vaccine should not be used along with the first distemper vaccination.

Puppies younger than eight to nine weeks of age should be revaccinated every two to four weeks until 16 weeks of age. Current recommendations are to revaccinate annually. A recombinant distemper vaccine is now available.

INFECTIOUS HEPATITIS VACCINE

The infectious hepatitis vaccine is a Modified Live Virus Vaccine containing CAV-2. This vaccine protects against canine hepatitis and two of the adenoviruses involved in the kennel cough complex (CAV-1 and CAV-2).

Hepatitis vaccines containing CAV-1 caused clouding of the clear window of the eye (called *blue eye*) two weeks after vaccination, and are no longer used. Hepatitis Vaccine is incorporated into the DHPP shot which is given at eight to 12 weeks of age and again at 16 weeks of age. Annual vaccination is recommended, although initial immunity may persist for life.

LEPTOSPIROSIS BACTERIN

Leptospira bacterin protects against two of the four subspecies of bacteria that cause leptospirosis. The bacterin is incorporated into a DHLPP shot given at 12 weeks of age and again at 16 weeks of age.

Leptospira bacterin is responsible for 70 percent of post-vaccination DHLPP anaphylactic shock reactions. In addition, the vaccine currently available does not protect against the two species that are currently responsible for the majority of cases. Accordingly, routine vaccination is now considerd optional by many veterinarians. It is still indicated in areas where the risk of the disease is greater than the risk of the vaccination.

A vaccine is being developed that will protect dogs against all four species, and should be available in the near future. This may change the recommendations given in the *Suggested Vaccination Schedule* on page 63.

Immunity following vaccination averages about four to six months. Therefore, if vaccination is undertaken, it may be advisable to revaccinate every six months. Discuss this with your veterinarian.

CANINE PARVOVIRUS VACCINE

Commercially available vaccines effectively cross-protect against all the current strains of parvo, including the recently identified variant strains. Because the age at which individual pups can respond to parvovirus vaccination varies, all puppies should receive a series of two to four vaccinations starting at eight weeks of age and concluding at 16 weeks of age.

New high titer–low passage vaccines are more effective than older vaccines even in the presence of maternal antibodies, and have narrowed the window of susceptibility that occurs between declining levels of maternal antibodies and acquired immunity produced by the vaccine. This has resulted in fewer vaccine failures.

Even after a pup has received his first series of vaccinations, he should not be exposed to dogs that may be a source of infection until after he receives his final vaccination at 16 weeks of age. Annual boosters are required to maintain immunity.

In unvaccinated dogs older than 16 weeks, give two doses of vaccine two weeks apart. Brood bitches should be vaccinated two to four weeks before breeding to ensure high levels of antibody in their colostrum.

CORONAVIRUS VACCINE

Vaccination against coronavirus does not prevent the disease, but may reduce the severity of the illness. This is a mild disease and is rarely fatal. Accordingly, many veterinarians do not routinely vaccinate against coronavirus. However, the vaccine may be incorporated into the other vaccines your dog is receiving.

Consider immunization for show dogs, dogs living and boarding in kennels, and others at high risk of exposure. Puppies should be vaccinated at 12 weeks of age and again at 16 weeks. Unvaccinated adults should receive two vaccinations four weeks apart. Annual boosters are required.

RABIES VACCINE

The first rabies vaccination should be given at three months of age, with the first booster shot given one year later (at 15 months of age). Thereafter, give boosters annually or every three years, according to state and local statutes.

CANINE PARAINFLUENZA VACCINE

Parainfluenza is the principal virus implicated in the kennel cough complex. Vaccines will decrease the prevalence and severity of the infection. Parainfluenza is incorporated into the canine distemper-measles-parainfluenza and DHPP shots. The first dose is given at five to six weeks of age; the second and third doses at eight to 12 and 16 weeks of age. An intranasal vaccine combined with bordetella vaccine is also available.

The injectable parainfluenza vaccine protects against disease but does not eliminate the virus from nasal secretions. That means dogs can still transmit the infection. The intranasal vaccine protects against both disease and infection, thus eliminating the possibility of transmitting the disease to other dogs.

Annual boosters are recommended by the manufacturer. However, evidence suggests that parainfluenza vaccines do not always protect for the full 12 months, and in many cases should be given twice a year, especially for dogs at increased risk.

BORDETELLA VACCINE

Bordetella bronchiseptica vaccines are of some help in controlling kennel cough and other respiratory infections caused by this bacteria. Show dogs, boarded dogs and dogs living in kennels may benefit from this optional protection.

There are two vaccine types available to prevent bordetella. One is an intranasal vaccine and the other is injectable. The intranasal vaccine, which protects against parainfluenza as well as bordetella, gives the most immediate immunity.

The injectable bacterin must be given twice. The first injection is given at five to six weeks of age and is repeated two to four weeks later. Puppies born in high-risk areas where bordetella is prevalent can be vaccinated with the intranasal vaccine at three weeks of age.

As with parvovirus, annual boosters are recommended by the manufacturer. But because of the short duration of immunity, semi-annual boosters may be more appropriate.

A VACCINATION SCHEDULE

This suggested vaccination schedule should provide adequate protection at minimum cost. Because of new and forthcoming developments in vaccination technology, these recommendations may well be subject to change in the near future. Follow the recommendations of your veterinarian in all cases.

Suggested Vaccination Schedule	
Age of Dog	**Vaccine Recommended**
5 to 6 weeks	Distemper-measles-parainfluenza, Bordetella*
8 to 12 weeks	DHPP (distemper, hepatitis, parainfluenza, parvovirus), Coronavirus*, Leptospirosis*, Bordetella*, Lyme disease*
12 weeks	Rabies
16 weeks	DHPP, Coronavirus*, Lyme disease*, Leptospirosis*
15 to 16 months (first booster)	Rabies, DHPP, Coronavirus*, Leptospirosis*, Bordetella*, Lyme disease*
Annual booster (12 months after first booster)	DHPP, Coronavirus*, Leptospirosis*, Bordetella*, Lyme disease*
Booster every 1 to 3 years	Rabies

* These vaccinations are optional, but may be advisable in dogs at high risk in endemic areas.

The above vaccination schedule should be modified under the following circumstances:

1. If the puppies receive no colostrum from the dam, start immunizations at three weeks of age.

2. Give females a DHPP booster two to four weeks before breeding.

3. Some rabies boosters are required at one-year intervals, others at three years. Follow the instructions of the manufacturer and those of your veterinarian. Local statutes often determine when the booster should be given.

4. Parainfluenza and leptospirosis vaccinations may be indicated twice a year in endemic areas.

5. Bordetella may be indicated for show dogs, kennel dogs, dogs that are boarded and others at high risk for exposure to the kennel cough complex. Boosters may be indicated twice a year in endemic areas.

Canine Bacterial Diseases

BRUCELLOSIS

This disease is caused by the bacteria *Brucella canis*. It is a major cause of sterility and spontaneous abortion in dogs. Puppies infected *in utero* are typically aborted at 45 to 59 days after conception. Suspect this disease in any bitch who aborts two weeks prior to term, and whenever a bitch delivers stillborn puppies or puppies that sicken and die.

Dogs with acute infection have enlarged lymph nodes in the groin and/or beneath the jaw. Fever is rare. The testicles of the male may swell in the initial stages, and then become smaller and *atrophic* as the sperm-producing cells are destroyed. Note, however, that this disease can infect a dog or bitch without producing any signs of illness.

During an acute infection, bacteria are found in the blood, urine, body secretions and the products of abortion. During chronic or inactive infection bacteria can be transmitted in vaginal secretions during estrus and in semen.

The most common mode of transmission is by contact with infected vaginal discharges following a spontaneous abortion, and by contact with the urine of infected dogs. The disease can spread rapidly throughout a kennel in this manner. Males can acquire the disease through oral and nasal contact with the vaginal secretions of an estrus females. Females can acquire the disease through breeding. This is of particular concern to breeders, because males can harbor the bacteria for life.

A positive blood culture obtained during the acute infection is the most conclusive diagnostic test. Bacteria can also be cultured from aborted tissue. Blood serum tests will determine if a dog has ever been infected.

Treatment: Brucellosis is difficult to eradicate. A course of intramuscular and oral antibiotics given for at least three weeks will eliminate the disease in 80 percent of dogs. As a further precaution, spay or neuter all infected animals to prevent the transmission of disease to other dogs. Since a cure is possible, an exception can be considered for a valuable breeding animal. Discuss the implications of this with your veterinarian.

Prevention: All animals should be tested before entry into a breeding program. Brood bitches should be re-tested one month before each breeding and stud dogs re-tested at least once or twice a year.

Rare instances of human infection have followed exposure to canine brucellosis. It is important to wear rubber gloves and take proper hygienic precautions when handling all aborted products of conception.

LEPTOSPIROSIS

Canine leptospirosis is a disease caused by a type of bacteria called *spirochetes*. There are four species that can infect dogs. Leptospira are found in wild and domestic animals. The bacteria are spread in the urine, often making their way into water sources and remaining infective in the soil for up to six months. Rats, pigs, cattle, skunks and opossums appear to be the primary reservoirs.

Spirochetes enter a dog's system through a break in the skin or when the dog drinks water contaminated by infected urine. Dogs that spend a lot of time in the water are at increased risk. Most infections are mild and do not show clinical signs.

Signs appear 4 to 12 days after exposure. Fever is present in the early stage. Other signs are loss of appetite for several days, vomiting, lethargy, depression, muscle pain and sometimes diarrhea or blood in the urine. Leptospirosis primarily affects the kidneys and liver.

In severe cases the whites of the dog's eyes turn yellow (*jaundice*). This indicates hepatitis with destruction of liver cells. Coagulation problems can ensue, with spontaneous bleeding from the mouth and the presence of blood in the stools. Following recovery, untreated dogs can become carriers and shed bacteria in their urine for up to a year.

Treatment: The diagnosis can be suspect based on the dog's clinical signs. Tests of kidney and liver function will be abnormal. Spirochetes can be detected in the urine and blood by fluorescent antibody staining. Blood tests are available to confirm the diagnosis.

Severely ill dogs should be hospitalized for public health reasons and to provide more intensive care. Antibiotic combinations involving penicillin and streptomycin are effective against the disease. Supportive measures include control of vomiting and diarrhea, correction of dehydration with intravenous fluids, and maintenance of nutrition.

Public Health Considerations: Leptospira cause a disease in humans called *Weil's disease*. People acquire the disease in the same way as dogs. Weil's disease is considered an occupational disease among dairy milkers and people who work around animals.

TETANUS (LOCKJAW)

This is a non-contagious disease caused by the bacteria *Clostridium tetani*. It affects almost all warm-blooded animals, although dogs possess some natural resistance.

The tetanus bacteria is present in the intestinal tract of some animals, where it does not cause disease. It is commonly found in soil contaminated by horse and cow manure. Bacteria enter the skin via a puncture or open wound (a rusty nail is the classic example).

Symptoms can appear as early as a few days after the injury, but are often delayed for several weeks. Tetanus bacteria grow best in tissue where the oxygen concentration is low. The ideal environment is a deep wound that has sealed over, or one in which there is devitalized tissue heavily contaminated with filth. The bacteria produce a toxin that affects the nervous system.

Signs of disease are caused by the neurotoxin. They include spastic contraction and rigid extension of the legs, difficulty opening the mouth and swallowing, retraction of the lips and eyeballs, and protrusion of the third eyelid. Contraction of the forehead muscles can cause the ears to stand erect. Muscle spasms are triggered by almost anything that stimulates the dog. These symptoms are similar to those of *strychnine poisoning*. Death is caused by dehydration, exhaustion and difficulty breathing.

Treatment: Fatalities can be avoided by early veterinary treatment. Tetanus antitoxins, antibiotics, sedatives, intravenous fluids and care of the wound alter the course for the better.

Prevention: The disease can be prevented by prompt attention to skin wounds (see *Wounds* in Chapter 1). Because natural resistance is high in dogs, vaccination is not usually necessary. However, vaccinating herding dogs and those that live around livestock may be advisable.

TUBERCULOSIS

This disease is rare in dogs, and is caused by the tubercle bacillus. It affects humans and all domestic animals. There has been a consistent increase in human tuberculosis in the United States during the past decade, in part due to increased immigration and in part because of the susceptibility of persons with HIV infection to pulmonary tuberculosis. Dogs in contact with infected animals and humans are at increased risk.

In dogs, tuberculosis is primarily a lung infection, and is acquired by inhaling tubercle bacilli. Respiratory tuberculosis causes a chronic cough, labored breathing, shortness of breath and the production of bloody sputum. Low-grade fever with chronic wasting and loss of condition, despite good care and feeding, is common. Diagnosis is made by a positive chest X-ray and the presence of tubercle bacilli in the sputum. An intradermal skin test is available for screening.

Treatment: Treating canine tuberculosis is extremely difficult. Although there have been reports of success with dogs hospitalized and treated with antibiotics over a long period of time, the uncertainty of the outcome, plus the obvious hazard to human health, makes euthanasia the wisest choice.

BORDETELLA BRONCHISEPTICA

Bordetella bronchiseptica is frequently found in dogs with the kennel cough complex and other respiratory diseases. In puppies and immune-compromised adult animals, secondary bacterial invasion of the lower respiratory tract following viral illness may cause life-threatening pneumonia. Accordingly, it is important to treat all upper respiratory infections by placing the animal in a warm, draft-free environment, humidifying the atmosphere and avoiding stressful activities that can interfere with a smooth recovery. Antibiotics are indicated if the dog develops fever and a mucopurulent nasal discharge.

Signs of upper respiratory illness caused by bordetella include a dry, hacking cough accompanied by a clear nasal or eye discharge. The bacteria can be cultured from nasal swabs or *trans-tracheal washings*.

Treatment: Treat bordetella as you would *Kennel Cough Complex* (see Chapter 10). Antibiotics are indicated for all cases of upper respiratory infection in which bordetella is isolated. Antibiotics given by nebulizer may be more effective than those given orally or by injection. This is because the bacteria attach to the mucosal surface of the respiratory tract and are difficult to reach with systemic antibiotics.

Prevention: Bordetella vaccinations are not routine, but may be advisable for show dogs, boarded dogs, and dogs living in kennels. See *Bordetella Vaccine* on page 62.

SALMONELLA

Several bacteria of the salmonella species are capable of producing acute infectious diarrhea in dogs. Salmonella are resistant to environmental factors and remain alive for many months or years in soil and manure. In dogs, the disease is acquired by consuming raw or commercially contaminated foods, by eating animal manure, or by making oral contact with surfaces contaminate by the diarrhea of an infected dog.

Puppies and young adults are most susceptible, as are dogs whose natural resistance has been compromised by a viral infection, malnutrition or being housed in crowded, unsanitary quarters.

Signs of illness include fever, vomiting and diarrhea. The stool may be bloody and foul smelling. Dehydration develops when vomiting and diarrhea are prolonged. Bacteria in the bloodstream can cause abscesses in the liver, kidneys, uterus and lungs. The acute illness, which lasts four to 10 days, may be followed by a chronic diarrhea that persists for more than a month. Dogs with chronic diarrhea shed salmonella in their feces and are a potential source of infection for other animals and humans.

Diagnosis is made by identifying salmonella bacteria in stool cultures when the dog is in the carrier state, or in the feces, blood and infected tissues of dogs suffering from acute infection.

Treatment: Mild cases respond well to fluid replacement. Many salmonella species demonstrate resistance to common antibiotics. In fact, antibiotics can favor the growth of resistant bacteria and prolong fecal shedding of bacteria.

Accordingly, antibiotics are used only for seriously ill dogs. Sulfa drugs and the quinolones are the antibiotics of choice.

CAMPYLOBACTERIOSIS

Campylobacteriosis is a disease that produces acute infectious diarrhea in puppies and kittens. It also occurs in kennel dogs and strays—most of whom are in poor condition and are suffering from other intestinal infections.

The bacteria is acquired by contact with contaminated food, water, uncooked meat (poultry, beef) and animal feces. Campylobacteria can survive for up to five weeks in water or unpasturized milk.

The incubation period is one to seven days. Signs of acute infection include vomiting and a watery diarrhea that contains mucus and sometimes blood. The disease usually runs its course in five to 15 days, but may be followed by chronic diarrhea in which bacteria is shed in the feces.

Treatment: Treat mild diarrhea as described in Chapter 9, *The Digestive System*. Keep the dog warm, dry and in a stress-free environment. More severely affected dogs will require veterinary management with intravenous fluids to correct dehydration. Antibiotics may be advisable. Erythromycin and ciprofloxin are the drugs of choice.

Public Health Considerations: Campylobacteriosis is a common cause of diarrhea in humans. The infection can be devastating, especially in people suffering from alcoholism, cirrhosis, diabetes, valvular heart disease and AIDS. Most human cases arise from contact with newly acquired kittens or puppies suffering from diarrhea. Parents should be aware that puppies and kittens with diarrhea may harbor a human pathogen. These pets should be kept away from small children and ill adults until the animals are cleared by a veterinarian.

COLIOBACILLOSIS *(E. COLI)*

Coliobacillosis is an infectious diarrhea caused by the bacteria *E. coli.* There are some strains of *E. coli* that are not part of the normal intestinal flora. When ingested, these strains are capable of producing acute diarrhea.

E. coli is an important cause of *puppy septicemia* (see Chapter 17). In dogs of all ages a concurrent viral infection of the intestinal tract can permit *E. coli* to become pathogenic and produce a life-threatening illness.

Treatment: Acutely ill dogs must be hospitalized for intensive veterinary management. It is important to maintain strict sanitary precautions when handling infected stools.

Prevention: In humans, outbreaks of severe *E. coli* have occurred after eating undercooked ground beef or unwashed vegetables. *E. coli* is also a prominent cause of traveler's diarrhea. Human infection can be prevented, in part, by washing all raw fruits and vegetables and by avoiding improperly cooked poultry and especially ground meat patties that are still red in the middle.

LYME DISEASE

Lyme disease is caused by the spirochete bacteria *Borrelia burgdorferi*. The spirochete is acquired by the bite of an infected tick. Lyme disease is now regarded as the most common tick-borne illness in the United States.

This disease was first recognized in 1975 following an outbreak of what appeared to be acute arthritis in several rural communities in southeastern Connecticut, including the town of Old Lyme. Currently most cases are found in wooded locations in the Northeast, upper Midwest (including much of Wisconsin and Minnesota), northern California and the Pacific Northwest.

The white-footed mouse is the principal reservoir for the spirochete. Birds can also harbor it. The white-tailed deer supports the tick, but not the spirochete. Lyme disease is spread during tick season (May through August), peaking in the month of July.

The disease in dogs is characterized by the sudden onset of lameness. In fact, lameness is often the only sign of infection. One or more joints may become swollen and painful to the touch. Some dogs run a fever and experience weakness, lethargy, loss of appetite and weight loss. The lameness may last only a few days, but in some cases it becomes chronic and persists or recurs for months.

Serological blood tests will indicate whether a dog has been exposed to the disease. Dogs may not test positive until a few weeks after exposure. False positives occur in dogs vaccinated against Lyme disease. They also occur in endemic areas. A rising antibody titer in the absence of recent vaccination, however, indicates active infection. X-rays of swollen joints show fluid without degenerative joint changes. *Synovial fluid analysis* (in which a needle is inserted into a joint to remove fluid for examination) may show spirochetes.

Treatment: Antibiotics are given for two to four weeks. Ampicillin and doxycycline are among the most effective.

Prevention: Ticks must attach for 5 to 20 hours before they are capable of transmitting infection. Accordingly, a daily inspection with removal of ticks will prevent many dogs from becoming infected.

Tick collars such as Preventic, and tick control on the premises help to reduce the occurrence of Lyme disease. Frontline Spot On is a flea control preparation that kills ticks for up to 30 days following a single application. For more information, see *Ticks* in Chapter 4.

A vaccine is now being widely used to prevent Lyme disease in dogs. The value of the vaccine has not yet been fully established. This optional vaccination may be advisable for dogs at risk for Lyme disease. Discuss this with your veterinarian.

Public Health Considerations: Dogs do not transmit Lyme disease to humans, although they can spread ticks carrying the spirochete. Ticks may transfer to people before feeding on the dog, although this is uncommon. Once a tick starts feeding on a dog, it will not seek a second host. Dispose very carefully of any ticks you remove from your dog. The best method is to put them in a jar with a bit of alcohol, seal the jar, and throw it away.

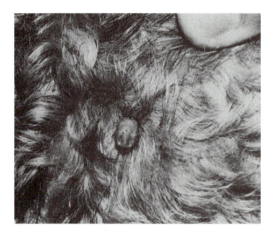

Check your dog daily for ticks during tick season. This is an engorged female tick. (J. Clawson)

More than 16,000 cases of Lyme disease were reported in humans in 46 states in 1996. In humans bitten by an infected tick, a flat or slightly raised skin patch (*macule*) appears at the site of the tick bite 7 to 10 days after exposure (it can range from 3 to 30 days). The macule is present in 75 percent of patients. The macule expands to four to eight inches; it is round or elliptical with a red border and clearing at the center. Shortly thereafter the person develops fever, chills, fatigue, headache, joint pain, backache, stiff neck and swollen lymph nodes. Early antibiotic treatment shortens the course of Lyme disease and helps to prevent late complications. It is important to maintain a high index of suspicion for Lyme disease and consult a physician if there is any question about exposure.

Canine Viral Diseases

DISTEMPER

Distemper is a highly contagious disease caused by a virus similar to the germ that causes measles in people. Worldwide, it is the leading cause of infectious disease deaths in dogs, although in the United States it occurs only sporadically. All unvaccinated dogs are at high risk of infection.

Infected animals shed canine distemper virus in all body secretions. Inhaling the virus is the primary source of exposure. The highest incidence occurs in unvaccinated puppies 6 to 12 weeks of age, at which time maternal antibodies fall below protective levels.

Half the dogs that become infected with canine distemper virus show mild signs of illness or no signs at all. The overall health of the dog has a lot to do with how ill he becomes. The disease is most severe in dogs that are poorly nourished and ill-kept.

The distemper virus has an affinity for attacking brain cells and cells that line the surfaces of the body, including the skin, conjunctiva, the mucous membranes of the breathing tubes and the gastrointestinal tract. The disease takes a variety of forms. Secondary infections and complications are common, partly attributable to the immunosuppressive effects of the virus.

The first signs of distemper appear six to nine days after exposure, and in mild cases go unnoticed:

First Stage. This stage is characterized by a fever spike of up to 103° to 105°F. A second fever spike is accompanied by loss of appetite, listlessness and a watery discharge from the eyes and nose. These symptoms may be mistaken for a cold.

Within a few days the eye and nasal discharge becomes thick, yellow and sticky. The dog develops a pronounced dry cough. Pus blisters may appear on the abdomen. Vomiting and diarrhea are frequent and may cause severe dehydration.

During the next one to two weeks, the dog seems to be getting better but then develops a relapse. This often coincides with the end of the course of antibiotics and the development of gastrointestinal and respiratory complications due to secondary bacterial invasion.

Second Stage. Two to three weeks after the onset of the disease, many dogs develop signs of brain involvement (*encephalitis*), characterized by brief attacks of slobbering, head-shaking, and chewing movements of the jaws (as if the dog were chewing gum). Epilepticlike seizures may occur, in which the dog runs in circles, falls over and kicks all four feet wildly. After the convulsive episode the dog appears confused, shies away from his owner, wanders about aimlessly and appears blind.

In cases with brain involvement and uncertain diagnosis, a spinal tap and analysis of cerebrospinal fluid may be of assistance. But this is not always diagnostic. Another indication of brain involvement is *distemper myoclonus*, a condition characterized by rhythmic contractions of muscle groups at up to 60 contractions per minute. The jerking can affect all parts of the body, but is most common in the head. Myoclonus is first seen when the dog is resting or sleeping. Later it occurs both day and night. Pain accompanies myoclonus, and the dog whines and cries. If the dog recovers, the jerking continues indefinitely—but becomes less severe with time.

Hard-Pad is a form of distemper in which the virus attacks the skin of the feet and nose, producing thick, horny skin on the nose and calluslike pads on the feet. It first appears about 15 days after the onset of the infection. At one time hard-pad and encephalitis were thought to be separate diseases, but they are now recognized as being caused by different strains of the distemper virus. Hard-pad is much less common than it was in the past.

Treatment: Distemper should be treated by a veterinarian. Antibiotics are used to prevent secondary bacterial infections, even though they have no effect on the distemper virus. Supportive treatment includes intravenous fluids to correct dehydration, medications to prevent vomiting and diarrhea, and anticonvulsants and sedatives to control seizures.

The thickened, callused pads of a dog with hard-pad, a form of distemper.

The outcome depends on how quickly the owner seeks professional help, the virulence of the distemper strain, the age of the dog, whether he has been vaccinated, and his ability to mount a rapid and effective immune response to the virus.

Prevention: Vaccination against canine distemper is almost 100 percent protective. All puppies should be vaccinated at five to six weeks of age. Brood bitches should be given a DHPP booster shot two to four weeks before breeding. This ensures that high antibody levels will be present in the colostrum. See *Canine Distemper Vaccine* on page 60.

CANINE HERPESVIRUS INFECTION

Canine herpesvirus is widespread in the dog population and produces a variety of illnesses. It causes a fatal disease in newborn puppies (see *Herpesvirus of Puppies* in Chapter 17). It is one of the agents implicated in the kennel cough complex. It causes vaginitis in bitches and infection of the penile sheath in males, and it can be transmitted between males and females during breeding.

Bitches with vaginitis develop hemorrhagic areas and blisterlike lesions of the vaginal mucosa. These lesions may reappear when the bitch comes into heat. Intrauterine infections that progress from the vagina are associated with early embryonic loss, abortions and stillbirths.

Herpesvirus infection can be confirmed by isolating the virus from infected tissue. There is no effective treatment. A vaccine is not available.

INFECTIOUS CANINE HEPATITIS

Infectious canine hepatitis is a highly contagious viral disease caused by canine adenovirus-1. In the United States the disease is rare and is seen almost exclusively in wild canids and unvaccinated dogs. Most cases occur in puppies under a year of age.

Following exposure, the virus multiplies in the dog's tissues and is shed in all body secretions. During this stage the dog is highly contagious and can spread infection to other dogs that make contact with infected urine, stool and saliva. After he has recovered, the dog remains infective and sheds the virus in the urine for up to nine months.

Infectious canine hepatitis affects the liver, kidneys and lining of the blood vessels, producing a mild infection at one extreme to a rapidly fatal infection at the other. Dogs with a mild or subclinical infection lose their appetite and simply appear lethargic. In the fatal form, the dog becomes suddenly ill, develops bloody diarrhea, collapses and dies within hours. Puppies may die without obvious illness.

A dog with acute infection runs a fever up to 106°F, refuses to eat, passes bloody diarrhea and often vomits blood. The dog has a tucked-up belly caused by painful swelling of the liver. Light is painful to the dog's eyes and causes tearing and squinting. Tonsillitis, spontaneous bleeding beneath the gums and under the skin, and yellowing of the whites of the eyes (*jaundice*) may occur.

About 25 percent of dogs recovering from infectious canine hepatitis develop a characteristic clouding of the cornea of one or both eyes known as *blue eye*. In most cases blue eye disappears within a few days.

Treatment: Infectious hepatitis can be suspected by the signs and symptoms and confirmed by virus isolation tests. Acute cases must be hospitalized for intensive veterinary treatment.

Prevention: Vaccination is highly effective in preventing infectious canine hepatitis (see *Infectious Hepatitis Vaccine*, page 60). Infectious canine hepatitis does not cause hepatitis in humans.

RABIES

Rabies is a fatal disease that occurs in nearly all warm-blooded animals, although rarely in rodents. In the United States, vaccination programs for dogs and other domestic animals have been remarkably effective. This has greatly reduced the risk of rabies in pets and their owners.

The major wildlife reservoirs for rabies (with substantial overlap) are the skunk in the Midwest, Southwest and California; raccoons in New England and the East; foxes in New York, neighboring Canada, Alaska and the Southwest; and coyotes and foxes in Texas. Bats, which are distributed widely, also carry rabies.

The main source of infection for humans outside the United States continues to be the bite from an infected dog or cat. In India, for example, a country that lacks an effective rabies control program, it is estimated that several thousand people die of rabies each year. Travelers to countries where rabies is endemic should be aware of the risk of dog bites.

The rabies virus, which is present in infected saliva, enters at the site of a bite. Saliva on an open wound or disrupted mucous membrane also constitutes exposure. The average incubation period in dogs is two to eight weeks, but it can be as short as one week or as long as a year. The virus travels to the brain along nerve

The eyes of a rabid dog, showing divergent gaze, protrusion of the nictitating membrane and a pasty eye discharge. (Courtesy American Veterinary Publications)

routes. The more distant the bite is from the brain, the longer the period of incubation. The virus then travels back along nerves to the mouth. Entry into the salivary glands occurs less than 10 days before the appearance of symptoms.

The symptoms of rabies are due to inflammation of the brain (*encephalitis*). During the *prodromal* phase, which lasts two to three days, the signs are subtle and consist of personality changes. Affectionate and sociable pets may become irritable and aggressive. Shy and less outgoing pets may become overtly affectionate. An infected dog often chews at the site where the virus entered the body. Soon, the animal becomes withdrawn and stares off into space.

There are two characteristic forms of encephalitis: the *furious* form and the *paralytic* or dumb form. A rabid dog may show signs of both forms as the disease progresses.

In the furious or "mad dog" type of rabies, the dog becomes frenzied and vicious, attacking anything that moves. The muscles of the face go into spasm, drawing the lips back to expose the teeth. When running free, the dog shows no fear and snaps and bites at any animal in his path.

In the paralytic form, the throat and jaw muscles become paralyzed, causing the mouth to drop open and the tongue to hang out. The dog is unable to swallow his own saliva and drools, coughs, gags and may foam at the mouth. As encephalitis progresses, the dog loses control of his body movements, staggers about and collapses. Death from respiratory failure occurs in one to two days. In some cases paralysis may be the only sign of rabies.

Treatment: There is no effective treatment. The disease is always fatal.

Any dog bitten by an animal not known to be free of rabies must be assumed to be rabid until proven otherwise. The recommendations are as follows: If the dog has previously been vaccinated against rabies, revaccinate immediately and observe the dog under leash confinement at home for 45 days. In the case of an unvaccinated dog, either euthanize the animal (this is preferable) or confine him under strict quarantine without human or animal contact for six months. Then vaccinate one month before he is released. If this seems harsh, keep in mind that it would not have been necessary if the pet had been vaccinated.

Prevention: Dogs should be vaccinated beginning at three months of age, with booster shots every one to three years, depending on the vaccine used and local and state ordinances. Regardless of the age at the initial vaccination, a second vaccination should be given one year later (see *Rabies Vaccine*, page 62).

When traveling with your pet, be sure to carry your rabies certificate signed by a veterinarian, or your pet's current rabies tag. If you enter a rabies quarantine area and are unable to prove vaccination, your pet could be impounded. In addition, you could be subject to a heavy fine.

Public Health Considerations: Preventive vaccinations are available for high-risk groups of humans, including veterinarians, animal handlers, cave explorers and laboratory workers.

Do not pet, handle or give first aid to any animal suspected of having rabies. All bites of *wild animals*, whether provoked or not, must be regarded as having rabies potential. Rodent bites should also be evaluated, but because rodents rarely carry rabies, these bites are of less concern.

The United States Public Health Service Advisory Committee has established certain guidelines for practitioners to follow in the appropriate management of people who are exposed to a potentially rabid animal. The treatment schedule depends upon the nature of the exposure (lick or bite), the severity of the injury, and the condition of the animal at the time of exposure and during a subsequent observation period.

Early laboratory confirmation of animal rabies is essential so that exposed humans can receive rabies prophylaxis as quickly as possible. Rabies is confirmed by finding rabies virus or rabies antigen in the brain or salivary tissues of the suspected animal. The animal must be euthanized and his head sent in a chilled (not frozen) state to a laboratory equipped to diagnose rabies.

Whenever you have contact with an animal that may conceivably be rabid, *immediately consult your physician and veterinarian*, and also notify the local health department. Biting dogs that appear healthy should be confined and kept under observation for 10 days. *This holds true even if the dog is known to be vaccinated for rabies.*

If You or Your Dog Are Bitten: It is extremely important to vigorously cleanse all animal bites and scratches, washing them thoroughly with soap and water. Studies in animals have shown that local wound cleansing greatly reduces the risk of rabies. The wound should not be sutured.

The introduction of inactivated vaccines grown in human diploid cell cultures has improved the effectiveness and safety of postexposure vaccination. Assuming the bite victim did not have a pre-exposure rabies immunization, both passive rabies immune globulin and human origin active diploid cell vaccine should be given. Up to 50 percent of the rabies immune globulin should be infiltrated around the wound.

Prophylaxis should begin as soon as possible (within 14 days of the lick or bite). Vaccination is not effective once signs of rabies appear.

PSEUDORABIES

Pseudorabies is an acute fatal disease of the central nervous system that affects dogs, cats and other mammals. It is rare in the United States and is not a hazard to human health. Pseudorabies is caused by a herpesvirus that predominantly infects pigs. Almost all cases are the result of a dog eating contaminated raw pork. Although pseudorabies bears no actual relationship to rabies, it may be confused with the furious form of that disease.

After an incubation period of three to five days, illness begins with restlessness and depression, followed almost immediately by intense itching with violent scratching and biting at the skin. The dog often drools excessively and acts as though something were caught in his throat. The most furious itching occurs about the head and shoulders, and inside the mouth. The dog staggers about, collapses and falls into a coma. Death occurs in a matter of hours.

Signs of pseudorabies suggest the possibility of rabies, but the shorter course (just a few hours), lack of vicious attacks, and intolerable itching distinguish the two diseases. There is no evidence that the disease is transmitted from dog to dog.

Treatment: There is no available treatment.

Prevention: The disease can be controlled by preventing pets from roaming and coming into contact with pigs. Never feed raw pork to dogs. Currently there are no vaccines available in the United States to protect dogs from pseudorabies.

KENNEL COUGH

Kennel cough is, in fact, not one but a group of highly contagious respiratory diseases of dogs that spread rapidly through a kennel or other area where many dogs are kept in close quarters. A harsh, dry cough is the characteristic sign of infection. The cough may persist for many weeks and become a chronic problem as the virus is replaced by secondary bacterial invaders.

A number of viruses and the bacteria *bordetella bronchiseptica* have been implicated in the kennel cough complex. Immunizing your dog with parainfluenza and CAV-2 vaccines—incorporated into the routine immunizations—will decrease the prevalence and severity of kennel cough. For more information, see *Kennel Cough Complex* in Chapter 10.

CANINE PARVOVIRUS

Canine parvovirus is an acute, highly contagious disease of dogs that was first described in the early 1970s. The virus has a special affinity for attacking rapidly reproducing cells, such as those lining the gastrointestinal tract. The disease is transmitted by oral contact with infected feces. The virus is shed in large amounts in the stools of acutely infected dogs for up to several weeks following infection. Parvo can be carried on the dog's hair and feet, as well as on contaminated crates, shoes and other objects.

Parvo affects dogs of all ages, but most cases occur in puppies 6 to 20 weeks of age. Doberman Pinschers and Rottweilers appear to acquire the infection more readily and experience more severe symptoms. The reason for lower resistance in these breeds is unknown.

Following an incubation period that averages four to five days, the acute illness begins with depression, vomiting and diarrhea. Some dog have no fever, while others have high fever (up to 106°F). Pups with severe abdominal pain exhibit a tucked-up abdomen. Diarrhea is profuse and contains mucus and/or blood. Dehydration develops rapidly.

Heart muscle involvement in neonatal puppies used to be common, but is now quite rare. This is because routine vaccination of brood bitches two to four weeks before breeding boosts maternal antibody levels and provides better protection for puppies.

Suspect parvo in all pups with the abrupt onset of vomiting and diarrhea. The most efficient way to diagnose parvo is to identify either the virus or virus antigens in stools. An in-office blood serum test (*ELISA*) is available for rapid veterinary diagnosis. False negatives do occur. Virus isolation techniques are more precise, but require an outside laboratory.

Treatment: This disease requires intensive veterinary management. In all but mild cases, hospitalization is essential to correct dehydration and electrolyte

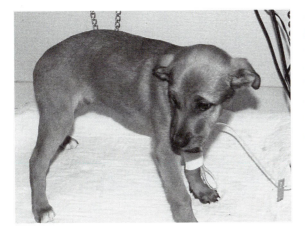

A puppy with parvovirus infection. Note the tucked-up belly indicative of abdominal pain. Dehydration developed rapidly, but was corrected with IV fluids. The pup recovered.

imbalances. Intravenous fluids and medications to control vomiting and diarrhea are often required.

Puppies and dogs should not eat or drink until the vomiting has stopped. This can take three to five days. Antibiotics are prescribed to prevent septicemia and other bacterial complications, which are the usual cause of death.

The outcome depends upon the virulence of the specific strain of parvovirus, the age and immune status of the dog, and how quickly the treatment is started. Most pups with good veterinary care recover without complications.

Prevention: Thoroughly clean and disinfect the quarters of infected animals. Parvo is an extremely hardy virus that resists most household cleaners and survives on the premises for months. The most effective disinfectant is household bleach in a 1:32 dilution. The bleach must be left on the contaminated surface for 20 minutes before being rinsed.

Vaccinations starting at eight weeks of age will prevent most (but not all) cases of parvovirus infection (see *Canine Parvovirus Vaccine*, page 61). During the first weeks of life, puppies are protected by high levels of maternal antibodies. As these levels decline, there is a period lasting from two to four weeks during which puppies are susceptible to infection because vaccinations have not yet fully taken effect. This susceptible period varies from pup to pup, which is why pups anywhere between 6 and 20 weeks age can be especially susceptible to parvo. Nearly all apparent vaccination failures are due to exposure during this susceptible period.

New high titer–low passage vaccines are narrowing the window of susceptibility. Nevertheless, it is still important to isolate young puppies as much as possible from other dogs and from potential sources of infection until they complete the parvo vaccination series at 16 weeks of age. Annual boosters are required.

CANINE CORONAVIRUS

Canine coronavirus is a contagious intestinal infection that usually produces a mild disease. However, it can be severe in young puppies and dogs stressed by concurrent infections. The distribution is worldwide, and dogs of all ages are affected.

Coronavirus is transmitted by contact with infected oral and fecal secretions. Following infection, the virus is shed in the stool for many months. Signs and symptoms vary from none (the most common form) to outbreaks of acute diarrhea, typically occurring in a community of dogs.

The early signs of illness are depression with loss of appetite, followed by vomiting and the passage of a foul-smelling, yellow to orange diarrhea that varies from soft to watery. The diarrhea may contain blood. Unlike parvovirus, fever is uncommon. Dehydration can occur if the diarrhea is severe.

There is no readily available test to diagnose coronavirus during the acute illness. A rise in antibody titer in paired serum (at the time of illness and two to six weeks later) can provide a retrospective diagnosis.

Treatment: Treatment is supportive, and includes maintaining hydration and controlling vomiting and diarrhea as described for the treatment of parvovirus. Antibiotics are not prescribed because of the mild nature of most infections.

Prevention: A vaccine is available to control coronavirus. Vaccination provides only partial immunity, however, and is optional. Immunization can be considered for show dogs and dogs living or boarding in kennels (see *Coronavirus Vaccine*, page 61).

Fungal Diseases

Fungal diseases can be divided into two categories. In one category, the fungus affects just the skin or mucous membranes. Examples are *ringworm* and *thrush*. In the other category, the disease is widespread and involves the liver, lungs, brain and other organs, in which case it is called *systemic*.

Fungi live in soil and organic material. Fungus spores, which resist heat and can live for long periods without water, gain entrance through the respiratory tract or a break in the skin.

Systemic fungal diseases are not common in dogs. They tend to occur in chronically ill or poorly nourished animals. Prolonged treatment with steroids and/or antibiotics may also change the dog's pattern of resistance and allow a fungal infection to develop. Suspect a fungus when an unexplained infection fails to respond to a course of antibiotics.

HISTOPLASMOSIS

This disease is found in the central United States near the Great Lakes, the Appalachian Mountains, Texas, and the valleys of the Mississippi, Ohio and Missouri Rivers. These areas have nitrogen-rich soil that facilitates growth of the causative fungus (*Histoplasma capsulatum*). Spores are found in soil contaminated by the dung of bats, chickens and other birds.

In most cases, histoplasmosis is *subclinical* or inapparent, occasionally producing a mild respiratory infection. There is an acute intestinal form, however, that attacks the small bowel and colon. The principal signs are weight loss and intractable diarrhea. A systemic form is characterized by fever, weight loss, vomiting, muscle wasting, enlargement of the tonsils and involvement of the liver, spleen, bone marrow, eyes, skin and, rarely, the brain.

The diagnosis is made by chest X-ray, blood studies, and recovery of the histoplasma organism in *cytology*, biopsy or culture specimens.

Treatment: Oral anti-fungal drugs of the imidazole group, including ketoconazole, itraconazole and fluconazole, are particularly effective in treating non–life-threatening histoplasmosis. In severe infections, Amphotericin B is often combined with one of the imidazoles. Amphotericin B is potentially damaging to the kidneys.

Antifungal therapy requires many months of drug use after the symptoms disappear. The disease will reappear if long-term suppression is not maintained. Antifungal drugs can be toxic and require close veterinary management.

Prevention: Keep dogs away from chicken coops, caves and other places inhabited by birds and bats.

COCCIDIOIDOMYCOSIS

This is the most severe and life-threatening systemic fungus disease. Coccidioidomycosis is found in dry, dusty parts of the southwestern United States, and in California and neighboring Mexico. Note that coccidioidomycosis is *not* the same disease as *coccidiosis*, a disease caused by an intestinal protozoan.

Infection occurs by inhaling spores. Most cases are subclinical or inapparent. A severe form affects the lungs and produces acute pneumonia. If the disease becomes systemic, it may involve the long bones (most common), liver, spleen, lymph nodes, brain and skin.

The diagnosis is made by identifying the organism (*Coccidioides immitis*) in cytology, biopsy or culture specimens.

Treatment: Coccidioidomycosis can be treated effectively by one of the imidazole group of antifungal agents (see *Histoplasmosis*). Prolonged treatment for up to a year is required to prevent recurrence.

CRYPTOCOCCOSIS

This disease, caused by the yeastlike fungus *Cryptococcus neoformans*, is acquired by inhaling spores found in soil contaminated by bird droppings, especially those of pigeons. In dogs, cryptococcosis involves the brain, eyes, lymph nodes and skin. Signs of brain involvement are an unsteady gait, head pressing, circling, seizures, blindness and dementia. Involvement of the inner structures of the eyes leads to blindness.

In the less common form that infects the skin, cryptococcosis produces firm nodules, primarily in the head area, that ulcerate and drain pus.

The diagnosis is made by fungal culture and/or tissue biopsy. A cryptococcus latex agglutination test is available.

Treatment: Oral antifungal drugs of the imidazole group (see *Histoplasmosis*) are partially effective when started early in the course of the disease. The response is uncertain and treatment is prolonged.

Public Health Considerations: There are no documented cases of transmission of cryptococcosis from dogs to people.

BLASTOMYCOSIS

This systemic fungal disease occurs along the Eastern Seaboard, in the Great Lakes region, and the Mississippi, Ohio and Missouri River valleys. The fungus is associated with moist, rotting organic debris protected from sunlight and enriched with bird droppings, particularly those of pigeons. The disease is acquired by inhaling infected spores. Dogs are considerably more susceptible to blastomycosis than are humans.

Most cases of acute canine blastomycosis involve the respiratory system and cause bronchopneumonia. About 40 percent of cases involve the eyes and skin, producing signs similar to those of cryptococcosis.

Microscopic identification of organisms in *trans-tracheal washings* or in fluid aspirated from infected tissues is the most efficient way to make the diagnosis. In difficult cases, biopsy and culture may be needed. Serologic tests also are available.

Treatment: A combination of Amphotericin B and one of the imidazoles appears to offer the best chance of successful treatment (see *Histoplasmosis*).

Public Health Considerations: Although the hazard to human health is minimal, humans can acquire the fungus from infected bandages and bedding. Use rubber gloves and take hygienic precautions when handling an infected dog.

SPOROTRICHOSIS

This is a skin and subcutaneous infection acquired by contact with spores in the soil. The spores gain access through puncture wounds caused by thorns and splinters; therefore, the disease is seen most often in hunting dogs. Most cases are reported in the northern and central portions of the United States.

A nodular, draining, crusted sore forms at the site of the skin wound, usually on the trunk or head. There may be several small firm nodules in the lymph glands that form a chain beneath the skin. On rare occasion the disease becomes systemic and spreads to the liver and lungs. The outlook for these dogs is guarded.

The diagnosis is made by removing a piece of tissue and examining it under the microscope; or more conclusively, by growing the fungus in culture. A fluorescent antibody test can be performed on infected tissue or serum.

Treatment: Response is excellent when the infection is limited to the skin and surrounding tissues. Potassium iodide (a saturated solution) is the agent of choice. Antifungals of the imidazole group (see *Histoplasmosis*) have also been used.

Public Health Considerations: Sporotrichosis is known to infect humans handling animals with infective drainage. It is important to wear rubber gloves and use strict hygienic precautions when handling all animals with draining wounds.

Protozoan Diseases

Protozoans are one-celled animals that are not visible to the naked eye, but are easily seen under the microscope. A fresh stool specimen is required to identify the adult parasite or its cysts (called *oocysts*).

TOXOPLASMOSIS

This disease is caused by a protozoan that infects warm-blooded animals. Cats are the definitive host, but other animals including dogs and humans can act as intermediate hosts. The principal mode of transmission in dogs and people is by ingesting raw or undercooked pork, beef, mutton or veal that contains *Toxoplasma gondii*.

The excretion of oocysts in the stools of cats and the ingestion of spores by dogs are other potential sources of infection. Oocysts require one to three days under ideal conditions of warm temperature and high humidity to produce spores. These infective spores can survive in the environment for months or years. Only cats excrete the oocytes in their stool. The dog is therefore not capable of infecting other dogs and humans in this way.

Most dogs with toxoplasmosis experience no symptoms. When symptoms do occur they include fever, loss of appetite, lethargy, cough and rapid breathing. Other signs are weight loss, diarrhea, lymph node enlargement and swelling of the abdomen. Young puppies with toxoplasmosis may show signs of pneumonia, hepatitis and encephalitis. In brood bitches, intrauterine infection can result in abortion, still-births and the birth of sick puppies that die within the first week of life.

The diagnosis is made by serology. An elevated IgM titer (by *ELISA* tests) is diagnostic for active or recent infection.

Treatment: Antibiotics are available to treat acute toxoplasmosis. Clindamycin is the drug of choice.

Prevention: Prevent the disease by keeping your pet from roaming and hunting. Cook all fresh meat (both yours and your pets') to a temperature of at least 150°F (medium well). Wash your hands with soap and water after handling raw meat. Always clean kitchen surfaces that make contact with raw meat.

Public Health Considerations: Cats are the definitive host but other animals including dogs and humans can act as intermediate hosts. The greatest hazard to human health is congenital toxoplasmosis. About 25 to 50 percent of the human adult population shows serologic evidence of having been infected. Men and women with protective antibodies are immune to reinfection.

The danger occurs when a pregnant woman without immunity is exposed to areas contaminated by cat feces and becomes infected with *T. gondii*, This can result in abortion, stillbirth and even the birth of babies with toxoplasma encephalitis.

Pregnant women should therefore avoid contact with fecal material from cats. Be sure to wear disposable plastic gloves when handling a cat's litter. Remove all stools from the litter box *daily*. Dispose of the litter carefully. Clean and disinfect litter boxes at least every three days using boiling water or 10 percent ammonia solution; even better, use disposable litter box liners. Sand boxes must be covered when not in use to keep cats from defecating in them.

A blood test can be requested to see if a cat has acquired immunity through prior exposure. A cat with a positive test that is not shedding oocysts in several stool specimens is considered safer than one who has not yet become infected. A cat without immunity should be confined in the home during her owner's pregnancy.

COCCIDIOSIS

This is a diarrhea disease caused by a species of coccidia commonly found in the feces of puppies and, occasionally, adult dogs. Because infection is mild, symptoms usually do not occur unless the pup's resistance has been lowered by a concurrent disease, malnutrition or immunosuppression.

Coccidiosis is a particular problem in neonatal puppies overstressed by filth, crowding, chilling and poor sanitation. An outbreak of coccidial diarrhea can occur in association with roundworm infestation or the trauma of shipping. Coccidiosis is an opportunist. Always look for another precipitating cause.

Puppies acquire the infection from contaminated premises or from their mother if she is a carrier. When kennel sanitation is poor, puppies reinfect themselves from their own feces.

Five to seven days after ingesting oocytes, infective cysts appear in the feces. The first sign is mild diarrhea that progresses until the feces become mucus-like and tinged with blood. The diarrhea is accompanied by loss of appetite, weakness and dehydration. Dogs that recover become carriers. Infected dogs and carriers can be identified by finding oocysts in a microscopic slide of fresh stool.

Treatment: Treatment in adult dogs usually is not necessary due to the mild nature of the diarrhea. Puppies with severe diarrhea may need to be hospitalized for fluid replacement. Antibiotics effective against coccidiosis include sulfadimethoxine, Trimethoprin-sulfa, furazolidone and amprolium.

Prevention: Known carriers should be isolated and treated. Wash down infected quarters daily with *boiling* water to destroy oocysts. Coccidiosis can be prevented by maintaining clean quarters and providing an appropriate whelping environment, as described in *Caring for the Newborn* in Chapter 17.

TRICHOMONIASIS

This is a protozoan infection caused by a species of trichomonas often associated with a mucoid (and occasionally bloody) diarrhea in puppies. Commonly, it is found in association with poor kennel sanitation. Prolonged infection leads to weak, debilitated, stunted puppies with rough coats. The diagnosis is made by finding protozoan cysts in fresh stool.

Treatment: The infection responds well to Flagyl (metronidazole).

GIARDIASIS

This disease is caused by a protozoan of the *giardia* species. Dogs acquire the infection from drinking water from streams and other sources contaminated with infective oocysts.

Most infections in adult dogs are subclinical. Young dogs can develop a diarrhea syndrome characterized by the passage of large volumes of foul-smelling, watery or "cow-pie" stools. The diarrhea may be acute or chronic, intermittent or persistent, and may be accompanied by weight loss.

Diagnosis is made by finding the protozoan or its characteristics oocysts in saline smears of fresh stool. Smears from rectal swabs are satisfactory. A negative smear does not exclude giardia, as oocysts are shed only intermittently. Three negative fecal smears collected at least two days apart should be obtained before the diagnosis is excluded. New serology tests (*ELISA, IFA*) are becoming available.

Treatment: Giardiasis responds well to Flagyl (metronidazole). Because Flagyl causes developmental malformations in the fetus, it should not be administered to pregnant bitches. Other effective drugs are available.

Public Health Considerations: There is no conclusive evidence that cysts shed by dogs or cats cause human infection. Contaminated water sources are the principal source of giardiasis in people. Water from private wells and untreated municipal water systems should be boiled, filtered or treated with disinfectants approved for potable water. Consult your public health department for specific information.

CANINE BABESIOSIS (NANTUCKET DISEASE)

This is an uncommon disease caused by a protozoan that destroys red blood cells, producing a *hemolytic anemia*. One mode of transmission is by the bite of a brown dog tick. Natural hosts of this tick are various wild animals, particularly the white-footed mouse and the white-tailed deer. As these animals are also implicated in Lyme disease, both diseases can occur at the same time. Babesiosis can also be transmitted by blood transfusions.

In humans, babesiosis is called Nantucket disease because most cases in the United States have been reported on Nantucket Island and nearby Martha's Vineyard. Outside the United States the disease is found in tropical and subtropical regions throughout the world. For reasons unknown, the Greyhound is particularly susceptible to babesiosis.

Most infections in dogs are subclinical. With acute illness the signs are fever, enlargement of the spleen and liver, and abnormal blood tests indicative of hemolytic anemia. The signs of anemia are shortness of breath, exercise intolerance and pallor of the gums and tongue. The bone marrow and liver can be affected.

Diagnosis is contingent upon finding the protozoan in blood smears. An *IFA* serum antibody test also is available.

Treatment: Antibiotics effective against canine babesiosis have not been approved by the FDA, but your veterinarian can obtain FDA permission to use a nonapproved drug. Prevent infection by controlling ticks as described in Chapter 4, *Ticks*.

CANINE HEPATOZOONOSIS

This is another protozoan disease transmitted by the brown dog tick. Its geographic distribution in the United States is limited to Oklahoma, Louisiana and the Texas Gulf Coast. Illness is most likely to occur in immunosuppressed dogs and pups younger than four months of age.

Signs of illness include diarrhea (often bloody), muscle and bone pain with reluctance to move, eye and nasal discharges, and severe loss of weight and condition.

Treatment: The disease can be treated with a variety of antiprotozoan medications, but a cure has not been established. Hepatozoonosis is best prevented by controlling ticks as described in Chapter 4, *Ticks*.

AMERICAN TRYPANOSOMIASIS (CHAGAS DISEASE)

Trypanosomiasis is caused by the protozoan *T. cruzi*. A small number of cases have been reported, principally in the southwestern United States, Texas and California. Raccoons, opossums, armadillos, rats, cats and dogs serve as the principal reservoirs.

Dogs (and humans) acquire the disease from a family of insects called kissing bugs, so named because they come out of cracks at night and bite the face of sleepers. Infection occurs through contamination of the bug bites by the insect's feces. Another source of infection in dogs is feeding on a host (such as a raccoon) that harbors encysted larvae in its tissues.

Signs include fever, weakness, enlargement of the lymph nodes and spleen, inflammation of the spinal cord and brain. Trypanosomiasis attacks the heart muscle, causing myocarditis with heart arrhythmias. This can lead to collapse and death. Another complication of myocarditis is congestive heart failure one to three years later.

The diagnosis is made by identifying the protozoan in blood smears. Serology tests also are available.

Treatment: Experimental drugs have been used, but the response is poor. Because this often fatal disease can be transmitted to humans, euthanasia is recommended. It is essential to take the utmost precautions when handling infected animals, as well as their blood and discharges.

Rickettsial Diseases

Rickettsiae are small parasites (about the size of bacteria) that live within cells. The majority are maintained in nature by a cycle that involves an insect vector, a permanent host and an animal reservoir.

CANINE EHRLICHIOSIS

This is a relatively common rickettsial disease caused by the organism E. canis, although several other rickettsiae are capable of causing ehrlichiosis. The disease is transmitted by the bite of a common brown dog tick. Ehrlichiosis occurs mainly in the Gulf Coast area, the Eastern Seaboard, the Midwest and California. Outside of the United States it is distributed worldwide.

Because of its chronic nature, cases of ehrlichiosis are seen year-round, not just during the tick season. Ticks acquire the rickettsia by feeding on an infected host. A variety of wild and domestic animals serve as reservoirs.

The disease occurs in three phases. During the *acute phase,* the dog develops fever, depression, loss of appetite, shortness of breath, lymph node enlargement and occasionally signs of encephalitis. These symptoms may suggest Rocky Mountain spotted fever, Lyme disease or canine distemper.

Two to four weeks after the onset of the acute phase, the dog enters a *subclinical phase* that lasts one to four weeks. Some dogs eliminate the infection during the subclinical phase; others progress to the chronic phase. There appears to be a breed disposition for developing chronic ehrlichiosis; German Shepherd Dogs and Doberman Pinschers, for example, are at increased risk.

During the *chronic phase,* which appears one to four months after the tick bite, the disease attacks the bone marrow and immune system, producing weight loss, fever, anemia, a hemorrhagic syndrome with spontaneous bleeding and nosebleeds, swelling of the limbs and various neurologic signs. These signs may suggest leukemia.

A serologic blood test (*IFA*) is sensitive for E. canis. However, the test may not be positive until two to three weeks after the tick bite.

Treatment: Tetracycline and doxycycline are highly effective against rickettsiae, and should be given for two to three weeks. Improvement in the acute phase begins within one to two days. Supportive treatment involves intravenous fluids and blood transfusions. The outlook for recovery is excellent if treatment is started before the dog develops bone marrow depression.

Prevention: Tick control is the mainstay of prevention (see *Ticks* in Chapter 4). Dogs living in areas where the disease is endemic can be protected by giving a low dose of oral tetracycline (1.3 mg per pound of body weight) or doxycycline (0.45 to 0.90 mg per pound of body weight) every 24 hours.

Using Frontline Spot On to control fleas has the advantage of killing ticks for up to 30 days following a single application. Collars containing amitraz (such as Preventic) are also effective in controlling ticks.

Prevention: Control of ticks is the mainstay of prevention (see *Ticks* in Chapter 4). Ticks do not infect dogs until they have been attached for 5 to 20 hours. Therefore, examining pets that have been roaming in tick-infested areas, and early removal of ticks, can prevent many infections.

ROCKY MOUNTAIN SPOTTED FEVER

Rocky Mountain spotted fever is a rickettsial disease caused by *Rickettsia rickettsii* and transmitted by several species of ticks. It is the most significant rickettsial disease in humans. Most cases occur in the southeastern United States, Midwest, Plains States and Southwest. The Rocky Mountain area, where the disease was first discovered at the turn of the 20th century, now accounts for only a small percentage of cases.

Unlike canine ehrlichiosis, Rocky Mountain spotted fever coincides with the tick season (the first of April through the first of September). The two main reservoirs for Rocky Mountain spotted fever are rodents and dogs. Adult ticks transmit the disease to dogs when they attach and feed.

Signs of acute infection appear during the tick season and include listlessness, depression, high fever, loss of appetite, cough, conjunctivitis, difficult breathing, swelling of the legs, and joint and muscle pains. These symptoms may suggest canine ehrlichiosis, Lyme disease or distemper. Central nervous system signs include unstable gait, altered mental state and seizures. Inflammation of the heart muscle (myocarditis) can cause cardiac arrhythmias, resulting in sudden death.

One to two weeks after the onset of illness some dogs develop a hemmorrhagic syndrome similar to that seen with canine ehrlichiosis. Various bleeding problems such as nosebleeds, subcutaneous hemorrhaging, and blood in the urine and stools may develop. This can cause shock, multiple organ failure and death.

Rocky Mountain spotted fever should be suspected in a sick dog with a history of tick infestation during April through September. Serologic diagnosis is best achieved by noting a rise in micro-IFA antibody titer in paired serum tests (at the time of illness and two to three weeks later).

Treatment: Tetracycline and its derivative, doxycycline, are the antibiotics of choice. Enrofloxacin is also effective. Antibiotics should be started as soon as Rocky Mountain spotted fever is suspected, even if the diagnosis is not confirmed. Mortality is high if treatment is delayed. Furthermore, dogs with Rocky Mountain spotted fever respond dramatically in one to two days, which confirms the presumptive diagnosis. Antibiotics are continued for two to three weeks. Supportive treatment is the same as that described for canine ehrlichiosis.

Using Frontline Spot On to control fleas has the advantage of killing ticks for up to 30 days following a single application. Collars containing amitraz (Preventic) are also effective in controlling ticks.

CANINE SALMON POISONING DISEASE

This is a severe rickettsial disease of dogs and wild canids that requires the presence of several intermediate hosts, including snails, flukes, fish and mammals. Humans are not affected.

Dogs acquire the infection when they eat raw freshwater or ocean salmon and related species containing encysted flukes that harbor rickettsiae. The disease is limited to the Pacific Northwest. This is because the first intermediate host is a small snail found only in streams along the coasts of Washington, Oregon and California.

A few days after a dog ingests contaminated fish, the larval fluke matures and attaches to the lining of the dog's intestine, where it inoculates the rickettsial organism. The incubation period is 5 to 21 days.

Illness begins with high fever, followed by hypothermia, loss of appetite, vomiting, diarrhea (usually bloody) and generalized lymph node enlargement. These signs are like those of canine distemper and parvovirus. However, a history of eating raw fish suggests a diagnosis of salmon poisoning.

Treatment: Death usually occurs in 7 to 10 days in untreated dogs. However, the illness does respond well to intravenous tetracycline. Supportive treatment with IV fluids and blood transfusions for hemorrhagic diarrhea, may be required. Praziquantel and mebendazole eliminate intestinal flukes.

Prevention: Do not allow dogs to eat raw fish. Thoroughly cooking fish (or freezing it for 24 hours) destroys encysted flukes and rickettsiae.

THE SKIN AND COAT

Skin disease is a common problem in dogs, and the condition of the skin can often tell you a great deal about your dog's general health. A dog's skin is thinner and more sensitive to injury than human skin. It is easily damaged by rough handling with the wrong type of grooming equipment, and once the surface of the skin is broken and disturbed by trauma or some other disorder, the condition tends to spread rather easily and become a major problem.

The outer layer of skin is the *epidermis*, a scaly layer that varies in thickness over different parts of the body. It is thick and tough over the nose and foot pads, and thin and most susceptible to injury in the creases of the groin and armpits.

The layer beneath the epidermis is the *dermis*. The dermis gives rise to the *skin appendages:* hair follicles, sebaceous glands, toenails and sweat glands. Sweat glands are found only in the foot pads of dogs.

Hair follicles produce three types of hair. *Primary hair* is exemplified by the long guard hair that makes up the top coat. Each guard hair grows from its own follicle. Muscles connected to the root of each guard hair enable the hair to stand erect, as happens when a dog raises his hackles. Within each guard hair follicle is a cluster of *accessory hair* that composes the undercoat. The function of the undercoat is to provide warmth and protection. Whiskers and eyelashes make up a third type of hair, which is modified to serve the sense of touch.

Sebaceous glands are located in the dermis, and are linked to the hair follicles. Sebaceous glands secrete an oily substance called *sebum*, which collects in the hair follicles and coats each strand of hair. This adds shine and, more important, enables the hair to shed water. Water-going breeds depend upon this skin oil to waterproof their coats. Sebum is also responsible for the characteristic doggy odor apparent in some dogs with oily coats.

The color of a dog's skin can vary from pink to light brown, or it may be dark with patches of black. The dark pigment in the skin is called *melanin*. It is produced by cells in the dermis called *melanocytes*.

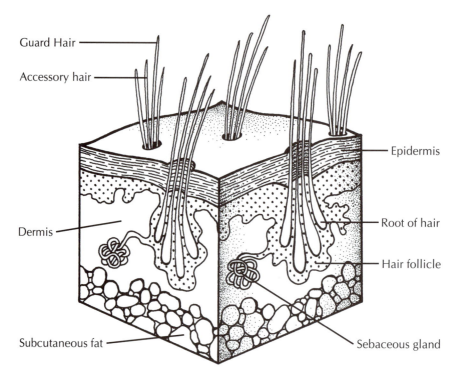

Cross Section of the Skin

The Dog's Coat

The quality of a dog's coat is controlled by a number of factors, including hormone concentrations, nutrition, general health, genetics and the frequency of grooming and bathing. Dogs living outdoors in cold weather grow a heavy coat for insulation and protection.

Hormonal diseases such as hypothyroidism, hyperestrogenism and Cushing's syndrome slow or suppress hair growth, making the coat appear thin or sparse. A protein deficiency caused by parasites or ill health may cause the coat to be dull, dry, brittle and thin.

If your dog's coat is below par, have him checked by your veterinarian. Poor coat quality is often an indication of a *systemic* disease.

HAIR GROWTH AND SHEDDING

Dog hair grows in cycles. Each follicle has a period of rapid growth (the *anagen phase*), followed by slower growth, and then a resting phase (the *catagen phase*). During the resting period, mature hair remains in the follicles and eventually detaches at the base. When the dog sheds his coat (the *telogen phase*), a young hair pushes out the old hair and the cycle begins anew. The average dog takes about four months to grow a coat, but there are individual and breed variations. The Afghan Hound, for example, grows his coat in about 18 months.

Most dogs shed or "blow" their coats at least once a year. Dams often blow their coats six to eight weeks after delivering puppies.

Many people assume that temperature changes govern when a dog sheds his coat. In fact, the seasonal length of daylight exerts the major influence. Longer periods of daylight in spring activate a shedding process that lasts four to six weeks. In fall, as the daylight hours grow shorter, many dogs may again shed their coats. Sensitivity to ambient light is most pronounced in dogs that live outdoors. Dogs that live primarily indoors are exposed to artificial light and a rather fixed photoperiod. These dogs may shed and grow a coat all year long.

Some breeds, such as Poodles, Bedlington Terriers and Kerry Blue Terriers, possess what is called a nonshedding curly coat. These breeds do not shed.

Some dogs have a double coat comprised of long, course, outer guard hair and a soft, fine, wooly undercoat. When a dog with a double coat begins to shed, the appearance of the coat can be quite alarming. The undercoat is shed in a mosaic or patchy fashion, giving the dog a moth-eaten appearance that may suggest a skin disease.

When shedding begins, remove as much of the irritating dead hair as possible by daily brushing. In breeds with a thick double coat, a bath will loosen the dead hair and make it easier to remove.

Avoiding Coat and Skin Problems

GROOMING

Grooming at regular intervals will keep your dog's coat and skin in good condition and prevent many problems. Establish a grooming schedule during puppyhood and stick to it throughout the dog's life. Initially, keep the sessions brief and make grooming a pleasurable experience. If the puppy grows to dislike the basic routine, a simple procedure will become most difficult.

How often to groom depends on the dog's coat type, breed, and the purpose for which he is being groomed. Show dogs, for example, usually require daily grooming. Long-haired dogs should be brushed frequently to prevent the coat from tangling and matting. Certain breeds require braiding, plucking and clipping. For these dogs it is a good idea to consult a breeder or professional pet groomer.

These are some useful grooming tools. The ones you will use most will depend upon your dog's breed and the nature of his coat.

- **Grooming table.** It should be solid with a nonslippery surface. Adjust it to a height where you can work without bending. Use for all grooming sessions lasting more than a few minutes.

- **Bristle brush.** This is a brush for all breeds. Removes loose hair and surface dirt and dresses the top coat. A brush with natural bristles produces less static electricity.
- **Pin brush.** This brush has long pins protruding from a rubber cushion. Especially effective for long-haired breeds.
- **Slicker brush.** This is a rectangular board with thin, bent wire teeth and a handle. A slicker brush is used to remove loose hair. Brush in short, deep strokes.
- **Hound glove (palm brush).** Intended for short-coated breeds, this removes dead hair and gives a polish to the coat.
- **Comb.** A standard *wide-toothed* metal comb with smooth, round teeth is used for short-haired areas and to set up hair for scissors. A *fine-toothed* comb is used to unsnarl fine hair. Many utility combs such as the *Greyhound* comb combine both features: the teeth are a quarter inch apart on the wide side and an eighth inch apart on the other. A *flea* comb is a very fine-toothed comb with 30 to 36 teeth per inch.
- **Scissors.** Used to trim the coat and cut out mats. The tips should be blunt or rounded. *Thinning shears* are scissors with spaces between the teeth that thin out hair but don't cut all of it.
- **Rake.** Long and short-toothed rakes are used to remove loose, dead hair during shedding. They will damage healthy hair if used too vigorously.
- **Mat splitter.** A single or multi-bladed tool for breaking up mats into smaller and smaller strands.
- **Nail clipper.** Nail clippers come with either two cutting edges and or a single blade that acts like a guillotine.
- **Nail file.** Handy after cutting nails to round the edges.
- **Towel.** Toweling short-haired breeds will remove loose dead hair. It tends to tangle long hair, however.

It is important that the bristles on the brush and the teeth on the comb be the right length for the dog's coat. For example, if the coat is thick and the bristles and teeth are too short, the top coat may look smooth for a time but the undercoat will mat. Eventually the top coat becomes involved and the dog may have to be shaved. On the other hand, if the dog has a thin undercoat, grooming with tools that have long bristles and teeth can scratch and injure the skin.

BRUSHING AND COMBING TECHNIQUES

A dog's coat is easily damaged by rough handling and improper grooming techniques. Hair has tiny scales that lie flat against the hair shaft. As the hair is pulled and stretched (which is not desirable), the scales project out like barbs. Adjacent hairs become snarled and eventually break during the unsnarling process.

The coat should be brushed with tools that pass smoothly through the hair. To avoid stretching, do not pull forcefully on a rake, slicker brush or comb—except when removing dead hair during the shedding stage. If you find that you are pulling hard, you are either taking too deep a bite or using a grooming tool with teeth or bristles that are too stiff or too close together. In general, a pin brush can be used safely without stretching the hair.

Dry hair attracts static electricity, which causes individual hairs to stick together. It is a good practice to use an antistatic coat conditioner before brushing. A number of popular products are available as pumps, aerosols and rub-on cremes.

In long-haired dogs, insert the bristle or pin brush all the way into the coat and twist it slightly. Using short strokes, brush *against* the lay of the hair. Avoid using long strokes, as this can break the hair.

For short-coated breeds, brush *with* the lay of the hair, starting at the head and working back toward the tail. In all breeds, pay particular attention to the hindquarters and back of the thighs, where dead hair is likely to mat.

If the dog is blowing his undercoat, remove loose hair with a rake. Start on the underside of the dog and work layer by layer up to the topside.

REMOVING MATS

Mats are solid lumps of fur that can form anywhere on the body but are usually found behind the ears, in the folds of the armpits, around the anus, on the backs of the thighs and between the toes. Mats are evidence of neglected grooming or grooming with the wrong tools.

To remove mats, first saturate the lumps of hair in coat conditioner for several minutes. This rehydrates the hair and closes the barbs. Then separate as much of the mat as you can with your fingers.

Some mats can be removed with the tip of a comb. However, most require the use of scissors or a mat splitter. Cutting into mats with scissors must be done with extreme care, because a dog's skin is not attached to the underlying muscle and tents up as the mat is pulled. Do not slide the scissors beneath the mat and attempt to remove it flush with the skin. You will almost certainly remove a piece of skin. When possible, slide a comb beneath the mat as a barrier between the scissors and the skin. Then hold the scissors *perpendicular* to the comb and carefully snip into the fur ball in narrow strips. Tease the mat out gently. After the mat has been removed, comb out residual snarls.

Beyond the Brush

A good care and maintenance program should include a schedule for examining the ears, cleaning the teeth, clipping the toenails, and, if necessary, emptying the anal sacs.

Be sure to groom beneath the *ear flaps* and inspect the openings of the ear canals at least once a month, and whenever your dog has been running in tall grass, weeds and brush. Plant matter can enter the ear canals by first clinging to the hair around the openings. An otic cleanser helps to dissolve wax and skin debris sticking to the inside surface of the ear flap. Use a cotton ball dampened with the cleanser.

Inspect the *ear canals* for dirt, debris, excess wax and a disagreeable odor. If any of these are present, clean as described in *Cleaning the Ears* in Chapter 6. If the ear canals are clean, leave them alone, as excessive cleaning can interfere with local immune defense mechanisms. Any discharge should be brought to the attention of your veterinarian.

Routinely inspecting and cleaning the teeth will prevent the build-up of tartar and calculus. For more information, see *Taking Care of Your Dog's Teeth* in Chapter 8.

Inspecting the anal sacs may disclose a buildup of secretions. To empty the anal sacs, see *Anal Sacs* in Chapter 9.

TRIMMING THE TOENAILS

Most dogs wear down their toenails by activity. If they are not worn down naturally, however, they can become extremely long and damage carpets and upholstery. Excessively long nails can splay the toes and interfere with traction by preventing the foot pads from making contact with the ground. Long toenails should be trimmed.

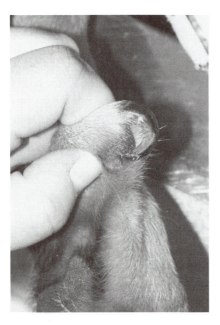

This neglected dewclaw has grown around into the pad.

Nails are also trimmed to prepare a dog for show. If trimming is done twice a month, the quick (the bundle of nerves and blood vessels inside the nail) will recede toward the base of the nail and the nail will remain permanently shorter.

Dogs with *dewclaws* must have these nails looked at frequently. Dewclaws are remnants of fifth toes and are found high on the inside of each foot. In many breeds the dewclaws are removed shortly after birth. In other breeds the presence of dewclaws is required by the breed standard. These nails do not contact the ground and thus can grow around in a circle and pierce the skin. Dewclaws should be trimmed regularly. This is particularly true for dogs with dewclaws on the rear legs. If you have a puppy with dewclaws, it is important to get him used to having them trimmed, even though trimming may not yet be necessary.

Some nail clippers for dogs have two cutting edges, while others of the guillotine type have one. Either type is satisfactory. Nail clippers designed for humans do not work well because a dog's nails are not flat like a person's.

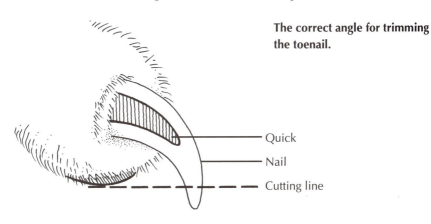

The correct angle for trimming the toenail.

Quick

Nail

Cutting line

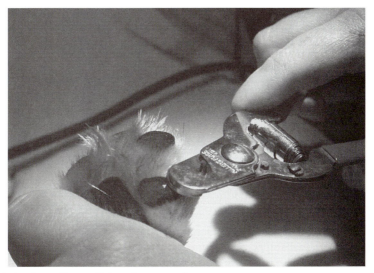

Trim the nails parallel to the toe pads.

Begin by lifting the dog's paw and extending the nail. Identify the *quick* (the pink part), which contains the nerves and blood vessels. If the toenails are white, it's easy to see the quick. Be sure to trim the nail in front of (but close to) the quick. When using a guillotine cutter, the blade should slice upward from the underside of the nail. If the toenails are dark and the quick is invisible, a good rule is to cut the nails parallel to the toe pads, so that the nails just clear the floor.

If you accidentally cut into the quick, the dog will feel a brief moment of pain and the nail will begin to bleed. Hold pressure over the end of the nail with a cotton ball. The blood will clot in a few minutes. If bleeding persists, pack with styptic powder or use a styptic pencil.

Bathing

There are no firm guidelines on how often to bathe a dog. The quality and texture of the dog's hair (whether it's long, silky, curly, smooth or wiry) will determine how much dirt it collects and how frequently the dog should be bathed. If you own a dog with special coat requirements, you may wish to consult a breeder or a professional groomer for specific recommendations.

The usual reasons for bathing a dog are to remove accumulated dirt and debris, to facilitate the removal of dead hair at shedding time, to eliminate doggy odor in dogs with oily coats, and to improve the appearance of the coat in preparation for a dog show. Routine bathing is not necessary for the health of the coat or the dog. In fact, frequent bathing can rob the coat of its natural sheen and make it harsh and dry. For most dogs, brushing at regular intervals will keep the coat and skin in good condition and eliminate the need for frequent baths.

Before bathing, brush out snarls and remove mats. If this step is omitted, the wet matted hair will set and be most difficult to manage.

It is important to select a shampoo labeled "for dogs." The pH of canine skin is neutral (7 to 7.4). Most human shampoos are on the acid side and are therefore unsuitable for dogs. There are a number of good commercial dog shampoos on the market for white dogs and dogs with other coat colors. *Household disinfectants must never be used on dogs.* These chemicals are absorbed through the skin and can cause death.

Except on warm sunny days, baths should be given indoors using a bathtub or basin. Place a rubber mat on the floor of the tub or basin to prevent the dog from slipping and panicking. Plug the ears with cotton to keep water out of the ears—wet ear canals are predisposed to infection.

Place the dog in the tub. Begin by washing his face with a damp cloth. Lift up the ear flaps and wipe the undersurface to remove dirt, wax and dead skin. Using a bath sprayer, wet the dog thoroughly with warm water. If necessary, bury the nozzle into his hair to get to the skin.

Then work the shampoo in by hand one section at a time. Be sure to lather all of the dog—not only his back and sides, but also his neck, chest, belly, legs, feet

Rinse the dog thoroughly to remove all soap and residue. As an option, apply coat conditioner to bring out the luster in the coat.

and tail. If the coat is badly soiled, rinse lightly and then repeat the sudsing process.

Remove the shampoo by rinsing the coat with the bath spray. Don't forget between the toes. It is essential to rinse and rinse until all the soap is out of the coat. Residual soap makes hair dull and tacky. It may also cause contact dermatitis if left on the skin.

Commercial coat conditioners are often used to bring out the beauty of the coat for show purposes. Do not use vinegar, lemon or bleaches. They are either too acid or too alkaline and will damage the coat. Some exhibitors add Alpha-Keri bath oil to the final rinse to give luster to the coat. The concentration is one teaspoonful per quart of water.

After the dog has been thoroughly rinsed, squeeze out as much water as you can by hand. Allow the dog to shake, and then blot dry with towels. You can complete the drying process with a good air blower. Commercial dog-drying units are very effective when used as directed. *Do not* use your own hair dryer on high heat. This damages the coat and may burn the skin. Use hand-held dryers only on low heat and slant them to keep the column of air from blowing directly on the dog's skin. Some dogs may be frightened by the noise and blowing air. If this is the case, do not force the dog to submit, as this can lead to psychological trauma and problems later on.

After the bath, keep the dog indoors until his coat is completely dry. This can take several hours.

DRY AND WATERLESS SHAMPOOS

Maintaining a clean coat between baths is highly desirable, especially for dogs with oily coats prone to collecting dirt. A number of household products have been used successfully as dry shampoos. Calcium carbonate, unscented talcum or baby powder, and cornstarch are all effective. They can be used frequently without damaging the coat or skin.

Work the substance into the coat and leave it for 20 minutes to absorb oils. Then remove the powder with a soft bristle brush. Remember that all traces of powder must be removed from the coat before entering the conformation ring for judging.

Commercial waterless shampoos (they require no rinsing) are sprays for quick cleaning problem spots. When used as an all-over spray, they are an excellent bath substitute. Apply and towel off.

SPECIAL BATH PROBLEMS

De-Skunking

The old remedy for removing skunk oil involved soaking the affected parts in tomato juice and then giving the dog a bath. Recently a new recipe appeared in *Chemical & Engineering* magazine and has been widely quoted on the Internet. It is said to be far more effective and does not require repeated use. It can be used on cats as well as dogs. The recipe is as follows:

> 1 quart 3 percent hydrogen peroxide (from the drug store)
>
> 1/4 cup baking soda (sodium bicarbonate)
>
> 1 teaspoon liquid soap (such as Ivory or dish soap)

Bathe the pet and work the solution into the coat. Follow with a tap water rinse. In long-haired dogs, most of the challenge is getting the solution down to the skin. Discard any unused formula because the release of oxygen caused by the chemical reaction could make the container explode.

Tar and Paint

When feasible, trim away any hair containing tar, oil or paint. To remove residual substances, saturate the effected parts in vegetable oil. Leave alone for 24 hours, then wash the coat with soap and water or give the dog a complete bath.

Do not use petroleum solvents such as gasoline, kerosene or turpentine to remove any substance from a dog's coat. These products are extremely harmful to the skin and are highly toxic if absorbed.

Sorting Out Skin Diseases

The following tables serve as an introduction to skin diseases, and suggest where to look to find the cause of a problem.

The *itchy skin diseases* in the first table are characterized by constant scratching, biting at the skin and rubbing up against objects to relieve the itch.

The next two tables list diseases characterized by *hair loss* with few if any other symptoms. Hair loss can mean impaired growth of new hair, in which case it usually involves specific areas or the entire coat. Or you may see patches of hair loss on various parts of the body. In general, hair loss caused by hormonal diseases is symmetric (the same on both sides of the body), while that caused by parasites and other causes is asymmetric.

The next table lists diseases in which the predominant sign is skin infection— *pyoderma*. Pyoderma is characterized by *pus, infected sores, scabs, ulcerations, papules, pustules, furuncles, boils* and *skin abscesses*. The skin infection is often secondary to some other skin disease, particularly an itchy skin disease that causes the dog to attack his own skin.

The table after that lists *autoimmune* and *immune-mediated* skin diseases, characterized by *blebs*. Blebs, also called *vesicles*, are blisters that contain clear fluid. Large ones are called *bullae*. All tend to progress through rubbing, biting and scratching, eventually producing skin erosions, ulcers and crusts. Look for these changes to appear first on the face, nose, muzzle and ears.

During the course of grooming, playing with or handling your dog, you may discover a lump or bump on or beneath the skin. To learn what it may be, see the last table on *lumps or bumps on or beneath the skin*.

Itchy Skin Diseases

Allergic contact dermatitis: Same as contact dermatitis, but rash may spread beyond area of contact. Requires repeated or continuous exposure to allergen (such as wearing a flea collar).

Canine atopy: Severe itching that occurs in young dogs and begins in late summer and fall. Caused by seasonal pollens. Occurs in mixed breeds as well as purebreds. Common.

Chiggers: Itching and severe skin irritation between toes, and around the ears and mouth. Look for barely visible red, yellow or orange chiggers.

Contact dermatitis: Red, itchy bumps and inflamed skin at the site of contact with chemical, detergent, paint or other irritant. Affects feet and hairless parts of the body.

Damp hay itch (*Pelodera*): Red pimplelike bumps on skin. Severe itching. Occurs in dogs bedded on damp hay and similar grass.

Flea allergy dermatitis: Red, itchy pimplelike bumps over the base of the tail, back of rear legs and inner thighs. Scratching continues after fleas have been killed.

Fleas: Itching and scratching along the back, around the tail and hindquarters. Look for fleas, or black and white gritty specks in hair (flea feces and eggs).

Fly-bite dermatitis: Painful bites at tips of erect ears and bent surfaces of floppy ears. Bites become scabbed, crusty-black and bleed easily.

Food allergy dermatitis: Nonseasonal itching with reddened skin, papules, pustules and wheals. Found over the ears, rump, back of the legs and undersurface of the body.

Grubs: Inch-long fly larvae that form cystlike lumps beneath the skin with a hole in the center for the insect to breathe. Often found beneath chin or along abdomen.

Lice: Two-millimeter-long insects, or white grains of "sand" (nits) attached to hair. Not common. Found in dogs with matted coats. May have bare spots where hair has been rubbed off.

Lick granuloma (*acral pruritic dermatitis*): Red, shiny skin ulcer caused by continuous licking at wrist or ankle. Mainly in large, short-coated breeds.

Maggots: Soft-bodied, legless fly larvae found in damp matted fur.

Scabies (*Sarcoptic mange*): Intense itching. Small red spots that look like insect bites on the skin of the ears, elbows and hocks. Typical crusty ear tips.

Ticks: Large insects attached to skin. May swell up to size of pea. Found beneath ear flaps and where hair is thin.

Walking dandruff (*Cheyletiella mange*): Occurs in puppies 2 to 12 weeks of age. Large amounts of dry, scaly, flaky skin over the neck and back. Itching is variable.

Hormone-Related Diseases with Hair Loss

Cortisone excess: Symmetric hair loss over trunk and body. Abdomen is pot-bellied and pendulous. Seen with Cushing's syndrome. In some cases the dog is taking steroids.

Growth hormone-responsive alopecia: Bilaterally symmetric hair loss. Begins around puberty. Breed specific involvement.

Hyperestrogenism (*Estrogen excess*): Occurs in females and males. Bilateral symmetric hair loss in perineum and around genitals. Enlarged vulva and clitoris; in males, pendulous prepuce.

Hypoestrogenism (*Estrogen deficiency*): Occurs in older spayed females. Scanty hair growth and thinning coat, initially around vulva and later over body. Skin is smooth and soft, like a baby's.

Hypothyroidism: Most common cause of bilaterally symmetric hair loss without itching. Coat is thin, scanty and falls out easily. Involves the neck beneath the chin to the brisket, sides of body, backs of thighs and top of tail.

Other Diseases with Hair Loss

Acanthosis nigrans: Mainly in Dachshunds. Hair loss begins in armpit folds. Black, thick, greasy, rancid-smelling skin.

Color mutant alopecia (*Blue Doberman syndrome*): Loss of hair over the body, giving a moth-eaten look. Papules and pustules appear in areas of hair loss. Also affects other breeds.

Demodectic mange: *Localized*—Occurs in puppies. Hair loss around eyelids, lips and corners of mouth, giving a moth-eaten look. Fewer than five patches, up to one inch in diameter. *Generalized*—Numerous patches that enlarge and coalesce. Severe skin problem complicated by pyoderma. Primarily affects young adults.

Nasal solar dermatitis (*Collie nose*): Loss of hair at junction of nose and muzzle. Can lead to severe ulceration. Affects dogs with lightly pigmented noses.

Pressure sores (*Calluses*): Gray, hairless, thickened pads of wrinkled skin, usually over elbows but may involve other pressure points. Caused by lying on hard surfaces.

Ringworm: A fungal infection. Scaly, crusty circular patches 1/2 to 2 inches across. Patches show central hair loss with a red ring at the periphery. Some cases show widespread involvement.

Sebaceous adenitis: Mainly in Standard Poodles. Symmertical loss of hair over face, head, neck and back. Dandruff-like scales and hair follicle infection can develop.

Seborrhea: Dry type—similar to heavy dandruff. Greasy type—yellow brown greasy scales that adhere to hair shafts; rancid odor.

Zinc-responsive dermatosis: Crusty, scaly skin with hair loss over the face, nose, elbows and hocks. Cracked feet. Caused by zinc deficiency. Arctic breeds most susceptible.

Skin Diseases with Pus Drainage

Actinomycosis and norcadiosis: Uncommon skin infections with abscesses and draining sinus tracts that discharge pus and respond slowly to treatment.

Acute moist dermatitis (*Hot spots*): Rapidly advancing patches of inflamed skin from which the hair falls out. The skin is covered with a wet exudate of pus. Progresses through self-chewing and results in pyoderma.

Cellulitis or abscess: Painful, warm, reddened skin, or pockets of pus beneath the skin. Look for a cause (such as a foreign body, bite wound, self-trauma from irritative skin disease).

Folliculitis (*Hair pore infection*): Hair shaft protrudes through center of pustule. *Superficial*—Similar to impetigo, but extends to involve armpit folds and chest. *Deep*—Pustules become larger and firmer. Pus, crusts and draining tracts in the skin.

Impetigo: Pimple-like bumps (*pustules*) and thin brown crust on hairless skin of abdomen and groin. Occurs in young puppies.

Interdigital cysts: A swelling between the toes that may open and drain pus.

Mycetoma: Painful swelling at the site of a puncture wound, usually on legs or feet. Pus drains through sinus tracts deep in the mass.

Puppy acne: Purplish red bumps (*pustules*) on the chin and lower lip. Not painful.

Puppy strangles (*Juvenile pyoderma*): Painful swelling of face (lips, eyelids, ears), followed by rapid appearance of pustules and draining sores. Occurs in puppies under four months of age.

Skin fold pyoderma (*Skin wrinkle infection*): Red, inflamed skin with a foul odor in lip fold, nose fold, vulvar fold and tail fold.

Autoimmune and Immune-Mediated Skin Diseases

Bullous pemphigoid: Similar to *pemphigus vulgaris* (see below), but usually begins at the junction of skin and mucous membranes. Mouth is commonly involved.

Discoid lupus erythematosus: Affects the flat surface of the nose. Ulceration and depigmentation are characteristic.

Erythema multiforme: Acute eruption of skin and mucous membranes. Often caused by drugs. Characteristic target-like eruptions with red rims and blanching at center.

Pemphigus erythematosus: Similar to pemphigus foliaceus, but restricted to face, head and foot pads.

Pemphigus foliaceus: Red skin patches (*macules*) that progress rapidly to pustules and then to dry yellow crusts. Usually limited to face (nose, muzzle, around eyes, ears). Crusts adhere to underlying skin and hair. Often becomes generalized. Depigmentation seen in late stages. The feet can become thickened and cracked. Occasionally only the foot pads are involved.

Pemphigus vegetans: Flat-topped pustules involving skin folds. Heals with wart-like growths.

Pemphigus vulgaris: Vesicles and bullae (small and large blisters) that ulcerate and form thick crusts. Usually found around the lips and in the mouth, but may be generalized. Ulceration of foot pads and shedding of nails are common.

Nodular panniculitis: Multiple lumps (like marbles beneath the skin) over the back and along the sides. Lumps open and drain, then heal by scarring.

Systemic lupus erythematosus: Skin involvement similar to pemphigus foliaceus. First sign may be wandering lameness. Ulceration of foot pads is common.

Toxic epidermal necrolysis: Severe, painful skin disease. Blebs and ulcers involve the skin, mucous membranes and foot pads. Large sections of skin are shed like a burn.

Lumps and Bumps on or Beneath the Skin (See Chapter 18)

Abscess: A painful collection of pus at the site of a bite or puncture wound.

Basal cell tumor: Solitary nodule, usually on a narrow base or stalk. Found on the head, neck and shoulders of older dogs.

Ceruminous gland adenoma: A pinkish-white dome-shaped growth in the ear canal less than one centimeter in size. May become ulcerated and secondarily infected.

Epidermal inclusion cyst: A firm lump beneath the skin. May discharge cheesy material and become infected.

Hematoma: A collection of clotted blood beneath the skin; often involves the ear flaps.

Histiocytoma: Rapidly growing dome-shaped (buttonlike) growth found anywhere on the body, usually in young adults.

Lipoma: Smooth round or oblong growth beneath the skin; feels somewhat soft.

Mast cell tumor: Solitary or multiple growths usually found on the trunk, perineum and legs. Breed specific predisposition.

Melanoma: A brown or black pigmented nodule found in areas of dark skin. Growths in mouth and nailbeds usually are malignant.

Perianal gland tumor: A solitary or multinodular growth in the perineum around the anus. Occurs in older intact males.

Sebaceous adenoma: Smooth, pink, wartlike growth less than one inch in size. Most common on the eyelids and limbs. Occurs in older individuals (average age 10).

Skin papillomas: These grow out from the skin and may look like a wart. Not painful.

Soft-tissue sarcomas: Ill-defined or well-demarcated masses of varying size and location. Often slow growing.

Squamous cell carcinoma: A nonhealing gray or reddish-looking ulcer found on the belly, scrotum, feet, legs, lips or nose; may resemble a cauliflowerlike growth.

Transmissible venereal tumors: Ulcerated often multiple cauliflower-like growths on the genitalia of dogs and bitches.

Fleas

The ordinary cat flea (*C. felis*) is the leading cause of itching and scratching in dogs and cats. Fleas survive by feeding on blood. In many dogs, the bites cause only a mild itch, but a heavy infection in a puppy or small dog can cause severe anemia and even death.

Some dogs develop a marked hypersensitivity to the saliva of fleas, and experience intense itching which results in skin abrasions, hair loss and secondary pyoderma (see *Flea Allergy Dermatitis*, page 119). Fleas are also an intermediate host for the dog tapeworm.

Flea infestation can be diagnosed by finding fleas on the dog or by seeing salt-and-pepperlike, black-and-white grains about the size of sand in the coat. These particles are flea feces (the "pepper") and flea eggs (the "salt"). Fecal material is made up of digested blood. When brushed onto a wet paper, it turns a reddish brown.

The adult flea is a small dark brown insect about 2.5 millimeters in size that can be seen with the naked eye. Although fleas have no wings and cannot fly, they do have powerful back legs and can jump great distances. Fleas move through the hair rapidly and are difficult to catch. Run a fine-toothed flea comb through the hair and look for fleas on your dog's back, in the groin, and around the tail and hindquarters. Itching is most pronounced in these areas.

THE FLEA LIFE CYCLE

An effective flea control strategy requires an understanding of the flea life cycle. Fleas need a warm, humid environment to flourish and reproduce. The higher the temperature and humidity, the more efficient their reproduction. The adult flea can live up to 115 days on the dog, but only one or two days when off.

After taking a blood meal, fleas mate on the skin of the dog. The female lays eggs within 24 to 48 hours, and may produce up to 2,000 eggs in a four-month life span. The eggs fall off and incubate beneath furniture and in carpets, cracks and bedding. Deep pile and shag carpets make an ideal environment for egg development.

In 10 days the eggs hatch into larvae that feed on local debris. Larvae spin a cocoon and go into a pupal stage that lasts for days or months. Under ideal temperature and humidity conditions, fleas can emerge rapidly. After hatching, immature adult fleas have two weeks to find a host.

At any given time, about 1 percent of the flea population is composed of adult fleas, while 99 percent remain in the invisible egg, larval and pupal stages. An effective flea control program must eliminate this large reservoir.

NEW METHODS OF FLEA CONTROL

New products such as Program, Advantage and Frontline Spot On have all but replaced the use of oral Proban and topical insecticides to treat and prevent fleas. The new products are more effective and safer than the traditional insecticides. They are also easier to administer.

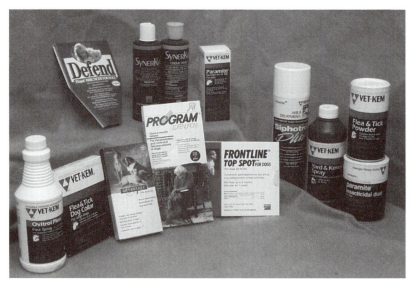

A host of new products have revolutionized flea control.

Program (*lufenuron*) was the first and remains the most popular agent for controlling fleas on dogs. Program is a tablet given once a month with a meal. The active ingredient accumulates in the dog's subcutaneous tissue and requires that the flea bite the dog in order to work.

Program works by inhibiting flea eggs from growing and hatching. This leads to a steady drop in the number of new fleas in the environment. However, as mature fleas are not affected, it can take 30 to 60 days or longer for the adult fleas on the dog to die of old age before you notice a reduction in itching and scratching.

For more immediate results, and especially if the dog is suffering from flea allergy dermatitis, Program should be combined with a flea shampoo or some other topical insecticide treatment. Advantage or Frontline can be added to Program to kill adult fleas within one to two days. It may be necessary to eliminate fleas on the premises using insecticides, as well (see *Eliminating Fleas on the Premises*, page 108).

Program should not be used on puppies younger than six weeks of age, but is safe to use on pregnant and lactating bitches.

A product called Sentinel combines Program with the heartworm preventive Interceptor. This broad-spectrum preventive not only controls fleas, but also protects against heartworms, ascarids, hookworms and whipworms.

Advantage (*imidacloyrid*) is a once-a-month liquid preparation that kills fleas by direct contact. Fleas don't have to bite the pet for the preparation to work. Advantage comes in a tube and is applied to the dog's skin between the shoulder blades (you must carefully part the hair to make sure you get the liquid on the skin). The amount to apply depends on the size of the dog, and will be prescribed by your veterinarian. One application protects a dog for up to 30 days. Advantage kills fleas on direct contact. Following application, 98 to 100 percent of adult fleas are killed within 12 hours. Thus, any new fleas that infest the dog should be killed before they have a chance to lay eggs. This breaks the flea life cycle and eventually eliminates fleas in the environment. Advantage is not absorbed into the dog's system, and therefore is nontoxic. Humans do not absorb the chemical after petting a treated dog.

One drawback of Advantage is that it loses some of its effectiveness if the coat becomes thoroughly wet more often than once a week. If this happens, the dog can be retreated as often as once a week.

Advantage should not be used on puppies under seven weeks of age, or on pregnant or lactating females.

Frontline Spot On and Frontline Spray contain the active ingredient *fipromil*, which acts on contact within 24 to 48 hours to kill fleas. The fleas do not need to bite the dog to be killed. Frontline is a liquid that comes in tubes and is applied as described for Advantage. On large dogs it is necessary to use more than one tube to get the correct dosage.

The effectiveness of Frontline is not diminished if the dog's coat becomes wet. The product has a residual effect that lasts up to 90 days in some dogs. Like Advantage, Frontline is not absorbed and thus appears to be nontoxic. One additional benefit is that it also kills ticks for up to 30 days.

Frontline Spot On should not be used on puppies under 10 weeks of age. The spray, however, can be used on puppies eight weeks and older. Frontline should not be used on pregnant or lactating females.

A newly released heartworm preventative called Selamectin (*Revolution*) is a once-a-month liquid preparation applied to the skin of the dog's neck between the shoulder blades, as described for Advantage. It also controls adult fleas and prevents flea eggs from hatching. It is discussed in Chapter 11 (see *Heartworms*).

TOPICAL INSECTICIDES FOR FLEA CONTROL

A variety of insecticide products are available to control fleas, but there are differences in safety and effectiveness. Be sure to read the label to make sure the product is specifically intended to control fleas on dogs. Better yet, consult your veterinarian and use the products he or she recommends as being most economical, effective and convenient.

Flea shampoos kill only when they are on the pet. Once rinsed off, they have no residual effect. They are best used in mild to moderate flea infestations when treatment of the environment has been thorough. In general, pyrethrin-based shampoos are safest, especially on puppies.

Powders and dusts have more residual killing activity, but must be worked thoroughly through the haircoat down to the skin. They tend to leave the coat dry and gritty. Dusting must be repeated two to three times a week, or as recommended by the manufacturer.

Sprays, foams and dips have the most effective killing action and are the best choices for severe flea infestations and for dogs with flea allergy dermatitis. Sprays and foams work best on dogs with short coats. Sprays come in pressurized cans and trigger-activated bottles. The hiss of the pressurized can may frighten some dogs, in which case the foam is preferable. Most sprays have a residual killing action that lasts up to 14 days.

Water-based sprays are preferable to alcohol-based sprays, which are flammable and can dry the coat. When using a spray, begin near the back of the dog's head and work toward the tail. This prevents fleas on the body from escaping the treatment by moving up onto the face.

Sprays and foams should not be used on puppies under two months of age, unless the manufacturer's label says it is safe to do so.

Insecticide flea dips applied to the coat and allowed to dry are extremely effective in getting rid of fleas. Dips penetrate the haircoat and have the most immediate killing action and the longest residual activity. They also have the greatest potential for toxicity. Before using a dip, read the instructions carefully. Use according to the manufacturer's recommendations. For information on how to use a flea dip, see *Insecticide Dips*, page 116.

Flea collars aid in flea control but do not eradicate all fleas. Most collars contain dichlorvos, which vaporizes and surrounds the dog. If the dog sleeps outdoors, the collar will not be effective. Flea collars lose their potency over time and must be changed every two months, or as recommended by the manufacturer. *Dog flea collars should not be used on cats.*

Dogs can become sensitive to the chemicals in flea collars and develop contact dermatitis. This can be prevented to some extent by airing the collar for 24 hours and applying it loosely. The collar should fit so that you can get at least two fingers between it and the dog's neck.

Using a dichlorvos flea collar along with a dichlorvos-containing dewormer could result in the absorption of a toxic concentration of dichlorvos. Remove the collar one week before deworming and replace it one week after deworming. Also, do not allow the dog to eat or chew his collar.

A SUGGESTED FLEA CONTROL PROGRAM

Start your dog on a monthly flea-prevention protocol (if possible, before the fleas attack), using a product such as Program or Sentinel. Prevention is the key to success.

When fleas have already become established, it is essential to kill them on the dog and prevent them from coming back. One way to do this is to shampoo or dip the dog to immediately eliminate the fleas. Twenty-four to 48 hours later, apply Frontline Spot On or Advantage to kill new fleas hatching from eggs on the premises. Some veterinarians combine Spot On or Advantage with Program or Sentinel for more rapid results. Because all of these products prevent fleas from reproducing, they eventually rid the environment of fleas.

For this approach to be successful, *it is essential to treat all the pets (dogs and cats) in the family.*

The following protocol for eliminating fleas can be used *if your dog is not on a monthly flea control program:*

- All pets (dogs and cats) must be treated.
- Dip every other week using a solution containing chlorpyrifos or permethrin. It is important to be sure that the product is labeled as safe for the pet in question.
- On alternate weeks, use sprays or foams containing pyrethrins and/or permethrin. Apply to the skin surface, not just the hair. (Note: If you are unable to treat every animal in the home, substitute sprays and foams at the maximum frequency allowed by the manufacturer.)
- For unaffected pets, a dip or spray application twice a month is sufficient.
- Mechanical removal of fleas using a flea comb (32 teeth per inch) is effective on short-haired dogs. The pet must be combed at least every other day. Comb the face as well as the body. Kill fleas on the comb by immersing it in alcohol or liquid detergent.
- Flea collars should not be used as the sole source of flea control.

ELIMINATING FLEAS ON THE PREMISES

If you are using a monthly flea control product such as Program or Sentinel (with or without Advantage or Frontline Spot On), the environment should eventually come under control as the fleas fail to reproduce. For this to be effective, all pets must be treated.

To immediately control fleas in the house, thoroughly clean the entire house and then apply insecticides in the form of carpet shampoos and house sprays. On carpeted floors, electrostatically charged sodium polyborate powder (Rx for Fleas is the brand name) is most effective, lasting up to a year.

In households with cats and/or young children, the safest insecticides are the *pyrethrins* (this includes *pyrethroids* and *permethrin*), and the insect growth regulators *methoprene* and *fenoxycarb*. Insect growth regulators prevent eggs and larvae from developing into adult fleas. Methoprene must come into contact with the egg within 12 hours after the egg is laid to be completely effective, while fenoxycarb can contact the egg any time during its development to be effective.

Insecticides must be applied monthly to all floor surfaces. If pyrethrins are used alone, weekly spraying for the first three weeks is necessary.

Foggers generally contain permethrin or synergized natural pyrethrins (pyrethroids). Some contain insect growth regulators. One disadvantage of foggers is that the mist settles on top of carpets and may not settle in the cracks of upholstery and beneath furniture. Flea larvae and pupae, however, burrow deep into the nap and also seek out cracks and crevices. To offset this disadvantage, shampoo carpets and spray beneath furniture before activating the fogger.

Do not use foggers in rooms where toddlers and young children live or play. Although labels on these products say that rooms should be vacated for one to three hours, studies show that high residue levels can remain for a week or longer. Especially dangerous are exposed plastic toys and stuffed animals, which seem to attract the pesticide.

Mechanical cleaning and insecticide applications must be repeated at three-week intervals. It may take nine weeks to eliminate all visible fleas. With a heavy infestation, it may be advisable to enlist the services of a professional exterminator.

Outdoor control involves treating the yard, kennel, pens, runs and favorite resting spots. For more information, see *Disinfecting the Premises* on page 116.

Other External Parasites

SCABIES (SARCOPTIC MANGE)

This disease is caused by tiny spiderlike mites. Scabies is highly contagious and is transmitted primarily by direct contact and through contaminated grooming equipment and kennels. Probably no other skin disease will cause your dog to scratch and bite at his skin with such intensity.

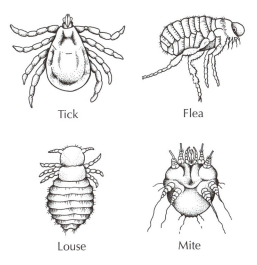

Common external parasites.

Tick   Flea

Louse   Mite

The severe itching is caused by female mites tunneling a few millimeters under the skin to lay their eggs. The eggs hatch in 3 to 10 days. The immature mites develop into adults and begin to lay eggs of their own. The entire life cycle occurs on the dog's skin, and takes just 17 to 21 days.

Signs: Scabies attacks the skin of the ears, elbows, hocks, and the underside of the chest and face. The onset is abrupt with scratching, hair loss and inflamed skin in these areas. Crusty ear tips are characteristic. A classic test for scabies is to rub the ear flap between your fingers and watch the dog scratch on the same side. In late stages the skin becomes thick, crusted, scaly and darkly pigmented.

Scabies in people can produce an itchy rash, typically found at the belt line. This rash is caused by insects that have transferred from the dog. Scabies mites, however, do not live on human skin for longer than three weeks. If the problem does not disappear in three weeks, look for a continuing source of infestation.

The diagnosis is made by examining skin scrapings under a microscope. In some cases the mites may not be identified. If the dog's syptoms strongly suggest scabies, your veterinarian may decide to begin treatment as a diagnostic test. A positive response to the treatment confirms the diagnosis of scabies.

Treatment: Scabies must be treated under veterinary supervision. Clip the hair away from scabies-affected areas on medium- and long-haired dogs and bathe the entire animal using a *benzoyl peroxide* shampoo (OxyDex or Pyoben). The shampoo loosens scales and allows an insecticide dip to penetrate the hair pores.

Scabies mites have developed resistance to a number of organophosphate dips. Two dips that remain active against them are *amitraz* (Mitaban) and two to four percent *lime-sulfur* (LymDyp). Only lime-sulfur is licensed by the FDA for treatment of scabies in dogs. LymDyp has an unpleasant odor, stains white coats and can irritate the skin.

Dip the dog once a week for six consecutive weeks (or until the symptoms resolve), using the dip recommended by your veterinarian. Continue treatment for two more weeks after the dogs appears to be cured. When using any dip, carefully

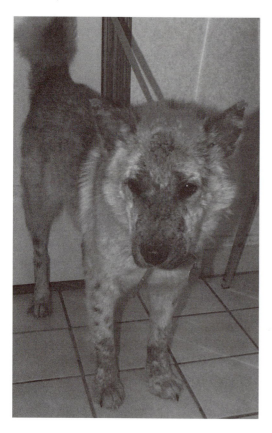

Scabies with extensive involvement of the face. Note the crusty ear tips characteristic of this disease.

follow the instructions on the label. For information on how to dip, see *Insecticide Dips*, page 116. It important to treat all dogs that have come into contact with the affected individual.

Oral ivermectin is effective against scabies and is frequently used as a diagnostic test when skin scrapings have been negative. Although not licensed by the FDA for treating scabies in dogs, it is used for this purpose by many veterinarians. Ivermectin, in doses used for scabies, has produced central nervous system problems and deaths in Collies, Shetland Sheepdogs, Old English Sheepdogs, Australian Shepherds and other herding breeds and their crosses. The drug is contraindicated in these breeds. Always have the heartworm status of your dog checked before giving ivermectin.

Recent reports suggest that Interceptor (*milbemycin oxime*) may also be effective against scabies mites, and could be used in place of ivermectin in breeds in which ivermectin is contraindicated.

Corticosteroids relieve severe itching and may be required for the first two to three days of treatment. Infected skin sores require oral and topical antibiotics. Adult mites can live for 21 days off the host. Treatment of the indoor environment (as described in *Eliminating Fleas on the Premises*, page 108) is advisable to prevent recurrence.

WALKING DANDRUFF (CHEYLETIELLA MANGE)

Cheyletiella mange is a highly contagious skin disease that affects young puppies. It is caused by large reddish mites that infest kennels and pet shops. These mites live on the surface of the skin and die within 10 days when off their host. Walking dandruff is becoming less prevalent because of the widespread use of flea control preparations that also kill cheyletiella mites.

Cheyletiella mange mites are usually found along the back, but occasionally infest other parts of the body. The signs are a red bumpy rash along with a large amount of flaky skin in the haircoat. Suspect this condition if you find a heavy dandruff over the neck and back of a recently acquired puppy or kitten. Itching may be intense or completely absent.

The diagnosis is made by finding mites or eggs in dandruff scrapings collected with a flea comb or sticky tape. In some cases the mites or eggs cannot be seen, and the diagnosis depends on the animal's response to therapy.

Cheyletiella mites can infect humans, producing an itchy papular rash (small red pumps with areas of central *necrosis*) found most often on the arms, trunk and buttocks. This rash, like that of scabies, should disappear when the pet is successfully treated.

Treatment: All animals that have been in contact with the affected dog must be treated to eliminate mites from the kennel and household. Pyrethrin shampoos and 2 percent lime-sulfur dips (LymDyp) are effective in killing cheyletiella mites. Follow the directions on the label (see *Using Insecticides*, page 115). If the mites are resistant, seek veterinary consultation; other treatments are available.

Clean and spray the dog's quarters with a residual insecticide appropriate for killing adult fleas.

CHIGGERS (TROMBICULID MITES)

Chiggers, also called harvest mites or red bugs, live as adults in decaying vegetation. Only their larval forms are parasitic. Dogs acquire the infestation while prowling in forest grasslands and fields in late summer and fall, when chiggers are reproducing.

Chigger larvae appear as red, yellow or orange specks, barely visible to the naked eye but easily seen with a magnifying glass. They tend to clump in areas where the skin is thin, usually between the toes or about the ears and mouth. The larvae feed by sucking on the skin. The result is severe itching with the formation of sores and scabs. The diagnosis is made by identifying the mites by visual inspection or by microscopic examination of skin scrapings.

Treatment: Chiggers respond well to a single application of a lime sulfur dip (LymDyp) or a pyrethrin shampoo. Corticosteroids may be required for two or three days to control intense itching. If the ear canals are involved, treat with thiabendazole drops (Tresderm). Prevent reinfestation by keeping your dog out of fields and grasses during the chigger season.

LICE (PEDICULOSIS)

Lice are uncommon in dogs. They occur primarily in dogs that are run-down and poorly kept. Lice are usually found beneath matted hair around the ears, head, neck, shoulders and in the perineal area. Because of the severe itching and constant irritation, bare spots may be seen where the hair has been rubbed off.

There are two species of lice: *biting lice*, which feed on skin scales, and *sucking lice*, which feed on the dog's blood and can cause severe protein deficiency and anemia.

Lice are tiny insects 2 to 3 mm in size, frequently found around the head and ears and beneath matted hair.

Adult lice are wingless, slow-moving, pale-colored insects about two to three millimeters long. The eggs, called *nits,* look like white grains of sand firmly attached to the hair. The diagnosis is made by visual identification of adult lice or nits. Nits may look something like flaky skin (dandruff), but inspection with a magnifying glass reveals the difference.

Treatment: Lice show little resistance to treatment and do not live long off the host. They are easily killed with most insecticides, including lime-sulfur, pyrethrins and pyrethroids. The infected dog and all animals that have been in contact with it should be treated once a week for four weeks with an insecticide shampoo, dip or powder. Infected bedding should be destroyed and the dog's sleeping quarters and grooming equipment disinfected.

Severely anemic dogs may require a blood transfusion or vitamins and iron supplements.

TICKS

Ticks are found in nearly all parts of the country and are especially prevalent in spring and fall. Ticks are vectors for several diseases in dogs, cats and humans: Rocky Mountain spotted fever, canine ehrlichiosis, canine babesiosis, canine hepatozoonosis and Lyme disease. The saliva of ticks can produce an allergic hypersensitivity reaction and, in the case of the female wood tick, a disease called tick paralysis.

The tick has a complicated life cycle involving three hosts, including wild and domestic animals and humans. The adult ticks drops onto the host as it walks through tall grass and brush. Ticks can fasten to any part of the dog's skin, but are commonly found around the ears and between the toes. A severely infested dog may have hundreds of ticks all over his body.

The male tick is a small, flat insect about the size of a match head. A blood tick is a pea-sized female tick that feeds on the dog. It is during feeding that diseases are transmitted. Males and females mate on the skin of the dog, after which the female takes a blood meal. This usually occurs 5 to 20 hours after the dog acquires the ticks. Thus, prompt removal of ticks is an effective method of preventing tick-borne diseases.

Ticks may drop off a dog and transfer to people, although this is not common. Once a tick starts feeding on a dog, it will feed until it is engorged and will not seek a second host.

Treatment: Always examine your dog after hiking in tick-infested areas. If you find only one or two ticks, the easiest thing to do is to remove them. Keep in mind that the blood of ticks can be dangerous to people. Therefore, do not crush or squeeze a tick with your bare fingers. Before removing the tick, put on disposable rubber or plastic gloves.

Ticks unattached to the skin are easily removed with a pair of tweezers. Once removed, the tick can be killed by putting it in rubbing alcohol.

A blood tick with its head buried in the skin should not be pulled loose, because the head may detach and remain behind. Before removing the tick, apply nail polish remover, rubbing alcohol or a commercial tick spray (available at pet supply shops or through your veterinarian) directly to the tick with a saturated cotton-tip applicator or a cotton ball. The tick will begin to back out in less than a minute. Then grasp the tick firmly with tweezers and lift it off. Dispose of the tick by putting it in rubbing alcohol to kill it and flushing it down the toilet.

If the head or mouth parts remain embedded in the skin, redness and swelling is likely to occur at the site of the bite. In most cases this reaction clears up in two to three days. However, if it does not do so—or seems to be getting worse—consult your veterinarian.

With numerous ticks, treatment involves an insecticide dip containing a natural or synthetic pyrethrins labeled for ticks, or an organophosphate dip such as Paramite. For information on how to dip, see *Insecticide Dips*, page 116.

With a heavy infestation, dip every week for four to six weeks. Be sure to eliminate ticks from the dog's sleeping quarters (see *Disinfecting the Premises*, page 116).

Ticks can work their way deep into the ear canals. These ticks should be removed by a veterinarian.

Prevention: Ticks must attach for several hours before they can transmit diseases. Therefore, if you remove ticks promptly after your dog has been running in the fields or woods, you can prevent many tick-borne infections.

Preventic tick collars containing *amitraz* are quite effective in controlling ticks. Frontline Spot On used to control fleas has some effectiveness in killing ticks for up to 30 days following a single application. Consider using this product along with an amitraz tick collar during the tick season.

For outdoor control, cut tall grass, weeds and brush. Treat the yard with an insecticide labeled for use with animals. Use according to directions.

PELODERA DERMATITIS (DAMP HAY ITCH)

This disease is caused by the larvae of a threadlike worm found in decaying rice hulls, straw, marsh hay and other grasses that are in contact with damp soil. The larvae burrow into the skin of the dog's chest, abdomen and feet, causing intense itching and pimplelike bumps. Later, you may see raw, crusted and inflamed areas where the dog has scratched and chewed the skin.

The condition is found in dogs bedded on damp hay and straw. The diagnosis is made by finding the worm larvae on microscopic examination of skin scrapings.

Treatment: Bathe the dog with a benzoyl peroxide shampoo such as OxyDex or Pyoben to remove scales and crusts. Follow with an organophosphate insecticide dip such as Paramite (see *Using Insecticides*, page 115). Repeat the dip in one week if the dog continues to itch. Apply topical antibiotic ointment to inflamed skin areas three times a day.

Wash the dog's bedding and spray the sleeping area with an organophosphate insecticide containing *malathion* or *diazinon*. Change the bedding from hay to cedar shavings or shredded paper; or provide the dog with a fabric-covered sleeping pad.

FLIES

Adult flies may at times deposit their eggs on raw or infected wounds, or in soil where larvae can penetrate the dog's skin.

Maggots

A maggot infestation, called *myiasis*, is a seasonal, warm-weather disease caused most often by the bluebottle or blow fly that lays its eggs on open wounds or on badly soiled, matted fur. Debilitated dogs and old dogs who are unable to keep themselves clean are susceptible to maggots.

The eggs hatch within three days. Over the next two weeks the larvae grow into large maggots that produce a salivary enzyme that digests the skin, causing "punched-out" areas. The maggots then penetrate the skin, enlarge the opening, and set the stage for a bacterial skin infection. With a severe infestation the dog could go into shock. The shock is caused by enzymes and toxins secreted by the maggots. This is a medical emergency and requires immediate veterinary attention.

Treatment: Clip the affected areas to remove soiled and matted hair. Remove all maggots with blunt-nosed tweezers. Wash infected areas with Betadine solution and dry the dog. Then spray or shampoo the dog using a nonalcohol-based product containing a pyrethrins. Repeat as described for *Fleas* and check closely for remaining maggots.

Dogs with infected wounds should be treated with oral antibiotics. If the dog is debilitated, his health and nutrition must be improved to bring about a cure.

Grubs (Cuterebriasis)

Grubs are the larvae of a large botfly that has a wide seasonal distribution in the United States. This fly lays its eggs near the burrows of rodents and rabbits. Dogs acquire the disease by direct contact with infested soil.

Newly hatched larvae penetrate the skin to form cystlike lumps with small openings to allow the grubs to breathe. Typical infestation locations are along the jaw, under the belly and along the flanks. Inch-long grubs may protrude from these breathing holes. In about one month, the grubs emerge and drop to the ground. Several grubs may be found in the same area of the body. In such cases, they form large nodular masses.

Treatment: Veterinary assistance is best. Clip away hair to expose the breathing holes. Grasp each grub with a fine-tipped forceps and gently draw it out. Do not crush or rupture the grub. This can produce anaphylactic shock in the dog.

If you are unable to grasp the grub, a small incision must be made under local anesthesia to remove the parasite. Grub wounds are slow to heal and often become infected. Antibiotics may be required.

Using Insecticides

Dealing effectively with external parasites often involves using insecticides on your pets, your home and your yard. Insecticides are incorporated into powders, sprays, dusts and dips for the elimination of fleas, lice, mites, ticks and other parasites on the dog. They are also used to disinfect bedding, houses, kennels, runs, gardens, garages and other spots where a dog could become reinfested.

There are four classes of insecticides in current use. In order of decreasing toxicity, they are: chlorinated hydrocarbons; organophosphates and carbamates; pyrethrins (natural and synthetic); and natural insecticides such as d-limonene. In addition, there are insect growth regulators that, although not insecticides, act to prevent insect reproduction.

Insecticides can be dangerous if not used properly, so it is important to follow all directions on the label and to use with them care. The diagnosis and treatment of insecticide poisoning is discussed in *Poisoning* in Chapter 1. For a discussion of insecticides used in flea control, see *Topical Insecticides for Flea Control,* page 106.

When you purchase an insecticide, be sure it is labeled as safe for use on dogs. Preparations manufactured for sheep and livestock can irritate the skin of dogs and even cause death.

Insecticides are poisons! *Before using any insecticide, be sure to read and follow the directions of the manufacturer.* This will prevent accidental poisoning from improper use.

INSECTICIDE DIPS

Dips are insecticide solutions that are sponged or rinsed onto the body and allowed to dry on the hair and skin. Choose a dip recommended by your veterinarian or, if you decide to use a commercial preparation, read the label to be sure the product is effective against the parasite in question. If your dog has recently been dewormed, check with your veterinarian before using a dip.

Before dipping, plug the dog's ears with cotton to prevent the insecticide from entering the ear canals. Begin by washing the dog with a gentle commercial dog shampoo, or, if prescribed by your veterinarian, a shampoo that loosens crusts and scales. Squeeze out excess water from the coat to keep it from diluting the dip. Make up the dip according to the directions on the package. Then apply as directed. Protect the dog's eyes from contact with the shampoo or dip to avoid eye burns (see *Burns of the Eyes* in Chapter 5).

Most dips must be repeated one or more times at intervals of 7 to 10 days to rid the dog of the parasite in question. Consult the label for recommended frequency. Do not exceed this frequency. Many dips should not be used on young puppies.

DISINFECTING THE PREMISES

The goal of premise control is to prevent reinfestation by ridding the environment of insects, eggs, larvae and other intermediate stages. This is accomplished by mechanical cleaning and the application of insecticides.

Indoor Control

To eliminate all sources of reinfestation, it is essential to treat all animals in the household. Destroy infected bedding. Blankets and rugs on which the dog regularly sleeps should be washed weekly at the hottest setting. Scrub the dog's quarters with a strong household disinfectant. To be effective, the quarters should receive at least two thorough cleanings with application of insecticides spaced three weeks apart.

A thorough housecleaning involves vacuuming carpets, curtains and furniture. Vacuum cleaner bags must be discarded immediately after use, as they provide an ideal environment for flea hatching. Floors should be mopped, giving special attention to cracks and crevices where eggs are likely to incubate.

Steam cleaning of carpets is highly effective in killing eggs and larvae. Insecticides can be used in the water of the steam cleaner. Specific products are available where you rent the equipment. With a heavy infestation, consider enlisting the services of a professional exterminator.

Insecticides are applied in the form of carpet shampoos and premise sprays (see *Eliminating Fleas on the Premises,* page 108). Remove all pets and children before you begin, and read all instructions carefully.

Outdoor Control

For outdoor control, first remove all decaying vegetation. Mow, rake and discard the debris.

For disinfecting kennels, runs and other areas, the liquid application of chlorpyrifos, permethrin or diazinon is preferred. Follow the directions in regard to mixing, preparation and application. When applying sprays, give special attention to favorite sleeping spots such beneath the porch or in the garage. Be sure the ground is dry before allowing pets outside.

Repeat the application twice at three-week intervals, or as recommended by the manufacturer. The residual activity of outdoor insecticides depends on weather conditions. In dry weather, it may remain effective for a month; in wet weather, for only one to two weeks.

Some insecticide dips can be used as sprays on gardens, lawns and kennels. Use according to the instructions on the label.

Lick Granulomas (Acral Pruritic Dermatitis)

A lick granuloma is an open sore at the ankle or wrist perpetuated by constant licking. It is seen most often in large short-coated dogs such as Doberman Pinschers, Great Danes, Labrador Retrievers and bird dogs.

At one time lick sores were thought to be *psychogenic* in origin and related to boredom and inactivity. It now appears that most cases are preceded by an itchy skin disease (such as canine atopy) that starts the lick cycle. Other possible initiating causes include demodectic mange, a bacterial or fungal infection, prior trauma and underlying joint disease. The precipitating event focuses the dog's attention on the area. The licking then becomes a habit that may be perpetuated by psychological events.

As the dog licks at his wrist or ankle, the hair is rubbed off and the surface of the skin becomes red and shiny. Eventually the skin becomes raised, thick, hard and insensitive to pressure. However, it remains fresh-looking from the constant licking.

Treatment: It is important to review the course of events in an attempt to identify the precipitating cause. If a disease such as canine atopy is diagnosed, medical treatment is directed toward that condition.

Local treatment involves the use of topical and injectable steroids, radiation therapy, surgical removal, cryotherapy and acupuncture. Results are variable. The lick granuloma is one of the most difficult skin problems to treat successfully.

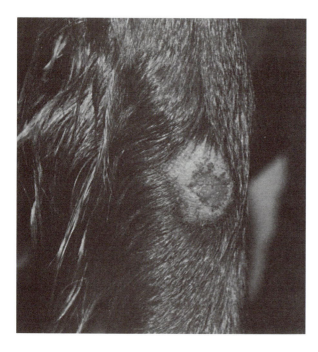

A lick granuloma near the ankle. The hair is rubbed off and the ulcer is clean and shiny.

Because lick sores are perpetuated by *psychogenic* factors, a change in the dog's routine or lifestyle should be part of the treatment program. For example, some arrangement may need to be made to provide company for the dog when the owner is away. A new puppy in the house may provide companionship and entertain an older dog. Behavior-modifying drugs may be beneficial in some cases.

Allergies

The number of dogs with allergies has increased dramatically in recent years. It is now estimated that one in seven dogs suffer from allergic symptoms. Heredity plays a role. Although certain breeds appear to be more allergy prone, all breeds and their mixes can be affected.

An allergy is in an unpleasant reaction caused by exposure to a food, inhalant or something in the dog's environment. What the dog is exposed to is called the *allergen*. The way in which the dog's immune system responds to the allergen is called the allergic or hypersensitivity reaction.

Before a dog can be allergic, exposure to the allergen must occur at least twice. The first exposure causes the immune system to manufacture antibodies to the allergen. A later exposure triggers an allergen-antibody reaction that releases histamine, the chemical mediator responsible for the reaction.

While humans tend to experience upper respiratory symptoms when an allergy is triggered, the target organ in dogs is the skin, with intense itching being the principal sign. Dogs with allergies often scratch continuously, are miserable, snappish and generally unpleasant to be around.

There are two kinds of hypersensitivity. The *immediate* type occurs minutes after exposure and usually produces hives. The *delayed* response occurs hours or days later and causes intense itching. *Anaphylactic shock* (discussed in Chapter 1) is a severe hypersensitivity reaction of the immediate type accompanied by diarrhea, vomiting, weakness, difficulty breathing with *stridor*, collapse and death.

Dog allergies fall into three categories:

- Those caused by fleas and other biting insects (*flea allergy dermatitis*).
- Those caused by inhaled allergens such as dust mites, grasses, molds, tree and weed pollens (*canine atopy*).
- Those caused and by foods and drugs (*food allergy*).

HIVES

Hives are an allergic reaction characterized by the sudden appearance of raised, circular, itchy wheals on the skin of the face and elsewhere. The hair sticks out in little patches. Frequently you will see swelling of the eyelids. Hives generally appear within 30 minutes of exposure and disappear within 24 hours.

Insect bites are a common cause of hives. Hives can occur after a vaccination. Penicillin, tetracycline and other antibiotics can produce hives. Topical insecticides and soaps are other causes. Hives that come and go usually are caused by an allergen in the dog's environment.

Treatment: When possible, identify the allergen and prevent further exposure. When a food allergy is suspected, modify the dog's diet (see *Food Allergy*, page 123). In the case of an acute reaction, you can give a dose of Milk of Magnesia to speed removal of the food from the intestinal tract (see *Common Drugs for Home Veterinary Use* in Chapter 20). When hives appear shortly after a shampoo or application of a topical insecticide, bathe the dog and rinse thoroughly to remove the chemical from the dog's coat and skin.

Hives usually respond well to an antihistamine such as Benadryl (see the table *Common Drugs for Home Veterinary Use* in Chapter 20 for dosage). Cortisone may be indicated to control a severe case. Consult your veterinarian.

FLEA ALLERGY DERMATITIS

This is the most common allergy in dogs. It is caused by a hypersensitivity reaction to one or more substances in the saliva of fleas. Flea allergy dermatitis is an allergic reaction of both the immediate and delayed type; *itching begins immediately and tends to persist long after fleas have been eliminated*. Symptoms are worse in midsummer during the flea season. However, dogs that live in the house may suffer all year long.

Flea allergy dermatitis is characterized by severe itching with inflamed skin and red pimplelike bumps (*papules*) found where fleas are heavily concentrated—over the rump and base of the tail, under the legs, on the groin and belly. Dogs chew and rub at these areas. Hair falls out and the skin becomes dry and scaly. In some cases the skin breaks down and develops raw areas that become crusted and infected. In time, the skin becomes thick and darkly pigmented.

The diagnosis can be suspected by finding fleas on the dog and seeing the characteristic skin rash. Check for fleas by standing your dog over a sheet of white paper and brushing the coat. White and black grains of sandy material that drop onto the paper are flea eggs and feces. An allergic response to flea saliva can be demonstrated by an intradermal skin test.

Hair loss over the rump and base of the tail due to excessive itching, scratching and rubbing caused by flea bites.

Treatment: The majority of dogs with flea allergy dermatitis can be cured by eliminating fleas on the dog and controlling fleas in the environment. All pets in the household, even those not affected, must be treated simultaneously to eliminate fleas. Antihistamines and/or corticosteroids may be required for two to three days to control itching. *Pyoderma* requires topical and oral antibiotics. Seek veterinary attention for these problems.

Prevention: The monthly application of a flea control product such as Frontline Spot On or Advantage will kill adult fleas before they bite the dog. Program inhibits reinfestation by preventing fleas from reproducing. The combination of Program with Frontline or Advantage should eventually eliminate fleas, but for a more rapid response it may be necessary to treat the environment as described in *Eliminating Fleas on the Premises*, page 108.

CANINE ATOPY (ATOPIC DERMATITIS)

Canine atopy is a disease in which there is an inherited tendency to develop IgE antibodies in response to exposure to *allergens* inhaled or absorbed through the skin. This extremely common allergic skin disease is second only to flea allergy dermatitis in frequency, and affects about 10 percent of dogs.

Atopy begins in dogs one to three years of age. Susceptible breeds include Golden and Labrador Retrievers, Lhasa Apsos, Wire Fox Terriers, West Highland White Terriers, Dalmatians, Poodles, English and Irish Setters, Boxers, Bulldogs, among others.

Signs first appear in conjunction with the weed pollens of late summer and fall. Later, other pollens begin to influence the picture: tree pollens in March and April; then grass pollens in May, June and early July. Finally, the dog starts to react to wool, house dust, molds, feathers, plant fibers and so forth. With prolonged exposure and multiple allergens, the condition becomes a year-round affair.

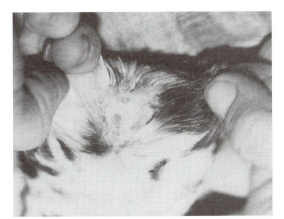

Itchy papules between toes, caused by atopy.

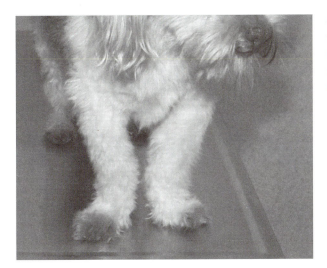

Canine atopy: Note the characteristic brown stains on the feet from licking at the paws.

In *early* canine atopy, itching is seasonal and the skin looks normal. Dogs scratch at the ears and underside of the body. The itching is often accompanied by face-rubbing, sneezing, a runny nose (*allergic rhinitis*), watery eyes and licking at the paws (leaving characteristic brown stains on the feet). In many dogs the disease does not progress beyond this stage.

When it does progress, an itch-scratch-itch cycle develops with deep scratches (called *excoriations*) in the skin, hair loss, scabs, crusts and secondary bacterial skin infection. These dogs are miserable. In time, the skin becomes thick and darkly pigmented. A dry or greasy seborrhea with flaky skin often develops in conjunction with skin infection.

Ear canal infections may accompany these signs, or may be the sole manifestation of atopy. The ear flaps are red and inflamed, and the canals filled with a brown wax that eventually causes bacterial or yeast otitis (see *Ear Allergies*, Chapter 6).

Canine atopy, especially when complicated by *pyoderma*, can be difficult to distinguish from flea allergy dermatitis, scabies, demodectic mange, food allergies and other skin diseases. The diagnosis can be suspected on the basis of the history, location of skin lesions and seasonal pattern of occurrence. Skin scrapings, bacterial and fungal cultures, and a trial on a hypoallergenic test diet should be considered before embarking on an involved course of treatment for atopy. It is important to treat and eliminate fleas. The majority of dogs with canine atopy are allergic to fleas and may have an associated flea allergy dermatitis complicating the picture.

The preferred method of diagnosing canine atopy is through intradermal skin testing, which means injecting small amounts of many known allergens and observing the skin reaction. This can be time consuming and expensive, because it requires many trips to the veterinarian. To be accurate, all supportive drugs must be withdrawn during the testing period. If intradermal skin testing is not available, a serologic blood test (*ELISA*) designed to detect group-specific IgE antibody may assist in making the diagnosis.

Treatment: The most effective long-term solution would be to change the dog's living circumstances to avoid the allergen. The atopic dog is usually allergic to many different allergens, however, and it often is not practical or feasible to avoid exposure to them all.

Most dogs with atopy respond well to treatment. A first and most important step is to reduce the threshold for scratching by treating and eliminating all associated irritative skin problems such as *seborrhea* and *pyoderma*.

Antihistamines control itching and scratching in 20 to 40 percent of atopic dogs. Corticosteroids are the most effective anti-itch drugs, but also have the most serious side effects. They are best used intermittently in low doses and for a limited time. Preparations containing hydrocortisone with Pramoxine are often prescribed for treating local areas of itching. Pramoxine is a topical anesthetic that provides temporary relief from pain and itching.

Derm Caps and other essential fatty acid products derived from fish oils have produced good results in some dogs. The are used as nutritional supplements in conjunction with other therapies. A variety of shampoos are available and may be prescribed by your veterinarian to rehydrate the skin, treat bacterial infection and control seborrhea.

Dogs that do not respond to medical treatment can be considered for immunotherapy with hyposensitization. This involves skin testing to identify the allergen(s) and then desensitizing the dog to the specific irritants through a series of injections given over a period of 9 to 12 months or longer.

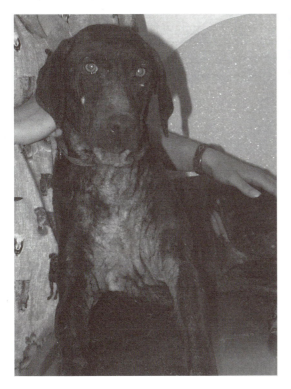

Severe allergic dermatitis with surface skin infection, in this case caused by canine atopy.

FOOD ALLERGY

Food allergy is the third most common cause of allergic itching and scratching. It occurs in dogs of all ages. Unlike canine atopy, food allergy has no seasonal incidence. Allergies can develop to meats, milk, eggs, fish, beef, pork, horse meat, cereal grains, potatoes, soy products and dietary additives. A dog must have been exposed to the allergen one or more times in order to become allergic. Typically, the dog has been on the same diet for at least two years.

The principal sign is severe itching, accompanied by the appearance of small red bumps, *pustules* and raised patches of skin. Characteristically, the rash involves the ears, feet, backs of the legs and underside of the body. Since food allergy is less common than canine atopy and flea allergy dermatitis, the dog is often thought to be suffering from one of those diseases.

Treatment: The diagnosis is made by placing the dog on a hypoallergenic test diet and watching for a definite reduction in itching and scratching. A hypoallergenic diet is one that has a very limited number of ingredients. It should be free of coloring, preservatives and flavorings. Most importantly, it should contain ingredients that the dog is unlikely to have encountered in the past. Your veterinarian can prescribe an appropriate hypoallergenic diet after carefully reviewing the composition of the dog's current diet. Switching from one commercial ration to another is not an adequate test, as these non-prescription diets contain too many ingredients.

A reduction in itching may occur within a few days of starting the test diet, but in many cases it takes several weeks. The test diet should be continued for at least 10 weeks. Once improvement is noted, various foods can be added one by one until the offending allergen is identified by seeing that it causes an increse in the amount of itching and scratching.

As an alternative, the test diet can consist of a commercial hypoallergenic prescription diet such as salmon/rice or duck/potato available through Hill's Pet Products. Once a good commercial hypoallergenic diet is found, the dog can be left on that diet indefinitely.

IRRITANT CONTACT AND ALLERGIC CONTACT DERMATITIS

Irritant contact dermatitis is caused by the direct effect of a chemical or irritant on the skin. It occurs in areas where the skin is not well protected by hair, such as the feet, chin, nose, hocks and stifles, and the undersurface of the body including the scrotum. Irritant contact dermatitis can occur after a single exposure or repeated exposure.

Irritant contact dermatitis produces itchy red bumps along with inflammation of the skin. You may notice moist weepy spots, blisters and crusts. The skin becomes rough and scaly and hair is lost. Excessive scratching damages the skin and sets the stage for secondary pyoderma. Chemicals producing irritant dermatitis include acids and alkalis, detergents, solvents, soaps and petroleum by-products.

Less commonly, the skin becomes sensitized to a certain chemical and a delayed type of hypersensitivity reaction develops. This is an *allergic contact dermatitis*. This rash is indistinguishable from that of an irritant contact dermatitis, but appears after repeated exposure and often spreads beyond the site of contact.

Chemicals causing allergic contact dermatitis are found in soaps, flea collars, shampoos, wool and synthetic fibers, leather, plastic and rubber dishes, grasses and pollens, insecticides, petrolatum, paint, carpet dyes, rubber and wood preservatives. Neomycin, found in many topical medications, can produce an allergic contact dermatitis, as can other drugs and medications.

Plastic and rubber food dish dermatitis affects the nose and lips (see *Plastic Dish Nasal Dermatitis* in Chapter 7).

Flea collar dermatitis is an allergic contact dermatitis associated with itching, redness, hair loss, and the development of excoriations, scabs and crusts beneath the collar. It can be prevented to some degree by airing the collar for 24 hours and applying the collar loosely. The flea collar should fit so that you can get at least two fingers beneath the ring.

Treatment: Consider the area of involvement and identify the chemical or skin allergen causing the problem. Prevent further exposure. Treat infected skin with a topical antibiotic ointment such as Triple Antibiotic. Topical and oral corticosteroids prescribed by your veterinarian relieve itching and inflammation.

Disorders in Which Hair Is Lost

The distinguishing feature of this group of skin diseases is hair loss without itching or scratching. Later, the initial problem can become complicated by seborrhea and pyoderma.

Hormone diseases are associated with hair loss. Although these diseases involve many systems, the skin and coat changes provide visual evidence that may lead to early recognition and treatment. Hormone skin disorders cause bilateral hair loss and skin changes that are symmetrical—one side of the body being the mirror image of the other.

HYPOTHYROIDISM

This is a disease of thyroid deficiency. The thyroid gland sits on the throat below the larynx. Its function is to produce thyroxine (T4), which controls the rate of metabolism. Thus dogs with hypothyroidism have metabolic rates below normal. Hypothyroidism, in nearly all cases, is caused by either *autoimmune thyroiditis* (also called lymphocytic thyroiditis), or *idiopathic thyroid gland atrophy*, both of which result in destruction of thyroid tissue. Autoimmune thyroiditis is known to be an inherited disease. The cause of thyroid gland atrophy is unknown.

The incidence of hypothyroidism in dogs is estimated to be less than 1 percent. The disease occurs most often in middle-aged dogs of the medium and large breeds. The breeds most commonly affected are the Golden Retriever, Doberman Pinscher, Irish Setter, Miniature Schnauzer, Dachshund, Cocker Spaniel, Airedale Terrier, Labrador Retriever, Greyhound, Scottish Deerhound and others. Currently only Golden Retrievers, Irish Setters and Cocker Spaniels are recognized as having a genetic predisposition.

Hypothyroidism is the most common endocrine skin disease in dogs—but it is still less common than other skin diseases. Coat and skin changes are bilateral and symmetrical. A typical sign is poor hair regrowth, which is most noticeable after the dog has been clipped.

It is also common to see hair loss that involves the front of the neck down to the chest, the sides of the body, the backs of the thighs and the top of the tail. The hair is excessively dry, brittle, and falls out easily. The exposed skin is dry, thick, puffy and darkly pigmented. Some dogs develop secondary *seborrhea*.

Other signs of hypothyroidism include weight gain, intolerance to cold, a slow heart rate, absence of heat cycles, lethargy and a variety of nonspecific symptoms that could be due to a number of other diseases. Hypothyroid dogs may develop blepharitis, corneal ulcers, deafness, adult-onset megaesophagus, chronic constipation and anemia. Hypothyroidism has been found in association with dilated cardiomyopathy, strokes, coronary artery disease (rare in dogs), von Willebrand's disease and myasthenia gravis. At least two-thirds of hypothyroid dogs have high serum cholesterol levels. Finding elevated serum cholesterol on routine blood screening warrants a workup for hypothyroidism.

The recommended blood test for screening purposes is the total T4. This test is indicated for dogs that have findings suggestive of hypothyroidism on physical examination. A normal T4 is fairly conclusive evidence that the dog does not have hypothyroidism. However, a low-normal or below normal level does not mean the dog is hypothyroid, because concentrations below normal are common for many reasons other than hypothyroidism.

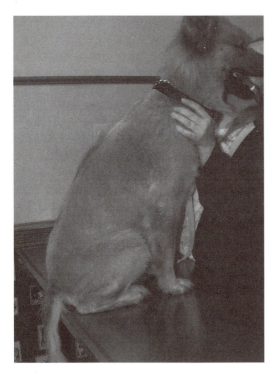

Poor hair regrowth after shearing, suggesting hypothyroidism.

To avoid overdiagnosing and overtreating the disease, it is important to confirm the significance of a low T4 using a more accurate thyroid function test, such as the FT4, by equilibrium dialysis. Other blood tests also are available for diagnosing hypothyroidism. One is an assay for *thyroglobulin autoantibodies*; these autoantibodies are present in about 50 percent of cases of autoimmune thyroiditis. This test must be sent to a special laboratory for analysis.

Treatment: Hypothyroidism is permanent, but can be effectively treated with daily or twice-daily thyroid hormone replacement using synthetic L-thyroxine (L-T4). The initial dose is based on the dog's weight. This should be adjusted for individual circumstances. Monitoring is accomplished by physical examination and measuring the total T4. This must be done frequently, particularly early in the course of treatment. Hair loss and other signs of hypothyroidism usually reverse with treatment.

The Orthopedic Foundation for Animals (OFA) maintains a hypothyroid registry to identify dogs as normal for breeding. A certificate and breed registry number is issued to all dogs found to be normal at 12 months of age, based on the results of FT4, cTSH and thyroid autoantibody screening by an OFA-approved laboratory (see Appendix C). Screening and registration is of value for dogs at risk of inherited hypothyroidism. If the test is positive, these dogs should not be used for breeding.

HYPERADRENOCORTICISM (CORTISONE EXCESS)

Overproduction of glucocorticoids by the two adrenal glands located just above the kidneys is called Cushing's syndrome. The diagnosis and treatment of this unusual disease is discussed in Chapter 9. Some cases of hyperadrenocorticism are iatrogrenic in origin—that is, they are caused by corticosteroids given for medical purposes.

Excess cortisone can cause hair loss over the body in a symmetric pattern, with darkening of the underlying skin. The remaining hair is dry and dull. Small blackheads may be found on the abdomen. The abdomen is pendulous, distended and pot-bellied. Dogs with hyperadrenocorticism lose body condition and develop severe problems such as hypertension, congestive heart failure and diabetes mellitus.

Treatment: If your dog is on long-term corticosteroids for a medical condition and develops signs of hyperadrenocorticism, your veterinarian may be able to reduce the dosage or find a substitute medication. The treatment of Cushing's syndrome caused by tumors of the pituitary and adrenal glands is discussed in Chapter 9.

ESTROGEN EXCESS (HYPERESTROGENISM)

Hyperestogenism is caused by the overproduction of estrogen from the ovaries or testicles. In females, it is associated with granulosa cell tumors and cysts of the ovaries. In males, it is caused by testicular tumors. These subjects are discussed in Chapter 18.

Signs of hyperestrogenism are feminization with enlargement of the mammary glands and nipples in both sexes; enlargement of the vulva and clitoris in females; and the development of a pendulous prepuce in males. Females may exhibit irregular heat cycles, false pregnancy and pyometra.

Skin and coat changes begin in the perineum around the genital areas and proceed to the underside of the abdomen. Typically, the hair becomes dry and brittle, falls out easily and fails to regrow. Later the skin becomes darkly pigmented. A dry, flaky seborrhea often develops, particularly in females. The coat and skin changes follow a symmetrical pattern.

The cause of the hyperestrogenism should be determined by physical examination, ultrasound, endocrine blood tests and, if necessary, *laparoscopy* or exploratory surgery.

Treatment: Hyperestrogenism in both sexes responds well to neutering.

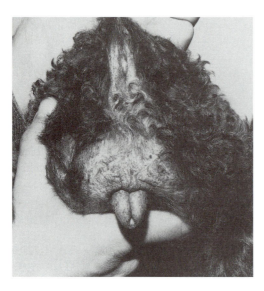

Hyperestrogenism: Excess estrogen causes enlargement of the vulva.

GROWTH HORMONE-RESPONSIVE ALOPECIA

This is a rare cause of bilateral symmetric hair loss. Growth hormone (somatotropin) is secreted by the pituitary gland. In some cases, for unknown reasons, the pituitary does not manufacture or release adequate concentrations of growth hormone, resulting in coat and skin changes similar to those described for hyerperestrogenism. Symptoms generally appear at puberty, but may occur at any age. This disease has been observed in Pomeranians, Chow Chows, Poodles, Samoyeds, Keeshonds and American Water Spaniels.

Treatment: It is important to exclude other hormone-dependent causes of hair loss. The treatment of choice for growth hormone-responsive alopecia is neutering. If the coat does not improve, the dog may respond to growth hormone administered subcutaneously three time a week for four to six weeks. Dogs receiving growth hormone must be monitored for the development of diabetes mellitus.

ESTROGEN DEFICIENCY (HYPOESTROGENISM)

This mild skin condition occurs in older females spayed as puppies. There is gradual loss of hair due to lack of new growth over the undersurface of the belly and around the vulva. Later, it involves the lower chest and neck. The skin becomes soft, smooth and nearly hairless. Affected females shed very little, do not collect much dirt and make excellent house pets.

Treatment: This is not a serious disease, and can be left untreated. If treatment is desired, estrogen can be given under veterinary supervision. The hormone must be given at least twice a week to affect hair growth. Note that estrogens may cause bone marrow suppression in dogs. This can be fatal if not recognized in time. Accordingly, all dogs receiving estrogen must be monitored with frequent blood counts.

TRACTION ALOPECIA

Hair loss with baldness occurs in dogs who have had barrettes, rubber bands and other devices used to tie up their hair. When these accessories are applied too tightly or for too long a time, traction on the hair effects the hair follicles, causing the roots to stop growing. This results in an area of hair loss that may be permanent.

Treatment: The only treatment for a permanent bald spot is to remove it surgically. This would only be done for cosmetic reasons. Alopecia can be prevented by applying traction devices loosely and for short periods, or preferably by not using them at all.

ACANTHOSIS NIGRANS

Acanthosis nigrans literally means thick, black skin. Primary acanthosis nigrans is seen principally in Dachshunds. The age of onset is less than one year. The exact cause is unknown. Secondary acanthosis nigrans occurs in all breeds in association with endocrine skin diseases, itchy skin diseases and obesity.

In Dachshunds, the disease affects the armpit folds and the skin folds of the groin. As the disease progresses, you will see extreme black pigmentation associated with a greasy rancid discharge on the surface of the skin. Secondary bacterial infections are common. Eventually the process extends over a considerable area, covering the brisket and legs. This disease causes considerable distress to the dog and his owner.

Treatment: Primary acanthosis should be treated by a veterinarian. The disease is controllable but not curable. Most dogs can be kept comfortable with potent topical (and occasionally oral) corticosteroids. Melatonin and vitamin E have been effective in some cases. Antibiotics are used to treat secondary skin infections. Use antiseborrhea shampoos to remove excess oil and bacteria (see *Seborrhea*, page 131). Weight reduction to reduce skin fold friction is desirable.

Secondary acanthosis nigrans responds to treatment of the underlying skin problem.

ZINC-RESPONSIVE DERMATOSIS

Zinc is a trace mineral required for hair growth and maintenance of the skin. A deficiency of zinc causes thinning of the hair and a scaly crusty dermatitis over the face, most noticeable on the nose and around the eyes, ears and mouth. Crusts also appear over pressure points such as the elbows and hocks. The feet become callused and crack easily.

Siberian Huskies, Doberman Pinschers, Great Danes and Alaskan Malmutes are predisposed to zinc-responsive dermatosis. A genetic defect involving zinc absorption from the intestine has been identified in Siberian Huskies and Malmutes. In these breeds the disease may occur even when the dog is eating a well-balanced diet.

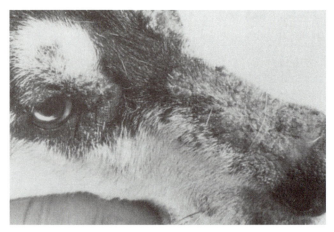

Crusty dermatitis over the face of a Siberian Husky, caused by zinc deficiency. (Courtesy Bristol-Myers Squibb)

Diets high in fiber and calcium may precipitate zinc deficiency by binding zinc in the gastrointestinal tract. A zinc deficiency syndrome occurs in large-breed puppies fed diets oversupplemented with vitamins and minerals (particularly calcium). A closely related condition has been observed in dogs fed dry, generic dog foods that are deficient in zinc.

Treatment: The diagnosis is confirmed by the response to therapy. Regardless of the cause, the dermatosis responds rapidly to zinc sulfate (10 mg/kg/day) or zinc methionine (1.7 mg/kg/day). Improvement begins almost at once. Alaskan Malmutes and Siberian Huskies usually require zinc supplements for life. Puppies with an acquired zinc deficiency respond to zinc supplements and a nutritionally balanced ration.

COLOR MUTANT ALOPECIA (BLUE DOBERMAN SYNDROME)

This hereditary skin disease is seen most often in fawn and blue-coated Dobermans, and occasionally in blue Great Danes, blue Newfoundlands, Chow Chows, Whippets and Italian Greyhounds.

Affected dogs are born with a healthy haircoat. At six months of age or later, the coat becomes thin, brittle, dry and takes on a moth-eaten appearance. The skin becomes rough and scaly. Blackheads, papules and pustules appear on the involved areas. Some blue Dobermans do not manifest the disease before three years of age.

Treatment: There is no cure. Treatment is directed toward relieving the surface condition, which involves shampoos that rehydrate the skin, remove scales and flush the hair follicles. These must be prescribed by your veterinarian. Because the affected hair is fragile and comes out easily, vigorous brushing and the use of harsh or inappropriate shampoos aggravates the problem and should be avoided. The coat mutantation has a genetic basis. Affected dogs should not be bred.

SEBACEOUS ADENITIS

This is an inherited skin disease controlled by an autosomal recessive gene that adversely affects the development of sebaceous glands. Predisposed breeds include the Standard Poodle, Akita, Samoyed and Vizsla. Symptoms usually appear in the first four years of life, but may develop later.

Long-coated breeds such as the Standard Poodle have areas of symmetric hair loss involving the muzzle, top of the head, ear flaps and the top of the neck, trunk and tail. The skin develops a scaly *seborrhea*, and in advanced cases a bacterial infection of the hair follicles. Short-coated breeds such as the Vizsla have circular areas of hair loss with scaling on the head, ears, trunk and legs.

Treatment: The diagnosis is confirmed by skin biopsy. Treatment involves corticosteroids, Accutane (isotretinoin) and a number of antiseborrhea and antifollicular drugs and shampoos that can be prescribed by your veterinarian.

The institute for Genetic Disease Control in Animals maintains a registry for sebaceous adenitis in Standard Poodles (see Appendix C). Dogs with sebaceous adenitis and those identified as carriers should not be bred.

SEBORRHEA

Seborrhea is a condition in which flakes of dead skin (scales) are shed from the epidermis and hair follicles. These flakes may be dry and dandrufflike, or oily and greasy. Oily seborrhea is due to excessive production of sebum by the sebaceous glands. Sebum is responsible for the rancid doggy odor that accompanies oily seborrhea.

Primary and secondary seborrhea are two different diseases.

Primary Seborrhea

This common disease is seen most often in American Cocker Spaniels, English Springer Spaniels, West Highland White Terriers, Basset Hounds, Irish Setters, German Shepherds, Labrador Retrievers, Chinese Shar-Pei and other breeds. Affected dogs may have dry flaky skin, greasy scaly skin, or a combination of both. The flakes of dry seborrhea are easy to lift off the skin. The scales of oily seborrhea stick to the hair. In oily seborrhea the hair follicles can become plugged and infected, resulting in the development of *folliculitis*.

The elbows, hocks, front of the neck down to the chest, and hair along the borders of the ears are commonly involved with primary seborrhea. With oily seborrhea, wax may accumulate in the ear canals, producing a condition called *ceruminous otitis*.

Secondary Seborrhea

This condition occurs when some other skin disease triggers the seborrheic process. Diseases often associated with secondary seborrhea include scabies, demodectic mange, canine atopy, food hypersensitivity dermatitis, flea allergy dermatitis, hypothyroidism, hormone-related skin diseases, color mutant alopecia, pemphigus foliaceus and others. *Primary seborrhea should not be diagnosed until secondary seborrhea has been eliminated.*

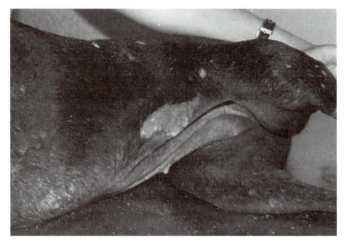

The dry flaky skin of secondary seborrhea, triggered by long-standing atopic dermatitis.

Treatment: Primary seborrhea is incurable but treatable. Therapy is directed toward controlling scale formation with shampoos and rinses. A number of commercial antiseborrheic products are available. The choice of shampoos and rinses and frequency of application vary with the specific problem, and should be determined by your veterinarian.

For *mild* dry flaking, moisturizing hypoallergenic shampoos and rinses that contain no dyes, fragrances or other added ingredients can help to rehydrate the skin. These products can be used frequently without causing harm.

For *severe* dry flaking, shampoos containing sulfur and salicylic acid are recommended to remove scales. For oily seborrhea, shampoos containing coal tar are effective and retard further scale production. Benzoyl peroxide shampoos have excellent hair-pore flushing activity and aid in removing greasy scales adhering to hair shafts.

Therapeutic shampooing may be more effective when preceded by a warm water shampoo. Rinse thoroughly and follow with the medicated shampoo. Leave on for 15 minutes. Then rinse thoroughly.

Systemic antibiotics are used to treat folliculitis and other skin infections. A short course of oral corticosteroids may be prescribed during periods of severe itching. Dietary supplements containing essential fatty acids derived from fish oil (such as DermCaps) are said to be beneficial in seborrhea and certainly can do no harm.

Secondary seborrhea is managed like primary seborrhea. It usually disappears with control of the underlying skin disease.

RINGWORM

Ringworm is a fungal infection that invades the hair and hair follicles. Most cases are caused by *Microsporum canis*. Ringworm in dogs is primarily a disease of puppies and young adults. Typical areas of involvement are the face, ears, paws and tail.

Ringworm is transmitted by spores in the soil, and by contact with the infected hair of dogs and cats, typically found on carpets, brushes, combs, toys and furniture. Humans can acquire ringworm from pets and vice versa. Children are especially susceptible.

Ringworm takes its name from its classic appearance: a spreading circle of hair loss with scaly skin at the center and a red ring at the periphery. Note, however, that many cases of circular hair loss thought to be ringworm are actually localized demodectic mange or hair follicle infection. Atypical ringworm is common, with irregular areas of hair loss associated with scaling and crusting.

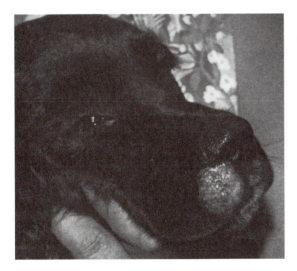

Ringworm on the muzzle of a Cocker Spaniel.

Ringworm by itself is not an itchy skin condition, but secondary bacterial infection with scabs and crusts can provoke licking and scratching. Ringworm can invade the toenails. This results in nails that are dry, cracked, brittle and deformed.

A *kerion* is a round, raised, nodular lesion that results from a combined fungal and bacterial infection that invades the roots of the hair. In most cases the fungus is *Microsporun gypseum* and the bacteria is a staphylococcus. Kerions occur on the face and limbs. Therapy involves treating the bacterial component as described in *Folliculitis*.

Ringworm mimics many other skin disease, so an accurate diagnosis is essential. Hair infected by *microsporum canis* may fluoresce green under ultraviolet light (called *Wood's light*), but false positive and false negative results are common. Ultraviolet light is used as a screening tool only. Microscopic examination of hairs plucked from areas that fluoresce can sometimes provide an immediate diagnosis, but the most reliable method of diagnosing ringworm is by fungal culture.

Kerions are deep-seated skin infections caused by a ringworm fungus in combination with a bacteria.

Treatment: Although mild cases regress spontaneously in three to four months, all cases of ringworm should be treated to prevent progression and spread to other pets and people in the household.

With only one or two areas of involvement, apply a topical antifungal agent containing miconazole 2 percent cream or 1 percent lotion twice a day in the direction of the lay of the hair. Continue treatment until the skin is healed. Prepare to treat for at least four to six weeks.

When several sites are involved, repeat the treatment just described, and add an antifungal shampoo containing Miconazole or another shampoo labeled for the treatment of ringworm. Continue to treat for two weeks beyond apparent cure.

In difficult cases your veterinarian may prescribe an antifungal drug called Griseofulvin. Ketoconazole and other drugs of the imidazole group are also effective, but may not be approved by the FDA for treating ringworm in dogs. Griseofulvin and ketoconazole have serious potential side effects and should not be given to pregnant bitches because they may cause birth defects. Antifungal drugs require close veterinary counseling and supervision.

Prevention: Ringworm spores can survive for up to one year and should be eliminated from the environment. Discard the dog's bedding. Sterilize grooming equipment in a 1:10 dilution of bleach. Vacuum the carpets at least weekly to remove infected hair. Mop and wash hard surfaces (floors, countertops, dog runs) using diluted bleach. Technical Captan can be used as a spray in a dilution of 1:200 in water to treat a kennel.

Strict hand-washing precautions are necessary to prevent human contamination. Children should not be allowed to handle pets with ringworm. Wash contaminated clothing and fabrics with bleach.

DEMODECTIC MANGE

Demodectic mange is caused by a tiny mite, *Demodex canis*, too small to be seen with the naked eye. Nearly all dogs acquire mange mites from their mothers during the first few days of life. These mites are considered normal skin fauna when present in small numbers. They produce disease only when an abnormal immune system allows their numbers to get out of control. This occurs primarily in puppies, and in adult dogs with lowered immunity. A high incidence of mange in certain bloodlines suggests that some purebred dogs are born with an inherited immune susceptibility.

Demodectic mange occurs in a *localized* and *generalized* form. The diagnosis is made by taking multiple skin scrapings and looking for the mites.

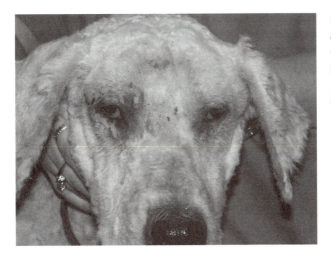

Localized demodectic mange with moth-eaten hair loss around the dog's right eye and on the forehead. The skin is red and inflamed.

Localized Demodectic Mange

This disease occurs in dogs under one year of age. The appearance of the skin is similar to that of ringworm. The principal sign is thinning of hair around the eyelids, the lips and the corners of the mouth, and occasionally on the legs and feet. The thinning progresses to patches of moth-eaten hair loss about one inch in diameter. In some cases the skin becomes red, scaly and infected.

Localized mange usually heals spontaneously in six to eight weeks, but may wax and wane for several months. If more than five patches are present, the disease could be progressing to the generalized form. This occurs in approximately 10 percent of cases.

Treatment: A topical ointment containing either benzoyl peroxide gel (OxyDex or Pyoben), or a mild topical preparation used to treat ear mites can be massaged into affected areas once daily. This *may* shorten the course of the disease. The medication should be rubbed with the lay of the hair to minimize further hair loss. Treatment may cause the area to look worse for the first two to three weeks. There is no evidence that treating localized mange prevents the disease from becoming generalized. The puppy should be checked again in four weeks.

Generalized Demodectic Mange

Dogs with the generalized disease develop patches of hair loss on the head, legs and trunk. These patches coalesce to form large areas of hair loss. The hair follicles become plugged with mites and skin scales. The skin breaks down to form sores, crusts and draining tracts, presenting a most disabling problem. Some cases are a continuation of localized mange; others develop spontaneously in older dogs.

When generalized demodectic mange develops in dogs under one year of age, there is a 30 to 50 percent chance that the puppy will recover spontaneously. It is uncertain whether medical treatment accelerates this recovery.

In dogs older than a year of age, a spontaneous cure is unlikely but the outlook for improvement with medical treatment has improved dramatically over the past decade. Most dogs can be cured with intense therapy. Most of the remaining cases can be controlled if the owner is willing to commit the necessary time and expense.

Treatment: Generalized demodectic mange must be treated under close veterinary supervision. Therapy involves the use of medicated shampoos and dips to remove surface scales and kill mites. Shave or clip hair from all affected areas to facilitate access to the skin.

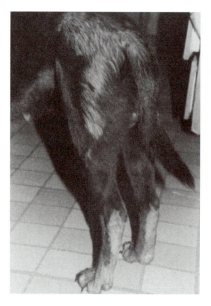

Generalized demodectic mange with extensive areas of hair loss, crusts and sores. Treatment is prolonged but is usually successful.

The FDA protocol involves first bathing the dog with a medicated benzoyl peroxide shampoo (OxyDex or Pyoben) to remove skin scales. Allow the shampoo to remain on the dog for 10 minutes before rinsing it off. Completely dry the dog.

Amitraz (Mitaban) currently is the only miticide approved by the FDA for use on dogs. Make up an amitraz dip by adding Mitaban to two gallons of water, according to the directions. Be sure to treat in a well-ventilated area and wear rubber or plastic gloves to keep the chemical off your skin. Sponge on the dip over a 10-minute period, allowing the dog's feet to soak in the rinse. Allow the dip to dry on the dog. Repeat every two weeks, or as directed by your veterinarian. Try to keep the dog from getting his coat and feet wet between dips.

Continue this protocol for 60 days beyond the day when skin scrapings first became negative. Side effects of Mitaban include drowsiness, lethargy, vomiting, diarrhea, dizziness and a staggering gait. Puppies are more susceptible than adults to these effects. Should such a reaction occur, immediately remove the miticide by thoroughly rinsing the coat and skin.

If the FDA protocol is not completely effective, your veterinarian may suggest an alternative treatment.

Secondary skin infections should be treated with antibiotics, based on culture and sensitivity tests. Corticosteroids, often used to control severe itching, lower the dog's immunity to the mites and should not be used to treat this disease.

Because of an inherited immune susceptibility, dogs that recover from demodectic mange should not be bred.

PRESSURE SORES (CALLUSES)

A callus is a gray, hairless, wrinkled pad of thickened skin overlying a bony pressure point. It is caused by lying on a hard surface. Calluses tend to occur in heavy dogs and dogs kenneled on cement floors. The most common site is the elbow. Other sites are the outside of the hocks, the buttocks and the sides of the legs.

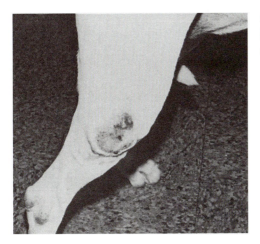

A callus on the outside of the back leg, caused by lying on a cement surface.

If the callus goes unchecked, the surface breaks down, forming an ulcer that can become infected. This then becomes a most difficult problem to treat.

Treatment: Provide the dog with a soft sleeping surface, such as a dog mattress or foam pad covered with fabric, to take pressure off the callus. An infected ulcer over bone must be treated by a veterinarian.

Pyoderma (Skin Infections)

Bacterial infections often develop in skin that has been traumatized and abraded by excessive rubbing, chewing and scratching. Pyoderma is therefore a frequent complication of other skin diseases, particularly those that cause intense itching.

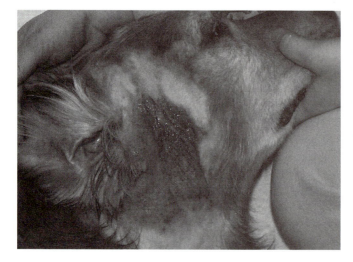

Pyoderma of the side of the face, caused by excessive scratching. The dog had a severe itchy ear disorder.

PUPPY DERMATITIS (IMPETIGO AND ACNE)

Impetigo and acne are mild surface skin infections that occur in puppies dogs under one year of age. *Impetigo* presents with pus-filled blisters on the hairless parts of the abdomen and the groin. The blisters rupture, leaving thin brown crusts. Puppies housed in unsanitary quarters are most likely to be infected.

Acne occurs in puppies three months of age and older. It can be identified by purplish red pustules and blackheads that come to a head and drain pus. These lesions are found on the chin and lower lip, and occasionally in the genital area, perineum and groin. Blockage of hair follicles by skin scales and sebum is a predisposing cause. Acne is more common among Doberman Pinschers, Boxers, Great Danes and Bulldogs.

Treatment: Topical therapy for impetigo and mild acne involves bathing the puppy with a benzoyl peroxide shampoo (OxyDex or Pyoben) twice a week for two to three weeks. Correct any predisposing causes, such as unsanitary puppy quarters.

Acne, however, is often a deep-seated skin infection and may not respond to topical therapy alone. Your veterinarian may add a course of oral antibiotics that are effective against staphylococcus. Acne usually disappears spontaneously at sexual maturity.

FOLLICULITIS

Folliculitis is an infection that begins in hair follicles. In mild folliculitis you typically will find many small pimplelike bumps (*pustules*) with a hair shaft protruding through the center of each. Once the follicles become infected, the infection can bore deeply into the dermis, forming large pustules and *furuncles* that rupture, discharge pus and crust over. Draining sinus tracts develop in deep folliculitis.

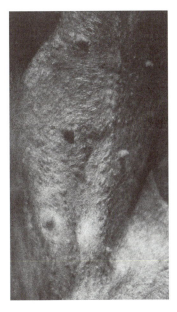

Small pimple-like pustules on the abdomen, typical of folliculitis.

Folliculitis usually involves the undersurface of the body, especially the armpits, abdomen and groin. A condition called *Schnauzer comedo syndrome* is common in Miniature Schnauzers. Dogs suffering from this have many large blackheads running down the middle of their backs.

Folliculitis often occurs as a secondary complication to scabies, demodectic mange, seborrhea, hormone skin disease and other problems. Some cases are caused by vigorous grooming, which traumatizes the hair follicles.

Treatment: It is important to identify and treat the underlying cause as well as the folliculitis.

Mild cases should be treated as described for acne. Deep folliculitis requires vigorous topical and systemic therapy. Clip away the hair from infected skin on long-haired dogs (don't clip short-haired dogs), and bathe the dog twice a day for 10 days with a povidone-iodine shampoo such as Betadine. As the skin infection improves, switch to a benzoyl peroxide shampoo such as Sulf OxyDex, OxyDex or Pyoben, used twice a week. Continue until healing is complete.

The dogs should also be placed on an oral antibiotic selected on the basis of culture and sensitivity tests. Continue oral antibiotics for six to eight weeks, including at least two weeks beyond apparent cure. Treatment failures occur when antibiotics are stopped too soon or used at too low a dosage. The prolonged use of corticosteroids should be avoided in folliculitis.

SKIN FOLD PYODERMA

When skin surfaces rub together, the skin becomes wet and inflamed. This creates ideal conditions for bacterial growth. Skin fold infection takes a variety of forms. It occurs as *lip fold pyoderma* in the spaniel breeds and St. Bernards; as *face fold pyoderma* in Pekingese and Chinese Shar-Pei; as *vulvar fold pyoderma* in obese females and as *tail fold pyoderma* in breeds with corkscrew tails (such as Bulldogs, Boston Terriers and Pugs).

The signs are irritation and inflammation of the skin. The moist skin gives off a foul odor.

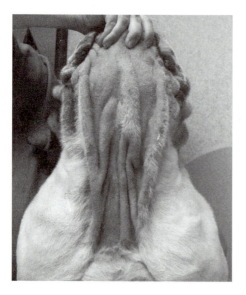

An English Bulldog with skin-fold pyoderma of the neck.

Treatment: The most effective treatment is to eliminate the skin fold by corrective surgery. When this is not feasible, the condition can be controlled by cleansing the infected skin fold with a benzoyl peroxide shampoo such as Sulf OxyDex, OxyDex or Pyoben. Dry the skin and then apply OxyDex or Pyoben gel twice a day for 10 to 14 days. An antibiotic-steroid cream (Panolog) can be used twice a day for two or three days to control inflammation and itching.

Once the infection has been successfully treated, use benzoyl peroxide gel as needed to prevent recurrence.

ACUTE MOIST DERMATITIS (HOT SPOTS)

A hot spot is a warm, painful, swollen patch of skin one to four inches in size that exudes pus and gives off a foul odor. Hair is lost rapidly. The infection progresses when the dog licks and chews the site. These circular patches appear suddenly and enlarge quickly, often within a matter of hours.

Hot spots can occur anywhere on the body, often in more than one spot. They occur most often in breeds with heavy coats, and tend to appear just before shedding, when moist dead hair is trapped next to the skin. Fleas, mites and other skin parasites, skin allergies, irritant skin diseases, ear and anal gland infections, and neglected grooming are other factors initiate the itch-scratch-itch cycle.

Treatment: Hot spots are extremely painful. The dog usually will need to be sedated or anesthetized for the initial treatment. Clip away hair to expose the hot spot. Gently cleanse the skin with a dilute povidone-iodine shampoo (Betadine) or a chlorhexidine shampoo (Nolvasan). Allow the skin to dry. Then apply an antibiotic steroid cream (Panolog or Neocort) twice a day for 10 to 14 days. Oral antibiotics are usually prescribed. Your veterinarian may also prescribe a short course of oral corticosteroids to control severe itching. Prevent the dog from traumatizing the area by applying an *Elizabethan collar*. Predisposing skin problems must be treated as well.

CELLULITIS AND SKIN ABSCESS

Cellulitis is an infection involving the skin and subcutaneous tissue. Most cases are caused by puncture wounds, deep scratches, bites and lacerations. Cellulitis can often be prevented by proper treatment of wounds, as described in Chapter 1, *Wounds*.

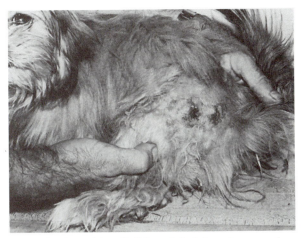

Skin infection with cellulitis and draining abscesses due to staphylococcus.

An area affcetd by cellulitis will be tender to pressure, feel hoter than normal, not be as soft as it would be normally, and appear redder than normal. As infection spreads out from the wound, you may feel tender cords beneath the skin, which are swollen lymphatic channels. Regional lymph nodes in the groin, armpit or neck may enlarge to contain the infection.

A *skin abscess* is a localized pocket of pus beneath the epidermis. Pimples, *pustules*, *furuncles* and boils are examples of small skin abscesses. A large abscess feels like fluid under pressure.

Treatment: Localize the infection by clipping away the hair. Apply warm soaks for 15 minutes three times a day. Saline soaks (1 teaspoon of table salt to 1 quart of water), or Epsom soaks (1/4 cup of Epsom salts to a quart of water) make a good poultice. Splinters and foreign bodies beneath the skin are a continuing source of infection and must be removed.

Pimples, pustules, furuncles, boils and abscesses that do not drain spontaneously may need to be lanced by your veterinarian. If a sizeable cavity is present, your veterinarian may ask you to flush it once or twice a day using a dilute antiseptic surgical solution such as chlorhexidine until healing is complete.

Oral and injectable antibiotics are indicated in the treatment of wound infections, cellulitis, abscess and other pyodermas.

PUPPY STRANGLES (JUVENILE PYODERMA)

Juvenile pyoderma occurs in puppies 4 to 16 weeks of age and often affects several puppies in the same litter. It can be recognized by a sudden swelling of the lips, eyelids, ear flaps or face, along with the rapid development of pustules, crusts, skin erosions and ulcers. The lymph nodes beneath the chin may become swollen and enlarged. These pups are quite sick and must be seen promptly by a veterinarian.

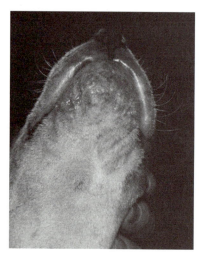

Puppy strangles with pustules and swollen lymph nodes beneath the chin.

Although bacteria have been implicated in some cases of puppy strangles, this is the exception rather than the rule. Most cases are considered to be an inflammatory immune process of unknown cause.

Treatment: Apply warm, moist packs for 15 minutes three times a day. Further treatment involves the use of oral corticosteroids and antibiotics for 14 days. Antibiotics alone are not effective.

Do not attempt to express the pus from the sores. This increases the likelihood of scarring.

MYCETOMA

A mycetoma is a tumorlike mass caused by several species of fungi that enter the body through wounds. This condition typically appears as a lump on the feet or legs beneath the skin with a tract to the surface that drains granular material. The granules are white, yellow or black, depending on the type of fungus involved. The condition resembles a chronic abscess that resists healing, despite prolonged treatment with antibiotics.

Treatment: Complete surgical removal is the treatment of choice. This is not always possible. Some of the newer antifungal drugs (ketoconazole, itraconazole) show promise in treating difficult cases. Treatment must be continued for at least two months beyond apparent cure.

INTERDIGITAL CYSTS (CYSTS BETWEEN THE TOES)

An interdigital cyst is an inflammatory reaction and not a true cyst. It appears as a swelling between the toes that may open and drain pus. The causes are numerous, and include trauma, foreign bodies such as thorns and plant awns, and the bites of ticks and other external parasites.

Treatment: Treatment may involve long-term antibiotics.

An interdigital cyst that has ruptured and formed a draining tract.

ACTINOMYCOSIS AND NORCADIOSIS

These skin infections, acquired by contact with infected soil, generally occur in hunting dogs. Both bacteria can produce a systemic infection that involves the lymph nodes, brain, chest cavity, lungs and bone. Subcutaneous abscesses with draining sinus tracts appear at the site of a puncture wound or break in the skin, usually in the head and neck area. The wound discharge often resembles tomato soup and/or contains material that looks like sulfa granules. Norcadiosis can be associated with gingivitis and mouth ulcers.

Treatment: The diagnosis is made by culturing the wound drainage. Treatment involves surgically opening infected abscesses and draining body cavities. Norcadiosis responds to sulfa drugs; actinomycosis to penicillin. Prolonged antibiotic treatment is necessary.

Autoimmune and Immune-Mediated Skin Diseases

Autoimmune skin diseases are caused by a specific antibody directed against a normal component of the skin. The antibody (called an *autoantibody*) destroys the cohesiveness of skin cells, resulting in the development of *blebs, pustules* and other skin changes typical of the disease. *Pemphigus* is an example of an autoimmune skin diseases.

Immune-mediated skin diseases (exemplified by lupus erythematosus) are systemic diseases in which the skin is but one site of attack. The autoantibody reacts with the antigen, and the two form a complex that is deposited in various locations including the kidneys, vessel walls and basement membrane of the skin. The deposited complexes trigger an inflammatory response that destroys the tissue.

PEMPHIGUS COMPLEX

In pemphigus, the autoantibody is directed against the wall of the skin cell. These cells lose their ability to remain attached and separate, forming *blebs, vesicles* and *pustules*. The exact stimulus for the pemphigus antibody is unknown. Four types of pemphigus are seen in dogs:

Pemphigus Foliaceus is the most common autoimmune skin disease of dogs. It generally occurs in dogs two to seven years of age. Predisposed breeds include Akitas, Bearded Collies, Newfoundlands, Chow Chows, Dachshunds, Doberman Pinschers and Schipperkes.

Pemphigus foliaceus is a pustular dermatitis that begins with red skin patches that involve the face and ears, but often becomes generalized. The patches rapidly progress to blisters and pustules, which then become dry yellow crusts. The crusts adhere to the underlying skin and hair. Areas of depigmentation occur as the disease progresses.

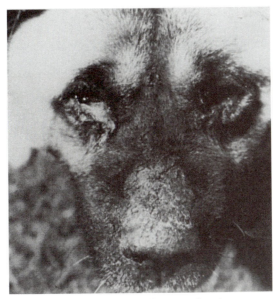

An Akita with pemphigus foliaceus, showing extensive face involvement. (Courtesy Bristol-Myers Squibb)

Pemphigus foliaceus can involve the feet, causing thickening and cracking of the foot pads, and pain when the dog puts weight on the feet. In some cases the disease involves *only* the foot pads. Pemphigus foliaceus should be considered whenever a dog with a painful limp exhibits thickened or cracked foot pads.

Pemphigus Erythematosus is a localized variant of pemphigus foliaceus with involvement limited to the face, head and foot pads. Collies and German Shepherds appear to be at greatest risk. The disease is easily confused with discoid lupus erythematosus.

Pemphigus Vulgaris is an uncommon disease in which blisters and ulcers form at the junction of the skin and the mucous membranes. It involves the lips, nostrils and eyelids. It can also attack the nailbeds, with subsequent shedding of the nails.

Pemphigus Vegetans is an extremely rare form of pemphigus vulgaris. It is characterized by flat-topped pustules involving the skin folds of the armpits and groin. Characteristically, the lesions heal with wartlike growths.

Pemphigus is best diagnosed by skin biopsy. Serologic blood tests are helpful, but false positives and false negatives are common.

Treatment: There is no cure for any form of pemphigus, but more than 50 percent of dogs with pemphigus foliaceus and pemphigus erythematosus can be kept relatively free of symptoms using corticosteroids alone, or corticosteroids in combination with azathioprine or chlorambucil. Treatment is life long. Sunscreen applied to the depigmented skin of the nose helps to prevent ultraviolet injury (see Chapter 7, *Collie Nose*).

Pemphigus vulgaris and pemphigus vegetans respond less well to treatment.

BULLOUS PEMPHIGOID

This is an uncommon autoimmune skin disease in which blisters, *bullae* and ulcerative erosions are found on the skin of the trunk, groin, armpit and abdomen. Collies and Doberman Pinschers appear to be predisposed. This disease also affects the foot pads, and 80 percent of cases ultimately involve the mouth.

Treatment: Treatment is similar to that for pemphigus foliaceus. The outlook for improvement is poor.

LUPUS ERYTHEMATOSUS COMPLEX

Lupus erythematosus is an immune-mediated disease in which the antigen/antibody complex lodges in the small vessels of many organs, including the skin. The exact stimulus for the antigen/antibody reaction is unknown. Two types of lupus occur dogs:

Systemic Lupus Erythematosus. This is a complex disease affecting several organs, including the skin, kidneys, heart and joints. The first indication may be a stilted gait or lameness that wanders from joint to joint.

Skin involvement is especially evident about the face and over the nose and muzzle, but may be found elsewhere. A vesicular, pustular, erosive dermatitis develops in these areas, and is followed by crusting, oozing and hair loss. The mucous membranes of the mouth are often involved. The foot pads can become thickened and ulcerated and may eventually shed. Secondary pyoderma is a major cause of death.

The diagnosis is difficult but is aided by skin biopsy and an antinuclear antibody (ANA) test. This test is positive in 90 percent of cases.

Treatment: Treatment depends on what organs are involved. Most cases require chemotherapy. Secondary pyoderma must be treated aggressively. The outlook for long-term control is guarded.

Discoid Lupus Erythematosus. This is the second most common immune skin disease, after pemphigus foliaceus. It is considered to be a milder form of systemic lupus and is limited to the face. Depigmentation of the nose is usually followed by the appearance of open sores and crusts. Collies, German Shepherds, Siberian Huskies and Shetland Sheepdogs are most often affected. The typical appearance and location of discoid lupus, and the absence of other sites of skin involvement, make the diagnosis almost certain.

Treatment: Discoid lupus can be successfully managed with oral and/or topical corticosteroids. Oral vitamin E in a dose of 400 IU given every 12 hours before or during meals is reported to be beneficial. Apply topical sunscreens during periods of exposure to sunlight (see Chapter 7, *Collie Nose*). Ultraviolet injury severely aggravates this problem.

Ulceration of the skin of the nose, with open sores and crusts, typical of discoid lupus erythematosus. (Courtesy Bristol-Myers Squibb)

TOXIC EPIDERMAL NECROLYSIS

Toxic epidermal necrolysis is a rare, ulcerative skin disease that appears to be triggered by various drugs, internal cancers, infections and unknown factors. Blebs, ulcers and erosions develop suddenly and progress rapidly. The mouth and foot pads are frequently involved. This is an extremely painful skin disease. The dog is severely depressed and refuses to eat. The death rate approaches 30 percent.

Treatment: Treatment involves stopping all suspect medications and correcting any underlying cause. Corticosteroids, intravenous fluids and antibiotics are required during the acute illness to support the circulation. Recovery takes two to three weeks.

ERYTHEMA MULTIFORME

Erythema multiforme is an acute eruption of the skin and mucous membranes. The characteristic skin lesion is a round or oval targetlike skin eruption with a red rim and central blanching. There is an association with drugs, infections, tumors and connective tissue diseases.

Erythema multiforme tends to be less severe than toxic epidermal necrolysis. Many cases recover spontaneously, especially if the predisposing cause can be found and corrected.

NODULAR PANNICULITIS

This is an uncommon inflammatory condition of subcutaneous fat in which lumps appear over the back and along the sides of the body, much like marbles beneath the skin. These lumps are more apparent in short-coated breeds. As the disease progresses, the lumps ulcerate and drain, then heal by scarring. The dog usually runs a fever and appears lethargic. The cause of the disease is unknown. Biopsy of a nodule confirms the diagnosis.

Treatment: Surgical excision is the treatment of choice for a solitary nodule. With multiple nodules, treatment involves corticosteroids and/or vitamin E. The outlook for long-term recovery is good.

THE EYES

The eye is an organ with several parts, each uniquely adapted to meet the special needs of the dog. The eyeball is seated in a bony socket and protected by a cushion of fat. Muscles surrounding the eyeball close the eye tightly in response to pain and irritation. This makes it difficult to inspect the surface of the eye for injuries and foreign bodies.

The large, clear window at the front of the eye is the cornea. Bordering it is a narrow rim of white connective tissue called the sclera, much less conspicuous in dogs than in humans. The sclera surrounds and supports the entire eyeball. In certain breeds the sclera may be pigmented or spotted.

The round opening at the center of the eye is the pupil. Around the pupil is a sphincterlike muscle called the iris. Like a shutter on a camera, the iris opens and closes to regulate the amount of light that enters the eye. The iris contains the pigment that gives the eye its color.

A pinkish membrane called the conjunctiva covers the white of the eye and doubles back to cover the inner surface of the eyelid. This membrane contains blood vessels and nerve endings. When inflamed, the conjunctiva appears red and swollen.

The eyelids are tight folds of skin that support the front of the globe. Eyelashes are always present on the upper eyelids, but not on the lower eyelids.

The dog has an important third eyelid, the *nictitating membrane*, located at the inner corner of the eye. This third eyelid is normally inconspicuous, but when it extends across the surface of the eye, it gives the impression that the eyeball has rolled back into its socket.

Tears are secreted by the lacrimal glands. Each eye has two lacrimal glands: one beneath the bony ridge at the top of the eye socket and the other incorporated into the third eyelid. Tears are conveyed to the surface of the eye by small ducts that empty behind the lids. Tears prevent the cornea from drying out. They also contain immune substances that fight infections. Tears gather at the inner corner of the eye and are carried by the nasolacrimal ducts into the nasal cavity near the front of the nose.

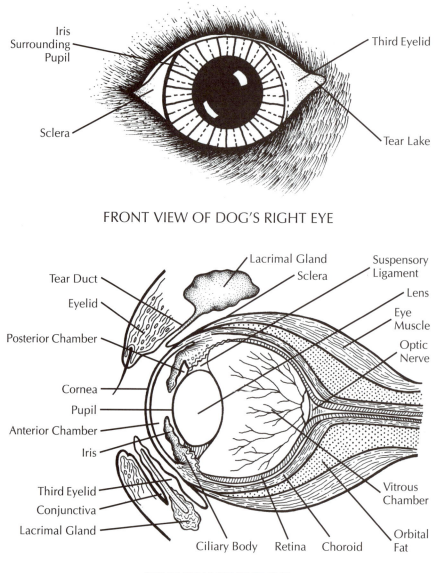

Iris Surrounding Pupil

Sclera

Third Eyelid

Tear Lake

FRONT VIEW OF DOG'S RIGHT EYE

Tear Duct

Eyelid

Posterior Chamber

Cornea

Pupil

Anterior Chamber

Iris

Third Eyelid

Conjunctiva

Lacrimal Gland

Lacrimal Gland

Sclera

Suspensory Ligament

Lens

Eye Muscle

Optic Nerve

Vitrous Chamber

Orbital Fat

Ciliary Body   Retina   Choroid

SIDE VIEW OF THE EYE

The inner eye has three fluid-filled chambers. The anterior chamber is found between the cornea and the iris. The small posterior chamber lies between the iris and front of the lens. The large vitreous chamber, containing a clear jelly, fills the cavity behind the lens and in front of the retina.

The lens is held in place by a series of strands called the suspensory ligaments. These attach to the ciliary body, a structure composed of muscle, connective tissue and blood vessels. The ciliary body secretes the fluid that fills the anterior and posterior chambers. Contraction of the ciliary muscles changes the curvature of the lens, which enables images of objects at different distances to be focused onto the retina.

Light enters the eye by passing through the cornea and anterior chamber and then through the pupil and lens. It then travels through the vitreous and is received by the retina. The retina is a layer of photoreceptor cells that converts light into electrical impulses. These impulses are then carried to the brain via the optic nerves.

How Dogs See

Dogs have relatively poor vision in some areas when compared with people. Dogs are near-sighted and *accommodate* poorly. Accommodation is the process during which the lens changes shape to focus light on the retina. Dogs accommodate poorly because the ciliary muscles that change the shape of the lens are relatively weak.

The dog's retina contains a small number of cone cells that distinguish between blue, yellow and gray. However, the dog's retina lacks photoreceptors for red and green, and thus is similar to the retina of people who are red-green color-blind. While dogs do perceive some colors, it is believed that the ability to perceive subtle shades of gray is the most important function of the cone cells.

On the positive side, dogs have large pupils and a wide field of vision, making them adept at following moving objects. Dogs also have an abundance of rods in the retina, which are the cells that detect light. Along with the cone cells that distinguish shades of gray, they enable dogs to see very well in relative darkness. Dogs also have a fair degree of binocular vision and depth perception. Furthermore, any deficiency that dogs may have in eyesight is more than made up for by their superior senses of hearing and smell.

What to Do if Your Dog Has an Eye Problem

If your dog has matter in his eye or if the eye waters, if the dog blinks, squints, paws at the eye and gives evidence that the eye is painful, you are faced with an eye problem. You must examine the eye and attempt to determine the cause.

SIGNS OF EYE AILMENT

Eye diseases are accompanied by a number of signs and symptoms. The most serious is pain. *A dog with a painful eye should be taken to the nearest veterinary hospital as soon as you notice the condition.* Irreversible damage can occur in a matter of hours.

Eye Pain. Signs of pain include excessive tearing, squinting, tenderness to the touch and sensitivity to light. Other signs of a painful eye are loss of appetite, lethargy, whining and crying. The nictitating membrane often protrudes in response to pain. The most common causes of severe eye pain are acute glaucoma, uveitis, keratitis and corneal injuries.

Eye Discharge. The appearance of discharge helps to define the cause of the problem. A clear discharge with no other symptoms suggests a problem with the tearing mechanism. A *painless* discharge accompanied by redness is typical of conjunctivitis. Any discharge accompanied by signs of pain should alert you to the possibility of corneal or inner eye problems.

Film Over the Eye. An opaque or whitish membrane that moves out over the surface of the eyeball from the inner corner of the eye is a protruded nictitating membrane. Causes are discussed in *The Third Eyelid*, page 162.

Cloudy Eye. Loss of clarity or transparency accompanied by signs of pain suggests keratitis, glaucoma or uveitis. Cataracts are the most likely cause when the eye is not painful. If the eye is entirely opaque you might think the dog is blind, but this is not necessarily the case.

Hard or Soft Eye. Changes in eye pressure and firmness of the eyeball are caused by diseases of the inner eye. A hard eye with a dilated pupil indicates glaucoma. A soft eye with a small pupil indicates uveitis.

Irritation of the Eyelids. Diseases that cause swelling, crusting, itching or hair loss are discussed in *Eyelids*, page 156.

Bulging or Sunken Eye. A bulging eye occurs with glaucoma, tumors and abscesses behind the globe, and with an eye out of its socket. A sunken eye occurs with dehydration, weight loss, eye pain and tetanus.

HOW TO EXAMINE THE EYE

An eye examination is best carried out in a dark room using a single light source, such as a flashlight. A magnifying glass will help you see fine details on the surface of the eye. Have an assistant restrain the dog, as described in Chapter 1, *Restraining for Examination and Treatment.*

First compare one eye to the other. Are they the same size, shape and color? Are the pupils equal in size? Is there a discharge, and if so is it watery or mucoid? Is the dog squinting? Is the nictitating membrane visible? Does the cornea look smoky,

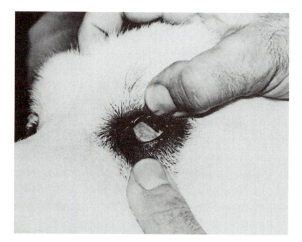

How to examine the eye. Note the third eyelid. It contains a tear gland that produces about half the tear volume. (J. Clawson)

hazy or cloudy? Is it painful to the dog when you press gently on the eyeball through closed eyelids? These maneuvers can be performed easily and do not require any technical expertise. Yet they provide the type of information you need to determine if this is an emergency.

To examine the surface of the eyeball, place one thumb against the skin of the cheek below the eye and the other thumb against the ridge of bone above. Gently draw down with the lower thumb and apply counter traction with the other. Because of the mobility of the skin of the dog's face, the lower eyelid will sag out and you can look in and see the conjunctival sac and most of the cornea behind it. Reverse the procedure to examine the eye behind the upper eyelid. Flash a light across the surface of the cornea to see if it is clear and transparent. Any dull or dished-out spot is an indication of corneal abrasion or ulcer.

Press gently on the surface of the eye through the closed eyelids to see if one eye feels harder or softer than the other. If the eye is tender, the dog will give evidence of pain.

To test the dog's vision, cover one eye and make a movement as if you are about to touch the other eye with your finger. If the dog has vision in that eye, he will blink as he sees your finger approaching.

Do not neglect minor eye ailments. If there is any doubt about the diagnosis, and particularly if the eye has been doctored at home but has not shown improvement in 24 hours, call your veterinarian.

HOW TO APPLY EYE MEDICINES

Place ointments into the space behind the lower eyelid (the conjunctival sac). Drops can be applied directly to the eyeball.

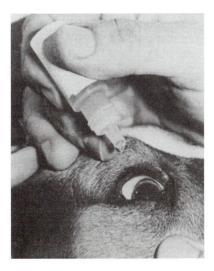

Drops are applied directly to the eyeball. (J. Clawson)

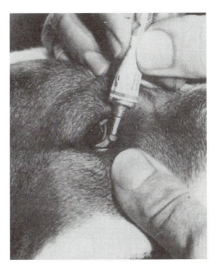

Apply ointment to the inner surface of the lower lid. (J. Clawson)

To apply ointment, steady your dog's head with one hand and draw down on the lower eyelid with your thumb to expose the conjunctival sac. Rest the hand containing the applicator against the dog's forehead, as shown in the photo. This way, if the dog jerks his head your hand will move with it, preventing the applicator from poking the eye. Slowly squeeze out a ribbon of ointment.

To instill drops, steady the hand holding the dropper against the side of the dog's head. Tilt the muzzle up; then drop the medication into the eye. Eye drops tend to wash out with tears and must be applied several times a day.

Only use drops and ointments that are specifically labeled for ophthalmic use. Be sure to check the expiration date on the product's label. Prolonged administration of antibiotics in the eye may lead to resistant infections.

The Eyeball

EYE OUT OF ITS SOCKET

This is an emergency. Dislocation of one or both eyeballs is a common problem in dogs with large bulging eyes such as Boston Terriers, Pugs, Pekinese, Maltese and some spaniels. It is generally caused by dog bites and other trauma. Struggling with these dogs while attempting to hold and restrain them for any reason can cause the eye to bulge out so far that the eyelids snap shut behind the eyeball. This prevents the eyeball from returning to its socket.

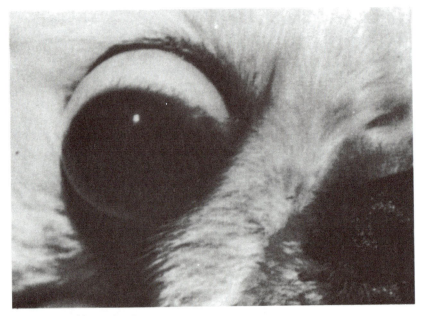

An eye out of its socket is an emergency.

A dislocated eyeball is an extremely serious condition that may cause loss of vision. Shortly after the eye dislocates, swelling behind the eye makes it extremely difficult to return the eyeball to its normal position. *Proceed at once to the nearest veterinary hospital.* Carry the dog, if possible. Cover the eye with a wet cloth. Prevent the dog from pawing at the eye.

If it appears that veterinary help will not be available within 30 minutes, consider attempting to reposition the eyeball yourself. This requires at least two people: one to restrain and hold the dog, and the other to reposition the eye. Lubricate the surface of the eye with K-Y or petroleum jelly and lift the eyelids out and over the eyeball, while maintaining gentle inward pressure on the globe with a wad of moist cotton. If not successful, make no further attempt. Seek professional assistance.

After the eye has been replaced, your veterinarian may suggest a surgical procedure to prevent a recurrence.

OTHER CAUSES OF A BULGING EYE

Abscesses, hematomas and tumors in the retrobulbar space behind the eye can push the globe forward and cause bulging.

A *retrobulbar abscess* is an extremely painful condition that comes on rapidly. The face around the eye is swollen and the globe is extremely tender to finger pressure. Dogs experience great difficulty opening and closing their mouths. A retrobulbar abscess must be surgically drained.

Retrobulbar hematomas (blood clots behind the eyeball) also develop suddenly. They occur with head injuries and can appear spontaneously in conjunction with some bleeding disorders.

Tumors in the retrobulbar space produce a gradual bulging. Unlike the two conditions just described, they are relatively painless.

Chronic glaucoma can lead to increased eye size and protrusion.

SUNKEN EYE (ENOPHTHALMOS)

When an eyes recedes, the third eyelid usually slides out over the surface of the eyeball and becomes visible. The treatment of a sunken eye is directed toward the underlying cause.

Both eyeballs may recede when there is loss of substance in the fat pads behind the eyes. This occurs with severe dehydration or rapid weight loss.

There is a retractor muscle which, when it goes into spasm, pulls the eyeball back into its socket. Tetanus produces spasms of the retractor muscles of both eyeballs, along with the characteristic appearance of the third eyelids.

When only one eye is involved, the most likely cause is a painful eye. Nonpainful causes include nerve damage following a neck injury or a middle ear infection. With this condition, called *Horner's syndrome*, the pupil is small on the affected side. Finally, after a severe eye injury, the eye can become smaller and sink into its socket.

HAIR GROWING FROM THE EYEBALL (DERMOID CYST)

Dermoid cysts are congenital growths usually found at the outer corners of the eyes. These cysts contain hair that often appears to be growing out of the surface of the eye. The dermoid is not a malignant tumor, but it should be removed because of the irritating effect of the hair.

Eyelids

SEVERE SQUINTING (BLEPHAROSPASM)

Severe squinting with spasm of the muscles around the eye is a symptom of a painful eye. Any painful eye condition can cause squinting. The tightening of the muscles rolls the eyelids in against the eye. Once rolled in, the rough edges of the lids rub against the eyeball, causing further pain and spasm.

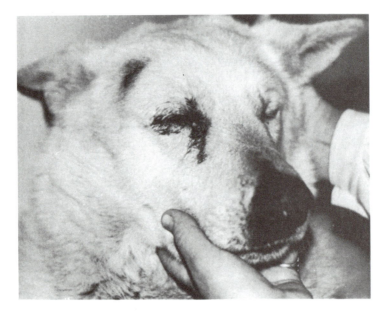

Severe squinting with shutting of the eye, indicative of a painful eye.

Anesthetic drops can be applied to the eyeball to relieve the pain and break the cycle. The relief is temporary, unless the irritating factor is identified and removed.

INFLAMED EYELIDS (BLEPHARITIS)

Bacterial blepharitis is a condition in which the eyelids become thick, reddened, inflamed and encrusted. Mucuslike pus may adhere to the lids. Blepharitis in puppies usually occurs primarily in association with puppy strangles. In older dogs it can be associated with various skin diseases including canine atopy, demodectic mange, autoimmune diseases and hypothyroidism.

Staphylococcal blepharitis occurs in both puppies and adults. It is identified by finding small white pimples on the edges of the eyelids. The pimples rupture and cause itching and redness. This disease occurs most often in Poodles.

The thickened, inflamed and encrusted eyelids of blepharitis.

Treatment: Blepharitis is treated with oral and topical antibiotics. Soak the eyelids daily with a warm washcloth to remove adherent crusts. Three or four times a day, apply a topical ophthalmic ointment or solution containing neomycin, bacitracin or polymyxin B. Your veterinarian may prescribe an ophthalmic ointment that contains corticosteroids. Blepharitis is difficult to cure. Some dogs require long-term treatment. Dogs with chronic blepharitis should be checked for hypothyroidism.

ALLERGIC BLEPHARITIS (CHEMOSIS)

Sudden swelling of the eyelids is an allergic reaction, most often to insect bites or ingredients in foods. The lids appear fluid-filled, soft and puffy, and the dog itches and rubs his face. The reaction may be accompanied by hives in which the hair stands out erect in little patches all over the body.

This is not a serious problem. It is of short duration and improves when the *allergen* is removed. Simple cases can be treated with eye drops or ointments containing a corticosteroid prescribed by your veterinarian.

FOREIGN BODIES IN THE EYES

Foreign material such as grass seeds, dirt and specks of vegetable matter can adhere to the surface of the eye or become trapped behind the eyelids. Dogs that ride in the open beds of pickup trucks and in cars with their heads out the windows are at high risk for getting dirt and debris in the eyes. Thorns, thistles and splinters can also penetrate the cornea. This is most likely to happen when a dog is running through dense brush and tall weeds.

Signs of a foreign body in the eye are tearing and watering, blinking, squinting and pawing. The third eyelid may protrude to protect the painful eye.

Examine the eye as described above. You may be able to see dirt or plant material on the surface or behind the upper and lower eyelids. If not, the foreign body may be caught behind the third eyelid. In that case, the dog will need a topical eye anesthetic before it can be removed.

Treatment: To remove foreign material on the surface of the eye or behind the eyelids, restrain the dog and hold the eyelids open as described in *How to Apply Eye Medicine*, page 153. Flush the eye for 10 to 15 minutes using cool water, or preferably a sterile saline eyewash. Soak a wad of cotton in the solution and squeeze it into the eye.

If the foreign body cannot be removed by irrigation, you may be able to remove it by gently touching it with a wet cotton-tipped swab. The foreign body may adhere to the cotton tip. Foreign bodies that penetrate the surface of the eye must be removed by a veterinarian.

If the dog continues to squint or tear after the foreign body has been removed, have him checked to see if the cornea has been damaged.

BURNS OF THE EYES

Chemical injuries to the conjunctiva and cornea can occur when acids, alkali, soaps, shampoos and topical insecticides are splashed into the eyes. Toxic fumes can also irritate and injure the eyes. The signs are tearing, squinting and pawing at the eye.

Treatment: Flush the eyes with cool water or a sterile saline solution, as described for *Foreign Bodies in the Eyes*. This must be done immediately after exposure to prevent damage to the eye. After you have completed the flushing, take your dog to the veterinarian for further evaluation and treatment.

Be sure to protect the eyes from shampoos and insecticides when bathing and dipping your dog.

STYS AND CHALAZIONS

The eyelid contains hair follicles and meibomian glands. The meibomian glands secrete an oil that acts as a barrier to the evaporation of tears. Infection occurring in either a hair follicle or a meibomian gland produces a sty, also called a *hordeolum*, which is a small abscess that comes to a head.

An uninfected meibomian gland may become plugged, resulting in the development of a nontender swelling on the eyelid called a chalazion. Chalazions tend to occur in older dogs. They remain relatively static and only require treatment if they are getting larger.

Treatment: A dog with a sty should be placed on oral and topical antibiotics as described for *blepharitis*. Applying warm compresses to the eyelid three or four times a day is beneficial in bringing the sty to a head. If the sty does not rupture, your veterinarian may puncture it with a sterile needle or a scalpel.

Chalazions are removed surgically. Do not squeeze the chalazion in an attempt to express its contents. If the chalazion ruptures into the eyelid, the oily contents set up a severe inflammatory reaction that is most difficult to treat.

EXTRA EYELASHES (DISTICHIASIS)

This is a congenital condition in which an extra row of eyelashes grows from the eyelid and is directed inward, rubbing against the surface of the eye. In untreated cases, the constant irritation leads to *corneal abrasion*. The condition may not be noticed until the puppy is grown. Extra eyelashes occur most often in Poodles, Cocker Spaniels and Pekingese, but all breeds can be affected.

Aberrant eyelashes that grow inward on the upper and lower eyelids produce the same type of problem.

Treatment: The offending eyelashes should be removed and their roots destroyed through *cryotherapy* (chemical freezing), electrolysis or surgery. Plucking them with blunt-nosed tweezers provides temporary relief, but the eyelashes grow back in about four weeks. Dogs that have had their eyelashes permanently removed cannot be shown in conformation.

FACIAL HAIR

Hair in the nasal folds may grow up against the eyeball and rub against the cornea. This tends to be a problem in Poodles, Maltese, Yorkshire Terriers and in short-nosed breeds such as Pekingese, Shih Tzu, Lhasa Apsos and Bulldogs. In Old English Sheepdogs and other breeds with long facial hair, a similar problem can occur. The involved hair will be stained reddish-brown by tears.

Treatment: The offending hairs should be removed by clipping, or, if the hair is in the nasal folds, by surgery.

Dogs with long hair about the face are subject to eye irritation. (Sydney Giffin Wiley)

ENTROPION

This condition, in which the eyelids roll inward, is the most common congenital defect of the eyelids. It can also be caused by injury and long-standing eyelid infections that cause scarring. The abnormal eyelids produce irritation with tearing and squinting. Corneal injuries are common.

It may be difficult to distinguish entropion from blepharospasm. The best way to tell them apart is to administer a topical eye anesthetic. If the inverted eyelids are caused by a blepharospasm, temporarily blocking the eye pain causes the inversion to disappear.

Breeds most commonly affected by entropion are the Chinese Shar-Pei, Chow Chow, Great Dane, Great Pyrenees, Saint Bernard, Bulldog and the hunting breeds. Most cases involve the lower eyelids. In dogs with large heads and loose facial skin such as Chinese Shar-Pei, Bloodhounds and Saint Bernards, the upper eyelids may be involved.

Treatment: Entropion requires surgical correction. Note that dogs who have had corrective surgery on their eyelids cannot be shown in conformation.

Shar-Pei puppies suffer from a condition called *neonatal entropion.* These puppies should have their eyelids everted with temporary sutures at three to five weeks of age. If they do not outgrow the problem, plastic surgery on the eyelids can be performed at a later date.

This Shar-Pei puppy's eyelids have been everted with temporary sutures. This may correct the entropion without need for permanent surgery.

ECTROPION

In dogs with this condition, the lower eyelid rolls out from the surface of the eye. This exposes the eye to irritants and leads to a high incidence of chronic conjunctivitis and corneal injury. Ectropion occurs in dogs with loose facial skin such as hounds, spaniels and Saint Bernards. It is also seen in older dogs whose facial skin has lost its tone. It can occur temporarily in hunting dogs, after a long day in the field.

Treatment: Mild ectropion that causes no symptoms needs no treatment. But in most cases, ectropionshould be corrected by a surgical procedure that tightens the eyelids.

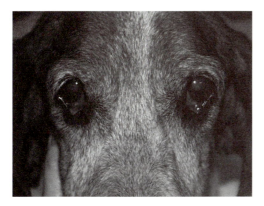

Ectropion exposes the eyes to irritants and leads to chronic eye infections and corneal injuries.

EYELID TUMORS

The most common tumor of the eyelid is a meibomian gland adenoma. Meibomian glands are found only on the eyelids. These glands secrete an oil that acts as a barrier to the evaporation of tears. Meibomian gland adenomas have a cauliflower-like appearance and may be single or multiple.

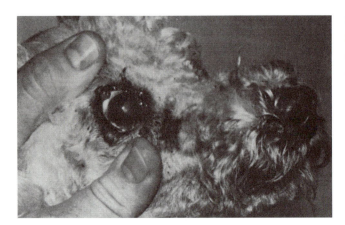

These growths on the eyelids are meibomian gland adenomas.

Among other eyelid tumors, the most common is the *sebaceous adenoma*. Most are benign, and are found in older dogs.

Papillomas are wartlike tumors caused by the canine oral papilloma virus. These tumors also grow on the surface of the eye.

Treatment: Eyelid tumors should be removed to prevent injury to the cornea.

The Third Eyelid (Nictitating Membrane)

FILM OVER THE EYE

An opaque third eyelid, normally not seen, may become visible across the front of the eye, in which case the nictitating membrane is said to be protruding. The appearance of the third eyelid indicates that the eyeball has sunken into its socket (see *Sunken Eye*, page 155), or that the eyeball has been pulled back into its socket by spasm of the retractor muscles in response to severe eye pain.

A dog may be born with visible third eyelids, called *haws*. In the show ring this is often considered undesirable, because it gives the animal a somewhat haggard look. Most breed standards (if they mention it at all) require that the haws be scarcely apparent. The haws is a concern only because it gives the dog an unsightly appearance. There is no medical reason to remove the third eyelids just because the haws is visible.

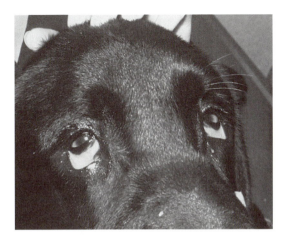

Protrusion of the third eyelids, showing the haws.

EVERSION OF THE CARTILAGE

This is a congenital condition among Weimaraners, Great Danes, Golden Retrievers, Saint Bernards and other breeds. The third eyelid appears to roll back upon itself like a dry leaf. Corneal irritation may occur.

Treatment: This can be treated surgically if it is causing a problem.

CHERRY EYE

There is a tear gland wrapped around the cartilage of the third eyelid that is a major source of tears for the eye. In cherry eye, the fibrous attachments to the undersurface of the third eyelid are weak. This allows the gland to prolapse, or bulge out from beneath the eyelid, exposing a cherrylike growth that is really a normal-sized tear gland. This growth can irritate the surface of the eye and produce recurrent conjunctivitis. Cherry eye is a congenital defect that occurs most commonly in Cocker Spaniels, Beagles, Boston Terriers and Bulldogs.

Cherry eye is a prolapse of the tear gland of the third eyelid.

Treatment: Removing the third eyelid or the tear gland seriously interferes with tear production and may result in a dry eye syndrome in breeds so disposed (see *The Tearing Mechanism*, page 166). Instead of removing the eyelid, surgery can be performed that repositions the third eyelid and the tear gland. This corrects the problem while maintaining tear production.

The Outer Eye

CONJUNCTIVITIS (RED EYE)

Conjunctivitis, sometimes called red eye, is an inflammation of the conjunctival membrane that covers the back of the eyelids and the surface of the eyeball, up to the cornea. It is one of the most common eye problems in dogs.

The classic signs of conjunctivitis are a red eye with a discharge. *Conjunctivitis is not painful.* If the eye is red and the dog is squinting and shutting the eye, consider the possibility of keratitis, uveitis or glaucoma. Any delay in treating these conditions can lead to blindness.

When the discharge involves both eyes, suspect an allergy or a systemic disease such as canine distemper. When it involves only one eye, consider a local predisposing cause such as a conjunctival foreign body or hair rubbing on the eye.

The eye discharge in conjunctivitis may be clear (*serous*), mucuslike (*mucoid*) or pus-like (*purulent*). A stringy mucoid discharge suggests the dog may have inadequate tear volume, a problem associated with *keratoconjunctivitis sicca.* In fact, this is the most common cause of conjunctivitis in dogs.

Serous Conjunctivitis is a mild condition in which the membranes look pink and somewhat swollen. The discharge is clear and watery. Serous conjunctivitis is caused by physical irritants such as wind, cold, dust and various allergens such as those causing allergic blepharitis. Allergic conjunctivitis is often accompanied by itching, and the dog will rub his face.

Follicular (Mucoid) Conjunctivitis is a condition in which the small mucous glands (follicles) on the underside of the nictitating membrane react to an eye irritant or infection by forming a rough, cobblestone surface that irritates the eye and produces a mucoid discharge. After the inciting factor has been treated, the follicles persist and the rough surface acts as a chronic irritant.

Purulent Conjunctivitis begins as serous conjunctivitis that becomes infected. The usual culprits are the bacteria streptococcus and staphylococcus. The conjunctiva is red and swollen. The eye discharge contains mucus and pus. Thick secretions may crust the eyelids.

Treatment: Any underlying cause of conjunctivitis should be corrected. Serous conjunctivitis can be treated at home. Flush the eye three or four times daily with an over-the-counter sterile saline eyewash. Notify your veterinarian if the eye appears to be getting worse.

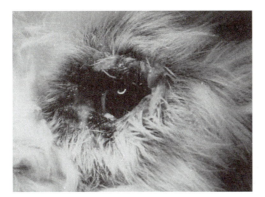

Chronic purulent conjunctivitis. The discharge is thick and tenacious. This condition is difficult to clear up.

Mild cases of follicular conjunctivitis respond to antibiotic/corticosteroid eye ointments prescribed by your veterinarian. In resistant cases, the follicles may need to be destroyed by chemical cauterization.

Purulent conjunctivitis requires veterinary examination and treatment. It is important to remove mucus and pus from the eyes, as well as pus and crusts that adhere to the eyelids. Moisten a cotton ball with sterile eyewash and gently cleanse the eye. Warm, moist packs may help loosen crusts. Repeat as necessary and apply topical antibiotics prescribed by your veterinarian (see *How to Apply Eye Medicines*, page 153). Continue topical antibiotics for several days beyond apparent cure.Note that corticosteroids and eye medications containing corticosteroids should not be used in purulent conjunctivitis, because they impair the local inflammatory response that fights infection. Bacterial culture and sensitivity tests are indicated if the conjunctivitis does not improve. Dogs with recurrent or persistent conjunctivitis should be tested for *keratoconjunctivitis sicca*.

NEONATAL CONJUNCTIVITIS

The eyes of newborn puppies open at 10 to 14 days of age. Infection behind the eyelids, called neonatal conjunctivitis, can occur before or after the eyelids separate. The conjunctivitis is caused by bacteria that gain access to the space behind the eyelids during or shortly after birth.

There is a condition called *ankyloblepharon* in which the eyelids do not open as widely as they should. This predisposes a puppy to neonatal conjunctivitis. Neonatal conjunctivitis may affect several puppies in the litter.

Suspect this problem if the eyelids appear swollen and/or the eyelids bulge. A purulent discharge may be present if the infection occurs when the eyes are beginning to open. The discharge may cause the eyelids to stick together.

Treatment: Notify your veterinarian immediately if you suspect neonatal conjunctivitis. Delay in treatment can lead to corneal damage and blindness.

The eyelids (if still fused) should be opened to allow pus to escape. With puppies older than seven days, this can usually be accomplished by gently pulling the eyelids apart. In puppies younger than seven days, your veterinarian may need to open the eyelids with a surgical instrument.

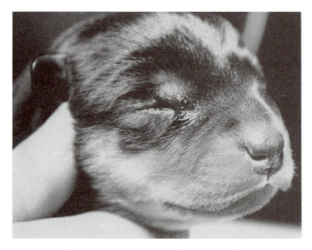

In a case of newborn conjunctivitis, the eyelids should be gently separated to evacuate the pus and treat the infection.

Once the lids are open, the surface of the eye and the eyelids should be cleaned to remove purulent discharge, as described for *conjunctivitis*. Repeat as necessary. Eyelids that stick together should be manually separated to facilitate drainage. Solutions or ointments prescribed by your veterinarian that contain broad-spectrum antibiotics should be instilled into the eyes several times daily. Artificial tears should also be used frequently, as newborns do not make tears before their eyes would naturally open. The artificial tears prevent drying of the cornea.

The Tearing Mechanism

Each eye has two lacrimal glands: one beneath the bony ridge at the top of the eye socket, and the other incorporated into the third eyelid. Each produces approximately half the aqueous tear volume. Excess tears are collected at the inner corner of the eye and drained by the nasolacrimal duct into the nasal cavity near the front of the nose.

The tear film actually comprises three layers. The outer layer is a lipid, or oily layer produced by meibomian glands in the eyelids. This layer acts as a barrier and prevents tears from evaporating and spilling over the eyelids. The middle, or aqueous layer consists of the watery tears produced by the lacrimal glands. The inner layer is composed of mucus secreted by the conjunctiva. Mucus is a wetting agent and holds the aqueous layer against the surface of the eye.

Diseases of the tearing mechanism produce either a dry eye or a watery eye.

KERATOCONJUNCTIVITIS SICCA (DRY EYE)

Keratoconjunctivitis sicca is a disorder of the tear glands that results in insufficient aqueous tear production and a correspondingly dry cornea. The tear film contains less of the aqueous layer and more of the mucus layer. In consequence, the classic sign of dry eye is a *thick, stringy, mucous to mucopurulent discharge*. Since this type of discharge can also be seen with conjunctivitis, dogs with dry eye may be treated for chronic conjunctivitis for long periods with little or no improvement.

In a dog with dry eye, the bright, glistening sheen normally seen in the eye is replaced by a lackluster appearance in which the cornea is dry, dull and opaque. Recurrent bouts of conjunctivitis are typical. Eventually the cornea becomes ulcerated or develops keratitis. Blindness may ensue.

Dry eye can have several causes. Immune-mediated diseases appear to play a major role. Other cases are idiopathic—that is, the cause is not known. Breeds predisposed to dry eye include Bulldogs, Cocker Spaniels, Lhasa Apsos, West Highland White Terriers and others.

Some specific conditions that predispose a dog to dry eye include:

- Injury to the nerves that innervate the lacrimal glands. A branch of the facial nerve that activates the tear glands passes through the middle ear. Infections in the middle ear can damage this branch, affecting the tear glands as well as the muscles on that side of the face. In this case, the opposite eye is not affected.

- Injury to the tear glands themselves. Partial or complete destruction of tear glands can follow *systemic* diseases such as canine distemper, Addison's disease and immune-mediated diseases such as rheumatoid arthritis. Bacterial blepharitis or conjunctivitis can destroy the tear glands or occlude the small ducts that carry the tears into the eye. A number of sulfonamide drugs are toxic to tear glands. Tear gland injuries may be partially reversible if the underlying cause is eliminated.

- Congenital absence of the tear glands is rare. It tends to occur in the smaller breeds.

The diagnosis of dry eye is made by measuring the volume of tears. The *Schirmer tear test* involves placing a commercial filter paper strip into the tear pool at the inner corner of the dog's eye and leaving it for one minute to see how much of the strip is wetted. Normally the strip should be wet to a distance of 20 mm. In dogs with dry eye, the strip wets less than 10 mm (often less than 5 mm).

Treatment: For many years, the frequent application of artificial tears was the only treatment available for dry eye. But the recent approval of ophthalmic cyclosporin by the FDA has revolutionized treatment and greatly improved results. Cyclosporin is an immunosuppressive drug that reverses immune-mediated destruction of the lacrimal glands.

Cyclosporin ointment is applied to the surface of the involved eye. The frequency of application must be determined by your veterinarian. The effect is not immediate. Artificial tears and topical antibiotics should be continued until the Schirmer tear test indicates that the volume of tears is adequate.

Treatment is life-long. Interrupting cyclosporin for as little as 24 hours cause symptoms to reappear in 90 percent of dogs. This can be reversed by resuming treatment.

When damage to the lacrimal glands leaves little or no functioning tissue, cyclosporin is not likely to be effective. Artificial tears (drops and ointments) prescribed by your veterinarian must then be instilled into the dog's eyes several times a day for life. Ointments are less expensive and do not need to be applied as frequently as drops. Saline drops should not be used because they aggravate the problem by washing away the lipid layer of the tear film.

A topical mucolytic agent containing acetylcystine may be recommended to reduce heavy mucus accumulation. Topical antibiotics are indicated whenever the mucus discharge becomes purulent. Topical corticosteroids may be prescribed by your veterinarian in some circumstances to decrease inflammation. In the presence of corneal ulceration, corticosteroids are contraindicated because they predispose a dog to rupture of the cornea.

Surgical treatment can be considered as a last resort when medical management fails. The operation involves transplanting the duct of the parotid salivary gland up into the corner of the eye. The saliva takes the place of the tears. The operation has several significant disadvantages. One is that the volume of tears may be more than the drainage system can handle. This can result in a watery eye and the accumulation of mineral deposits on the cornea and face.

EPIPHORA (WATERY EYE)

There are many conditions in which a watery or mucus discharge overflows the eyes and runs down the face. With a severe watery eye there is constant wetness

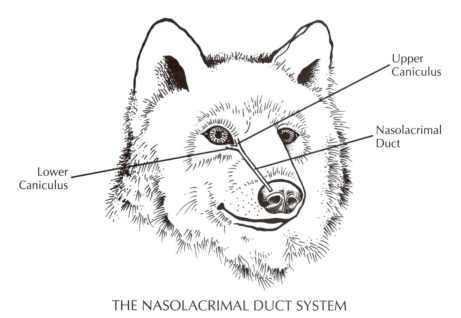

THE NASOLACRIMAL DUCT SYSTEM

and the skin may become inflamed and infected, adding to the dog's unsightly appearance and physical discomfort.

Epiphora is primarily a cosmetic problem unless it is a symptom of a painful eye. For example, entropion, conjunctivitis, foreign bodies, corneal ulcers, anterior uveitis and acute glaucoma are all accompanied by excessive tearing. Excessive tearing may also be caused by eye irritation due to extra eyelashes or facial hair that rub on the surface of the eye.

Treatment: For treatment of epiphora, see *Poodle Eye*, below.

NASOLACRIMAL OCCLUSION (BLOCKAGE IN THE TEAR-DRAINAGE SYSTEM)

The tear-drainage system is composed of a nasolacrimal duct that collects tears at the tear lake and empties them into the nasal cavity near the front of the nose. The duct branches at the corner of the eye into two smaller collecting ducts—the upper and lower canaliculi—whose openings (called punctums) are located in the upper and lower eyelids.

A puppy can be born with a defective tear drainage system. In one condition, called *imperforate inferior punctum*, the duct system is normal except for a conjunctival membrane across the punctum of the lower eyelid. The problem occurs most often in Cocker Spaniels.

Other causes of nasolacrimal occlusion include entropion, in which the eyelid rolls inward and blocks the punctum; scarring of a punctum following a bout of purulent conjunctivitis; infection in a duct that causes cellular debris to plug the duct; and foreign bodies such as grass seeds that lodge in the ducts. These conditions usually cause tearing in only one eye.

The drainage system is first tested to see if it is open by staining the pool of tears with fluorescein dye. If the dye does not appear at the nostril, the system is blocked on that side. Nasolacrimal probes can be inserted into the ducts and various flushing techniques used to establish the point of obstruction. The flushing often removes the blockage and opens the duct.

Treatment: Nasolacrimal duct infection is treated with antibiotics, in some cases by instilling them directly into a duct. The dosage, type and route of administration must be determined by your veterinarian.

A minor operation on a duct opening may be needed to clear a blockage. Follow-up treatment includes the use of topical antibiotics and corticosteroids to reduce inflammation.

POODLE EYE

This problem, in which brown stains appear at the corner of the eye, is common to several toy breeds including Poodles, Lhasa Apsos, Maltese, Pomeranians, Pekingese and other small breeds.

The exact cause of tear overflow in these breeds is unknown. One theory is that susceptible breeds have a pooling space that is too small to collect a lake of tears. Tears contain chemicals that react with light to produce reddish-brown stains. The staining will be more apparent in dogs whose haircoat is light colored or white.

Treatment: Poodle eye often improves when the dog is given a course of tetracycline, which is secreted in the tears and binds the photochemicals that cause the staining. The face remains wet, but is not discolored. Tetracycline is given orally for three weeks. If the staining returns after the antibiotic is stopped, long-term antibiotics can be considered. One option is to add low-dose tetracycline to the daily food ration.

Surgery is another alternative. The operation involves removing part of the tear gland of the third eyelid. While this reduces tear volume and makes a better tear lake, it does carry the risk of producing a dry eye as discussed in *Cherry Eye*. Removal of the tear gland should be considered only if the Schirmer tear test shows that the strip wets more than 15 mm per minute (see *Keratoconjunctivitis Sicca*, page 167).

The dog's appearance can be improved for cosmetic purposes by plucking the stained hairs or clipping them close to the face. Stains can be removed by bathing with a dilute solution of hydrogen peroxide (1:10). Be sure peroxide does not get into the eyes. A minor problem can be improved with a piece of white chalk. If you are planning to show the dog, note that all powder or chalk must be removed from the hair before the dog is brought into the conformation ring for judging.

Do not use chlorine bleaches for eye stains! The fumes are painful and may cause chemical conjunctivitis.

The Cornea

The cornea is the clear part of the eye. Corneal injuries are extremely painful and require immediate veterinary attention. Affected dogs will squint, tear and avoid light. The third eyelid often comes out to protect the injured eye. Breeds with bulging eyes, such as the Pekingese, Maltese, Boston Terriers, Pugs and some spaniels, are particularly susceptible to corneal injuries.

Corticosteroids incorporated into many common eye preparations used in treating conjunctivitis should not be used in an eye suspected of having a corneal injury, because of the danger the cornea will rupture into the anterior chamber.

CORNEAL ABRASION

The cornea is covered by a protective surface layer of epithelial cells. Any irritation, such as a scratch or foreign body, damages this surface layer. Swelling at the site of the injury causes the area to appear hazy and opaque when viewed under magnification. The opaque area also stains positive with fluorescein dye.

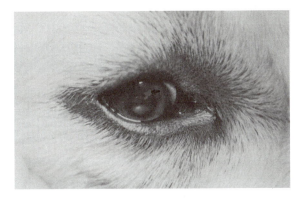

Note the opaque area on the surface of the cornea at the site of a healed corneal abrasion.

Corneal abrasions in the upper part of the cornea may be caused by misdirected eyelashes. Lower corneal opacities suggest an imbedded foreign body. Abrasions near the inner corner of the eye suggest a foreign body beneath the third eyelid.

A corneal abrasion heals in about three to five days by a process in which the adjacent epithelial cells enlarge and migrate over the defect. The injury will not heal, however, if a foreign body is imbedded in the cornea or beneath one of the eyelids. It is important to check for a foreign body in all cases of corneal abrasion.

Treatment: All corneal injuries must be seen and treated by a veterinarian to avoid complications, including keratitis and corneal ulcer. Broad-spectrum topical antibiotic drops or ointments are prescribed every four to six hours to prevent infection. A topical atropine preparation is used to keep the pupil dilated, which reduces eye pain. The eye is examined periodically to monitor progress. Treatment is continued until the abrasion is healed.

CORNEAL ULCER

An ulcer is similar to a corneal abrasion, except that an ulcer is deeper and involves the middle and sometimes the inner layer of the cornea.

Most corneal ulcers are caused by trauma, but some are associated with kerato-conjunctivitis sicca, corneal dystrophy, diabetes mellitus, Addison's disease and hypothyroidism.

Corneal ulcers are extremely painful and cause severe tearing, squinting and pawing at the eye. Dogs frequently avoid light. Large ulcers are visible to the naked eye as dull spots or dished-out depressions on the surface of the cornea. Small ulcers are best seen after the eye has been stained with fluorescein.

Treatment: Early veterinary consultation and treatment is vital to prevent serious complications and even loss of the eye. Medical treatment is similar to that described for a corneal abrasion, except that ulcers take more time to heal. Your veterinarian may recommend injecting antibiotics directly into the eye beneath the conjunctiva.

Surgical treatment involves suturing the third eyelid or a flap of conjunctiva over the surface of the eye to protect the cornea during healing. Soft contact lenses and collagen shields are other methods of protecting a damaged cornea. The advantage of a contact lens is that it can be changed weekly to observe and treat the ulcer. Collagen shields need to be replaced periodically because they degrade and disappear within a few days.

Rupture of the eye into the anterior chamber can be anticipated if the cloudy central portion of a deep ulcer begins to clear, or the endothelial layer protrudes like a bulging tire. This can be recognized by your veterinarian. It is an emergency. Immediate surgery is necessary to prevent loss of the eye.

INDOLENT CORNEAL ULCERS IN BOXERS

A specific type of slow-healing (indolent) ulcer is found in Boxers and other breeds, including the Samoyed, Dachshund, Miniature Poodle, Pembroke Welsh Corgi, Wire Fox Terrier and Shetland Sheepdog. Most affected dogs are neutered males or females over the age of six.

The indolent ulcer is caused by lack of a binding substance or "glue" normally present in the basement membrane of the cornea. (The basement membrane is a thin layer of cells between the outer and middle layers of the cornea.) The missing substance allows the epithelium to peel away, leaving a concave ulcer.

Treatment: The treatment is prolonged. It involves paring away the poorly adherent corneal epithelium and treating the ulcer as described in *Corneal Ulcer*, above.

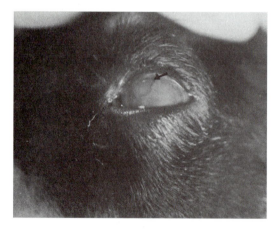

A large corneal ulcer of the type often seen in Boxers.

KERATITIS (CLOUDY EYE)

Keratitis is inflammation of the cornea in which the cornea becomes cloudy, resulting in loss of transparency. The signs are excessive tearing, squinting, pawing at the eye, avoiding light and protrusion of the third eyelid. There are different types of keratitis; all are serious diseases and can lead to partial or complete blindness. All types of keratitis must be treated by a veterinarian.

Ulcerative Keratitis. This is a painful corneal inflammation that occurs as a complication of keratoconjunctivitis sicca or corneal ulcer. The cornea appears dull and hazy, then cloudy, and finally milky white and relatively opaque. Treatment is similar to that described for *Corneal Ulcer*.

Infectious Keratitis. Bacterial infection may complicate ulcerative keratitis, keratoconjunctivitis sicca or corneal ulcer. The most common invading bacteria are staphylococcus, streptococcus and pseudomonas. In addition to eye pain, infectious keratitis is characterized by a purulent discharge from the eye. The eyelids are swollen and matted. This might, at first, suggest conjunctivitis (which could seriously delay diagnosis and treatment), but recall that conjunctivitis is not accompanied by signs of a painful eye.

Treatment is similar to that described for *Corneal Ulcer*. It is important to use topical antibiotics selected on the basis of culture and sensitivity tests.

A fungal keratitis is uncommon in dogs, but may occur with the prolonged use of topical antibiotics. The diagnosis is made by fungal culture. It is treated with antifungal drugs.

Interstitial Keratitis (Blue Eye). This is a corneal inflammation in which a bluish-white film appears over the clear window of the eye. It is caused by the virus of infectious hepatitis, and at one time it occurred after vaccination with CAV-1. Signs appear 10 days after exposure. The eyes begin to water and the dog squints and avoids light. Most dogs recover completely within a few weeks. In some cases the eye remains permanently clouded.

Vascular and Pigmentary Keratitis. Vascular keratitis is caused by neovascularization—the process by which the transparency of the cornea is lost due to an ingrowth of blood vessels and connective tissue. In pigmentary keratitis, melanin pigment is deposited in the cornea. This is a separate but often associated process. Both conditions interfere with vision and may progress to blindness.

Blood vessels growing on the surface of the eye (pigmentary keratitis), in this case caused by lack of tears (keratoconjunctivitis sicca).

Vascular and pigmentary keratitis may, in some cases, be the result of a chronic corneal irritation such as that caused by entropion or *lagophthalmos* (inability to completely close the eyes). Removing the initiating process may reverse the keratitis.

Pannus is a specific type of nonpainful pigmentary keratitis found in German Shepherd Dogs and their crosses, and also in Belgian Tervurens, Border Collies, Greyhounds, Siberian Huskies, Australian Shepherds and other breeds. It occurs in dogs over two years old. An immune-mediated disease is suspected to be the cause. A distinguishing feature of pannus is redness and thickening of the third eyelid, but this may not always be present.

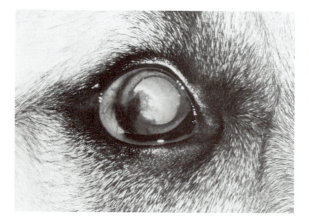

Pannus in a German Shepherd Dog. Note the blood vessels and pigment in the cornea and the thickening of the third eyelid.

Treatment: Vascular and pigmentary keratitis not related to chronic eye irritation is progressive and incurable. The goal of treatment is to arrest the disease and maintain remission.

Neovascularization responds well to high-dose topical corticosteroids. These preparations must be monitored closely by your veterinarian, because prolonged use of corticosteroids in the eyes can lead to a mild form of Cushing's syndrome and other problems. Improvement begins in two to six weeks. Treatment is life-long. Stopping the eye drops even for a short time is followed by relapse.

Ophthalmic cyclosporin instilled into the eyes twice daily may reduce the deposition of melanin pigment.

CORNEAL DYSTROPHIES

Corneal dystrophies are diseases of the cornea that occur in both eyes, are not related to inflammation, and are inherited. In most cases a dystrophy appears as a gray-white crystalline or metallic opacity in the substance of the cornea. These opacities are usually oval or round. They often become progressively larger, but in some cases remain the same size. Rapid progression usually leads to blindness. Slow progression may or may not lead to blindness.

Corneal dystrophy is a genetic disorder affecting many breeds, including the Collie, Siberian Husky, Cavalier King Charles Spaniel, Beagle, Airedale Terrier, Cocker Spaniel, Alaskan Malamute, Bearded Collie, Bichon Frise, German Shepherd Dog, Lhasa Apso, Shetland Sheepdog, Chihuahua, Miniature Pinscher, Weimaraner, Pointer and Samoyed. The age of onset, rate of progression, appearance and location of the opacities and mode of inheritance vary with the breed and the individual dog. In some breeds, such as the Siberian Husky, the disease is evident as early as four months of age; in others, such as the Chihuahua, it appears as late as 13 years.

Some cases of corneal dystrophy are complicated by the development of a corneal ulcer.

Treatment: There is no effective treatment. A corneal dystrophy that threatens eyesight can be removed surgically. This may temporarily improve vision, but the opacity will reform.

Prevention: Corneal dystrophies can be identified by veterinary eye examination. Affected individuals should not be used for breeding. The mode of inheritance has been determined for some breeds. This may make it possible to project which dogs in the pedigree are carriers. For more information, see *Canine Eye Registry Foundation* in *Retinal Diseases*.

The Inner Eye

BLINDNESS

Any condition that blocks light from getting to the retina impairs a dog's vision. Corneal diseases and cataracts fall into this category. Glaucoma, uveitis and retinal diseases are other important causes of blindness in dogs.

Most causes of blindness will not be evident on general observation of the eye itself. But there are some signs that suggest a dog may not be seeing as well as before. For example, a visually impaired dog may step high or with great caution, tread on objects normally avoided, bump into furniture and carry his nose close to the ground. The inactivity of older dogs is often attributed simply to old age, but failing eyesight may also be a cause.

Shining a bright light into the dog's eye to test for pupillary constriction is not an accurate test for blindness, because the pupil can become smaller from a light reflex alone. This doesn't tell you whether the dog is able to form a visual image.

One way to test eyesight is to observe the dog in a dark room in which the furniture has been rearranged. As the dog begins to walk about, see if he moves with confidence or hesitates and collides with furniture. Turn on the lights and repeat the test. A completely blind dog will perform the same way on both tests. A dog with some sight will show more confidence when the lights are on. Performance tests such as these give qualitative information about eyesight, but the degree of impairment can be determined only by veterinary examination.

After a diagnosis of blindness or irreversible loss of eyesight has been made, the dog's life is not necessarily over. The fact is that most dogs, even those with normal eyesight, do not really see very well. They rely to a greater extent on their keen senses of hearing and smell. These senses take over and actually become more acute as eyesight fails. This makes it relatively easy for visually impaired dogs to get around in areas they know. However, a blind dog should not be turned loose in unfamiliar surroundings or he could be injured. When left outdoors, confine a visually impaired dog to a fenced yard or run. Walking on a leash is safe exercise. The dog learns to rely on his master as a "seeing-eye person."

It is important to be aware of impending blindness while the dog is still able to see. This allows time for retraining in basic commands such as stop, stay and come. When the dog actually does go blind, obedience training can be a lifesaver.

CATARACTS

A cataract is a loss of normal transparency of the lens. Any opaque spot on the lens, regardless of its size, technically is a cataract. A cataract visible to the naked eye appears as a milky-gray film behind the pupil.

The majority of cataracts in dogs are genetically determined, but the mode of inheritance varies among breeds. Congenital (*juvenile*) cataracts have been described in more than 75 breeds, including Cocker Spaniels, Bichons Frises, Boston Terriers, Wire Fox Terriers, West Highland White Terriers, Miniature Schnauzers, Standard Poodles, Siberian Huskies, Golden Retrievers, Old English Sheepdogs and Labrador Retrievers. Juvenile cataracts appear in dogs before six years of age and involve both eyes, although not necessarily at the same time. A genetic test for many of the above breeds is under development through *Vetgen* (see Appendix C).

Acquired cataracts occur as a consequence of aging and other eye diseases, most notably uveitis. Dogs with diabetes can develop cataracts in a matter of weeks. Puppies fed milk-replacement formula deficient in arginine can develop bilateral cataracts.

Senile cataracts are a major cause of blindness in dogs six to eight years of age and older. These cataracts begin at the center of the lens and gradually spread out toward the periphery like spokes of a wheel. When the lens becomes uniformly opaque, the cataract has reached its mature stage. Senile cataracts seldom develop at the same rate. One cataract generally matures before the other.

Senile cataracts should be distinguished from *nuclear sclerosis*, a normal aging of the lens in which new fibers are continually forming at the periphery of the lens and pushing inward toward the center. These changes cause a bluish haze in the lenses of older dogs. This haze does not interfere with vision.

Juvenile cataract in the right eye.

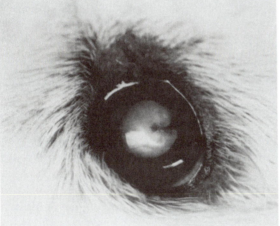

Acquired cataract associated with a displaced lens.

Treatment: Senile cataracts do not need to be treated unless both eyes are involved and the degree of blindness is such that the dog is having difficulty getting around. Visual impairment can be corrected by removing the lens, an operation called phacoemulsification. Without a lens the image is blurred and the edges are indistinct, but objects can be seen. Replacement with an artificial lens (intraocular lens replacement) is an option.

Some juvenile cataracts will be spontaneously reabsorbed, usually within one year of their appearance. Complete resorption results in vision comparable to that of successful lens surgery. Cataract extraction is not recommended in the presence of resorption.

Prevention: Hereditary cataracts can be prevented by not breeding affected dogs and those that carry the gene. Dogs with congenital cataracts can be identified by annual eye examinations carried out by veterinary ophthalmologists affiliated with The Canine Eye Registry Foundation (CERF, see Appendix C and *Retinal Diseases*, page 180).

ANTERIOR UVEITIS (SOFT EYE)

This disease is caused by an inflammation of the iris and ciliary body. The iris is the shutter that controls the size of the pupil. The ciliary body produces the fluid that nourishes the structures in front of the lens and maintains intraocular pressure.

Most cases of anterior uveitis are caused by autoimmune complexes that gain access to the anterior chamber. Thus anterior uveitis may occur with a long list of bacterial infections and systemic diseases in dogs. Local diseases associated with anterior uveitis include corneal ulceration, rupture of the lens and trauma to the eye. In some cases of uveitis the cause is unknown.

Anterior uveitis, a painful eye condition with tearing and squinting.

Anterior uveitis is painful and is accompanied by a red eye, severe tearing and squinting, avoidance of light and protrusion of the third eyelid. The pupil is small and reacts sluggishly to light. It may appear hazy or cloudy due to inflammation in the anterior chamber. A distinguishing feature of anterior uveitis (but one that is not always present) is that the affected eye feels softer than the normal eye.

The diagnosis is made by a complete veterinary eye examination. It is important to measure intraocular pressure to rule out glaucoma.

Treatment: Any systemic or local disease must be identified and treated. The treatment of uveitis is complex and involves the use of local and systemic corticosteroids, NSAIDs, immunosuppressants and drugs that dilate the pupil. Problems that can occur along with or after an episode of anterior uveitis include secondary glaucoma, cataract, sunken eye and blindness. The likelihood of such complications can be minimized by early diagnosis and treatment.

GLAUCOMA

Glaucoma is a serious eye disease associated with a high incidence of blindness. There is a continuous (although very slow) exchange of fluid between the chambers of the eye and the systemic venous circulation. Fluid in the eye is produced by the ciliary body and leaves the eye at the angle formed by the iris and cornea. Glaucoma occurs when fluid in the eye is produced faster than it can be removed. This leads to a sustained increase in intraocular pressure. High intraocular pressure causes degenerative changes to the optic nerve and retina.

Glaucoma is described as primary or secondary. *Primary glaucoma* is a hereditary disease that affects Beagles, Cocker Spaniels, Basset Hounds, Samoyeds and other breeds. In 50 percent of cases the second eye is involved within two years of the first.

Secondary glaucoma is a complication of some other eye disease such as uveitis, displacement of the lens or trauma to the eye. Treatment of secondary glaucoma is directed toward the underlying eye problem.

An eye with *acute glaucoma* is exquisitely painful, with tearing and squinting. The affected eye feels harder than the normal eye and has a fixed, blank look due to the hazy and steamy appearance of the cornea and enlarged pupil.

Glaucoma in the *chronic stage* is associated with enlargement of the globe and protrusion of the eyeball. The eye may be tender to pressure and feel harder than the unaffected eye. In nearly all cases the eye is blind.

The diagnosis of glaucoma can be made only by veterinary eye examination and measurement of intraocular pressure.

Chronic glaucoma with enlargement of the globe and protrusion of the eyeball. Note an associated cataract.

Treatment: *Acute glaucoma is a veterinary emergency that can produce blindness in a matter of hours.* This is one reason why it is so important to take your dog to a veterinary hospital *immediately* on suspicion of a painful eye. Medical treatment involves the use of drugs to rapidly lower intraocular pressure.

The initial drug of choice is intravenous mannitol. Mannitol increases serum osmotic pressure and draws fluid out of the anterior chamber into the circulatory system. Other drugs used in treating glaucoma include carbonic anhydrase inhibitors that block the enzyme that produces the intraocular fluid. Topical medications increase outflow by constricting the pupil. This widens the angle between the iris and the cornea.

If medical treatment is not effective, a surgical procedure can be considered. Cryosurgery involves freezing and destroying a portion of the ciliary body to reduce the production of intraocular fluid. The operation can also be done with a laser, but this requires referral to a special canine eye center.

In chronic glaucoma the eye is blind and thus susceptible to corneal injuries and other problems, including intense pain. If these develop, the eye should be removed. If desired, a prosthesis can be inserted for cosmetic reasons.

Prevention: Eye examinations (such as the CERF exam discussed below in *Retinal Diseases*) will detect small increases in intraocular pressure, thereby allowing sufficient time to start prophylactic treatment before glaucoma develops. Annual eye examinations should be performed on all dogs with a hereditary predisposition to primary glaucoma.

A dog with glaucoma in one eye must be watched carefully for signs of glaucoma in the other eye. Intraocular pressure should be measured every four months in these high-risk individuals. Dogs with primary glaucoma should not be used for breeding.

Retinal Diseases

The retina is a thin, delicate membrane that lines the back of the eye. It is supported and nourished by the choroid, a layer of pigmented vascular tissue behind the retina. In retinal diseases, the retina loses some or all of its capacity to perceive light.

The majority of retinal diseases in dogs are inherited and are transmitted when an affected or carrier dog is used for breeding. In order to control the prevalence of retinal disease, it is important to determine *before a dog is used for breeding* whether or not that dog is affected. Inherited eye disease can be identified at an early age by a routine eye examination performed by a veterinary ophthalmologist, most of whom are affiliated with CERF.

CERF was established in 1974 with two purposes:

- To screen purebred dogs for inherited eye diseases and issue certificates to those free of disease.
- To collect research data on the incidence of various inherited eye diseases.

In 1989, the activities of CERF were combined with those of the Veterinary Medicine Data Bank at Purdue University. More recently, the Canine DNA Registry has been added to the Data Bank.

All types of hereditary eye disease are screened for during a CERF examination. There are more than 180 board-certified veterinary ophthalmologists affiliated with CERF throughout the United States and Canada. A dog receives a certification based on the appearance of the eyes at the time of the examination. Because some inherited eye diseases develop later in life, certification is good for one year only and must be repeated annually. Furthermore, certification does not imply clearance for the carrier state. Dogs that are unaffected by disease may or may not be carriers.

Because the CERF registry is closed (that is, the identity of affected dogs remains confidential), CERF information cannot be used to determine which ancestors in a pedigree may have been affected. CERF maintains a Website that contains the names of all dogs that have a current CERF certification. The site is updated at the beginning of each month. Your veterinarian can refer you to a CERF specialist in your area, or you can contact CERF directly (see *Appendix C*).

The *Institute for Genetic Disease Control in Animals* (GDC) also maintains a registry for hereditary eye diseases. This open registry allows breeders to share the results of eye examinations on all dogs registered with the GDC. Knowing which ancestors are affected makes it possible to determine which progeny may be carriers. This knowledge can be of value in selecting breeding stock at low risk for transmitting the disease. For information on the GDC, see Appendix C.

COLLIE EYE ANOMALY SYNDROME

This disease was originally described in the Collie, but also affects Shetland Sheepdogs and some other breeds. The disease attacks the choroid that nourishes the retina. The eye abnormalities include retinal degeneration and retinal detachment. Both conditions cause loss of vision.

Collie eye can be detected by a veterinary ophthalmologist in puppies as young as four to eight weeks of age, after the bluish puppy film disappears from the eye. The retina is graded 1 to 5, depending on the degree of degeneration. Grades 1 and 2 do not affect eyesight; grades 3, 4 and 5 are associated with increasing visual impairment. The grade does not change as the dog grows older, but retinal detachment with sudden blindness can occur at any time.

The inheritance of Collie eye has been investigated in the Collie and found to be a simple recessive trait. There is no treatment.

PROGRESSIVE RETINAL ATROPHY

Progressive retinal atrophy (PRA) was first discovered in the Gordon Setter in 1911 and is now recognized in more than 86 breeds. PRA includes several specific inherited types of the disease. In most instances the mode of inheritance is an autosomal recessive gene. In all cases there is destruction of retinal cells in both eyes, leading to loss of eyesight. There is no treatment for PRA.

The initial sign of PRA is night blindness. The dog hesitates to go out at night and won't jump on or off furniture in a dark room. As blindness progresses, the dog develops other signs of visual impairment. For example, the dog may go up, but not down, a flight of stairs. Other behavioral changes also suggest loss of visual acuity.

With the specific type of PRA called *early onset slow progression*, afflicted dogs exhibit night blindness during the first year of life but retain daylight vision for a year or longer. Breeds affected by this type of PRA include the Akita, Miniature Schnauzer, Norwegian Elkhound, Tibetan Terrier, Dachshund and Gordon Setter.

With the type of PRA called *early onset rapid progression*, visual impairment begins during the first year of life and progresses to complete blindness in a matter of months. Breeds affected by this type include the Collie, Irish Setter and Cardigan Welsh Corgi.

In *late onset PRA*, night blindness is noted after two years of age. Complete blindness occurs by age four. This variant affects the Afghan Hound, Border Collie, Cocker Spaniel and Labrador Retriever.

Sudden acquired retinal degeneration is a disease of unknown cause found most often in healthy, middle-aged female dogs 6 to 14 years of age. It produces rapid and complete loss of vision in both eyes in a matter of hours to several days.

Prevention: It is important to certify all breeding stock and register all offspring with CERF or the GDC. Breed only those dogs that are free of PRA and that are at low risk for carrying and transmitting the gene. Carrier dogs can be identified by pedigree analysis—if it is known which ancestors in the pedigree had PRA. For example, knowing that a dog has PRA (an autosomal recessive trait) automatically tells you that both parents were at least PRA carriers and may even have been affected. Pedigree information may be available through open registries such as the GDC's or through those sponsored by breed clubs; or in specific instances through conscientious breeders who keep meticulous records and are willing to share the information. In the Irish Setter, affected dogs and carrier dogs can be identified by a DNA blood test administered through CERF.

CENTRAL PROGRESSIVE RETINAL ATROPHY

Central progressive retinal atrophy (CPRA) is a degenerative retinal disease that also affects both eyes. It is less common than PRA and occurs in older dogs. CPRA affects the pigment cells at the center of the retina. It is recognized in Labrador Retrievers, Golden Retrievers, Shetland Sheepdogs, Border Collies, Rough Collies, Redbone Coon Hounds and other breeds.

Because the central part of the retina (where the dog sees best) is the primary target of the disease, a dog with CPRA is unable to see stationary objects well, especially in bright light. However, the dog is still able to see moving objects because motion is perceived at the periphery of the retina. Although vision decreases as the disease progresses, complete blindness is rare.

THE EARS

Hearing is one of the dog's most keen senses. Dogs can hear sounds too faint for us to detect, and can also hear noises pitched at a much higher frequency. Because their hearing is so acute, dogs rely much more on their hearing than on their eyesight.

Dogs' ears come in all sizes and shapes, and can be carried erect, bent or flopped over. The outside is covered by hair that matches the rest of the coat. Hair is also present on the inside of the ear flap, although it is sparsely distributed. The skin on the inside of the ear flap is light pink in some breeds, and spotted in others.

Sound, which is really vibrations of the air, is collected by the ear flap, or pinna, and directed down the comparatively large ear canal. The ear canal descends in a vertical direction and then angles horizontally to end at the eardrum (tympanic membrane). Movements of the tympanic membrane are transmitted via a chain of small bones (the auditory ossicles) to the bony canals of the inner ear.

Within the bony canals lies the cochlea. The cochlea, which is the receptor organ for hearing, contains a lymphlike fluid that converts sound vibrations into fluid waves. The fluid waves are transformed into nerve impulses and conducted by the cochlear nerve to the auditory nerve.

Within the bony canals also lies the vestibular apparatus, an organ of balance composed of the semicircular canals, the utricle and saccule. The purpose of the vestibular apparatus is to synchronize eye movements and maintain posture, balance and coordination. The vestibular nerve joins the cochlear nerve to form the auditory nerve that connects to the hearing and balance centers in the brain.

Also found in the middle ear is the opening of the auditory tube. The auditory tube connects the middle ear cavity to the nasopharynx. The purpose of the auditory tube is to equalize air pressure on each side of the eardrum.

Ear diseases make up 20 percent of the average veterinary practice.

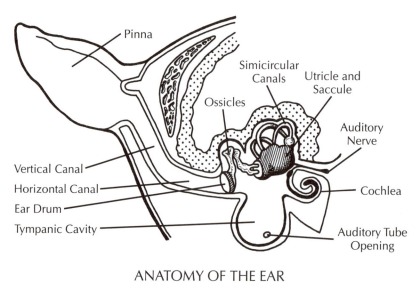

ANATOMY OF THE EAR

Basic Ear Care

AVOIDING EAR PROBLEMS

Wet ear canals can predispose a dog to ear infections. When bathing your dog, keep water out of the ears by inserting cotton wadding into the canals. Similarly, it is important to dry your dog's ears after he has been swimming. If water gets into an ear, wipe the opening gently with a cotton ball. If you know from prior visits to your veterinarian that your dog's eardrums are intact, you can instill an ear solution containing a drying agent (see *How to Apply Ear Medicines*, page 185). Commonly used drying solutions include ClearX and Panodry.

Foreign material in the ears causes irritation and, later, infection. Grass seeds and awns frequently cling to the hair surrounding the ear openings and then drop into the canals. Always groom under the ear flaps, especially after your dog has been running in tall grass, weeds and brush.

It is common in professional grooming parlors to pluck hair out of the ear canals. Serum then oozes from the hair pores. The serum makes an excellent medium for bacterial growth. This may be one reason why ear infections are more common among Poodles, Schnauzers and other breeds that are professionally groomed. It is recommended that you do not allow hair to be plucked from this area unless there is a medical reason to do so. In some cases, the hair forms a wad that obstructs air flow and keeps the ear canals moist; avoiding this would be a valid medical reason to remove the offending hair. Mats at or above the external opening should be removed as described in Chapter 4, *Removing Mats*. Wads of hair that are actually in the ear canals should be removed by a veterinarian.

CLEANING THE EARS

Routine ear cleaning is not required. A small amount of light brown waxy secretion in the ear canals is normal, and some ear wax is necessary for the health of the ears. However, the inside of the ear flaps should be cleaned whenever there is a accumulation of wax, dirt or debris. Gently wipe the skin with a cloth dampened with mineral oil, or better yet, with an ear cleansing solution such as Oti-Clens, Epi-Otic or a similar product. Ear cleansers can be purchased at pet supply stores or through your veterinarian. Do not use alcohol, ether or other irritating solvents; they can cause intense pain and inflame the tissues.

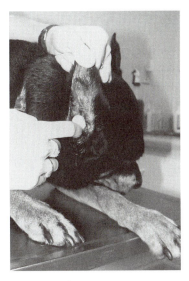

Clean the ears with a damp cotton ball. Do not insert cotton-tipped swabs into the ear canals.

If there is an excessive accumulation of wax in the ear canals that appears to be the blocking air flow, or if there is discharge from the ear, take your dog to the veterinarian for treatment. These ears are either infected or likely to become so. After an initial cleaning, you may be instructed to instill a cleansing solution at home. Apply a few drops to the canal and massage the base of the ear to loosen wax and debris. Then gently wipe out the ear canal with cotton balls.

Never insert cotton-tipped applicators or swabs down into the ear canals, because this pushes wax and cellular debris further into the ear. This is a common cause of ear infection. However, cotton-tipped applicators and swabs can be used to clean the skin folds of the outer ear.

HOW TO APPLY EAR MEDICINES

Ear medicines should be applied only to clean, dry ear canals. Some ear preparations come in tubes with long nozzles; others use medicine droppers. Restrain the dog so that the tip of the applicator does not accidentally tear the wall of the ear

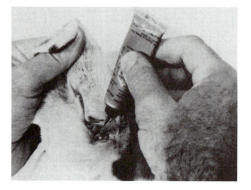

To apply ear medication, insert the tip of the applicator into the canal only as far as you can see. (J. Clawson)

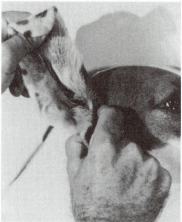

Massage the base of the ear to disperse the medication. (J. Clawson)

canal (see *Restraining for Examination and Treatment* in Chapter 1). Fold the ear flap over the top of the dog's head. Insert the end of the nozzle or medicine dropper into the ear canal only as far as you can see. Squeeze in a small amount of ointment, or instill three or four drops of liquid.

Most infections involve the part of the ear canal next to the eardrum. It is important that the medicine reach this area. Massage the cartilage at the base of the ear for 20 seconds to disperse the medicine. This makes a squishy sound.

Do not use ear preparations or drying solutions unless you know for sure that the eardrums are intact as determined by a veterinary exam using an otoscope. If a preparation is inserted into a canal with a perforated eardrum, it will enter the middle ear and damage structures essential to hearing.

ANTIBIOTICS FOR THE EAR

Antibiotic preparations commonly prescribed for the treatment of external ear infections include Panolog (neomycin, nystatin, cortisone), Liquichlor (chloramphenicol), Tresderm (neomycin, thiabendazole, cortisone) and Gentocin Otic (gentamicin). Preparations containing miconazole and clortrimazole are also available for treating yeast and fungal infections. Allergic skin reactions can occur with any of these products. Ear medications should be instilled once or twice daily, or as directed by your veterinarian.

Prolonged use of antibiotics in the ear predisposes the dog to the development of antibiotic-resistant bacteria and the overgrowth of yeast and fungi. When bacterial and fungal cultures are indicated, your dog must be off antibiotics for at least three days.

The Ear Flap

The ear flap, or pinna, is an erect sheet of cartilage covered on both sides by a layer of skin and hair. The pinna is often involved in diseases as part of a generalized process, especially in the case of allergic and autoimmune skin diseases, as discussed in Chapter 4.

BITES AND LACERATIONS

The pinna is commonly injured during fights with other animals.

Treatment: Control bleeding and treat the wound as described in Chapter 1 (see *Wounds*). Apply a topical antibiotic ointment such as triple antibiotic or Neosporin. Leave the ear uncovered. Wounds caused by animal bites are often complicated by infection and must be watched carefully. Large lacerations, and those involving the edges of the ears or the ear cartilage, should receive prompt veterinary attention. Surgical repair is necessary to prevent scarring and deformity.

EAR ALLERGIES

Dogs with canine atopy and food hypersensitivity dermatitis are predisposed to develop inflamed ears. In fact, ear involvement may be the only indication of an allergy. In dogs with ear allergies, an itch-scratch-itch cycle develops resulting in excoriations, hair loss, scabs and crusts about the ears. The ear canals are filled with a brown wax.

An allergic contact dermatitis can develop in ear canals that have been medicated with an ear preparation. The antibiotic neomycin is a frequent cause of this problem.

Treatment: Any underlying allergic skin disease must be treated to eliminate the ear symptoms. Treatment for itching involves the use of antihistamines and topical and oral corticosteroids. Discontinue any ear preparation that may be allergenic. An allergic otitis is often complicated by a bacterial or yeast infection that must also be treated.

SWOLLEN EAR FLAP

Sudden swelling of the ear flap can be caused by an abscess or hematoma. Abscesses frequently occur after dog fights. A hematoma is an accumulation of blood beneath the skin. One cause of hematoma is violent head shaking and scratching at the ear. Look for an underlying itchy ear disorder.

Treatment: Blood must be released from a hematoma to prevent scarring and ear deformity. Removing it with a needle and syringe (something your veterinarian must do) is effective in about 50 percent of cases. If serum accumulates in drained blood pocket, treatment involves removing a window of skin to provide open and continuous drainage. Sutures are then made through both sides of the ear to pull the skin down and eliminate the pocket.

The treatment of abscess is discussed in Chapter 4 (see *Cellulitis and Skin Abscess*).

FLY-BITE DERMATITIS

Biting flies can attack the face and ears of dogs, sucking blood and inflicting painful bites over the tips or bent folds of the ears. These bites are typically scabbed, crusty black and bleed easily. German Shepherd Dogs, Collies and other breeds with erect ears are most susceptible.

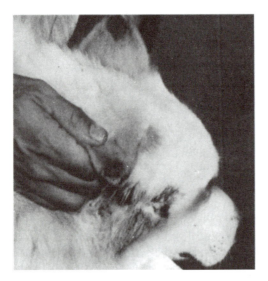

Fly-bite dermatitis affects the ear tips of dogs with erect ears.

Treatment: Keep the dog indoors during the day until the wounds are healed. If you are unable to do so, apply insect repellant to the ear tips and keep them clean and dry to discourage flies. Infected ear tips should be treated with a topical antibiotic ointment such as triple antibiotic.

FROSTBITE

Frostbite affects the ear tips of dogs left outdoors in severe winter weather, particularly under conditions of high wind and humidity. The ears are especially vulnerable to frost bite because they are so exposed.

Initially, the skin of frostbitten ears appears pale or even blue. All of the frostbitten tissue may survive, or a sharp line of demarcation may develop between normal skin and black, dead skin. If this happens, seek veterinary help.

The emergency treatment of frostbite is discussed in Chapter 1.

EAR FISSURE

Ear fissure occurs in breeds with floppy ears. It results from intense scratching along with violent head-shaking, which causes the ears to snap. The ear tips are denuded of hair and often become bloody. With continued trauma, the tips of the ears split and a crack in the skin, called a fissure, appears.

Treatment: The underlying irritation, often an external otitis, should be sought and treated to eliminate the head-shaking. Treat the ear tips by applying an antibiotic-steroid ointment such as Panolog once or twice daily. If the fissure does not heal, it may need to be surgically repaired.

MARGINAL SEBORRHEA

This is a skin disease caused by a buildup of skin oil (sebum) on the hair along the edges of the ear flaps. The hair has a greasy feel. When rubbed with a thumbnail, the hair falls out. The disease is most common in Dachshunds.

Treatment: Marginal seborrhea is incurable, but can be controlled by bathing the ears with benzoyl peroxide or a sulfur-tar shampoo (see *Seborrhea* in Chapter 4). Soak the ear margins in warm water before shampooing. Repeat every 24 to 48 hours until all the greasy material has been removed. Use a moisturizer to keep the ears soft and pliant. Repeat the treatment as necessary. If the skin is severely inflamed, apply 1-percent hydrocortisone ointment.

The Ear Canal

EXTERNAL OTITIS

External otitis is an infection of the ear canal. The ear canals are delicate structures, and are easily infected. Eighty percent of infections occur in breeds with long, dropped ears. This is fascially a function of air circulation, since open erect ears dry out more easily than dropped ears, and therefore provide less favorable conditions for bacterial growth.

Many factors contribute to the development of external otitis. Some breeds (such as the Chinese Shar-Pei) are predisposed because of narrow or *stenotic* ear canals. Other breeds may be predisposed because they have an abundance of hair that blocks the circulation of air. Many dogs with allergic skin diseases, particularly canine atopy and food hypersensitivity dermatitis, are predisposed to ear infections as part of the generalized skin response. Similarly, dogs with primary and secondary seborrhea often have ear canal involvement characterized by a buildup of yellowish oily wax that provides an excellent medium for bacterial growth. Foreign bodies such as grass seeds and foxtails, and growths in the ear canal, are other predisposing causes. Ear mites, discussed later in this chapter, can precede bacterial otitis.

Iatrogenic causes of infection include using cotton-tipped applicators to clean the deep recesses of the ears, allowing water to get into the ears during bathing, excessive and improper cleaning of the ears, and a grooming routine that calls for plucking or clipping hair in the external canals. (Iatrogenic disease is an unintended problem that results from a medical treatment or procedure.)

Signs of external otitis are head-shaking, scratching and rubbing at the affected ear. The ear is painful. The dog often tilts or carries his head down on the painful side and cries or whines when the ear is touched. Examination reveals redness and swelling of the skin folds. There usually is a waxy or purulent discharge with a bad odor. Hearing can be affected.

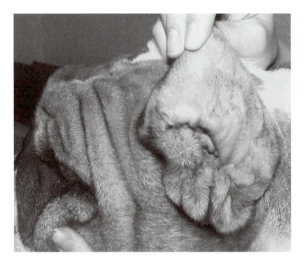

Severe external otitis with a swollen, inflamed ear canal. Note the skin abrasions from scratching at the ear.

Ceruminous Otitis. This condition occurs with primary seborrhea, discussed in the skin chapter. There is an extensive buildup of oily, yellowish wax in the ear canals, which provides an excellent medium for bacteria and yeast. Treatment is directed toward control of the *seborrhea* (see Chapter 4).

The waxy and greasy appearance of ceruminous otitis associated with primary seborrhea.

Bacterial Otitis. Acute bacterial infections are usually caused by staphylococci. The discharge is moist and light brown. Chronic infections usually are caused by proteus or pseudomonas. The discharge is yellow or green. There are exceptions. More than one species of bacteria may be involved, which complicates antibiotic treatment.

Fungal and Yeast Infections. Secondary yeast infections follow antibiotic treatment of bacterial otitis. Yeast infections also occur commonly in dogs suffering from atopic dermatitis, food hypersensitive dermatitis and seborrheic skin diseases. A brown waxy discharge with a rancid odor is characteristic. These infections tend to persist until the underlying disease is controlled.

Because external ear infections often progress to the middle ear, *it is extremely important to take your dog to a veterinarian as soon as you suspect an ear problem.* Veterinary examination of the deep portions of the ear canal using an otoscope is the most important step in making the diagnosis and planning the treatment.

It is essential to know whether the eardrums are intact, since it is not safe to medicate the ears if the drums are perforated. It is also important to be sure the problem is not caused by a foreign body or tumor. A specimen of waxy material is taken with a cotton-tipped applicator, rolled onto a glass slide and examined under the microscope looking for bacteria, yeast, ear mites and any other predisposing factors.

Otoscopic examination cannot be attempted if the canal is dirty and filled with wax and purulent debris. First, the ear must be cleaned. This may require sedation or anesthesia.

Treatment: The first step is to clean and dry the ear canals. This requires ear cleaning solutions, a syringe, an ear curette and cotton balls. It should be done at the veterinary clinic. Cleaning creates a less favorable environment for bacteria to grow and allows the medication to treat the surface of the ear canal. Medication can't penetrate the debris of a dirty ear.

Follow-up care at home involves medicating the ear with a preparation prescribed by your veterinarian (see *How to Apply Ear Medicines*, page 185). If the ear continues to produce wax and exudate, a cleansing and flushing solution such as Oti-Clens or Epi-Otic, and/or a drying solution such as ClearX or Panodry, may be recommended. These solutions are used immediately before medicating the ear with an antibiotic or antifungal medication. Topical and/or oral corticosteroids may be recommended to control pain and decrease swelling and inflammation.

Bacterial infections that continue to progress produce thickening and narrowing of the ear canal and chronic pain. These ears are difficult to clean and treat. As a last resort, your veterinarian may advise a surgical operation called an ear resection that re-establishes air circulation and promotes drainage.

EAR MITES (OTODECTIC MANGE)

Otodectic mites are tiny insects that live in the ear canals and feed by piercing the skin. They are highly contagious to cats and dogs, but not to humans. Ear mites are the most common cause of ear symptoms in puppies and young adult dogs. Suspect ear mites when both of the dog's ears are involved.

Ear mites should not be confused with the mites that cause sarcoptic mange. This is an entirely different disease, but one whose signs can include crusty ear tips (see *Scabies* in Chapter 4).

It takes only a few ear mites to produce a severe hypersensitive reaction that leads to intense itching with scratching and violent head shaking. The ear flaps become red, excoriated, crusted and scabbed. The canals contain a dry, crumbly, dark brown, waxy discharge that looks like coffee grounds and may have a bad odor due to secondary infection.

Ear mites can be identified by removing a specimen of wax with a cotton-tipped applicator and looking at it under a magnifying glass against a black background. Mites are white specks, about the size of the head of a pin, that move.

Treatment: Once the diagnosis has been made, all dogs and cats in the household should be treated to prevent reinfestation. The ears must be cleaned as described for external otitis. *This is essential.* Dirty ear canals provide wax and cellular debris that shelter mites and make it difficult for ear medications to contact and destroy them.

Medicate the ears using a miticide ear preparation prescribed by your veterinarian. Most preparations contain pyrethrins and thiabendazole. Commonly used ones are Nolvamite, Cerumite and Tresderm. Tresderm contains a miticide, an antibiotic and a steroid to relieve itching. Use according to instructions.

It is important to complete the entire course of treatment. If treatment is stopped too soon, a new crop of mites will reinfest the dog.

During treatment, mites escape from the ear canals and temporarily take up residence elsewhere on the dog, causing itching and scratching. In addition to treating the ear canals, the entire dog and all animals that come in contact with it should be treated weekly for four weeks using a pyrethrins-based shampoo and/or a pyrethrins-based flea powder (see *Fleas*, Chapter 4).

Mite infections are often complicated by secondary bacterial otitis. When present, treat as described for *external otitis*.

FOREIGN BODIES AND TICKS IN THE EAR

Foreign bodies in the ear canal cause irritation and, later, infection. Most are the result of grass seeds and awns that first cling to hair surrounding the ear opening and then drop down into the canal. Always examine the ears after a dog has been running in tall grass, weeds and brush.

Foreign bodies near the opening can be removed with blunt-nosed tweezers, taking care not to push them deeper into the ear canal. Foreign bodies in the deep recesses of the ear generally go undetected until they produce an external otitis and are found and removed during veterinary examination.

Ticks may be found on the ear flaps or in the ear canals. When a tick is accessible, remove it as described in Chapter 4 (see *Ticks*). Recall that ticks carry diseases; they should not be squeezed or crushed with the bare fingers. Ticks deep in the ear canal should be removed by a veterinarian.

CERUMINOUS GLAND TUMORS

These tumors arise from wax-producing glands in the ear canal. They are pinkish-white dome-shaped growths less than 1 cm in size. Most are pedunculated (on a stalk), with the base attached to the wall of the ear canal. The length of the stalk allows the tumor to extend outward and become visible. Ceruminous gland tumors may become infected and bleed. Small tumors tend to be benign. Large tumors are usually malignant and invasive.

Treatment: Surgical removal is the treatment of choice. Surgery, combined with radiation therapy, is recommended for invasive tumors.

The Middle Ear

OTITIS MEDIA (MIDDLE EAR INFECTION)

Otitis media is an infection of the eardrum and the cavity of the middle ear, including the three bony ossicles. Most cases are caused by outer ear infection that involves the eardrum and then progresses to the middle ear. In fact, about 50 percent of cases of chronic external otitis are associated with otitis media. Bacteria can also gain entrance to the middle ear through the opening of the auditory tube that connects the middle ear to the nasopharynx. Occasionally, the infection is blood borne.

The early signs of otitis media are the same as those of external otitis. However, as the middle ear becomes infected the pain increases dramatically. The dog often tilts his head down on the affected side, holds it as still as possible, and exhibits increased pain sensitivity when the head is touched or the mouth is opened. Hearing can be affected, but the loss may not be noticed unless both ears are involved.

An otoscopic examination performed after the dog has been sedated or anesthetized reveals a bulging eardrum. If the drum is ruptured, pus may be seen draining from the middle ear. X-rays occasionally show fluid or inflammatory tissue in the middle ear cavity.

Injury to a branch of the facial nerve that crosses the eardrum causes drooping of the upper lip and ear on the affected side. Another sign of facial nerve injury is *Horner's syndrome*, a symptom complex of the eye that consists of a small pupil, drooping upper eyelid, protrusion of the nictitating membrane and retraction of the eyeball into the orbit.

Treatment: This involves thoroughly cleansing and flushing the ear, as described for *external otitis*. If the eardrum is intact but bulging, pus and fluid in the middle ear can be aspirated using a syringe and needle. This reduces pressure and relieves pain.

Right-sided facial paralysis caused by otitis media. The dog is able to move his left ear down, but the right ear is paralyzed.

The exudate is cultured. Oral antibiotics are started and can be changed pending the results of sensitivity reports. Antibiotics are continued for at least three weeks, or until the problem resolves. Recurrent or chronic otitis media may require middle ear surgery.

Prevention: Most cases of otitis media can be prevented by treating ear canal infections at an early stage. This is why it is so important to take your dog to a veterinarian as soon as you suspect an ear problem.

The Inner Ear

INTERNAL OTITIS (INNER EAR INFECTION)

Internal otitis is an inflammation and infection of the inner ear. Most cases are preceded by outer ear infections. Suspect internal otitis if the dog suddenly develops signs of *labyrinthitis*, described in the next section.

Treatment: This is an emergency. Take you dog to the veterinarian. Treatment is similar to that described for otitis media.

LABYRINTHITIS

Diseases of the inner ear are characterized by labyrinthitis, or dizziness. The labyrinth is part of a complex organ of balance composed of the semicircular canals, the utricle and saccule (see the drawing *Anatomy of the Ear* at the beginning of this chapter). The labyrinth is like a gyroscope. It's purpose is to synchronize eye movements and maintain posture, balance and coordination. A major cause of labyrinthitis is inner ear infection.

A dog with labyrinthitis will often assume an abnormal posture, with his head tilted down on the affected side. Dizziness, lack of coordination and loss of balance are evident. The dog circles and leans toward the affected side and may exhibit rapid jerking movements of the eyeballs, a condition called *nystagmus*. Vomiting occurs in some cases.

The typical posture of a dog with labyrinthitis. The head is tilted down on the affected side.

The prolonged administration of aminoglycoside and neomycin antibiotics can produce labyrinthitis, as well as deafness. Most ear preparations are capable of causing labyrinthitis and ear damage if they make contact with the sensitive structures of the inner ear. This is why the ears should never be flushed or medicated without first making sure that the eardrums are intact.

Other diseases that can cause labyrinthitis include head trauma, brain tumor, poisoning, drug intoxication and a condition called idiopathic vestibular syndrome. Suspect one of these if your dog develops labyrinthitis without having had a prior ear infection.

Idiopathic vestibular syndrome is a disease of unknown cause that affects middle-aged and older dogs. It is the second most common cause of labyrinthitis, after inner ear infection. The onset is sudden. The dizziness, staggering and vomiting can be incapacitating. Vomiting may last for several days, in which case the dog may require intravenous fluids. Signs peak in 24 hours, but some degree of imbalance persists for three to six weeks. Recovery occurs in all cases. After recovery, some dogs experience a slight but permanent head tilt.

Deafness

Hearing loss can be caused by congenital deafness, changes of old age, middle and inner ear infections, head injuries, wax and debris blocking the ear canals, tumors of the middle ear, and certain drugs and poisons. The antibiotics streptomycin, gentamicin, neomycin and kanamycin can damage the auditory and vestibular nerves, causing both deafness and labyrinthitis. Hypothyroidism can be associated with a type of deafness that may respond to treatment with thyroid hormone.

Congenital deafness is caused by developmental defects in the hearing apparatus. Although present from birth, it is not evident until puppies are old enough to respond to sound. This happens from 11 days onward. There is a connection between hereditary deafness and a gene for coat color. Dogs with predominantly white coats, and those with *merle* hair coats, are at increased risk for congenital deafness. The highest incidence occurs in Dalmatians, but at least 35 breeds and their crosses are affected. Deafness may involve one or both ears.

Senile deafness develops gradually, beginning at about 10 years of age. It is seldom total. Old dogs with deafness often retain some ability to hear high-pitched sounds, such as a dog whistle. The deafness may not be particularly noticeable unless there is also loss of vision.

A dog with significant hearing loss is less active, moves more slowly, is difficult to arouse from sleep and fails to respond to commands. Shouting, clapping loudly when the dog is not looking, blowing a whistle and other attention-getting sounds can be used to test the dog's hearing. Stamping on the floor attracts their attention, as they can feel the vibrations.

Hearing tests can be conducted in puppies and adult dogs. Hearing is tested using an electroencephalogram (*EEG*) to record the brain waves produced in response to sounds of different frequencies. If the brain wave pattern remains unchanged, the sound was not heard. This procedure, called a brain stem auditory evoked response (BAER), is particularly useful for screening puppies that are at risk for congenital deafness. It is available at referral centers.

The Institute for Genetic Disease Control in Animals (*GDC*) maintains an open registry for inherited deafness. Results are used to better understand the mode of inheritance and develop data that can help in selecting normal breeding stock. Testing is done at a minimum age of 35 days, according to a BAER protocol. For information on contacting the GDC, see Appendix C.

THE NOSE

A dog's nose is made up of the nostrils (also called nares) and the nasal cavity, which runs the length of the muzzle. The nasal cavity is divided by a midline partition into two passages, one for each nostril (see the figure *Anatomy of the Head* on page 210). These passages open into the throat behind the soft palate. The dog has two major sinuses that connect with the nasal cavity: the maxillary and the frontal. Infections of the nasal cavity may involve the sinuses, and vice versa.

The nasal cavity is lined by a mucous membrane called the mucociliary blanket, which is abundantly supplied with blood vessels. This blanket acts as a defense against infection by trapping bacteria and foreign irritants and conveying them to the back of the throat through the actions of tiny hairlike structures called cilia. At the back of the throat, the particles are trapped in mucus and either coughed out or swallowed. Dehydration or exposure to cold air stops the motion of the cilia and thickens the layer of mucus. This reduces the effectiveness of the mucociliary blanket.

The keen sense of smell of the Basset Hound is perhaps 100 times greater than that of humans.

There is a rich supply of nerves in the nasal cavity of dogs—far greater than in most other animals. These nerves ultimately connect with the highly developed olfactory center in the dog's brain. The abundant nerve supply and the large olfactory center account for the dog's keen sense of smell—perhaps 100 times greater than ours.

The nasal cavity is extremely sensitive and bleeds easily when traumatized. An otoscope and nasal forceps are used to remove foreign bodies. Instruments passed into the nasal passages cause violent sneezing, however, so heavy sedation or anesthesia is required to conduct a thorough examination.

The moisture at the tip of the nose is secreted by mucous glands in the nasal cavity. A dog's nose is normally cool and moist, but may be warm and dry depending on activity, temperature, humidity and state of hydration. A warm dry nose does not necessarily indicate that a dog has a fever. If you suspect fever, confirm it with a rectal thermometer.

Most dogs have darkly pigmented noses, but brown, pink and spotted noses are normal for some breeds.

Signs of Nasal Irritation

NASAL DISCHARGE

A runny nose indicates an irritant in the nasal passages. Because irritants also produce sneezing, these two signs tend to occur together.

Excited and nervous dogs often secrete a clear, watery mucus that drips from the nose. This type of discharge is not accompanied by sneezing and disappears when the dog relaxes.

Any nasal discharge that persists for several hours is significant. A clear, watery discharge is typical of allergic and viral rhinitis, while a thick discharge suggests a bacterial or fungal infection. A nasal discharge accompanied by gagging and retching indicates a postnasal drip. A discharge from one nostril is seen with oral-nasal fistulas and foreign bodies and tumors in the nose.

Foreign bodies, tumors and chronic bacterial and fungal infections can erode the mucous membranes and produce a blood-streaked mucus discharge or a nosebleed. Nosebleeds also occur with bleeding disorders such as von Willebrand's disease and hemophilia. If you see blood in the nasal discharge, notify your veterinarian.

Human cold viruses don't affect dogs. However, dogs are afflicted by a number of serious respiratory diseases that initially produce symptoms like those of the human cold. A runny nose along with an eye discharge and coughing and sneezing is an indication that you should seek veterinary attention for your dog.

SNEEZING

Sneezing is an important early sign of nasal irritation. Occasional sneezing is normal, but if the sneezing is violent, uninterrupted or accompanied by a nasal discharge, it's a serious condition and you should consult your veterinarian.

Sneezing with a watery nasal discharge and rubbing the face with the paws is typical of *canine atopy* (see Chapter 4). A sudden bout of violent sneezing, along with head shaking and pawing at the nose, suggests a foreign body in the nose. Nosebleeds can occur after particularly violent bouts of sneezing.

Prolonged sneezing causes swelling and congestion of the nasal membranes. The result is a sniffling or noisy character to the breathing.

MOUTH BREATHING

Dogs are nose breathers and usually do not breathe through their mouths except when panting. Mouth breathing indicates that both nasal air passages are blocked. This may not be obvious until the dog becomes excited or begins to exercise.

The Nose

COLLAPSED NOSTRILS (STENOTIC NARES)

Collapsed nostrils occur in puppies of the brachycephalic (short-nosed) breeds, including Pugs, Pekingese, Bulldogs and others. In these puppies the nasal cartilages are soft and floppy, so that as the puppy breathes in the nostrils come together and obstruct the nasal openings. This causes various degrees of respiratory obstruction, which can seriously compromise the puppy's health and development.

Collapsed nostrils are a congenital problem often accompanied by other manifestations of the *brachycephalic syndrome* described in Chapter 10.

Collapsed nostrils is a common problem in short-nosed breeds. These dogs snort, sniffle and have a foamy nasal discharge.

COLLIE NOSE (NASAL SOLAR DERMATITIS)

This is a weepy, crusty dermatitis that affects Collies, Australian Shepherds, Shetland Sheepdogs and related breeds. It is seen most commonly in sunny regions such as Florida, California and the mountainous regions of the West. It is caused by lack of pigment on the nose and prolonged exposure to ultraviolet sunlight. Lack of pigment is hereditary in some dogs, but it can be acquired through skin diseases and scarring.

Initially, the skin appears normal except for the lack of black pigment. With exposure to sunlight, the skin at the border between the muzzle and nose becomes irritated. As the irritation continues, hair falls out and the skin begins to ooze and crust. With continued exposure, the skin breaks down. In advanced cases, the whole surface of the nose becomes ulcerated and the tip itself may disappear, leaving unsightly tissue that bleeds easily. A skin cancer may develop.

Crusts and ulcerations of the skin of the nose caused by nasal solar dermatitis.

Nasal solar dermatitis must be distinguished from discoid lupus erythematosus, pemphigus foliaceus and zinc responsive dermatosis—skin diseases discussed in Chapter 4. All three diseases produce a skin reaction similar to nasal solar dermatitis. A distinguishing feature of nasal solar dermatitis is that pigment was lacking *before* the disease developed. In the other three, the pigment disappears as the disease progresses. Note that once depigmentation occurs in these diseases, the damaging effects of sunlight add to the problem.

Treatment: Prevent further exposure by keeping your dog indoors as much as possible during the most intense period of sunlight, between 9 a.m. and 3 p.m. Letting the dog out on cloudy days does not address the problem, because ultraviolet rays penetrate clouds. Sunscreens are of some aid in protecting dogs who spend time outdoors. Use products containing an SPF greater than 15. Apply the sunscreen 30 to 60 minutes before exposure and again later in the day.

Treat an irritated nose with a skin preparation such as Cortaid that contains 0.5 to 1.0 percent hydrocortisone.

Tattooing the nose with black ink is another consideration, but to be effective it must be repeated at least once. Note that tattooing does not eliminate the need to apply sunscreens and to prevent exposure to sunlight.

VITILIGO

Vitiligo is a condition in which pigment is lost from the nose, lips and eyelids. Black pigment is present early in life in affected dogs, but it gradually fades to a chocolate brown. The exact cause of vitiligo in dogs has not yet been determined. There is no treatment.

NASAL DEPIGMENTATION

Nasal depigmentation, also called *Dudley nose*, is a syndrome of unknown cause that may be a form of vitiligo. Depigmentation primarily effects the skin of the nose where hair is absent. It tends to occur in Afghan Hounds, Samoyeds, white German Shepherd Dogs, Doberman Pinschers, Irish Setters, Pointers and Poodles. In this condition, a nose that is solid black at birth gradually fades to a chocolate brown, or in the case of complete depigmentation, to pinkish white. Some dogs experience a remission in which the nose spontaneously becomes darker.

Depigmentation of the nose can occur as a seasonal abnormality.

Snow nose is a separate but common condition in which dark pigment on the nose fades during the winter months and darkens again in spring and summer. Complete depigmentation does not occur. Snow nose is seen in Siberian Huskies, Golden Retrievers, Labrador Retrievers, Bernese Mountain Dogs and other breeds.

Lack of pigment on the nose is primarily a cosmetic problem, and is considered to be a conformation fault in the show ring. A number of home remedies have been advocated, but their success is questionable. Sunscreen, as described for nasal solar dermatitis, helps prevent ultraviolet injury to dogs lacking pigment.

PLASTIC DISH NASAL DERMATITIS

This is a localized form of depigmentation that affects the nose and lips. It is caused by eating out of plastic and rubber dishes that contain the chemical p-benzylhydroquinone. This chemical is absorbed through the skin and inhibits the synthesis of melanin, the chemical that produces dark pigment in the skin. The involved skin also becomes irritated and inflamed. The problem can be corrected by feeding from a glass, ceramic or stainless steel bowl.

NASAL CALLUS (HYPERKERATOSIS)

This disease occurs in old dogs. The cause is unknown. The skin of the nose becomes dry, thickened and hornlike. The callused nose may crack and develop fissures, then become irritated and infected. Hyperkeratosis can also occur in *zinc-responsive dermatosis, pemphigus foliaceus* and *discoid lupus erythematosus* (see Chapter 4).

A related condition involving the nose and foot pads occurs as a sequel to canine distemper. This disease is called *hard pad*. As the dog recovers from distemper, the nose often regains its normal appearance.

Treatment: There is no cure for idiopathic nasal callus. Control is aimed at softening the nasal callus with wet dressings and keeping the nose well lubricated with mineral oil or petroleum jelly. Local infection is treated with topical antibiotics such as triple antibiotic ointment.

The Nasal Cavity

NOSEBLEEDS (EPISTAXIS)

Nosebleeds are caused by foreign bodies, infections, tumors or parasites that erode the nasal mucous membranes. Some are caused by lacerations of the nostrils or puncture wounds from thorns or barbed wire.

A spontaneous nosebleed may be a manifestation of a generalized clotting disorder such as hemophilia or von Willebrand's disease. Vitamin K deficiency is another cause of spontaneous bleeding. It occurs most often with poisoning by rodenticide anticoagulants.

Treatment: Nosebleeds are often accompanied by bouts of sneezing that aggravate the bleeding. Keep the dog as quiet as possible. Apply an ice pack wrapped in cloth to the bridge of the nose. If the nostril is bleeding and the bleeding site is visible, apply steady pressure with a gauze square.

Most nosebleeds subside rather quickly when interference is kept to a minimum. If the bleeding does not stop, or if there is no obvious cause, take your dog at once to the veterinary clinic.

FOREIGN BODY IN THE NOSE

Nasal foreign bodies include blades of grass, grass seeds and awns, bone and wood splinters. The principal sign is a sudden bout of *violent sneezing*, accompanied by pawing at the nose, and occasionally bleeding from one nostril. The sneezing is first continuous and later intermittent. When a foreign body has been present for hours or days, there is a thick discharge (often bloody) from the involved nostril.

Treatment: A foreign body may be visible close to the opening of the nostril, in which case it can be removed with tweezers. In most cases it will be located farther back. If the foreign body is not removed in a short time, it tends to migrate even deeper into the nasal cavity. Do not poke blindly in your dog's nose, as this causes further injury. Take your dog to the veterinarian. Removal of most foreign bodies requires heavy sedation or general anesthesia.

After the foreign body has been removed, your veterinarian may prescribe an oral antibiotic to treat secondary bacterial infection.

ORAL-NASAL FISTULA

In this condition, food and water regurgitate out the nose when the dog eats and drinks. The most common congenital cause is *cleft palate*, discussed in Chapter 17. An infected tooth is the most common acquired cause. The canine teeth and fourth premolars in the upper jaw lie beneath the nasal passages. An abscessed tooth (usually a canine) can rupture into the nasal cavity. The tooth falls out and the space occupied by the tooth opens a passage through the hard palate that allows food to pass from the mouth into the nose. The signs of oral-nasal fistula are a unilateral nasal discharge accompanied by sneezing, especially after eating.

Treatment: The problem is treated surgically by creating a flap of mucous membrane from the inside of the mouth and suturing it across the defect.

Prevention: Proper dental care, and prompt attention to any dental problems while they are still minor, will help prevent oral-nasal fistula caused by tooth decay.

ALLERGIC RHINITIS

An allergic nasal discharge occurs in dogs with *canine atopy* (see Chapter 4). Signs are the abrupt onset of sneezing with a clear nasal discharge. Itching around the eyes may cause the dog to rub its face on the carpet. With repeated exposure to different allergens, the allergic response becomes a year-round problem.

Treatment: An episode of allergic rhinitis responds well to an antihistamine such as Benadryl (see the table *Common Drugs for Home Veterinary Use* in Chapter 20 for dosage). Definitive treatment is directed toward the underlying atopy.

RHINITIS AND SINUSITIS

The frontal and maxillary sinuses are extensions of the nasal cavity and are lined by a mucous membrane similar to the one that lines the nose. Accordingly, infections in the nasal cavity may spread to the sinuses and vice versa. A nasal infection is called rhinitis and a sinus infection is called sinusitis.

The signs of rhinitis and sinusitis are sneezing, nasal discharge and gagging or retching from a postnasal drip. The discharge is thick, creamy and foul smelling.

In young dogs, bacterial rhinitis and sinusitis usually do not occur unless the mucous membrane has been damaged by an upper respiratory infection, foreign body in the nasal cavity or trauma to the nose. Respiratory infections caused by the herpesvirus, adenovirus and parainfluenza virus are the most common causes of acute rhinitis. These infections may be followed by secondary bacterial involvement.

Canine distemper is a serious cause of secondary bacterial rhinitis. The discharge is mucoid and purulent. Other signs of distemper will be present.

In older dogs, tumors and infected teeth are the most common causes of rhinitis and sinusitis. Both are characterized by a chronic, long-standing purulent discharge from one nostril, along with sneezing and sniffling. Tumors and abscessed teeth may cause a blood-streaked discharge.

The diagnosis of rhinitis and sinusitis is based on X-rays, cultures, direct visualization of the nasal cavity using a flexible endoscope and, in some cases, by tissue biopsy.

Treatment: Bacterial rhinitis following upper respiratory infection is treated with broad-spectrum antibiotics that are continued for at least two weeks. Fungal infections usually respond to one of the newer antifungal agents, such as itraconazole. Antifungal drugs are given for six to eight weeks.

Chronic infections are difficult to clear up. Inflammatory debris builds up, causing further obstruction of air flow. Treatment involves using an antibiotic selected on the basis of sensitivity tests. In some cases exploratory surgery will be required to clean out the nasal cavity and/or an infected sinus.

NASAL POLYPS AND TUMORS

A polyp is a growth that begins as an enlargement of one of the mucous glands in the nose. It looks something like a cherry on a stalk. It is not cancer. Polyps cause symptoms by bleeding and blocking the flow of air. They can be removed by your veterinarian. Recurrence is possible.

Other tumors are found in the nasal cavity and sinuses. Most are malignant. They tend to occur in older dogs. Breeds reported to be at increased risk include the Airedale Terrier, Basset Hound, Old English Sheepdog, Scottish Terrier, German Shepherd Dog, Keeshond and German Shorthaired Pointer. The leading sign is discharge or bleeding through one nostril, accompanied by sneezing and sniffling.

The diagnosis is suspected on X-rays and confirmed by biopsy of the tumor through an endoscope. A *CT scan* may be useful in evaluating the extent of bone involvement. Large tumors can make one side of the face protrude. If they extend behind the eye, the eye will bulge. These tumors are far advanced.

Treatment: Benign tumors are cured by complete surgical removal. Malignant tumors are invasive and generally not curable, but survival can sometimes be prolonged using a combination of surgery and radiation therapy.

THE MOUTH AND THROAT

The oral cavity is bounded on the front and sides by the lips and cheeks, above by the hard and soft palate, and below by the tongue and muscles of the floor of the mouth. Four pairs of salivary glands drain into the mouth, the two largest being the parotid and mandibular glands.

The saliva of dogs is alkaline and contains antibacterial enzymes. There is also a normal flora of bacteria in the mouth that keep harmful bacteria from gaining a foothold. These factors reduce the frequency of mouth infections in dogs.

The pharynx is a space formed by the joining of the nasal passages with the back of the mouth. Food is prevented from entering the respiratory tree by the epiglottis, a flaplike valve that closes over the larynx as the dog swallows.

Signs of Mouth and Throat Disease

An important sign of mouth pain is a change in eating behavior. A dog with a tender mouth eats slowly and selectively, dropping food that is particularly coarse and large. Dogs with pain on one side of the mouth often tilt their heads and chew on the opposite side. With an extremely painful mouth, the dog stops eating altogether.

Excessive drooling is common in all painful mouth diseases. It is often accompanied by bad breath. Any form of halitosis is abnormal. Periodontal disease and gingivitis are the most common causes of halitosis in dogs.

Sudden gagging, choking, drooling and difficulty swallowing suggest a foreign object in the mouth or throat.

Difficulty opening and closing the mouth is characteristic of head and neck abscesses and jaw injuries.

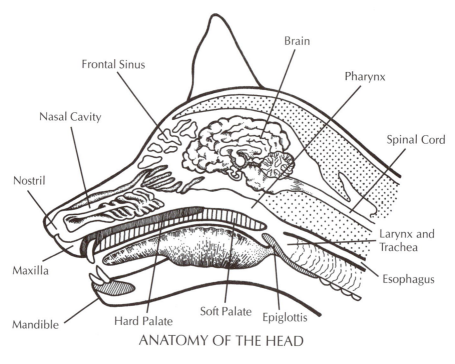

Brain

Frontal Sinus

Pharynx

Nasal Cavity

Spinal Cord

Nostril

Larynx and Trachea

Maxilla

Esophagus

Mandible

Hard Palate

Soft Palate

Epiglottis

ANATOMY OF THE HEAD

How to Examine the Mouth

Most mouth problems can be identified by inspecting the lips, gums, teeth and throat. To open the mouth, slip a thumb into the space behind the canine tooth and press upward on the roof of the mouth. As the mouth begins to open, press down on the lower jaw with the opposite thumb. To see the throat and tonsils, depress the tongue with a finger.

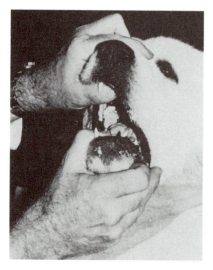

To examine the mouth, place your thumbs in the spaces behind the canine teeth and open the mouth.

To examine the dog's bite or occlusion, close the mouth and raise the upper lip while drawing down on the lower lip with your thumb. The bite is determined by seeing how the upper and lower incisor teeth come together (see *Incorrect Bite*, page 221). Raising the lips also exposes the mucous membranes of the gums. The appearance of the gums gives an indication of anemia and state of the circulation.

The Mouth

INFLAMMATION OF THE LIPS (CHEILITIS)

Cheilitis usually results from an infection inside the mouth that extends to involve the lips. In hunting dogs chapped lips can be caused by contact with weeds and brush. Dogs with canine atopy may irritate their lips by constantly rubbing and pawing the face.

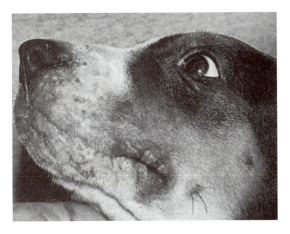

Inflammation of the lips.

Cheilitis can be recognized by the serum crusts that form at the junction of the haired and smooth parts of the lips. As the crusts peel off, the skin becomes raw and denuded and is sensitive to touch. Involvement of the hair follicles produces a localized folliculitis.

Treatment: Clean the lips daily using benzoyl peroxide shampoo (OxyDex or Pyoben), or hydrogen peroxide diluted 1:5 with water, and then apply an antibiotic-steroid cream such as Neocort. As the infection subsides, apply petroleum jelly to keep the lips soft and pliable. Periodontal disease or canine atopy, if present, should be treated to prevent recurrence.

LIP FOLD PYODERMA

In breeds with pendulous lips, folds on the lower lip that make contact with the upper incisors may become inflamed and infected. This tends to occur in Saint

Bernards, Cocker Spaniels and some hounds. The skin folds often contain pockets that trap food and saliva, creating a constantly wet environment that favors bacterial growth. When the folds are flattened, a raw surface is visible. The foul odor is often the reason for seeking medical attention.

Treatment is described in Chapter 4 (see *Skin Fold Pyoderma*).

MOUTH LACERATIONS

Lacerations of the lips, gums and tongue are common. Most occur during fights with other animals. Occasionally a dog accidentally bites his own lip, usually because of a badly positioned canine tooth. Dogs can cut their tongues picking up and licking sharp objects, such as the top of a food can. An unusual cause of tongue trauma is freezing to metal in extremely cold weather. When the tongue pulls free, epithelium strips off, leaving a raw bleeding surface.

Treatment: Control lip bleeding by applying pressure to the cut for five to 10 minutes. Grasp the lip between the fingers using a clean gauze dressing or a piece of linen. Bleeding from the tongue is difficult to control with direct pressure. Calm the dog and proceed to the nearest veterinary clinic.

Minor cuts that have stopped bleeding do not need to be sutured. Stitching should be considered when the edges gape open, when the laceration involves the lip border, or when bleeding persists after the pressure dressing is removed.

During healing, clean the dog's mouth twice a day with an antiseptic mouth wash, as described in the treatment of stomatitis. Feed a soft diet for one week.

If the laceration was caused by a poorly positioned tooth, the tooth should be extracted or realigned.

MOUTH BURNS

Electrical burns are caused by chewing on electric cords (see Chapter 1, *Electric Shock*). Most heal spontaneously, but in some cases a grayish ulcer develops at the site of the burn. Surgical removal of the ulcer may be required for cure.

Chemical burns are common. They are caused by licking a corrosive substance such as lye, phenol, phosphorus, household cleaners and alkalis. If the dog swallows the chemical, the esophagus or stomach may also be burned.

Treatment: The emergency treatment of oral chemical burns involves sponging and rinsing the mouth with copious amounts of tap water. Then transport the dog as quickly as possible to the nearest veterinary clinic for treatment of poisoning. In the event of delay, follow the instruction given in Chapter 1 on poisoning (see *Corrosive Household Products*). The aftercare for burns of the mouth is the same as that described below for stomatitis.

STOMATITIS (SORE MOUTH)

Stomatitis is inflammation of the mouth, gums and tongue. It usually is caused by periodontal disease and foreign bodies caught between the teeth or imbedded in the tongue. Occasionally it follows mouth lacerations and burns of the mucous membranes.

Stomatitis is an extremely painful condition accompanied by drooling, bad breath, refusal to eat, difficulty chewing and reluctance to permit an examination of the mouth. The inside of the mouth is red, inflamed and sometimes ulcerated. The gums often bleed when rubbed.

Stomatitis can be a local manifestation of a systemic disease. It is seen with kidney failure and uremia, diabetes mellitus, hypothyroidism, leptospirosis, distemper and autoimmune skin diseases. Specific types of stomatitis are:

Trench Mouth (Vincent's Stomatitis; Necrotizing Ulcerative Stomatitis). This is an exceptionally painful stomatitis caused by a variety of bacteria. There is a characteristic serious mouth odor, accompanied by a brown, purulent, slimy saliva that stains the front of the legs. The gums are beefy red and bleed easily. Ulcerations occur in the mucous membranes. Some cases are initiated by periodontal disease.

Thrush (Yeast Stomatitis). This is an uncommon stomatitis seen chiefly in dogs receiving broad-spectrum antibiotics that destroy normal bacterial flora and allow the growth of yeast. Thrush also occurs in dogs with compromised immunity associated with chronic illness. The mucous lining of the gums and tongue are covered with soft, white patches that coalesce to produce an adherent white membrane. Painful ulcers appear as the disease progresses.

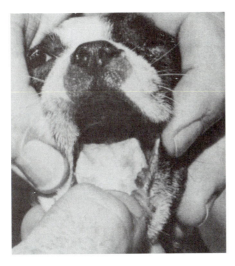

With thrush, the tongue is covered by soft white patches.

Recurrent Stomatitis. With this condition, traumatic ulcers of the mouth occur where jagged, broken or diseased teeth make repeated contact with the mucous lining of the lips, cheeks or gums. A bacteria and a fungus are quite commonly cultured from these ulcers.

Treatment: In most cases periodontal disease is present as a cause or a contributing factor. Your veterinarian may recommend a through cleaning of the dog's mouth under anesthesia. This affords the opportunity to treat dental calculus, decayed roots and broken teeth, treatments that are all essential to cure the problem. The dog is then placed on an appropriate antibiotic.

After-care at home involves rinsing the mouth with a 0.1 or 0.2 percent chlorhexidine solution (Peridex or Nolvadent) once or twice a day. Soak a cotton ball and gently swab the gums, teeth and oral cavity. You can use a plastic syringe and squirt the mouth wash directly onto the gums.

Feed a soft diet consisting of canned dog food diluted with water to a mushy consistency. Buffered or enteric coated aspirin helps to control pain (see *Common Drugs for Home Veterinary Use* in Chapter 20). B-complex vitamins containing niacin may be of benefit.

Thrush is treated with topical Nystatin or an antifungal drug such as ketoconazole.

It is important to diagnose and treat any systemic cause of the stomatitis.

ORAL PAPILLOMATOSIS (WARTS IN THE MOUTH)

Oral papillomas are painless warts that grow on the lips and in the mouths of dogs younger than two years old. They are caused by the canine oral papilloma virus. Initially, papillomas are small and pink. Over four to six weeks they increase in size and assume a rough, grayish-white, cauliflowerlike appearance. As many as 50 to 100 papillomas may be present. Skin papillomas caused by the same virus are common and occur on the surface of the eyelids and the skin of the body.

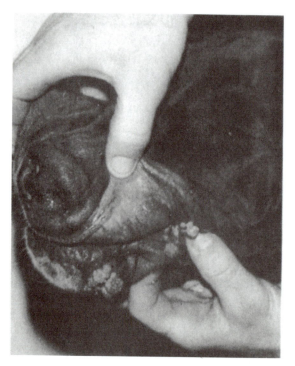

Mouth warts are caused by a canine virus. They usually disappear spontaneously in a few months.

Treatment: Oral papillomas usually disappear spontaneously in 6 to 12 weeks. If they fail to do so, they can be removed by surgery, freezing or electrocautery. Chemotherapy is effective in the case of numerous lesions. The dog's immune system makes antibodies that prevent reinfection.

FOREIGN OBJECTS IN THE MOUTH

Foreign objects in the mouth include bone splinters, slivers of wood, sewing needles and pins, porcupine quills, fish hooks and plant awns. Sharp objects can penetrate the lips, gums and tongue. Other objects can become caught between the teeth or wedged across the roof of the mouth. Pieces of string can become wrapped around the teeth and tongue.

A common place for a penetrating foreign body is beneath the tongue. On lifting the tongue, you may see a grapelike swelling or a draining tract. This means the foreign body has been present for some time.

In areas where cockle and sand burrs are prevalent, many small spines can become imbedded in the tongue and gums as the dog grooms burrs from his coat and feet.

The signs of a foreign body are pawing at the mouth, rubbing the mouth along the floor, drooling, gagging, licking the lips repeatedly and holding the mouth open. When a foreign object has been present for a day or longer, the principal signs may be lethargy, bad breath and refusal to eat.

Treatment: Obtain a good light source and gently examine your dog's mouth as described earlier in this chapter. A good look may reveal the cause. It is possible to directly remove some of the foreign bodies. Others will require a general anesthetic.

A thread attached to a needle should not be pulled out, as it can be used to locate the needle.

Foreign bodies present for a day or longer are difficult to remove and may cause infection. After removal, the dog is placed on an antibiotic for one week.

Fish Hooks

To remove a fish hook with a visible barb, cut the shank next to the barb with wire cutters and remove the hook in two pieces. When the barb is imbedded in the lip, determine which direction the barb is pointed and push the hook through until the barb is free. Cut and remove as described. Treat the puncture wound as described in Chapter 1 (*Wounds*).

Do not attempt to remove a fish hook imbedded in the mouth, or one that has been swallowed with the line attached. Take your dog to the veterinarian at once.

Porcupine Quills

Porcupine quills can penetrate the face, nose, lips, oral cavity, feet and skin of the dog. The decision to remove quills at home is based on the number of quills, their location, how deeply they are imbedded and whether professional help is readily available. Quills inside the mouth are difficult to remove without an anesthetic.

To remove quills at home, restrain the dog as described in Chapter 1 (*Restraining for Examination and Treatment*). Using a surgical hemostat or pliers (needle-nosed if possible), grasp each quill near the skin and draw it straight out in the long axis of the quill. If the quill breaks off a fragment will be left behind, causing a deep-seated infection requiring veterinary treatment.

After removing quills, observe your dog for about one week, looking for signs of infection, abscess or deeply imbedded quills working their way out.

String Around the Tongue

Swelling and bluish discoloration of the tongue may be caused by a rubber band or a string around its base. Occasionally a dog swallows one end of a string and the other end loops around the tongue. The harder the dog swallows, the more the string cuts into the tongue. Depending on how tightly the tongue is constricted, the venous and/or arterial blood supply may be cut off, resulting in irreversible tissue damage.

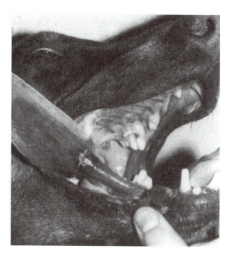

A string from a piece of baloney became wrapped around the base of this dog's tongue, causing ulceration. It was not seen until the tongue was raised.

Signs of tongue strangulation are similar to those of a foreign object in the mouth. It is easy to overlook a constriction because the band cuts into the tissue. A close inspection may be necessary to find the string and divide it using blunt-nosed baby scissors.

GROWTHS IN THE MOUTH

A common tumor in the mouth is the *epulis*, seen most often in Boxers and Bull-dogs. These benign tumors grow from the periodontal membrane in response to gum inflammation. They appear as growths on a flap of tissue. There are often multiple growths. Rarely, an epulis undergoes malignant transformation. Treatment is by surgical removal.

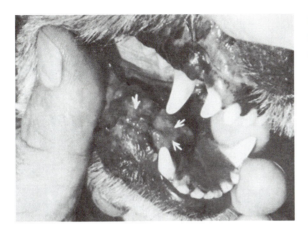

Cancer in the mouth. Note the growth behind the lower canine tooth.

Gingival hyperplasia is a condition in which the gums grow up alongside or over the teeth. A familial inheritance has been identified in Boxers, and is suspected in Great Danes, Collies, Doberman Pinschers and Dalmatians. The enlarged gums can interfere with eating and are easily traumatized. They also predispose the dog to periodontal disease. In any of these occur, the enlarged gums should be surgically removed.

Malignant tumors in the mouth are rare. In order of frequency they include melanoma, squamous cell carcinoma and fibrosarcoma. These tumors tend to occur in older dogs. Biopsy is required to make an exact diagnosis.

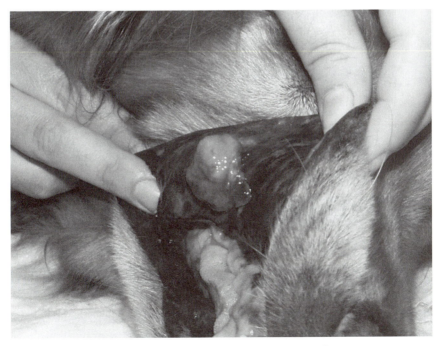

A melanoma growing on the inside of the upper lip.

Treatment: Early aggressive treatment of mouth tumors with wide local excision and/or radiation therapy offers the best chance for a cure. Surgery may involve removing part of the upper or lower jaw.

In many cases the tumor is already too far advanced for treatment. The prognosis is best for squamous cell carcinomas. Fifty percent of treated dogs survive a year or longer.

Teeth and Gums

DECIDUOUS AND ADULT TEETH

With rare exceptions, puppies are born without teeth. The first teeth to erupt are the incisors at two to three weeks of age. Next are the canines and premolars. The last premolar erupts at about eight weeks of age. As a rule, the teeth of larger breeds erupt more rapidly than those of smaller breeds.

The average puppy has 28 deciduous (temporary or baby) teeth. These are the incisors, canines and premolars. Puppies don't have molars.

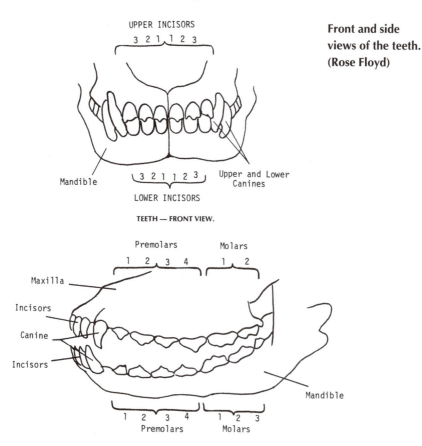

**Front and side
views of the teeth.
(Rose Floyd)**

UPPER INCISORS
3 2 1 1 2 3

Mandible

3 2 1 1 2 3
LOWER INCISORS

Upper and Lower
Canines

TEETH — FRONT VIEW.

Premolars
1 2 3 4

Molars
1 2

Maxilla

Incisors

Canine

Incisors

Mandible

1 2 3 4
Premolars

1 2 3
Molars

The deciduous teeth remain for only three to seven months. Beginning at about three months of age, the baby incisors are shed and replaced by adult incisors. By five months, a puppy should have all his adult incisors. The adult canines, premolars and molars come in between four and seven months of age. Thus, by seven to eight months of age, a puppy should have all his adult teeth. Knowing this teething sequence can give you an approximate idea of the age of a puppy.

The adult dog has 42 teeth: 22 in the mandible or lower jaw, and 20 in the maxilla or upper jaw. In each jaw there are six incisors, two canines and eight premolars. There are six molars in the lower jaw but only four in the upper jaw (see the figure *Front and Side Views of the Teeth*). The wear on the incisors is used to judge the age of the adult dog.

HOW DOGS' TEETH REVEAL THEIR AGE

To determine the age of puppies by time of dental eruption, see *Deciduous and Adult Teeth*.

In adult dogs, age is determined by checking the wear on the incisors. This method is relatively reliable up to about six years of age, but individual variations do occur.

The edges of the incisors are called the cusps. The amount of wear on the cusps is the most important factor in determining the age of the dog. The upper and lower incisors are identified by numbers, as shown in the figure *Front and Side Views of the Teeth*. Wear patterns are described for each age, but individual variations do occur. Beyond seven years, using the teeth to determine age is unreliable.

Typical Wear Patterns of Canine Teeth	
Age	Wear Pattern
1 year	Cusps are worn off lower incisors #1. Tartar begins to form on the canines.
2 years	Cusps are worn off lower incisors #2. Tartar is quite noticeable on the canines.
3 years	Cusps are worn off upper incisors #1.
4 years	Cusps are worn off upper incisors #2.
5 years	Cusps are worn slightly (at the corner) on lower incisors #3. The canines begin to show wear.
6 years	Cusps are worn off lower incisors # 3. The canines are becoming blunted.

RETAINED BABY TEETH

Normally, the roots of the baby teeth are reabsorbed as the adult teeth take their place. When this fails to happen, you will see what appears to be a double set of teeth. Toy breeds, in particular, tend to retain baby teeth as their adult teeth erupt. The adult teeth are then pushed out of line, producing a malocclusion or bad bite.

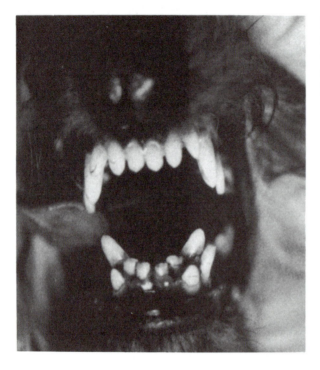

Retained baby teeth can force adult teeth out of line, causing malocclusion and gum injury.

Treatment: Puppies three to four months of age should be checked from time to time to see that their adult teeth are coming in normally. Whenever baby teeth interfere with adult teeth, the baby teeth should be pulled. If this is done by four to five months of age, the bite should correct spontaneously.

ABNORMAL NUMBER OF TEETH

The number of adult teeth in the dog, while usually 42, varies with the breed. In Bulldogs and other breeds with short faces, the last molars may be absent because of the short jaw.

Some dogs carry a mutation for missing teeth. Doberman Pinschers may have fewer than the normal eight premolars. This is considered a show fault but has no real significance in terms of the dog's health. Genetic variations of this type usually are hereditary.

You may find that your dog has more teeth than normal. This occurs most often in spaniels and hounds (especially Greyhounds). The extra teeth may crowd, twist or overlap the normal teeth. The offending teeth should be removed.

INCORRECT BITE (MALOCCLUSION)

An incorrect bite causes breeders more concern than any other mouth problem. Bad bites interfere with the ability to grasp, hold and chew food. Teeth out of alignment may injure the soft parts of the mouth.

A dog's bite is determined by how the upper and lower incisor teeth meet when the mouth is closed. The ideal occlusion is one in which the upper incisors just overlap and touch the lower incisors. This is called the *scissors* bite. In the *even* or *level* bite, the incisors meet edge to edge. This is a common occlusion, but is not considered ideal because the edge-to-edge contact wears the teeth. The correct bite for a given breed is described in the standard for that breed.

Most malocclusions are hereditary, resulting from genetic factors that control the rate of growth of the upper and lower jaws. Some incorrect bites are caused by retained baby teeth which push the erupting adult teeth out of line.

Overshot Bite. In the overshot bite, the upper jaw protrudes beyond the lower jaw, causing the upper teeth to overlap the lower teeth without touching. This condition is also called a *parrot mouth*, or *prognathism*. The overshot bite may correct itself spontaneously in young puppies if the gap is no greater than the head of a wooden match. Improvement can continue until the puppy is 10 months old, at which time the jaws stop growing.

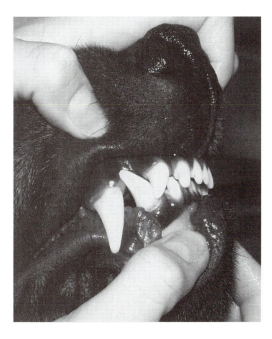

An overshot bite in an adult dog.

Puppies with severe overshot bites may have problems, because as the adult teeth come in they can injure the soft parts of the mouth. This requires treatment.

**With a seriously undershot bite, the teeth can
injure the soft tissues of the mouth.**

Undershot Bite. This is the reverse of the overshot bite, with the lower jaw protruding beyond the upper jaw. It is considered normal for brachycephalic breeds such as the Bulldog and Pug. Undershot bite is also called *brachygnathism*.

Wry Mouth. This is the worst of the malocclusion problems. In a wry mouth, one side of the jaw grows faster than the other, twisting the mouth. This can be a severe handicap in grasping and chewing food.

Treatment: Puppies should be examined by the veterinarian at two to three months of age to identify bite problems. In most cases treatment will not be necessary. If there is overcrowding or displacement of permanent teeth, however, the problem should be corrected by tooth extractions or orthodontic procedures such as crown-height reductions or the use of spacers.

The overshot bite is definitely hereditary and may be passed on to members of the next generation. The undershot bite is hereditary in some breeds. Dogs with hereditary dental malocclusions should be eliminated from breeding programs. This does not apply to brachycephalics, in which malocclusion is a breed characteristic.

UNSTABLE JAW

This condition, seen in Pekingese, Chihuahuas and some other toy breeds, occurs when the cartilage that joins the two sides of the lower jaw at the chin fails to calcify. The lower incisors that set in this soft cartilage become loose and unstable. Infection descends to the roots of these teeth and destroys the cartilage. This allows the two sides of the jaw to detach and move independently.

Treatment: The unstable jaw can be treated by removing the diseased teeth, administering antibiotics and stabilizing the joint with wires or screws.

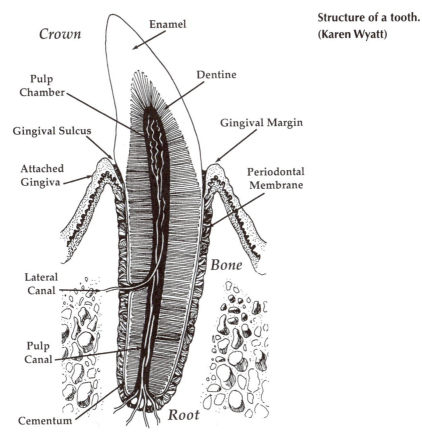

Crown

Enamel

Dentine

Pulp Chamber

Gingival Sulcus

Gingival Margin

Attached Gingiva

Periodontal Membrane

Bone

Lateral Canal

Pulp Canal

Cementum

Root

Structure of a tooth.
(Karen Wyatt)

PERIODONTAL DISEASE

Periodontal disease is one of the most common problems in veterinary practice. It occurs in two forms: The first is gingivitis, a reversible inflammation of the gums. The second is periodontitis, an inflammation of the deeper structures supporting the teeth. Treatment is directed toward preventing gingivitis from progressing to periodontitis, and delaying the progress of periodontitis once it is established.

Gingivitis. The edges of healthy gums fit tight around the teeth. In gingivitis, rough *calculus* builds up in an irregular fashion along the gum line, producing points at which the gum is forced away from the teeth. This creates small pockets that trap food and bacteria. In time, the gums become infected.

Dental calculus (also called tartar) is composed of calcium salts, food particles, bacteria and other organic material. It is yellow-brown and soft when first deposited. At the soft stage it is called *plaque*. The plaque quickly hardens into calculus. Calculus collects on all tooth surfaces but is found in the greatest amounts on the cheek side of the upper premolars and molars.

This buildup of calculus on the teeth is the primary cause of gum inflammation. This occurs to some extent in all dogs over the age of two. Certain breeds, such as Poodles, and smaller dogs seem to form calculus more readily. Dogs that eat dry kibble and chew on bones or dog biscuits have less calculus buildup than dogs that eat only soft, canned foods.

A characteristic sign of gingivitis is bad breath. The halitosis may have been present for some time—even accepted as normal. The gums appear red, swollen and bleed easily when touched. Pressing on the gums may cause pus to ooze from the gum line.

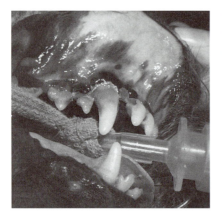

The formation of dental plaque is the first step in the development of periodontal disease.

Periodontitis. This develops as a continuation of gingivitis. The teeth are held in their bony sockets by a substance called cementum and a specialized connective tissue called the periodontal membrane. As the gum infection attacks the cementum and periodontal membrane (see the figure *Structure of a Tooth* on page 223), the roots become infected, the teeth begin to loosen and eventually detach. This is a painful process. Although the dog's appetite is good, it may sit by the food dish, eat reluctantly and drop food from his mouth. Drooling is common. A root abscess can rupture into the maxillary sinus or nasal cavity, producing a purulent unilateral nasal discharge or an *oral-nasal fistula* (see Chapter 7).

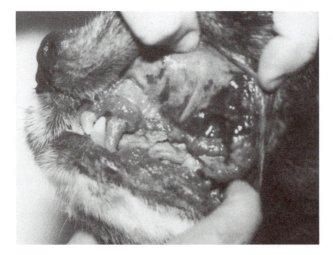

Severe periodontal disease with swollen, infected gums and heavy calculus deposits on the teeth.

Treatment: The teeth should be professionally cleaned, scaled and polished to remove all plaque and calculus. Many veterinarians now use ultrasonic dental units for cleaning teeth. For optimum results, the dog should be heavily sedated or given a general anesthetic.

Severe infections may necessitate removing a portion of the diseased gum (gingivectomy). In advanced periodontitis it may be necessary to extract some or all of the teeth before healing can begin. Once the gums are healed, a dog without teeth is able to eat surprisingly well. Antibiotics are dispensed and continued for one to three weeks, depending on the severity of the disease.

After-care at home involves rinsing the mouth with 0.2 percent chlorhexidine solution (Peridex or Nolvadent) once or twice a day. Soak a cotton ball and gently swab the gums and teeth, or use a plastic syringe and squirt the antiseptic directly onto the teeth and gums. You can also brush the dog's teeth with a dog tooth brush and a toothpaste containing chlorhexidine, as described in *Taking Care of Your Dog's Teeth*. Massage the gums with your finger or a piece of linen, using a gentle circular motion, while pressing on the outside surface of the gums. Continue the mouth washes and massages until the gums are healthy. Feed a soft diet consisting of canned dog food mixed with water to make a mush. Once healing is complete, switch to a good home dental program.

A new product called *Stomadhex*, available through your veterinarian, may prove to be an effective substitute for the after-care just described. Stomadhex is a small adhesive patch that sticks to mucous membranes. The patch is applied to the inside surface of the upper lip. It stays in place for several hours and slowly releases chlorhexidine and a vitamin called nicotinamide that promotes oral hygiene. The sustained release delivery system helps to prevent dental plaque and tartar and aids in controlling bad breath. The patch is applied daily for 10 days following a dental procedure, or as recommended by your veterinarian.

CAVITIES

Cavities are uncommon in dogs. When present, they usually form at the gum line and are related to periodontal disease. They can also occur on the crown of a molar. They appear as a black spot on the tooth. Cavities are painful and eventually lead to root abscesses.

Treatment: The quickest and easiest way to treat a cavity is to extract the tooth. The cavity can be filled and the tooth saved, but most veterinarians do not have the supplies and the equipment to fill cavities and will refer the dog to a veterinarian who specializes in dentistry. Root canal therapy is also being done for dogs that have deep cavities exposing the tooth pulp.

ABSCESSED ROOTS

Root abscesses can affect all the teeth, but the ones most commonly involved are the canines and the upper fourth premolars. Tooth abscesses are extremely painful and are accompanied by fever, reluctance to eat and depression. You may see pus oozing around the tooth.

An abscessed upper fourth premolar causes a characteristic swelling of the face below the eye. Eventually the abscess breaks through the skin and drains pus over the side of the face. A diseased tooth may break through the skin of the lower jaw and produce a similar condition. An abscessed tooth can result in an *oral-nasal fistula* (see Chapter 7).

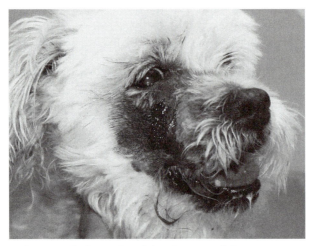

A ruptured abscess involving the root of the upper fourth premolar, with pus and blood draining over the side of the face.

Treatment: X-rays confirm the diagnosis and show whether bone is involved. The abscessed tooth is extracted under anesthesia and the tooth cavity is cleaned and drained. In some cases the tooth can be saved by doing a root canal procedure. Antibiotics are used to treat infection. After-care at home involves the use of chlorhexidine mouthwashes as described for periodontal disease and tooth decay.

BROKEN TEETH

Broken teeth are common. They are caused by chewing on hard objects such as stones and hard bones, and by catching the teeth on the wire of kennels and cages.

If the fracture involves only the enamel, the tooth is not painful and no treatment is necessary. However, a break in the crown that extends into the dental pulp can be extremely painful, and the dog may become depressed and refuse to eat. Restorative dentistry or extraction of the tooth will be necessary to prevent an abscessed root.

Taking Care of Your Dog's Teeth

Most dogs should receive professional dental care by age two to three years. The frequency of dental examinations, scaling and polishing depends on how quickly calculus forms on the dog's teeth. A good program of home dental care will cut down on how often your dog's teeth need to be professionally cleaned.

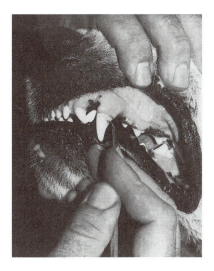

Tooth and gum disease can be prevented by home dental care, along with professional scaling and polishing as needed.

In fact, dental disease in dogs can be almost completely avoided by following these guidelines:

- Feed a dry kibble diet. Dry foods are abrasive and keep the teeth clean. Feed once or twice a day rather than allowing the dog to nibble all day. If you prefer to feed canned dog food, offer some dry biscuits, such as Milk Bones, daily.

- Brush the teeth and gums three times a week using a toothpaste made for dogs. Start the program when the dog is young and the gums are still healthy. If the dog develops periodontal disease, you will need to brush the teeth every day.

- Avoid giving your dog objects to chew that are harder than his teeth. High-impact rubber balls and rawhide chew toys are less likely to split or break teeth than knuckle bones. Avoid feeding chicken bones and long bones that splinter. They provide no benefit and may cause constipation and other problems. In fact, it is best to avoid all bones.

- Schedule annual veterinary visits for cleaning and scaling. A yearly check-up is the best prevention against dental problems.

BRUSHING THE TEETH AND GUMS

There are a number of good toothpastes and dental products designed for pets. Some contain abrasives such as calcium and silicates. An example is CET Dentifrice. Others use oxygenating substances to limit the growth of anaerobic bacteria (CET dental products and Oxyfresh). Nolvadent and Peridex contain chlorhexidine, which is both antibacterial and antiviral. Maxi/Guard contains zinc ascorbate, which promotes healing of diseased gums. Your veterinarian may suggest that you use one of these products, particularly if your dog has gum disease.

For routine cleaning, a satisfactory toothpaste can be made by mixing one tablespoon of baking soda with one teaspoon of water. If the dog is on a salt-restricted diet, substitute a salt replacer (potassium chloride) for the baking soda.

Do not use toothpaste made for humans. Its foaming action is unpleasant to dogs, and dogs cannot spit and rinse after using it.

The gums and teeth can be brushed with a finger or a soft nylon toothbrush with a 45-degree angle. Toothbrushes designed specifically for dogs are available at pet supply stores.

Finger brushing is done with a cloth or gauze wrapped around the finger. Apply the toothpaste to your wrapped finger. Lift the lips to expose the outside surface of the teeth. It is not necessary to open the mouth, as the self-cleaning action of the tongue will keep the inside surface of the teeth relatively free of calculus. Gently rub the teeth and gums in a circular motion.

With a toothbrush, hold the brush at a 45-degree angle, parallel to the gums and brush in small circles, overlapping the teeth and gums. The most important part to brush is the gingival sulcus, where the gum attaches to the tooth (see *Structure of a Tooth* on page 223). Bleeding may occur with vigorous brushing. This indicates gum disease. Daily brushing should tighten the gums and stop the bleeding in one to two weeks.

The Throat

SORE THROAT (PHARYNGITIS) AND TONSILLITIS

These two conditions have a common cause and thus often occur together. In fact, sore throats usually do not occur in dogs as isolated infections, the way they do in people. Most sore throats are associated with infections in the mouth, sinuses or respiratory tract. They can also occur with systemic diseases such as parvovirus, distemper, herpesvirus and pseudorabies.

The group A streptococcal sore throat (commonly known as strep throat) that occurs commonly in young children can produce mild or inapparent sore throat in dogs and cats, who may then harbor the bacteria in the respiratory tract. To eliminate the bacteria in households with recurrent strep throats, consider treating pets as well as family members.

The signs of sore throat are fever, coughing, gagging, pain on swallowing and loss of appetite. The throat looks red and inflamed. A purulent drainage may be seen coating the back of the throat.

The tonsils are aggregates of lymph tissue located at the back of the throat in dogs, as they are in people. They may not be visible unless they are inflamed. This generally occurs as a secondary symptom of a sore throat.

Primary bacterial tonsillitis is rare. It occurs in young dogs of the smaller breeds. Symptoms are similar to those of a sore throat, except that fever is more pronounced (over 103°F) and the dog appears depressed. The tonsils are bright red and swollen. Localized abscesses may be visible as white spots on the surface of the tonsils.

Chronic tonsillitis with tonsil enlargement is caused by persistent infection or by mechanical irritation from prolonged coughing, retching or regurgitation of stomach acid into the throat.

Treatment: Acute pharyngitis and tonsillitis respond to treatment of the underlying condition. When a primary cause cannot be identified, treatment involves giving a broad-spectrum antibiotic for 10 days. Feed a soft diet consisting of canned dog food mixed with water to make a mush. Aspirin relieves pain (see *Common Drugs for Home Veterinary Use* in Chapter 20).

Enlarged tonsils must be distinguished from lymphoma and squamous cell carcinoma—the most common cancers of the tonsil. This is accomplished by biopsy. Tonsillectomy for chronically inflamed tonsils is seldom necessary.

FOREIGN BODY IN THE THROAT (GAGGING)

Dogs gag on small rubber balls and other objects that can lodge in the back of the throat. Bones that lodge sideways in the throat are another cause of gagging. The signs of a foreign body in the throat are sudden anxiety, pawing furiously at the mouth, drooling, gagging and attempting to vomit.

Foreign bodies in the throat should be distinguished from objects in the larynx. Objects in the larynx cause coughing, choking and *respiratory distress*.

Treatment: Soothe and quiet the dog. Proceed directly to the nearest veterinary clinic. *If the dog is coughing and choking—or has fainted—the object has moved from the throat into the larynx and is blocking the airway.* Administer emergency treatment as described for *Choking* in Chapter 10, page 287.

Salivary Glands

The dog has four pairs of salivary glands that drain into the mouth. Only the parotid gland, located below the dog's ear on the side of the face, can be examined from the outside. The salivary glands secrete an alkaline fluid that lubricates the food and aids in digestion.

DROOLING (HYPERSALIVATION)

Some degree of drooling is normal in dogs, particularly in breeds with loose, pendulous lips. Excessive drooling is called hypersalivation. Hypersalivation is commonly triggered by psychological events such as fear, apprehension and nervous anxiety.

Drooling also occurs in response to mouth pain caused by periodontal disease, abscessed teeth and stomatitis. A dog that drools excessively and acts irrationally should be suspected of having rabies. Distemper, pseudorabies and heat stroke are other diseases associated with drooling. Another common cause of drooling is motion sickness. Tranquilizers cause drooling, as do many poisons. When a dog drools for no apparent reason and appears healthy, look for a foreign body in the mouth.

Treatment: This depends on the cause of the drooling.

SALIVARY GLAND CYSTS, INFECTIONS AND TUMORS

The salivary glands can be injured as a result of dog fights and lacerations of the head and neck. The damaged duct or gland may leak saliva into the surrounding tissue, forming a fluid-filled cyst called a *mucocele*. This occurs most often in the mandibular glands, located in the floor of the mouth. Mucoceles in this location are known as a honey cysts or *ranulas*. A ranula presents as a large, smooth, rounded swelling in the floor of the mouth on the right or left side of the tongue,

Mucoceles cause problems when they become large enough to interfere with eating or swallowing. If a needle is inserted into the swelling, a thick, mucuslike, honey-colored material is extracted. This may eliminate the problem, but more often surgery is required. It involves draining the cyst into the mouth. If this is not successful, the salivary gland can be removed.

Salivary gland infection is uncommon. Most cases are associated with preexisting mouth infections. The zygomatic gland, located beneath the cheek bone, is the gland most often involved. The signs of zygomatic gland infection are a bulging eye, tearing and pain on opening the mouth. Treatment involves removing the gland.

Tumors of the salivary glands are rare. Most are malignant. They appear as slowly enlarging lumps or masses located beneath the tongue or on the side of the face. Small tumors can be cured by surgical removal.

The Head

HEAD AND NECK ABSCESSES

Head and neck abscesses are caused by infected animal bites and sharp objects such as wood splinters, pins, chicken bones and quills that work their way back into the soft tissues. Some are preceded by a sore throat, tonsillitis, mouth infection or abscessed tooth.

Head and neck abscesses appear suddenly and are accompanied by fever. They are extremely tender and may give a lop-sided look to the head, face or neck. Opening the mouth may cause extreme pain. Affected dogs refuse to eat and drink.

A *retrobulbar* abscess occurs in the space behind the eyeball. It is accompanied by tearing and protrusion of the eye. A *submandibular* abscess is a swelling in the floor of the mouth that extends beneath the jaw bone. An abscess in the frontal sinus causes swelling beneath the eye.

Treatment: Head and neck abscesses should receive immediate veterinary attention. You may be asked to apply warm moist packs for 15 minutes four times a day to bring the abscess to a head. Antibiotics help to localize the infection. Once the swelling becomes soft, it is ready to be drained.

After incision and drainage, a wick may be used to keep the edges apart so that the abscess cavity can heal from below. After-care is similar to that described for *Cellulitis and Skin Abscess* (see Chapter 4).

CRANIOMANDIBULAR OSTEOPATHY (SWOLLEN JAW)

This condition of unknown cause occurs predominantly in young West Highland White Terriers, Scottish Terriers and Cairn Terriers, and has also been reported in Boston Terriers, Boxers, Labrador Retrievers, Great Danes and Doberman Pinschers. A recessive mode of inheritance has been described.

The disease begins in puppies four to 10 months of age. It is characterized by the deposition of excess bone along the underside of the lower jaw and on other parts of the jaw and skull. The swollen jaw is extremely painful. The hinge joints of the jaw may be involved, making it extremely difficult for the dog to open his mouth. Fever, drooling, and loss of appetite are characteristic. When the mouth is forcefully opened, the dog cries in pain.

Treatment: There is no effective treatment for the abnormal bone deposits. Tube feeding may be required during periods of appetite loss to support nutrition. Pain is controlled with buffered aspirin. The disease usually stabilizes at one year of age. Partial or complete regression of the excess bone may then occur. Although complete recovery is uncommon, most dogs are able to eat and maintain their weight.

The *Orthopedic Foundation for Animals* and the *Institute for Genetic Disease Control in Animals* maintain CMO registries for terriers in an attempt to diagnose and track the disease. For information on contacting these organizations, see Appendix C.

THE DIGESTIVE SYSTEM

The digestive tract begins at the mouth and ends at the anus. The lips, teeth, tongue, salivary glands, mouth and pharynx are considered in other chapters of the book. The remaining digestive tract organs are the esophagus, stomach, duodenum (the first part of the small bowel), small intestine, colon, rectum and anus. The organs that aid in digesting and absorbing foodstuffs are the pancreas, gall bladder and liver. The pancreas is located next to the duodenum. The pancreatic enzymes drain into the pancreatic duct, which joins the bile duct from the liver; both ducts empty into the duodenum.

The esophagus is a muscular tube that carries food down to the stomach through a series of rhythmic contractions. The lower esophagus enters the stomach at a sharp angle, which prevents food and liquids from refluxing back up into the esophagus.

Food can remain in the stomach for up to eight hours before passing through the pylorus into the duodenum and small intestine. Digestive juices from the pancreas and small intestine break the food down into amino acids, fatty acids and carbohydrates. The products of the meal are absorbed into the intestinal circulation and are carried to the liver, where they are converted to stored energy.

Fiber and undigested food continue on through the small intestine into the colon. The function of the colon is to remove water and store waste material as feces.

The adrenal glands, found in the adbomen above the kidneys, are important in the production of corticosteriods and other hormones that regulate body funtions. They will also be discussed in this chapter.

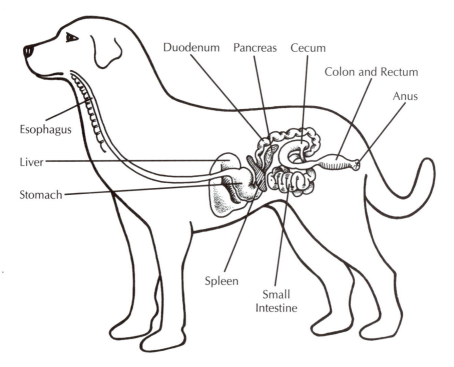

Duodenum Pancreas Cecum

Colon and Rectum

Anus

Esophagus

Liver

Stomach

Spleen

Small
Intestine

ANATOMY OF THE DIGESTIVE SYSTEM

Endoscopy

An endoscope is an instrument used for viewing the interior of a body canal or a hollow organ such as the stomach or colon. Its use as a diagnostic tool is invaluable for disgestive tract disorders, and more veterinary hospitals have acquired endoscopes.

While the dog is under general anesthesia, the flexible endoscope is inserted into the mouth or anus and fed through the gastrointestinal tract. A powerful light and either a fiber optic cable or a minature video camera is used to view the interior of the bowel. Tiny instruments passed through the scope are used to take biopsies and perform other minor procedures.

GASTROSCOPY

Gastroscopy, also called esophagogastroduodenoscopy or *EGD*, is the endoscopic procedure for exploring and biopsying the upper gastrointestinal (GI) tract. It is the best way to diagnose gastritis, stomach and duodenal ulcers, tumors and foreign bodies. The endoscope is inserted into the mouth and passed through the esophagus into the stomach and duodenum. Foreign bodies, if encountered during the examination, can be removed from the esophagus and stomach.

COLONOSCOPY

Colonoscopy is a procedure in which the endoscope is passed through the anus into the rectum and colon. The ability to visualize the interior of the lower GI tract and biopsy the intestine has greatly simplified the diagnosis of colitis and other colon diseases.

The Esophagus

The esophagus is a muscular tube that propels food and water into the stomach. This is accomplished by a series of rhythmic contractions called peristaltic waves, which are coordinated with the act of swallowing.

Signs of esophageal disease include regurgitation, painful swallowing (called dysphagia), drooling and weight loss.

REGURGITATION

Regurgitation is the relatively effortless expulsion of undigested food, without retching. It occurs because either the esophagus is physically blocked or it lacks peristaltic activity. In either case the food accumulates until the esophagus is overloaded, after which the food is passively expelled.

Regurgitation should not be confused with vomiting. Vomiting is the *forceful* expulsion of stomach contents, preceded by drooling and retching. The material vomited is usually sour smelling, partly digested and stained with yellow bile.

The sudden onset of regurgitation in a previously healthy dog is almost certainly due to a foreign body caught in the esophagus. Drooling indicates that the dog cannot swallow saliva.

Chronic regurgitation (the kind that comes and goes but seems to be getting worse) suggests a partial obstruction caused by megaesophagus, stricture or tumor.

A serious complication of regurgitation is *aspiration pneumonia*, in which the lungs become infected as a result of food being aspriated into the lungs. When regurgitated food ends up in the lungs, aspiration pneumonia is the result. Another important complication is nasal cavity infection. This occurs when food is regurgitated into the nose.

DIFFICULT, PAINFUL SWALLOWING (DYSPHAGIA)

A dog with a painful esophagus eats slowly, stretches his neck and makes repeated efforts to swallow the same mouthful. As the condition becomes more painful, the dog stops eating and begins to lose weight.

Difficult, painful swallowing indicates a partial blockage caused by an esophageal foreign body, stricture or tumor. Pain on swallowing also occurs with mouth infections, sore throats and tonsillitis.

MEGAESOPHAGUS (ENLARGED ESOPHAGUS)

Megaesophagus means enlarged esophagus. When an esophagus is partially obstructed over a period of time, it gradually enlarges like a balloon and becomes a
storage organ. This process, called megaesophagus, is accompanied by regurgitation, loss of weight and recurrent episodes of aspiration pneumonia.

There are two causes of megaesophagus. The first is a failure of the esophagus to
contract and propel food into the stomach. This impaired motility occurs as a
hereditary disorder in puppies and as an acquired disease in adults. The second
cause of megaesophagus is a physical blockage, such as a foreign body.

Congenital Megaesophagus. A hereditary form of megaesophagus occurs in
puppies. It is caused by a developmental disorder involving the nerve plexus in the
lower esophagus. Peristaltic activity stops at the level of the paralyzed esophagus,
and food can go no further. In time, the esophagus above the inert segment enlarges and balloons out. This can be demonstrated by lifting the puppy by his back
legs and looking for a bulging out of the esophagus at the side of the neck.

Congenital megaesophagus has been described in German Shepherd Dogs, Golden
Retrievers, Great Danes, Irish Setters, Greyhounds, Labrador Retrievers, Newfoundlands, Miniature Schnauzers, Chinese Shar-Pei and Wire Fox Terriers. *Hereditary
myopathies* (see Chapter 12) are other causes of congenital megaesophagus.

Puppies with congenital megaesophagus show signs at weaning when they begin to eat solid foods. Characteristically, they approach the food dish with enthusiasm but back away after a few bites. They often regurgitate small amounts of
food, which they eat again. After repeatedly eating the food, it becomes quite
liquid and passes into the stomach. Repeated inhalation of food causes bouts of
aspiration pneumonia.

Another type of congenital megaesophagus is caused by retained fetal arteries
in the chest. The arteries produce a constriction around the esophagus (known as
vascular ring anomaly) that prevents swallowing. The most common anomaly is a
persistent right aortic arch. Regurgitation and difficulty swallowing appear at 4 to
10 months of age. These puppies are stunted and malnourished.

Adult-Onset Megaesophagus. This is an acquired condition that occurs with
several rare neuromuscular diseases, including *myasthenia gravis*. Other known causes
are hypothyroidism, esophagitis, autoimmune diseases and heavy metal poisoning.
In most cases the cause is unknown.

A chest X-ray may show an enlarged esophagus, opaque material in the esophagus or aspiration pneumonia. The diagnosis can be confirmed by administering a
barium meal and taking an X-ray of the chest.

Treatment: The primary goals are maintaining nutrition and preventing complications. Divide a puppy's daily ration into four or more small feedings. *It is important to provide both food and water from a raised bowl to maximize the effects of
gravity.* A semi-liquid or gruel mixture is easier for some dogs to swallow. Others do
better with solids. This should be determined by trial and error.

Episodes of aspiration pneumonia require antibiotics, selected on the basis of
culture and sensitivity tests. Signs of pneumonia are coughing, fever and rapid,

labored breathing (see *Pneumonia*, Chapter 10). Puppies with congenital megae-sophagus may eventually outgrow the condition. Surgical correction of some vascu-lar ring anomalies is possible. Dogs with congenital megaesophagus should not be used for breeding.

Adult-onset megaesophagus is irreversible, but some dogs do well for many years with careful attention to feeding and prompt treatment of respiratory infections.

FOREIGN BODY IN THE ESOPHAGUS

Foreign bodies in the esophagus are common. The most common are bones and bone splinters. Other objects that obstruct a dog's esophagus include string, fish-hooks, needles, wood splinters and small toys. Suspect an esophageal foreign body when a dog suddenly begins to gag, retch, drool and regurgitate. A history of regurgitation and difficulty swallowing for several days or longer suggests a partial obstruction.

Sharp foreign bodies are particularly dangerous, as they can perforate the esopha-gus. A dog with a perforated esophagus exhibits fever, cough, rapid breathing, dif-ficulty swallowing and a rigid stance.

Treatment: An esophageal foreign body is an emergency. Take your dog to a veterinarian at once.

The diagnosis can usually be made by taking X-rays of the neck and chest. Ingesting a contrast material such as Gastrografin, followed by an X-ray of the esophagus, may be required.

Many foreign bodies can be removed by *gastroscopy*. The dog is given a general anesthetic, after which an endoscope is passed through the mouth and into the esophagus. The object is located visually and removed with a grasping instrument. If the object cannot be withdrawn, it can often be pushed down into

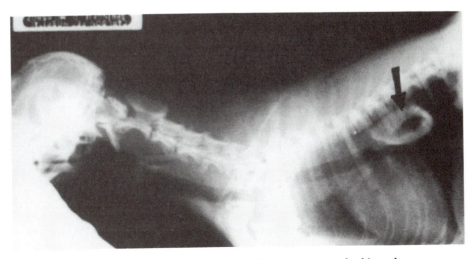

A steak bone lodged in the lower esophagus. The bone was pushed into the stomach using an endoscope and then surgically removed.

the stomach and removed by an abdominal operation. Foreign bodies that cannot be dislodged using the endoscope require open esophageal surgery. The same is true for esophageal perforations.

ESOPHAGITIS

Only a few conditions cause inflammation of the esophagus. One is a mucosal injury caused by a foreign body. Another is a burn caused by ingesting a caustic liquid (see *Corrosive Household Products*, Chapter 1). Finally, there are cases caused by gastroesophageal reflux.

Gastroesophageal Reflux. This is the process in which stomach acid backs up into the esophagus, resulting in chemical burns of the mucosal lining. This can occur when a dog is tilted in a head-down position during general anesthesia. It also occurs with a stomach tube, after chronic vomiting and with a hiatal hernia.

Hiatal Hernia. With this type of hernia, the stomach protrudes through an abnormally large esophageal opening in the diaphragm. The opening allows part or all of the stomach to slide up into the chest. Hiatal hernias are not common in dogs. Most of them are congenital, with an increased incidence among Chinese Shar-Pei. The major concern with hiatal hernia is that it causes gastroesophageal reflux.

Signs of moderate to severe esophagitis are dysphagia, repeated swallowing, regurgitation and drooling. With chronic esophagitis the dog loses appetite and weight. The diagnosis is made by *gastroscopy*, which reveals an inflamed, swollen esophageal mucosa.

Treatment: It is directed toward correcting the underlying condition. Hiatal hernias can be surgically repaired. Medications used to treat chronic gastroesophageal reflux in people are also effective in dogs.

ESOPHAGEAL STRICTURE

A stricture is a circular scar that forms after an injury to the wall of the esophagus. Most injuries are caused by esophageal foreign bodies. Swallowed caustic liquids and gastroesophageal reflux are other causes. Tumors of the esophagus can produce a stricturelike narrowing.

The principal sign of esophageal stricture is regurgitation. The diagnosis can be made by X-ray after the dog has been given a barium solution, or by an esophageal endoscopy. The stricture appears as a fibrous ring that narrows the esophagus.

Treatment: Early strictures can be treated by stretching the wall of the esophagus with a balloon catheter passed through the endoscope. When this is not successful, surgery may be considered to remove the strictured segment. The operation is difficult and has a high complication rate. After successful surgery, most dogs are able to swallow normally. Those who continue to have problems may have developed a motility disorder due to enlargement of the esophagus (see *Megaesophagus*, page 236).

GROWTHS

Primary tumors of the esophagus are rare and most are malignant. A common benign tumor is a leiomyoma. Tumors that have spread to lymph nodes around the esophagus can press on the esophagus, creating a physical obstruction. Growths on the esophagus caused by a worm parasite (*Spirocerca lupi*) occur in the southwestern United States. The disease is uncommon. A few of these growths can transform into cancers.

Treatment: Surgical removal of benign tumors (and malignant tumors that have not spread) offers the best chance for cure. Worm parasites are treated with anthelmintics.

The Stomach

VOMITING

Vomiting is common in dogs. All vomiting is the result of activating the vomiting center in the brain. The vomiting center is well-developed in dogs, so dogs vomit more readily than most other animals. As a dog perceives a need to vomit, he becomes anxious and may seek attention and reassurance. He then begins to salivate and swallow repeatedly.

Vomiting begins with a simultaneous contraction of the muscles of the stomach and abdominal wall. There is an abrupt increase in intra-abdominal pressure. The lower esophagus relaxes, allowing the stomach contents to travel up the esophagus and out the mouth. The dog extends his neck and makes harsh gagging sounds. This sequence should be distinguished from the passive act of *regurgitation*, already discussed.

The most common cause of vomiting is eating indigestible substances such as grass that irritate the lining of the stomach. Another cause of vomiting is overeating. Puppies that gobble their food and immediately exercise are likely to vomit. This after-meal vomiting frequently is caused by feeding a group of puppies from a common food pan. Since they are all competing for food, each one eats as much as he possibly can. Separating puppies, or feeding frequent small meals, eliminates the problem of gorging.

Dogs may vomit when upset, excited or suffering from a phobia (for example, during a thunderstorm). Phobic dogs drool, whine, paw and tremble.

Vomiting occurs with most acute infectious disease. It also occurs with many chronic diseases, including kidney and liver failure, Cushing's syndrome and diabetes mellitus.

To determine the cause of vomiting, note whether it is repeated, and if so, whether it is sporadic or persistent. How soon after eating does it occur? Is it projectile? Inspect the vomitus for blood, fecal material, foreign objects and worms.

Persistent Vomiting

If the dog vomits or retches repeatedly, bringing up a frothy, clear fluid, this suggests a stomach irritation such as *acute gastritis*. However, persistent vomiting also occurs with life-threatening diseases such as *acute pancreatitis, gastric outflow obstruction, intestinal obstruction* and *peritonitis*. Persistent retching without bringing up any vomitus is typical of *bloat*. Repeated vomiting *along with diarrhea* suggests *acute infectious enteritis*.

Sporadic Vomiting

Sometimes a dog vomits off and on over a period of days or weeks. There is no relationship to meals. The appetite is poor. The dog has a haggard look and appears listless. Suspect liver or kidney disease, or an illness such as *chronic gastritis, stomach or duodenal ulcer*, a heavy worm infestation or *diabetes mellitus*. In an older dog, suspect a *gastric tumor*. A veterinary checkup is in order.

Vomiting Blood

Red blood in the vomitus indicates an active bleeding point somewhere between the mouth and upper small bowel. (Blood from the nasopharynx and esophagus may be swallowed.) Common causes are *stomach and duodenal ulcers, gastrointestinal foreign bodies* and *gastric tumors*. Material that looks like coffee grounds is old, partially digested blood. This also indicates a bleeding point between the mouth and upper small bowel. Any dog that vomits blood should be seen by a veterinarian.

Fecal Vomiting

A dog that vomits foul material that looks and smells like feces is suffering from *intestinal obstruction* or *peritonitis*. Seek immediate professional treatment.

Projectile Vomiting

Projectile vomiting is forceful vomiting in which the stomach contents are ejected a considerable distance. Typically it occurs in *gastric outflow obstructions*. Diseases that cause pressure on the brain (tumors, encephalitis, blood clots) also cause projectile vomiting.

Vomiting Foreign Objects

Dogs may also vomit foreign objects, including rubber balls, pieces of toys, sticks and stones. Puppies with a heavy roundworm infestation may vomit adult worms. These pups should be treated as described in *Ascarids* in Chapter 2.

HOME TREATMENT OF VOMITING

If there is any question about the cause or seriousness of the vomiting, seek veterinary help. Vomiting dogs can dehydrate rapidly as they lose body fluids and electrolytes. Home treatment is appropriate only for normal, healthy adult dogs. Puppies and old dogs are less able to tolerate dehydration and should be treated by a veterinarian.

An important initial step is to rest the stomach by withholding food and water for a minimum of 12 hours. If the vomiting stops with stomach rest, the dog can be permitted to lick a few ice chips every three to four hours. If the vomiting has stopped, offer 1/4 to 1/2 cup of water (depending on the size of the dog) every two to three hours. A pediatric electrolyte solution (see *Home Treatment of Diarrhea,* page 250) can be given in small amounts in addition to the water.

After 12 hours with no vomiting, start the dog on a bland diet such as two parts boiled rice mixed with one part hamburger. (Boil the hamburger to remove the fat—fat delays stomach emptying.) Other bland foods that may be substituted are cottage cheese, strained meat baby food and chicken and rice soup. Begin by offering small amounts (one or two tablespoons at a time) every two to three hours. Increase the volume over the next two days and gradually return the dog to his customary diet.

Stop all food and water and obtain immediate veterinary assistance when:

- Vomiting persists despite the fact that the dog has received no food or water for several hours.
- Vomiting recurs during attempts to introduce food and water.
- Vomiting is accompanied by diarrhea.
- The dog vomits fresh blood or material that looks like coffee grounds.
- The dog becomes weak and lethargic or shows signs of systemic illness.

MOTION SICKNESS

Many young dogs suffer from car sickness and become sick when traveling by boat or air. The signs are restlessness followed by salivation, yawning, nausea and then vomiting. Motion sickness is caused by overstimulation of the labyrinth in the inner ear.

If your dog is susceptible to motion sickness, your veterinarian may prescribe a drug, such as Dramamine (see *Common Drugs for Home Veterinary Use* in Chapter 20), to control symptoms. Give the first dose one hour before traveling. Remember, *do not* medicate your dog on the day of a dog show, as Dramamine causes drowsiness.

Dogs travel best on an empty stomach, so it is best to withhold food and water before taking a trip. Most dogs with motion sickness become accustomed to riding in the car and eventually outgrow the problem.

ACUTE GASTRITIS (ACUTE VOMITING)

Acute gastritis is an irritation of the lining of the stomach that comes on suddenly. The principal sign is severe and continuous vomiting. Keep in mind that persistent vomiting is also associated with life-threatening diseases such as intestinal obstruction and peritonitis. Seek professional consultation in all cases where the cause of persistent vomiting is not known.

Common stomach irritants are spoiled food and garbage, stools, grass, plastic wrappings, hair and bones. Certain drugs (notably aspirin, but also cortisone, butazolidine and some antibiotics) produce gastric irritation. Common poisons are antifreeze, fertilizers, plant toxins and crabgrass killers.

A dog with an acute gastritis vomits shortly after eating. Later the dog appears lethargic and sits with his head hanging over the water bowl. The dog's temperature remains normal unless he is suffering from *acute infectious enteritis*, a disease that also causes diarrhea.

Treatment: Acute nonspecific gastritis is self-limiting and usually resolves in 24 to 48 hours if the stomach is rested and protected from excess acid. Follow the instructions given above in *Home Treatment of Vomiting*.

CHRONIC GASTRITIS (SPORADIC VOMITING)

Dogs with chronic gastritis vomit from time to time over a period of days or weeks. These dogs appear lethargic, have a dull hair coat and lose weight. The vomitus sometimes contains foreign material and food eaten the day before.

A common cause of chronic gastritis is a food allergy (see *Food Allergy* in Chapter 4). Other causes are persistent grass eating, repeated consumption of drugs, chemicals or toxins, and ingesting cellulose, plastic, paper or rubber products. Also consider the possibility of hair balls. Hair is shed more heavily in the springtime, and is swallowed as the dog licks and pulls it out. Hair and other foreign materials can be incorporated into hard masses called *bezoars*. Bezoars may grow to a size that makes it impossible for them to pass out of the stomach (see *Gastrointestinal Foreign Bodies*, page 255). *Note that in many cases of chronic vomiting the cause is not known.*

A condition called *hypertrophic gastropathy* is a thickening of the mucous membranes of the lower half of the stomach, which can lead to gastric obstruction and food retention. Vomiting occurs three to four hours after eating. Hypertrophic gastropathy occurs most often in middle-aged dogs of the small breeds. The cause is unknown.

Eosinophilic gastritis is a chronic condition characterized by the accumulation of *eosinophils* (a type of white blood cell) in the mucous lining of the stomach, along with thickening and scarring of the stomach wall. The cause is unknown, although a food allergy has been proposed. Eosinophilic gastritis is more likely than other types of gastritis to be associated with ulcers and bleeding.

Stomach and duodenal ulcers also produce sporadic vomiting. Finally, if there is no obvious explanation for the sporadic vomiting, the dog may be suffering from a systemic disease, such as liver or kidney failure, which can be diagnosed by blood tests.

Treatment: Dogs with chronic vomiting should be seen by a veterinarian. Gastroscopy with biopsy of the stomach wall is the quickest way to make a diagnosis of chronic gastritis.

The treatment of chronic gastritis involves switching to a bland, high-carbohydrate diet such as Hill's Prescription Diet i/d. Alternatively, you can feed a homemade diet of boiled rice and cottage cheese. Offer frequent small feedings and avoid large meals. As the dog recovers, gradually introduce a high-quality commercial dog food.

Eosinophilic gastritis responds well to a course of corticosteroids and a hypoallergenic diet prescribed by your veterinarian. Gastritis associated with *gastric outflow obstruction* is treated as described for *stomach and duodenal ulcers*.

STOMACH AND DUODENAL ULCERS

Stomach and duodenal ulcers are being diagnosed more frequently in dogs due to the wider use of gastroscopy. Seen through the endoscope, superficial ulcers are patches of inflamed and eroded mucosa covered by white or yellow pus. Deep ulcers are punched-out areas involving all layers of the stomach wall. Ulcers can be single or multiple, and can range in size from less than one inch to several inches in diameter. Ulcers occur more often in the stomach than in the duodenum.

Ulcers in dogs are not believed to be caused by stomach bacteria. The usual cause is consumption of a corticosteroid or nonsteroidal anti-inflammatory drug such as aspirin or Motrin. Dogs are even more susceptible than people to the ulcer-producing effects of these drugs.

Other conditions that predispose a dog to ulcers include all forms of liver disease, kidney failure, stress (severe illness, major surgery), chronic gastritis (particularly the eosinophilic type) and shock.

Mast cell tumors of the skin (discussed in Chapter 18) can cause ulcers. This is because these tumors produce and release histamine, which is a powerful stimulant to acid secretion. In fact, ulcers occur in up to 80 percent of dogs with mast cell tumors.

The principal sign of an ulcer is sporadic or chronic vomiting. Dogs may also lose weight and be anemic. Occasionally the vomitus contains old blood (which looks like coffee grounds) or fresh blood and blood clots, although the bleeding in many ulcers is microscopic. With rapid bleeding the dog goes into shock, passes black tarry stools. Stomach and duodenal ulcers can rupture into the abdomen, causing *peritonitis*.

Treatment: Dogs with gastrointestinal bleeding should be hospitalized for observation and further tests. Severe anemia is treated with blood transfusions. If possible, discontinue all ulcer-producing medications.

In dogs with nonspecific signs, such as chronic vomiting, the diagnosis is made by *gastroscopy*. It is important to identify and eliminate predisposing causes. Anti-ulcer drugs used in people are effective in dogs. They include the H-2 blockers Tagamet and Zantac, the mucosal protectants sucralfate (Carafate) and misoprostol (Cytotec), omeprazole (Prilosec), and antacids such as Mylanta, Maalox and Amphogel. These drugs are best taken in combination (an antacid along with an H-2 blocker), several times a day. A veterinarian should determine the most effective drug combination and schedule. Treatment is continued for at least three to four weeks. A follow-up gastroscopy is advisable to ensure that healing is complete.

Perforated ulcers require emergency surgery.

GASTRIC OUTFLOW OBSTRUCTION

At the outlet of the stomach is the pyloric canal. Scarring and contraction of the pyloric canal prevents the stomach from emptying. Stomach and duodenal ulcers close to the pyloric canal are the most common cause of inflammation and scarring. Other causes of scarring and contraction include hypertrophic and eosinophilic gastritis (see *Chronic Gastritis*, page 242), and gastric tumors. Foreign bodies and *bezoars* are other causes of gastric outflow obstruction (see *Gastrointestinal Foreign Bodies*, page 255).

Gastric outflow obstruction can be partial or complete. Dogs with partial obstruction vomit intermittently, often 12 to 16 hours after eating. The vomitus usually contains undigested food and, occasionally, blood. When obstruction is complete, vomiting occurs immediately after eating and is often projectile. Other symptoms of gastric outflow obstruction include loss of appetite, weight loss, bloating and belching.

The diagnosis can sometimes be made by an X-ray of the abdomen or an ultrasound showing an enlarged, fluid-filled stomach. Gastroscopy or an upper GI series may be required for more complete diagnosis. Treatment involves surgically removing the blockage.

GASTRIC TUMORS

A stomach tumor should be suspected in an older dog with sporadic vomiting. The vomitus often contains old, partially digested blood. Anemia and weight loss frequently found. Tumors in the pyloric canal region often cause *gastric outflow obstruction*.

Adenocarcinoma is the most common malignant tumor of the stomach. Benign tumors such as leiomyomas and polyps also occur. The diagnosis is made by gastroscopy and biopsy of the tumor.

Treatment: Surgical treatment involves removing the part of the stomach containing the tumor. The prognosis for benign tumors is excellent. Malignant tumors are difficult to cure.

BLOAT (GASTRIC DILATATION VOLVULUS)

Bloat is a life-threatening emergency that affects dogs in the prime of life. The mortality rate for gastric volvulus approaches 50 percent. Early recognition and treatment are the keys to survival.

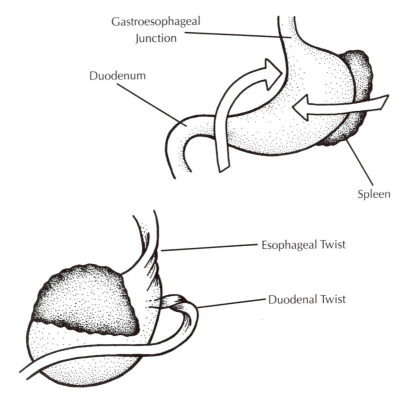

Gastroesophageal Junction

Duodenum

Spleen

Esophageal Twist

Duodenal Twist

In a dog with volvulus, the twists at the gastroesophageal junction and duodenum trap gas and fluids in the stomach. The dog is unable to belch or vomit.

Anatomy of Bloat

Bloat actually refers to two conditions, The first is *gastric dilatation*, in which the stomach distends with gas and fluid. The second is *volvulus*, in which the distended stomach rotates on its long axis. The spleen is attached to the wall of the stomach, and therefore and rotates with the stomach. Gastric dilatation may or may not be complicated by volvulus. If volvulus occurs, the stomach may twist 180° or less (technically called a torsion). An actual volvulus is a twist of 180° to 360° or more.

During volvulus, the pylorus is pulled out of position and becomes displaced to the left of the gastroesophageal junction (as shown in the diagram). This pinches off the duodenum and prevents fluid and air from escaping from the stomach through the pyloric canal. Simultaneously, the gastroesophageal junction becomes twisted and obstructed, preventing the dog from belching and vomiting. Gas and fluid are trapped in the closed-off stomach, which becomes hugely distended as the material ferments. Interference with blood circulation results in necrosis (death) of the wall of the stomach.

This sequence produces a number of other problems, including acute dehydration, bacterial *septicemia*, circulatory shock, cardiac arrhythmias, gastric perforation, peritonitis and death.

Bloat can occur in any dog at any age, but typically occurs in middle-aged to older dogs. There may be a familial association with other dogs who have bloated. Large-breed dogs with deep chests are anatomically predisposed. These breeds include the Great Dane, German Shepherd Dog, Saint Bernard, Labrador Retriever, Irish Wolfhound, Great Pyrenees, Boxer, Weimaraner, Old English Sheepdog, Irish Setter, Bloodhound and Standard Poodle. Chinese Shar-Pei and Basset Hounds have the highest incidence among midsize dogs. Small dogs are rarely affected.

Bloat develops suddenly, usually in a healthy, active dog. The dog may have just eaten a large meal, exercised vigorously before or after eating, or drank a large amount of water immediately after eating. There is no evidence that the protein or soy content in the diet contributes to bloat; research has shown the majority of gas associated with bloat is due to swallowed air.

Signs of Bloat

The classic signs of bloat are restlessness and pacing, salivation, retching, unproductive attempts to vomit and enlargement of the abdomen. The dog may whine or groan when you press on his belly. Thumping the abdomen produces a hollow drum sound.

Unfortunately, not all cases of bloat present with typical signs. *In early bloat the dog may not appear distended, but the abdomen usually feels slightly tight.* The dog appears lethargic, obviously uncomfortable, walks in a stiff-legged fashion, hangs his head, *but may not look extremely anxious or distressed.* Early on it is not possible to distinguish dilitation from volvulus.

Late signs (those of impending shock) include pale gums and tongue, *delayed capillary refill time,* rapid heart rate, weak pulse, rapid labored breathing, weakness and collapse.

If the dog is able to belch or vomit, quite likely the problem is not due to a volvulus, but this can only be determined by veterinary examination.

Treatment of Bloat

In all cases where there is the slightest suspicion of bloat, take your dog at once to a veterinary hospital. Time is of the essence.

Uncomplicated gastric dilatation is relieved by passing a long rubber or plastic tube through the dog's mouth into the stomach. This is also the quickest way to confirm a diagnosis of bloat. As the tube enters the dog's stomach, there should be a rush of air and fluid from the tube, bringing relief. The stomach is then washed out. The dog should not be allowed to eat or drink for the first 36 hours, and will need to be supported with intravenous fluids. If symptoms do not return, the diet can be gradually restored.

Passing a stomach tube is a procedure normally done by a veterinarian. In extreme circumstances when professional help is not available, you may be asked to perform the procedure at home. If you live in a remote location where fast access to veterinary services is limited, you may wish to acquire a stomach tube and add it to your home emergency medical kit.

To pass a stomach tube, first mark the tube by measuring the distance from the nose to the first rib. Then, lubricate the tube with K-Y or petroleum jelly. Insert

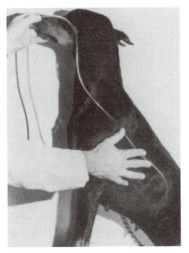

Before passing a tube into the stomach, the tube is marked by measuring the distance from the nose to the first rib.

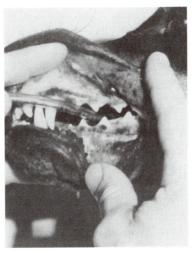

The tube is inserted in back of the canine teeth and advanced to the level of the mark.

the tube behind one of the canine teeth and advance it into the throat until the dog begins to swallow. If the dog gags, continue to advance the tube. If the dog coughs, the tube has entered the windpipe. Withdraw the tube a few inches and start again. *If the tube will not pass into the stomach, discontinue further attempts,* as it is possible to harm the dog.

Being able to pass a tube does not always rule out volvulus. Occasionally the tube passes even though the stomach is twisted. A diagnosis of dilatation or volvulus is best confirmed by X-rays of the abdomen. Dogs with simple dilatation have a large volume of gas in the stomach, but the gas pattern is normal. Dogs with volvulus have a "double bubble" gas pattern.

Emergency therapy is directed toward correcting shock and dehydration with intravenous fluids and corticosteroids. Antibiotics may be indicated to control infection. Ventricular arrhythmias are common. They require heart monitoring and the use of anti-arrhythmic drugs.

If the dog has a volvulus, emergency surgery is required as soon as the dog is able to tolerate the anesthetic. The goals are to reposition the stomach and spleen, or to remove the spleen and part of the stomach if these organs have undergone necrosis. Future recurrence can often be prevented by suturing the wall of the stomach to the abdominal wall (a procedure called gastropexy). This important step keeps the stomach in position and prevents it from twisting.

Preventing Bloat

Dogs that respond to non-surgical treatment have a 70 percent chance of having another episode of bloat. Some of these episodes can be prevented by following these practices:

- Divide the day's ration into three equal feedings.
- Restrict access to water for one hour before and after meals.
- Never let your dog drink a large amount of water all at once.
- Avoid strenuous exercise on a full stomach.
- Be aware of the early signs and seek prompt veterinary attention whenever you suspect bloat.

The Small and Large Bowel

Problems in the small and large bowel are associated with three common symptoms: diarrhea, constipation and passing blood. Diarrhea is by far the most common. Diarrhea in puppies is discussed in *Dehydration* in Chapter 17.

CAUSES OF DIARRHEA

Diarrhea is the passage of loose, unformed stools. In most cases there is a large volume of stool and an increased number of bowel movements. The two most common causes of diarrhea in dogs are dietary indiscretion and intestinal parasites. Many canine infectious diseases are also associated with acute diarrhea.

Food takes about eight hours to pass through the small intestine. During passage, the bulk of the food and 80 percent of the water is absorbed. The colon concentrates the remainder. At the end, a well-formed stool is evacuated. A normal stool contains no mucus, blood or undigested food.

With rapid transit through the bowel, food arrives at the rectum in a liquid state, resulting in a loose, unformed bowel movement. This type of rapid transit accounts for the majority of temporary diarrhea in dogs.

Dietary indiscretion is a common cause of rapid transit. Dogs are natural scavengers, and tend to eat many indigestible substances including garbage and decayed food, dead animals, grass, wild and ornamental plants, and pieces of plastic, wood, paper and other foreign materials. Many of these are irritating to the stomach as well as to the bowel, and are partially eliminated through vomiting.

Food intolerance can also cause rapid transit. Foods that some dogs seem unable to tolerate can include beef, pork, chicken, horsemeat, fish, eggs, spices, corn, wheat, soy, gravies, salts, spices, fats, and some commercial dog foods. Note that food intolerance is not the same as *food allergy* (discussed in Chapter 4), which causes dermatitis but rarely causes diarrhea.

Some adult dogs are unable to digest milk and milk by-products because of *lactase deficiency*. Lactase is an intestinal enzyme that breaks down the lactose in milk into small-chain sugars. Undigested lactose cannot be absorbed and remains in the bowel and holds water with it. This increases motility and causes large-volume diarrhea.

Intestinal parasites are a common cause of acute and chronic diarrhea in puppies and adults. The greatest problems are caused by roundworms, hookworms, whipworms, threadworms and giardia.

Diarrhea is a common side effect of many drugs and medications, particularly the *NSAIDs*, which include aspirin. Heart preparations, some dewormers and most antibiotics also can cause diarrhea.

Dogs can experience diarrhea when they're excited or upset—for example, when they're going to the veterinary hospital or a dog show. In fact, any sudden change in a dog's diet or living circumstances may cause emotional diarrhea.

In trying to figrue out the cause of a diarrhea, it is important to decide whether the diarrhea originates in the small bowel or the large bowel. The characteristics of the diarrhea, as well as the condition of the dog, will help to make this determination. The chart below details what to look for.

Characteristics of Diarrhea

	Likely Cause	Likely Location
Color		
Yellow or greenish	Rapid transit	Small bowel
Black, tarry	Upper GI bleeding	Stomach or small bowel
Red blood or clots	Lower GI bleeding	Colon clots
Pasty, light	Lack of bile	Liver
Large, gray, rancid	Inadequate digestion or absorption	Small bowel
Consistency		
Watery	Rapid transit	Small bowel
Foamy	Bacterial infection	Small bowel
Greasy, often with oily hair around the anus	Malabsorption	Small bowel, pancreas
Glistening or jellylike	Contains mucus	Colon
Odor		
Foodlike, or smelling like sour milk	Rapid transit and inadequate digestion or absorption (suggests overfeeding, especially in puppies)	Small bowel
Rancid or foul	Inadequate digestion with fermentation	Small bowel, pancreas

continues

Characteristics of Diarrhea

	Likely Cause	Likely Location
Frequency		
Several small stools in an hour, with straining	Colitis	Colon
Three or four large stools a day	Inadequate digestion or absorption	Small bowel, pancreas
Condition of the dog		
Weight loss	Inadequate digestion or absorption	Small bowel, pancreas
No weight loss, normal appetite	Large bowel disorder	Colon
Vomiting	Enteritis	Small bowel, rarely colon

Diarrhea can be classified as acute or chronic, depending on its duration. Acute diarrhea comes on suddenly and is over in a short period. Chronic diarrhea often comes on gradually and persists for three weeks or longer—or has an episodic pattern of recurrence.

Chronic diarrhea requires veterinary investigation. Routine tests include stool examinations for parasites (hookworms, whipworms, giardia), bacteria (salmonella, camphylobacter, clostridia) and occasionally fungi (histoplasmosis, aspergillosis, candida). A number of immune assays and fecal absorption tests are available for diagnosing maldigestion and malabsorption syndromes.

Colonoscopy with direct visualization of the interior of the colon is an important diagnostic test for large bowel diarrhea. Liquid stool can be aspirated for culture and *cytology*, and biopsies taken of the bowel wall or any suspicious lesions. *Gastroscopy* with biopsy of the duodenum and sampling of small bowel secretions helps in diagnosing small bowel diarrhea.

HOME TREATMENT OF DIARRHEA

Diarrhea that does not cause dehydration can be treated at home. Adult dogs with no fever will drink enough water to remain hydrated if moderate to severe diarrhea does not persist for more than 24 hours. Young puppies and elderly dogs with acute diarrhea are at risk for dehydration and should be seen by a veterinarian.

Acute Diarrhea

The most important step in treating acute diarrhea is to rest the GI tract by withholding all food for 24 hours. The dog should be encouraged to drink as much water as he wants. With persistent diarrhea, consider giving a supplemental electrolyte solution such as Pedialyte, available over-the-counter in pharmacies and grocery stores. Dilute it one-half with water and add it to the dog's drinking bowl. If the dog won't drink the electrolyte solution, offer water only.

With persistent diarrhea, an antidiarrheal drug is a good way to slow intestinal motility. Pepto-Bismol and Kaopectate are safe and effective when used as directed (see *Common Drugs for Home Veterinary Use* in Chapter 20).

Acute diarrhea usually responds within 24 hours to intestinal rest. Start the dog out on an easily digestible diet that's low in fat. Examples are boiled hamburger (one part drained meat to two parts cooked rice) and boiled chicken with the skin removed. Cooked white rice, cottage cheese, cooked macaroni and soft-boiled eggs are other easily digestible foods. Feed three or four small meals a day for the first two days. Then slowly switch the diet back to the dog's regular food.

Obtain immediate veterinary care if:

- The diarrhea continues for more than 24 hours.
- The stool contains blood or is black and tarry.
- The diarrhea is accompanied by vomiting.
- The dog appears weak or depressed, or has a fever.

Chronic Diarrhea

The first step is to find and remove the underlying cause. Diarrhea resulting from a change in diet can be corrected by switching back to the old diet and then making step-by-step changes to pinpoint the cause. When *lactase deficiency* is suspected, eliminate milk and dairy products from the diet, particularly as they are not required for adult dogs.

Diarrhea caused by overeating (characterized by large, bulky, unformed stools) can be controlled by tailoring the diet more accurately to the caloric needs of the dog and feeding the daily ration in three equal meals.

Chronic, intermittent diarrhea that persists for more than three weeks requires veterinary attention.

INFLAMMATORY BOWEL DISEASE

This is a group of diseases of the small and large intestine characterized by chronic and protracted diarrhea, malabsorption, weight loss, anemia and malnutrition. They are all treatable, but seldom cured. In each case a different type of inflammatory cell is found in large numbers in the lining of the small and/or large intestine. These cells distinguish the specific diseases. Diagnosis is made by endoscopy and biopsy of the bowel wall, or by exploratory surgery.

Lymphocytic-Plasmacytic Enterocolitis

This is the most common inflammatory bowel disease in dogs. LPE has been associated with giardiasis, food allergy and overgrowth of intestinal bacteria. Lymphocytes and plasma cells are the target cells seen on biopsy. Certain breeds are predisposed, suggesting a genetic influence. They are the Basenji, Soft Coated Wheaton Terrier and Chinese Shar-Pei. In the Basenji, the disease is known to be related to an immune disorder.

LPE produces a small bowel–type diarrhea. Vomiting is common. Involvement of the colon produces signs of *colitis*.

Hypoallergenic diets cause partial or complete resolution of symptoms in some dogs. Antibiotics are used to treat bacterial overgrowth and giardiasis. Immuno-suppressant drugs such as azathioprine (Imuran) and/or prednisone are used if other treatments are not successful.

Eosinophilic Enterocolitis

This is a relatively uncommon form of inflammatory bowel disease. On biopsy, *eosinophils* may be found in the stomach, small intestine or colon, and an elevated eosinophil count may be present in the blood. Some cases are thought to be asso-ciated with food allergy or the tissue migration of roundworms and hookworms.

High-dose corticosteroids are used to treat this diesease. They are tapered off as symptoms respond. The dog should be tested for intestinal parasites and placed on a hypoallergenic diet.

Granulomatous (Regional) Enteritis

This is a rare disease, similar to Crohn's disease in humans. There is thickening and narrowing of the terminal small bowel due to inflammation of surrounding fat and lymph nodes. Macrophages, which are tissue white cells, are found on biopsy of the colon. The diarrhea is the chronic large-bowel type, containing mucus and blood. Biopsies are processed with special stains to exclude histoplasmosis and in-testinal tuberculosis.

Treatment involves the use of corticosteroids and immunosuppressive drugs to reduce inflammation and scarring. A course of metronidazole may be of benefit. A strictured bowel requires surgery.

Neutrophilic Enterocolitis

This inflammatory bowel disease produces acute and chronic large-bowel diarrhea. The inflammatory infiltrate is composed of mature white cells. Diagnosis is based on colon biopsy and stool cultures to exclude bacterial infection. Treatment in-volves the use of antibiotics and/or corticosteroids.

Histiocytic Ulcerative Colitis

This inflammatory bowel disease occurs almost exclusively in Boxers. Signs appear before age two. Affected dogs develop severe, unrelenting diarrhea containing mucus and blood. The diagnosis is based on colon biopsy. Treatment is similar to that described for lymphocytic-plasmacytic enterocolitis.

ACUTE INFECTIOUS ENTERITIS

Enteritis is an infection of the gastrointestinal tract characterized by the sudden onset of vomiting and diarrhea, rapid pulse, fever, apathy and depression. The vomitus and diarrhea may contain blood. Dehydration occurs rapidly. Dogs under one year of age and those over 10 are particularly susceptible to the effects of dehydration and shock.

The most common cause of infectious enteritis in dogs is *parvovirus* (see Chapter 3). Salmonella, *E. coli,* camphylobacter and other bacteria are also responsible for some cases.

The bacteria *Clostridium perfringens* produce a disease called *canine hemorrhagic gastroenteritis.* The disease begins suddenly with vomiting, followed in two to three hours by a profuse, bloody diarrhea. Small breeds, particularly Miniature Schnauzers and Toy Poodles, have a predisposition for hemorrhagic gastroenteritis.

Garbage poisoning and ingesting poisons and toxic chemicals produces signs and symptoms similar to those of acute enteritis. When diarrhea and vomiting occur together, the dog's condition is serious and warrants an immediate trip to the veterinarian.

Treatment: This is directed toward prompt replacement of fluids and electrolytes. Antibiotics effective against the causative bacteria may also be administered.

MALABSORPTION SYNDROME

Malabsorption is not a specific disease, but rather occurs as a consequence of some underlying small-bowel or pancreas disorder. In malabsorption syndrome, the dog either does not digest food or does not absorb the products of disgestion from the small intestine. Dogs suffering from malabsorption are underweight and malnourished despite a voracious appetite. Diarrhea occurs three or four times a day. The stools are typically large, rancid smelling and contain a great deal of fat. The hair around the anus may be oily or greasy.

Predisposing causes of malabsorption include *exocrine pancreatic insufficiency,* permanent damage to the intestinal mucosa following *infectious enteritis, inflammatory bowel disease* with inflamed or destroyed intestinal mucosa, surgical removal of a major portion of the small bowel, and primary diseases of the small intestine.

One primary disease of the small intestine is *idiopathic villous atrophy.* Villi are microscopic hairlike structures that make up the absorptive surface of the small bowel. In villous atrophy these structures are blunted and poorly developed. Idiopathic villous atrophy occurs most often in German Shepherd Dogs. A similar hereditary disease is *wheat-sensitive enteropathy,* described in Irish Setters in Great Britain.

Small intestinal bacterial overgrowth has been identified as another important cause of malabsorption. German Shepherd Dogs, Basenjis and Chinese Shar-Peis have an increased incidence. Affected dogs develop an abundant and abnormal bacterial flora in the small intestine, which causes foul-smelling diarrhea. Some cases have been associated with exocrine pancreatic insufficiency, inflammatory bowel disease or stagnant loops of bowel caused by intestinal surgery. In German Shepherd Dogs and Chinese Shar-Peis, the condition may be related to a specific immune deficiency. In the majority of cases the cause of the bacterial overgrowth is unknown.

In many cases the cause of malabsorption can be identified through special diagnostic tests, including stool analysis and intestinal biopsies.

Treatment: Treatment of is directed toward the specific disease. Dogs with villous atrophy are managed with gluten-free prescription diets. Small intestinal bacterial overgrowth usually responds to one or more courses of an oral broad-spectrum antibiotic. Treatment of *exocrine pancreatic insufficiency* is discussed elsewhere in this chapter (see page 271).

COLITIS

Colitis is an inflammation of the colon. It is responsible for about 50 percent of cases of chronic diarrhea in dogs. The signs of colitis are painful defecation, prolonged squatting and straining, breaking wind, and passing many small stools mixed with blood and mucus. These signs can easily be mistaken for constipation.

The usual cause of colitis is one of the *inflammatory bowel diseases* already discussed. *Whipworms* are another frequent cause. *Fungal colitis* is uncommon. It targets dogs with immune deficiency and lowered resistance. *Prototheca colitis* is a rare disease caused by an algae. It produces a severe form of colitis and can become systemic. Treatment has not been successful.

Irritable bowel syndrome describes a diarrhea motility disorder often associated with stress. It tends to occur in high-strung, nervous dogs. Dogs with irritable bowel syndrome have frequent small stools, often mixed with mucus. The diagnosis is based on exclusion of other causes of colitis. The problem can be helped by a high-fiber diet (see *Constipation*, page 257).

Colitis is diagnosed by *colonoscopy* and colon biopsy. Stool specimens are examined for parasites and fungi. Treatment is directed toward the underlying condition, often an inflammatory bowel disease.

INTESTINAL OBSTRUCTION (BLOCKED BOWEL)

Any problem that interferes with the passage of intestinal contents through the GI tract results in a blocked bowel. The most common cause is a *gastrointestinal foreign body*. The second most common cause is *intussusception*. This term describes a situation in which the bowel telescopes in upon itself, like a sock pulled inside out. Most cases of intussusception occur at the cecum, where the small bowel joins the colon. As the small bowel inverts into the cecum and colon, the lead point travels a considerable distance, dragging the small intestine after it. Intussusceptions generally occur in puppies and young dogs.

Other causes of intestinal obstruction are tumors and strictures, adhesions following abdominal surgery, and navel and groin hernias that trap loops of bowel in the hernia sac.

An intestinal obstruction can be partial or complete. Partial obstructions cause intermittent vomiting and/or diarrhea, which tends to occur over several weeks. Complete obstructions produce sudden abdominal pain and vomiting that continues without relief. When the blockage is in the upper small bowel, the vomiting may be projectile. Blockages in the lower GI tract cause abdominal distension and the vomiting of brown, fecal-smelling material. Dogs with complete obstruction pass no stool or gas.

Intestinal *strangulation* occurs when the obstruction interferes with the blood supply to the bowel. Within hours the bowel becomes gangrenous. The dog's condition deteriorates rapidly (see *Peritonitis*, page 256).

The diagnosis of intestinal obstruction is made by abdominal X-rays showing distended gas-filled loops of bowel.

Treatment: This involves surgical exploration and relief of the blockage. Gangrenous bowel is resected back to viable bowel, and intestinal continuity is restored with end-to-end suturing of the bowel.

GASTROINTESTINAL FOREIGN BODIES

Dogs have been known to swallow bones, toys, sticks, stones, pins and needles, wood splinters, cloth, rubber balls, rawhide, leather, string, peach pits and other objects. With string, one end often knots up while the other gets caught in food. Tension on the string then causes it to cut through the wall of the bowel.

The esophagus in the dog is larger than the outlet of the stomach. Thus dogs may swallow objects too large to pass out of the stomach. Gastric foreign bodies are therefore associated with *chronic gastritis* and episodes of *gastric outflow obstruction*.

If an object makes it into the small intestine, it usually passes through the entire GI tract without causing problems. Those that do obstruct usually do so at the ileocecal valve or in the colon and rectum. Foreign bodies in the rectum cause *anorectal obstructions*. Sharp objects such as pins, splinters and bone chips can lodge anywhere in the GI tract and obstruct or perforate the bowel, causing *intestinal obstruction* or *peritonitis*.

Unless it also causes ingestion, a swallowed foreign body will go unnoticed until it produces symptoms. Many foreign bodies can be seen on X-rays of the abdomen.

Treatment: Foreign bodies producing symptoms should be removed. This usually involves abdominal surgery. Gastric foreign bodies can sometimes be removed through an endoscope.

FLATULENCE (PASSING GAS)

Dogs that pass large amounts of gas often embarrass or distress their owners. The most common cause of flatulence is swallowing large amounts of air while gulping food. The next is eating highly fermentable foods such as onions, beans, cauliflower, cabbage and soybeans. Flatulence also occurs with *malabsorption syndromes*. The excess gas is related to incomplete digestion of carbohydrates.

A sudden bout of flatulence accompanied by abdominal discomfort, loss of appetite or diarrhea, and is an indication to seek veterinary attention.

Treatment: Change the dog's ration to a highly digestible low-fiber diet, and avoid giving table scraps. Feed three small meals instead of one large meal to keep the dog from gulping food and swallowing air. If this does not stop the flatulence, consider switching to a prescription diet such as Hill's i/d or k/d, available through your veterinarian. If further treatment is desired, simethicone can be given to absorb intestinal gas. Simethicone is available in over-the-counter preparations for people in liquid and tablet formulations. The dose for dogs is 40 mg once or twice a day after meals.

EATING STOOLS (COPROPHAGIA)

Coprophagia is the name given to the habit of eating stools—either the dog's own or some other animal's. Cats' stools seem particularly tempting to dogs.

Most dogs with coprophagia are well nourished and show no evidence of a nutrient deficiency that would account for the compulsion to eat stools. These individuals may have acquired a taste preference for stools beginning in puppyhood. Other reasons sometimes suggested stool-eating include boredom, unresolved conflict and confinement in close quarters, such as a kennel. Once established, the habit is difficult to break.

A minority of dogs have a medical reason for coprophagia. Dogs with *malabsorption syndrome*, in particular, have a ravenous appetite and eat stools in an attempt to acquire additional calories. Coprophagia has also been described with corticosteroid therapy, Cushing's syndrome, diabetes mellitus, hyperthyroidism and intestinal parasites.

Stool-eating is undesirable, not only for aesthetic reasons but because ingesting animal feces can bring in intestinal parasites. Dogs that eat large amounts of horse manure can develop severe vomiting and diarrhea.

Treatment: Veterinary examination is warranted to check for parasites and other medical problems. Management included removing stools from the environment as quickly as possible, making cat litter boxes inaccessible to dogs, and distracting the dog by providing extra exercise and interaction with pets and humans.

A number of ingredients have been suggested as additives to the dog's food in order to improve digestion or render the stools unappetizing. A partial list includes meat tenderizers, crushed pineapple, Viokase, B-complex vitamins, sulfur, glutamic acid, monosodium glutamate, sauerkraut and canned pumpkin. Forbid is a frequently recommended product made from alfalfa that gives the stool a disagreeable odor and taste. There are no scientific studies to confirm or deny the effectiveness of any of these additives, but anecdotal reports suggest they may be of benefit in some cases.

PERITONITIS

Inflammation of the cavity containing the abdominal organs is called peritonitis. Peritonitis occurs when digestive enzymes, food, stool, bacteria, blood, bile or urine leak into the peritoneal cavity. Common causes are bloat, ruptured ulcers, perforations caused by gastrointestinal foreign bodies, intestinal obstructions, rupture of the uterus, rupture of the bladder, acute pancreatitis, penetrating wounds of the abdomen, and breakdown of suture lines following intestinal surgery.

Peritonitis can be localized or diffuse. In localized peritonitis an apron of fat (the omentum) seals off and contains the source of contamination. In diffuse or generalized peritonitis, the infection spreads rapidly throughout the abdominal cavity.

Dogs with generalized peritonitis have severe abdominal pain and are reluctant to move. Vomiting is common. Pressing on the abdomen causes the dog to groan. The abdomen has a tucked-up appearance and feels rigid or boardlike, owing to reflex spasm of the abdominal wall muscles.

Dehydration, infection and shock ensue rapidly. The pulse is weak and thready, breathing is rapid and labored, and the gums are cool and pale. The *capillary refill time* is prolonged over three seconds. Collapse and death occur in a matter of hours.

Treatment: Immediate veterinary treatment is essential for survival. Intravenous fluids and broad-spectrum antibiotics are given to treat dehydration and shock. Surgical exploration is needed as soon as the dog is able to tolerate a general anesthetic.

After the source of the peritonitis is repaired, the peritoneal cavity is repeatedly flushed to remove all foreign material. The surgeon may decide to pack the abdominal wound open with gauze pads to facilitate drainage of infected peritoneal fluid. An incision left open can be closed at a later date.

Localized peritonitis may respond to fluid replacement and antibiotics alone.

CONSTIPATION

Constipation means absent, infrequent or difficult defecation. Most healthy dogs have one or two stools a day. This varies with the individual and the diet. A day or two without stools is not a cause for concern if the stools remain normal in size and pass without difficulty. But when feces are retained in the colon for two or three days, they become dry and hard, and require forceful straining to pass.

Note that straining also occurs with *colitis, obstructed bladder* and *anorectal obstructions*. It is important to be sure the dog is not suffering from one of these other problems before treating him for constipation. Colitis, in particular, is often confused with constipation. Remember that a dog with colitis will pass many small stools containing mucus and/or blood.

Causes of Constipation

Many middle-aged and older dogs are prone to constipation. A common predisposing cause is failure to drink enough water. With mild dehydration, water is withdrawn from the colon, which dehydrates the feces.

Ingesting foreign materials, such as bone chips, hair, grass, cellulose, cloth, paper and other substances, is a well-recognized cause of acute and chronic constipation. The indigestible material mixes with feces to form rock-like masses in the colon. Many drugs commonly used in dogs cause constipation as a secondary side effect. Discuss this possible correlation with your veterinarian. Hypothyroidism is an occasional cause of chronic constipation.

The urge to defecate can also be voluntarily overridden. Dogs develop such inhibitions during house-training. When left alone in the house for long periods, they often override the urge to defecate. Dogs also may be reluctant to empty their bowels when hospitalized, boarded or taken on a trip.

Dogs with constipation of recent onset should be examined by a veterinarian. Other reasons to seek veterinary consultation are painful defecation, straining during defecation and passing blood or mucus.

Treating Constipation

Eliminate or control predisposing causes. Be sure to provide access to clean, fresh water at all times. Constipation associated with ingesting foreign materials such as bone chips can be corrected by eliminating the source and giving dog biscuits to chew on instead. Older dogs with reduced bowel activity can be helped by soaking the kibble with equal parts of water and letting the mixture stand for 20 minutes.

Dogs that voluntarily retain their stool can be helped by providing frequent opportunities for the dog to eliminate. Take the dog outside several times a day, preferably to an area where he is accustomed to going. A mild laxative may be needed when the dog is traveling.

Laxatives

There are a number of laxatives available for treating constipation. *Osmotic laxatives* draw water into the intestine and liquefy the feces. Products containing lactulose prescribed by your veterinarian are among the safest and most effective. A mild osmotic laxative effect can also be obtained by adding milk to the diet in amounts that exceed the capacity of the intestinal enzyme lactase to break down lactose into absorbable sugars. The lactose molecule pulls fluid into the bowel and stimulates intestinal motility.

The mild saline laxative Phillips Milk of Magnesia (magnesium hydroxide) acts in a manner similar to osmotic laxatives. (See *Common Drugs for Home Veterinary Use* in Chapter 20.) Magnesium hydroxide is contraindicated in dogs with kidney failure.

Stimulant laxatives increase the force of intestinal peristalsis. They are highly effective in treating constipation, but repeated use can interfere with colon function. A commonly used stimulant laxative is bisacodyl (Dulcolax). The dose for dogs is five to 20 mg per day.

These laxatives are used for *treating* constipation. They are not the laxatives of choice for *preventing* constipation and should not be used on a daily basis. Consult your veterinarian before you give your dog any laxative.

Preventing Constipation

This is best accomplished through good hydration, a non-constipating diet, regular exercise and the adding fiber to the diet. Nearly all dogs can benefit from a high-fiber diet. A convenient way to provide the fiber is to feed a commercial food formulated for senior dogs. You can also obtain a high-fiber diet, such as Hill's Prescription w/d, from your veterinarian.

Another way to provide additional fiber is to add a *bulk-forming laxative* daily to the dog's food. Bulk laxatives soften the feces and promote more frequent elimination. Commonly used bulk laxatives are unprocessed wheat bran (one to five tablespoons per day) and Metamucil (one to five teaspoons per day). Bulk laxatives can be used indefinitely without causing problems.

Emollient laxatives containing docusate are indicated when the feces are dry and hard, but should not be used if the dog is dehydrated. Examples are Colace (50 to 200 mg per day), Surfak (100 to 240 mg per day) and Dialose (100 mg per day). These products promote water absorption into the feces, thereby softening the stool. They can be used daily.

Mineral oil is a lubricant laxative that facilitates the passage of hard stool through the anal canal. However, mineral oil interferes with the absorption of fat-soluble vitamins, so daily or frequent administration may cause vitamin deficiency. Mineral oil also reacts adversely with docusate and thus should not be used in conjunction with Colace and the other emollient laxatives. The best way to give mineral oil is to add it once or twice a week to the dog's meal at a dose of 10 to 50 mL, depending on the weight of the dog. *Never administer mineral oil by syringe because it is tasteless and can be inhaled into the lungs.*

FECAL IMPACTIONS

A fecal impaction is a mass of hard stool in the rectum and colon. There may be a predisposing condition such as an enlarged prostate that compresses the rectal canal (see *Anorectal Obstructions*, page 260).

Dogs with fecal impactions pass little or no stool despite repeated and forceful straining, are lethargic, have no appetite, experience abdominal distension and vomiting, and may have a hunched-up appearance. Digital rectal examination reveals a large tubular mass.

Treatment: Veterinary examination and treatment is needed. A severe fecal impaction requires rehydration with intravenous fluids prior to removal. Most will need to be removed under general anesthesia using finger extraction and forceps.

Mild fecal impactions may respond to a combination of an osmotic or stimulant laxative (see *Constipation*, above) and a small enema. A safe and effective small enema is warm tap water administered at 2.5 to 5.0 mL per pound of body weight. Tap water enemas can be repeated every few hours.

Tap water enemas are given through a rubber catheter connected to a plastic syringe or enema bag. Lubricate the tip of the catheter and insert it one to two inches into the rectum. Administer the enema. After the enema has been expelled, administer 10 to 20 ml mineral oil (5 to 10 mL for a small dog) through the catheter to facilitate passage of the remaining stool.

Packaged saline laxative enemas containing sodium phosphate (such as Fleet) also are effective for treating constipation and fecal impactions. Phosphate, however, has the potential to cause toxicity in small dogs and dogs with kidney disease, and should not be used in these individuals. Fleet enemas are safe to use in midsize and large dogs with normal kidney function. The recommended dose is one-half unit of a Fleet enema, or one unit of a Fleet Children's enema. Do not repeat.

Fleet enemas come in plastic bottles equipped with nozzles. Lubricate the tip of the nozzle and insert it far enough into the anal canal to retain the fluid. Squeeze the bottle to administer the enema.

The Anus and Rectum

The signs of anorectal disease are pain on defecation, straining to pass stool, rectal bleeding, scooting and biting and licking at the rear. Dogs with anorectal pain often attempt to defecate from a standing position.

Bleeding from the anal canal is recognized by finding blood on the outside of the stool rather than mixed in with it.

Scooting is rubbing the bottom along the ground. It indicates anal itching. Anal itching can be caused by flea bites, inflammation of the anal skin, anal sac disease, roundworms and tapeworms.

ANORECTAL OBSTRUCTIONS

A common cause of an anorectal obstruction is an enlarged prostate that bulges backward and compresses the rectum. This occurs in older male dogs. Foreign bodies that pass through the upper GI tract may obstruct the rectum. Pelvic fractures that have undergone malunion can narrow the rectum, causing a mechanical blockage. Boston Terriers and Bulldogs with *screw tails* often have a rigid extension of the tail that extends down upon the anal canal, pinching it against the pelvic floor. Other cause of blockage are fecal impactions, matted stool around the anus, rectal strictures, perianal gland tumors, perianal hernias, and rectal polyps and cancers.

Rectal strictures result from perianal infections, fistulas and surgical attempts to treat them. *Perineal hernias* are bulges that occur alongside the anus. They weaken the muscular support of the rectum and interfere with the mechanics of elimination. The bulge becomes larger as the dog strains. Perineal hernias occur in elderly sexually intact males.

The principal sign of anorectal obstruction is straining to defecate. The stool may be flat or ribbonlike. The dog may or may not pass blood. The diagnosis is made by digital rectal examination and occasionally by colonoscopy.

Treatment: It varies with the cause of the obstruction. Most foreign bodies can be removed by digital extraction under sedation or anesthesia. Neutering is the treatment of choice for an *enlarged prostate* (see Chapter 14). Perineal hernias are treated by hernia repair plus neutering, or by neutering alone. Strictures are corrected through surgery. Perianal gland tumors and polyps and cancers are discussed later in this chapter. Constipation associated with the screw tail usually requires surgical correction of the screw tail.

For conditions for which surgical treatment is not feasible, the goal is to maintain normal defecation by using laxatives and stool-softening diets (see *Constipation*, above).

MATTED STOOL AROUND THE ANUS (PSEUDOCONSTIPATION)

Pseudoconstipation is caused by hair around the anus that becomes densely matted with dried stool and forms a barrier to defecation. It occurs in long-haired dogs, usually following a bout of diarrhea. The skin becomes irritated, painful and infected. This introduces an element of voluntary retention.

Dogs with pseudoconstipation are restless and bite and lick at the anus. Other signs are scooting, whining and attempting to defecate while standing. There is an extremely offensive odor.

Treatment: Clip away the matted hair to remove the cause of the blockage. If the area is painful, this is best done under a general anesthetic by your veterinarian. Keep the area clean and apply a topical ointment such as triple antibiotic or Cortaid to the inflamed skin. If the dog strains and does not eliminate easily, see *Constipation*, above. Dogs prone to pseudoconstipation should have the hair around the anus regularly clipped short.

PROCTITIS (INFLAMED ANUS AND RECTUM)

Inflammation of the anal skin is caused by pseudoconstipation discussed above. Repeated bouts of diarrhea, especially in puppies, can cause an inflamed anus. Other causes are insect bites and worms. Irritation of the anal canal is caused by the passage of bone chips and hard stools.

Straining is a common sign of proctitis. Other signs are scooting, licking and biting at the rear.

Treatment: Irritated anal skin can be soothed by applying an ointment such as that described for *pseudoconstipation*. Treat constipation and diarrhea as described earlier in this chapter.

PROTRUSION OF ANAL TISSUE (ANORECTAL PROLAPSE)

Anorectal prolapse is the protrusion of rectal tissue through the anus. It occurs as a sequel to forceful and prolonged straining. Conditions associated with forceful straining include severe constipation, fecal impaction, diarrhea, an anorectal obstruction, labor and delivery, and an obstructed bladder.

A *mucosal prolapse* is confined to the lining of the anal canal. It appears as a red, swollen, doughnut-shaped ring of tissue. This might be mistaken for prolapsed hemorrhoids, but dogs don't get hemorrhoids. In a *complete rectal prolapse*, a segment of rectum several inches long protrudes through the anus, appearing as a pink or red cylindrical mass.

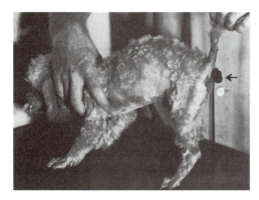

Complete rectal prolapse.

Treatment: A mucosal prolapse disappears spontaneously when the underlying cause of straining is corrected. The dog should be placed on a stool softener such as Colace and fed a highly digestible, *low-residue* diet until symptoms resolve.

A rectal prolapse requires veterinary management to reduce the prolapse. A temporary purse-string suture may be taken around the anal opening to prevent immediate recurrence. If the prolapsed bowel is necrotic (the tissue is dead), it will have to be surgically removed. Bowel continuity is restored through end-to-end suturing.

MALFORMATION OF THE ANUS

Imperforate anus is a rare congenital condition in which the anus, or the anus and rectum, do not develop. In female puppies there may be a passage between the colon and vagina called *rectovaginal fistula*. Newborn puppies without an anus are unable to pass gas or meconium—the dark green fecal material that is usually excreted at birth.

Imperforate anus in a newborn puppy.

Abdominal distention and vomiting appear during the first 24 hours. If the colon opens into the vagina, gas and stool may pass out through the vulva, temporarily averting a bowel obstruction.

Treatment: Imperforate anus and rectovaginal fistula require surgical correction for survival.

ANAL SACS

The dog has two anal sacs or glands located at five and seven o'clock in reference to the circumference of the anus. They can be seen by drawing down on the skin of the lower part of the anus and looking in those locations.

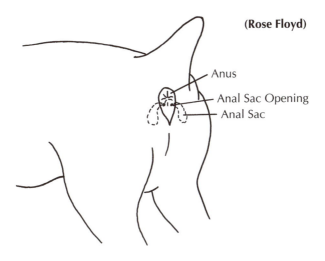

(Rose Floyd)

Anus
Anal Sac Opening
Anal Sac

THE ANAL SACS

The anal sacs are similar to scent glands. In skunks they serve a defensive purpose. In dogs they produce an odor that identifies the individual and marks the stool to establish territory. This is why dogs greet each other by sniffing at the rear.

The anal sacs are emptied by the pressure of stool passing through the anus. They can also be emptied by forceful contractions of the anal sphincter—something that may happen when a dog is frightened or upset.

How to Empty the Anal Sacs

Manually emptying the anal sacs is called expressing them. It is not necessary to express the anal sacs unless the dog has an anal sac disease, or when frequent malodor poses a problem. Begin by putting on a disposable latex or plastic surgical glove. Raise the dog's tail and locate the openings as shown in the figure above. If they're full, the anal sacs can be felt as small, firm lumps in the perianal area at the five and seven o'clock positions.

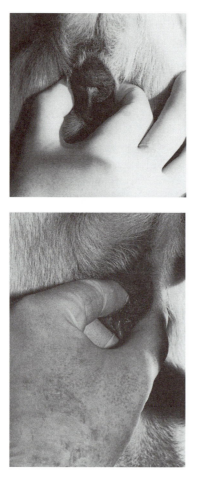

The anal sacs can be emptied by squeezing the skin surrounding the sacs between the thumb and forefinger.

When impacted, the anal sacs are best emptied with a finger in the anal canal and a thumb on the outside.

Grasp the skin surrounding the sacs between your thumb and forefinger and squeeze. When an anal sac is impacted (blocked), it usually is best to empty the sacs with a finger in the anal canal and a thumb on the outside.

As the sac empties, you may smell a strong odor. Wipe the secretions with a damp cloth. Normal secretions are liquid and brown. If the discharge is yellow, bloody or pus-like, the sac is infected and you should seek veterinary attention.

Anal Sac Disease

Anal sac disease is a cycle that begins with impaction and progresses through infection to abscess and rupture.

Anal Sac Impaction. Impaction is the accumulation of pasty secretions in the anal sacs. The sacs become distended and mildly tender. The expressed secretions are thick and dark brown or grayish brown. The sacs become impacted when they don't empty completely. This may be due to insufficient pressure on the sacs during defecation because of small, soft stools; inadequate sphincter pressure; or blockage of the openings by thick dry secretions. Impactions tend to occur most often in small-breed dogs.

Treatment: Impaction is treated by manually expressing the secretions. Dogs with recurrent anal sac impactions should have their sacs emptied at regular intervals. Place the dog on a high-fiber diet or a bulk laxative to increase the size of the stools (see *Constipation* on page 257).

Anal Sac Infection. Anal sac infection (*sacculitis*) complicates impaction. Infection is recognized by a painful swelling on one or both sides of the anus. The secretions are thin, yellowish or blood-tinged. The dog will scoot, lick and bite at the rear.

Treatment: Begin by expressing the sacs. Repeat in one to two weeks. For recurrent infection, empty the sacs weekly. After emptying, an antibiotic is instilled into the sacs. This procedure is difficult to perform and should be done by your veterinarian.

Anal Sac Abscess. Abscess is recognized by fever and the signs of anal sac infection described above. The swelling, usually on one side, is at first red, then later turns a deep purple. Unlike anal sac infection, the swelling of an abscess cannot be reduced by emptying the sac. An abscess often ruptures through the adjacent skin, producing a draining tract.

An anal sac abscess located below and to the left of the anus. The abscess must be incised and drained.

Treatment: If the abscess has not ruptured spontaneously, it should be lanced when it becomes soft and fluidlike. The cavity is flushed repeatedly and the dog is placed on an oral antibiotic. Your veterinarian may ask you to flush the cavity twice a day with a topical antiseptic such as dilute Betadine solution for one to two weeks.

Dogs with recurrent anal sac infections should have their anal sacs surgically removed. This is best done during a period between infections.

PERIANAL FISTULAS

Fistulas are draining tracts in the perianal skin caused by infection of the skin glands in and around the anus. Initially they appear as draining puncture holes. Later they coalesce to form open sores and draining tracts. The discharge is foul-smelling. Occasionally fistulas connect internally with the anal sacs.

Perianal fistulas occur most often in German Shepherd Dogs, but are found in Irish Setters, English Setters, Labrador Retrievers and other breeds. There may be an association with breeds that have a low-slung, broad-based tail.

Symptoms are similar to those of anal sac infection. There may be a foul-smelling discharge. The diagnosis is made by visual inspection of the perianal area.

Treatment: Surgery is the most effective treatment. Perianal fistulas are difficult to cure and are associated with postoperative complications and recurrences. Early treatment offers the best chance for success.

RECTAL POLYPS AND CANCERS

Polyps are benign, grapelike growths that occur in the rectum and may protrude from the anus. They are not common, but when present they should be removed.

Adenocarcinoma is the most common malignant colorectal growth, followed by *lymphoma*. Adenocarcinomas are slow growing gastrointestinal tumors found predominantly in older dogs, usually in the lower colon and rectum. These tumors can obstruct, ulcerate and bleed. The diagnosis is made by colonoscopy and biopsy of the tumor. Surgical resection is the treatment of choice for colon and rectal cancers. Lymphomas can be treated with chemotherapy.

Cancers can also arise from the anal sacs. This occurs primarily in older females. *Anal sac adenocarcinomas* have the unique property of producing parathyroid hormone, and thus may be associated with a severe form of hypercalcemia (see *Hyperparathyroidism*, Chapter 13). These tumors vary in size from small lumps that are barely palpable to large masses protruding from the rectum. Anal sac adenocarcinomas are best treated by surgical excision. Chemotherapy is a consideration for large tumors.

PERIANAL GLAND TUMORS (ADENOMAS AND ADENOCARCINOMAS)

These common tumors, often multiple, arise from glands located around the anus and at the base of the tail. They occur primarily in intact males over seven years of age, and require the presence of testosterone. Adenomas can be recognized by their typical location and rounded, rubbery appearance. A minority undergo malignant transformation to adenocarcinoma. These cancerous neoplasms can grow to a large size, break through the skin, become secondarily infected and cause anorectal obstruction. Metastases to the lungs occur frequently.

Perianal gland adenocarcinoma, locally advanced with spread to the abdomen.

Treatment: The diagnosis is confirmed by tissue biopsy. For small tumors, this is best done by completely excising the tumor. If the tumor is found to be malignant, a chest X-ray should be taken to rule out metastatic spread.

Perianal gland tumors may regress completely following removal of the testicles. Thus neutering should be performed for all perianal tumors whether benign or malignant. Benign tumors should be removed with a rim of normal tissue. Malignant tumors should be removed as widely as possible at the time of neutering, providing the operation can be performed without causing rectal incontinence. Radiation and chemotherapy are other treatment options.

The Liver

The liver performs many vital functions, including synthesizing enzymes, proteins and metabolites; removing ammonia and other wastes from the bloodstream; manufacturing blood-clotting factors; and detoxifying the blood of drugs and poisons.

LIVER FAILURE

The early signs of liver disease are nonspecific. They include loss of appetite, weight loss and chronic intermittent vomiting and diarrhea. Vomiting is more common than diarrhea. Drinking and urinating more often than normal may be the first signs, and the principal reason for seeking medical attention.

In the early stages of liver disease the liver swells and enlarges. As the disease progresses, the liver cells die and are replaced by scar tissue. The liver then becomes rubbery and firm. This condition is called *cirrhosis*. It is not reversible.

Eighty percent of liver cells must die before the liver begins to fail. The signs of liver failure are jaundice, hepatic encephalopathy, ascites, spontaneous bleeding and dependent edema.

Jaundice. With impaired liver function, bile accumulates in the blood and tissues, staining the tissues yellow. This can be seen in the yellow appearance of the white of the eyes and in the mucous membranes of the gums and tongue. Bile excreted in the urine turns the urine dark brown (the color of tea).

Hepatic Encephalopathy. This is a type of brain inflammation caused by high levels of ammonia and other toxins in the blood. Ammonia is a by-product of protein metabolism, and is normally removed from the bloodstream by a healthy liver. When the liver is sick, ammonia accumulates to toxic levels and exerts a poisonous effect on the brain.

Dogs with hepatic encephalopathy develop incoordination, sporadic weakness, disorientation, head-pressing, behavioral changes, drooling, stupor and mental dullness. Symptoms tend to wax and wane. They become more severe after a high-protein meal. Seizures and coma occur when hepatic encephalopathy is advanced.

Ascites. Ascites is the accumulation of fluid in the abdomen. In liver disease, it is caused by low serum proteins and increased pressure in the veins that supply the liver. A dog with ascites has a swollen or bloated look. Thumping on the abdomen produces a dull, flat sound.

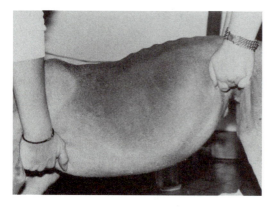

A swollen abdomen resulting from ascites.

Bleeding. Spontaneous bleeding occurs with advanced liver disease. Common sites of bleeding are the stomach, intestine and urinary tract. Blood may be noted in the vomitus, stools or urine. Punctate (pinhead-sized) hemorrhages may be seen on the gums. Bruises can appear under the lips and skin. Major blood loss from spontaneous bleeding is relatively uncommon, but uncontrollable bleeding can be a serious problem if the dog is injured or requires surgery.

Dependent Edema. Swelling of the abdominal wall and lower legs is related to malnutrition and low serum protein levels. It is not as common in liver disease as it is in congestive heart failure.

Treatment: Treatment of liver failure is directed toward treating the liver disease causing it.

CAUSES OF LIVER DISEASE

A number of diseases, chemicals, drugs and toxins can damage the liver. The liver is directly affected by infectious canine hepatitis and leptospirosis. It is frequently involved in heartworm infection, Cushing's syndrome and diabetes mellitus. Primary and metastatic tumors are a major cause of liver failure in dogs.

Chemicals known to produce liver toxicity include carbon tetrachloride, insecticides, and toxic amounts of lead, phosphorus, selenium, arsenic and iron. Drugs capable of damaging the liver include anesthetic gases, antibiotics, antifungals, dewormers, diuretics, analgesics (aspirin and Tylenol), anticonvulsants, testosterone preparations (Cheque Drops) and corticosteroids. Most drug reactions are associated with excessive dosage and/or prolonged usage.

A blockage of the bile duct by gallstones, liver flukes, tumors or pancreatitis is uncommon, but becomes a consideration when a dog has unexplained jaundice.

Liver Shunts. Liver shunts, also called *portosystemic shunts*, are abnormal veins that allow blood from the intestine to bypass the liver. Ammonia and other toxins are not metabolized or removed from the circulation, resulting in signs of hepatic encephalopathy.

The majority of portosystemic shunts are congenital. Multiple shunts outside the liver may be congenital but are more often caused by cirrhosis. Miniature Schnauzers and Yorkshire Terriers appear to be at increased risk for congenital shunts that develop outside the liver. Large-breed dogs are at increased risk for shunts inside the liver that occur because of a fetal vein that normally closes at birth fails to do so.

Most dogs with congenital liver shunts develop symptoms of hepatic encephalopathy by six months of age, although some dogs may not develop symptoms until middle age or older. The diagnosis is confirmed by X-ray studies where contrast dyes are injected into the liver circulation, and by bile acid assays. These studies are available at referral centers.

Idiopathic Chronic Hepatitis. This is not one disease, but a group of poorly understood liver diseases that culminate in cirrhosis. With the exception of copper-associated hepatitis, these diseases appear to have an autoimmune basis: The dog's immune system is somehow stimulated to manufacture antibodies against its own liver. This establishes an inflammatory process that progresses to liver failure. The basis for the autoimmune reaction is unknown.

Copper-Associated Hepatitis. Hepatitis related to high levels of copper occurs in the Doberman Pinscher, Bedlington Terrier, West Highland White Terrier and Skye Terrier. In Bedlingtons and Westies there is an inherited defect in copper metabolism that allows toxic concentrations of copper to accumulate in the liver.

In Dobermans, copper concentrations are increased in most but not all affected dogs. It is unclear in the Doberman (and Skye Terrier) whether high copper levels are the cause of the hepatitis or the result. Copper can accumulate in the liver as a consequence of hepatitis alone. As a rule, the higher the copper concentration, the more likely it is that copper is the cause. Genetic testing for copper toxicosis in Bedlington Terriers is available through the University of Pennsylvania.

Treatment: Blood tests, ultrasounds and CT scans provide useful information, but the only definitive test is biopsy of the liver. The prognosis for recovery depends on how long the dog has been ill, the extent of liver damage, and whether the disease can be surgically cured or controlled with medications.

Infectious diseases respond to treatment of the underlying condition. Drugs and poisons frequently exert temporary effects that reverse when the exposure is stopped.

Bile duct obstructions and some primary tumors of the liver can be corrected by surgery.

The treatment of idiopathic chronic hepatitis involves the use of corticosteroids and immunosuppressants such as azathioprine (Imuran). The prognosis varies. Some dogs respond well and can be taken off medications; others require life-long treatment. Dogs that respond poorly generally have advanced liver disease with cirrhosis.

The treatment of choice for liver shunts is partial or complete surgical ligation of the shunt. This is not always possible. Medical management is directed toward controlling hepatic encephalopathy.

Treatment of copper-associated hepatitis varies with the affected breed. Medications can be given to move copper out of the liver into the circulation, where it can be excreted in the urine. The absorption of copper can be decreased by giving oral zinc products that bind copper in the gut. Dogs with inherited defects in copper metabolism should not be used for breeding.

In addition to treating the liver disease, it is important to control and prevent complications, particularly hepatic encephalopathy and bleeding. This may involve feeding special diets low in protein, lowering blood ammonia levels, maintaining blood-clotting factors, preventing seizures, correcting electrolyte abnormalities, and administering antacids to prevent stomach and duodenal ulcers.

The Pancreas

The pancreas has two functions. The first is to provide digestive enzymes; the second is to make insulin for sugar metabolism. Digestive enzymes are manufactured by the acinar cells and insulin by the islet cells.

PANCREATITIS

Pancreatitis is inflammation and swelling of the pancreas. It can occur in a mild or severe form. The cause of spontaneous pancreatitis in dogs is not well understood. Dogs receiving corticosteroids are at increased risk. There is a higher incidence of pancreatitis in dogs with *Cushing's syndrome, diabetes mellitus, hypothyroidism* and *idiopathic hyperlipemia* (a disease of Miniature Schnauzers). These diseases are associated with high serum lipid levels. Pancreatitis is also more prevalent in overweight spayed females and dogs on high-fat diets. An attack may be triggered by eating table scraps or a fatty meal.

The signs of *acute pancreatitis* are the abrupt onset of vomiting and severe pain in the abdomen. The dog may have a tucked-up belly and assume a prayer position. Abdominal pain is caused by the release of digestive enzymes into the pancreas and surrounding tissue. Diarrhea, dehydration, weakness and shock may ensue.

Mild pancreatitis produces loss of appetite, depression, intermittent vomiting and diarrhea and weight loss.

Following an attack of pancreatitis, the pancreas may be permanently damaged. When it is, the dog may develop *diabetes mellitus* if the islet cells have been destroyed or *exocrine pancreatic insufficiency* if the acinar cells have been destroyed.

Treatment: Dogs with acute pancreatitis require hospitalization to treat shock and dehydration. The diagnosis can be suspected based on a physical examination. It is confirmed by blood tests showing elevated amylase and/or lipase levels. Abdominal ultrasonography may reveal an enlarged and swollen pancreas.

The most important step in treating pancreatitis is to rest the gland completely. This is accomplished by giving the dog nothing by mouth for several days and maintaining fluid and electrolyte balance with intravenous saline solutions. Antibiotics are used to prevent secondary bacterial infections. Pain is controlled with narcotics. Cardiac arrhythmias, if present, are treated with anti-arrhythmic drugs.

Dogs that do not respond to medical treatment may require surgery to drain an infected pancreas. The prognosis for dogs with shock and spreading peritonitis is poor.

Dogs that recover from pancreatitis are susceptible to recurrent attacks, which can be mild or severe. These episodes can be prevented, in part, by eliminating predisposing factors. For example, place overweight dogs on a weight-loss program (see *Weight Reduction*, page 281). Feed the total daily ration in two or three small servings to avoid overstimulating the pancreas. Do not feed table scraps. Dogs with high serum lipid levels (determined by your veterinarian) should be placed on a fat-restricted diet.

EXOCRINE PANCREATIC INSUFFICIENCY

The acinar cells in the pancreas manufacture digestive enzymes that empty into the duodenum in response to the stimulation of a meal. These enzymes empty into the duodenum. Without them, food cannot be adequately digested, and nutrients therefore cannot be adequately absorbed. For reasons that are unknown, the acinar cells may *atrophy* (shrink and become useless) and stop producing enzymes. This condition is called *pancreatic acinar cell atrophy* (PAA), and it is one of the major causes of pancreatic insufficiency.

PAA begins in dogs under two years of age. All breeds are affected, but there is a predisposition in large breeds, particularly German Shepherd Dogs, in whom the disease may be inherited as an autosomal recessive trait.

A less common cause of pancreatic insufficiency is pancreatitis. Following a bout of inflammation, the pancreas may become scarred and contracted. This produces the same effect as acinar cell atrophy. This form of pancreatic insufficiency tends to affect middle-aged and older dogs of the small breeds.

Dogs with pancreatic insufficiency lose weight despite a voracious appetite and increased food consumption. The unabsorbed food produces a diarrhea with large, gray, semi-formed cow-pie stools with a rancid odor (see *Malabsorption Syndrome*, page 253). The hair around the anus is often oily from undigested fat. Intense hunger may cause the dog to eat his own stool.

The diagnosis of pancreatic insufficiency can be suspected from the appearance of the stool and other observations. The best and most accurate test is the serum trypsin-like immunoreactive assay (TLI), available to veterinarians through special mail-out laboratories.

Treatment: Most dogs respond well to having the missing enzymes added to their meals. Powered pancreatic extracts (Viokase-V and Pancrezyme) are superior to enteric-coated and uncrushed tablets. Divide the daily food intake into two or three meals. Add one or two teaspoons of powdered extract to each meal just before feeding. As the diarrhea comes under control, reduce the enzyme replacement to the minimum effective maintenance dose. One teaspoon to each of two meals is adequate for most dogs.

Dogs that do not respond completely to pancreatic enzymes may do so when the maintenance diet is switched to a highly digestible, fat-restricted diet such as Hill's Prescription Diet i/d. An acid-blocker such as Tagamet or Zantac may be prescribed by your veterinarian to prevent destruction of the pancreatic enzymes by acid in the stomach.

Vitamin absorption is reduced in pancreatic insufficiency. Vitamin supplements (oral and subcutaneous) may be advisable, at least for the first three months. Discuss this with your veterinarian.

DIABETES MELLITUS (SUGAR DIABETES)

Diabetes mellitus, sometimes called sugar diabetes, is a common disease in dogs. Golden Retrievers, German Shepherd Dogs, Keeshonden and Poodles have the highest incidence, but all breeds can be affected. Females with the disease outnumber males by three to one. The average age of onset is six to nine years.

Diabetes is due to inadequate production of insulin by the islet cells in the pancreas. There may be a genetic predisposition for this in some dogs. Islet cell destruction also occurs as a sequel to pancreatitis.

Insulin enables glucose to pass into cells, where it is metabolized to produce energy for metabolism. Insulin deficiency results in *hyperglycemia* (high blood sugar) and *glycosuria* (high urine sugar). Glucose in the urine causes the diabetic animal to excrete large volumes of urine. In turn, this creates dehydration and the urge to drink large amounts of water. Ultimately, diabetes is a disease that affects all organs.

Initially, dogs that do not metabolize enough sugar have an increase in appetite and a desire to consume more food. Later, with the effects of malnourishment, the appetite drops.

In summary, the signs of early diabetes are frequent urination, drinking lots of water, a large appetite and unexplained loss of weight. The laboratory findings are high glucose levels in the blood and urine.

In more advanced cases there is lethargy, loss of appetite, vomiting, dehydration, weakness and coma. Cataracts are common in diabetic dogs.

Diabetic ketoacidosis is a condition associated with severe hyperglycemia in which ketones (acids) build up in the blood. Ketones are by-products of the metabolism of fat. In diabetic ketoacidosis, fats are metabolized for energy because sugar is unavailable. Diabetic ketoacidosis can be recognized by weakness, vomiting, rapid breathing and the odor of acetone on the breath (it smells like nail polish remover). Diabetic ketoacidosis is a life-threatening emergency. If you suspect diabetic ketoacidosis, take your dog at once to the veterinarian.

Treatment: Dietary control and daily injections of insulin can regulate most diabetic dogs, allowing them to lead active, healthy lives. Oral hypoglycemic agents used for treating diabetes in people have not been effective in dogs.

Insulin requirements cannot be predicted solely on the basis of the dog's weight, because the degree of pancreatic failure is different in every dog. The daily insulin dose must be established for each individual. In the newly diagnosed diabetic, insulin therapy is started at home. After a week of treatment, the dog is brought back to the clinic and a blood glucose curve (a series of blood sugar tests drawn over 12 to 24 hours) is obtained to see when the blood glucose peaks and hits its lows. Refinements are then made in the dosage and timing of the injections. How to prepare and inject the insulin will be explained to you by your veterinarian.

Dietary Management. Obesity greatly reduces tissue responsiveness to insulin and makes diabetes difficult to control. Accordingly, an overweight diabetic dog should be put on a high-fiber, high-carbohydrate diet until it reaches an ideal weight. Examples of such diets are Hill's Prescription Diets r/d and w/d, Fit and Trim Dry, and Cycle 3 Light Dry. See also *Weight Reduction*, page 281.

Hyperglycemia is less likely to occur if the dog is fed canned and dry kibble foods containing high concentrations of fiber and complex carbohydrates. Both of these components slow absorption and help minimize fluctuations in blood sugar after eating. Some commercially available diets meeting these requirements are Hill's Prescription Diets w/d and r/d (canned and dry), and Fit and Trim Dry.

Daily caloric requirements are determined by the weight and activity of the dog. Once established, the amount to feed is determined by dividing the daily caloric requirement by the amount of calories per cup or can of food. It is important to keep the number of calories constant from day to day, because insulin requirements are computed on that basis.

It is equally important to maintain a strict schedule for insulin injections. To prevent severe hyperglycemia after eating, do not give all the day's calories at one sitting. Divide the ration into equal parts and feed two or three meals a day, or as directed by your veterinarian.

A thin dog that has lost weight should be fed a *low-fiber* diet (low-fiber diets have higher caloric density) such as Alpo Light (canned) and Iams Less Active (dry) until weight is regained.

Insulin Overdose. An overdose of insulin causes the blood sugar to drop to levels well below normal. This is called *hypoglycemia*. Suspect this if your dog appears confused, disoriented, drowsy, shivers, staggers about, collapses, falls into a coma or has seizures. Insulin overdoses are associated with improper administration, using the wrong syringe (resulting in too high a dose) or changing the type of insulin. To treat an insulin overdose, see *Hypoglycemia* in Chapter 17.

The Adrenal Glands

The adrenal glands are small, paired structures located just above each kidney. The outer zone of the adrenal gland (the cortex) is composed of glandular cells that manufacture and release corticosteroids. There are two types of corticosteroids: mineralcorticoids and glucocorticoids. Mineralcorticoids regulate electrolyte concentrations. Glucocorticoids reduce inflammation and suppress the immune system. These latter are the corticosteroids used in nearly all steriod medications. The output of corticosteroids from the adrenal glands is controlled by the pituitary gland through the production of adrenocorticotropic hormone (ACTH).

CUSHING'S SYNDROME (HYPERADRENOCORTICISM)

Cushing's syndrome is a disease caused by long-term exposure to high levels of glucocorticosteroids, either manufactured by the body or given as medications.

Tumors of the pituitary gland that secrete ACTH stimulate the adrenal glands to produce large amounts of adrenal hormones. This sustained overproduction in response to pituitary stimulation accounts for 85 percent of cases of spontaneous Cushing's syndrome. The remaining 15 percent are caused by corticosteroid-producing tumors of the adrenal glands themselves.

Spontaneous Cushing's syndrome occurs primarily in middle-aged and older dogs, although dogs of all ages can be affected. Poodles, Boston Terriers, Dachshunds and Boxers have the highest incidence.

A number of cases of Cushing's syndrome are caused by long-term therapy with drugs containing corticosteroids. This is called *iatrogenic* Cushing's syndrome.

The signs of Cushing's syndrome include bilaterally symmetrical hair loss, a pot-bellied abdomen, lethargy with reduced activity, infertility in females, testicular atrophy in males, loss of muscle mass and weakness. Excessive thirst and frequent urination also occur. Other complications include increased susceptibility to infections, blood clots in the circulatory system (*thromboembolism*), high blood pressure, congestive heart failure, and central nervous system signs including behavioral changes and seizures.

The diagnosis of Cushing's syndrome is based on laboratory tests, especially those than measure serum cortisol concentrations before and after the injection of ACTH and dexamethasone. Advances in *CT scans* and magnetic resonance imaging (*MRI*) techniques have made it possible to visualize small tumors of the pituitary and adrenal glands.

This dog has Cushing's syndrome. Note the symmetrical loss of hair over the body.

Three months after treatment, the hair has regrown and the coat looks a lot better.

Treatment: Spontaneous Cushing's syndrome is treated with a drug called mitotane. The medication acts on the adrenal cortex to selectively suppress the production of glucocorticoids. The drug protocol is complex and requires close veterinary monitoring. The prognosis is guarded. The average life span with medical treatment is about two years.

A drug called Anipryl (deprenyl) recently has been approved for treating spontaneous Cushing's syndrome of pituitary origin. It appears to be effective in improving some of the symptoms of Cushing's syndrome, particularly the reduced activity level.

Pituitary tumors often respond to radiation therapy, but the availability of equipment is limited and the cost is high. Benign and malignant tumors of the adrenal glands can be surgically removed in some cases. Iatrogenic Cushing's syndrome is reversible if the causative drug can be tapered and, preferably, discontinued.

ADDISON'S DISEASE (HYPOADRENOCORTICISM)

This uncommon disease is caused by inadequate production of corticosteroids. Some cases are caused by diseases that destroy the adrenal gland, including infections, tumors and toxic drugs. An autoimmune reaction, in which antibodies are directed against the cells of the adrenal cortex, may be responsible for cases in which the cause is not known.

An *iatrogenic* form of Addison's disease occurs after the administration of corticosteroids to treat medical conditions. The corticosteroids have the side effect of putting the adrenal glands at rest. An abrupt withdrawal of the drug can produce a temporary deficit of hydrocortisone and cause an acute Addisonian crisis with shock and circulatory collapse. Another common iatrogenic cause of Addison's disease is the use of mitotane to treat Cushing's disease, as decribed above.

The signs of Addison's disease are lethargy, muscle weakness, intermittent vomiting and diarrhea and slow pulse. The disease should be considered when a dog unaccountably collapses. The diagnosis is made by an ACTH stimulation test. In a positive test, the adrenal cortex does not respond to an injection of ACTH by increasing the concentration of cortisol in the serum.

Treatment: Shock associated with acute adrenal insufficiency responds rapidly to corticosteroids and intravenous fluids. Chronic adrenal insufficiency can be controlled by giving an oral cortisone preparation daily. Treatment is life long. The dosage varies with the severity of the disease, and must be determined by your veterinarian.

Feeding and Nutrition

DOG FOOD BASICS

Dogs have fewer taste buds than humans do (about 2,000, compared with our 12,000), and thus have relatively insensitive palates. Dogs can discern sweetness, sourness, bitterness and saltiness. It is probably accurate to describe a dog's sense of taste as pleasant, unpleasant and indifferent.

Nonetheless, dogs do show a preference for certain dog foods. In side-by-side product comparisons, 80 percent of dogs showed definite likes and dislikes. Incidentally, the more expensive foods were not necessarily the most tasty.

Pet food manufacturers have made feeding your dog a relatively simple task. An owner need only decide which brand to buy, how much to feed and whether the dog likes the food. The cost is often the final consideration.

Federal law requires that all pet food manufacturers provide a list of ingredients on the package. However, a list by itself gives only a rough idea of the quality of the food. For example, protein in dog food is derived from meat by-products, poultry by-products, fish by-products, soybean meal and cereal grains such as corn or wheat. These various protein sources are not all of the same quality and digestibility. The mere fact that beef or some other protein is mentioned on the package is no guarantee of quality—it may indicate levels as low as 3percent. However, if the *product's name* contains the words "beef," "chicken," "lamb," "fish" and so on, 95 percent of the dry weight of the product must be derived from that protein source.

A high-quality diet should furnish a proper balance of *essential amino acids*. Ten amino acids cannot be manufactured by the dog, and are considered dietary essentials. The quality of the protein depends on the right combination of essential amino acids. In general, a good balance of amino acids is accomplished using a combination of protein from plant and animal sources, because the amino acids deficient in one source are usually present in the other.

Symptoms of *amino acid deficiency* include depressed appetite, impaired growth, gray haircoat, low hemoglobin levels, immune deficiency and lowered reproductive performance.

COMMERCIAL DOG FOODS

Brands of commercial dog foods can be classified as generic, popular and premium. Generic foods are more expensive than popular ones, and premium foods are the most expensive.

Generic dog foods do not carry a brand name. Closely related to generics are the *private-label pet foods* that carry the names of the stores in which they are sold. These foods provide a list of ingredients as required by law, but cannot make claims that the food is nutritionally balanced or complete. Generic products are less expensive than popular and premium brands, because the food is manufactured using low-cost ingredients. Furthermore, the ingredients vary from package to package, depending on which nutrient sources were available at the time the food was manufactured. In feed tests many of the generic products were found to have lower digestibility, due to the addition of indigestible fibers.

Popular dog foods are the recognizable brands from major food manufacturers. They are available at most supermarkets and grocery stores. These companies spend a good deal of time and energy testing and advertising their products.

To show that their foods contain all the protein, fat, vitamin and mineral requirements needed for dogs to grow and thrive, popular dog food makers cite one of two established standards on the label. Both standards are set by the Association of American Feed Control Officials (AAFCO), a nonprofit association of federal and state officials that develops guidelines for the production, labeling and sale of animal feeds.

One standard requires that the food meet an AAFCO profile that is based on a calculation of all the nutrients dogs are theoretically known to require to maintain health and fitness. The other standard involves feeding tests that show dogs can live and thrive on the product.

The calculation approach is limited in its usefulness because current knowledge is not firm for all nutrients dogs require. In addition, there is no guarantee that the dog can digest and absorb all the nutrients in a specific food.

Feeding trials are superior to the calculation method because they show that the product actually works and delivers the desired results. The drawbacks are that only a six-month feeding trial is required for a manufacturer to make the claim. Furthermore, once one product is labeled as having been successfully tested on dogs, the pet food company is allowed to claim that other products in a similar "family" or class have also passed a feeding trial. Therefore which products were actually tested is uncertain. This information remains proprietary.

Nevertheless, in order for a pet food company to represent its product as "complete," "balanced," "perfect," "scientific," or "formulated for growth, pregnancy or lactation," the product must conform to one of the AAFCO profiles for that stage of life. Any food marketed "for all life stages" must have the extra protein and calories needed to support growing young puppies as well as maintain elderly dogs. Because of these constraints, the nutrient content of these products remains fairly constant even though different sources may be used in the formulation.

Premium dog foods are available only through veterinarians, pet supply stores and feed stores. In general, the ingredients used in these products are highly digestible and have good to excellent nutrient availability. In contrast to popular brands, premium foods are produced using fixed formulas. The ingredients used do not fluctuate in response to availability or market price. Manufacturers of these foods validate their claims through AAFCO feeding studies (not calculations). Because these products contain high-quality food sources that are easily digested, smaller amounts can be fed. Therefore, even though a big bag may cost more, the cost per serving may be comparable to many popular brands.

Dog food is available as canned, semi-moist and dry kibble. It makes little difference from a nutritional point of view which of these you choose. Some dogs find canned food more palatable because it generally has a higher percentage of moisture and fat. Dry kibble is least expensive and has the advantage of maintaining the health of the teeth and gums. You can leave dry food out all day for free-choice consumption. Canned food should be left out for short periods only because it spoils quickly. Any unused portion should be refrigerated.

Commercial foods contain instructions on the label about how much to feed based on the weight of the dog. The manufacturer's recommended serving size is often greater than many dogs require. Follow the directions at first, but monitor your dog's weight. Feed more if the dog starts to lose weight and less if he gains weight or leaves food in the dish.

In summary, while the standards set by AAFCO do have some limitations, they still provide the best guidelines available for selecting a dog food. Look on the package for the AAFCO statement that the nutritional adequacy of the product has been confirmed by a feeding trial. This shows that the product is complete and balanced for the intended life stage. Avoid generic and private-label foods that do not contain the AAFCO feeding trial statement.

Once you have narrowed the field, select a product that your dog finds especially tasty. Choosing between a popular or premium brand is a matter of convenience, expense and palatability of the ration. Premium foods may be more digestible and consistent from batch to batch, but these considerations may not be significant for most dogs.

FEEDING ADULTS

When a puppy reaches a year of age, his diet should be changed to one appropriate for maintaining an adult dog. Adult foods are less expensive than puppy foods and those foods formulated for all stages of life, because they have less protein.

From a nutritional point of view, there is no harm in leaving an adult dog on a puppy ration as long as the amount fed is trimmed back to the amount appropriate for adult maintenance. Failure to reduce the daily caloric intake is one of the main reasons for excessive weight gain in early adulthood.

Although feeding once a day is fine for many dogs, dividing the daily ration into two equal servings is probably healthier and more satisfying. If you are feeding dry kibble, you can leave the food out during the day for free-choice consumption. Discard unused food at the end of the day. Canned and semimoist products should be fed twice daily, at the same time each day, and the unused portion should be picked up after 15 minutes and refrigerated.

Caloric requirements differ from dog to dog, but in general, dogs need fewer calories as they grow older. They also need less in warm weather and during periods of inactivity. Once again, feeding instructions should be taken as guidelines only. These instructions are only rough estimates and are not always applicable to a specific breed or individual. The goal is to maintain normal body weight. Feed the dog whatever is necessary to maintain ideal weight.

Hard-working dogs require a highly digestible diet with increased fat content to maintain stamina and body condition. This is one area where a premium dog food formulated for working dogs may be particularly beneficial. In the off season when the dog is not working, feed less of the high-calorie food or gradually change to a less nutrient-dense dog food.

Feeding during pregnancy and lactation is discussed in Chapter 16, *Care and Feeding During Pregnancy*, page 421. Feeding the elderly dog is discussed in Chapter 19, page 499.

TABLE SCRAPS AND EXTRAS

Table scraps and "people food" compete for a dog's appetite. Calories obtained through extra foods ordinarily are not of the same quality as those obtained through the dog's regular food. If you are feeding a high-quality commercial product, additional calories will unbalance the food and lead to obesity.

Attacks of *pancreatitis* have occurred following the feeding of table scraps. Feeding table scraps can also lead to unwanted behavior problems, such as begging or stealing food from the table.

If you decide to feed table scraps or treats, limit the amount to no more than 5 to 10 percent of the dog's daily caloric requirement. Meats, fish and poultry should be well cooked and all bones should be removed. Note that many adult dogs are lactose intolerant. Feeding dairy products such as milk and cheese may result in diarrhea. These foods should be strictly avoided.

SUPPLEMENTS

Calcium, phosphorus, iron, microminerals and vitamins are supplied in ample quantity in good-quality dog food. Vitamin and mineral supplements are not necessary and can be detrimental to a dog's health. They not recommended unless there is a medical indication for their use.

SWITCHING DIETS

Dogs do not seem to object to eating the same food day after day. But if you believe, as many people do, that variety is the spice of life, you may wish to change your pet's diet from time to time. Note that when you change flavors you may change the nutritional value of the food as well. The new flavor (because of the flavor additive) may contain more or less protein, fat or fiber, although this might not be reflected by the label.

A change in diet may be indicated for medical reasons, in which case the new diet will be prescribed by your veterinarian.

When changing diets, gradually mix the new diet in with the old over 7 to 10 days. Observe how well your dog eats the new diet. A change in the appearance of the stool (loose or increased bulk) suggests that the new diet may not agree with the dog as well as the old one did.

FEEDING GROWING PUPPIES

Most breeders supply a diet sheet with a new puppy, detailing what the pup has been fed, how much and at what times of the day. Follow this, at least for the first few days, since an abrupt change in diet can cause digestive upsets.

The caloric requirements of growing puppies are shown in the table in Chapter 17 (page 460). Pups up to six months of age require twice as many calories per pound of body weight per day as they will as adults. Protein requirements are also higher. After six months, these requirements begin to decline as the puppy's growth rate decelerates.

These requirements are best met by feeding a product labeled "for growth of puppies" or marketed as "for all stages of life." The information on the label should show that on a dry matter basis the product:

- has at least 25 percent protein
- has at least 17 percent fat
- has less than 5 percent fiber
- has 1.0 to 1.8 percent calcium
- has 0.8 to 1.6 percent phosphorus
- is 80 percent digestible
- provides 1,750 metabolizable calories per pound weight of feed

Labels provide recommended daily feeding amounts. They are useful as guidelines, but are not applicable for every pup, nor for every stage of the puppy's life.

Puppies should be fed at least three times a day from weaning to six months of age. After six months of age, puppies can be fed twice a day. *Do not* feed puppies table scraps or snacks between meals, as this will unbalance the diet.

Overfeeding is a much more common problem than underfeeding. Overfeeding can lead to obesity and may worsen the symptoms of *hip dysplasia* and other inherited bone diseases. Overfeeding is particularly undesirable in heavy-boned, rapidly growing puppies of the large breeds. In fact, in larger breeds a *slower* growth rate has been found to be more healthy, because it allows the muscles and tendons to develop at the same rate as the bones.

If you own a large breed puppy, you may want to feed somewhat less than the amount recommended on the package. Some packages have instructions for feeding large-breed puppies. These may be more accurate than following general guidelines. Special formulas that are lower in calories, fat and calcium are available through your veterinarian. Feed as prescribed.

WEIGHT REDUCTION

It has been estimated that about 20 percent of dogs in the United States are overweight. Obesity is due to overfeeding, particularly feeding snacks and treats between meals, and failing to reduce the caloric intake of puppies when they reach adulthood. Adding table scraps to a nutritionally balanced diet is another cause of weight gain.

Obesity greatly complicates many diseases including diabetes, hypertension, heart disease, arthritis and other musculoskeletal problems. It also shortens the quality and duration of the pet's life. For these reasons it is important to prevent excessive weight gain and to return an overweight dog to a more normal body condition.

Determine your dog's body condition by his appearance and the amount of fat distributed over the ribs. You should be able to feel the ribs as individual structures. From above, you should see a well-defined narrowing or waistlike effect below the rib cage and above the hips. If you are unable to feel the individual ribs and the dog has lost his waist, he is carrying too much fat.

Breed standards give the ideal weight for males and females of each breed. If your dog is of the typical height, he or she should fall within the standard range for weight.

The two dietary approaches to weight reduction are to feed less of the current food or to feed another food that is less dense in calories. A disadvantage of feeding less of the maintenance food is that it can lead to nutritional deficiencies. This is because maintenance foods meet daily nutrient requirements only if the dog consumes the full amount recommended. Furthermore, because the dog is eating less, he doesn't feel as full and is more apt to beg or steal food.

Special reducing dog foods that are less dense in calories are advantageous because the volume of food does not need to be significantly reduced. Commercial dog foods marketed as "lean," "light" or "low-calorie" that conform to AAFCO feeding trial standards supply all the nutrient requirements when fed as directed. Nutrient deficiencies should not occur.

These reducing foods provide fewer calories by reducing the amount of fat. This is accomplished by replacing some of the fat with either digestible carbohydrate or indigestible fiber. Those that use carbohydrate are preferable to those that use fiber. Diets with even sharper calorie restrictions than commercial products can be obtained through your veterinarian.

To begin a reduction program, weigh your dog to establish his current weight. Chart the weight at weekly intervals. Compute the amount to feed based on the dog's ideal weight—not his current weight. The dog should lose no more than two percent of his body weight per week. Use the feeding directions on the package as a good reference, but adjust the size of the feedings to maintain gradual weight loss. *Avoid feeding snacks or table scraps.* After the dog reaches his ideal weight, feed a balanced ration to maintain that weight.

Combine weight-reducing diets with more exercise. Increase the length of the exercise gradually, to avoid overtaxing the dog.

C h a p t e r 10

THE RESPIRATORY SYSTEM

The upper respiratory system is made up of the nasal passages, throat, larynx and trachea (see the figure *Anatomy of the Head* at the start of Chapter 8). The bronchi and lungs make up the lower respiratory tract. The breathing tubes branch into progressively smaller passages until they open into the air sacs (alveoli). The lungs are composed of the bronchi, air sacs and blood vessels. The ribs and muscles of the chest, along with the diaphragm, function as a bellows, moving the air into and out of the lungs.

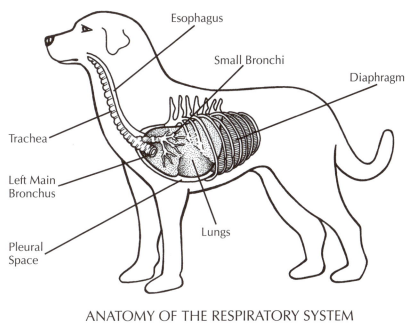

ANATOMY OF THE RESPIRATORY SYSTEM

283

Abnormal Breathing

RAPID LABORED BREATHING

A dog at rest takes about 10 to 30 breaths per minute. Breathing at a faster rate suggests fever, pain or anxiety. Rapid breathing should be distinguished from *panting*. Panting is the chief way a dog lowers his body temperature; water evaporates from the mouth, tongue and lungs, and warm air in the body is exchanged for cooler air in the atmosphere.

Rapid breathing, when accompanied by labored or difficult breathing, is a sign of distress. Dogs with congestive heart failure and/or lung disease often have rapid labored breathing at rest or with only mild exertion. Other causes of rapid labored breathing are shock, heat stroke, dehydration, and *ketoacidosis* associated with diabetes, kidney failure and some poisonings.

Dogs with rapid labored breathing should be seen by a veterinarian.

NOISY BREATHING

Noisy breathing indicates an obstruction in the nasal passages, the back of the throat or the larynx. Snorting and snoring are typically heard with the *brachycephalic syndrome* discussed on page 285.

CROUPY BREATHING (STRIDOR)

Croupy breathing, or *stridor*, is a high-pitched raspy sound caused by air passing through a narrowed voice box. It may be heard only when the dog exercises. When the onset is sudden, the most likely cause is a foreign body in the voice box. When croupy breathing has been present for some time, consider vocal cord paralysis.

WHEEZING

A wheeze is a whistling sound heard when the dog inhales or exhales, or both. Wheezing indicates spasm or narrowing in the trachea or bronchi. Wheezes in the lungs are best heard with a stethoscope. Some causes of wheezing are chronic bronchitis, congestive heart failure and tumors of the larynx, trachea and lungs.

SHALLOW BREATHING

Shallow breathing is seen with broken ribs and severe bruising of the chest wall. Blood, pus or serum in the chest cavity (called *pleural effusion*) restricts breathing by interfering with the range of motion of the chest. A dog with shallow breathing compensates by breathing more rapidly.

Obstructed Breathing

BRACHYCEPHALIC SYNDROME

Bulldogs, Pugs, Pekingese, Chow Chows and dogs with broad skulls and short muzzles frequently show some degree of airway obstruction, manifested by mouth breathing, snorting and snoring. These difficulties become more pronounced when the dog is exercising or is overheated, and tend to get worse as the dog grows older.

The obstructed breathing in these dogs is caused by deformities that include collapsed nostrils, an elongated soft palate and eversion of the laryngeal saccules. These deformities often occur together. Collapsed nostrils and elongated soft palate are congenital. Eversion of the laryngeal saccules is acquired.

Collapsed Nostrils (Stenotic Nares)

In puppies with stenotic nares, the nasal openings are small and the nasal cartilage is soft and floppy, causing the nostrils to collapse as the puppy breathes in. This produces varying degrees of airway obstruction, manifested by mouth breathing, noisy breathing and occasionally a nasal discharge. In severe cases the chest is flattened from front to back. These pups fail to thrive and are poorly developed.

Treatment: Stenotic nares can be treated successfully by enlarging the nasal openings. This is accomplished by removing a wedge of nasal skin and cartilage. Not all dogs with stenotic nares require surgery. In some dogs the cartilages firm up satisfactorily by six months of age. If there is no urgency in symptoms, your veterinarian may delay treatment to see if this happens.

Elongated Soft Palate

The soft palate is a flap of mucosa that closes off the nasopharynx during swallowing (see the figure *Anatomy of the Head* on page 210). Normally, it touches or slightly overlaps the epiglottis. In dogs with an elongated soft palate, the palate overlaps the epiglottis to a considerable degree, partially obstructing the airway during breathing. This is manifested by snorting, snoring, *stridor*, gurgling and gagging. The obstruction is worse with exercise. In time, stretched ligaments in the larynx leads to labored breathing and *laryngeal collapse*.

Treatment: An elongated soft palate is treated by surgically shortening the palate so that the edge opposes or slightly overlaps the epiglottis. Results are good if the operation is done before destructive changes occur in the larynx.

Eversion of the Laryngeal Saccules

Laryngeal saccules are small mucosal pouches that project into the larynx. In long-standing upper airway obstruction the saccules enlarge and turn out (*eversion*), narrowing the airway even further.

Treatment: Everted laryngeal saccules often accompany an elongated soft palate. If present, they should be removed. This operation is done at the same time as shortening of the palate.

The Larynx (Voice Box)

The larynx is an oblong box located in the throat above the windpipe. Just above the larynx is the epiglottis, a leaflike flap of cartilage that closes over the larynx and protects the airway during swallowing.

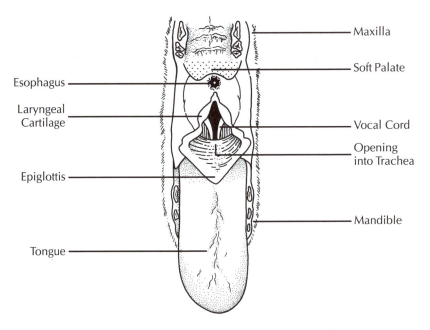

OPEN MOUTH VIEW OF THE LARNYX

The larynx is composed of cartilage held together by ligaments. Within the larynx are the vocal cords, which is why the larynx is sometimes called the voice box. A dog's vocal chords are thick and prominent, enabling them to bark loudly. The interior of the larynx is lined with a mucous membrane. The mucosa of the larynx, unlike the rest of the respiratory tract, does not contain cilia—hairlike structures that help move things through the passage. Therefore, mucus tends to pool in the larynx. Exaggerated throat-clearing is required to bring up the phlegm.

The larynx is the most sensitive cough area in the respiratory tract. Pressure over the larynx, such as that caused by a tight choke collar, can cause episodes of explosive coughing.

Diseases of the larynx cause hoarseness and progressive loss of the ability to bark. Choking, gagging and coughing may be observed, especially while eating or drinking. Laryngeal obstructions such as those caused by laryngeal collapse, vocal cord paralysis and a foreign body in the airway produce shortness of breath on exertion, *stridor*, *cyanosis* and collapse.

LARYNGITIS

Laryngitis is inflammation and swelling of the vocal cords and surrounding laryngeal mucosa. The signs are hoarseness and the inability to bark. The most common cause of laryngitis is voice strain caused by excessive barking or coughing. In the absence of these, suspect vocal cord paralysis. Laryngitis can accompany tonsillitis, throat infections, kennel cough and tumors in the throat.

Treatment: Laryngitis due to excessive barking usually responds to removing the stimulus for the barking (see *Excessive Barking*, Chapter 17). When voice strain is due to prolonged coughing, seek veterinary consultation to investigate and eliminate the cause of the coughing.

LARYNGEAL EDEMA

Sudden swelling of the larynx and vocal cords can result in marked narrowing or complete obstruction of the airway. Signs are *stridor*, rapid labored breathing, *cyanosis* and collapse.

Insect bites can cause an anaphylactic reaction with sudden swelling of the larynx. Another cause of laryngeal edema is excessive panting, particularly when it is associated with heat stroke. Similarly, any process that results in forced breathing across a narrowed airway (such as vocal cord paralysis) can lead to swelling that exacerbates the original disease.

Treatment: Sudden stridor and difficulty in breathing is an acute emergency. Proceed as quickly as possible to the nearest veterinary clinic. Corticosteroids are given to reduce swelling and inflammation. Adrenalin is a specific antidote for an allergic reaction (see *Anaphylactic Shock*, Chapter 1). Antihistamines also are beneficial. Sedatives help to relieve anxiety and panting.

CHOKING (FOREIGN OBJECT IN THE VOICE BOX)

The sudden onset of forceful coughing, pawing at the mouth and respiratory distress in a healthy dog suggest a foreign body caught in the larynx. This is an emergency! If the dog is conscious and able to breathe, proceed at once to the nearest veterinary clinic.

If your dog is gagging and retching but is not experiencing *difficulty in breathing*, assume that a foreign object such as a bone splinter or rubber ball is caught in his mouth or in the back of his throat. These subjects are discussed in Chapter 8, *Foreign Body in the Throat*, on page 229.

Fortunately, a foreign body in the voice box is not a common occurrence. Most objects are expelled by the forceful coughing that results from laryngeal stimulation.

Treatment: If the dog collapses and is unable to breathe, place him on his side with his head down. Open his mouth, pull out his tongue as far as you can, sweep your fingers from side to side, grasp the object and remove it. Then administer artificial respiration or CPR as necessary (see *CPR* in Chapter 1, page 7).

If the object cannot be easily removed, do not try to get around it with your fingers. This will force it further down the throat. Instead, proceed to the Heilich Maneuver.

The Heimlich Maneuver

1. **Abdominal compressions.** It may be easiest to hold the dog in your lap upside down with his back against your chest. Place your arms around the dog's waist from behind. Make a fist and grasp it with the other hand. Place the fist in the dog's upper mid-abdomen close to the breast bone at the apex of the V formed by the rib cage.

    Compress the abdomen by forcefully thrusting up and in with the fist four times in quick succession. This maneuver pushes the diaphragm upward and forces a burst of air through the larynx. This usually dislodges the object. Proceed to step 2.

2. **Finger sweeps.** Pull out the tongue and *sweep the mouth.* Remove the foreign body and proceed to step 5. If you are unable to dislodge the object, proceed to step 3.

3. **Artificial respiration.** *Give five mouth-to-nose respirations.* Even a small volume of air getting past the obstruction is beneficial. Proceed to step 4.

4. **Chest thumps.** Deliver a sharp blow with the heel of your hand to the dog's back between the shoulder blades. Repeat the finger sweeps. If the object is still not dislodged, repeat steps 1 through 4 until the object is dislodged.

5. **Ventilation.** Once the object is dislodged, check for breathing and heart rate; administer artificial respiration and cardiac massage if necessary. When the dog revives, proceed to the veterinary hospital for further treatment.

LARYNGOSPASM (REVERSE SNEEZING)

This uncommon condition can be alarming because it sounds as if the dog can't catch his breath. During an attack the dog produces a loud snorting noise caused by violent attempts to draw in air. This may occur several times in succession. After the attack the dog appears completely normal.

Reverse sneezing is believed to be caused by a temporary spasm of the muscles of the larynx, possibly the result of a drop of mucus that falls on the vocal cords from the soft palate. The attack can be ended by making the dog swallow. This is accomplished by massaging the front of the neck in the region of the pharynx just beneath the jaw.

If the attack does not stop and the dog collapses, suspect a foreign body in the larynx. See *Choking* on page 287.

LARYNGEAL PARALYSIS (VOCAL CORD PARALYSIS)

This is an acquired disease that occurs in older dogs of the large and giant breeds, particularly Labrador Retrievers, Golden Retrievers, Irish Setters, Saint Bernards and Great Pyrenees. In Siberian Huskies, Bouviers des Flandres, Bull Terriers and Dalmatians it occurs as a hereditary defect.

A classic sign of laryngeal paralysis is a characteristic croupy or "roaring" noise heard as the dog inhales. Initially it appears during or after exercise. Later it occurs at rest. Another sign is progressive weakening of the bark, which ends in a croaky whisper. In time the dog develops noisy breathing, labored breathing, reduced exercise tolerance and fainting spells. *Laryngeal edema* may develop and further compromise the airway, causing respiratory collapse and even death.

The diagnosis is made by examining the vocal cords with a laryngoscope. Paralyzed vocal cords come together in the middle instead of remaining well apart. This produces a tight air passage through the larynx.

Treatment: A number of surgical procedures have been used to enlarge the airway. The technique used most often involves removing both vocal cords and their supporting cartilage. This relieves the obstruction, but the dog is unable to bark.

LARYNGEAL TRAUMA

Choke chain injuries can fracture the hyoid bone and/or cause compression damage to the nerves of the pharynx and larynx. Other causes of trauma to the larynx include bite wounds and sharp foreign objects such as bones and pins that penetrate the larynx. Dogs with laryngeal injuries often breathe normally at rest but show respiratory distress during exertion.

Treatment: Treatment of laryngeal trauma involves confining and resting the dog and administering anti-inflammatory medications. If the larynx is severely traumatized, a *tracheostomy* (an operation in which an opening is made through the skin into the windpipe to establish a new airway) may be required. Choke chain injuries can be prevented by using a head halter or chest harness.

LARYNGEAL COLLAPSE

This is a late stage in airway obstruction. Pressure changes in the upper airway caused by stenotic nares, an elongated soft palate, laryngeal paralysis or everted laryngeal saccules stretching the ligaments that support the laryngeal cartilages. These cartilages gradually collapse inward and block the airway. At this stage any change in the dog's need for air can cause acute respiratory insufficiency and cardiac arrest.

Treatment: The first step is to surgically correct predisposing factors. If symptoms persist, the dog may benefit from a permanent *tracheostomy*.

Coughing

Coughing is a reflex initiated by an irritation in the airway. Coughs are caused by respiratory infections, inhaled irritants such as grass seeds and food particles, congestive heart failure, chronic bronchitis, respiratory tract tumors and pressure from tight collars.

Coughs are self-perpetuating. Coughing dries out the mucous membranes and irritates the breathing tubes—leading to further coughing.

DIAGNOSING A COUGH

The type of cough often suggests the diagnosis:

- A deep, dry hacking cough made worse by exercise or excitement is characteristic of kennel cough.
- A moist, bubbling cough indicates fluid or phlegm in the lungs and suggests pneumonia.
- A high, weak, gagging cough, followed by swallowing and licking the lips, is characteristic of tonsillitis and sore throat.
- A spasm of prolonged coughing thst occurs at night or while lying on the sternum suggests heart disease.
- A "goose-honk" cough in a toy breed dog indicates a collapsing trachea.

The diagnostic workup of a dog with a chronic cough includes a chest X-ray and *trans-tracheal washings*. Washings are cells obtained by flushing the trachea with saline solution. This can be done with a sterile tube passed down the windpipe while the dog is sedated, or by direct penetration of the windpipe through the skin of the neck using a needle and catheter. The washings are processed for *cytology* and bacterial culture. The information usually leads to a specific diagnosis.

Bronchoscopy is particularly useful in the investigation of chronic coughs and coughs with the production of mucus and blood. The procedure requires sedation or general anesthesia. A rigid or flexible endoscope is passed into the trachea and bronchi. This allows the verterinarian to see the interior of the respiratory tract. Biopsies can be taken with accuracy, and washings collected for examination and culture. Bronchoscopy is also the procedure of choice for removing bronchial foreign bodies.

Treatment of Cough: Only minor coughs of brief duration should be treated at home. Coughs accompanied by labored breathing, a discharge from the eyes or nose, or the production of bloody sputum should be seen and treated by a veterinarian.

It is important to identify and correct any contributing factors. Eliminate any irritating atmospheric pollutants such as cigarette smoke, aerosol insecticides, house dust and perfumes from the home environment.

Breaking the cough cycle is an important part of treating irritant coughs. A variety of children's cough medicines are available over-the-counter. Robitussin is an effective cough medicine that contains an expectorant called guaifenesin. It does not suppress the cough reflex, but does liquefy mucus secretions so they can be brought up more easily. Robitussin is safe to use for all coughs.

Robitussin-DM and Benylin Expectorant, also available over-the-counter, contain the cough suppressant dextromethorphan. The correct dosage for all these cough preparations is given in the table *Common Drugs for Home Veterinary Use* on page 512 in Chapter 20.

When stronger cough suppressants are needed, preparations containing the narcotics Hycodan and Torbutrol are available by prescription through your veterinarian.

Cough suppressants should be used selectively and only for short periods. Although they decrease the frequency and severity of the cough, they do not treat the condition causing it. Overuse may delay diagnosis and treatment. Cough suppressants (but not expectorants) should be avoided in bacterial infections, and when phlegm is being brought up or swallowed. Productive coughs are clearing unwanted material from the airway.

The Trachea and Bronchi

KENNEL COUGH COMPLEX (ACUTE TRACHEOBRONCHITIS)

The kennel cough complex is a group of highly contagious respiratory diseases in dogs. The name comes from the fact that the infection tends to spread rapidly, especially among dogs in boarding kennels. Several viruses and bacteria, alone or in combination, can cause the disease. The organisms most frequently involved are canine parainfluenza virus and the bacteria *Bordetella bronchiseptica*, both discussed in Chapter 3. Canine adenovirus types CAV-1 and CAV-2, as well as canine herpesvirus, canine distemper and mycoplasma are other causes of kennel cough.

A *harsh, dry, hacking cough* is the characteristic sign of tracheobronchitis. The cough is unproductive and is often accompanied by gagging and retching. Except for the cough, the dog is bright and alert, has a good appetite and a normal temperature. In most cases kennel cough is a mild disease. With rest and a stress-free environment, most adult dogs recover completely in seven to 14 days.

Kennel cough may be complicated by secondary bacterial pneumonia. This is most likely to occur in dogs with bronchitis, collapsing trachea and diseases that lower their resistance to infection. In puppies, kennel cough can be accompanied by nasal congestion. These puppies require frequent care to loosen thick secretions, improve breathing and prevent pneumonia. This is also true for toy breeds.

A severe form of tracheobronchitis that can lead to pneumonia is characterized by low-grade fluctuating fever, loss of appetite and depression. These dogs have a moist productive cough, nasal discharge, exercise intolerance, wheezing and rapid breathing. This form of kennel cough requires hospitalization.

Treatment: Kennel cough should be treated by a veterinarian. Isolate dogs to prevent spreading the diease. The quarters should be warm, dry and *well ventilated*. Humidification is beneficial. A cool mist vaporizer offers some advantage over a heat vaporizer, because it is less likely to add excessive heat to the atmosphere.

Moderate daily exercise is beneficial in that it assists bronchial drainage. Strenuous exertion off leash should be avoided.

Antibiotics are routinely used for treating kennel cough. The drugs of choice are the tetracyclines and trimethoprim-sulfa. Continue the antibiotics for 7 to 10 days. Excessive coughing is controlled with cough suppressants.

Dogs with severe tracheobronchitis or pneumonia are hospitalized and treated intensively with intramuscular antibiotics and drugs that dilate the breathing passages.

Prevention: CPI and CAV-2 vaccines—incorporated into the routine immunizations—will decrease the prevalence and severity of kennel cough. Show dogs, boarded dogs, and dogs that go to grooming parlors may benefit from an optional bordetella vaccination. For more information, see *Vaccinations* in Chapter 3.

FOREIGN BODY IN THE LUNGS

Grass seeds and food particles are the most common foreign materials inhaled by dogs that are big enough to lodge in the smaller breathing tubes. Most of these are quickly coughed up. If the object becomes fixed in the airway it causes intense irritation and swelling of the air passage. Mucus collects below the obstruction and forms an ideal medium for bacterial growth and infection. Objects that remain in the lungs for several weeks can cause pneumonia.

Sudden attacks of coughing that occur immediately after vomiting or after a dog has been running in tall grass and weeds suggest inhalation of a foreign body. *Lungworms* in the bronchi also cause severe coughing spasms.

Treatment: Unexplained coughing should be investigated by a veterinarian. Avoid cough medicines, since they delay treatment. *Bronchoscopy* is usually successful in locating and removing bronchial foreign bodies, particularly if the procedure is done within two weeks of inhalation.

COLLAPSING TRACHEA

This condition occurs primarily in older toy breeds, particularly Chihuahuas, Pomeranians and Toy Poodles, and occasionally in young dogs as a congenital defect.

Tracheal collapse occurs because the C-shaped tracheal rings do not possess normal rigidity. As a result, the involved wall of the trachea collapses as the dog inhales. Obesity is a predisposing factor, as is chronic bronchitis.

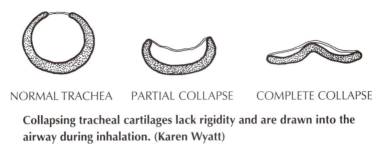

NORMAL TRACHEA   PARTIAL COLLAPSE   COMPLETE COLLAPSE

Collapsing tracheal cartilages lack rigidity and are drawn into the airway during inhalation. (Karen Wyatt)

The principal sign of tracheal collapse is a characteristic "goose-honk" cough. The cough is made worse by stress and exertion. Coughing may also occur when the dog eats or drinks. Respiratory insufficiency develops as the disease progresses.

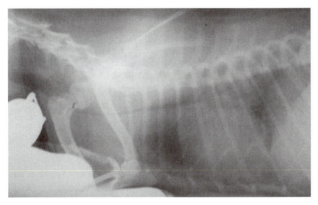

This chest X-ray shows an enlarged air column (dark shadow) in the neck indicating a normal-sized trachea, and a narrow air column in the chest indicating a collapsed trachea.

Treatment: Veterinary examination is the first step. Diseases of the heart and lungs should be ruled out before making the diagnosis. Dogs with mild to moderate symptoms respond to proper nutrition and a low-stress routine that avoids situations that trigger episodes of coughing. Moderate exercise is beneficial.

Overweight dogs should be put on a weight-loss diet as described for chronic bronchitis. Eliminate cigarette smoke and other atmospheric pollutants that can trigger coughing.

Bronchodilator drugs such as Aminophylline or Theophylline are beneficial for many small dogs. Mild low-dose sedatives during stressful periods also are helpful. Cough suppressants and corticosteroids may be prescribed at times when the coughing is particularly severe. Respiratory infections require prompt treatment with antibiotics.

Surgery can be considered in severe cases. It involves placing a rigid tubular polypropylene splint around the trachea and suturing the collapsing rings to the splint. Complications are possible.

CHRONIC BRONCHITIS

Chronic bronchitis should be considered whenever a cough persists for more than two months. This disease affects middle-aged dogs of both sexes. It is characterized by an acute inflammatory reaction of the interior of the smaller breathing tubes.

In most cases the cause is unknown. Although some cases are preceded by kennel cough, infectious agents usually do not play a role except as secondary invaders. House dust, cigarette smoke and other atmospheric irritants contribute to but do not cause the bronchial inflammation.

The hallmark of chronic bronchitis is a harsh, dry cough that may or may not be productive. Coughing is triggered by exercise and excitement. Episodes often end with gagging, retching and the expectoration of foamy saliva. This can be mistaken for vomiting. The dog's appetite and weight are well maintained.

Unchecked chronic bronchitis damages the breathing tubes and leads to the accumulation of infected mucus and pus in dilated bronchi. This is called *bronchiectasis*. Chronic coughing can also lead to enlargement of the alveoli (lung air sacs), a condition called *emphysema*. These two diseases are not reversible and gradually progress to chronic lung disease and congestive heart failure.

The diagnostic workup for bronchitis is the same as that described in *Diagnosing a Cough* (page 290).

Treatment: General measures include eliminating atmospheric pollutants such as dust and cigarette smoke. Minimize stress, fatigue and excitement. Overweight dogs should be put on a weight-loss diet (see *Weight Reduction* in Chapter 9). Prescription diets such as Hill's r/d are available through your veterinarian.

Walking on a leash is good exercise, but don't overdo it. To avoid pressure on the larynx, switch from a collar to a chest harness or head halter.

Medical management is directed toward reducing bronchial inflammation. Your veterinarian may prescribe a course of corticosteroids for 10 to 14 days. If this is beneficial, the dog may be placed on a maintenance dose given daily or every other day. Bronchodilators such as Theophylline relax the breathing passages and reduce respiratory fatigue. They are beneficial for dogs with associated wheezing and airway spasm.

If the cough gets worse there is probably a secondary bacterial infection. Seek veterinary attention, as antibiotics will be required. Cough suppressants are beneficial for episodes of exhaustive coughing, but should be used for short periods only, as they interfere with host defenses and prevent the elimination of purulent secretions. Expectorants can be used as often as needed.

The response to treatment varies. Some dogs make a near-normal recovery while others require frequent medication adjustments.

The Lungs

PNEUMONIA

Pneumonia can be caused by viruses, bacteria, fungi and parasites. Bacterial and viral pneumonia are often preceded by infection in the nasopharynx or breathing tubes.

Pneumonia is uncommon in healthy adult dogs. It tends to target the very young and the very old, and those whose immune systems have been compromised as a result of corticosteroid therapy, chemotherapy or chronic illness. Dogs with chronic bronchitis, collapsing trachea and foreign bodies in the lower airway frequently develop bacterial pneumonia.

Inhalation or *aspiration pneumonia* occurs with megaesophagus, gastroesophageal reflux, paralysis of the swallowing mechanism, and reflux of gastric contents into the lungs during general anesthesia or vomiting. Chemical pneumonia is caused by inhaling smoke or ingesting hydrocarbons such as gasoline or kerosene.

Signs of pneumonia are cough, fever, depression, rapid breathing, rapid pulse and occasionally a nasal discharge that is thick with mucus. The cough is moist and bubbling, indicating fluid in the lungs. Dogs with severe pneumonia frequently sit with their heads extended and elbows turned out to allow for greater expansion of the chest.

The diagnosis is made by chest X-ray and blood tests. Bacterial culture and sensitivity tests aid in selecting the most effective antibiotic.

Treatment: Dogs with fever and signs of respiratory infection should receive urgent veterinary care. Take the dog to the hospital as soon as possible. *Do not give cough suppressants.* Coughing is beneficial because it clears the airway and facilitates breathing.

Bacterial infection responds well to antibiotics selected specifically for the bacteria causing the diease. Your veterinarian will select the most appropriate drug. The antibiotic should be continued for at least three weeks, or until the follow-up chest X-ray shows clearing.

Any predisposing causes, such as gastroesophageal reflux or a bronchial foreign body, should be treated to prevent recurrence.

PULMONARY INFILTRATES OF EOSINOPHILS

This is an uncommon respiratory disease in dogs, caused by the presence of numerous *eosinophils* (a type of white blood cell) in the blood, respiratory secretions and lungs. Eosinophils usually indicate a hypersensitivity reaction. Accordingly, an allergic basis for PIE has been proposed. What the dog is allergic to is usually unknown.

Before a diagnosis of PIE can be made, other causes of eosinophilia, such as heartworms, lungworms, migrating intestinal parasites, fungal infections and lymphosarcoma, must be excluded.

The signs of PIE are fever, cough, rapid breathing and weight loss. Listening to the chest with a stethoscope reveals dry, crackling sounds. The diagnosis is made by finding eosinophils in the blood and *trans-tracheal washings*.

Treatment: Treatment involves large doses of corticosteroids that are tapered gradually over several weeks. Many dogs recover fully, but relapses can occur.

PLEURAL EFFUSION

A pleural effusion is an accumulation of serum or blood in the chest. The most common cause is congestive heart failure. Other causes include liver disease, kidney failure, pancreatitis and primary and metastatic tumors of the lungs. Bacterial pneumonia can extend to the pleural space, producing an infected pleural effusion called empyema. Blood in the pleural space (called *hemothorax*) occurs with chest trauma, malignant lung tumors and spontaneous bleeding disorders.

Large pleural effusions press on the lungs and cause respiratory distress. Severely affected dogs have rapid labored breathing and often stand or sit with elbows out, chest fully expanded, and head and neck extended. Breathing is open-mouthed. The lips, gums and tongue may appear blue. The least bit of effort can cause collapse.

Treatment: *Urgent veterinary attention is required.* The fluid in the lungs must be removed as soon as possible to facilitate breathing. This is accomplished by inserting a needle or catheter into the pleural space and withdrawing the fluid by syringe. The dog should be hospitalized for further studies.

Tumors of the Larynx, Trachea and Lungs

Benign and malignant tumors occur in the larynx, trachea, bronchi and lungs. The diagnosis of laryngeal, tracheal and lung tumors is based on chest X-rays, *bronchoscopy* and/or *trans-tracheal washings* and *cytology* (see *Diagnosing a Cough*, page 290). Tissue biopsy provides an accurate diagnosis and helps in planning treatment.

LARYNGEAL TUMORS

Laryngeal tumors are uncommon and occur in middle-aged to older dogs. Most are malignant (squamous cell carcinomas). Signs are noisy breathing, change in voice and loss of bark. A characteristic *stridor* may be heard when the dog inhales. Sudden death can occur from respiratory obstruction.

TRACHEAL TUMORS

Tracheal tumors are rare. In older dogs they tend to be malignant (osteosarcomas). In young dogs they are more likely to be benign (osteochondromas). The most common sign is a productive cough. Stridor on inhalation may be noted during exercise or panting. Cyanosis and collapse can occur when the tumors get very large and cause severe respiratory obstruction.

LUNG TUMORS

Lung tumors account for about 1 percent of all neoplasms in the dog. Most arise from cells lining the bronchi. They tend to occur in older dogs of both sexes. Most primary lung tumors are malignant and will have already spread to other parts of the body by the time they are diagnosed.

A harsh, nonproductive cough is the most common sign. *Pleural effusion* may occur as a late complication.

METASTATIC LUNG TUMORS

Metastatic lung tumors—that is, tumors that spread to the lungs from other parts of the body—are more common than primary lung tumors. Tumors that metastasize to the lungs include mammary gland cancers, osteosarcomas, thyroid cancers, melanomas and squamous cell carcinomas.

Treatment: Surgical exploration and removal of small tumors offers the best chance for cure. Larger tumors usually cannot be cured, but may respond to chemotherapy. The advanced age of many dogs with respiratory tract tumors usually makes aggressive treatment impractical.

THE CIRCULATORY SYSTEM

The circulatory system is comprised of the heart, the blood and the blood vessels.

The heart is a pump made up of four chambers: the right atrium and right ventricle, and the left atrium and left ventricle. The two sides of the heart are separated by a muscular wall. Blood cannot get from one side of the heart to the other without first going through the general or pulmonary circulation. Four heart valves keep blood flowing in one direction. When the valves are diseased, blood can leak backward, creating difficulties.

In normal circulation, blood is pumped out of the left ventricle, through the aortic valve and into the aorta. It passes through arteries of progressively smaller size until it reaches the capillary beds of the skin, muscles, brain and internal organs. From the capillaries blood is carried back through veins of progressively larger diameter, finally reaching two large veins called the *anterior and posterior vena cavae*.

From these large veins, the blood enters the right atrium. It passes from the right atrium through the *tricuspid valve* and into the right ventricle. As the right ventricle contracts, the *pulmonary valve* opens, allowing the blood to enter the main pulmonary artery. The pulmonary artery branches into smaller vessels and finally into capillaries around the air sacs. It is here that carbon dioxide is exchanged for oxygen. The blood then returns via the pulmonary veins, passes through the *mitral valve* and into the left ventricle. As the left ventricle contracts, the *aortic valve* opens and blood is pumped into the general circulation—thus completing the cycle.

The beating of the heart is controlled by its own internal electrical system, but also responds to outside influences. Thus, the heart beats faster when a dog exercises, becomes frightened, is overheated or requires greater blood flow to the body. The arteries and veins can expand or contract to maintain correct blood pressure.

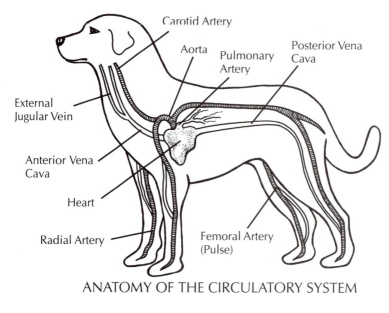

ANATOMY OF THE CIRCULATORY SYSTEM

The Normal Heart

There are outward physical signs that help to determine if a dog's heart and circulatory system are working normally. Familiarize yourself with what is normal, so you can recognize any abnormal signs.

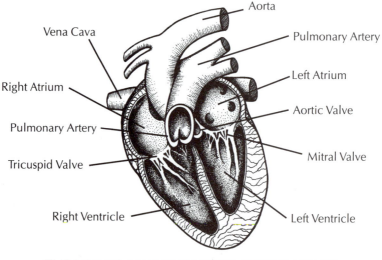

THE VALVES AND CHAMBERS OF THE HEART

PULSE

The pulse, a transmitted heartbeat, is easily detected by feeling the femoral artery, located in the groin. With your dog standing, or preferably, lying on its back, feel along the inside of the thigh where the leg joins the body. Press with your fingers until you locate the pulse.

You can also take a dog's pulse by pressing against the rib cage over its heart. Feel the heartbeat just below the elbow joint. If the heart is enlarged or diseased, you may be able to detect a buzzing or vibration over the chest wall.

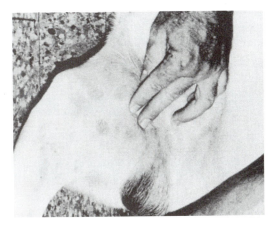

Feel for the femoral pulse in the thigh, where the leg joins the body. (J. Clawson)

The pulse rate is determined by counting the number of beats per minute. Most adult dogs at rest maintain a rate of 60 to 160 beats per minute. In large dogs the rate is somewhat slower and in toy dogs it's somewhat faster. In puppies the heart rate is 220 beats per minute.

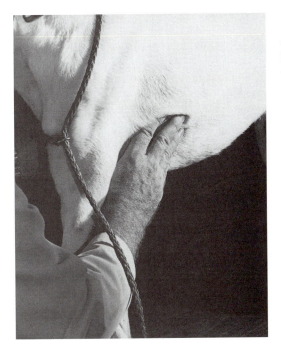

Another way to take the pulse is to feel the heartbeat behind the left elbow. (J. Clawson)

HEART SOUNDS

Veterinarians use a stethoscope to listen to the heart. You can listen to the heart by placing your ear against the chest. The normal heartbeat is divided into two sounds. The first is a *lub*, followed by a slight pause and then a *dub*. Put together the sound is *lub-dub*…in a steady, evenly spaced manner.

The heartbeat should be strong, steady and regular. A slight alteration in rhythm as the dog breathes in and out is normal. An exceedingly fast pulse can indicate anxiety, fever, anemia, blood loss, dehydration, shock, infection, heat stroke or heart (and lung) disease. A slow pulse can indicate heart disease, pressure on the brain, or an advanced morbid condition causing collapse of the circulation.

An erratic, irregular or disordered pulse indicates a *cardiac arrhythmia*. Many arrhythmias are associated with a sudden drop in blood pressure as the arrhythmia begins. In turn, the drop in blood flow to the muscles and brain is accompanied by sudden weakness or collapse, often giving the impression of a fainting spell.

When the heart sounds can be heard all over the chest, the heart is probably enlarged.

Murmurs. Heart murmurs are common. Murmurs are caused by turbulence in the flow of blood through the heart. Serious murmurs are caused by heart disease. Anemia can cause a heart murmur.

Not all murmurs are serious. Some are said to be innocent; that is, there is no disease, just a normal degree of turbulence. To determine whether a murmur is serious or of little consequence, your veterinarian may request diagnostic studies such as a chest X-ray, electrocardiogram and an echocardiogram (ultrasound of the heart).

Thrills. A thrill is caused by turbulence of such a degree that you can feel a buzzing or vibration over the chest. It suggests an obstruction to the flow of blood—for example, a constricted valve or a hole in the wall between two chambers of the heart. A thrill indicates a serious heart condition.

CIRCULATION

You can determine the adequacy of your dog's circulation and the presence or absence of anemia by examining the gums and tongue. A deep pink color is a sign of good circulation and a normal red blood cell volume. A pale color indicates anemia. A gray or bluish tinge is a sign of insufficient oxygen in the blood (called cyanosis). With severe circulatory collapse, the mucous membranes are cool and gray.

The adequacy of the circulation can be tested by noting how long it takes for the gums to "pink up" after being firmly pressed with a finger. This is called *capillary refill time*. The normal response is one second or less. More than two seconds suggests poor circulation. When the finger impression remains pale for three seconds or longer, the dog is in shock.

Canine Heart Disease

The leading cause of heart failure in dogs is chronic valvular disease. Next is dilated cardiomyopathy, followed by heartworms and congenital heart disease. Infrequent causes are bacterial endocarditis and myocarditis. Coronary artery disease is rare in dogs. It occurs only in dogs with severe hypothyroidism accompanied by extremely high serum cholesterol levels.

CHRONIC VALVULAR DISEASE

This common heart disease of unknown cause affects 20 to 40 percent of dogs. It occurs most often in *toy and small breed dogs*, particularly Cavalier King Charles Spaniels, Miniature and Toy Poodles, Chihuahuas, Lhasa Apsos, Yorkshire Terriers, Schnauzers and Cocker Spaniels.

Chronic valvular disease is characterized by degenerative changes in the heart valves. The mitral valve is affected in nearly all cases; the tricuspid valve in about one-third of cases. The valve leaflets become thickened and distorted so that the free edges of the valves no longer make contact. The cords that attach the valve leaflets to the lining of the heart may rupture, allowing the valve to float freely in the bloodstream.

These changes result in loss of valve function and a fall in cardiac output. When the ventricles contract, some blood is ejected backward into the corresponding atrium. This is called regurgitation. Regurgitation increases the blood pressure in the atrium and causes it to enlarge. Because the mitral valve is invariably involved, chronic valvular disease is also sometimes called mitral valve disease or mitral regurgitation.

The hallmark of mitral regurgitation is a loud heart murmur heard over the left side of the chest. A chest X-ray, ECG and *echocardiogram* (cardiac ultrasound) may show an enlarged left atrium, thickened valves or a ruptured cord. If the tricuspid valve is involved, there will be a loud heart murmur heard over the right side of the heart. It is important to exclude heartworms as a cause of the right-sided heart murmur.

Signs of congestive heart failure can be attributed to low cardiac output and lung congestion. They include a dry cough that occurs after exercise and is worse at night; lethargy and tiring easily; and fainting spells often related to cardiac arrhythmias.

Treatment: Many dogs with uncomplicated heart murmurs associated with chronic valvular disease remain asymptomatic for years. The disease, however, is chronic and progressive. Treatment should be started at the first signs of impending heart failure (coughing, easy tiring). The outlook depends on how far the disease has progressed and the general health and age of the dog. For more information on treatment, see *Congestive Heart Failure*, page 307.

DILATED CARDIOMYOPATHY

Dilated cardiomyopathy is a disease in which the heart chambers enlarge and the walls of the ventricles become thin. The heart muscle weakens and begins to fail.

Dilated cardiomyopathy is the most common cause of congestive heart failure in *large and giant breed dogs*. It is rare in toy breeds and small dogs. A high incidence is found in Boxers, Doberman Pinschers, Springer Spaniels and American and English Cocker Spaniels. Other breeds affected include German Shepherd Dogs, Great Danes, Saint Bernards and Schnauzers. Most dogs are two to five years of age at the onset of symptoms. The majority are males.

In most cases the cause of dilated cardiomyopathy is unknown (*idiopathic*). *Myocarditis*, an inflammation of the heart muscle, may precede dilated cardiomyopathy in some dogs. *Hypothyroidism* has been associated with dilated cardiomyopathy. A genetic or familial basis has been proposed for giant and large-breed dogs.

The signs of dilated cardiomyopathy are the same as those of congestive heart failure and cardiac arrhythmias. Weight loss can occur in a matter of weeks. Affected dogs are lethargic, tire easily, breathe rapidly and cough frequently, sometimes bringing up bloody sputum. Coughing is especially common at night. A swollen abdomen (called *ascites*) may be noted. Cardiac arrhythmias can cause weakness and collapse.

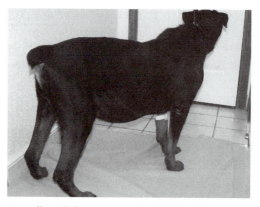

A swollen abdomen associated with dilated cardiomyopathy and congestive heart failure.

The diagnosis of dilated cardiomyopathy is based on *ECG* changes showing cardiac arrhythmias, a chest X-ray showing enlarged heart chambers, and an *echocardiogram* showing the characteristic pattern of a failing heart muscle.

Treatment: Treatment is directed at improving the force of the heart muscle, controlling arrhythmias and preventing the buildup of fluid in the lungs and abdomen (see *Congestive Heart Failure*, page 307). The prognosis for long-term survival is guarded.

With excellent medical control, some dogs may live for a year or more. Death usually occurs as the result of a sudden cardiac arrhythmia.

CONGENITAL HEART DISEASE

All forms of congenital heart disease occur in dogs. The most common defects are valve malformations (called *dysplasias*), valve narrowing (*stenosis*), abnormal openings between the heart chambers (*septal defects*), patent ductus arteriosus and Tetralogy of Fallot.

Patent ductus arteriosus is a persistent arterial connection between the aorta and pulmonary artery that normally closes at birth or shortly thereafter. In the uterus, the ductus plays an important role in shunting blood away from the nonfunctioning lungs. Many large and small breeds are affected by patent ductus arteriosus.

Tetralogy of Fallot is a congenital defect of the heart consisting of four abnormalities that result in insufficiently oxygenated blood pumped to the body.

Most dogs with *severe* congenital heart defects die within the first year of life. Dogs with *moderate* defects may survive but usually exhibit exercise intolerance, fainting episodes and stunted growth. In these individuals heart failure can occur suddenly and unexpectedly. Dogs with *mild* valvular disease or small septal defects are often asymptomatic; the only indication of congenital heart defect being a heart murmur discovered on physical examination.

The diagnosis of congenital heart defect is based on ECG, chest X-rays and *echocardiogram*. An ultrasound study called Doppler echocardiography measures the velocity and direction of blood flow in the heart chambers. This information makes the diagnosis of congenital heart defects extremely accurate. Cardiac catheterization with angiocardiography is the "gold standard" for diagnosing congenital heart defects, but it carries a small risk and is available only at advanced veterinary hospitals. Doppler echocardiography, being accurate and noninvasive, has largely replaced cardiac catheterization for routine diagnosis.

Treatment: Dogs with minor heart defects have a good prognosis and do not benefit from surgery. Patent ductus arteriosus is an example of a defect that does benefit from surgery. Without surgery, 60 percent of affected puppies die within the first year. With surgery, the death rate is less than 10 percent.

Moderate atrial and ventricular septal defects can be repaired surgically with varying degrees of success. This requires open heart surgery and cardiopulmonary bypass.

Valve dysplasias and large septal defects have a poor prognosis, regardless of the method of treatment. Affected dogs are at risk of congestive heart failure and sudden death.

The treatment of congestive heart failure and cardiac arrhythmias is discussed later in this chapter.

Prevention: Most congenital heart defects have a hereditary basis. Breeds with a known predisposition for specific congenital heart defects are shown in the accompanying chart. This list is by no means comprehensive.

Breed Predispositions for Congenital Heart Defects	
Atrial septal defects	Samoyed
Ventricular septal defects	Bulldog
Aortic and subaortic stenosis	Newfoundland, Golden Retriever, German Shepherd, Rottweiler
Tricuspid dysplasia	Labrador Retriever, Great Dane, Weimaraner
Mitral dysplasia	Great Dane, German Shepherd Dog, Bull Terrier
Patent ductus arteriosus	Poodle, Pomeranian, Collie, Shetland Sheepdog, German Shepherd Dog
Tetralogy of Fallot	Keeshond

It is important to identify affected individuals when treatment is most likely to be successful and before the dog is used for breeding. The best time to screen puppies for congenital heart defects is when they are six to eight weeks of age, before being released to their new homes. Screening is done by carefully listening for murmurs with a stethoscope over the four valve areas. The examination is best performed by a veterinarian experienced in recognizing heart murmurs. Murmurs heard at this age may not be associated with disease; some will disappear as the pup matures. If the murmur is present at 16 weeks, however, the puppy should be screened using cardiac ultrasound.

The Orthopedic Foundation for Animals (OFA) maintains a cardiac registry to gather data on congenital heart defects. (See Appendix C for information on how to contact OFA.) Dogs are screened at 12 months of age or later, and if found to be unaffected, are issued a certificate and a registration number. For bloodlines with an increased incidence of congenital heart defects, it is highly desirable to seek OFA certification before selecting breeding animals.

BACTERIAL ENDOCARDITIS

Bacterial endocarditis is an infection of the heart valves and the lining of the heart. The disease is not common. It is caused by bacterial species that gain entrance to the circulation from wounds and infections elsewhere in the body. In many cases the actual source of infection is unknown. Dogs on corticosteroids and immunosuppressant drugs are at increased risk, as are midsize and large dogs.

As the bacteria invade the heart valves, they produce ulcerations and small wartlike bumps called vegetations. The effects on the valves are similar to those of chronic valvular disease. In addition, parts of infected vegetations can break off and spread the infection to other organs. This seeding process causes a variety of signs, including fever, shaking chills, joint swelling and lameness, spontaneous bleeding, blindness, behavioral and personality changes, unstable gait, stupor and seizures. These signs are nonspecific and may suggest a number of other diseases.

The presence of a heart murmur, particularly a new or changing murmur, suggests a diagnosis of bacterial endocarditis. This can be confirmed by ECG, chest X-rays and *echocardiography*. Blood cultures identify the causative bacteria.

Treatment: Antibiotics must be selected based on blood culture and sensitivity tests. To eliminate vegetations, long-term antibiotic therapy (two to four months) is required. The dog should be monitored closely for signs of congestive heart failure, which may appear suddenly, and for the development of antibiotic-resistant organisms.

Dogs with less severe valve disease may recover with only mild permanent damage. The prognosis is guarded for dogs with mitral valve involvement and poor for those with aortic valve involvement.

MYOCARDITIS

Myocarditis is an inflammation of the heart muscle. It is an uncommon cause of heart disease in dogs. Myocarditis occurs with American trypanosomiasis, Lyme disease, viral diseases including distemper, and bacterial, fungal and protozoan infections. Parvovirus produces a fatal form of myocarditis in neonatal puppies. It is rarely seen now because of the practice of routinely immunizing brood bitches against parvo.

One of the first signs of myocarditis is weakness and fainting caused by cardiac arrhythmias. It can also be suspected by the sudden appearance of congestive heart failure, along with abnormal findings on an ECG and *echocardiogram*. If necessary, the diagnosis can be confirmed by a heart muscle biopsy. This must be done at a medical center. Treatment and prognosis are similar to those described for *dilated cardiomyopathy*. If a specific cause is found, it should be treated.

Congestive Heart Failure

Heart failure is the inability of the heart to provide adequate circulation to meet the body's needs. It is the end result of a weakened heart muscle. The health of the liver, kidneys, lungs and other organs is impaired by the circulatory failure, resulting in a problem involving multiple organs.

A diseased heart can compensate for many months or years without signs of failure. When failure does occur, it may appear suddenly and unexpectedly—sometimes immediately after strenuous exercise, when the heart is unable to keep up with the body's demands.

In toy and small-breed dogs, *chronic valvular disease* with mitral regurgitation is the most common cause of congestive heart failure. In large-breed dogs it is *dilated cardiomyopathy*.

The early signs of congestive heart failure are easy tiring, a decrease in activity level and intermittent coughing. The coughing occurs during periods of exertion or excitation. It also tends to occur at night, usually about two hours after the dog goes to bed.

These early signs are nonspecific and may even be considered normal for the dog's age. As heart failure progresses the dog develops other signs, such as lack of appetite, rapid breathing, abdominal swelling and a marked loss of weight.

Because the heart no longer pumps effectively, blood backs up in the lungs, liver, legs and other organs. Increased pressure in the veins causes fluid to leak into the lungs and peritoneal cavity. Fluid in the lungs is the cause of the coughing. A rapid accumulation of fluid in the small breathing tubes can cause the dog to cough up a bubbly red fluid, a condition called *pulmonary edema*. Pulmonary edema indicates *failure of the left ventricle*.

With *failure of the right ventricle*, fluid leaks into the abdomen, giving the belly a characteristic swelling or pot-bellied appearance (called *ascites*). This may be accompanied by swelling of the legs (*dependent edema*). An accumulation of fluid in the chest cavity (*pleural effusion*) also occurs with right-sided heart failure.

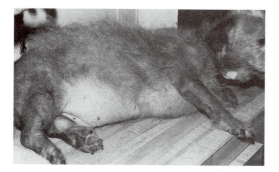

Right-sided congestive heart failure with ascites and dependent leg edema.

In the late stages of congestive heart failure the dog sits with its elbows spread and its head extended. Breathing is labored. The pulse is rapid, thready and often irregular. The mucous membranes of the gums and tongue are bluish-gray and cool. A thrill may be felt over the chest. Fainting can occur with stress or exertion.

An accurate diagnosis is established through chest X-ray, ECG, echocardiography and other tests (such as a heartworm antigen test) as indicated.

Treatment: It is important to correct any underlying cause whenever possible. *Heartworms, bacterial endocarditis* and some forms of congenital heart disease are potentially curable if they are treated before the heart is damaged.

Treatment of congestive heart failure involves feeding a low-salt diet, restricting exercise and giving appropriate medications to increase heart function and prevent cardiac arrhythmias.

Most commercial diets contain excessive amounts of salt. Your veterinarian may prescribe a low-salt prescription diet such as Hill's h/d or CV Heart Diet. In dogs with mild symptoms, salt restriction may be the only treatment required.

Exercise is beneficial—but only for dogs that are not symptomatic. If symptoms such as easy tiring, coughing or rapid breathing appear with exercise, *do not allow your dog to engage in activities that elicit these symptoms.*

Various drugs are available that increase the force and contraction of the heart muscle or decrease the workload. They include the digitalis glycosides, calcium channel blockers, angiotensin-converting enzyme (ACE) inhibitors, beta blockers and anti-arrhythmics. These are the same drugs used in people. ACE inhibitors such as enalapril maleate (Enacard) may prolong the life of dogs with valvular heart disease and cardiomyopathy, and are commonly used in dogs with these diseases. Fluid accumulation in the lungs and elsewhere is managed by diuretics such as Lasix. Potassium supplements may be necessary when giving diuretics. Dogs with congestive heart failure may benefit from vitamin-B supplements.

When treating cardiac arrhythmias, it is important to search for and correct any underlying electrolyte or metabolic problems that might trigger an attack. A number of cardiac drugs, including digitalis, lidocaine, diltiazem, procainamide, atropine and propanalol, are used to control arrhythmias in dogs.

With proper treatment, a dog can live a longer and more comfortable life. Heart disease, however, requires close monitoring. You will need to return to your veterinarian regularly for checkups.

Heartworms

Heartworm disease, so named because the adult worms live in the right side of the heart, continues to be a major problem. Heartworms are spread by mosquitoes, and thus are found throughout the world. In the United States the prevalence is highest along the southeastern Atlantic and Gulf Coasts. The disease is less prevalent along the northern borders and at higher elevations. The overall incidence among dogs is 15 to 20 percent, but in areas where the disease is highly endemic, virtually all unprotected dogs will become infected.

Large and medium dogs are at increased risk. This reflects the greater outdoor exposure of larger dogs. In fact, dogs living outdoors are four to five times more likely to develop heartworms than those living indoors.

HEARTWORM LIFE CYCLE

A knowledge of the life cycle of this parasite (*Dirofilaria immitis*) is needed to understand its prevention and treatment. Infection begins when L_3 infective larvae in the mouthparts of a mosquito enter the dog's skin at the site of a bite. The larvae burrow beneath the skin and undergo two molts that eventually lead to the development of small immature worms. The first molt (L_3 to L_4) occurs one to 12 days after inoculation. The larvae remain in the L_4 stage for 50 to 68 days, and then molt into the L_5 stage (immature worms).

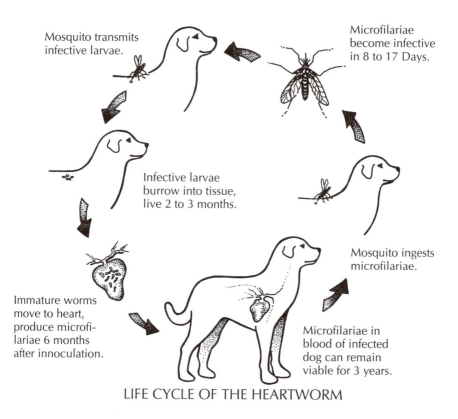

Mosquito transmits infective larvae.

Microfilariae become infective in 8 to 17 Days.

Infective larvae burrow into tissue, live 2 to 3 months.

Mosquito ingests microfilariae.

Immature worms move to heart, produce microfilariae 6 months after innoculation.

Microfilariae in blood of infected dog can remain viable for 3 years.

LIFE CYCLE OF THE HEARTWORM

It is only during the brief L_3 stage, 1 to 12 days after the larvae enter the dog's body, that they are susceptible to the killing effects of diethylcarbamazine. However, throughout the L_3 and L_4 stages the larvae are susceptible to two other drugs: ivermectin and milbemycin. This knowledge is used in prevention programs.

Immature worms make their way into a peripheral vein and are carried to the right ventricle and pulmonary arteries, where they await further maturation. Approximately six months after entering the dog's body, they become adults. Adults can reach lengths of 4 to 12 inches and live up to five years. As many as 250 worms may be found in a heavily infested dog.

Sexual reproduction occurs if worms of the opposite sex are present. Females give birth to live young called *microfilaria*; 5,000 microfilariae can be produced in one day by a single worm. Microfilaria are able to remain alive in the dog's circulatory system for up to three years.

Before the microfilariae can become infective to another dog, the L_1 larvae must go into a secondary host, the mosquito. This occurs when the mosquito bites the dog. The L_1 larvae in the mosquito molt to L_3 larvae. In warm southern climates this process takes less than 10 days; in northern climates it can take up to 17 days. The L_3 larvae then move to the mouthparts of the mosquito and are ready to infect a new host.

HEARTWORM DISEASE

When there are fewer than 50 adult worms in the average size dog, the worms live primarily in the pulmonary arteries and the right ventricle of the heart. When the numbers are greater than 75, the worms usually extend into the right atrium. With a heavier infestation the worms may migrate into the superior and inferior *vena cavae* and the veins of the liver.

This model shows heartworms in the right atrium and right ventricle.

Worms in the pulmonary circulation can migrate into the terminal branches of the pulmonary arteries, where they obstruct the flow of blood and cause the vessels to clot. This is known as *pulmonary thromboembolism*. Even after treatment, dead worms can be carried by the bloodstream into the pulmonary circulation, resulting in a similar severe and sometimes fatal reaction. Chronic pulmonary thromboembolism causes loss of lung tissue and right-sided congestive heart failure. Dogs with thromboembolism may cough up bloody sputum.

Worms entwined about the heart valves can interfere with the mechanics of the heart and produce effects similar to those of chronic valvular disease.

Worms clumps in the *vena cavae* or hepatic veins are responsible for a condition called *vena cava syndrome*, which causes liver failure with jaundice, swelling of the abdomen (*ascites*), spontaneous bleeding and anemia. Collapse and death can occur in two to three days.

SIGNS

The signs of heartworm disease depend on the number of worms and the size of the dog. Dogs with a light infection involving only a few worms may remain asymptomatic.

The typical early signs of heartworm infestation are easy tiring, intolerance to exercise and a soft, deep cough. As the disease progresses these symptoms become more severe and the dog loses weight, breathes more rapidly and may cough after exercise to the point of fainting. The ribs become prominent and the chest starts to bulge. An acute *vena cava syndrome* or episode of *thromboembolism* can lead to collapse and death.

DIAGNOSIS

A number of blood tests are available for diagnosing heartworms. The most accurate is the *heartworm antigen test*, which identifies an antigen produced by the adult female heartworm. False negatives occur in early infections (before the appearance of mature worms), in light infections with fewer than five adult worms and in infections in which only males are present. False positives are rare.

Another important heartworm test is the *microfilarial concentration test*, in which parasites in a sample of blood are identified under the microscope. Although a positive test definitely indicates heartworms, a negative test does not rule out the diagnosis because typically 10 to 25 percent of infected dogs do not have microfilariae circulating in the peripheral blood.

Dogs with a negative microfilarial concentration test who indeed do have heartworms are said to be suffering from an *occult infection*. There are a number of explanations for occult infection. One is that the dog is receiving a heartworm preventive. Preventives kill microfilariae but not adult worms. Thus these dogs will have a positive heartworm antigen test and a negative microfilarial concentration test.

There is yet another type of microfilaria that can be present in dogs tested for heartworms. It is called *Dipetalonema*. It is a harmless worm living under the skin. Its importance rests in the fact that its microfilariae may be mistaken for those of heartworm.

A chest X-ray is the best test for determining the severity of the infection. Dogs with a heavy burden of worms in the pulmonary artery have X-rays that show enlargement of the right ventricle and/or pulmonary arteries.

An *ECG* may show right ventricular enlargement and cardiac arrhythmias. An *echocardiogram* may show worms in the main pulmonary artery or the right ventricle. In the *vena cava syndrome*, heartworms can be seen in the vena cava. Blood and urine samples are obtained to check for anemia and assess kidney and liver function.

TREATING HEARTWORM DISEASE

When and how to treat depends on the number of heartworms, their location, any medical complications (congestive heart failure, liver or kidney disease), the age and condition of the dog and the presence of circulating microfilariae. After a thorough medical examination, your veterinarian will discuss these options and recommend a treatment program based on the findings.

For dogs with uncomplicated heartworm disease, the objectives are to eliminate all adult worms, kill microfilariae (if present) and initiate preventive measures. At the same time, it is important to avoid complications associated with drug toxicity and the passage of dead worms into the lungs.

The first step in dealing with uncomplicated heartworm infection is to administer an agent to kill the adult worms. Two drugs commonly used are thiacetarsamide (Caparsolate) and melarsamine (Immiticide). Both compounds contain arsenic. Caparsolate is given intravenously twice a day for two days. Significant toxic reactions can occur, and include loss of appetite, vomiting, diarrhea, jaundice, kidney failure and death. Caparsolate does not always kill all the worms. Immature worms, especially females, are relatively resistant. The drug is not safe to use on high-risk dogs with congestive heart failure, or liver or those with kidney impairment.

Immiticide eliminates over 90 percent of worms, making it more effective than Caparsolate. It has a higher margin of safety and can be given to dogs at high risk. Immiticide is given by intramuscular injection once a day for two days. If the dog is severely debilitated by heartworms, the drug can be given in divided doses 30 days apart. Complications are similar to those of Caparsolate, but occur less often. Both drugs can cause a local reaction at the site of injection. Thromboembolism is a complication associated with the death of adult worms, and can occur with either drug.

Approximately 10 percent of dogs are poor candidates for immediate drug treatment because of severe pulmonary artery infestation and congestive heart failure. These dogs will benefit from complete rest and confinement for two to three weeks before and after drug therapy. Aspirin, a mild anticoagulant, is given to prevent respiratory failure due to worm thromboembolism.

Elderly dogs with heartworms are at high risk of death from therapy to kill the adult worms. Some old dogs may be better off without treatment. An acceptable alternative is to restrict exercise and administer a low dose of aspirin daily to prevent further damage to the lungs.

Surgical removal of worms is reserved for critically ill dogs with the *vena cava syndrome* who are not candidates for drug therapy because of the risk of liver failure or thromboembolism. To remove the worms with this method, an incision is made over the jugular vein in the neck. The vein is opened and a long grasping instrument is passed down through the superior vena cava into the right atrium and the inferior vena cava. The worms are grasped one by one and removed. The procedure requires X-ray equipment and special skills. Residual worms are eliminated with drug therapy after the dog improves.

A heartworm antigen test should be performed three to five months after drug therapy. If all worms have been eliminated, the test will be negative. If the test is positive, retreatment can be considered.

The next step is to kill circulating microfilaria. This step is omitted if parasites are not found on a microfilaria concentration test.

Most veterinarians wait four weeks to allow the dog to recover from the effects of killing the adult worms before beginning therapy to kill the microfilaria. Currently there are two drugs used to kill microfilaria, although neither is licensed for this purpose. They are ivermectin (Ivomec) and milbemycin (Interceptor). Ivomec is the most effective and has the fewest complications.

Dogs undergoing treatment with Ivomec are admitted to the hospital on the morning of treatment. The drug is given orally and the dog is observed for 10 to 12 hours for signs of toxicity, including vomiting, diarrhea, lethargy, weakness and shock. Most reactions are mild and respond to intravenous fluids and corticosteroids. Shock and death have occurred in Collies, Shetland Sheepdogs, Australian Shepherds, Old English Sheepdogs and other herding breeds and their crosses. Ivomec should not be used in these dogs.

Dramatic declines in microfilaria counts occur over the next few days. Ninety percent of dogs are microfilaria free at three weeks. At this time the dog should return for a microfilaria concentration test. If positive, the protocol is repeated. If negative, begin heartworm prevention.

A positive microfilaria concentration test after two treatments strongly suggests that adult worms are still present in the dog. Confirm this with a heartworm antigen test and treat accordingly.

HEARTWORM PREVENTION (PROPHYLAXIS)

If you live or travel with your dog in an area where heartworm is endemic, your dog should be on a heartworm prevention program. Ask your veterinarian about local prevalence and follow his or her recommendations for prevention.

A prevention program should be started at six to eight weeks of age in endemic areas, or as soon thereafter as climate conditions dictate. In the deep South, where mosquitoes are a year-round problem, dogs should be kept on preventive drugs all year long. In areas where it is unnecessary to administer the drug year round, start the drug one month before the mosquito season and continue it for one month beyond the first frost (generally from May or June to November or December). Continue heartworm prevention for life.

All dogs seven months or older should have an antigen test for heartworms before starting a prevention program. If the test is positive, a microfilaria concentration test should be performed. The antigen test should be repeated annually or as frequently as your veterinarian recommends—even if the dog is on a heartworm prevention program.

There are a number of drugs currently in use as heartworm preventives. They include diethylcarbamazine (Filarabits), the macrolide agents which are ivermectin (Heartgard), milbemycin oxime (Interceptor) and moxidectin (ProHeart), and a newly released heartworm preparation called Selamectin (Revolution).

Heartgard is an effective preventive that is given once a month. This drug acts on the L$_4$ larvae. Heartgard has the advantage that dogs do not have to be heartworm free to initiate therapy; dogs infected for as long as two months before treatment will not develop heartworms. If a monthly dose is missed, restart the drug and obtain a heartworm antigen test seven months later. Heartgard is marketed in chewable tablets of different sizes, depending on the weight of the dog. Heartgard in the recommended dose is safe to use on Collies and other herding breeds.

Heartgard Plus is a popular chewable tablet that combines ivermectin with pyrantel pamoate. This combination prevents heartworms and also controls roundworms and hookworms.

Interceptor (milbemycin oxime) and ProHeart (moxidectin) are other orally administered once-a-month heartworm preventives that also act on the L_4 larvae. Like Heartgard, these drugs are marketed in different dosages based on the weight of the dog. Interceptor also controls hookworms, roundworms and whipworms. Both drugs are safe to use on Collies and Collie crosses.

Diethylcarbamazine (DEC) has proven over many years to be extremely safe and effective when given daily. It is less convenient that the macrolide agents, and unlike the macrolides does not protect if two or three days are missed. DEC is available as a liquid (Nemacide Oral Syrup) and as a chewable tablet (Filaribits Plus and other brands). Your veterinarian will determine the appropriate dose for the weight of the dog. *Dogs over six months of age must be tested for microfilaria before starting on DEC.* If microfilaria are found in the blood, the drug should not be given because anaphylactic reactions of varying severity, including death, may develop.

DEC kills L_3 infective larvae before they molt to L_4. Since molting can occur in as short a time as 24 hours, DEC must be given daily to be effective. If more than two days of treatment are missed, stop the drug and consult your veterinarian for further instructions.

Drugs containing DEC have an extremely bitter taste. Filaribits is a chewable tablet that combines DEC with a formula for masking the bitterness. Filarbits Plus is a combination of DEC and oxibendazole. This product has the advantage of controlling hookworms and roundworms as well as heartworms.

Selamectin (*Revolution*) is a once-a-month liquid heartworm preventative applied to the skin of the dog's neck between the shoulder blades. It is available from your veterinarian in premeasured doses according to the dog's size and age. A principal advantage of selamectin is that it controls adult fleas and prevents flea eggs from hatching for one month. In addition, it treats ear mites and the mites that cause *scabies*. The drug has received limited usage at the time of this writing. It may well prove to be as effective as oral products, and if so may become a popular alternative because of ease of application and the advantages listed above.

In theory, the best way to prevent heartworms is to keep your dog from being bitten by a mosquito. Unfortunately, preventing mosquito bites can never be 100 percent effective. Dogs can be reasonably protected if they remain indoors in the late afternoon and evenings when mosquitoes are feeding.

Areas of most frequent heartworm infestation are along coastal regions, where swamps or other brackish water provide ideal conditions for mosquitoes to breed. Since mosquitoes have a flight range of one quarter mile, spraying around the yard and kennel and removing standing water can be partially effective.

Anemia and Clotting Disorders

Anemia is a defined as a deficiency of red blood cells (*erythrocytes*) in the circulatory system. Adult dogs are anemic when the concentration of red cells in whole blood is less than 37 percent by volume. The normal is 45 percent. Red cells are produced by the bone marrow and have an average life span of 110 to 120 days. Old red cells are trapped by the spleen and removed from the circulation. The iron they contain is recycled to make new erythrocytes.

The purpose of red cells is to carry oxygen. Thus, the symptoms of anemia are caused by insufficient oxygen in the organs and muscles. Signs include lack of appetite, lethargy and weakness. The mucous membranes of the gums and tongue become a pale pink to white. With severe anemia, the pulse and respiratory rate are rapid and the dog may collapse with exertion. A heart murmur may be heard.

Anemia can be caused by blood loss, hemolysis and inadequate red cell production.

BLOOD LOSS ANEMIA

In adult dogs the most common cause of blood loss is slow gastrointestinal bleeding associated with stomach and duodenal ulcers, worm parasites and tumors in the gastrointestinal tract. Chronic blood loss also occurs through the urinary system (see Chapter 14, *Blood in the Urine*). Hookworms and fleas are common causes of chronic blood loss in puppies. Blood in the urine or stools may be associated with a spontaneous bleeding disorder such as von Willebrand's disease.

Treatment: Treatment must be directed toward the cause of the anemia. Gastrointestinal bleeding can be detected by checking the stools for microscopic traces of blood. Other tests can also be used to determine the cause of the *occult* (microscopic) bleeding.

HEMOLYTIC ANEMIAS

Hemolysis is an acceleration in the normal process of red cell breakdown. Red cells break down to form bile and hemoglobin. With severe hemolysis, these breakdown products accumulate in the body. Accordingly, in an acute hemolytic crisis you would expect to see *jaundice* (a yellow cast to the eyes and mucous membranes) and *hemoglobinuria* (passage of dark-brown urine containing hemoglobin). In addition, the dog appears weak and pale, and has a rapid pulse. The spleen, liver and lymph nodes may be enlarged.

Causes of hemolysis include immune-mediated hemolytic anemia, congenital hemolytic anemia, infectious diseases (canine babesiosis or leptospirosis), drug reactions to acetaminophen and poisonous snake bites. A number of bacteria produce toxins that destroy red cells, so hemolysis can also occur with severe infections.

Neonatal isoerythrolysis is a hemolytic disease of newborn puppies; it is discussed in Chapter 17.

Immune-Mediated Hemolytic Anemia. This is the most common cause of hemolysis in adult dogs. Red cell destruction is caused by *auto-antibodies* that attack antigens present on the surface of red cells. The weakened cells are trapped in the spleen and destroyed.

Poodles, Old English Sheepdogs, Irish Setters and Cocker Spaniels are predisposed to immune-mediated hemolytic anemia, but all breeds are susceptible. Affected dogs are usually between two and eight years of age; females outnumber males four to one.

Most cases of immune-mediated hemolytic anemia are idiopathic. That is, the reason why the auto-antibodies developed in that particular dog is unknown. In some cases there is a history of recent drug therapy. An immune-mediated hemolytic anemia also occurs with *systemic lupus erythematosus*.

Congenital Hemolytic Anemias. There are several inherited abnormalities in erythrocyte structure that result in premature destruction of red cells. *Phosphofructokinase deficiency* is an autosomal recessive trait that occurs in English Springer Spaniels and Cocker Spaniels. A deficiency of this enzyme results in changes in the pH of erythrocytes, causing the cells to periodically fragment and produce bouts of hemoglobinuria.

Pyruvate kinase deficiency is another erythrocyte enzyme deficiency caused by an autosomal recessive gene. This disease is recognized in several breeds, including the Basenji, Beagle and West Highland White Terrier. Puppies usually develop the hemolytic anemia at 2 to 12 months of age. Death by age three is the usual outcome.

Genetic tests for phosphofructokinase and pyruvate kinase deficiency are available or in development at the University of Pennsylvania.

OFA maintains a voluntary diagnostic service and registry for dogs with phosphofructokinase deficiency, and Basenjis with pyruvate kinase deficiency—in cooperation with the respective national breed clubs (see Appendix C).

Treatment of Hemolytic Anemia: The diagnosis is made by microscopic examination of blood smears, looking for specific changes in the appearance of the erythrocytes and other blood elements; and by serologic blood tests.

Treatment of idiopathic immune-mediated hemolytic anemia is directed toward preventing further red cell destruction by blocking the antigen-antibody reaction using corticosteroids and immunosuppressants. Severe anemia is corrected with blood transfusions. Splenectomy (removal of the spleen) may be beneficial, but only when tests prove that the spleen is contributing to the hemolytic process.

The response to treatment depends on the rate of hemolysis and whether an underlying cause can be found and corrected. In immune-mediated hemolytic anemia the outlook is guarded. Even with appropriate medical treatment, the mortality rate is close to 40 percent.

INADEQUATE RED CELL PRODUCTION

When the metabolic activity of the bone marrow is depressed, new erythrocytes are not manufactured as fast as old ones are destroyed. This results in an anemia due to inadequate red cell production. A common cause of bone marrow depression is chronic illness, especially that associated with kidney and liver disease.

Iron, trace minerals, vitamins and fatty acids are all incorporated into red cells. Thus a deficiency of one or more of these nutrients could slow down or stop erythrocyte production. This is an unusual cause of anemia in dogs, because commercial dog foods contain more than adequate amounts of essential vitamins and minerals.

Iron deficiency is an exception. It occurs when iron is lost from the body faster than it can be replaced through the diet. The two situations in which this is most likely to happen are chronic gastrointestinal bleeding and a heavy infestation of blood-sucking insects (such as fleas, ticks and lice).

Erythrocyte production can be depressed by certain drugs. Estrogen is an important cause of bone marrow depression. This includes estrogens given for medical purposes as well as those produced by testicular and ovarian tumors. Other drugs that depress the bone marrow include chemotherapy agents, chloramphenicol, butazolidin, thiacetarsamide, quinidine and trimethoprim-sulfadiazine.

Primary and metastatic cancer can invade the bone marrow and crowd out normal cells.

Treatment: The diagnosis of inadequate red cell production is made by bone marrow biopsy. Treatment is directed toward eliminating the cause of the bone marrow deficiency. The dog should be screened for kidney and liver disease. Iron deficiency anemia warrants stool examination and a further medical workup. Many drug-related causes of bone marrow depression reverse when the drug is stopped. Estrogen-producing tumors of the ovary or testicle should be sought and treated.

CLOTTING DISORDERS

Clotting disorders are caused by an absence of one of the coagulation factors needed to complete the clotting sequence. Severe deficiencies are associated with spontaneous bleeding.

Von Willebrand's Disease (vWD)

This is the most common inherited bleeding disorder in dogs. It has been described in more than 50 breeds. Both males and females can transmit and express the genetic trait. vWD is inherited as an autosomal dominant gene with variable expression. That is, the severity of the bleeding is related to the degree to which the gene is expressed.

The bleeding is caused by a deficiency of a plasma protein called the von Willebrand factor, which is critical for normal platelet function in the early stages of clotting.

In most cases the bleeding in vWD is mild or inapparent, and lessens with age. Severe problems include prolonged nosebleeds, bleeding beneath the skin and into the muscles, and blood in the stool and urine. There is often a history of bleeding from the gums following tooth eruptions, and oozing from wounds following tail docking and dewclaw removal.

Breeds at risk for vWD in which bleeding is likely to be mild include the Doberman Pinscher, Golden Retriever, Standard Poodle, Pembroke Welsh Corgi, Manchester Terrier, Miniature Schnauzer, Akita and others. Breeds in which bleeding is likely to be more severe include the Scottish Terrier, Shetland Sheepdog, German Shorthaired Pointer and Chesapeake Bay Retriever.

Hypothyroidism is common in dogs with vWD, and may contribute to the bleeding.

The diagnosis is made by specific blood tests, including a bleeding time. A quantitative test for von Willebrand's disease involves measuring the vWD antigen. Dogs with vWD antigen levels below the normal range are at risk for expressing and/or carrying the trait.

OFA maintains a vWD registry for many of the breeds mentioned above. A DNA test for identifying affected dogs and carriers is available through *VetGen* (see Appendix C).

Hemophilia

This is a sex-linked recessive trait occurring only in males who inherit a maternal X chromosome carrying a defective gene. Females always inherit two X chromosomes, at least one of which contains a normal dominant gene. Thus females can carry the trait but do not develop the disease—the exception being a female who inherits two recessive genes: one from a hemophiliac father, and the other from a mother who is either a hemophiliac or a carrier.

Hemophilia A (most common) is a deficiency of coagulation factor VIII. Hemophilia B is a deficiency of factor IX. Hemophilia occurs in all breeds, with a predisposition for the German Shepherd Dogs, Airedale Terrier and Bichon Frise. Hemophilia produces bleeding into the chest and abdominal cavities, muscles and subcutaneous tissues. Bleeding into the joints is common.

Other coagulation deficiencies involve factors VII, X, XI and prothrombin. These deficiencies are inherited as single factor autosomal traits, and affect males and females alike. They are less common than hemophilia. Affected breeds include the Boxer, English and American Cocker Spaniel, English Springer Spaniel, Beagle and Kerry Blue Terrier.

The diagnosis of a coagulation factor deficiency is based on a number of clotting tests, plus an analysis for the specific factor that is deficient.

Disseminated Intravascular Coagulation (DIC)

This is an acquired bleeding disorder triggered by shock and infection, certain tumors (particularly *hemangiosarcomas*, osteosarcomas and cancers of the prostate and mammary glands), and severe injuries such as crush wounds and burns. DIC is characterized by intravascular clotting throughout the entire capillary circulation, followed by spontaneous bleeding when all the clotting factors have been consumed. The bleeding associated with DIC involves the nose, mouth, gastrointestinal tract and body cavities. Dogs with DIC are extremely ill and often die.

Another acquired bleeding disorder is caused by vitamin K deficiency. It is discussed in Chapter 1 (see *Rodent Poisons*).

Treatment of Coagulation Disorders

Successful treatment of spontaneous bleeding requires rapid diagnosis. Dogs with severe blood loss are given fresh, whole blood containing red cells, platelets and active coagulation factors. Dogs with less severe blood loss that don't require blood transfusions are given fresh-frozen plasma or concentrates containing the missing coagulation factor.

Treating vWD hypothyroid dogs with thyroid replacement therapy may prevent subsequent bleeding episodes. An important additional step in treating DIC is to control the underlying cause of the intravascular coagulation.

Dogs with inherited coagulation disorders, and those that may be carriers, should not be used for breeding.

THE NERVOUS SYSTEM

The brain is comprised of the cerebrum, cerebellum, midbrain and brain stem. The cerebrum is the largest part of the brain. It is the center of learning, memory, behavior and voluntary movement. Diseases affecting the cerebrum are characterized by depression, alterations in personality and behavior, and seizures.

The cerebellum has two lobes. Its primary function is to integrate motor pathways, coordinate movements and maintain balance. Diseases of the cerebellum result in lack of coordination, unstable gait and muscle tremors.

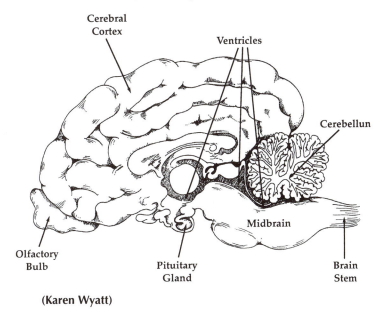

(Karen Wyatt)

CROSS SECTION OF THE BRAIN

In the midbrain and brain stem are the centers that control the respiratory rate, heart beat, blood pressure and other vital functions. At the base of the brain and closely connected to the midbrain and brain stem are the hypothalamus and pituitary gland. These structures are important in regulating the dog's body temperature and hormone systems. They are also the centers for primitive responses such as hunger, thirst, anger and fright.

The spinal cord passes down a bony canal formed by the arches of the vertebrae. The cord sends out nerve roots that combine with one another to form the peripheral nerves. Diseases of the spinal cord produce various degrees of weakness and paralysis.

The cauda equina is the termination of the spinal cord. Diseases of the cauda equina produce paralysis of the tail, loss of bladder and bowel control, and paralysis of the anal sphincter.

The paired cranial nerves, 12 total, arise from the midbrain and brain stem and pass directly out into the head and neck through openings in the skull. The optic nerves to the eyes, the otic nerves to the ears and the olfactory nerves to the nasal cavity are examples of paired cranial nerves.

Neurologic Evaluation

A complete health history is of paramount importance in diagnosing unexplained neurologic symptoms. Your veterinarian will want to know if the dog has been in an accident. Did he receive a blow to the head? Is he taking any medications? Has he been exposed to other dogs exhibiting similar signs? When did you first notice the symptoms? Did they come on suddenly or gradually? Have they progressed? If so, has the progression been rapid or gradual? The age, sex and breed of the dog are important, because some neurologic diseases are genetically determined and appear in certain breeds or at certain ages.

Diagnostic tests used in evaluating neurologic include X-rays of the skull and vertebral column, electroencephalography (*EEG*), and muscle and nerve conduction studies. A spinal tap is a procedure in which a needle is inserted into the spinal canal to remove cerebrospinal fluid for laboratory analysis. A myelogram is a spinal tap in which dye is introduced into the spinal canal so signs of spinal cord compression will be visible on X-rays. Computed tomography (*CT scan*) and magnetic resonance imaging (*MRI*) allow a radiologist to see a computerized image of the structures in the brain, spinal canal and body cavities. These examinations are now available at veterinary schools and many large veterinary hospitals.

Head Injuries

A dog's head can be injured in many ways, including a car accident, a fall, a blow to the head or a gunshot wound. Since the brain is encased in bone and surrounded by a layer of fluid, it takes a major blow to the head to fracture the skull and injure the brain.

SKULL FRACTURES

A skull fracture can be linear, star shaped, compound (a compound fracture opens to outside the body) or depressed (forming a depression). Skull fractures often extend into the middle ear, nasal cavity or sinuses, creating pathways for bacteria to gain access to the brain and cause infection. In general, the larger the skull fracture the greater the likelihood of brain injury. However, the brain can be injured even if the skull is not broken.

BRAIN INJURIES

Injuries severe enough to fracture the skull are often associated with bleeding into and around the brain. Brain injuries are classified according to the severity of brain damage.

Contusion (Bruising). With a contusion, there is no loss of consciousness. After a blow to the head the dog remains dazed, wobbly and disoriented. The condition clears gradually.

Concussion. By definition, a concussion means the dog was knocked unconscious. With a mild concussion there is only a brief loss of consciousness, while with a severe concussion the dog may be unconscious for hours or even days. When he returns to consciousness, the dog exhibits the same signs as for a contusion.

A severe concussion causes the death of millions of neurons. Recent information indicates that brain cell death does not cease within a few hours of injury, but can continue for weeks or months.

Seizures. Seizures can occur at the time of injury or any time thereafter. Seizures at the time of injury are particularly detrimental because they increase pressure in the skull and compromise blood flow. This worsens the effects of the injury. Seizures that occur weeks after injury are caused by scars that form in areas where brain tissue has died.

Brain Swelling and Bleeding. Severe head injuries result in brain swelling and bleeding into and around the brain.

Brain swelling, technically called *cerebral edema*, is always accompanied by a depressed level of consciousness and often coma. Since the brain is encased in a rigid skull, as the brain swells the cerebellum is slowly forced down through the large opening at the base of the skull. This squeezes and compresses the vital centers in the midbrain. Death occurs from cardiac and respiratory arrest.

Blood clots can form between the skull and the brain or within the brain itself. A blood clot produces localized pressure that does not, at least initially, compress the vital centers. Like cerebral edema, the first indication is a depressed level of consciousness. One pupil may be dilated and unresponsive to a light shined in the eye. Another sign is weakness or paralysis involving one or more limbs.

TREATING HEAD INJURIES

Treating shock takes precedence over managing the head injury. If the dog is unconscious, establish an open airway by extending the head and pulling the tongue forward as far as you can beyond the level of the canine teeth.

Signs of death are no pulse, no effort to breathe, dilated pupils and soft eyes. Usually it is impossible to tell at the time of an accident whether such signs are reversible. Accordingly, begin administering CPR immediately if you suspect the dog is dead (see *CPR* in Chapter 1, page 7).

Some things you should do at the scene of the accident before transporting the dog to the nearest veterinary hospital are:

* Handle the dog with extreme care and gentleness. Pain and fright deepen the level of shock. Cover the dog with a warm blanket.

* Control bleeding as described in *Wounds* in Chapter 1, page 36.

* Place the dog on a flat stretcher as described in the treatment of *Spinal Cord Injuries*, page 337.

* Stabilize all fractures, if possible (see *Broken Bones* in Chapter 13, page 351).

* Record a baseline neurologic exam (level of consciousness, limb movements, pupil size).

* Transport the dog with his head higher than his hindquarters; this helps to lower intracranial pressure.

Signs of cerebral edema can appear at any time during the first 24 hours after a blow to the head. The most important thing to observe is the dog's level of consciousness. An *alert* dog is easily aroused (no apparent brain swelling). A *semicomatose* dog is sleepy but arousable (mild to moderate brain swelling). A *comatose* dog cannot be aroused (severe brain swelling).

Cerebral edema is treated with intravenous corticosteroids, oxygen and diuretics such as Mannitol and Lasix. Seizures are controlled with an intravenous or oral anticonvulsant such as Valium.

Open skull fractures require surgical cleansing and removal of devitalized bone. Depressed bone fragments may need to be elevated to relieve pressure on the brain. Antibiotics are often necessary with open fractures to prevent infection.

Only dogs that are fully alert, are not having seizures and exhibit no neurologic signs should be permitted to return home. Awaken the dog every two hours for the first 24 hours at home to check his level of responsiveness. Any change from an alert status is an indication to return at once for veterinary evaluation. In addition, be sure to check the dog's pupils. They should be of equal size. An enlarged pupil that does not constrict when light is shined in the eyes indicates pressure on the brain. Also notify your veterinarian if the dog's breathing becomes rapid or irregular, if he exhibits any form of muscle weakness or if he has a seizure.

The prognosis for recovery depends upon the severity of the brain injury. When the dog remains in a coma for more than 48 hours the outlook is poor. However, if the dog steadily improves throughout the first week, the outlook is good.

Dogs that recover may exhibit a post-traumatic syndrome that can include seizures, behavior changes, head tilt and blindness.

Brain Diseases

ENCEPHALITIS (BRAIN INFECTION)

Encephalitis is an inflammation of the brain. Symptoms include fever, depression, behavior and personality changes (especially aggression), uncoordinated gait, seizures, stupor and coma.

Canine distemper is the most common cause of encephalitis in dogs. Signs develop two to three weeks after the onset of the disease. Other causes of viral encephalitis include rabies, pseudorabies and herpesvirus. Rabies is a very serious disease, but with present-day vaccination programs the disease is uncommon. Canine herpesvirus produces an encephalitis in puppies younger than two weeks of age.

Bacterial Encephalitis is caused by organisms that enter the brain via the circulatory system or by direct extension from an infected sinus, nasal passage or an abscess in the head or neck. Fungal brain infections (caused by cryptococcosis, blastomycosis and histoplasmosis) are rare causes of encephalitis, as are protozoan infections. Tick-borne rickettsial diseases, notably Rocky Mountain spotted fever and canine ehrlichiosis, are infrequent causes. These diseases may also involve the spinal cord.

Post-Vaccination Encephalitis occurs with the use of modified live virus vaccines. It is most likely to occur when modified live virus distemper vaccine is administered at the same time as modified live parvovirus vaccine in puppies less than six to eight weeks old.

Lead Encephalitis is seen primarily in young dogs that chew on materials that contain lead, such as paint and drywall. Lead alters brain metabolism and causes inflammation and swelling. Central nervous system signs are often preceded by vomiting, diarrhea or constipation. The diagnosis is confirmed by an elevated blood lead level.

Meningitis is an infection of the surface of the brain and spinal canal. It is caused by infected bite wounds about the head and neck and bacterial infections that travel to the brain from the sinuses, nasal passages or middle ears. *Aseptic meningitis* is a nonbacterial disease of unknown cause. It affects large-breed dogs 4 to 24 months of age.

The diagnosis of encephalitis and meningitis is based on analysis of cerebrospinal fluid obtained by spinal tap. Serologic tests may identify the cause of the inflammation.

Treatment: Corticosteroids are used to reduce inflammation and swelling of the brain. Seizures are controlled with anticonvulsants. Antibiotics are used to treat bacterial infections. Rickettsia are extremely sensitive to tetracycline. Dogs that recover from encephalitis may develop seizure disorders and other neurologic symptoms.

GRANULOMATOUS MENINGOENCEPHALITIS

GME is a common inflammatory brain disease in dogs. The cause is unknown. Female dogs of small breeds, especially terriers, Poodles and Poodle crosses, are predisposed. Although GME can occur at any age, most affected dogs are two to six years of age.

A chronic form of GME called *Pug encephalitis* occurs as an inherited disease in Pugs between the ages of nine months and four years. It often begins with seizures, confusion and loss of memory.

GME can affect all parts of the brain (the disseminated form), or only specific areas (the focal form). There is a rare ocular form that targets the optic nerves of the eyes.

The *disseminated disease* appears suddenly and progresses over a matter of weeks. It is characterized by incoordination, stumbling and falling, circling, head tilt, seizures and dementia.

The *focal disease* begins with symptoms such as those of a brain tumor. Behavior and personality changes may predominate. The focal disease progresses to the disseminated disease over a period of three to six months.

Ocular disease is characterized by sudden blindness with a dilated pupil. It progresses to the disseminated disease more slowly that focal disease.

GME can be suspected when a toy dog such as a Poodle inexplicably develops confusion, disorientation, seizures or other neurologic signs that progress rapidly over a matter of weeks. A spinal tap with analysis of cerebrospinal fluid helps to confirm the diagnosis. A CT scan or MRI is useful in determining the form and location of the disease.

Treatment: Corticosteroids and immunosuppressive drugs may slow the progression of GME and provide temporary relief for several months. However, GME is almost invariably a progressive and fatal disease.

BRAIN TUMORS AND ABSCESSES

Brain tumors are not common. They tend to occur in middle-aged and older dogs. The highest incidence is found in the short-nosed breeds that have large-domed heads, including the Boxer, Bulldog and Boston Terrier. Tumors that can *metastasize* to the brain include cancers of the mammary glands, prostate and lungs.

Symptoms depend on the tumor's location and rate of growth. Tumors in the cerebrum produce seizures and/or behavioral changes. The dog may exhibit a staggering gait, head tilt, *nystagmus* (rhythmic movement of the eyeballs) and limb weakness or paralysis. These signs are progressive and continue to worsen. Late signs are stupor and coma.

A brain abscess is a collection of pus in or around the brain. The signs are similar to those of a brain tumor. There may be a prior infection in the oral cavity, inner ear or respiratory tract.

Treatment: The diagnosis of tumor or abscess is made by neurologic examination and special tests including *EEG*, cerebrospinal fluid analysis, *CT scan* or *MRI*. Surgical removal of benign brain tumors may be possible in some cases. Chemotherapy and radiation therapy have not proven to be effective in dogs. There may be temporary improvement with corticosteroids and anticonvulsants.

Abscesses are treated with high doses of antibiotics. Corticosteroids are usually contraindicated. The outlook for recovery is guarded.

STROKE

Strokes are not common in dogs. A stroke can be caused by bleeding into the brain, obstruction of an artery caused by an *embolus*, or clotting of a cerebral artery. An embolus is a clot that develops at another site and travels through the vascular system to a smaller vessel where it becomes lodged and interrupts blood flow to the area served by that artery. This results in death of tissue in the affected area, a condition called infarction. Most strokes in dogs are caused by emboli.

Bleeding in the brain is seen with ruptured cerebral blood vessels and brain tumors. Spontaneous bleeding may occur with coagulation disorders. Disseminated intravascular coagulation is a cause of both bleeding and infarction. Some hemorrhagic strokes occur for unknown reasons.

Infarctions can occur with Rocky Mountain spotted fever, hardening of the arteries associated with hypothyroidism, and for unknown reasons.

The onset of stroke is sudden. The signs depend on the location and extent of the bleeding or brain infarction. They include behavioral changes, disorientation, seizures, weakness or paralysis on one side of the body, stupor and coma. Large strokes are often accompanied by cardiac arrhythmias and collapse. The diagnostic work up is similar to that for a brain tumor.

Treatment: Treatment involves the use of corticosteroids to prevent brain swelling and anticonvulsants to control seizures. Dogs that survive the first few days have a good prognosis for recovery. The long-term outlook depends on controlling or eliminating the underlying disease.

Hereditary Diseases

Hereditary nervous system diseases are not common. Most run in families. Affected individuals should not be used for breeding.

HEREDITARY MYOPATHIES (MUSCULAR DYSTROPHY)

Muscular dystrophy is actually a group of genetically determined diseases in which there is a progressive degeneration of skeletal muscle (the muscles that are attached to the skeleton). Weakness is the predominant sign. The diagnosis can be suspected by finding high serum CPK levels. It is confirmed by muscle biopsy.

Hereditary Myopathy of Labrador Retrievers. This disease is inherited as an autosomal recessive trait. Signs of weakness begin between six weeks and seven months of age. There is a marked decrease in exercise tolerance. An affected pup may have difficulty holding up his head, bunny hop when running and collapse after brief exertion. The disease may affect the muscles involved in chewing and swallowing, resulting in drooling and the development of *megaesophagus*. Exposure to cold greatly exacerbates the symptoms.

Diazepam (Valium) given twice a day benefits some puppies. It is important to prevent stress and chilling, and to warm a pup quickly if he is exposed to cold. The disease often stabilizes or improves by 6 to 12 months of age. Many dogs are able to live a normal life. If drooling and megaesophagus develop, however, the outlook is guarded.

Sex-Linked Muscular Dystrophy. This disease affects Golden Retrievers, Irish Terriers, Samoyeds, Rottweilers, Belgian Tervurens and Miniature Schnauzers. It is transmitted on the X chromosome from the dam. Affected pups are weak at birth and often die. Those that survive develop a stilted gait, drooling, wasting of muscle and stunted growth. The condition may stabilize temporarily by six months of age, but later progresses. There is no effective treatment and the long-term prognosis is poor.

Bouvier des Flandres Myopathy. This disease affects only the muscles of swallowing, resulting in regurgitation and megaesophagus. Signs appear at about two years of age. With severe megaesophagus the outlook is guarded.

Distal Myopathy of Rottweilers. This disease affects the legs and feet, producing an abnormal stance with splayed toes and weak hocks.

Myotonia. This disease affects Chow Chows, Staffordshire Terriers, Rhodesian Ridgebacks, Cavalier King Charles Spaniels, Great Danes, Golden Retrievers and Irish Setters. Signs appear when the pups begin to walk. They include stiffness upon rising and walking. This is followed by a progressive stiffening of the gait as the dog exercises.

DEGENERATIVE MYELOPATHY

This is a degenerative disease of the spinal cord that appears to run in families. It occurs primarily in middle-aged German Shepherd Dogs. It is the most common cause of hindquarter weakness in German Shepherds and their crosses. The Siberian Husky and other large breeds are also affected.

The disease manifests itself as a slowly progressive weakness or paralysis of the hind limbs, along with an unsteady gait suggestive of hip dysplasia. The toenails on the hind feet may show abnormal wear from dragging on the ground.

Treatment with corticosteroids and/or vitamin supplements has not proven to be effective. About 50 percent of dogs will show some improvement when given aminocaproic acid.

INHERITED NEUROPATHIES

There are a number of rare diseases in which sensory and motor nerves degenerate. With loss of sensation and motor function, an affected dog does not feel the position of his limbs, is unable to position them correctly to prevent stumbling, and fails to withdraw a leg from a painful stimulus.

The diagnosis is made by sensory and motor nerve conduction studies. There is no cure, but because of the slow progression of the disease some dogs live comfortably for many years. Most of these neuropathies are inherited as autosomal recessive traits.

Neuropathy of German Shorthaired and English Pointers. Signs of this sensory neuropathy are first noted at three to four months of age. The pup begins to lick and bite at his paws, which become swollen, reddened, ulcerated and eventually mutilated. Loss of sensation can extend up the limb and involve the trunk.

Dachshund Sensory Neuropathy. This disease begins in Longhaired Dachshunds at three months of age. It is characterized by uncoordinated gait, urinary incontinence and loss of sensation over the entire body. Self-mutilation of the penis may be the first sign.

Global Cell Leukodystrophy. This disease is caused by an enzyme deficiency that results in degeneration of nerve cells. It occurs in West Highland White Terriers, Cairn Terriers, Beagles, Pomeranians and Poodles. Signs are unsteady gait, head tremors, nystagmus (a rhythmic movement of the eyeballs) and blindness.

Hypertrophic Neuropathy in Tibetan Mastiffs. This disease begins at 7 to 12 weeks of age and is characterized by hind-limb weakness that progresses to generalized weakness and, ultimately, an inability to stand. Some dogs maintain a degree of strength.

Motor Neuron Disease in Brittanys and Rottweilers. In this disease muscle weakness is progressive. Megaesophagus and head tremors have been observed in Rottweilers.

Hypomyelination Diseases. In these diseases, myelin, which forms a sheath around nerve fibers, is not completely developed at birth. The result is that nerve impules are conducted very slowly. Hypomyelination occurs in Chow Chows, Weimaraners, Samoyeds and Bernese Mountain Dogs. One form, called the *shaking puppy syndrome*, is a sex-linked recessive trait affecting only males.

The characteristic sign of hypomyelination is muscle tremors involving the limbs, trunk, head and eyes of newborn puppies. The tremors get worse with activity and disappear with sleep. Severely affected puppies show uncoordinated body movements and are unable to stand. There is no cure for the disease. Tremors in Chow Chows and Weimaraners may improve gradually and disappear by one year of age.

WHITE DOG SHAKER SYNDROME

This syndrome occurs primarily in adult small-breed dogs with white coats, although dogs with other coat colors are occasionally affected. The disease occurs most often in West Highland White Terriers, Maltese, Bichons Frises and white Poodles. It is characterized by the sudden appearance of tremors that involve the entire body and head, often accompanied by wild and random movements of the eyes. These tremors can be disabling. The cause is unknown, but an autoimmune basis has been suggested.

Treatment: Corticosteroids reverse the shaking within a few days. Some dogs require extended treatment. About 25 percent of dogs retain some degree of tremor for life.

CEREBELLAR DISEASES

Cerebellar Degeneration is a slowly progressive disease in which there is death of nerve cells in the cerebellum. The disease has been described in numerous breeds, including the Kerry Blue Terrier, Gordon Setter, Rough-Coated Collie, Great Dane, Labrador Retriever, Golden Retriever, Cocker Spaniel, Airedale Terrier, Samoyed, Cairn Terrier and Bullmastiff.

Affected puppies appear normal for the first two months of life, but then begin to show uncoordinated body movements such as jerking, stumbling, falling and overreaching with the paws. Although there is no cure, cerebellar degeneration stabilizes in some puppies, allowing them to remain active.

Cerebellar Hypoplasia is a condition in which the cerebellum is abnormally small at birth. A hereditary form has been reported in Airedales, Gordon Setters and Chow Chows. A nonhereditary form has been described in Bull Terriers, Weimaraners, Dachshunds and Labrador Retrievers. Signs are similar to those of cerebellar degeneration, but are observed shortly after birth when puppies first begin to crawl. Some puppies compensate and make good pets.

HYDROCEPHALUS

Hydrocephalus is caused by the excessive accumulation of cerebrospinal fluid in the *ventricles* of the brain. The enlarged ventricles damage the cerebral cortex by compressing it against the skull. Most cases are congenital. Some are acquired through trauma, brain infections and tumors.

Breeds with an increased risk of congenital hydrocephalus include the Maltese, Yorkshire Terrier, Chihuahua, Lhasa Apso, Pomeranian, Toy Poodle, Cairn Terrier, Boston Terrier, Pug, Pekingese and Bulldog.

Hydrocephalus produces seizures, partial or complete blindness and *dementia*. The diagnosis is made by skull X-rays, ultrasound of the ventricles and, in difficult cases, by CT *scan* or MRI. A characteristic enlargement of the dome of the skull occurs in congenital hydrocephalus, but this may not be seen until the puppy is several months old.

An increase in ventricular size without clinical signs has also been noted. This is called subclinical hydrocephalus. In certain lines of toy breeds with a high incidence of clinical and sub-clinical hydrocephalus, *EEG* screening and breeding only dogs with normal EEGs has reduced the incidence of hydrocephalus.

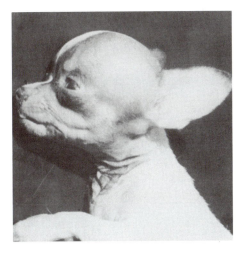

The enlarged dome of a hydro-cephalic Chihuahua puppy.

Treatment: This is directed toward decreasing the production of cerebrospinal fluid with corticosteroids and diuretics. Surgery has been beneficial is some cases. The long-term prognosis is favorable if diagnosis and treatment is begun before the brain is damaged. Nonetheless, affected dogs often appear dull and have a limited ability to learn.

Seizure Disorders

A seizure is caused by an abnormal burst of electrical activity within the brain, commonly in one of the cerebral hemispheres. The electrical activity sometimes spreads out and involves other areas, including the midbrain.

A typical *grand mal seizure* is preceded by a period of altered behavior, called the *aura*. During the aura dogs may be restless and anxious, cry out, demand affection or seek seclusion. The actual seizure lasts less than two minutes, and is characterized by collapse with rigid extension of the legs. The dog becomes unconscious and stops breathing for 10 to 30 seconds. This is followed by rhythmic jerking of the legs (which resembles running or paddling). Some dogs also champ, chew, drool or urinate and defecate. As the dog regains consciousness there is a post-seizure state characterized by disorientation and confusion. The dog may stumble into walls and appear blind. The post-seizure state can persist for minutes or hours. Grand mal seizures are typical of epilepsy.

A *focal motor or partial seizure* is one in which the jerking or twitching is limited (at least initially) to a particular part of the body. A focal seizure usually indicates a specific brain *lesion*, such as a scar, tumor or abscess.

Seizures are commonly associated with brain injury, encephalitis, heat stroke, brain abscess, brain tumor, stroke, poisoning, kidney failure and liver failure. Seizures associated with a concussion frequently occur weeks or months after the head injury, and are caused by a focus of scar tissue in the brain.

Post-encephalitic seizures occur three to four weeks after the onset of encephalitis. Distemper, in particular, is characterized by attacks that begin with champing, tongue chewing, foaming at the mouth, head shaking and blinking, all followed by a dazed look.

Post-vaccination seizures have been described in puppies under six weeks of age following vaccination with a combined distemper-parvovirus vaccine.

A sudden drop in blood sugar (*hypoglycemia*) can trigger a seizure. This occurs in newborn pups with *cardiopulmonary syndrome* (discussed in Chapter 17, *Why Puppies Die*). A common cause of hypoglycemia is giving too much insulin to a diabetic dog.

Common poisons that cause seizures are animal baits such as strychnine, antifreeze (ethylene glycol), lead, insecticides (organophosphates) and chocolate. Seizures caused by organophosphates are preceded by drooling and muscle twitching. Exposure to a spray, dip or premise treatment suggests the diagnosis.

There are a number of conditions that, while not true seizures, are often mistaken for them. *Bee stings*, for example, can cause frenzied barking followed by fainting or collapse. *Cardiac arrhythmias* can be mistaken for seizures because they cause loss of consciousness and collapse.

Narcolepsy and *cataplexy* are uncommon disorders of the sleep mechanism in which a dog is excessively sleepy all day (narcolepsy) or experiences sudden muscle paralysis and collapse (cataplexy). Between attacks the dog is completely normal. Narcolepsy can occur without cataplexy, and vice versa, although narcolepsy alone is difficult to recognize in dogs. A dog may have one or many episodes of collapse in a day, each lasting a few seconds or up to 30 minutes. The attacks can usually be reversed by petting the dog or making a loud noise. There are several effective drugs available to prevent narcolepsy and cataplexy. Dogs afflicted with the inherited form (mainly Doberman Pinschers and Labrador Retrievers) often improve as they grow older.

Treatment: If the dog is in a dangerous location at the time of the seizure, move him to a safe site. Otherwise, do not disturb the dog during or after the seizure, as this may trigger further seizures. Despite the old wives' tale, do not pull out the dog's tongue or wedge something between his teeth. Note the length of the seizure. As soon as the seizure is over, notify your veterinarian, as he or she will want to examine the dog in order to diagnose and treat the underlying cause.

Seizures lasting more than five minutes (called *status epilepticus seizures*) or *cluster seizures* (several seizures one after the other without a return to consciousness) are emergencies. They must be stopped with intravenous Valium to prevent permanent brain damage or death. Seek immediate veterinary attention. Status epilepticus has a poor prognosis, because it is usually caused by poisoning or a serious brain disease.

EPILEPSY

Epilepsy is a recurrent seizure disorder that may be *idiopathic* or acquired. Acquired epilepsy has an identifiable cause, such as a mass of scar tissue in the brain following a head injury.

Idiopathic epilepsy occurs in up to 3 percent of dogs and accounts for 80 percent of recurrent seizures. The cause is unknown, although an imbalance in chemicals that transmit electrical impulses in the brain has been suggested. Seizures, usually of the *grand mal* type, begin between six months and five years of age.

Breeds in which the condition is inherited include Beagles, Dachshunds, Keeshonden German Shepherd Dogs and Belgian Tervurens. Breeds with a high incidence, but in which inheritance has not been established, include Cocker Spaniels, Collies, Golden Retrievers, Labrador Retrievers, Irish Setters, Poodles, Miniature Schnauzers, Saint Bernards, Siberian Huskies and Wire Fox Terriers.

If the diagnosis is truly epilepsy, the attacks must be recurrent and similar. Also epileptic seizures usually become more frequent with time. Your veterinarian will ask you to keep a log of the frequency of seizures, and to provide a description of the dog's behavior before, during and after the seizure.

A typical epileptic seizure has three phases: an aura, a generalized grand mal seizure and a post-seizure state—as described above. All three phases may not be seen because many seizures occur while the dog is resting or asleep. Furthermore, in some cases the seizure is atypical. Instead of a classic grand mal convulsion, the dog exhibits strange behavior such as frenzied barking, licking or chewing at itself, staring into space or snapping at invisible objects. This is called a *psychomotor seizure* and is believed to arise from a center lower in the brain (not the cerebrum).

Focal motor seizures, as already discussed, indicate a lesion in the brain. An abnormal neurologic exam or *EEG* during a period when there have been no recent seizures also indicates a lesion in the brain. These findings eliminate the diagnosis of epilepsy. Further work up includes a spinal tap with cerebrospinal fluid analysis, skull X-rays, CT scan or MRI.

Treatment: A number of new drugs are available for treating epilepsy. However, anti-epileptic drugs, either singly or in combination, are not 100 percent effective. The best one can hope for is that treatment will significantly decrease the number and severity of the seizures while increasing the free interval between them. In general, treatment is indicated if there are two or more seizures a month, or more than 10 to 12 seizures a year. Cluster seizures and status epilepticus are other indications to start treatment.

Phenobarbital continues to be the single most effective drug for treating epilepsy in dogs. Its principal side effect is sedation. Most dogs, however, develop a tolerance to the sedative effects within a few weeks.

If seizures cannot be controlled with phenobarbital alone, other drugs, such as potassium bromide, Clonazem, Valporic Acid or Clorazepate, can be added. The dosages and rates of action of all anticonvulsants are variable. Regular monitoring of serum drug levels is essential—both to control seizures and to avoid toxicity. The two common causes of treatment failure are not maintaining adequate drug levels and not giving the drugs as often as directed. *It is important to work closely with your veterinarian.*

Coma

Coma is a depressed level of consciousness. It begins with confusion, progresses through stupor and ends in complete loss of consciousness. Following a head injury with cerebral concussion, coma can occur without progressing through the earlier stages. A dog in a coma is insensitive to pain and cannot be awakened.

Coma occurs with oxygen deprivation, brain swelling, brain tumor, encephalitis, poisoning and death. Many diseases that cause seizures progress to coma.

Low blood sugar (*hypoglycemia*) is a common cause of coma. It tends to occur in toy-breed puppies and adult hunting dogs after a long day in the field. A common *iatrogenic* cause is giving too much insulin to a diabetic dog (see *Diabetes Mellitis* in Chapter 9). Another cause of coma is prolonged *hypothermia* (see *Cold Exposure* in Chapter 1).

Coma related to high fever and heat stroke is a serious complication that leads to permanent brain damage. Vigorous efforts must be made to bring down the fever (see *Heat Stroke* in Chapter 1). Coma is also especially ominous when it is associated with brain trauma or when it occurs in the late stages of kidney and liver disease.

Common poisons that cause coma are ethylene glycol (antifreeze), barbiturates, kerosene, turpentine, arsenic, cyanide, organophosphates, plants, chocolate and lead. A dog found in a coma in the trunk of a car or in an airtight space may have smothered or developed carbon monoxide poisoning (see *Drowning and Suffocation* in Chapter 1).

Treatment: First determine the level of consciousness and whether the dog is alive. If the dog shows no signs of life, begin *CPR* (as described in Chapter 1). An unconscious dog can choke on his vomitus, so pull out the tongue and clear the airway with your fingers. If the dog has a foreign body such as a piece of meat obstructing the airway, treat as described for *Choking* in Chapter 10, page 287. Wrap the dog in a blanket and proceed at once to your veterinarian.

Weakness or Paralysis

There are several diseases—none of them very common—that attack the motor nerves, causing weakness and paralysis but leaving the sensory nerves intact. These diseases resemble one another and are difficult to tell apart.

TICK PARALYSIS

The saliva of some common female wood ticks contains a poison that affects the motor nerves, producing weakness and paralysis. Signs appear about one week after a dog has been exposed to a wooded area. Over the next 48 to 72 hours the dog grows progressively weaker. Sensation to a pin prick is normal. In time, the paralysis reaches a level where the dog collapses and is unable to lift his head. Death can occur from respiratory arrest.

Treatment: Seek veterinary attention whenever a dog exhibits unexplained weakness. Tick paralysis can be prevented by removing ticks promptly from the dog and the methods of tick control described in Chapter 4 (see *Ticks*).

BOTULISM

Botulism is a paralytic disease caused by neurotoxins produced by the bacteria *Clostridium botulinum*. The disease is acquired by eating spoiled carcasses or improperly canned vegetables and meats.

The outlook for recovery is good if the disease does not progress rapidly. Antitoxins are available. Mildly affected dogs recover without treatment.

COONHOUND PARALYSIS

The cause of this disease is unknown. It is believed to be an immune-mediated disease with antibodies directed at the dog's own peripheral nerves. The agent triggering the immune reaction may be a virus or a bacteria. It occurs most often in hunting dogs one to two weeks after having had contact with a raccoon.

Paralysis begins as weakness in the hindquarters and progresses forward until the dog is unable to stand. During this time the dog remains anxious but alert. The paralysis can affect the muscles involved in respiration and swallowing. It reaches its peak at about 10 days.

Treatment: Good nursing care is the main treatment. Full recovery may take weeks or months.

MYASTHENIA GRAVIS

This is a rare disease caused by a deficiency of acetylcholine receptors, normally present at the junction of nerve endings and muscle cells. When an animal decides to move a muscle, the nerve endings release acetylcholine, which is a neurotransmitter. The acetylcholine carries the nerve impulse acros the junction, where acetylcholine receptors respond and send the nerve impulse on its way. A reduction in the number or function of these receptors produces generalized muscle weakness, made worse by exercise. Weakness is most apparent in the hindquarters. Dogs with myasthenia gravis have difficulty getting up, and exhibit a swaying or staggering gait.

There is a *focal form* of myasthenia gravis that affects only the muscles involved in swallowing. The dog is unable to swallow solid food and develops an enlarged, dilated megaesophagus. Aspiration pneumonia often follows.

A *congenital form* of myasthenia gravis is inherited as an autosomal recessive trait. It occurs in Jack Russell Terriers, Springer Spaniels and Smooth Fox Terriers.

An *acquired form* of myasthenia gravis occurs in all breeds, but is seen most often in Golden Retrievers, German Shepherd Dogs, Labrador Retrievers, Dachshunds and Scottish Terriers, often occurring at one to four years of age or 9 to 13 years of age. Acquired myasthenia gravis is an immune-mediated disease in which *auto-antibodies* are directed at and destroy the acetylcholine receptors.

Hypothyroidism can occur at the same time as autoimmune myasthenia gravis. Occasionally, myasthenia gravis is related to a tumor of the thymus gland, but this is rare.

The diagnosis of myasthenia gravis is based on neurologic examination. One test involves injecting a drug called edrophonium chloride. This drug blocks the enzyme that breaks down acetylcholine, resulting in higher concentrations of this neurotransmitter at the receptor sites. The test is positive if muscle strength improves after the injection. A serologic test for diagnosing autoimmune myasthenia gravis is available.

Treatment: Drugs are available that increase the concentration of acetylcholine at receptor sites, thereby reversing muscle weakness. These drugs can be given by syrup or injection. The dose varies according to the dogs activity and stress levels. Close veterinary monitoring is required.

Megaesophagus is treated as described in Chapter 9. Thymus gland tumors are treated by surgical removal. *Hypothyroidism* responds to thyroid replacement therapy. With appropriate treatment, the outlook for complete recovery and the return of normal swallowing is good.

HYPOKALEMIA (LOW SERUM POTASSIUM)

Hypokalemia, a condition in which the dog has low serum potassium, is a metabolic cause of generalized muscle weakness. Loss of potassium occurs with severe vomiting. It also occurs with the long-term use of diuretics that cause the kidneys to excrete potassium. Other causes of hypokalemia include bloat, diabetic ketoacidosis and Cushing's syndrome.

Treatment: The diagnosis is made by measuring serum potassium levels. Weakness disappears as potassium is replaced and the underlying cause is corrected.

Spinal Cord Diseases

Injuries and diseases of the spinal cord generally produce weakness and paralysis in one or more limbs and/or the tail. Spinal cord diseases do not cause seizures, nor do they produce changes in personality or behavior. This sets them apart from brain diseases. However, injuries to peripheral nerves may be difficult to distinguish from spinal cord injuries.

SPINAL CORD INJURIES

Spinal cord injuries are associated with ruptured discs and vertebral fractures and dislocations caused by accidents such as automobile accidents, gunshot wounds and falls.

Immediately after a spine injury, there may be neck or back pain, weakness or paralysis of the legs, a stumbling gait, loss of feeling in the limbs and urinary or fecal incontinence. Signs that progress after an injury are often caused by tissue swelling, which interferes with the blood supply to the spinal cord and may cause permanent paralysis.

A pelvic fracture can be mistaken for a spinal fracture. In both cases the dog is unable to bear weight on his hindquarters and shows pain when handled in the injured area. Thus it might appear as if the outlook is poor, even though a dog with a broken pelvis often makes a complete recovery.

Treatment: Dogs with spinal cord trauma usually have life-threatening injuries that take precedence and require immediate attention (see *Treating Head Injuries,* page 324). All dogs that are unconscious or unable to stand should be considered to have spinal cord injuries until proven otherwise. Handle these animals with extreme care to protect the spine. Vertebral fractures are unstable. Flexing the neck or back may compress the spinal cord and worsen the injury.

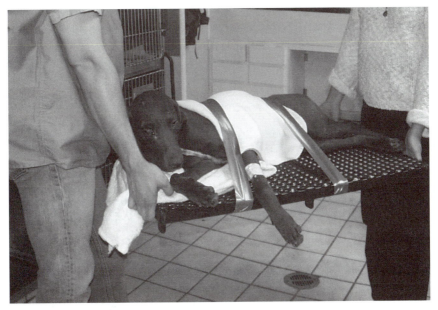

A dog with a lower back injury. Duct tape over the shoulder and hip prevents back movement. Transport on a flat surface.

At the scene of the accident, *move the dog as gently as possible onto a flat surface, such as a piece of plywood, and transport to the nearest veterinary clinic.* Sliding the dog onto a blanket and lifting the corners is an acceptable way to transport him if a make-shift stretcher is not available.

Spinal cord injuries are treated with corticosteroids and diuretics such as Mannitol to prevent further swelling at the site of the injury. Good nursing care and physiotherapy are extremely important in preventing complications and hastening recovery. Surgery may be necessary to relieve pressure on the spinal cord or to stabilize a fractured vertebra.

A dog with mild bruising of the spinal cord begins to recover in a few days. However, if the cord has been lacerated or severely damaged, then paralysis or death may be the result.

INFECTIONS AND TUMORS

Infections of the vertebral bodies, discs and spinal cord are uncommon. Most bacterial infections occur after trauma or by extension from infected wounds close to the spine. Viral, fungal, rickettsial and protozoan diseases that cause encephalitis can also cause spinal cord infections (known as *myelitis*).

The diagnosis of myelitis is made by spinal tap and cerebrospinal fluid analysis. Treatment involves the long-term use of antibiotics, selected on the basis of culture and sensitivity tests. Surgery may be necessary to remove a foreign body, drain an abscess, obtain material for testing or relieve pressure on the spinal cord.

Tumors can involve the spinal cord, nerve roots or structures around the cord. Symptoms are caused by the compression of the cord or the nerves coming out from the cord. Benign neoplasms include meningiomas and osteophytes (see *Bone Spurs*, page 341). Malignant tumors include osteosarcomas and lymphosarcomas. Some benign tumors can be cured by surgery. Malignant tumors usually are not removable, but may respond temporarily to radiation and/or chemotherapy.

RUPTURED DISCS

A disc is a cushion of cartilage that sits between the vertebrae and acts as a shock absorber. It is composed of a rim of tough, fibrous connective tissue that surrounds a gel-like center called the nucleus. When a disc ruptures, one of two things may happen. The first is that the fibrous capsule breaks, allowing the inner nucleus to push out through the opening and impinge on the spinal cord or a nerve root. This type of rupture is called a *Hansen Type 1*. The second is that the entire disc, surrounded by an unbroken capsule, can bulge outward. This is called a *Hansen Type 2*.

Ruptured Discs in the Back. The Hansen Type 1 rupture occurs in small breeds such as the Dachshund, Beagle, Cocker Spaniel, Pekingese and small mixed breeds. In fact, ruptured discs are more frequent in Dachshunds than in all other breeds combined.

The capsule begins to degenerate at about two to nine months of age, and signs of impingement on the spinal cord appear at three to six years of age. About 80 percent of Type 1 ruptured discs occur in the lower back between the last thoracic and the first two lumbar vertebrae. Most of the remainder occur in the neck. There is often a history of mild trauma, such as jumping off a sofa, but normal movements are sufficient to cause a Type 1 extrusion. Occasionally, more than one disc becomes ruptured.

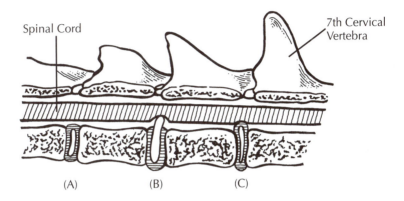

Ruptured discs. (A) is a normal disc; (B) is an acute Hansen Type 1 disc rupture; (C) is a Hansen Type 2 disc rupture.

The symptoms of a Type 1 rupture usually come on gradually but can appear with sudden explosiveness. The main sign is pain. The dog holds his back stiffly and may cry or whine when patted or handled in the injured area. He usually refuses to walk up stairs or jump into a car. Neurologic signs include weakness, lameness, and a wobbly gait. A dog experiencing the severe back pain of an acute rupture will have a hunched-up position and a tight abdomen. The dog may pant and tremble. Sudden disc ruptures can produce complete hindquarter paralysis.

Hansen Type 2 discs ruptures occur in the larger breeds, including German Shepherd Dogs and Labrador Retrievers. The entire disc, surrounded by its capsule, gradually impinges on the spinal canal. Symptoms appear in dogs 5 to 12 years of age. Because the process is gradual, symptoms progress slowly.

Ruptured Discs in the Neck. Dogs with ruptured Hansen Type 1 neck discs carry their heads low and rigidly, making the neck look shorter. These discs are extremely painful. Dogs often cry out when patted on the head and refuse to lower their heads to eat and drink. Weakness and lameness involve the front legs. Complete paralysis of all four legs does occur but is rare. Hansen Type 2 neck discs occur with the *wobbler syndrome*, discussed below.

The diagnosis of ruptured disc is made by neurologic examination and imaging studies including spine X-rays, a *myelogram*, and possibly a *CT scan* or *MRI*.

Treatment: Most disc problems improve with rest and medication. The dog should be closely confined for two to four weeks to allow the disc to return to its

Hindquarter paralysis caused by a type 1 back disc rupture.

former position. Corticosteroids reduce swelling and inflammation. Analgesics relieve pain.

Dogs with neck disc problems should be walked with a chest harness rather than a collar.

Disc injuries that cause paralysis require special handling and transporting, as described for *Spinal Cord Injuries* (page 337). Surgical intervention may be necessary.

WOBBLER SYNDROME

The wobbler syndrome is a disease that results from compression of the spinal cord in the neck. The compression is caused by vertebral instability related to either a malformed cervical vertebrae or a ruptured Hansen Type 2 neck disc. Both may be accompanied by *hypertrophy* (enlargement) of the ligament that runs down the vertebral canal beneath the vertebrae. Ligament enlargement is believed to be a reaction to instability of the spine.

Most cases of wobbler syndrome occur in Doberman Pinschers over five years of age, and to a lesser extent in Great Danes under two years of age, but other breeds can also be affected. Ruptured discs are more common in Doberman Pinschers, while vertebral malformations predominate in Great Danes. The malformed vertebrae may be related to the long neck and rapid rate of growth in Great Danes.

The principal sign of both conditions is a progressive loss of coordination in the rear legs accompanied by a peculiar, wobbly gait. Weakness or partial paralysis affects the front legs as the disease progresses. Manipulating the neck up and down is painful and may exacerbate the paralysis. The diagnosis is made by lateral X-rays of the cervical spine and by a *myelogram*.

Treatment: Medical treatment is similar to that described for ruptured discs above. Dogs with mild symptoms may respond to medical management. More severely affected dogs respond best to a surgical procedure that decompresses the spinal cord and stabilizes the vertebral column.

Breed factors and genetic influences appear to contribute to the wobbler syndrome. Until more is known about the exact cause, affected individuals should not be used for breeding.

CAUDA EQUINA SYNDROME

The cauda equina is composed of nerves that form the terminal extension of the spinal cord. Injuries to the cauda equina can be caused by ruptured discs, *spina bifida* (a developmental defect in the bones of the lower back), infections of the spinal cord and disc spaces, spinal cord tumors, and lumbosacral vertebral canal stenosis.

Lumbosacral vertebral canal stenosis is an acquired disorder in which there is instability of the spine in the lower back. There may be a congenital component that produces narrowing of the bony canal. German Shepherd Dogs are most often affected.

The early signs of the cauda equina syndrome include pain in the lower back (lumbosacral area), difficulty getting up, and recurring lameness in one or both hind legs. Testing for sensation in the lumbosacral area reveals an increased sensitivity to touch and pinprick. This is the key to early diagnosis.

In more advanced cases there is weakness or partial paralysis in the hind limbs, and urinary and/or fecal incontinence. The anal sphincter may be completely relaxed.

Treatment: Medical management is similar to that described for ruptured discs. It is most successful when symptoms are mild. Surgical decompression and bone fusion can be considered for dogs that do not respond to medical management, and for those with progressive hind limb weakness. Dogs with a paralyzed bladder or rectum are unlikely to benefit from treatment.

BONE SPURS (SPONDYLOSIS)

Spondylosis is characterized by the presence of *osteophytes*—bone spurs that form around intervertebral discs as dog ages. They usually do not produce symptoms. On rare occasions, spurs project into the spinal canal and cause symptoms like those of a ruptured disc. A fusion of the osteophytes, called *spondylosis deformans*, restricts movement of the vertebral column and causes pain and stiffness. Large-breed dogs are most often affected.

Treatment: Dogs with the pain and stiffness of spondylosis deformans respond well to analgesics. Surgery to remove osteophytes and decompress the spinal cord may be of benefit in dogs that are not helped by analgesics.

Peripheral Nerve Injuries

An injury to a nerve results in loss of sensation and/or muscle movement in the structures affected by that nerve. With complete paralysis the leg hangs limply. With partial paralysis, the dog stumbles when attempting to put weight on the leg. Common injuries are stretches, tears and lacerations.

Stretches involving the brachial and radial nerves are usually caused by auto accidents or falls in which the front leg is jerked away from the trunk. A similar stretching of the femoral or sciatic nerves can cause a paralyzed back leg. Nerves can be crushed when a vehicle rolls over the leg. Bone fractures and muscle injuries often occur at the same time.

Another cause of nerve paralysis (usually temporary) is the injection of an irritating medication into the tissue surrounding a nerve. This problem does not occur frequently, but can be a cause of concern when it does. The correct procedure for giving injections is described in Chapter 20.

Lacerated nerves do not regenerate. The paralysis is permanent. Stretched nerves may (but do not always) return to normal. Those that do recover begin to improve in three weeks and may continue to improve for 12 months. If recovery does not occur, the dog may benefit from amputation of the paralyzed leg.

THE MUSCULOSKELETAL SYSTEM

The dog's skeleton is made up of 319 bones—about 100 more than humans have. Although the number of bones is roughly the same in all breeds, there is considerable variation in size and shape as the result of selective breeding.

The place where two bones meet is called a joint, or articulation. In some joints there is a cushioning pad of cartilage interposed between the bones. This pad is called a meniscus. A damaged meniscus can deteriorate and inflame the joint. Abnormal wear and tear on joint surfaces and joint cartilages leads to arthritis. In many cases the abnormal wear and tear is the result of poor joint conformation associated with inherited orthopedic diseases such as hip dysplasia.

Joint position is maintained by ligaments, tendons and a tough fibrous capsule surrounding the joint. Together, these structures provide stability and hold the joint together. Joint looseness (called *laxity*) is caused by stretching of these ligaments. Laxity allows the ends of the bones to slip partly out of joint. When the joint capsule ruptures, the bones slip completely out of joint. This is called dislocation.

The skeletal anatomy of humans and dogs has much in common, including a similar terminology. However, there are significant differences in the angles, lengths and position of bones. The hock, for example, is actually the heel bone in humans. While people walk on the soles of their feet, dogs walk on their toes. Humans carry all their weight on their hips. Dogs carry 75 percent of their weight on their shoulders and front legs.

Veterinarians, dog breeders and judges use certain terms to describe a dog's overall composition and structure. *Conformation* is how the various angles, shapes and parts of the dog's body conform to the breed standard. Standards for purebred dogs

SKELETAL ANATOMY

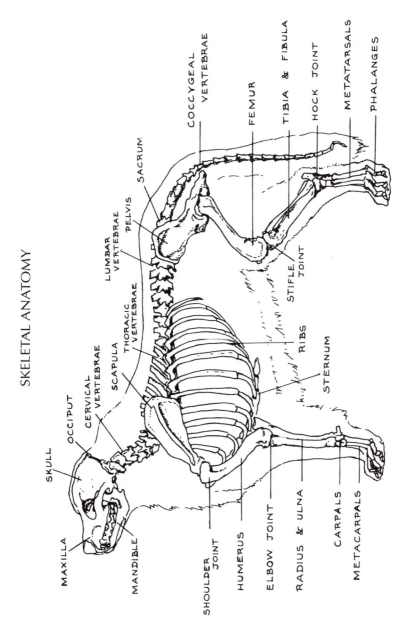

SKULL

MAXILLA

MANDIBLE

OCCIPUT

CERVICAL VERTEBRAE

SCAPULA

THORACIC VERTEBRAE

LUMBAR VERTEBRAE

PELVIS

SACRUM

COCCYGEAL VERTEBRAE

FEMUR

TIBIA & FIBULA

HOCK JOINT

METATARSALS

PHALANGES

STIFLE JOINT

RIBS

STERNUM

SHOULDER JOINT

HUMERUS

ELBOW JOINT

RADIUS & ULNA

CARPALS

METACARPALS

(Bridget Olerenshaw)

describe the ideal conformation for each breed. These standards are based to a certain extent upon aesthetic considerations, but they also take into account the breed's original working purposes.

Most breed standards provide some information on the desired angle or slope of the bones of the shoulder, pelvis and limbs. These angles are determined using imaginary lines drawn horizontally and vertically through the plane of the standing dog.

Another term used to judge the physical attributes of a dog is *soundness*. When applied to the musculoskeletal system, it means that in a sound dog all the bones and joints are in correct alignment and are functioning as intended. In particular, in a dog with good skeletal conformation the alignment of the legs allows equal distribution of weight, equal bone pressure and equal strain on the supporting ligaments when the dog is standing naturally or moving at a trot.

Limping (Lameness)

Limping indicates pain or weakness in the involved leg. It is a common sign of bone and joint disease, but it also occurs with muscle and nerve injuries.

FINDING THE CAUSE

Consider the history and circumstances surrounding the appearance of lameness. Did the lameness appear spontaneously or was there a history of injury? Which leg is involved? A dog often holds up the paw or places less weight on a painful leg, especially one that has been recently injured. This may not be evident in chronic lameness. A dog usually takes shorter steps on a painful or weak leg. You may notice that his head bobs or drops as his weight comes down on the painful leg.

Having identified which leg is involved, try to identify the specific site and possible cause. First examine the foot and look between the toes. Many cases of lameness are due to foot injuries such as sprains, pad lacerations and penetrating puncture wounds caused by thorns and splinters. Carefully feel the leg from the toes up. Locate areas of tenderness by applying gentle pressure. Next, flex and extend all joints from the toes to the shoulder looking for resistance (lack of easy movement). Resistance is a sign of joint pain, which will be evident when the dog attempts to pull the leg free.

Having located the site of pain, the next step is to try to determine the cause of the pain. Consider the following:

- *Infected areas* are red, warm and tender, and are often associated with skin lacerations or bite wounds. There may be purulent drainage from the wound. The limp grows steadily worse. An abscess may be developing.

- *Sprains and strains* occur suddenly and are often accompanied by swelling and bruising. Usually the dog is able to bear some weight on the leg. The lameness may persist for days or weeks.

- *Fractures and dislocations* cause severe pain and the dog is unable to bear weight on the leg. Some degree of deformity is present. The tissues are swollen and discolored from bleeding.

- *Inherited orthopedic diseases* generally come on gradually. Young dogs are affected. There may be few local findings to explain the lameness. Swelling, if present, is often slight. The lameness persists and grows worse with time.

- *Degenerative joint disease*, also called arthritis or osteoarthritis, is the most common cause of lameness in older dogs. The lameness is worse when the dog wakes up and improves as it moves about.

- *Spinal cord injuries* and *peripheral nerve injuries* (discussed in Chapter 12) produce weakness or paralysis (*without pain*) in one or more limbs.

- A firm mass or swelling without signs of inflammation suggests a *bone tumor* (discussed in Chapter 18). Pressure over a bone tumor causes varying degrees of pain. Consider this diagnosis in a mature dog with an unexplained limp.

DIAGNOSTIC TESTS

X-rays of the bones and joints are used to diagnose fractures and dislocations. They are also helpful in distinguishing bone growths from soft tissue swellings. Note that many cases of lameness occur without positive findings on conventional X-rays.

Bone Scan (Nuclear Scintography). This is an imaging technique that uses intravenous radioactive isotopes and X-ray equipment to form a picture of the bone and surrounding tissue. Because of the cost and the restrictions on the use of radioactive isotopes, bone scans are performed only at medical centers and schools of veterinary medicine.

CT Scan and MRI. These studies may be of benefit in special circumstances, but their availability and cost limit their usefulness.

Synovial Fluid Analysis. Synovial fluid is a viscous joint lubricant that contains hyaluronic acid. The fluid can be removed using a sterile needle and syringe. Analysis helps to determine the cause of the joint swelling. Normal synovial fluid is clear and pale yellow. Blood in the fluid indicates recent joint injury. Pus indicates joint infection (*septic arthritis*).

Bone and Joint Injuries

JOINT SPRAINS

A sprain is an injury caused by sudden stretching or tearing of the ligaments in and around the joint. Signs are pain over the joint, swelling of the tissues and temporary lameness.

Treatment: If the dog is unable to put weight on the leg, seek veterinary consultation to rule out a fracture or dislocation. This is true for any injury that fails to improve in 24 hours. X-rays should be taken.

It is most important to prevent further injury by resting the affected part. Restrict activity by confining the dog in a small area. Apply cold packs to the injured joint for 15 to 30 minutes, three or four times a day for the first 24 hours. Use a chemical cold pack or put crushed ice in a plastic bag. Wrap the pack in a towel and secure it in place over the injured joint with a loose gauze wrap.

After the first 24 hours, switch to warm, moist compresses for 15 to 30 minutes three times a day for the next two to three days. Apply as described for cold packs. Avoid hot compresses, which can burn the skin.

Analgesics may be prescribed by your veterinarian to relieve pain (see *Common Drugs for Home Veterinary Use* in Chapter 20). One disadvantage of pain relievers is that they may allow the dog to begin using the leg while the injury is still fresh. This can delay healing. Keep the dog off the leg by confining him in a small, closed area. Take him out on a leash only to eliminate. Allow at least three weeks for successful healing. Incomplete healing is associated with prolonged lameness and the later development of degenerative arthritis in the joint.

TENDON INJURIES

Tendons can be stretched, partly torn or ruptured. Strained tendons follow sudden wrenching or twisting injuries. The tendons of the forepaws (front and back) are strained most often. The signs of tendon injury are lameness, pain on bearing weight and painful swelling over the course of the tendon.

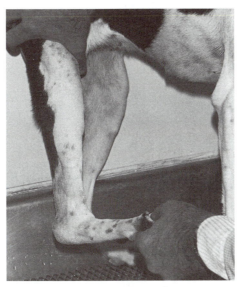

The Achilles or heel tendon is the one most often ruptured in the dog.

Rupture of the *Achilles tendon* at the hock joint can be caused by sudden and extreme flexion of the hock. This injury tends to occur in Greyhounds and sporting and performance breeds. The Achilles tendon is the one most often severed in dog fights and car accidents. Rupture of the Achilles tendon causes a dropped hock.

Inflammation of a tendon is called tendonitis. This injury follows strenuous field or road work and overuse of the limb.

Treatment: It is the same as described for *joint sprains*. A ruptured Achilles tendon should be surgically repaired.

MUSCLE STRAINS AND CONTUSIONS

Muscle strains are caused by stretching or tearing the muscle fibers, or by overuse of a muscle following strenuous field or road work. Signs are lameness, swelling of the muscle, tenderness over the injured part and bruising. Bruising may be difficult to see beneath the fur.

Treatment: Initial treatment is similar to that described for *joint sprains*. The dog should be rested for at least three weeks.

DISLOCATED JOINTS

A strong force is necessary to rupture a joint and displace the bones. Such injuries are usually caused by auto accidents and falls from a height. Signs of a dislocated

Subluxation of the left hip, with outward rotation of the knee and inward rotation of the heel.

joint are sudden pain and inability to use the limb. The elbow or knee may be bent, with the leg pointing either toward or away from the body. The affected leg may be either shorter or longer than the opposite leg.

Subluxations (also called *luxations*) are dislocations in which the bones are only partly out of joint. Some subluxations are congenital, but most are caused by trauma. The limb does not shorten and joint deformity is minimal. Dislocations and subluxations affect the hips, stifles, shoulders, elbows and the small joints that make up the hocks and wrists. Subluxations of these smaller joints can be caused by a sudden force such as jumping from a height.

Treatment: Veterinary examination is necessary to rule out associated fractures and to replace the dislocated bones, a procedure that requires anesthesia. The treatment of other life-threatening injuries may take precedence. After reduction (replacement of the dislocated joint), the limb is immobilized in a sling or splint. Depending on the extent of the injury, the dog is placed on strict crate rest or allowed limited exercise on a short leash. Physical therapy with exercises that move the joint passively through a limited range of motion, and activities such as swimming, help the dog recover strength and joint flexibility.

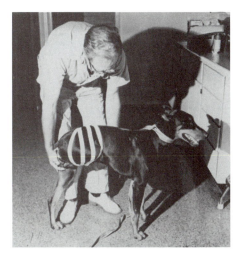

A restriction bandage used to immobilize the leg after reduction of a dislocated hip. (J. Clawson)

Joint surgery is necessary for dislocations that cannot be reduced by manipulating the limbs. Surgery gives the best results for recurrent dislocations and for subluxations of the wrists and hocks.

STIFLE INJURIES

The stifle joint is stabilized by a number of ligaments. The two large ligaments that cross in the middle of the joint are the cranial and caudal cruciates. The ligaments that stabilize the sides of the joints are the medial and lateral collaterals. The meniscus is a cushion of cartilage between the femur and the tibia and fibula.

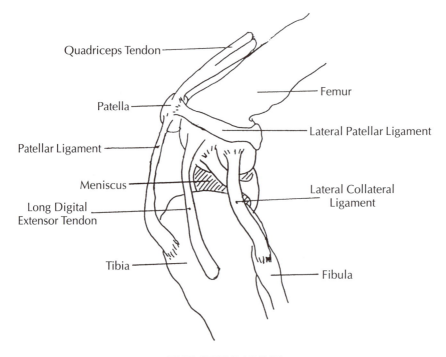

THE STIFLE JOINT

Torn Knee Ligaments. Rupture of the cranial cruciate is a common and serious injury of the stifle. It occurs in all breeds at all ages, but is more likely to occur in younger, active dogs. A congenital or developmental predisposition may exist.

The sudden onset of rear leg lameness suggests a rupture. The lameness may disappear with rest, then recur with exercise. In some cases the presenting sign is persistent lameness in one or both hind legs. The diagnosis is confirmed by palpating the stifle joint. In many cases the medial collateral ligament is also damaged.

Rupture of the medial or lateral collateral ligament usually is caused by a severe blow to the side of the joint. The affected ligament may be stretched, partially torn or completely severed. Diagnosis is made by manipulating the joint and looking for a degree of looseness. Severe blows to the stifle may also cause joint fractures.

Torn Meniscus. Injuries to the meniscus are associated with injuries to the cruciates. If a cruciate injury goes untreated, secondary damage to the meniscus occurs in the weeks and months that follow. The end result is degenerative arthritis and permanent lameness. Isolated meniscus injuries are rare in dogs.

Treatment: The treatment of choice for ruptured cruciate ligaments is surgical repair. If repair is not done, the joint becomes unstable and is subject to further damage. Following surgical repair, physical therapy and restricted exercise (as described above for *Dislocated Joints*) are important for successful recovery.

Collateral ligaments that have been stretched but not torn usually heal satisfactorily with rest and restricted activity.

Meniscal injuries respond well to surgical removal of the damaged part of the cartilage.

BROKEN BONES (FRACTURES)

Most fractures are caused by automobile accidents and falls from a height. The bones most commonly broken are the femur, pelvis, skull, jaw and spine. Fractures are classified as *open* or *closed*. In an *open fracture* (also called a *compound fracture*), a wound exposes the bone. Often the bone is seen sticking through the skin. These fractures are contaminated by dirt and bacteria and thus are accompanied by a high rate of bone infection.

Signs of bone fracture include pain, swelling, inability to bear weight and deformity with shortening of the leg.

Treatment: Injuries that cause fractures can also cause shock, blood loss and trauma to internal organs. Controlling shock takes precedence over treating any fractures (see *Shock* in Chapter 1). A dog in pain is often uncooperative and self-protective. Take precautions to avoid being bitten. If necessary, muzzle the dog (see *Handling and Restraint* in Chapter 1).

Open wounds over bones should be covered with a sterile dressing, using several gauze pads, if available. If you cannot get gauze pads, cover the wound with a clean cloth or towel and wrap loosely.

The splinting of fractures relieves pain and prevents shock and further tissue damage while the dog is being transported to the veterinary hospital. The decision to splint is based on a number of factors including the severity and location of the injury, the time it will take to get professional help, the presence of other injuries and the availability of materials. Note that improper splinting can cause more harm than good. Do not attempt to splint the leg if the dog resists.

Always splint the limb in the position you find it. Do not attempt to straighten a crooked leg.

An effective splint is one that crosses the joints above and below the fracture. When the fracture is below the knee or elbow, fold a magazine, a newspaper or a piece of thick cardboard around the leg and extend the splint from the toes to a point well above the knee or elbow. Hold the splint in place by wrapping it with a roll gauze, necktie or tape. Do not wrap tightly. Fractures above the elbow and knee are difficult to splint. The best way to prevent further damage is to keep the dog as still as possible.

Dogs in shock should be transported lying down, either on a flat surface or in a hammock stretcher, to facilitate breathing and prevent a drop in blood pressure. *Head injuries* and *spinal cord injuries* require special handling and transport. See Chapter 12.

Fractures where the ends of bones are at angles or far apart must be reduced under general anesthesia to bring the ends together and realign the bone. This is accomplished by pulling on the leg to overcome the musclular forces causing the displacement. Once reduced, the position of the bones must be maintained. In

A magazine makes a good temporary splint for fractures of the leg below the elbow or knee. (J. Clawson)

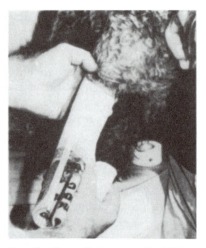

An effective splint crosses the joints above and below the fracture site. (J. Clawson)

general, with fractures above the knee or elbow the position is held with pins and metal plates, while fractures below the knee or elbow are immobilized with splints and casts. Fractures involving joints usually require open surgery and repair with pins, screws and wire.

Displaced *jaw fractures* cause malposition of the teeth. The jaw should be adjusted and the teeth wired together to maintain the correct position until healing is complete. Depressed skull fractures may require surgery to elevate the depressed fragments.

OSTEOMYELITIS (BONE INFECTION)

Bacterial contamination with subsequent infection is a hazard whenever bone is exposed. It occurs most often with open fractures. Other causes are gunshot wounds and animal bites that become infected and progress to adjacent bone. In rare cases osteomyelitis is caused by blood-borne bacteria and fungi. This occurs in dogs receiving chemotherapy and in those suffering from illnesses that impair immunity.

Signs of acute osteomyelitis are excessive pain, lameness, fever and swelling. In chronic osteomyelitis there is an intermittent purulent discharge through sinus tracts connecting the bone to the skin. The diagnosis is confirmed by X-rays and a culture of the bone. Bone scans are highly diagnostic but rarely indicated.

Treatment: Bone infection is a most difficult problem to treat. It is essential to remove all devitalized bone and leave the wound open for daily dressing changes and wound irrigations. Bacterial cultures of the infected bone aid in selecting appropriate antibiotics. Osteomyelitis associated with nonhealing fractures is treated by stabilizing the fracture with plates and screws and implanting a bone graft.

Inherited Orthopedic Diseases

Inherited bone and joint diseases have a genetic basis despite the fact that only a certain number of offspring will be affected. If, after a careful veterinary examination, one of these conditions is diagnosed in your dog, do not breed the animal.

HIP DYSPLASIA

Hip dysplasia is the most common cause of rear leg lameness in dogs. The highest incidence occurs in large-breed dogs, including Saint Bernards, Newfoundlands, Rottweilers, Chesapeake Bay Retrievers, Golden Retrievers, German Shepherd Dogs and many others. Smaller breeds are also affected, but are less likely to show symptoms. According to statistics compiled by the *Orthopedic Foundation for Animals*, the risk of hip dysplasia in many of the large-breed dogs presented to them for certification over the last 25 years ranged from 20 to 40 percent.

Hip dysplasia is a polygenic trait. That is, more than one gene controls the inheritance. The hip is a ball-and-socket joint; the ball is the head of the femur and the socket is the acetabulum of the pelvis. In a dysplastic hip, the head of the femur fits loosely into a poorly developed, shallow acetabulum. Joint instability occurs as muscle development lags behind the rate of skeletal growth. As the stress of weight-bearing exceeds the strength limits of the supporting connective tissue and muscle, the joint becomes loose and unstable. This allows for free play of the femoral head in the acetabulum, which promotes abnormal wear and tear.

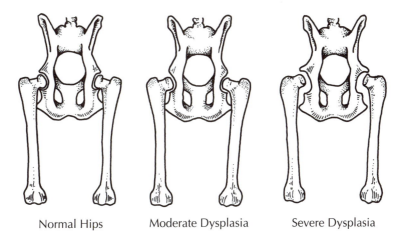

Normal Hips   Moderate Dysplasia   Severe Dysplasia

Hip dysplasia showing progressive increase in joint space and joint wear.

Feeding a very high-calorie diet to growing dogs can exacerbate a predisposition to hip dysplasia, because the rapid weight gain places increased stress on the hips. Being overweight supports the genetic potential for hip dysplasia, as well as other skeletal diseases. Another factor that can bring on the symptoms of hip dysplasia is inappropriate exercise during the period of rapid bone growth. Young dogs should be discouraged from jumping up and down from heights and from standing up on their back legs (which dogs do when they stand up against a fence or window to get a better view).

Dogs with hip dysplasia are born with hips that appear normal but progressively undergo structural changes. The age of onset is 4 to 12 months. Affected puppies may show pain in the hip, walk with a limp or a swaying gait, bunny hop when running and experience difficulty in the hindquarters when getting up. Pressing on the rump can cause the pelvis to drop. With the puppy on its back, the rear legs may not extend into the frog-leg position without causing pain.

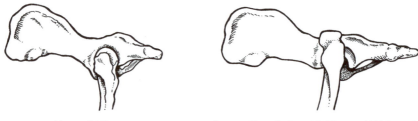

Normal Hip   Severe Dysplasia with Upward Dislocation

Upward displacement is the most common joint type of subluxation in hip dysplacia.

An X-ray of the hips and pelvis is the only reliable way of determining whether a dog has hip dysplasia. Good X-rays require heavy sedation or anesthesia. The standard view is taken with the dog lying on his back with his rear legs parallel and extended. The knees (stifles) are rotated internally. Care is taken to be sure that the pelvis is not tilted.

Hip dysplasia is graded according to the severity of X-ray findings. With normal hips (graded *excellent*), the femoral head fits tightly into a well-formed hip socket with a minimum of space between the head of the femur and the acetabulum. The hip ball is almost completely covered by the socket. With *mild hip dysplasia*, the X-rays will show mild subluxation (increased space in the joint) with the hip ball part-way out of the socket. There are no changes associated with degenerative arthritis.

In *moderate dysplasia* the hip ball is barely seated into a shallow acetabulum. Arthritic changes begin to appear. These include wear and flattening of the femoral head, a rough appearance to the joint surfaces and the beginning of bone spurs. In *severe dysplasia* the head of the femur is completely out of the joint and arthritic changes are marked.

Once arthritis is noted, the condition is irreversible. But even with arthritis, some dogs are not lame. The onset of lameness is unpredictable, and some dogs may go most of their lives with dysplastic hips but no lameness. Others develop lameness as puppies.

The OFA provides a hip dysplasia registry for purebred dogs (see Appendix C). For a nominal fee, an OFA-certified radiologists will review hip X-rays taken by your veterinarian and, if the conformation of the hips is normal for the breed,

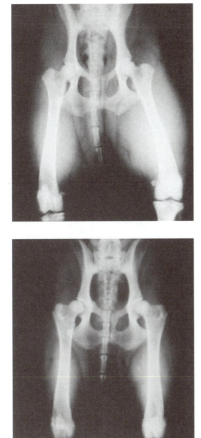

An X-ray of normal hips. The femoral heads fit tightly into well-formed sockets.

Moderate dysplasia. These loose hips are partly out of their sockets, and the femoral heads are beginning to flatten.

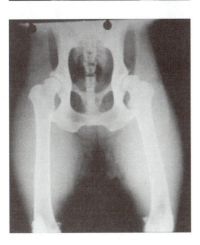

Severe dysplasia with degenerative arthritis. Note bilateral subluxations and bone spurs on the femoral heads and rims of the sockets.

certify the dog by assigning it an OFA number. As an optional step, you can have the OFA number added to your dog's AKC registration papers.

Dogs must be 24 months of age or older to be certified. Some female dogs will show subluxation when X-rayed around an estrus cycle, so OFA recommends not X-raying females around a heat period or within three to four weeks of weaning a litter.

The OFA registry is closed. That means if the dog is found to have hip dysplasia, the information remains confidential.

Dog breeders often request preliminary evaluations on hip status before selecting puppies for show and breeding stock. The OFA accepts preliminary X-rays on puppies as young as four months of age. Their own analysis reveals that these evaluations are about 90 percent accurate when compared with follow-ups at 24 months of age.

Another method of evaluating hips was developed at the University of Pennsylvania Veterinary School and is now administered by *PennHip* (see Appendix C). PennHip X-rays are taken in a different position than X-rays for OFA certification. They are used to guage joint laxity, which can be measured in puppies, starting at 16 weeks of age. The joint laxity does not change as the dog ages.

Dogs X-rayed for PennHip measurements are compared only to other dogs of the same breed. Your dog then receives a joint laxity distraction index (DI) number. PennHip suggests that only dogs in the top half for their breed with respect to joint laxity (that is, those with the tightest joints) be used for breeding. Those dogs who fall into the lower half, which are the ones with the loosest hips, have a greater chance of developing hip dysplasia in the future.

Finally another organization, the Institute for Genetic Disease Control in Animals, also maintains a hip dysplasia registry (see Appendix C). The GDC certifies dogs starting at 12 months of age. The GDC's registry is open. That is, the GDC provides information on affected as well as normal dogs to anyone making an inquiry.

The GDC requests that veterinarians palpate the stifle joints for *patella luxation* at the time of hip X-rays. They also request that copies of pedigrees be submitted with X-rays. The goal of the GDC is to build a large integrated database on the orthopedic conditions it registers.

A genetic test for hip dysplasia applicable for a number of breeds is under development through *VetGen* (see Appendix C).

Treatment: Treatment of hip dysplasia is both medical and surgical. Medical treatment includes restricting activity and giving a NSAID analgesic such as Rimadyl, and a joint *chondroprotectant* such as Adequan to relieve pain and inflammation and to repair damaged cartilage. These agents are discussed in more detail in *Degenerative Joint Disease,* page 363.

It is important to exercise lame dogs on a leash and not allow them to run, jump or play as long as they exhibit pain. Swimming is an excellent exercise that improves muscle mass and joint flexibility without overstressing the hips. Feed a quality food in amounts appropriate for normal (but not accelerated) growth. Overweight puppies should be given a calorie-restricted diet. Discuss this with your veterinarian. Vitamin and mineral supplements have no proven benefit in preventing or treating hip dysplasia, and may even be detrimental if given in excess.

After reviewing the X-rays, your veterinarian may recommend hip surgery. Early surgery in selected puppies can prevent some cases of degenerative joint disease. Surgery is also indicated for dogs who continue to experience pain and lameness despite medical treatment.

Five surgical options are available. Technical factors govern the choice. *Triple pelvic osteotomy* and *femoral osteotomy* are two operations performed on puppies that do not have degenerative joint changes. The goal of both operations is to position the femoral head more deeply in the acetabulum. Normal joint function is maintained with these operations and arthritis may not develop, although this is variable.

Pectineus myectomy is a relatively simple operation in which all of the pectineus muscle is removed on both affected sides. This operation does not slow the progress of joint disease but does afford pain relief for some time.

Femoral head and neck excision arthroplasty is an effective operation for the relief of intractable hip pain. The head of the femur is removed, allowing a fibrous union to replace the ball-and-socket joint. The operation is usually reserved for dogs weighing less than 36 pounds.

Total hip replacement is the most effective procedure for dogs nine months and older that have disabling degenerative joint disease in one or both hips. The operation removes the old joint and replaces it with a new, artificial joint. The procedure requires special equipment and is usually performed by an orthopedic specialist. Good results are obtained in more than 95 percent of cases.

Prevention: Preventing excessive weight gain in puppyhood and keeping the puppy from placing undue stress on the hips will delay the onset of hip dysplasia in many dogs with a genetic predisposition. It may also lead to a less severe form of the disease. Puppies at risk for hip dysplasia should be fed a calorie-controlled diet, as described in *Feeding Weaned Puppies* in Chapter 9.

Preventing hip dysplasia in a bloodline is based on selective breeding practices. *Hip dysplasia is a moderately heritable condition.* It is twice as common among littermates having one dysplastic parent. Experience shows that repeated selection of normal dogs for breeding stock significantly reduces the incidence of hip dysplasia in susceptible bloodlines.

Information on breed risk is available through the OFA and PennHip. In breeds where hip dysplasia is a particular problem, prospective puppy buyers are advised to check pedigrees for OFA, PennHip or GDC certifications, particularly for sires and dams.

LEGG-PERTHES DISEASE

Legg-Perthes disease is caused by avascular necrosis of the femoral head. Avascular necrosis means death of bone in the head of the femur resulting from an interruption in the blood supply. It is not clear what causes this, but genetic factors may be involved.

The disease occurs most often in toy-breed puppies between four and 11 months of age. Large breeds are occasionally affected. Avascular necrosis occurs in both hips in about 15 percent of cases. Occasionally, it is the result of a traumatically dislocated hip as the result of a trauma such as an auto accident or a fall from a height.

Weight bearing causes the dead bone beneath the cartilage of the femoral head to collapse. This fractures the cartilage and causes a gradual destruction of the hip joint.

Signs are severe lameness and sometimes the inability to bear weight on the leg. Muscle wasting is pronounced, and the joint loses some range of motion. The affected leg may be shorter than the opposite normal leg. A standard X-ray of the hips and pelvis establishes the diagnosis.

Treatment: Medical therapy involves restricting activity and administering analgesics. Some dogs may improve, but surgery generally produces the best results. Surgery involves either a femoral head and neck excision arthroplasty or a total hip replacement, as described in *Hip Dysplasia.*

The GDC maintains a Legg-Perthes registry for breeds in the Terrier Group.

LUXATING PATELLA (SLIPPING KNEECAP)

The patella or kneecap is a small bone that protects the front of the stifle joint. The patella is anchored in place by ligaments and slides in a groove in the femur called the trochlea. If the groove is too shallow, the patella will slip out when the knee bends. When the patella slips out to the inside of the knee joint, it's called *medial luxation.* When it slips out to the outside, it's called *lateral luxation.*

Luxating patella is usually an inherited developmental defect. Rarely, it is acquired through trauma.

Medial luxation is more common. It occurs in toy, miniature and large breeds, and is apparent in some pups when they begin to walk. In others it appears later. The patella may slip in and out of place, resulting in a gait that is sometimes normal and sometimes not. When the patella is out of place, the affected leg is usually carried with the stifle joint bent and the foot turned inward. The condition is bilateral in about 25 percent of cases.

Lateral luxation occurs in large and giant breeds at five to six months of age. A knock-kneed stance is the most noticeable sign. The foot often twists outward as weight is placed on the limb. Both knees are almost always involved.

The diagnosis of luxation is made by attempting to push the patella out of the trochlear groove. The degree of luxation is graded 1 to 4, depending on how easy it is to dislocate the patella and whether the patella returns spontaneously to the trochlear groove.

Treatment: This involves surgery to deepen the trochlear groove and repair any loose or torn ligaments. The specific operation depends on the age of the dog and the type of luxation.

Preliminary veterinary screening for medial patella luxation should be done on Toys and small breeds at six to eight weeks of age, before these pups are sent to their new homes.

The OFA maintains a patellar luxation registry and issues certificates to all dogs that palpate normal at 12 months of age or older. The GDC maintains a medial patella luxation registry for breeds in the Terrier Group and also issues certificates to dogs that palpate normal at 12 months of age or older. The GDC is attempting to accumulate information on patella luxation based on palpating patellas when dogs are X-rayed for hip dysplasia.

Dogs with genetically determined patella luxation should not be bred.

ELBOW DYSPLASIA

Elbow dysplasia is a common causes of front-leg lameness in large-breed dogs. Breeds predisposed to elbow dysplasia include the Golden Retriever, Labrador Retriever, English Setter, English Springer Spaniel, Rottweiler, German Shepherd, Bernese Mountain Dog, Chow Chow, Chinese Shar-Pei, Newfoundland and others.

The elbow joint is composed of the humerus, which articulates with the radius and ulna. The *anconeal process* unites with the ulna at about six months of age. It forms a curved depression in the ulna. The *coronoid process* forms part of the lower curved bone of the ulna. Dogs with elbow dysplasia have one or more of the following inherited developmental defects, which may occur singly or in combination: *ununited anconeal process, fragmented medial coronoid process, osteochondritis dissecans of the medial condyle* of the head of the humerus, and *incongruity of growth rate* between the radius and ulna resulting in curvature of the radius. The first three defects are related to osteochondrosis (discussed below in this chapter). The fourth is related to an enlargement of the epiphyseal growth plate at the head of the radius.

Signs of elbow dysplasia appear in puppies at 4 to 10 months of age. They consist of varying degrees of front-leg lameness that worsens with exercise. Characteristically, the elbow is held outward from the chest and may appear swollen.

The diagnosis is made using detailed X-rays of the elbow joint taken in extreme flexion. Radiologists are particularly interested in the appearance of the anconeal process of the ulna. In elbow dysplasia, the anconeal process has a rough, irregular appearance due to arthritic changes. Another sign of dysplasia is widening of the joint space associated with a loose, unstable joint. X-rays may be difficult to interpret before a pup is seven months of age. A CT scan may be required to demonstrate a fragmented coronoid process.

The wide stance and swollen elbow joints of a dog with bilateral elbow dysplasia.

Both the OFA and the GDC evaluate X-rays and maintain registries for elbow dysplasia (see Appendix C). Dogs must be 24 months of age or older to be certified by OFA, and 12 months or older to be certified by GDC. OFA accepts preliminary X-rays on growing pups for interpretation only.

Treatment: Medical treatment is similar to that described for hip dysplasia. Surgery is the treatment of choice for most dogs. Several factors, including the age of the dog and number and severity of the defects, govern the choice of surgical procedure. The more defects in the elbow, the greater the likelihood that the dog will develop degenerative arthritis—with or without surgery.

OSTEOCHONDROSIS

Osteochondrosis is a common disease of rapidly growing large-breed puppies. The first signs show up at between four and eight months of age.

Bone lengthening is a continuous process in which rapidly growing cartilage at the ends of bones becomes calcified and is gradually incorporated into the bone. Osteochondrosis is a disease caused by a defect in the calcification process of this growing cartilage. In osteochondrosis, the cartilage is calcified in an *irregular* instead of a uniform fashion. This creates areas of uncalcified, defective cartilage over the ends of the bones. With stress on the joint, the defective cartilage breaks into loose fragments called *joint mice*. This process, which is accompanied by joint pain and swelling, is called *osteochondritis dissecans*.

Osteochondrosis most often involves the head of the humerus in the shoulder joint. It also occurs in the elbow, where it is responsible for many of the defects of *elbow dysplasia*. Osteochondrosis occurs less commonly in the stifle and hock joints. In the stifle, osteochondrosis involves the femur at its articulation with the tibia. Symptoms of intermittent lameness may look like *luxating patella*. In the hock, osteochondrosis involves the articulation between the tibia and the talus (first bone of the hock).

The symptoms of osteochondrosis may resemble those of *panosteitis*, another disease that causes lameness in growing puppies. Panosteitis is described below.

Symptoms of osteochondrosis may appear following a traumatic episode such as jumping down stairs. The typical presentation is gradual lameness that seems to stem from the shoulder, elbow, stifle or hock in a young dog of one of the large breeds. Lameness often gets worse with exercise. Pain is present on flexing and extending the joint. X-rays may show fragmentation of joint cartilage or a loose piece of cartilage in the joint. The diagnosis may not be made definitively until the dog is 18 months of age.

Treatment: Medical treatment involves restricting activity and prescribing analgesics and *chondroprotectants*, as described for the treatment of degenerative joint disease. Preparations that contain polysulfated glycosaminoglycan (Adequan) may be of benefit in limiting further cartilage degeneration and relieving pain and inflammation.

In most cases surgery will be required to scrape away defective cartilage and remove any joint mice. The best results are obtained in the shoulder and elbow joints. The results are less favorable for the hock, which is a small joint, and for the stifle, which is a more complex joint. In the hock and stifle, degenerative joint disease is likely to occur over time.

PANOSTEITIS (WANDERING LAMENESS)

Panosteitis is a disease of large, rapidly growing puppies between 5 and 12 months of age. The disease has been described in German Shepherd Dogs, Doberman Pinchers, Great Danes, Irish Setters, Saint Bernards, Airedale Terriers, Basset Hounds, Miniature Schnauzers and other breeds. The cause is unknown, but an inherited polygenic trait is suspected. Males are affected four times more often than females. Suspect this disease if your puppy exhibits intermittent lameness in one or more legs that is unrelated to trauma.

A characteristic sign is the tendency for pain and lameness to shift from one limb to another over a course of several weeks or months. That's why this disease is sometimes called wandering leg lameness. Pressure over the shaft of an affected bone elicits pain. X-rays show a characteristic picture of increased density in a long bone. Panosteitis must be distinguished from other causes of lameness in growing puppies, including osteochondrosis, elbow dysplasia and hip dysplasia.

Treatment: The disease is self-limiting, but lameness may persist for several months. Symptoms usually disappear by the time the dog is 20 months old. Analgesics prescribed by your veterinarian can be given to relieve pain. If the dog is severely affected, restrict exercise.

Arthritis

Arthritis is a degenerative condition that affects one or more joints. Most cases occur among dogs with an inherited orthopedic disease such as osteochondrosis or hip dysplasia, or those with a joint injury. Some cases of arthritis are related to an immune-mediated joint disease or a joint infection.

DEGENERATIVE JOINT DISEASE (OSTEOARTHRITIS)

Degenerative joint disease, also called osteoarthritis, is a common disease that affects one out of five dogs during their lifetime. It isn't just a problem among older dogs. Hip dysplasia, ruptured cruciate ligaments, patella luxation, joint trauma and other joint conditions can cause degenerative arthritis, even in young dogs. Large-breed dogs are affected more often than small dogs. Heavy dogs are more likely to experience symptoms because of the extra strain placed on ligaments and joints.

Dogs with degenerative arthritis experience varying degrees of lameness, stiffness and joint pain, which is more apparent in the morning and after getting up from a nap. They often exhibit irritability and behavioral changes associated with increasing disability. Cold and damp surroundings increase pain and stiffness. Degenerative arthritis is progressive, and in time makes the dog's life miserable.

The diagnosis is made by joint X-rays that show bone spurs at points where the ligaments and the joint capsule attach to the bone. There may be varying degrees of joint space narrowing and increased density of bone around the joint.

Treatment: Degenerative joint disease is incurable, but treatment can substantially improve the dog's life. Treatment involves physical therapy and weight control, the use of analgesics to relieve pain and improve function, and the use of *condroprotective* agents to repair joint cartilage and prevent further damage. All of these should be used at the same time.

Physical Therapy. Moderate exercise is beneficial because it maintains muscle mass and preserves joint flexibility. Excessive exercise, however, is counterproductive. Arthritic dogs should not be allowed to jump up and down and should never be encouraged to stand up on their back legs. Dogs with pain and lameness should be exercised on a leash. Swimming is an excellent exercise that improves muscle mass without overstressing the joints. Exercise can be increased as the dog improves with medications.

Overweight dogs should be encouraged to lose weight, as described in *Weight Reduction* in Chapter 9. Being overweight seriously complicates the treatment of arthritis.

Analgesics. A few NSAIDs possess *chondroprotective* characteristics, which means that they protect against the breakdown of cartilage. Others such as aspirin actually destroy cartilage in the dosage required for pain relief. This is one reason why aspirin is used less frequently for treating osteoarthritis.

Another reason is that newer canine NSAIDs have been developed that offer significant advantages over aspirin and the older NSAIDs. Rimadyl (carprofen) is an excellent drug with a low incidence of gastrointestinal side effects that has proven itself over time. It must be given twice a day. Rimadyl provides good pain relief and seems to slow the arthritic process. There are no detrimental effects on cartilage. Etogesic (etodolac) is a newly approved NSAID. It requires only one dose a day. This drug may prove as effective as Rimadyl. These drugs are available through your veterinarian by prescription.

Note that many over-the-counter NSAIDs used for pain control in people are dangerous when given to dogs. *Do not use any drugs without veterinary approval, and never use more than one NSAID at the same time.*

Oral glucocorticoids (corticosteroids) are used for their anti-inflammatory effects. They have variable and opposite effects on the joint, depending on the dosage. Low concentrations appear to protect cartilage, while high concentrations (those needed to relieve pain) destroy cartilage. Future preparations may have better protective effects and a wider margin of safety. Until these drugs become available, glucocorticoids are best used for short periods in dogs with osteoarthritis who have failed to respond to NSAIDs. Long-term therapy should be reserved for dogs with immune-mediated arthritis.

Unfortunately, dogs are unusually sensitive to the adverse effects of both the NSAIDs and glucocorticoids. The most common side effect is GI bleeding. This can be difficult to diagnose and quite extensive before signs become apparent (see *Stomach and Duodenal Ulcers*, Chapter 9). Misoprostol (Cytotec) is a drug that prevents ulceration and helps to heal ulcers caused by NSAIDs. Sulcrafate (Carafate) is another drug that protects against mucosal damage. Your veterinarian may prescribe one of these stomach protectants if your dog is taking an NSAID for chronic arthritis.

Chondroprotectants. These compounds appear to modify the progression of osteoarthritis by preventing further breakdown of cartilage. Breakdown of cartilage is the first step in the development of degenerative joint disease. Chondroprotectants are most effective when used early in the course of arthritis.

Adequan is a chondroprotective given intramuscularly twice a week for four or more weeks. It can be used as a preventative in dogs that are at high risk of developing degenerative joint disease, such as those with hip dysplasia.

Other chondroprotective agents are *nutraceuticals*, products that lie somewhere between a nutrient and a drug. Nutraceuticals are believed to have medical value based on subjective evidence of their effectiveness, although clinical evidence based on controlled studies is lacking. Nutraceuticals do not undergo an approval process and are not regulated by a federal agency.

Most nutraceuticals used for osteoarthritis contain glucosamines, polysulfated glycosaminoglycans (PSGAG), and chondroitin sulfates—compounds know to be involved in the synthesis and repair of joint cartilage. Examples include Cosequin and Glyco-flex. These compounds are given orally and can be considered as follow-up therapy after Adequan, or in any condition in which joint damage is anticipated or expected, such as trauma, surgery, degenerative joint disease or immune-mediated arthritis. Chondroprotectives should be given along with an NSAID. The combination reduces pain and alleviates joint inflammation.

Surgical fusion of painful joints, such as the hock or elbow, relieves pain and restores limb movement in some dogs.

IMMUNE-MEDIATED ARTHRITIS

This is an unusual group of diseases in which antibodies are directed against the dog's own connective tissue, resulting in either an erosive or non-erosive arthritis. In erosive arthritis, cartilage and joint surfaces are destroyed. In nonerosive arthritis, there is inflammation but no tissue destruction.

Rheumatoid Arthritis is an *erosive arthritis* that occurs primarily in Toy breeds and other small breeds at approximately four years of age. It is characterized by morning stiffness, shifting lameness and swelling of the smaller joints, particularly the wrists and hocks. Fever, loss of appetite and lymphadenopathy are accompanying features.

Nonerosive Arthritis tends to occur in midsize and large-breed dogs at about five to six years of age. The cause is unknown. Signs are intermittent fever, loss of appetite, joint swelling and a lameness that often shifts from limb to limb. A form of non-erosive arthritis occurs with *systemic lupus erythematosus.*

The diagnosis of immune-mediated arthritis is made by joint X-rays and specific laboratory tests. *Synovial fluid analysis* helps to distinguish immune-mediated arthritis from infectious arthritis and degenerative joint disease.

Treatment: Immune-mediated arthritis responds to anti-inflammatory and immunosuppressive drugs, including corticosteroids and chemotherapy agents. Treatment must be continued for eight weeks or longer. Your veterinarian may use several drugs or drug combinations before determining which protocol works best for your dog. Rheumatoid arthritis is less responsive than non-erosive arthritis to drug therapy.

Light to moderate activity is beneficial, but vigorous exercise, which is most likely to occur during periods of remission, can injure the joints and should be restricted. Overweight dogs should be placed on a calorie-restricted diet. In fact, it may be advantageous if the dog is somewhat lean. Discuss this with your veterinarian.

INFECTIOUS ARTHRITIS

Infectious diseases can produce arthritis. Rickettsial arthritis is seen with Rocky Mountain spotted fever and canine ehrlichiosis, and spirochetal arthritis with Lyme disease. Fungal arthritis is a rare complication of a systemic fungal infection.

Septic arthritis is caused by bacteria that gain access to joints through open wounds, soft-tissue infections around joints, and via the bloodstream. Injecting steroids into a joint carries a small risk of introducing bacteria.

Treatment: This involves opening the joint and removing all infected and devitalized tissue. This is followed by a long-term course of antibiotics.

Metabolic Bone Diseases

HYPERPARATHYROIDISM

The parathyroids are four small glands in the neck located near the thyroid gland. The parathyroid glands secrete the hormone PTH, which is essential to bone metabolism and blood calcium regulation.

Primary Hyperparathyroidism. This disease is rare in dogs. It is caused by tumors of the parathyroid glands that cause them to secrete excessive amounts of PTH. Middle-aged and older dogs are affected. The average age of onset is 10. Signs are nonspecific and include loss of appetite, lethargy, excessive thirst and frequent urination. Constipation, weakness, vomiting, muscle twitching and a stiff gait have all been reported. The disease may not be suspected until a chemistry panel reveals a high serum calcium.

Anal sac adenocarcinomas have the unique property of producing PTH, and thus are a rare cause of hyperparathyroidism (see Chapter 9, *Anal Sacs*).

The diagnosis of primary hyperparathyroidism can be confirmed by measuring PTH. The serum PTH is above normal in dogs with this disease. Surgical removal of the affected glands is the only possible treatment.

Renal Secondary Hyperparathyroidism. This is the end result of long-standing kidney disease that causes retention of phosphorus. The high serum phosphorus and low serum calcium stimulates the parathyroids to produce PTH. Symptoms similar to those of primary hyperparathyroidism are usually overshadowed by the kidney problem. Treatment is directed toward correcting the kidney disease, as described in Chapter 14, *Kidney Failure*.

Nutritional Secondary Hyperparathyroidism. This disease (now rare) is caused by an excess of phosphorus or a deficiency of calcium in the diet. Vitamin D is required for calcium to be absorbed from the small intestine. Thus a deficiency of vitamin D produces a deficiency of calcium. Any of these problems can cause the parathyroid glands to produce more PTH.

One cause of nutritional secondary hyperparathyroidism is feeding a diet that consists primarily of organ meats such as beef heart, liver or kidney. Such diets are too high in phosphorus and too low in calcium and vitamin D. Other diets low in calcium are all-vegetable diets, corn bread diets and diets containing leftover table scraps. The disease does not occur in dogs that eat a nutritionally balanced diet.

In puppies and young dogs, signs suggest skeletal problems, and include lameness, bone pain, stunted growth and spontaneous fractures. In adult dogs, nutritional secondary hyperthyroidism produces periodontal disease. Thinning of the jaws exposes the roots of teeth. The teeth then loosen and fall out.

Treatment: Correct the diet by feeding a high-quality balanced food—in the case of puppies, one advertised as supporting growth. Vitamin and mineral supplements should not be given unless prescribed by a veterinarian.

Affected puppies should be kept quiet and confined for the first few weeks to prevent fractures. Older dogs with advanced periodontal disease or intractable eating habits may not eat enough of their balanced food. These dogs need restorative dentistry, and may require supplements.

HYPERTROPHIC OSTEODYSTROPHY

Hypertrophic osteodystrophy is a developmental disease that affects large and giant-breed dogs two to eight months of age. The cause is unknown.

Hypertrophic osteodystrophy targets the long bones close to the growth plates at the wrists and hocks. These areas become painful and give rise to lameness. The lameness ranges from mild to incapacitating. It often affects both front or both rear limbs. The bones are extremely warm, swollen and painful to the touch. Affected dogs are reluctant to move. Some dogs develop high fever, depression, weight loss and loss of appetite.

Bone X-rays show enlargement of the affected growth plate and increased density of bone adjacent to the growth plate. These findings distinguish hypertrophic osteodystrophy from *panosteitis* and other causes of lameness in growing pups.

Treatment: There is no specific treatment for hypertrophic osteodystrophy. Symptomatic therapy involves resting the dog and giving an NSAID such as Rimadyl, available through your veterinarian. Review the pup's diet to be sure he is not being overfed, and if so, reduce caloric intake. Discontinue all vitamin supplements the pup may have been receiving. Most affected puppies have one to two episodes of hypertrophic osteodystrophy and then recover, but permanent bone changes and physical deformities may develop.

Vitamin and Mineral Supplements

Contrary to popular belief, puppies do not need vitamin or mineral supplements for their normal growth and development. Modern name-brand commercial puppy foods are formulated to supply all the nutrients required to sustain normal growth—provided the puppy or young dog consumes the puppy food as the sole or main source of calories. More vitamins and minerals added to the diet will not add more substance or coat to the growing animal.

When calcium, phosphorus and vitamin D are given in excess of a dog's capacity to use them, growth and development can be adversely affected. Overdosing with vitamin D causes bones to calcify in an uneven fashion. In addition, calcium may be deposited in the lungs, heart and blood vessels.

Vitamin and mineral supplements are most effective when given to elderly dogs with poor eating habits that may have developed a specific deficiency. The appropriate dose of any supplement should be determined by your veterinarian.

THE URINARY SYSTEM

The urinary tract is made up of of the kidneys, ureters, bladder and, in the male, the prostate and urethra. (The male genitourinary system is seen below and the female system is shown in the figure that begins Chapter 15.) The kidneys are paired organs located on either side of the backbone just behind the last rib. Each kidney has a renal pelvis, or funnel, that siphons the urine into a ureter. The ureters transport urine to the bladder. The bladder empties into the urethra. The opening of the urethra is found at the tip of the penis in the male and between the folds of the vulva in the female. In the male, the urethra also serves as the channel for semen. The prostate envelops the urethra just below the bladder. The top surface of the prostate can be felt by rectal examination.

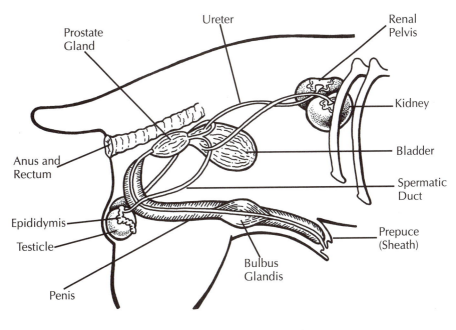

THE MALE GENITOURINARY SYSTEM

The chief functions of the kidneys are to regulate fluid, electrolyte and acid-base balance and to excrete the wastes of metabolism. This is accomplished by millions of nephrons, the basic working units of the kidneys. A nephron is composed of a globe of blood vessels (called the glomerulus) that filters urine from the plasma and passes it through a system of tubules that reabsorb water and electrolytes. This concentrates the urine. The leftover urine contains the waste products. Urine is normally yellow and clear. However, its appearance can be altered by the state of hydration and various drugs and diseases.

The decision to void is under the conscious control of the brain. Teaching a dog when to void is the basis for successful house-training. Once the dog decides to urinate, the actual mechanism of emptying the bladder is carried out by a complicated spinal cord reflex.

Signs of Urinary Tract Disease

Most urinary tract disorders cause some disturbance in the normal pattern of voiding. There are a number of things to look for.

PAINFUL URINATION (DYSURIA)

Signs are obvious distress during urination with straining, dribbling, licking at the penis or vulva, crying out in pain, voiding frequently in small amounts, squatting but not passing urine after many tries and passing mucus, blood clots or bloody urine. These symptoms indicate a disorder of the bladder, urethra or prostate. Pain and swelling in the lower abdomen suggest an overdistended bladder. A dog that does not pass urine after prolonged squatting or lifting of the leg is obstructed. This is usually caused by a stone.

BLOOD IN THE URINE (HEMATURIA)

Blood in the first portion of urine that clears with voiding indicates a problem in the urethra, penis, prostate, uterus or vagina. Blood that appears at the end of voiding suggests a disease of the bladder or prostate. A uniformly bloody urine is seen with diseases of the kidneys, ureters and bladder.

Bleeding without pain suggests kidney disease. Vaginal bleeding may give a false impression of hematuria. Microscopic hematuria is finding red blood cells on microscopic examination of the urine.

EXCESSIVE URINATION (POLYURIA)

Frequent passage of large volumes of urine suggests kidney disease. The dog compensates by drinking large amounts of water. You may notice this symptom first.

Other common causes of polyuria include diabetes mellitus, Cushing's syndrome, a pituitary tumor, hyperparathyroidism and some types of poisoning. Polyuria should be distinguished from dysuria and urinary incontinence.

URINARY INCONTINENCE

Incontinent dogs void inappropriately, in many cases because they have lost voluntary control. Characteristic signs are bedwetting, dribbling, sometimes frequent voiding and loss of urine when excited or stressed. Incontinence is discussed below.

DIAGNOSING URINARY TRACT DISEASES

Because of overlapping symptoms and the fact that more than one organ may be involved, it is difficult to make an exact diagnosis based on the symptoms alone. The laboratory can be of considerable help. Routine tests are a urinalysis, which tells your veterinarian whether your dog has a urinary tract infection, and blood chemistries, which provide information about the function of the kidneys.

Your veterinarian may ask you to bring in a urine specimen, which you can easily obtain by collecting a sample midstream in a plastic specimen container as the dog voids. Sterile urine specimens are obtained by aspirating urine from the bladder with a sterile needle and syringe, or by passing a sterile catheter into the bladder through the urethra. This will be done by your veterinarian when it is important to culture the urine.

X-ray films of the abdomen are particularly useful in diagnosing stones. Abdominal *ultrasonography* is an excellent noninvasive test that images the kidneys, ureters and bladder. An intravenous pyelogram (IVP) is an X-ray examination in which a dye is injected into a vein. The dye is excreted by the kidneys and outlines the renal pelvis and ureters. Other selective studies include *CT scans* and surgical exploration and biopsy of the kidneys.

Diseases of the Bladder, Urethra and Prostate

There are four basic problems, often interrelated, in the lower urinary tract. They are infection, obstruction, stones and urinary incontinence.

CYSTITIS (BLADDER INFECTION)

Cystitis is a bacterial infection of the lining of the bladder. Urethral infections in both males and females often precede bouts of cystitis. Other predisposing causes include increasing age, diabetes mellitus and being on long-term corticosteroid therapy. In sexually intact males there may be a pre-existing prostatitis.

Urinary stones can occur as a result of cystitis. The bacteria form a nidus around which the stone develops.

The principal sign of cystitis is frequent, painful urination. The urine may appear cloudy and have an abnormal odor. Females with cystitis may lick at the vulva and have a vaginal discharge. The diagnosis is confirmed by a urinalysis showing bacteria, white blood cells and often red blood cells in the urine.

Treatment: Cystitis should be treated promptly to prevent kidney infection. Your veterinarian will prescribe an oral antibiotic effective against the bacteria in question. Antibiotics are administered for two to three weeks, after which the urine should be checked again to be sure the infection has been eliminated.

A second attack suggests a secondary problem such as bladder stones and the need for a veterinary workup. The second attack is treated with antibiotics selected on the basis of culture and sensitivity tests. A follow-up urine culture is obtained one to two months after discontinuing treatment. Chronic forms of cystitis may require the use of urinary antiseptics or long-term antibiotics given at bed time.

BLADDER AND URETHRAL STONES

Bladder stones are common. Stones that form in the bladder may pass into the urethra. All dogs can develop bladder stones. Breeds with an increased incidence include the Miniature Schnauzer, Dalmatian, Shih Tzu, Dachshund and Bulldog.

Bladder and ureteral stones may be large or small, single or multiple, and may pass spontaneously or obstruct the lower urinary tract. Stones in the bladder eventually cause painful urination and blood in urine. Kidney stones are rare in dogs.

Most bladder stones are struvites (magnesium ammonium phosphate). They form in an alkaline urine and are usually preceded by a bladder infection. The bacteria and urinary sediment form a nidus around which the ammonium phosphate is deposited.

Uric acid stones form in an acid urine, and are frequently associated with inherited alterations in urate metabolism. Dalmatians and Bulldogs are genetically predisposed. Other stones are calcium oxalate and cystine stones. Silica stones are rare; they occur most often in male German Shepherd Dogs. These stones are usually not associated with a pre-existing bladder infection.

Stones that are large or numerous can sometimes be palpated through the abdomen. In most cases the diagnosis is made by X-ray. Stones not visible on an abdominal X-ray can often be demonstrated by *ultrasonography* or IVP. A urinalysis is routinely obtained. Stones that pass spontaneously and those that are removed surgically should be analyzed, if possible, since the composition of the stone influences the treatment of any remaining and future stones.

Treatment: Bladder infection, if present, is treated as described for *cystitis*. In many cases the stones can be dissolved over weeks or months by feeding the dog a

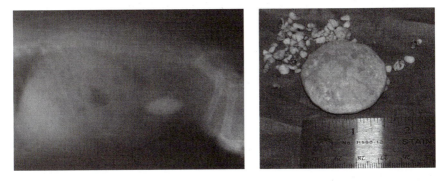

A large stone in the bladder of an
11-year-old terrier.

Struvite stones, removed from
the bladder of this dog.

special diet. Struvite stones dissolve in an acid urine low in magnesium and protein, accomplished by feeding Hill's Prescription Diet s/d. Uric acid stones respond to a low purine diet (Hill's u/d), along with the drug allopurinol. Cystine stones also respond to Hill's u/d, along with drugs that dissolve cystine. There are no available methods for dissolving calcium oxalate and silica stones.

Surgical removal is the treatment of choice for urethral stones causing obstruction (see *Obstructed Bladder* below), and for bladder stones that fail to respond to dissolution. Surgery is also indicated when medical treatment is contraindicated because of congestive heart failure, or when there is need for a more rapid resolution of symptoms.

The formation of new stones occurs in up to 30 percent of cases. The dog should be seen and checked at regular intervals.

OBSTRUCTED BLADDER (URINARY RETENTION)

A stone is the most common cause of an obstructed bladder. Tumors and strictures are less common causes. Enlargement of the prostate gland is a rare cause of bladder obstruction in dogs.

A dog with an obstructed bladder is acutely uncomfortable or in dire distress. Males and females often assume a peculiar splay-legged stance while attempting to void. A partial blockage can be suspected when the dog dribbles urine, voids frequently, and has a weak, splattery stream.

A partial obstruction may become a complete obstruction. With a complete obstruction no urine is passed. The lower abdomen becomes swollen, tender to pressure and feels as if there is a large ball in front of the pelvis. Note that the continuous straining associated with an obstructed bladder can be mistaken for constipation.

Treatment: A dog with a partial obstruction due to a urethral stone is likely to pass the stone spontaneously. Treatment thereafter is like that described for bladder and uretheral stones.

A *complete obstruction is an acute emergency.* Take your dog at once to the veterinarian. If the blockage is not relieved, the dog will go into kidney failure. Often the stone can be pushed back into the bladder using a sterile catheter, or by infusing water under pressure into the urethra. If not, surgical removal will be necessary.

URINARY INCONTINENCE

Incontinence is loss of voluntary control over the act of voiding. Incontinent dogs wet the bed, make mistakes in the house, sometimes dribble urine and may void more frequently than normal. There may be an ammonia-like odor about the dog's bedding. The skin around the penis or vulva may be scalded. There are several types of incontinence:

Hormone-Responsive Incontinence

This common incontinence is seen most often in middle-aged and older spayed females, and less commonly in young females and older neutered males. It is caused by a deficiency of estrogen in females and testosterone in males. Both these hormones are important in maintaining muscle tone of the urethral sphincter. Hormone-responsive incontinence is much like bed-wetting. The dog urinates normally, but wets when relaxed or asleep.

Treatment: Hormone-responsive continence in spayed females is treated by giving phenylpropanolamine, a drug that increases the tone of the urethral sphincter. Diethylstilbestrol (estrogen) can be given if phenylpropanolamine is not successful. Diethylstilbestrol is no longer the first choice because of the risk of bone marrow suppression. Incontinence in neutered males responds well to giving testosterone. Phenylpropanolamine has also been used successfully in males.

Submissive Urination

This is another common problem, characterized by the involuntary release of urine caused by contraction of the abdominal wall muscles along with relaxation of the muscles that support the urethra. The dog passes small amounts of urine when upset or in a stressful situation. It has also been called stress incontinence.

Treatment: Submissive urination is treated with phenylpropanolamine and/or other drugs that increase urethral tone. Keep stress-provoking sessions low key and brief, and avoid making direct eye contact with the dog. Do not punish the dog, as this makes the incontinence worse.

Neurogenic Incontinence

Spinal cord injuries, infections and tumors, and inherited neuropathies, can interfere with the nerves that control the bladder. A bladder with a compromised nerve supply lacks muscle tone and the ability to contract. The bladder continues to fill until the pressure exceeds the resistance of the sphincter mechanism that closes the urethra. This results in intermittent, uncontrolled dribbling.

Neurogenic incontinence can be confirmed with a cystometrogram. This is a test that measures how forcefully the bladder contracts in response to the introduction of incremental volumes of fluid into the bladder through a catheter. The results also suggest the site of the neurologic deficit (the spinal cord or the bladder).

Treatment: Neurogenic incontinence is treated with long-term catheterization and antibiotics to treat and suppress infection. Drugs that act on the bladder may be of help. This type of incontinence is difficult to treat.

Incontinence from Overdistension of the Bladder

This type of incontinence is due to a partially obstructed bladder caused by urethral stones, tumor or stricture. The signs and symptoms are similar to neurogenic incontinence, but the nerve supply to the bladder is undamaged.

Treatment: Dribbling associated with an overdistended bladder is treated by correcting the cause of the obstruction and placing an indwelling catheter until the bladder regains its muscular tone. Drug therapy is also beneficial. Since the bladder is neurologically normal, treatment may eliminate the problem entirely.

Kidney Failure

Dogs with failing kidneys are unable to concentrate their urine. They have a large urinary output and must drink more than usual to replace fluid losses. If they are not allowed to go outside as often as necessary, they may begin to make mistakes in the house. It is important to check kidney function in all incontinent dogs to be sure the incontinence does not have a medical basis.

Treatment: Treatment of *kidney failure* is discussed later in this chapter.

Other Causes of Incontinence

Other causes of incontinence are ectopic ureters and pelvic adhesions. One or both ureters may enter the vagina instead of the bladder. There is then continuous drainage of urine into the vagina. The incontinence of ectopic ureter is present from birth.

Incontinence shortly after spaying is usually caused by postoperative pelvic adhesions. Both an ectopic ureter and pelvic adhesions are potentially curable by surgery.

ENLARGED PROSTATE

The prostate is an accessory sex gland in males that completely surrounds the urethra at the neck of the bladder. The three conditions that cause prostatic enlargement are benign prostatic hyperplasia, prostatitis (discussed later in this chapter), and cancer of the prostate.

The diagnosis of prostate enlargement is made by digital rectal examination, during which the size, position and firmness of the prostate gland is assessed. *Ultrasonography* provides additional information and may be helpful in guiding a needle into the prostate to obtain a biopsy—a procedure indicated when cancer is suspected.

Benign Prostatic Hyperplasia is an increase in the size of the prostate gland. The disease is hormone dependent and is under the influence of testosterone. Benign prostatic hyperplasia begins in sexually intact males at about five years of age and progresses as the dog grows older. Thus, older dogs are more likely to have symptoms.

As the prostate enlarges, it gradually expands backward and may eventually obstruct the rectum, causing constipation and straining while defecating (see *Anorectal Obstructions* in Chapter 9). The feces may appear flat or ribbonlike. Defecation is difficult. Fecal impactions are common.

Rarely, the prostate pushes forward and presses on the urethra, causing straining during urination. Blood in the urine can be a sign of benign prostatic hyperplasia.

Prostate Cancer is rare in dogs. It is not influenced by testosterone.

Treatment: Treatment for benign prostatic hyperplasia is not necessary unless the dog has symptoms. Neutering eliminates the stimulus for prostatic enlargement and is the treatment of choice for dogs not intended for breeding. A significant decrease in the size of the prostate gland occurs shortly after neutering.

An alternative to neutering is to administer megestrol acetate (Megace), a synthetic derivative of progesterone. Megace decreases the size of the prostate without impairing fertility, but long-term use can cause a dog to develop diabetes mellitus. Note that estrogens, owing to their potentially serious side effects, are no longer recommended for treating benign prostatic hyperplasia.

The treatment of prostate cancer involves surgery and/or radiation therapy. In most cases the disease is far advanced by the time it is diagnosed. Because prostate cancer in dogs is not testosterone dependent, neutering does not slow the progress of the disease. Similarly, neutering does not protect against the development of prostate cancer.

PROSTATITIS

Prostatitis is a bacterial infection of the prostate gland, usually preceded by a bout of cystitis. Signs of acute prostatitis are fever, depression, vomiting, diarrhea and painful urination. The dog may have an arched back or tucked-up abdomen. Blood-tinged or purulent secretions may drip from the prepuce. The prostate gland is enlarged, swollen and tender. The disease can become chronic, with periodic flare-ups. Chronic prostatitis is a significant cause of male infertility.

Treatment: The diagnostic workup is like that described for benign prostatic hyperplasia. Your veterinarian can use techniques to collect prostatic secretions for culture and *cytology*. Once the diagnosis is made, the dog is placed on an oral antibiotic selected on the basis of culture and sensitivity tests. Antibiotics have difficulty penetrating the swollen prostate, so long-term administration is necessary.

Following treatment, the prostatic fluid should be recultured to ensure that the infection has been eliminated. Neutering helps to resolve symptoms and decreases the likelihood of recurrent prostatitis.

Prostate surgery may be necessary for dogs with serious complications, such as prostatic abscess.

Kidney Disease

PYELONEPHRITIS (KIDNEY INFECTION)

Pyelonephritis is a bacterial infection of the kidney, including the renal pelvis and ureter. Most cases are caused by an ascending bladder infection. There may be a predisposing blockage or congenital malformation of the urinary tract. Occasionally the infection is blood borne.

Acute pyelonephritis begins with fever, loss of appetite, vomiting and pain in the lower back. A stiff-legged gait and a hunched-up posture are characteristic. Some dogs exhibit signs of painful urination. On microscopic examination, the urine contains white blood cell casts, which are plugs of cells expelled from kidney tubules. An IVP or renal ultrasound may show an enlarged kidney or a dilated renal pelvis.

The arched back and hunched-up posture of a dog suffering from acute pyelonephritis.

Chronic pyelonephritis is an insidious disease that may or may not be preceded by an acute pyelonephritis. Signs are loss of appetite, weight loss and excessive urination and thirst. This disease smolders for months or years, eventually culminating in kidney failure. Early treatment of acute pyelonephritis may prevent this.

Treatment: Kidney infection is difficult to eliminate and relapse is common. Any underlying predisposing causes should be dealt with. Pyelonephritis is treated with antibiotics selected on the basis of bacterial sensitivity tests. Antibiotics should be continued for six to eight weeks. The urine should be recultured during treatment to be sure the antibiotic selected is still effective against the bacteria in question.

After treatment, it is important to reculture the urine on three separate occasions at six- to eight-week intervals before concluding that the dog is cured.

NEPHRITIS AND NEPHROSIS

Nephritis and nephrosis are names given to diseases of the kidneys that produce scarring and kidney failure.

Nephritis is an inflammatory process associated with certain infectious diseases, including canine hepatitis, canine ehrlichiosis, Lyme disease, Rocky Mountain spotted fever and others. Dogs with systemic lupus erythematosus and chronic pancreatitis can develop nephritis. A familial predisposition for a condition called *glomerulonephritis* occurs in Doberman Pinschers, Samoyeds and Bull Terriers.

Nephrosis is the result of degenerative changes caused by toxins and poisons that target the kidneys. The most important nephrotoxins are aspirin, ibuprofen and butazolidin. Certain antibiotics are nephrotoxic, particularly when given for prolonged periods or in high doses. They include polymyxin B, gentamicin, amphotericin B and kanamycin. The diagnosis of nephritis or nephrosis is established by kidney biopsy.

Dogs with nephritis or nephrosis may develop a condition called the *nephrotic syndrome*. Large amounts of protein are excreted into the urine from the damaged kidneys. In consequence, serum protein levels are low. This results in loss of fluid into the legs (*edema*), the abdominal cavity (*ascites*) and the chest cavity (*pleural effusion*). The swollen limbs and pot-bellied appearance of the nephrotic syndrome suggest right-sided congestive heart failure, but laboratory studies will distinguish between these two conditions.

Treatment: Nephritis, if caught in time, responds to elimination of the predisposing cause. For treatment of the nephrotic syndrome, see *Kidney Failure* below.

KIDNEY FAILURE (UREMIA)

Kidney failure is defined as the inability of the kidneys to remove waste products from the blood. The buildup of toxins produces the signs and symptoms of uremic poisoning. Kidney failure can appear suddenly (acute kidney failure) or come on gradually over months. Most cases are of the gradual onset type, and are caused by nephritis and nephrosis.

Causes of *acute kidney failure* include:

- Complete urinary tract obstruction caused by a stone.
- Rupture of the bladder or urethra.
- Shock, with inadequate blood flow to the kidneys.
- Congestive heart failure with low blood pressure and reduced blood flow to the kidneys.
- Poisoning, especially from antifreeze.

Dogs with kidney failure do not show signs of uremia until 75 percent of functioning kidney tissue is destroyed. Thus a considerable amount of damage occurs before the signs are noticed.

Signs of Kidney Failure

One of the first things you may notice is that your dog drinks and urinates more than usual and indicates his need to go outside several times a day. If not allowed to do so, the dog may begin to make mistakes in the house. These symptoms are due to failure of the kidneys to concentrate the urine. This results in a large urine output over which the dog has no control, with subsequent dehydration and thirst.

As kidney function declines, the dog retains ammonia, nitrogen, acids and other chemical wastes in his blood and tissues. This is called uremia. The degree of uremia is determined by measuring serum blood urea nitrogen (BUN), creatinine and electrolytes.

Signs of uremia are apathy and depression, loss of appetite and weight, a dry haircoat, a brownish discoloration to the surface of the tongue and an ammonia-like odor to the breath. Ulcers may occur in the mouth. With the *nephrotic syndrome* the dog develops *ascites* and *edema*. Vomiting, diarrhea and gastrointestinal bleeding may occur. At the end stages of failure, the dog falls into a coma.

A condition called *rubber jaw* may be seen with chronic kidney failure. It is characterized by loosening of the teeth and ulcerations of the mouth and gums.

Your veterinarian may wish to make an exact diagnosis by performing exploratory surgery and biopsy of the kidney. This helps to guide treatment and determine whether the disease is treatable.

Treatment of Kidney Failure

Dogs with kidney failure require periodic monitoring of blood chemistries in order to detect changes in kidney function that may require medical intervention.

A most important step is to restrict salt intake. This helps to prevent edema, ascites and hypertension. Another important step is to restrict protein intake. Protein is poorly metabolized by dogs with kidney failure. A diet rich in meat, or one that contains poor-quality protein, creates an increased nitrogen load that must be handled by the liver and kidneys. Dogs with weak kidneys can be thrown into failure by feeding them more protein than they can handle. Also restrict phosphorus intake. The best way to accomplish all of the above is to feed a highly digestible, low-protein, low-salt diet such as Hill's Prescription Diet k/d, available through your veterinarian.

It is extremely important to provide fresh water at all times. The dog must be able to take in enough water to compensate for his large urine output. B vitamins are lost in the urine of uremic dogs. These losses should be replaced by giving vitamin B supplements. Sodium bicarbonate tablets may be prescribed by your veterinarian to correct an acid-base imbalance. A phosphorous binder, such as Amphogel, may be recommended to lower the serum phosphorus.

A dog that becomes dehydrated because of illness or failure to drink enough water may decompensate suddenly, a condition called a uremic crisis. The dog should be hospitalized and rehydrated with intravenous fluids and balanced electrolyte solutions.

SEX AND

REPRODUCTION

Selective breeding for many centuries has resulted in the establishment of well-defined breeds based on features such as head type, size and body structure. The development of different breeds has been possible because of a phenomenon called *genetic mutation*. Mutations occur spontaneously, often for reasons unknown. A mutation changes encoded information in a gene, which results in the addition or deletion of an enzyme or protein that may perform an important cellular function. When a mutation arises in an egg or a sperm cell, it affects all the cells in the embryo and, if the animal survives, the mutation is passed on to future generations. In practice, the majority of mutations are detrimental in that they do something that interferes with the animal's ability to adapt to its environment. In nature, such mutations usually do not become part of the genetic pool, because the individuals possessing them do not survive to pass on their genes.

As wild dogs became dependent on humans for survival, matings between the most highly adapted and competitive animals gave way to a system in which breeding partners were selected by their masters for specific reasons. When mutations occurred, they often changed the appearance of the dog, but may also have given the dog a better sense of smell or the ability to burrow after rodents. By selectively breeding such dogs to others of similar type or attribute, over a long period of time humans were able to create hundreds of breeds as diverse as Saint Bernards, Chihuahuas, Pugs and Salukis.

Unfortunately, selective breeding has also resulted in the appearance of a number of genetic diseases involving most of the organs and systems discussed throughout this book. Sadly, these diseases are accepted and tolerated as part of the breed package, even though they weaken the species and have ethical as well as financial consequences to dog breeders and owners. Inherited diseases can, however, be controlled (and in some cases even eliminated) through informed breeding practices.

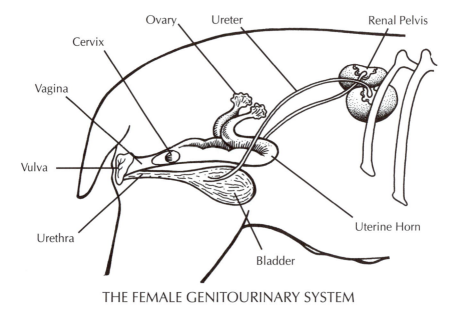

THE FEMALE GENITOURINARY SYSTEM

The Basics of Genetics

Heredity is the result of random combination of countless genes. In the canine *genome* there are 39 chromosome pairs (for a total of 78 chromosomes) and about 80,000 genes. Chromosomes are strands of DNA protein that contain a sequence of genes. When chromosomes pair up, their corresponding genes also pair up. The gene pair then determines the expression of a particular trait.

The sire and dam contribute equally to the genetic makeup of their offspring. Unlike other cells in the body, the egg and sperm cells each contain only 39 chromosomes. As these germ cells are formed, 39 chromosomes are retained and 39 are discarded. It is a matter of chance which chromosomes will be retained and which discarded. When the egg and sperm combine during fertilization, the 39 chromosomes in the egg and 39 in the sperm join up to form 39 pairs in the fertilized embryo.

Because the egg and the sperm each contribute one of two chromosomes to every pair, the number of theoretical combinations for a given chromosome pair is four. Similarly, the number of gene pair possibilities at any specific site is limited to four. However, if you consider the genetic potential of the breed as a whole, the number of different pair combinations that theoretically could occur at a specific site is twice the number of reproducing individuals in the breed. This is what is meant by *genetic diversity*.

A breed with a large population of unrelated dogs is genetically diverse. This is good, because reproductive efficiency and survival are high in genetically diverse populations. It also means breed clubs with only a few foundation animals, who have not been able to bring in new blood, face problems.

INHERITING PROBLEM GENES

Overall, about one out of every 100 puppies will express a demonstrable congenital defect. Some undesirable hereditary traits commonly seen in dogs include: undescended testicles; inguinal and navel hernias; abnormally short or absent tails; congenital heart defects; diabetes mellitus; canine hip and elbow dysplasia; patella luxation; wobbler's syndrome; malocclusion and incorrect bite; bleeding diseases; congenital deafness; entropion and ectropion; Collie eye anomaly and progressive retinal atrophy (PRA); glaucoma; congenital cataracts; idiopathic epilepsy; and behavioral disorders such as inherited aggression and shyness. This list is by no means complete.

A number of undesirable traits are expressed by *recessive genes*. A recessive gene can be carried down through many generations of offspring, causing no problem until it is combined with a like recessive gene. Simple recessive disorders are relatively easy to control if there is a genetic test for the carriers. If there is no test, control is difficult.

Disorders caused by *dominant genes* are much easier to control, because all carriers of the genes are clinically affected. Breeders can choose not to breed such individuals and their offspring, thus eliminating the problem from their breeding stock.

However, simple dominant or recessive genes do not cause the majority of hereditary problems in purebred dogs. Most of the traits that breeders are interested in are *polygenic*—that is, they are controlled by multiple genes, the majority of which are unknown. Hip dysplasia, for example, is considered to be a polygenic trait because defects in muscles, ligaments and bones must be present for dysplasia to occur.

Genetic disorders can be identified and their mode of inheritance determined through test breedings and pedigree analysis. Knowing which animals in a pedigree were affected by an inherited disease makes it possible to predict whether a specific individual is at high or low risk for transmitting the disease. This helps greatly in selecting breeding stock. For example, in progressive renal atrophy, which is controlled by a simple autosomal recessive gene, both parents must carry a defective gene for a puppy to be affected. Therefore, if a puppy does have PRA, it can be deduced that both parents were at least carriers and may even have had the disease. Other offspring of either of the two parents, and any siblings or half-siblings of the affected puppy, would be highly suspect of carrying the defective gene.

For genetic disorders caused by more than one gene, there is no way to tell whether a dog that tests normal for the disease is or is not a carrier. The probability that the dog is a carrier increases if some of his or her immediate relatives have the disease. It is important to know whether the littermates, the sire and dam and their littermates were affected. The breadth of the pedigree is more important than its depth. In other words, you want to know more about the *extended family*, as opposed to looking many generations into the past.

One problem is that even when the frequency of a disease is high in immediate relatives, some offspring that test normal will be carriers and some will not. If there is no genetic test for the carrier state, some genetically normal dogs that may be superior examples of the breed may not be used for breeding. In addition, in breeds where the gene pool is rather small, eliminating normal dogs from breeding can adversely affect genetic diversity.

Pedigree information on normal and affected animals is difficult to obtain, but may be available through open registries such as the Institute for Genetic Disease Control in Animals (GDC), registries sponsored by breed clubs, or in specific cases through the records of dedicated breeders who are willing to share that information.

In an open registry the results of a dog's tests are available to anyone making an inquiry. This provides a real service to the public, but many breeders are understandably reluctant to be the only ones to come forword with information that might reflect badly on their breeding programs. Further education and acceptance of the fact that hereditary problems are a concern for all should result in more widespread sharing of this information. Enlightened breed clubs are already moving in this direction.

Certification by the Orthopedic Foundation for Animals (OFA), Canine Eye Registry Foundation (CERF) or the GDC indicates that a dog shows no clinical signs of having the diseases for which he or she has been tested (see Appendix C). A pedigree that contains such certifications indicates a low probability of transmitting the disease. As a rule of thumb, *the greater the number of normal relatives in a dog's pedigree, the less likely it is that the dog will carry and transmit a heritable disease*.

Carrier dogs can sometimes be identified by a blood-based DNA test, such as the test used for PRA in Irish Setters. However, these tests are available only for certain diseases in certain breeds. As more is known about the canine genome (and this will take several years), newer methods should become available to test for and treat genetic diseases.

Breeding Purebred Dogs

It is important to begin with a mental picture of what you are trying to accomplish. A through knowledge of the breed standard is the most basic requirement. Beyond the standard, however, there is an elusive something extra; a certain almost extrasensory perception that gives success to those who have it.

A successful breeder is one who knows the virtues and faults of all the dogs in a pedigree for four generations. He or she will have the judgment to pick the best puppies and the willingness to eliminate as breeding stock all defective or substandard specimens.

Knowledge of this sort does not come quickly or easily. You need to learn everything you can about your breed, especially the bloodlines from which you plan to choose your stock. Visit as many kennels as you can, talk to the owners and see the tried-and-true producers, the winners and the retired dogs.

Keep in mind that a pedigree ensures only that the dogs are registered with the AKC or a similar organization. It does not testify to the quality of the dogs in question. Pedigrees are important because they are the means to study bloodlines and learn the relationships among dogs of a particular breed. They are of greatest value when the dogs are known or have actually been seen. The contribution of a superior dog who appears several times in a pedigree can be determined mathematically.

You will notice that the successful breeder is the one who sees faults in his or her own dogs as readily as those in a rival's. Perhaps the little "something extra" is the good sense to breed with the *whole* dog in mind—not to emphasize one particular attribute at the expense of the overall dog.

FOLLOWING BLOODLINES

A conscientious breeding program seeks to maintain and improve the quality of the breed. Dogs that are poor examples of breed type should be avoided in favor of those that are excellent. *When outstanding dogs are bred repeatedly to dogs of similar type, the type becomes fixed and the line breeds true.*

In essence, this is the strategy behind most planned breeding programs. The relationship between the various breeding individuals is kept relatively close in order to concentrate the desired genes in the offspring. This method is called *inbreeding*.

Inbreeding involves mating parent to offspring and full brother to sister. A variation on inbreeding, called linebreeding, breeds individuals that are closely related in line through a common ancestor. *Skillful linebreeding is the best method for perpetuating desired characteristics.*

Inbreeding and linebreeding expose both good and bad qualities in the stock. If the strain carries undesirable traits, this becomes evident after a few generations. While this may seem a disaster, in the long term the exposure of such traits is in the best interests of the breed. By choosing not to breed affected animals and their relatives, the undesirable trait can be eliminated from the bloodline.

A common misconception is that inbreeding causes high-strung, nervous or aggressive dogs. However, it is not the breeding process but the genetic potential in the bloodline that determines the animal's temperament. A kennel that uses unstable dogs is likely to have problems. One that uses fundamentally sound dogs produces sound dogs.

Close breeding for three or four generations generally fixes type in a line, after which further improvement becomes more difficult because of uniformity and loss of genetic diversity. In fact, the effect of uninterrupted linebreeding is a decline in reproductive fitness. Fewer litters are produced, the number of pups in the litter decreases and some of the puppies fail to thrive. Most breeders have found that it is wise at this stage to bring in new blood.

Using a stud dog from a totally different line may be considered. This produces an *outcrossed* litter and reshuffles the genes that have tended to become more or less fixed. Many times, particularly with an overly refined bitch, an outcross gives surprisingly good results. An improvement in the health and vigor of the resulting puppies is noted from birth.

While an outcross litter sometimes lacks uniformity, some very good show dogs have been produced in this manner. Puppies from such matings usually are bred back into one of the two lines, thereby recapturing the benefits of previous line-breeding.

The third and final strategy is to breed a dog and a bitch that are unrelated and of varied ancestry. In other words, neither animal has a linebred background. With this approach, it is essential that the breeder have a definite goal in mind. One dog may carry an attribute or quality totally lacking in the other. However, mating animals of such genetically diverse backgrounds in the hope of finding show qualities is rarely rewarding. Even if outstanding puppies are produced from such matings, it is unlikely their offspring will be of similar quality.

THE BROOD BITCH

In general, it is best to begin your breeding program with a show-quality bitch rather than a male. This way, you have the flexibility to breed to studs that best complement her qualities. In addition, if the litters are outstanding, you have foundation stock on which to base your bloodlines.

Before making a decision to breed your female, carefully consider the effort and expense that goes into producing a litter of healthy and active puppies. It can be both time consuming and expensive. Many pedigreed puppies cannot be sold locally. This means advertising and the effort and cost of finding just the right home in which to place them.

Also consider your bitch's overall conformation, disposition and the qualities she may pass along to her puppies. *If the bitch is not of breeding quality, she should be spayed.* Despite popular belief, a bitch does not need to have a litter in order to be psychologically fulfilled.

A bitch should not be bred until her second or third season, at which time she is physically and emotionally mature and able to adjust to motherhood. This usually does not occur before 18 to 24 months of age.

Be sure to check local and state laws concerning dog breeding. In some areas there are new regulations designed to control the explosion in the dog and cat populations. They may only apply to commerical establishments, but they may apply to all breeders regardless of how many litters they have a year.

Brood bitches should be kept in excellent physical condition. Overweight bitches and those depleted by improper diet, excessive breeding and unsanitary living conditions often do not come into season regularly, are difficult to breed and experience problems during delivery. They should not be bred until all such problems have been corrected.

The Prebreeding Examination

Schedule a veterinary examination at least one month before the date you plan to breed the bitch. Maiden bitches over 15 pounds should be examined with a gloved

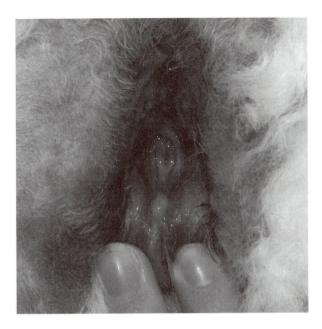

This bitch has a developmental anomaly of the vulva in which the rectum (above) opens into the vagina (below). This leads to reproductive failure from recurrent vaginal infections.

finger to make sure the vaginal canal is normal and that there are no constrictions or abnormalities that could interfere with breeding or conception.

Be sure to have her checked for dental infections. Bacteria from the mouth can be transmitted to newborn puppies when the mother bites and severs the umbilical cord. A stool test will show whether she has intestinal parasites. If found, they should be treated with appropriate medications (see Chapter 2, *Deworming Adult Dogs*).

Because of the seriousness of the sexually transmitted disease *brucellosis*, it is extremely important to obtain a brucellosis blood test on all bitches one month before breeding. Repeat this test before each subsequent breeding. Other blood tests that may be necessary include *canine herpesvirus* serology, a screen for *von Willebrand's disease* and a test for *hypothyroidism*.

Bitches living in areas where *heartworm* is a problem should have a heartworm antigen test, unless they are already receiving heartworm preventives. If the test is negative, begin the preventive medication. Most heartworm preventives are safe to use during pregnancy. As an added benefit, many control intestinal parasites.

A prospective brood bitch should be screened for hereditary diseases for which she may be at risk. For example, if her breed places her at increased risk for *hip dysplasia, elbow dysplasia* or *patella luxation*, it is highly desirable to obtain certification from the OFA or GDC before breeding. Breeds at risk for inherited eye diseases should be screened by CERF. *If any of these tests are positive, do not breed the bitch.*

A brood bitch should be given a DHPP booster shot two to four weeks before breeding. This boosts immunity to the common infectious diseases. In addition, high antibody levels will be transmitted to her pups. These maternal antibodies are the primary protection for puppies during the first three months of life.

Choosing the Right Stud Dog

Part of the preparation for breeding your bitch is to choose the stud dog well in advance. If your bitch comes from a show or breeding kennel, it is clearly a good idea to talk to her breeder before making a final decision. The breeder will be familiar with the bloodlines that lie behind your bitch. If you have an outstanding bitch from that bloodline, you should seriously consider using a stud from that same kennel to reinforce her best qualities.

The show record of a prospective stud dog may include a Championship, multiple breed wins, Group placings or even Bests in Show. Unfortunately, not all great show dogs are outstanding producers. A show record beyond a Championship is not as important as the record of the dog's offspring. If the dog has sired outstanding puppies, particularly out of several bitches, you have evidence that he is a good producer. Much of the credit, however, may belong to the breeder for using the dog wisely and with bitches that complement his attributes.

It is the responsibility of the breeder (that is, the owner of the bitch) to come to a clear understanding with the owner of the stud dog concerning the breeding terms. Usually a stud fee is paid at the time of the mating, or the stud's owner may agree to take a puppy of his or her own choosing. If the bitch does not conceive, the stud's owner may offer a return service at no extra charge. However, this is not obligatory. Terms vary with the circumstances and policies of the kennel. If the terms are in writing, there will be no misunderstandings later.

THE STUD DOG

The age at which a male dog reaches sexual maturity and begins to produce sperm varies from six to 12 months, the average being about nine months. Physiologically, a male could be used at stud at about one year. Most male dogs, however, do not achieve physical maturity before 18 to 24 months of age, and should not be used before that time. It is not until they reach physical maturity that their full breeding potential becomes apparent.

A stud dog should be kept at an ideal weight with regular exercise and a sound diet. Exercise maintains physical condition, endurance and muscle tone. Regular health check-ups are important. Vaccinations must be kept current, as the stud will have close contact with a number of bitches (see the *Vaccination Schedule* in Chapter 3).

The Prebreeding Examination

Before a male is used at stud he should undergo a complete physical examination with laboratory tests similar to those described for the brood bitch. Parasites, if present, should be treated. *Heartworm* preventives are important in areas where the disease is known to occur. Screening tests for *von Willebrand's disease* and *hypothyroidism* may be necessary for certain breeds.

It is extremely important that all prospective stud dogs undergo screening and certification for hereditary orthopedic and eye diseases, as well as other genetic disorders for which they may be at risk. *Dogs with any of these diseases should not be used at stud.*

All prospective male stud dogs should have a *brucellosis* test. Repeat the test every 6 to 12 months, depending on how active the dog is at stud. Once introduced into a kennel, brucellosis can cause widespread sterility and ruin a breeding program.

The reproductive tract examination includes an inspection of the penis, the prepuce and testicles, and digital rectal examination of the prostate. A semen analysis is not necessary unless there is some reason to suspect infertility. Inspection of the penis may reveal a sheath infection, phimosis or paraphimosis. A retained fold of skin (called frenulum) may prevent protrusion of the penis. This can be treated by your veterinarian. Some males have a long, flexible forepart to the penis that can bend backward and make intromission difficult or impossible without assisted breeding.

Solitary or multiple ulcerated cauliflower-like growths up to an inch in size that appear on the shaft of the penis may be *transmissible venereal tumors* (see Chapter 18). They will not be found on virgin dogs, because they occur as a consequence of breeding. All growths on the penis should receive veterinary attention. Lacerations and erosions tend to bleed when the penis is erect. If blood gets into the ejaculate, it can reduce the motility of the sperm.

Both testicles should be present in the scrotum. They should be of similar size and have a rather firm consistency. A dog with two undescended testicles is sterile. A dog with one undescended testicle may still be fertile, but should not be used at stud because the condition is heritable.

THE ESTROUS (HEAT) CYCLE

Bitches become sexually mature when they exhibit their first heat period, usually between 6 and 12 months of age, although there is considerable variation. Toy breeds become sexually mature several months earlier than giant breeds. Sexual maturity does not correspond to physical maturity—the attainment of adult height and weight—which generally happens at about 14 months of age.

Ovarian activity begins to decline after six years of age and ceases at around 10 years of age. By eight years of age it is marginal. Most bitches are not used for breeding after seven to eight years of age.

Females generally come into heat every five to nine months. The heat cycle is specific for each individual. Unlike some other animals, the heat cycle in dogs is not controlled by outside influences such as the number of hours of daylight.

The estrous, or heat, cycle is divided into four stages, each corresponding to the principal hormonal influence governing that stage. The combination of proestrus and estrus, which breeders refer to as the *heat period*, lasts an average of 21 days.

Proestrus

The initial stage of the heat cycle lasts an average of nine days (the range is three to 17 days). The first sign is a bloody discharge from the vulva. In early proestrus, the discharge may be light pink to yellow. If you are not sure about the discharge, wipe a tissue across the vulva. If you see a pinkish color, the bitch is in heat. Along with a discharge there is firm swelling of the vulva.

During proestrus the female makes chemical substances called *pheromones*. These substances attract males, although many experienced stud dogs will not show strong sexual interest in a bitch until she is in standing heat.

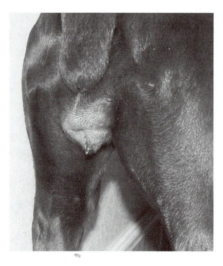

This bitch is in the proestrus stage. Note the swelling and enlargement of the vulva.

During the first four to five days of proestrus the female shows no interest in breeding. If mating is attempted, she will sit down, jump away, growl or snap at the male. A few days before estrus, the next phase, she may be willing to let the male mount her but she won't stand for breeding. Proestrus ends when the bitch becomes receptive to the male.

Estrus

The second phase of the heat cycle is called estrus, or *standing heat*. It is when the female is willing to breed. Estrus lasts seven to nine days (the range is 2 to 20 days). It ends when the bitch refuses to stand for the stud.

As estrus begins, the vulva softens and becomes pliable in preparation for *intromission*. The discharge becomes watermelon-colored or pink. At this time the female begins to flirt with the male, raises her tail and flags it to the side, lifts her pelvis and presents her vulva when touched in the rear.

Ovulation usually occurs on the second day of estrus, or about the 12th day of the heat cycle as measured from the first day of proestrus. *Keep in mind that ovulation may occur sooner or later than expected, owing to variations in the lengths of proestrus and estrus.*

A microscopic examination of vaginal secretions (a test called *vaginal cytology*) helps to pinpoint the beginning of estrus. There are characteristic changes in the appearance of vaginal cells that tell your veterinarian when the bitch is in estrus; and later, when she is in diestrus.

Vaginal cytology, however, is not an accurate method of predicting when ovulation will take place. A more accurate method is to measure serum progesterone levels. The serum progesterone level remains low during early proestrus (less than 2 ng/mL). As ovulation approaches, the serum progesterone begins to rise. The reason progesterone rises is that it is stimulated to do so by the rise in luteinizing hormone (LH), as shown on the accompanying graph. Note that LH peaks rapidly and drops precipitously. The LH surge triggers ovulation, which occurs two days after the peak. As LH peaks, the serum progesterone rises above 2 ng/mL. Thus, when the progesterone measures above 2 ng/mL, one can predict that ovulation will occur within the next 24 to 48 hours.

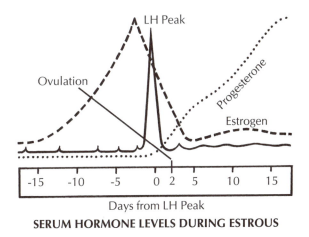

SERUM HORMONE LEVELS DURING ESTROUS

Progesterone levels can be measured by your veterinarian using a rapid in-house assay kit (*ELISA*). The test is not done for routine uncomplicated breedings. A radioimmunoassay test also is available, but blood must be sent to a reference laboratory.

Timing the breeding with ovulation increases the probability of breeding at the most fertile time in the estrous cycle—72 hours after ovulation. This is particularly important in planning artificial insemination and in attempting to impregnate bitches with infertility related to abnormal heat cycles or failure to show heat.

Diestrus

This third stage in the estrous cycle, also called the *luteal phase*, begins when the female refuses to stand for breeding. The male also loses interest at this time. Diestrus can be confirmed by *vaginal cytology*. It lasts about 60 days, and then merges with anestrus. If the bitch becomes pregnant, diestrus last 56 to 58 days and is followed by whelping.

Anestrus

The fourth phase of the estrous cycle is a period of sexual quiescence during which the progesterone-stimulated endometrium undergoes repair. Progesterone levels are low, indicating little if any ovarian activity. The length of anestrus varies, lasting on average 130 to 150 days. Anestrus is followed by the beginning of a new heat cycle.

HORMONAL EFFECTS DURING ESTROUS

Heat begins when the pituitary gland releases follicle stimulating hormone (FSH), which causes the ovaries to develop egg follicles and begin to produce estrogen. Estrogen causes the vulva to swell and the lining of the uterus to shed blood. This is responsible for the bloody discharge of proestrus.

During proestrus there is a steady increase in estrogen concentration, which peaks one to two days before the beginning of estrus and then drops precipitously (see the graph above). LH follows a similar course, but peaks a day or two after estrogen and then drops precipitously. The surge and drop in LH signals the onset of estrus and triggers ovulation two days later. Fertile matings can occur three days before the LH peak through six to seven days after the peak.

LH also ensures that the ovulatory follicles convert to corpora luteal cysts and begin to produce progesterone. The serum progesterone level parallels the rise in LH. It begins to rise during the last two days of proestrus, rises above 2 ng/mL as the LH peaks, continues to rise during estrus, remains elevated for 8 to 10 weeks during diestrus, and returns to baseline levels during anestrus. Progesterone is essential for keeping the uterine lining receptive to the implantation and growth of embryos. Removal of the ovaries during early pregnancy, or failure of the corpora luteal cysts to produce progesterone, results in spontaneous abortion.

The hormonal effects of the estrous cycle have implications for preventing pregnancy (see *Contraceptive Drugs*, page 406). If progesterone (Ovaban) is given during the first three days of proestrus, it blocks the release of pituitary FSH and aborts the heat cycle. Testosterone works by blocking the release of LH from the pituitary gland. It must be given 30 days before estrous to abort the heat cycle.

WHEN TO BREED

The most common cause of an unsuccessful mating is bad timing. Many dog owners do nothing more than count the days in a cycle. They attempt to breed on the 10th through the 14th day of the heat cycle. But, as noted earlier, each female is an individual with her own breeding timetable—a timetable that can vary according to the lengths of proestrus and estrus. Ovulation cannot always be predicted just by counting the days of the heat cycle. Furthermore, counting will not be accurate if you miss the early signs of heat, or if your bitch shows very little evidence of being in heat.

Fortunately, nature provides a safety factor: Sperm are able to survive for up to seven days in the female oviducts. An offsetting factor is that eggs must mature in the oviducts for three days before they can be fertilized. This still leaves a window of opportunity of several days before and after ovulation for successful breeding. In fact, the peak of female fertility occurs three days after ovulation.

There are reports of bitches being bred as early as the fourth day and as late as the 21st day of the heat cycle—and still conceiving a litter. When the heat cycle is this atypical, a combination of *vaginal cytology* and progesterone measurements can be used to determine estrus and predict the time of ovulation (see *The Estrous Cycle*, above).

Multiple breedings are more likely than a single breeding to produce pregnancy, and may even have an influence on the size of the litter. Accordingly, most veterinarians recommend breeding a bitch every other day (or every third day) for as long as she remains in standing heat. If, for any reason, a bitch cannot be bred more than once, consider timing that breeding using progesterone assays to predict the exact time of ovulation.

THE TIE

Male dogs differ from humans in that they do not have seminal vesicles in which to store sperm. Sperm flows directly into the urethra from the spermatic ducts and does not mix with prostatic fluid first. The first part of the male's ejaculate is clear. The second part is cloudy and contains the sperm. The third part is prostate fluid that washes out the urethra and neutralizes the acidity of the vagina.

After the penis enters the vagina, a bulb of erectile tissue at the base of the penis, called the *bulbus glandis*, enlarges and is held inside the vagina by powerful vulvar constrictor muscles. This tight union between the two animals is called the tie. For dogs to mate, the bulbus glandis must become enlarged *after* intromission.

The exact function of the tie is unknown. Its purpose may be to hold the penis in place while sperm flows up from the testicles. To be effective, a tie must last for at least two to three minutes. Many ties last 30 to 40 minutes. Contrary to popular belief, the length of the tie has no effect on the likelihood of pregnancy or the number of puppies conceived.

If the knot at the base of the penis swells up *before* intromission (an external tie), the penis cannot fully penetrate and will be withdrawn. Some inexperienced males have premature swelling of the bulbus glandis. These dogs should be lead away from the female until the bulb returns to its normal size.

Mating Procedures

Breeding dogs can be surprisingly stressful, particularly when there is a great deal of emotion invested in the outcome. If you do not feel confident in handling the mating, ask your veterinarian or an experienced breeder to be present to lend support and assist if necessary.

GETTING READY

When a bitch is due in season, she should be watched carefully for signs of proestrus. As soon as she shows color, notify the owner of the stud. He or she may want the bitch at once. This gives her time to settle into her new surroundings after a nerve-wracking trip. In addition, the stud's owner can follow her progress by exposing her to the male to see if she will stand for breeding.

If the female has a heavy or matted coat, trim the hair away to expose the vulva. On long-coated male dogs, it is a good idea to clip the hair around the penis before mating. Long hair near the head of the penis may catch on the penis during erection. As the penis returns to the sheath, the prepuce may be rolled under, causing a constriction (see *Paraphimosis*, page 414).

NORMAL MATING

Neither animal should be fed for several hours before mating. Avoid the heat of the day. In hot weather, bring both dogs into the house or kennel where it is relatively cool. Normally, the bitch should be taken to the stud's enclosure, as the male is more confident and assertive in his own surroundings. If the bitch is shy and retiring and the male is strong and assertive, it may be better to take the male to the enclosure of the bitch.

Keep the number of observers to a minimum. The fewer distractions the better. Both dogs should be introduced to each other on leads. Once it is certain that the bitch's behavior is friendly, the dogs can be let off leash for a short period to romp and flirt. If the stud is not interested, and particularly if the female rejects the male, she is not in standing heat. Separate the dogs and try again in 48 hours. *Do not persist when it is apparent that the bitch is not receptive.* This can confuse or frighten the female and frustrate the male, making future attempts more difficult.

If the bitch is ready to mate, she will hold her tail to the side and stand quietly. As the male mounts and penetrates, he clasps her around the loins with his forelegs and thrusts forward. At full penetration he treads up and down instead of thrusting forward. The bulbus glandis swells and is clasped by the vulva. This produces the tie and stimulates the male to ejaculate.

After ejaculation the male unclasps his forelegs and places both feet on the ground on one side of the bitch. He may lift his hind leg over the back of the bitch and swing around so that the two stand rump to rump. The dogs usually remain joined for 10 to 30 minutes.

Bitches may cry, whine or grunt during a tie. It is a good idea to have someone posted at the head of the bitch to calm her so she doesn't become frightened and try to pull free. As the dog and bitch separate, it can be momentarily painful. Be prepared for either to turn and snap.

HELPING THE MATING ALONG

Maiden bitches, nervous bitches and bitches that do not show strong signs of estrus can be difficult to breed. With these individuals it is often necessary to hold or restrain the bitch.

The procedure for assisting large dogs requires two or three people. One person sits on a stool at the bitch's side and supports her with a knee beneath the belly. This handler also draws the tail around the outside of the hind leg, exposing the vulva. A second person holds the leash of the male. If the dog mounts at the side or front, this handler gently pulls him off and encourages him to mount from the rear. An optional third person steadies the bitch from in front.

A cooperative female raises her vulva so that the male can make a straight entry into the vagina. The individual holding the bitch can make this easier for the male by raising the vulva with a hand between the bitch's legs.

Young and inexperienced males may become so excited that they ejaculate before intromission. This is more likely to happen if attempts are made to guide the male by taking hold of his penis behind the bulb.

A mating between a tall dog and a short bitch can present mechanical problems. The solution is to stand the male in a ditch or breed on a slope to equalize the difference.

Small dogs can be mated on a table with a piece of carpet on it for good footing. Support the female with a hand beneath her pelvis.

A PROLONGED TIE

A prolonged tie is one that lasts for an hour or longer. The problem is caused by a spasm of the constricting vulvar ring. The ring maintains the dog's erection by preventing the blood from leaving the bulbus glandis and returning to the body. Eventually the animals become frustrated and begin to tug against each other, aggravating the problem.

Do not throw water on the dogs or try to pull them apart. Instead, turn the male so that he mounts the female and then push on his rump to increase the depth of penetration. This relieves the constricting effect of the vulvar ring on the penis and allows the bulb to subside.

SHY BREEDERS AND DOGS THAT WON'T MATE

The most common reason why dogs refuse to mate is that it is the wrong time in the estrous cycle. If mating is attempted too early in the cycle, the bitch may growl and snap at the dog, or she may allow the male to mount, only to sit down or jump away as he starts to thrust. This is normal proestrus behavior, but some breeders may misinterpret it as a sign that mating won't take place.

A simple test to check for estrus is to stroke the female's vulva when she is relaxed. A bitch in estrus raises her vulva and flags her tail to the side. These signs indicate that she is hormonally ready for breeding. If it is the right time and she continues to refuse the male, then quite likely the problem is psychological. Psychological factors are much more common than hormonal or physical ones.

A female raised as a house pet may be a shy breeder because of inadequate social contact with members of her own species. Mate preference, too, can be a determining factor. A bitch that runs with a certain dog may mate willingly with that dog but refuse another. Some females are willing to mate only with very aggressive males.

In males, sexual aggressiveness may be influenced by unpleasant associations with sex. Some owners scold or punish a dog for showing sexual behavior toward dogs or people. Thus the dog comes to believe he will be punished if he attempts mating. A stud may fear mating because of a traumatic experience with an aggressive bitch.

Inadequate canine socialization can be a problem in males as well as females. This is especially true for dogs that live almost exclusively with people and have little or no opportunity to form social relations with others of their own kind. Finally, and least likely, a dog with a low libido may be suffering from a testosterone deficiency (see *Impotence*, page 399).

Treatment: Reluctance to mate is a problem that should be referred to your veterinarian for further evaluation. If an outgoing bitch consistently refuses to receive a stud, it is a good idea to have her examined for an abnormal heat cycle or a reproductive tract abnormality.

In the case of a frightened or completely uncooperative bitch, breeding by artificial insemination is preferable to a forced mating (see *Artificial Insemination*, below). Because the bitch won't display the usual signs of sexual receptivity, *vaginal cytology* and progesterone determinations should be used to time artificial insemination with ovulation (see *The Estrous Cycle*, page 389). Breeding by artificial insemination will not spoil a dog or bitch for natural breeding in the future.

A male may regain his self-confidence if he is allowed to run with an easygoing bitch that likes to be dominated. An experienced brood matron that is a willing breeder can help a bashful dog overcome his sexual inhibitions. Once he has bred successfully, usually his problems are over.

Artificial Insemination

Artificial insemination (AI) is a procedure in which semen is collected from the male and introduced into the reproductive tract of the female. The American Kennel Club has regulations concerning the registration of dogs produced by artificial insemination. Before breeding, check with the AKC or your country's kennel club for information on how to properly register the litter.

Procedures for collecting and processing the semen and inseminating the bitch are well standardized, and must be followed exactly or the breeding will not be successful. Accordingly, AI should be performed by veterinarians or those who have acquired expertise under veterinary supervision. When properly performed, conception rates using fresh semen are equal to those attained by natural breeding.

AI using *fresh semen* is best used when natural mating is impossible or has been unsuccessful. Usually this is for psychological reasons, anatomical reasons or problems associated with heat detection.

Cooled transported semen can be used to inseminate a bitch in another state or country who could not otherwise breed to a particular stud. Frozen semen can be stored for weeks, months or years, possibly increasing in value as the importance of a particular stud dog is recognized through his progeny.

The success rate for AI has improved dramatically with the ability to time the insemination with ovulation using progesterone assay kits (see *The Estrous Cycle*, page 389). Predicting ovulation is particularly important when the bitch does not display the typical signs of estrus.

Semen is obtained by stimulating the male and collecting the ejaculate in a rubber conical sheath connected to a receptacle such as a glass tube or syringe. When inseminating with fresh semen, the bitch must be present. The semen is introduced immediately into her vagina using a sterile flexible insemination pipette connected to a syringe. The semen is deposited at the entrance to the cervix.

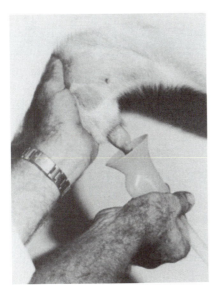

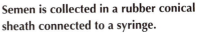
Semen is collected in a rubber conical sheath connected to a syringe.

The best results are obtained by collecting semen and inseminating the bitch every 48 to 72 hours, beginning at the first indication of standing heat and continuing until she refuses to breed. When insemination is timed with ovulation, insemination should be done two to three days after ovulation, as determined by progesterone assays. After AI, the bitch should be confined until she goes out of heat.

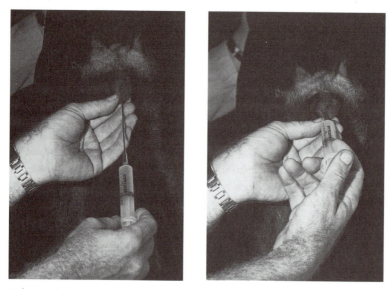

Using an insemination pipette, the semen is deposited into the vagina at the entrance of the cervix.

Cooled semen must be handled and shipped according to strict protocols to maintain the viability of the sperm. Properly prepared cooled semen from a fertile stud can be preserved for two to four days. Cooled semen should be inseminated twice, either on days three and five or days four and six—as measured from day zero, or the first day of estrus (standing heat). Day zero is determined by progesterone assay and the receptive behavior of the bitch.

Conception rates for frozen semen are not as high as they are for fresh or cooled semen. Frozen-thawed sperm are unable to traverse the cervix and must be inseminated directly into the uterine body. This is best accomplished by a needle injection directly into the uterus through the abdominal wall. It can also be done by passing a long stainless steel catheter through the cervix into the uterine body, but this is not as effective.

Advanced reproductive techniques using embryo transfers currently have a low rate of success.

Male Infertility

Male infertility means the inability to sire a litter. It can be congenital or acquired. A stud dog that has never sired a litter despite several matings should be considered congenitally infertile. Congenital causes of infertility include chromosomal abnormalities (*intersex*), underdeveloped testicles (*testicular hypoplasia*), undescended testicles, and abnormalities of the penis and prepuce that prevent mating.

Acquired infertility occurs in a proven stud dog that subsequently becomes infertile. This follows testicular injuries and infections, and may occur as a consequence of *prostatitis* and infections of the male genital tract, such as *brucellosis*. Drug therapy, *testicular degeneration* and *immune-mediated orchitis* are other causes of acquired infertility.

Hormone diseases of the pituitary and thyroid gland can cause both congenital and acquired infertility. Hypothyroidism is the most common hormonal cause of infertility. It affects both the dog's sex drive and his sperm count.

Retrograde ejaculation is an acquired cause of infertility. It is caused by failure of the internal urethral sphincter to contract during ejaculation. As a consequence, the sperm are ejaculated into the dog's bladder.

A significant cause of reduced fertility in males is excessive use. Dogs used at stud for three consecutive days should be rested for two days. Males with high fertility can be used every other day, but should be given periods of sexual rest to prevent overuse and loss of libido.

When a stud dog is used a great deal, a single mating may not be enough to cause pregnancy. Alternatively, a dog that has not been used for some time may have a low sperm count because of reduced production. During a second mating, two days after the first, the quality of the semen may be much improved.

Prolonged elevation of body temperature damages the sperm-producing cells. Some dogs are less fertile in the summer, especially if they live outdoors where the weather is very hot. A dog with a high fever may take several weeks or months to regain a normal sperm count. An age-related decline in sperm production occurs in older dogs.

IMPOTENCE

Impotence is loss of sex drive (libido). Most cases are caused by overuse, and by physiological factors already discussed above in *Shy Breeders and Dogs That Won't Mate* (page 395).

The male sex drive is under the influence of testosterone, produced by the testicles. A dog with a normal libido is easily aroused when presented with a bitch in standing heat. A dog with a poor libido exhibits little interest in sex, despite the overtures of a willing female. Lack of libido and a low sperm count occur together in testicular diseases, hypothyroidism and pituitary gland disorders.

In rare cases, a Sertoli cell tumor of the testicle may be responsible for impotence. These tumors manufacture estrogen, which neutralizes the effects of testosterone. Feminization of the male occurs, with enlargement of the mammary glands, a pendulous foreskin and bilateral symmetric hair loss (see *Tumors of the Testicles* in Chapter 18).

THE STUD DOG'S INFERTILITY EVALUATION

A thorough exam should include a comprehensive review of the past breeding performance, as well as a family history looking for predisposing hereditary causes. Other factors to consider are recent illnesses, medications, vaccinations and diet.

Collecting and evaluating semen is a most important part of the infertility exam. How semen is collected is described earlier in this chapter in *Artificial Insemination* (page 397). The number of sperm per millimeter and the quality of the semen are the two most important considerations. When the sperm count is low (a condition called *oligospermia*), there may be a problem with the epididymis or testicles. The complete absence of sperm (*azospermia*) suggests severe testicular degeneration, a blockage in the spermatic ducts, testicular tumor, testicular hypoplasia or retrograde ejaculation. In retrograde ejaculation, sperm will be found in urine collected from the bladder shortly after ejaculation. The semen and prostatic fluid are cultured to rule out infection.

Baseline laboratory tests screen for chronic diseases. Measuring the sex and thyroid hormones (testosterone, FSH, LH and T4) provides information on possible endocrine causes of infertility. Testicular biopsy gives information on causes of low sperm count, as well as the likelihood the dog will respond to medical treatment.

TREATMENT OF MALE INFERTILITY

Stress, sexual overuse, heat and temporary injury to sperm-producing cells are potentially reversible and often improve with a period of prolonged sexual rest. The treatment of prostatitis, sheath infections, orchitis and undescended testicles is discussed later in this chapter.

A male of marginal fertility should be bred at the peak of female fertility (72 hours after ovulation), as determined by *vaginal cytology* and progesterone measurements (see *The Estrous Cycle*, page 389).

Hormone therapy, and drugs to correct retrograde ejaculation and immune-mediated orchitis, have been of benefit in some cases. Genetic and chromosomal abnormalities associated with *intersex* may be accompanied by abnormal appearing genitalia. The diagnosis is made by *karyotyping* (analyzing the number, size and shape of the paired chromosomes).

Dogs with congenital infertility, and those with acquired infertility who do not produce sperm after six months of treatment, usually do not become fertile.

Female Infertility

The most common cause of reproductive failure is improper breeding management—particularly in detecting the heat cycle, determining when to breed and the number of breedings per cycle. These topics have been discussed earlier in this chapter. Other important factors that influence the outcome are the general health and nutrition of the bitch, the effectiveness of vaccination and parasite control programs, the maintenance of wholesome surroundings and the avoidance of overcrowding.

Diseases of the uterus (*endometritis, cystic endometrial hyperplasia* and *pyometra*), discussed elsewhere in this chapter, are other important causes of female infertility.

THE BITCH'S INFERTILITY EVALUATION

This involves a comprehensive review of the bitch's past breeding performance, as well as a family history of breeding problems. Other factors to consider are recent illnesses and any medications she may be taking. The physical exam is like that described for the prebreeding examination. Additional studies include *ultrasonography*, *vaginal cytology* and hormone assays such as FSH, LH, T4, estrogen and progesterone.

Infertility in bitches is often associated with abnormal heat cycles, but can be caused by other factors as well.

INFERTILITY WITH A NORMAL ESTROUS CYCLE

If the bitch fails to conceive after successful matings, the most probable cause is uterine infection: either *pyometra* or *cystic endometrial hyperplasia*. Other possible causes are *brucellosis* and *canine herpesvirus*. These two sexually transmitted diseases produce infertility by preventing conception, or by causing early pregnancy loss or spontaneous abortion.

Infertility may result from vaginal strictures and neoplasms that prevent intromission or the ability to tie. A blockage in the oviducts can prevent the union of egg and sperm. Tumors and congenital anomalies of the uterus can interfere with conception and embryo implantation. Lethal genes and chromosomes produce defective embryos and malformed fetuses that are reabsorbed or expelled.

ABNORMAL ESTROUS CYCLES

Abnormalities of the heat cycles can include silent heat, split heat, prolonged heat, absent heat and irregular heat. Occasionally a bitch will skip an entire heat period. Young bitches frequently have irregular or silent heat periods. Generally their cycles become regular by two to three years of age.

Silent Heat

Silent heat is a fertile heat cycle that escapes detection because of minimal vulvar swelling and vaginal bleeding. A bitch with silent heat may show no interest in the stud, except during a short period around the time of ovulation. Small breeds that achieve early sexual maturity may have one or two silent heats before exhibiting an obvious cycle. When heat goes undetected, the bitch is often given the mistaken diagnosis of *absent heat*.

Vaginal bleeding may go unnoticed if the female is fastidious and licks herself clean. If you are not familiar with the size of the normal vulva, you may not notice the swelling of proestrus. However, you should be able to recognize the mild vulvar enlargement and slight bloody discharge of proestrus if you carefully inspect the vulva once or twice a week. You can also expose the bitch to a stud dog twice a week and observe the behavior of both animals.

Veterinary examination using *vaginal cytology* and progesterone measurements is an accurate method of determining whether the bitch is cycling.

Split Heat

In this abnormality, the heat appears to be split into two separate cycles. In the first, or false, cycle the bitch attracts the male and develops the vulvar swelling and vaginal bleeding typical of proestrus. Because she does not proceed to estrus, however, she goes out of heat without becoming receptive. A second heat cycle occurs 2 to 10 weeks later. This cycle often proceeds to standing heat.

Split heat typically occurs in young females. It is caused by lack of pituitary output of LH. Because the LH does not rise, the ovaries do not produce ovulatory follicles and serum progesterone remains low (see *Hormonal Effects During Estrous*, page 392). In most cases no treatment is required. The next heat cycle usually is normal.

Prolonged Heat

This occurs when a bitch remains in heat for more than 21 days. During the prolonged heat she continues to display vaginal bleeding and remains attractive to males. Prolonged heat may occur in maiden bitches during the first heat cycle. It normalizes with maturity.

In all other cases, the hormonal basis is a persistent elevation of estrogen, caused by an estrogen-producing *ovarian cyst* or occasionally by a granulosa cell tumor of the ovary (see *Tumors of the Ovaries* in Chapter 18). *Vaginal cytology* and serum estrogen measurements will confirm the diagnosis of prolonged estrus. *Ultrasonography* may show an ovarian cyst or tumor. Ovarian cysts may regress. If they do not, surgery is required. Ovarian tumors must be surgically removed.

Heat can be terminated by giving an androgen preparation such as mibolerone (Cheque Drops) for three to four months. Bitches that respond to androgens usually begin a new heat cycle four to five months later and can often be bred at that time. As an alternative, an attempt can be made to breed the bitch on the same cycle by inducing ovulation with human chorionic gonadotropin (hCG) or gonadotrophin-releasing hormone (Gn-RH). If further breeding is not desired, spaying is the treatment of choice.

Absent Heat

Absent heat is due to a failure to cycle. Bitches younger than two years of age may not cycle because of sexual immaturity. Some large-breed dogs do not attain sexual maturity and experience their first heat until they are two years old. If a bitch does not go into heat by 24 to 30 months of age, have her examined by a veterinarian.

Heat will not occur if a female has been spayed. This becomes a consideration if the medical history is unknown. Inspect the lower abdomen to find a scar that indicates she was spayed. Females that have been treated with androgens or progesterones will not cycle during treatment and for some time thereafter. The same is true for bitches receiving corticosteroids.

Bitches that are malnourished or debilitated from recent illness often do not cycle until they are in a better state of health. *Hypothyroidism* is a common cause of absent heat. Other signs of hypothyroidism may or may not be present. The diagnosis is made by a thyroid blood test. *Cushing's syndrome* is an uncommon cause. Most bitches with Cushing's are over eight years of age and are no longer in their reproductive years.

Ovarian hypoplasia is a disease in which the ovaries do not develop to sexual maturity and are incapable of producing adequate amounts of estrogen. The mammary glands and vulva remain small and underdeveloped. Ovarian hypoplasia may be the result of sex chromosome abnormalities. An immune-mediated inflammation of the ovaries may be responsible for some cases of absent heat. Tumors of the ovary have also been associated with absent heat.

The diagnosis of absent heat is confirmed by weekly *vaginal cytology* and progesterone assays that show no hormonal effects of estrous. An elevated LH is present in bitches with ovarian hypoplasia and those with absent ovaries. *Ultrasonography* may reveal an immature uterus or an ovarian tumor. *Karyotyping* is recommended for bitches who show no evidence of cycling after six months of study. If the chromosomes are normal and the bitch has not cycled by 30 months of age, estrus and ovulation often can be induced by FSH and hCG in a protocol determined by your veterinarian.

Interestrous Interval

This is the interval between one heat cycle and the next. The average interval is five to nine months. Often a bitch's interestrous interval is either longer or shorter than normal, or occurs at irregular intervals. Some bitches come into heat every four months and others every 10 to 12 months. This may be genetically influenced. Basenjis and wolf-dog crosses, for example, come into heat once a year. An abnormal interestrous interval is one in which the interval between two heat cycles is either less than four months or greater than one year.

Prolonged Interestrous Interval

This condition, also referred to as *prolonged anestrus*, occurs in previously cycling bitches that do not come into heat after 16 or more months. A common cause is cessation of ovarian activity due to an *ovarian cyst* that produces progesterone. The administration of progesterone and androgenic drugs produces a similar effect. *Hypothyroidism* and *Cushing's syndrome* also produce prolonged anestrus.

Hypothyroidism can be diagnosed by a thyroid blood test. Cushing's syndrome generally occurs in elderly females and is not a common reproductive problem.

Bitches with normal ovaries that are slow to come into heat will often do so when kenneled with other cycling females and regularly exposed to a male. If this is not successful, and the bitch has a low serum progesterone level and no discernible medical cause for the prolonged anestrus, consider *karyotyping* to rule out *intersex*. If the karyotype is normal, an attempt can be made to induce estrus and ovulation as described above for *Absent Heat*.

Shortened Interestrous Interval

In this condition the interval between one cycle and the next is four months or less. A shortened interestrous interval should be distinguished from split heat, in which the first cycle does not progress beyond proestrus, and thus is incomplete.

The problem with a shortened interval is that the lining of the uterus has not had sufficient time to repair the progesterone-induced damage caused by the previous heat cycle. Thus the endometrium is not hormonally receptive to embryo implantation and the bitch with a shortened interestrous interval cannot become pregnant.

Treatment may not be necessary. Most young females develop normal interestrous intervals as they mature. In a mature bitch with a shortened interestrous cycle, the process of uterine repair can be expedited by using an androgen such as mibolerone (Cheque Drops) to terminate heat before ovulation, thus paving the way for a normal endometrium on the next heat cycle.

Premature Ovarian Failure

Ovarian function begins to decline at about six years of age and ceases, on average, when a bitch is 10 years old. This usually is not a problem, because most bitches are not bred beyond seven to eight years of age. The ovaries of some bitches, however, may cease to function as early as six years of age, resulting in permanent anestrus. This can be confirmed by FSH and LH concentrations; both will be extremely high in premature ovarian failure. There is no treatment for premature aging of the ovaries.

FETAL LOSS DURING PREGNANCY

Early embryonic loss may take place even before the embryos implant in the lining of the uterus because of unfavorable environmental conditions caused by endometritis or cystic endometrial hyperplasia, both discussed below. Other causes of early embryonic loss are chromosomal abnormalities and fatal genetic defects in the pups.

Pregnancy can be diagnosed at three to four weeks gestation by palpating the bitch's abdomen. Using *ultrasonography*, it is possible to diagnose pregnancy as early as 18 days after the first breeding. If a bitch is found to be pregnant and later does not deliver puppies, one of two things must have happened: either her puppies were resorbed or she miscarried (aborted).

Fetal resorption can occur at any time from fertilization through about the 40th day of gestation. The products of conception are absorbed back into the mother's body. Some bitches exhibit malaise, fever, loss of appetite and a thin, bloody or purulent vaginal discharge. In early fetal reabsorption, symptoms usually are absent and the pregnancy and resorption go unnoticed. Thus the problem is often mistaken for failure to conceive.

Abortion is defined as death of the fetus followed by expulsion of the products of conception. Abortion generally occurs during the last three weeks of gestation.

The signs of abortion are vaginal bleeding and the passage of tissue. These signs may not be observed if the bitch is fastidious.

A well recognized cause of third-trimester abortions and stillbirths is *brucellosis*. Another cause of late abortions, stillbirths, a decrease in the number of pups per litter and female infertility is *herpesvirus infection*. Occasionally, a bacterial infection will cause an abortion. Culprit bacteria include *E. coli*, camphylobacter and streptococcus. Drugs that can produce abortion include corticosteroids and chloramphenicol.

Bitches that suffer repeat early pregnancy losses or abort on successive pregnancies should be suspected of having uterine infection or a progesterone deficiency. Progesterone deficiency (called *hypoluteoidism*) is caused by failure of the corpora lutea of the ovaries to secrete adequate progesterone sufficient to support placental attachment. The condition recurs with subsequent pregnancies and becomes a likely consideration when a bitch repeatedly fails to maintain a pregnancy.

Causes of *sporadic abortion* include a serious illness during pregnancy with a high fever (such as *distemper* or *leptospirosis*), violent activities such as jumping from heights, a blow to the abdomen, and improper feeding and prenatal care.

Treatment: A bitch that has passed fetal tissue should be examined by a veterinarian. *Ultrasonography* may be needed to make sure the bitch has not retained fetal or placental tissue. Infectious abortions are treated with antibiotics and supportive measures, as necessary.

It is important to identify and correct the underlying cause whenever possible. Laboratory examination of the fetus and placenta, along with appropriate cultures, will reveal the cause of an abortion in about 50 percent of cases. When such studies are not done, the cause usually is never discovered. For safety, assume that all abortions are infectious. Maintain kennel hygiene and handle all discharges and tissues with disposable rubber gloves.

Bitches that abort should be screened for *brucellosis* and *herpesvirus*—if these tests were not already done in preparation for breeding. The investigation of chronic uterine infection is discussed in *Diseases of the Female Genital Tract*, page 410.

Hypoluteoidism is associated with low plasma progesterone levels in early pregnancy. Although conclusive studies are lacking, treatment with a progesterone supplement may prevent recurrent abortion in some bitches with apparent hypoluteoidism. The progesterone must be carefully monitored because of serious risks associated with its use during pregnancy.

False Pregnancy (Pseudocyesis)

False pregnancy (also called *pseudocyesis*) is a fairly common condition in which a nonpregnant female acts as if she were pregnant. The condition is caused by progesterone, which is manufactured by corpora luteal cysts in the ovaries. Signs appear about six to eight weeks after estrus.

A bitch with pseudopregnancy may exhibit some or all of the physical and behavioral signs of a true pregnancy, including abdominal distension, enlargement of the mammary glands and even lactation. Some females make a nest and become attached to small Toys and other puppy substitutes, occasionally guarding them aggressively. Bitches may vomit off and on and become depressed; a few develop diarrhea. The mammary glands may become caked and can be a source of pain.

Treatment: Most cases do not require treatment. Pseudocyesis disappears spontaneously in 12 weeks or less. Bitches with aggressive behavior or severe symptoms can be treated with hormones such as Ovaban, Cheque Drops or prolactin inhibitors. These drugs have significant side effects and are therefore not routinely used. For the treatment of caked mammary glands, see *Mastitis* in Chapter 16.

A female with pseudocyesis is likely to have other false pregnancies. If breeding is not intended, she should be spayed. This should be done after the pseudocyesis resolves.

Unwanted Pregnancy

Accidental pregnancy is common in dogs. Male dogs are remarkably adept at getting to females in heat. The usual measures, such as confining a female in a run or pen, are not always sufficient to protect her from a determined male.

To be absolutely safe, keep your bitch indoors when in she's in heat; take her out on a leash only. *Do not let her out of your sight for one minute.* She should be confined throughout the entire estrous cycle, which begins with the first show of color and continues for at least three weeks.

Chlorophyll tablets, which you can purchase from your veterinarian or at pet supply stores, may help to mask the odor of a female in heat, but are not effective in preventing mating.

If you witness a tie or suspect for any reason that your bitch may have been bred, take her at once to your veterinarian. The stage of the heat cycle can be determined by *vaginal cytology* and a serum progesterone assay. The bitch may not have been in her fertile period, in which case pregnancy is unlikely.

Sperm in the vagina can often be identified during the first 24 hours after mating, but absence of sperm does not rule out breeding or pregnancy.

If it appears that the bitch has indeed been bred and is likely to become pregnant, there are two alternatives: One is to wait and see if she becomes pregnant, then allow her to go through with her pregnancy; the other is to treat for termination, either before or after the pregnancy is confirmed.

The first alternative, allowing the bitch to carry her litter, is the safest and best if she is valuable and you are planning to breed her in the future. However, if she is not of breeding quality and you do not have the time and facilities to raise a litter of puppies and find suitable homes for them all, your best choice is to have her spayed. This can be done during the early stages of pregnancy without added risk. During the second half of pregnancy, hysterectomy becomes more difficult.

Note that there is no uniformly safe and effective medical alternative for preventing or terminating pregnancy in dogs. Preventing pregnancy using estradiol cyprinate (ECP), the *mismate shot*, is no longer recommended because of the high risks of estrogen-induced bone marrow suppression and pyometra. In addition, the shot is not reliable, even when given during the required three to five days after breeding.

Terminating pregnancy with prostaglandin $PGF_{2\alpha}$ (Lutalyse), although associated with significant complications including rupture of the uterus and gastrointestinal and respiratory distress, may be the best medical alternative currently available for inducing abortion. There are early and late treatment protocols. The late protocol, with which there has been the most experience, uses ultrasonography or abdominal palpation to diagnose pregnancy at 30 to 35 days after breeding. If the bitch is found to be pregnant, she is hospitalized and given Lutalyse injections daily for four to seven days.

Lutalyse causes the corpora lutea in the ovaries to disappear. The corpora lutea manufacture the progesterone that maintains the pregnancy. Although treatment is successful in the majority of cases, it is important to verify that pregnancy has indeed been terminated by obtaining a follow-up ultrasound and serum progesterone level.

Early pregnancy termination using Lutalyse uses a similar protocol, but the hormone is given 10 days after breeding, before pregnancy is actually confirmed. The advantage of early treatment is that no dead puppies are aborted. The disadvantage is that some nonpregnant bitches may be subjected to unnecessary treatment.

Several other drugs are available for inducing abortion in bitches. The drug RU-486 is under investigation and may prove to be an effective and relatively safe drug for inducing abortion in the first half of pregnancy. Currently, it is not available in the United States for use in dogs. Dexamethasone (a cortisone preparation) terminates pregnancy in mid-gestation, but specific protocols have not yet been established.

The inconvenience of a pregnancy must be weighed against the potential risks and complications associated with terminating the pregnancy. Discuss all these options fully with your veterinarian before making a decision.

Birth Control

SPAYING (OVARIOHYSTERECTOMY)

The best way to prevent conception in a female dog is to spay her. In this operation, called an ovariohysterectomy, the entire uterus including the body, horns and uterine tubes, is removed along with the ovaries. The operation is done through the abdomen. Spaying prevents the bitch from coming into season and eliminates the problems of cystic ovaries, false pregnancies, pyometra, irregular heat cycles and the need to keep her confined during estrus.

Spaying before the first heat greatly reduces the frequency of mammary (breast) tumors. Finally, with a spayed female there is no inconvenient heat to go through twice a year.

A bitch does not need to have a litter of puppies to be psychologically fulfilled. Dogs are people-oriented. They seek human companionship and look to their owners for happiness and personal fulfillment. Spaying will not change a female's basic personality, except perhaps to make her less irritable at certain times of the year. Nor will it affect her basic breed instincts, such as hunting, pointing, retrieving, herding, coursing or protecting livestock and property.

Spaying does not make a bitch fat and lazy. Obesity is caused by overfeeding and lack of exercise. By coincidence, a bitch is often spayed as she enters adulthood, at which time her caloric requirements diminish. If she continues to eat a high-calorie puppy food and puts on weight, the tendency is to blame the operation.

Traditionally, bitches have been spayed at about six months of age, before they go into heat for the first time. The American Veterinary Medical Association, the Humane Society of the United States and other organizations agree that it is safe to spay or neuter most puppies as early as eight weeks of age. Research has shown that there are no adverse effects on growth and development with early spaying. The operation is not difficult to perform at this time, provided good anesthetic equipment and expertise are available. The risk of complications is small. Early spaying before the puppies are placed in their permanent homes ensures that individuals with genetic or conformation defects will not be used for breeding. Early spaying is often practiced at animal shelters to insure that the dog will indeed be spayed.

When you've made arrangements to have your female spayed, be sure to withhold all food and water the evening before the surgery. A full stomach may result in vomiting and aspiration while the dog is under general anesthesia. Check with your veterinarian concerning other instructions or precautions to be taken before and after the surgery.

CONTRACEPTIVE DRUGS

Megestrol acetate (Ovaban) and mibolerone (Cheque Drops) currently are the only contraceptive drugs approved for use in dogs in the United States.

Ovaban is a long-acting progesterone. It inhibits the estrous cycle by suppressing the pituitary output of FSH (see *Hormonal Effects During Estrous*, page 392). The drug is safe and effective when used according to the manufacturer's recommendations. Veterinary examination is advised to rule out diabetes, pyometra, pregnancy and mammary gland tumors before starting the drug. If any of these are present, Ovaban should not be used. The first heat cycle in puppy bitches frequently is unreliable. To ensure proper drug performance, do not use Ovaban until the second heat.

To bring a bitch out of heat, start the pill at the first signs of proestrus. *It must be started within the first three days of the heat cycle* in order to prevent estrus and possible pregnancy. Ovaban is given for eight days. The next heat cycle will occur in two to nine months.

It is essential to adhere to a strict schedule with any contraceptive drug. Always confine your bitch during the first eight days of heat, since you might have missed the first signs of proestrus and started the drug too late. If an unplanned mating does take place and the bitch has not been on Ovaban for three full days, stop the pill and consult your veterinarian (see *Unwanted Pregnancy*, above). If mating occurs after the bitch has been on the pill for more than three days, complete the course. She will not become pregnant.

To postpone heat for a hunting trip, pleasure trip or dog show, start the pill at least one week before leaving and continue it for 32 days. Ovaban must be started at least one week before proestrus.

Bitches taking Ovaban may become hungry or lazy, gain weight, experience personality changes or show mammary gland enlargement. These changes disappear when the drug is stopped. Because of the risk of *pyometra* associated with the prolonged use of progesterone, Ovaban should not be used to postpone heat or to take a bitch out of heat for more than two consecutive heat cycles.

Cheque Drops are a liquid birth control preparation containing testosterone. The drug works by blocking the release of LH from the pituitary gland. Cheque Drops must be started at least 30 days before proestrus to reliably abort the heat cycle (see *Hormonal Effects During Estrous*, page 392). They definitely will not prevent heat if started after proestrus. After stopping the drug, the next heat cycle will occur in 70 days (on average), but this varies widely (the range is seven to 200 days).

Cheque Drops are given *daily*, either by mouth or mixed directly with the food. Your veterinarian will recommend an appropriate dose. Masculinization, vaginal discharge, excessive tearing and a musty body odor occasionally accompany its use. In most cases, these side effects disappear when the drug is stopped. Cheque Drops also have the potential to damage the liver (see *Causes of Liver Disease* in Chapter 9), but this is rare.

Discontinue Cheque Drops after 24 months of continuous use.

NEUTERING (CASTRATION)

Neutering is an operation in which both testicles are removed from a male dog. It can be performed at any age. The operation is not difficult and the dog can usually go home the same day. Instructions before surgery are the same as those for *spaying*.

Neutering has a number of health benefits. It eliminates the risk of testicular tumors and greatly reduces the risk of prostate enlargement and perianal adenomas. Neutered males are less territorial, more congenial with other dogs and less likely to roam. Neutering does not, however, affect the dog's basic instincts, including his willingness to guard and protect his family.

When a dog is neutered before puberty, his sexual urges do not develop. If he is neutered after sexual maturity, his interest in estrus females may persist, although this is uncommon.

Neutering may be advised to eliminate unmanageable behavior such as some forms of aggression. Unfortunately, many behavior problems arise from causes other than male hormones. Thus, neutering may not improve the dog's basic behavior.

Traditionally, it has been held that dogs should not be neutered until after attaining most of their adult stature at about six to nine months of age. It is now known that early neutering and spaying does not adversely affect growth and development. The American Veterinary Medical Association, the Humane Society of the United States and many veterinarians agree that neutering as early as 8 to 12 weeks is safe and may be preferable, particularly when there are genetic or conformation reasons why the individual should not be used at stud. Note that if neutering is done before the puppies are placed in their permanent homes, there will be no concern about future breeding misuse. Early neutering is often practiced at animal shelters to insure that the dog will indeed be neutered.

Diseases of the Female Genital Tract

VAGINITIS (VAGINAL INFECTION)

Vaginitis is an inflammation of the vagina. It is not necessarily accompanied by an infection. *Adult vaginitis* usually is caused by an anatomic abnormality of the vagina that results in urine pooling in the vaginal canal. A viral vaginitis caused by the herpesvirus is transmitted during breeding. A mycoplasma vaginitis may result from an overgrowth of mycoplasma organisms, which are normally present in the vagina in small numbers.

Signs of vaginitis are licking at the vulva and staining of the hair about the vulva. A vaginal discharge may not be visible if the bitch keeps herself clean. Vaginal examination is painful and may require sedation.

Male dogs are sometimes attracted to bitches with vaginitis. This can give the impression that the bitch is in heat. Vaginitis can ascend into the uterus or bladder, causing endometritis or, more commonly, a urinary tract infection.

The diagnosis is confirmed by speculum examination of the interior of the vagina. Cultures and *cytology* are obtained. A urinalysis is taken to rule out an associated urinary tract infection.

Juvenile vaginitis is seen in puppies less than a year of age. It is often asymptomatic. In some cases there is a light purulent vaginal discharge.

Treatment: Bacterial vaginitis is easier to clear up if an underlying cause can be identified and removed. In the absence of an underlying cause, treatment involves oral antibiotics selected on the basis of culture and sensitivity tests, along with an initial Betadine or chlorhexidine lavage to remove the accumulated discharge.

Bitches with bacterial vaginitis should not be bred until the infection has been eliminated. There is no effective treatment for herpesvirus vaginitis.

Juvenile vaginitis does not require treatment other than to keep the vulva clean to prevent skin inflammation caused by excessive licking. Most cases disappear when the female enters her first heat cycle. Spaying, if planned, should be postponed until after that time.

VAGINAL HYPERPLASIA AND PROLAPSE

Vaginal hyperplasia is an exaggerated swelling of the vaginal lining that occurs during proestrus and estrus in response to the influence of estrogen. When the swollen vaginal mucosa can no longer be contained within the vagina, it bulges out through the vaginal lips. The principal sign is the protrusion of a tongue-shaped mass through the vulva. Other signs include painful urination and excessive licking at the vulva. The protruding mass prevents mating. Vaginal hyperplasia occurs most often in young bitches of the larger breeds, particularly Boxers and Saint Bernards.

Severe hyperplasia may progress to prolapse. In vaginal prolapse, the apex of the vagina drops out through the vulva, resembling a donut-shaped mass. This can be mistaken for a *vaginal tumor* (see Chapter 18).

Vaginal prolapse can also be caused by prolonged straining, such as that associated with *anorectal obstructions* and difficult labor and delivery. Another unrelated cause of vaginal prolapse is forcefully separating dogs during the tie (see A *Prolonged Tie*, page 395).

Treatment: Vaginal hyperplasia subsides during diestrus but tends to recur with each new heat cycle. For mild hyperplasia, no treatment is necessary other than to keep the vaginal membranes clean and well lubricated with antibiotic ointment to prevent drying.

If breeding is desired, artificial insemination is the method of choice. If breeding is not intended, the bitch should be spayed. This cures the problem.

For severe hyperplasia or vaginal prolapse it may be possible to push the everted tissue back into the vagina and hold it in place with sutures until it regresses during diestrus. Surgical excision may be required to remove devitalized tissue and to prevent hyperplasia in future cycles.

PYOMETRA AND CYSTIC ENDOMETRIAL HYPERPLASIA

Pyometra is a life-threatening infection of the uterus that occurs most often in intact females over six years of age. The disease begins with a condition called cystic endometrial hyperplasia.

In cystic endometrial hyperplasia, the inner glandular layer of the uterus becomes thickened, fills with fluid and forms spaces like those in Swiss cheese. These endometrial changes are caused by the sustained effect of high levels of progesterone that occur during the 8 to 10 weeks of diestrus (see *Hormonal Effects During*

Estrous, page 392). Cystic endometrial hyperplasia provides ideal conditions for bacterial growth. The bacteria gain access to the uterus when the cervix is relaxed during estrus. The subsequent infection leads to pyometra.

Although estrogen does not cause cystic endometrial hyperplasia, it does increase the effects of progesterone. Estrogen given in the form of a *mismate shot* to prevent unwanted pregnancy has been associated with a greatly increased risk of pyometra and is no longer recommended for that purpose.

Signs of pyometra appear one to two months after the heat period. A bitch with pyometra appears depressed and lethargic, may refuse to eat, drinks a great deal of water and urinates frequently. Vomiting and diarrhea also can occur. Her temperature may be normal or even below normal. *Suspect pyometra in any intact bitch that appears ill without obvious cause.*

There are two types of pyometra: open and closed. In *open-cervix pyometra*, the cervix relaxes and releases a large amount of pus that often resembles tomato soup. These bitches usually do not appear as ill as those with closed-cervix pyometra.

In *closed-cervix pyometra*, the undrained uterus enlarges, often producing a painful swelling in the lower abdomen. This type of pyometra is more likely to be accompanied by vomiting and diarrhea, and may produce signs of toxicity such as high fever, rapid pulse and shock. The diagnosis of closed-cervix pyometra is made by an X-ray of the abdomen showing an enlarged uterus. *Ultrasonography* distinguishes pyometra from the enlarged uterus of pregnancy.

Treatment: Pyometra requires immediate veterinary attention to prevent shock and death. Hysterectomy, along with antibiotics, is the treatment of choice. It is best to do this operation before the bitch becomes septic.

When it is important to preserve the reproductive potential of a valuable bitch, an alternative to hysterectomy can be considered—providing that the cervix is open and the bitch is not septic. It involves the use of antibiotics along with prostaglandin. Prostaglandin $PGF_{2\alpha}$ (Lutalyse) relaxes the cervix, stimulates uterine contractions and evacuates the pus. Lutalyse is administered by subcutaneous injection daily for three to five days. If evacuation is not complete, a second course is given. Antibiotics are selected on the basis of sensitivity tests and are continued for one to three weeks after evacuation of the uterus. Lutalyse is not licensed by the FDA for use in small animals, but is nevertheless widely used for this purpose.

Prostaglandin treatment is accompanied by a number of dose-related side effects, including shock. Uterine rupture may occur when the cervix is closed. Many veterinarians regard closed-cervix pyometra as a contraindication to the use of Lutalyse.

Bitches that recover from pyometra are at increased risk for developing it again on subsequent heat cycles. They should be bred on the first estrus after recovery to maximize their chances for fertility.

ENDOMETRITIS

Endometritis is a low-grade bacterial infection of the uterus that occurs as a sequel to a postpartum infection of the uterus (see *Acute Metritis* in Chapter 16), and occasionally as a result of a *vaginitis* that ascends to the uterus. Endometritis is a significant cause of female infertility. Unlike pyometra, the infection is limited to the lining of the uterus. Little pus is produced, but the endometrium becomes inflamed and harbors bacteria. This creates an unfavorable environment for fertilization and the implantation of embryos.

A bitch with endometritis appears in good health, has a normal heat period and mates successfully, yet fails to become pregnant or is found to be pregnant but does not deliver puppies. The diagnosis should be considered whenever a bitch is bred at the right time but fails to conceive on two or more heat cycles.

Endometritis is difficult to diagnose. Abdominal palpation or ultrasonography during diestrus or anestrus may reveal a uterus somewhat larger or thicker than normal. Uterine biopsy confirms the diagnosis, but requires abdominal surgery.

Treatment: There is no effective treatment for endometritis. Hysterectomy is recommended for bitches not intended for breeding. This eliminates the risk of pyometra.

If future breeding is desired, consider using oral antibiotics and/or topical antibiotics infused into the uterus. Antibiotics are selected on the basis of cultures taken from the cervix. There may be benefit in starting an antibiotic seven days before breeding and continuing it until the bitch develops the behavioral signs of heat.

Diseases of the Male Genital Tract

There are several diseases of the male genital tract that can lead to mating problems and, in some cases, infertility. Among them are orchitis, balanoposthitis, phimosis, paraphimosis, undescended testicles, testicular degeneration, testicular tumors and prostatitis. *Prostatitis* is discussed in Chapter 14 and *testicular tumors* are discussed in Chapter 18.

INFECTION OF THE PREPUCE AND HEAD OF THE PENIS (BALANOPOSTHITIS)

The prepuce (foreskin) is a sheath of skin that folds over the head of the penis (see the figure *Anatomy of the Male Genitourinary System* on page 369). A small amount of yellow-green discharge from the opening of the prepuce is normal. A copious discharge indicates infection (called balanoposthitis).

Awns or pieces of straw can get caught beneath the foreskin and cause irritation, followed by infection and abscess within the sheath. *Herpesvirus* produces a chronic sheath infection that can be transmitted to the female during breeding. A strictured foreskin may cause a sheath infection.

Signs of sheath infection are excessive licking at the penis and a foul-smelling discharge from the prepuce.

Treatment: A purulent discharge from the prepuce should be investigated and treated by a veterinarian. Antibiotics are selected on the basis of culture and sensitivity tests. *Herpesvirus* is difficult to culture, but serology testing is available. A rising antibody level suggests the diagnosis.

STRICTURED FORESKIN (PHIMOSIS)

In this condition the opening of the sheath is extremely small, preventing the penis from extending and in some cases interfering with the flow of urine. Neonatal phimosis is a birth defect that occurs most often in German Shepherd Dogs and Golden Retrievers. Several pups in the litter may be affected. Adult phimosis can be caused by a sheath infection or a congenital defect.

Some cases of phimosis resolve with treatment of the associated sheath infection. Most will require surgery to enlarge the opening. Neonatal phimosis causing urinary tract obstruction requires immediate relief.

PENIS TRAPPED OUTSIDE THE SHEATH (PARAPHIMOSIS)

In this condition the extended penis is unable to return to its former position inside the sheath. It is caused by long hair on the skin around the sheath that causes the foreskin to roll under so that the sheath cannot slide. This usually happens after the penis has been extended during mating. The sheath then serves as a constricting ring around the shaft of the penis, causing sustained engorgement. A rubber band maliciously placed around the shaft of the penis produces a similar result.

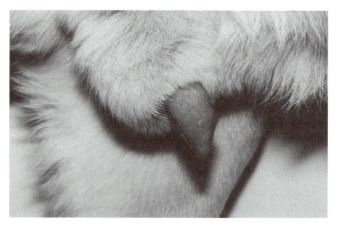

A dog with paraphimosis. Always check the male after mating to be sure the penis has returned to its sheath.

Treatment: The penis must be returned to its normal position inside the prepuce as quickly as possible to prevent further swelling and permanent damage. First lubricate the shaft with K-Y Jelly, mineral oil or olive oil. Push the prepuce back on the shaft of the penis while rolling it out to release the trapped hair. With one hand, gently draw the head of the penis toward you. With the other, slide the prepuce forward over the head of the penis. If these measures are not successful, proceed at once to the veterinary clinic. Surgery may be required to relieve the constriction.

Paraphimosis can be prevented by cutting the long hair around the foreskin before breeding. Always check the male after mating to be sure the penis has returned to its sheath.

UNDESCENDED TESTICLES

A dog with one or both testicles missing from the scrotum is said to be *cryptorchid*. If one testicle is missing and the other is present, the dog is *monorchid*. Cryptorchidism is inherited as an autosomal recessive trait. Mature dogs with two undescended testicles are sterile. A monorchid dog may be fertile, but should not be used for breeding.

The testicles usually descend into the scrotum by six to eight weeks of age, but may not descend until six months of age. Occasionally a testicle can be felt in the scrotum at one time but not at another. The testicles can retract up into the inguinal canal when a puppy is cold, excited or actively playing. These puppies are not cryptorchid.

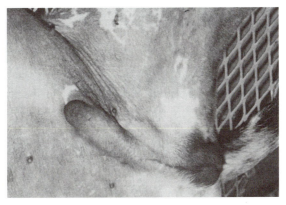

The smaller scrotum on the right is indicative of an undescended testicle.

Treatment: Hormone injections have been used to stimulate testicular descent in puppies, but the rationale is questionable. In some cases descent would have occurred spontaneously. Furthermore, cryptorchid dogs are not candidates for breeding because the condition is heritable.

Removing both testicles is the treatment of choice because of the risk of developing testicular neoplasms, which may be as high as 50 percent in undescended testicles (see *Tumors of the Testicles* in Chapter 18). During surgery, it is important to find and remove the cryptorchid testicles. This may involve making an abdominal incision.

TESTICULAR HYPOPLASIA AND DEGENERATION

The normal testicle is smooth, oval and has a regular outline. Both testicles should be of similar size and feel rather firm. The size of the testicle is related to its sperm-producing capacity. Accordingly, small testicles in a sexually mature dog produce a smaller number of sperm.

Testicular hypoplasia is a developmental disorder in which one or both testicles fail to reach normal size at sexual maturity. The small size and flabby consistency of these testicles is caused by poor development of sperm-producing tissue. An ejaculate will show either no sperm or a low number of sperm with numerous abnormal forms. There is no effective treatment.

Testicular degeneration is an acquired disease that can result in either permanent or temporary sterility. Unlike testicular hypoplasia, the testicles were normal before they became small. A common cause of reversible testicular degeneration is high fever. Effective sperm production requires that the scrotal temperature be at least two to three degrees below the core body temperature. Fever raises both body and scrotal temperatures. Diseases associated with fever that can cause temporary testicular degeneration are canine distemper, parvovirus and leptospirosis.

An *immune-mediated orchitis* occurs following testicular biopsy and trauma in which sperm escape and enter the bloodstream. The escaped sperm cause the body to produce antisperm antibodies. The antibodies destroy the sperm in the dog's own testicles.

In all these conditions the testicles become small and flabby like those of testicular hypoplasia.

Irreversible sterility follows diseases that destroy the testicles. These diseases are testicular trauma and acute bilateral orchitis. In these testicles, the sperm-producing tissue is replaced by fibrous connective tissue. The testicles become small and hard.

Treatment: The diagnosis of testicular disease can be confirmed by biopsy. Testicular degeneration is treated by correcting the underlying disease and allowing time for spontaneous recovery. Sexual rest is essential. Semen examinations are used to monitor the return of spermatogenesis. It takes 50 to 60 days for regenerating sperm to reach the ejaculate, so any improvement in sperm quality will not be seen for at least two months

INFECTION OF THE TESTICLES (ORCHITIS)

Infections and injuries of the testicle are common causes of male infertility. Scrotal and testicular injuries can be caused by dog bites; puncture wounds; frostbite; and weed, chemical and thermal burns. Infections are caused by bacteria that infect scrotal injuries or are spread through the spermatic ducts from the bladder or prostate. *Distemper* or *brucellosis* may be the causative agent.

Signs of orchitis are pain and swelling of the testicle and licking at the scrotum. The testicle becomes enlarged and hard. The dog assumes a spread-legged stance and walks with a stilted gait. Frequently, the epididymis is also involved.

Treatment: Testicular infection is treated with antibiotics selected on the basis of culture and sensitivity tests. Corticosteroids, NSAIDs and cold packs to the scrotum reduce swelling and inflammation. Following resolution, the testicle may shrink and become small and firm. These testicles no longer produce sperm. A persistent low-grade infection may occur in some cases. Removal of the testicle is then recommended.

Dog bites and injuries to the scrotum are quite likely to become infected. To prevent orchitis, all scrotal injuries (even ones that appear minor) should be examined and treated by a veterinarian.

PREGNANCY AND WHELPING

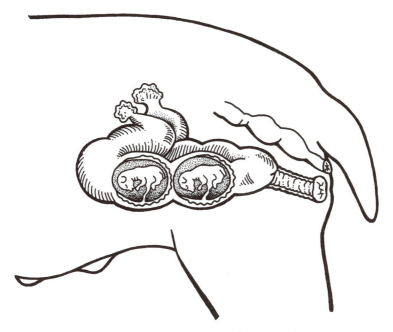

Puppies growing in the uterine horns at 35 days' gestation.

Pregnancy

GESTATION

Gestation is the period from conception to birth. It averages 63 days *from the day of ovulation* (the normal range is 56 to 66 days). Note that the day of ovulation is not always the same as the day of breeding.

Many people use the day of first breeding as the basis for determining when the bitch will whelp. However, a bitch may not ovulate until after her second or third breeding, so a more accurate determination of the whelping date can be obtained by using serum progesterone assays during estrus to determine ovulation. Ovulation coincides with the LH surge (see *The Estrous Cycle* in Chapter 15). The expected date of whelping is 62 to 64 days after the LH surge.

Whelping usually occurs earlier in bitches with large litters and later in those with small litters and single pups. Puppies born on the 56th day after ovulation are likely to be of low birth weight and physiologically immature. If they are born on the 55th day or before, they are premature and probably will not survive. Any gestation beyond 65 days from the day of first breeding *may be* postmature and require veterinary examination.

CONFIRMING PREGNANCY

During the first few weeks of gestation there are few signs of pregnancy, except for a slight gain in weight. Occasionally a bitch may experience morning sickness. This usually happens during the third to fourth week of pregnancy, and is caused by the effects of progesterone, combined with the stretching and distention of the uterus. You may notice that your bitch appears apathetic, lacks appetite and may vomit from time to time. *Morning sickness* lasts only a few days. Unless you are particularly attentive, you may not notice it at all. If vomiting occurs, feed several small meals spaced throughout the day.

By day 40, the nipples begin to darken and enlarge, and the belly is increasing in size. As birth approaches, the breasts enlarge and a milky fluid may be expressed from the nipples. Note that many bitches have breast enlargement after a normal heat period (see *False Pregnancy* in Chapter 15), so this alone should not lead you to conclude she is pregnant.

The uterus in dogs is Y-shaped with a horn on each side. The puppies grow and develop in the uterine horns. By palpating the abdomen, a veterinarian can tell by the 26th day after the last breeding whether a bitch is pregnant. The embryos can be felt as evenly spaced swellings about the size of walnuts in the average-size dog. After day 35, the fetuses are floating in capsules of fluid and can no longer be detected by palpation.

Abdominal palpation requires experience and a gentle hand. There are other structures in the abdomen that may feel lumpy. Excessive poking and prodding can damage the delicate fetal-placental units and cause a miscarriage. If you would like to learn how to palpate for puppies, ask your veterinarian to demonstrate the procedure to you.

Abdominal *ultrasonography* can detect puppies throughout pregnancy, beginning as early as 18 or 19 days after ovulation. The technique is safe and effective, and does not use radiation.

Abdominal X-rays will show fetal bone structure at about day 45. X-rays are used as an alternative to ultrasonography, to distinguish among pregnancy, false pregnancy and *pyometra*. They should be avoided in early pregnancy.

In late pregnancy, the abdomen becomes enlarged and pendulous. The movements of the puppies can be seen and felt during the last two weeks.

PRENATAL CHECKUPS

The first prenatal visit should be scheduled for two to three weeks after breeding. Any questions about activity and feeding during pregnancy can be answered at this time. Your veterinarian might schedule additional tests. Intestinal parasites, if present, should be treated.

Make an appointment to have the expectant mother seen again two weeks before her due date. Your veterinarian will want to discuss normal delivery procedures, alert you to potential problems and give you instructions on how to care for the newborn puppies. Be sure to ask where you can get emergency service after hours, if it's needed.

CARE AND FEEDING DURING PREGNANCY

A pregnant bitch needs little in the way of special attention. During the first half of pregnancy it is not necessary to restrict her activity. Moderate exercise is beneficial, because it helps to prevent undue weight gain and maintains muscle tone. Activities such as climbing fences, roughhousing with other dogs and children, and leaping up and down stairs should be avoided during the last two weeks of pregnancy.

Deworming

Panacur is a deworming agent effective against roundworms, hookworms and whipworms. It is safe to use during pregnancy. It is a good practice to deworm expectant mothers during the last two weeks of gestation and during lactation. This reduces environmental exposure to roundworm eggs (a human health hazard) and helps to control puppy roundworm infection.

Drugs During Pregnancy

Vaccinations, most medications, some flea and insecticide preparations, most hormones (including cortisone) and many dewormers are inadvisable during pregnancy.

Antibiotics that can effect fetal development include the tetracyclines, kana-mycin and Griseofulvin. Live-virus vaccines should not be given to pregnant fe-males because of the risks of abortion and birth defects. Always check with your veterinarian before giving any drug during pregnancy.

Diet and Feeding

During the first four weeks of pregnancy, continue to feed the usual adult mainte-nance food. Protein and calorie requirements increase during the second half of pregnancy. More than 75 percent of puppy weight and at least 50 percent of puppy length is attained during the last three weeks of gestation. Beginning on day 35, gradually increase the amount of food so that by whelping time the dam is consum-ing 1.5 times her maintenance ration.

Also at this time, consider switching to a commercial food formulated for growing puppies. These products are especially suitable for pregnant and nursing females because ounce for ounce they contain more protein, calcium and other essential nutrients. An appropriate food is one that contains at least 1,600 metabolizable kcals per pound of food and at least 21 percent protein. Nutrient information is given on the package label. Divide the day's ration into equal parts and feed two or three times a day. Avoid supplementing the bitch's diet with treats, table scraps or canned meat. To the extent that other foods supply additional calories, the dam may not eat enough of the pregnancy food to get all the nutrients she and her puppies need for a successful and healthy pregnancy.

Do not increase the caloric intake if the bitch is overweight. How to determine the ideal weight is discussed in *Weight Reduction* in Chapter 9. Excessive weight gain should be strictly avoided. Overweight bitches are notorious for having whelp-ing problems. An expectant mother should gain no more than 15 to 25 percent of her body weight by the end of gestation, and should weigh no more than 5 to 10 percent above her normal weight after whelping.

Vitamin and mineral supplements are not required unless the dam is below par from an earlier litter or recovering from an illness. In fact, excessive supplementa-tion can cause soft tissue calcifications and physical deformities in the developing puppies.

An expectant dam may lose her appetite a week or two before whelping. Her abdomen is crowded and she may have difficulty taking in large meals. Feed her several small meals spaced throughout the day.

PREPARING FOR WHELPING

Dams should deliver at home in familiar surroundings where they are at ease. The best place care for newborn puppies is in a whelping box. The box should be lo-cated in a warm, dry, out-of-the-way spot free from drafts and distractions.

An adequate wooden box for large dogs should be at least four to five feet on a side and 12 inches tall. A box two to three feet on a side and eight inches tall is sufficient for toy breeds. The sides should be tall enough to keep puppies from crawling out while allowing the dam to step (not jump) over. If necessary, one side can be made shorter than the others. This side can be replaced by a taller board when the pups are older. The sides of the whelping box should not be nailed to the floorboard. Instead, they should be held in grooves made by nailing one-by-two-inch-molding around the edges. The sides are then joined and held in place by hook-and-eye latches. The floor is much easier to clean and the box easier to store if the sides are removable.

Make a shelf around the inside of the box a few inches from the floor by nailing three- to six-inch wide boards to all four sides. Puppies will instinctively crawl under these ledges and thus are less likely to be stepped or rolled on by their mother.

Lay several sheets of newspaper in the bottom of the box to absorb moisture. Because newspapers offer little traction and do not provide a good surface for crawling, cover the newspapers with heavy towels, mattress pads or some other material that gives good traction and is either washable or disposable. Disposable baby diapers are excellent for toy breeds. Newborn puppies should never be placed in deep, loose bedding, such as blankets, in which they can smother. Also do not use straw or wood chips. These substances can be inhaled.

Introduce the dam to her whelping box about two weeks before she is due to deliver, and encourage her to sleep in it. By the time she whelps, she will understand that she is to do so in the box and not in her owners' bed.

Cold, damp quarters are a leading cause of newborn puppy deaths. The whelping room should be free of drafts and kept at a temperature of 85°F for the first seven days after delivery. During the second week, reduce the temperature to 80°F. Thereafter, progressively reduce the temperature to 72°F by the time the litter is six weeks old. Keep a constant check on the temperature using a thermometer placed on the floor of the whelping box.

Additional heat can be supplied by using 250-watt infrared heat bulbs, either suspended above the floor of the whelping box or mounted in a photographer's flood light reflectors (or plant lights). Be sure to leave an area of the box out of the direct source of heat, so the mother can rest in a cooler area.

One week before the dam is due to deliver, clip the long hair around her mammary glands and vulva.

In addition to the whelping box and a good heat source, you should keep these supplies on hand in case they are needed:

- A small box in which to place newborn puppies
- Sterile disposable latex gloves
- An eyedropper or small bulb syringe to aspirate mouth and nose secretions
- Dental floss or cotton thread to tie the umbilical stumps
- An antiseptic, such as iodine, to apply to the umbilical stumps
- Scissors
- Clean, laundered towels
- Plenty of fresh newspapers

Whelping

SIGNS OF WHELPING

Two to three days before the dam is due to deliver, take her rectal temperature each morning. Twelve to eighteen hours before labor begins, the rectal temperature drops from a normal of 101.3° to 99.5°F or below. This two-degree drop may not occur; if it does occur, it can easily be missed. Don't assume that a normal rectal temperature means she won't deliver soon. As the day of whelping approaches, restrict her to the house.

Twelve to twenty-four hours before whelping the dam loses her appetite, becomes more active and restlessness, perhaps rummages in closets, digs in the garden or scratches up her owners' bed. Now is the time to introduce her to the whelping box if you have not already done so. An experienced dam usually takes to it without difficulty. But if she decides to have her puppies in some other spot, move the entire family to the whelping box as soon as she finishes delivering.

LABOR AND DELIVERY

The dog's uterus has two horns that meet in a central uterine cavity. Developing puppies, encircled by their placentas, lie within the uterine horns. The cervix opens into the vaginal birth canal.

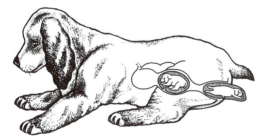

In this birth, the first puppy is being delivered in the common presentation with nose and feet first. The second puppy will be born backward. This ordinarily does not cause problems (see *Physical Blockage*).

The entire birthing process is seldom difficult and normally proceeds without human intervention. During *stage one*, which lasts 6 to 12 hours, involuntary uterine contractions dilate the cervix. The bitch may appear restless or uncomfortable, but exhibits no other signs.

In *stage two*, involuntary uterine contractions become more forceful. One uterine horn contracts and expels a puppy into the body of the uterus. The uterus contracts and pushes the presenting part of the puppy against the cervix. This stimulates active labor, with voluntary tightening of the abdominal wall muscles and purposeful straining. At this point the dam may become anxious and begin to pant and lick at her vulva. She may vomit. This is a normal reflex and should not be taken as a sign that something is wrong. Bitches usually deliver lying down, but some may stand or squat.

At complete cervical dilatation, the puppy slides into the vagina and the water bag around the puppy can be seen bulging through the lips of the vulva. In some cases the bag ruptures before the puppy is born. If so, a yellow or straw-colored fluid is passed. After the water bag breaks, the puppy should be delivered within a few minutes.

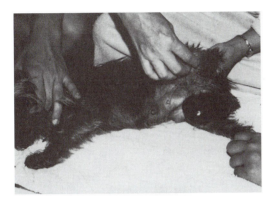

This puppy is being born surrounded by the water bag. Remove the membranes if the mother does not do so.

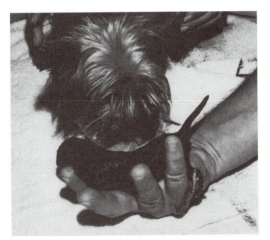

Present the puppy to the mother to lick and cuddle. This establishes the mother-puppy bond.

Encourage puppies to nurse between deliveries. This stimulates the dam's uterine contractions and helps bring down her milk. (JoAnn Thompson)

About 70 percent of puppies are born in the diving position, with feet and nose first. After the head is delivered, the rest of the puppy slides out easily. The mother instinctively removes the fetal membranes and vigorously licks the puppy's face to clear fluid and mucus from his nose and mouth. As the puppy gasps, the lungs inflate and breathing begins. The dam now severs the umbilical cord by *shredding* it with her teeth.

No attempt should be made to interfere with this normal maternal care. It is an important part of the recognition process and mother-puppy bonding. However, if the mother is occupied with another puppy and fails to remove the sac around the puppy, you should step in and strip away the fetal membranes to allow the puppy to breathe (see *Helping a Puppy to Breathe*, below). Similarly, if the cord is severed too cleanly or too close to the puppy's navel, it may continue to bleed. Be prepared to clamp or pinch off the cord and tie a thread around the stump. *After the mother severs the cord, the stump of each puppy should be disinfected with iodine or some other suitable antiseptic.* This step helps to prevent umbilical stump infection.

During *stage three* labor, the placenta is expelled. A placenta is passed within a few minutes after the birth of each puppy. The dam may consume some or all of the placentas. This instinctive reaction may stem from behavior in the wild, where it is important to remove the evidence of birthing. Consuming the placentas is not essential from a health point of view. Ingesting several placentas can produce diarrhea. You may wish to remove some or all of the placentas. However, be sure to count them. If the number of placentas is less than the number of puppies, notify your veterinarian. A retained placenta can cause acute postpartum metritis.

The next puppy will be born from the opposite uterine horn. As the dam prepares for the second puppy, remove the first puppy and place him in a warm box. This way, the mother will not accidentally roll on the pup while distracted by the next birth. Between births put the puppies back on the dam's nipples. Their sucking action stimulates uterine contractions and helps bring on the *colostrum*, or first milk of the dam. This colostrum contains maternal antibodies that protect against infectious diseases.

Most puppies are born at intervals of 15 minutes to 2 hours apart, but this is variable. The average time to whelp a litter of four to six puppies is six to eight hours, but large litters can take considerably longer. Active straining returns 5 to 30 minutes before the delivery of the next pup. Occasionally the interval between puppies is as long as three to four hours. But if you suspect that the mother has not finished delivering all her puppies and she rests for more than four hours, or if she actively strains for 30 to 60 minutes without delivering a puppy, notify your veterinarian without delay.

Twelve to twenty-four hours after the dam has delivered her last puppy, have her examined by your veterinarian to be sure there are no retained puppies or placentas. An oxytocin injection (breeders call this a pit shot) may be given to clear the uterus. This also stimulates the let-down of milk.

ASSISTING THE NORMAL DELIVERY

When labor is going well, there is no need to interfere. But on occasion a large puppy may get stuck in the vaginal birth canal. The head or presenting part appears during a forceful contraction and then slips back when the dam relaxes.

In most cases this can be corrected by lubricating the birth canal liberally with K-Y Jelly. If the dam does not deliver the puppy within 15 minutes, proceed as follows:

Put on a pair of sterile disposable latex gloves. As the presenting part appears at the vaginal opening, place your thumb and index finger on either side of the perineum, just below the anus, and push down gently to keep the puppy from slipping back into the mother. Next, grip the puppy in the birth canal and slide the lips of the vulva back over his head. Once this has been accomplished, the lips will hold the puppy in place, giving you a chance to get another grip.

Now grip the skin of the puppy with a clean piece of cloth behind his neck or along the back. As the mother strains, apply traction to the skin—not to the legs or head—and draw the puppy out. It may be helpful to rotate the puppy first one way and then the other. If these measures are not successful, see *Physical Blockage* in the section below.

HELPING A PUPPY TO BREATHE

The amniotic sac that surrounds the newborn puppy should be removed within 30 seconds so the puppy can breathe. If the mother fails to do this, tear open the sac and remove it, starting at the mouth and working it back over the body. Remove the secretions from the puppy's mouth and nose with a cotton swab, or gently suction the secretions using an eyedropper or a bulb syringe. Rub the puppy briskly with a soft towel.

Another good way to clear secretions is to hold the puppy in your hands while supporting his head. Then slowly swing him in a downward arc, stopping when his nose is pointed toward the floor. This expels water from the nostrils. Present the puppy to the mother to lick, sniff and cuddle.

Swing the puppy down with his nose pointing to the floor to clear secretions from his nostrils. Make sure you support his head.

After a difficult delivery, a puppy may be too weak or too limp to breathe on his own. Squeeze the puppy's chest gently from side to side and then from front to back. If the puppy still does not draw a breath, place your mouth over his nose and blow gently until you see his chest expand. *Do not blow forcefully, because this can rupture the lungs.* Remove your mouth to allow the puppy to exhale. Repeat this several times until the puppy breathes on his own.

Prolonged or Difficult Labor (Dystocia)

Prolonged labor at any stage is called dystocia. Dystocia is caused by a *physical blockage* or *uterine inertia*. The latter is a condition in which the uterus does not contract forcefully enough to expel the puppy. Dystocia usually affects the first puppy in the litter.

Dystocia rarely occurs in healthy, well-conditioned dams. However, it does occur in fat, overweight brood bitches. This is one reason why it is so important to prevent excessive weight gain in pregnancy.

PHYSICAL BLOCKAGE

The two common causes of physical blockage are a very large puppy and a puppy that is not positioned correctly in the birth canal.

Oversized Puppies. Large puppies occur in litters with just a few puppies, and particularly in litters with a single puppy. Relatively large puppies also occur when the sire was much larger than the dam. Prolonged gestation, and a puppy with a congenital defect such as hydrocephalus, are other reasons why a pup might be oversized relative to the size of the birth canal.

Physical blockage is often caused by a combination of a large puppy and a relatively narrow birth canal. Maternal causes of a narrow birth canal include a small pelvis, occasionally seen in terriers and the brachycephalic breeds; vaginal stenosis or a persistent hymen; a tumor of the vagina; and a previously fractured pelvis.

Incorrectly Positioned Puppy. Most puppies come down the birth canal nose and feet first, in the diving position, with their backs along the top of the vagina. When a puppy comes down backward, his hind feet or rump present first. The hind-feet presentation occurs about 20 percent of the time. It is probably not accurate to call this an incorrect presentation, because it seldom causes a problem. The breech position, however, in which the rump is the presenting part, does cause problems—particularly when it occurs with the first puppy. Another presentation that can complicate delivery is when the head is bent forward or to the side.

Treatment: Physical blockage can be suspected if the mother actively strains (bears down) for more than 30 to 60 minutes without delivering a puppy, or if she exhibits weak ineffectual labor for more than two hours instead of resting quietly between births. The obstruction must be unblocked by a veterinarian to prevent complications and allow labor to resume.

Veterinary obstetrics for an incorrect position involves manually correcting the presentation. Sterile gloves are used and the vaginal canal is lubricated with Betadine solution and K-Y Jelly. With one hand beneath the abdomen in front of the pelvis, the body of the uterus is lifted to align the puppy with the birth canal. A finger is slipped into the vagina to feel for a head, tail or leg. A tilted head can be corrected by inserting a finger into the puppy's mouth and gently guiding the head into correct alignment.

To correct a breech (rump first) presentation, first one leg and then the other is hooked with the finger, slipping the legs over the pelvic brim and into the vagina. This converts the breech to a hind-foot presentation. The vaginal opening is gently stretched to stimulate a forceful push by the mother. When the puppy is part way out, delivery is assisted as described for assisting a normal delivery.

Occasionally a blockage is caused by a retained placenta. The placenta can be hooked with the fingers and then grasped with a sterile gauze pad. Steady traction is maintained until the placenta passes out of the vagina.

If the obstruction cannot be relieved by medical means, an emergency cesarean section is required.

UTERINE INERTIA

Uterine inertia is an important cause of ineffective labor. Inertia is classified as *primary* (insufficient stimulation to start uterine contractions) or *secondary* (caused by uterine muscle fatigue after prolonged straining).

Primary Uterine Inertia

The two conditions associated with primary uterine inertia are failure to go into labor before 67 days after ovulation, and failure to progress from Stage One to stage two labor within 24 hours. Causes of failure to initiate labor include a small litter (particularly a single puppy), overstretching of the uterus by a large litter, the stress and anxiety of being a first-time mother (dams can voluntarily prolong, delay and even interrupt the normal birthing process for up to 24 hours), and occasionally a calcium deficiency, which is called *hypocalcemia*.

If more than 65 days have passed from the date of first breeding and the mother shows no signs of whelping, notify your veterinarian because gestation may be prolonged. (Alternatively, the pups may not yet be mature.) An X-ray can be taken to determine the number of puppies and their sizes.

Treatment: Hypocalcemia can be diagnosed by a blood test and treated by giving oral or intravenous calcium. If *postmaturity* is suspected, your veterinarian may wish to confirm this with a progesterone level test and then do a cesarean section.

With nervous dams, stage two labor can often be started by giving small doses of the tranquilizer acepromazine. If the cervix is dilated, oxytocin may be effective. Oxytocin should never be used when the cervix is closed, or in cases of suspected physical blockage, because of the danger of uterine rupture. If primary uterine inertia does not respond to medical treatment, a cesarean section is required.

Secondary Uterine Inertia

After a mechanical blockage has been removed, the uterus may be too tired for labor to resume. Treatment usually involves cesarean section.

WHEN TO CALL THE VETERINARIAN

It is better to call your veterinarian with a false alarm, if only to gain reassurance, than to hope the problem will disappear with time. Most whelping problems can be dealt with rather simply when they are attended to at once. However, the same problem, when neglected, becomes complicated—often leading to emergency surgery.

Signs of birthing problems are:

- 30 to 60 minutes of active straining without birth of a puppy
- Four hours between births with more puppies expected
- Two hours of weak, ineffectual labor without birth of a puppy
- A purulent or hemorrhagic vaginal discharge
- Apathy or weakness, with a rectal temperature above 104°F or below 97°F.
- Passing dark green or bloody fluid *before* the birth of the first puppy.

A dark green vaginal discharge indicates that the placenta is separating from the wall of the uterus. When this happens, the first puppy should be born within a few minutes. After the first puppy, the passage of dark green fluid is not a concern.

CESAREAN SECTION

Cesarean section is the treatment of choice for all dystocias that can't be relieved by drugs or obstetrics. Common indications for c-section include *primary uterine inertia* associated with *postmaturity, physical blockage* and *death of puppies in utero.*

The decision of when to proceed with an emergency c-section rests with your veterinarian. It is based on the condition of the dam, the length of labor, results of X-rays, the size of the puppies in relation to the pelvic outlet, the dam's response to oxytocin and whether the vaginal canal has lost its lubrication. Because of anatomical makeup, certain breeds such as the Bulldog, Chihuahua, Pekingese, Toy Poodle and Boston Terrier are prone to whelping difficulties. C-section may be indicated as an elective procedure as soon as the bitch goes into labor.

The operation is done under general anesthesia in the veterinary hospital. The risk of an elective c-section to a healthy dam is small. However, when labor has been prolonged, when the puppies are dead and beginning to decompose, or when the uterus has ruptured, the risk of surgery becomes significant.

Most dams are awake and able to nurse puppies within three hours of surgery and can be discharged from the hospital shortly thereafter.

A dam who has had a c-section may or may not require one with her next litter. This depends upon the reasons for the first c-section.

Cesarean section may be indicated as an elective procedure in Bulldogs and some other breeds. (Patty Rungo)

Postpartum Care of the Dam

Twelve to twenty-four hours after the dam delivers, ask your veterinarian to do a postpartum checkup. Many veterinarians prescribe an injection of oxytocin to help expel all the products of conception and return the uterus to its normal size. Take the mother's temperature at least once a day for the first week. A temperature of 103°F or higher indicates infection. The most likely causes are acute metritis and acute septic mastitis.

Some bloody or dark green discharge (called lochia) is normal for the first few days. The lochia changes to a watery pink or a bloody discharge that may persist for four to six weeks. A dark brown or foul-smelling discharge is abnormal and suggests a retained placenta or uterine infection (see *Acute Metritis*, page 433). A pink or bloody discharge that persists for more than six weeks indicates *subinvolution of placental sites* (SIPS). Be sure to consult your veterinarian if you see either of these discharges.

FEEDING A NURSING DAM

A nursing dam's calorie requirements increase steadily as her puppies grow. By the third or fourth week, she needs two to three times more calories than she did before pregnancy. If her diet is not adjusted to supply these calories, she may not be able to produce enough milk to nourish her puppies. Inadequate milk production is a common cause of puppy mortality.

Many commercial dog foods do not provide enough calories to support lactation. It is important to switch to a food advertised as formulated "for growing puppies" (see *Feeding and Nutrition* in Chapter 9). You may have already done this during the second half of pregnancy. Ounce for ounce, these foods contain more calories, protein and calcium. The food should contain at least 1,600 metabolizable kcals per pound of food and at least 21 percent protein. Nutrient information is given on the package label.

Do not use table scraps or treats to supply additional calories. The calories provided will not be of the same quality and may cause the dam to eat less of the high-quality food. Kibble can be left down continuously and fed free-choice. Canned foods should be fed at least three times a day.

How much should you feed a nursing dam? During the first week, feed one and a half times the manufacturer's recommended daily maintenance ration. Increase this to twice the daily ration during the second week. By the third week, a nursing dam should be eating three times the normal maintenance ration. Slowly reduce the size of the portions after the fourth week in preparation for weaning. *Be sure to keep clean, fresh water available at all times.*

Vitamin and mineral supplements are not necessary, and can even be harmful. Avoid them, unless the dam refuses to eat her food or has a pre-existing deficiency or a chronic illness. In these circumstances, seek veterinary consultation.

DRUGS AND LACTATION

Note that many drugs are passed on to puppies in the mother's milk. The amount depends on the blood concentration and whether the drug is soluble in fat. Fat-soluble drugs are stored in fat and will be secreted in the milk for prolonged periods. Keep in mind that a newborn's liver and kidneys are immature and cannot detoxify and eliminate drugs as readily as those of an adult. Avoid giving drugs during lactation, unless they are prescribed by your veterinarian.

Postpartum Problems

Problems that can affect the dam after delivery include subinvolution of placental sites, acute metritis, acute mastitis, caked mammary glands, absent milk supply and milk fever. Occasionally, a mother has problems accepting and caring for her puppies.

SUBINVOLUTION OF PLACENTA SITES (SIPS)

The uterus normally returns to near-normal size (a process called involution) by four to six weeks after whelping, and completes the entire process by 12 weeks postpartum. During the first four to six weeks the dam will have a light pink to bloody vaginal discharge called the lochia.

A vaginal discharge that persists for more than six weeks is caused by subinvolution of placental sites. These sites, where the placenta formerly attached to the wall of the uterus, are invaded by placenta-like tissue called trophoblasts. The trophoblasts prevent the uterus from completing the process of involution. The associated vaginal bleeding is usually mild but may be heavy enough to cause anemia.

SIPS tends to occur in bitches younger than three years of age. There is no breed predisposition. The condition does not cause discomfort. SIPS can be complicated by acute metritis or perforation of the uterus, but this is not common. The diagnosis is made by palpating the uterus and feeling lumpiness in the uterine horns. Ultrasonography shows the enlarged horns. *Vaginal cytology* may disclose trophoblast-like cells.

Treatment: The SIPS-related discharge usually resolves spontaneously. If it persists and you don't plan to breed the bitch again, have her spayed. When SIPS disappears spontaneously, future fertility is not affected. There is no predisposition for developing SIPS on subsequent litters.

ACUTE METRITIS (INFECTED UTERUS)

Acute metritis is a bacterial infection that spreads upward into the uterus during the birthing process or shortly afterward. Some cases are caused by a retained placenta or a mummified fetus. Others are caused by contamination of the birth canal during or after delivery. Unsanitary whelping quarters and failure to dispose of the placentas and change the bedding immediately after whelping predispose a bitch to bacterial growth.

Many cases of acute metritis can be prevented by a postpartum checkup 24 hours after delivery. The veterinarian will usually give an injection of oxytocin to clear the uterus.

Signs of metritis appear two to seven days after whelping. A dam with acute metritis is lethargic, refuses to eat, has a fever of 103° to 105°F, is not attentive to her puppies and may vomit and have diarrhea. There is a foul-smelling vaginal discharge, which should be distinguished from the normal greenish or bloody discharge common for the first few days. A normal discharge is not accompanied by high fever, excessive thirst and other signs of toxicity such as vomiting and diarrhea. Abdominal palpation and *ultrasonography* help to determine whether there has been a retained fetus or placenta. Cultures are taken to determine the pathogens involved and their antibiotic sensitivities.

Be sure to take the dam's rectal temperature daily after whelping and notify your veterinarian if she develops fever or any of the signs just described. Acute metritis is a life-threatening illness that can rapidly progress to *toxemia* and shock.

Treatment: Treatment involves administering intravenous fluids and antibiotics to support the circulation and treat toxemia. Oxytocin or prostaglandin $PGF_{2\alpha}$ (Lutalyse) is given to empty the uterus. Your veterinarian may insert a small catheter through the cervix and flush the uterus with sterile saline or Betadine solution. A severely ill dam may require a life-saving operation to remove the uterus and ovaries.

Most dams with acute metritis are too ill to nurse puppies. The puppies should be taken off the mother and raised by hand as described in Chapter 17. Bitches that recover from acute metritis may develop a persistent low-grade infection of the lining of the uterus (see *Endometritis* in Chapter 15).

MASTITIS

The bitch normally has five pairs of mammary glands, or a total of 10 individual breasts. There are two types of mastitis that can affect the nursing dam. They are caked breasts and acute septic mastitis.

Caked Breasts (Galactostasis)

Milk accumulation in late pregnancy and during lactation may increase to the point where the breasts become distended, painful and warm. They are not infected and the dam does not appear sick. Caking of the mammary glands also occurs during false pregnancy when there are no puppies to remove the milk. Caked breasts should be distinguished from the swollen breasts that develop when milk fails to let-down after whelping (see *Agalactia*, below).

Treatment: Withhold water for 6 to 10 hours. Also withhold food for 24 hours and modestly restrict food intake for the next three days. Your veterinarian may prescribe a diuretic such as Lasix.

False-pregnant bitches often exhibit an excessive mothering instinct that includes licking and stimulating the breasts, which makes matters worse. This can be prevented, in part, by giving a mild tranquilizer prescribed by your veterinarian. Hormonal therapy to dry up the breasts may be considered in cases of false pregnancy.

Acute Septic Mastitis

Acute mastitis is an infection or abscess of one or more of the mammary glands caused by bacteria that gain entrance from a scratch or puncture wound in the skin of the breast. Some cases are bloodborne and are associated with acute metritis. Breast infection can occur any time from day one to six weeks postpartum.

Dams with acute mastitis run a high fever, are depressed and refuse to eat. The affected breasts, usually the two largest ones close to the groin, are swollen,

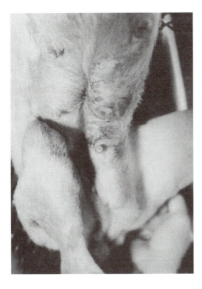

The inflamed mammary gland of a dam with acute septic mastitis.

extremely painful and usually reddish blue in appearance. The milk may be blood-tinged, thick, yellow or stringlike. In some cases the milk appears normal.

Treatment: Acute mastitis should be treated under veterinary supervision. Routine measures include appropriate antibiotics and the application of warm compresses for 30 minutes three times a day, followed by gentle stripping of the infected gland to express the milk. Early treatment may prevent abscess.

The milk of an infected breast is of poor nutritional quality, and puppies usually refuse to nurse from these teats. It is seldom necessary to tape a nipple or bind the breast to prevent nursing. A mammary gland that is not suckled stops producing milk in three days.

If the dam is septic, her overall milk production may decline. She may show little interest in tending her puppies. If this happens, remove the puppies and raise them by hand. If they are three weeks or older, wean them and dry up the breasts as described in Chapter 17.

Prevention: Puppies should have their nails trimmed weekly beginning at two to three weeks of age to keep them from scratching the skin of the dam.

ECLAMPSIA (MILK FEVER)

Eclampsia is a seizurelike condition caused by a low serum calcium (*hypocalcemia*). It usually appears two to four weeks postpartum. At this time there is a heavy drain on the mother's calcium stores as a consequence of nursing.

Small dogs, particularly Toys, are most likely to suffer from eclampsia. Large breeds are seldom affected. Eclampsia is also more likely to occur in dams on a low plane of nutrition during pregnancy. It also occurs among dams with large litters and, paradoxically, in brood bitches given calcium supplements during pregnancy.

Signs of eclampsia are restlessness, anxiety, rapid breathing and pale mucus membranes. The dam frequently leaves her puppies and paces up and down. Her gait may be stiff-legged, uncoordinated and jerky. Tightening of the face muscles exposes the teeth and gives her face a pinched look. In severe cases, she falls down on her side, kicks all four legs and salivates profusely. The rectal temperature may be elevated to 106°F.

Treatment: *Eclampsia is an emergency.* Notify your veterinarian at once. Intravenous calcium gluconate is a specific antidote. It is indicated at the first signs of muscle spasms or tremors. If the rectal temperature is over 104°F, treat as described for *Heat Stroke* in Chapter 1.

Puppies should be removed from the dam and fed by hand. If the puppies are three weeks or older, wean as described in Chapter 17. After 24 hours, young puppies can be permitted to return to the mother—if she has completely recovered. For the first week, restrict nursing to 30 minutes two or three times a day. If the dam remains asymptomatic, these restrictions can be lifted.

Mothers that continue to nurse should be supplemented with an oral calcium preparation such as calcium carbonate. Continue the supplement for as long as the dam is nursing.

AGALACTIA (ABSENCE OF MILK)

Milk may be absent because it has failed to let down or because the dam is not producing milk.

Failure of Milk Let-Down

This condition, which resembles *caked breasts*, should be suspected if the mammary glands are firm and swollen but no milk is found in the teat canals.

Most mothers instinctively encourage their puppies to suckle soon after delivery. Suckling stimulates the release of oxytocin from the pituitary gland. Oxytocin is responsible for milk let-down. A nervous, frightened or stressed mother may discourage her puppies from suckling, or may release a hormone (epinephrine) that blocks the action of oxytocin.

Puppies that are not receiving milk should be supplemented as described in Chapter 17, *Raising Puppies by Hand*. Between supplements, it is important to encourage suckling to continue breast stimulation. Once the milk comes down, the dam readily accepts her puppies.

Examine all the nipples to be sure they are open, fully formed and erect. A deformed nipple may cause difficulty in suckling. A recessed nipple can be improved by massaging it to stimulate the flow of milk and then putting a vigorous suckler directly on that nipple.

Treatment: A low-dose tranquilizer (acepromazine) often relieves stress-related agalactia. The problem can also be solved by giving oxytocin. It may be necessary to repeat the oxytocin during the first 48 hours.

Failure to Produce Enough Milk

True agalactia can be suspected if the bitch's breasts do not develop in late pregnancy. This condition may have a genetic basis. There is no treatment. These puppies must be hand fed using artificial bitch's milk (see *Raising Puppies by Hand* in Chapter 17).

Occasionally, a dam with a large litter is incapable of making enough milk to satisfy all her puppies. The most common cause of insufficient milk production is failure to feed the mother an adequate number of calories, especially during the second and third weeks after whelping, when nursing demands are greatest. This problem is entirely preventable (see *Feeding a Nursing Dam*, page 431).

If the mother is constitutionally unable to produce enough milk, her puppies should be supplemented with artificial bitch's milk.

MATERNAL NEGLECT

Mothers can neglect or injure their puppies for a number of reasons. The best way to prepare for quality nurturing is to create an atmosphere conducive to a contented nest. The whelping quarters should be clean, dry, in a quiet, out-of-the-way location and well heated to avoid chilling the puppies.

The mother-puppy bond begins during and shortly after birth. The mother recognizes each puppy by his distinctive scent. During the process of licking, cleaning and nursing the puppy, she establishes a supportive relationship that remains until the puppy is weaned.

This bond may be less secure when puppies are born by c-section. Such mothers can have difficulty accepting their puppies for the first 24 hours. This is less likely to happen when some of the puppies are born before the surgery, or when the puppies are put to her nipples before the sedation wears off.

A bitch whelping her first litter should be watched closely. She may confuse the puppy with the placenta, or injure a puppy while attempting to sever the cord and remove the membranes. Breeds with an undershot jaw or malocclusion problems are particularly prone to severing the cord too closely or accidentally biting the puppy.

A novice mother may have difficulty coping with a litter of squirming puppies for the first few hours. With a little help, she can be shown how to nurse her puppies and keep from stepping on them. Some house pets are extremely people-oriented and show little interest in being a mother if it means loss of family attention. Spend a good deal of time in the whelping area and allow the dam to have the run of the house. Lavishly praise the dam for being a good mother.

A dam may neglect her puppies if her milk does not come down during the first 24 hours. Treatment of delayed milk let-down is described earlier in the chapter. Once the milk does comes down, the puppies begin to nurse and the bond is established.

It is important to keep visitors out of the whelping area for the first three to four weeks, especially when the dam is a novice or is high-strung. Letting children and strange people handle the pups is stressful for the dam.

An overprotective dam could injure her puppies by picking them up and carrying them to another nest. Return the entire family to the box and stay with the mother, talking softly and stroking her often, until she settles in. Do not allow her to become frightened while carrying a puppy. Nest seeking can be prevented, in part, by introducing the dam to her whelping box two weeks before she is expected to deliver and encouraging her to sleep in it.

Other causes of puppy rejection are postpartum infections and complications such as *milk fever, mastitis* and *acute metritis*. In these cases puppies may have to be removed and reared by hand. A fading puppy whose body temperature has dropped below normal due to sickness or constitutional weakness may be pushed out of the nest. This is nature's way of culling.

Dams that continue to ignore or reject their puppies can sometimes be helped by tranquilizers.

PEDIATRICS

Healthy newborn puppies are the picture of contentment, sleeping much of the time and awakening only to eat. For the first 48 hours, puppies sleep with their heads curled under their chests. While sleeping, they jerk, kick and sometimes whimper. This is called activated sleep. It is the puppy's only way to exercise and helps develop muscle tone.

A good mother instinctively keeps her nest and puppies clean. By licking the belly and rectum of each puppy, she stimulates the elimination reflex.

Puppies can raise their heads at birth, but are unable to maintain an upright posture. Their eyes and ears are open at 10 to 14 days. Most puppies can stand at 14 days and by 21 days can eat from a bowl. Puppies are fully oriented to sight and sound by 25 days.

The heart of a newborn puppy beats at 160 to 200 beats per minute. The puppy takes 15 to 35 breaths per minute, and has an internal temperature ranging from 94° to 97°F. By two weeks of age, the normal heart rate is above 200 beats per minute and the respiratory rate 15 to 30 breaths per minute. The temperature gradually increases to 100°F by four weeks of age.

Contented newborns. (Sydney Giffin Wiley)

It is best to disturb newborn puppies as little as possible—at least until they are a few weeks old. Some dams get anxious when their puppies are handled. There is a theory that too much handling interferes with the process by which puppies learn to identify and relate to their mothers and littermates. These interactions are important in establishing normal canine behavior. When these early imprints do not proceed as they should, a puppy could develop problems with shyness or aggression at a later date.

After six weeks of age, positive interactions with humans and exposure to new and nonthreatening situations are important for the development of a happy, well-adjusted pet. For more information, see *The Importance of Early Socialization*, page 460.

Caring for the Newborn

Newborn puppies are born with very little capacity to adapt to environmental stresses. They are extremely vulnerable. But with proper care and attention to the special needs of these infants, many neonatal deaths can be avoided.

Two crucial factors to watch closely are the puppy's body temperature and his weight. A puppy's appearance, strength of suckle, sound of cry and general behavior also are important indicators of his health and well-being.

GENERAL APPEARANCE AND VITALITY

Healthy puppies are round and firm. They nurse vigorously and compete for nipples. Their mouths and tongues are wet. When you insert a finger into their mouths, they have a strong, vigorous suckle.

A newborn's skin is warm and pink. When pinched, it springs back in a resilient fashion. Pick up a puppy and he stretches and wiggles energetically in your hand. When removed from his mother, the puppy crawls back. Newborn puppies pile together for warmth.

A sick puppy presents a dramatically different picture. This puppy is limp, cold and hangs like a dishcloth. He shows little interest in nursing and tires easily. If you insert a finger into his mouth, his suckle response is poor.

Newborn puppies seldom cry. Crying indicates that a puppy is cold, hungry, sick or in pain. A distressed puppy crawls about looking for help and falls asleep away from the life-sustaining warmth of his mother and littermates. Later, he moves slowly and with great effort. He sleeps with his legs splayed apart and his head bent to the side. His cry is plaintive and piercing. Such a puppy is often rejected by the dam, who senses that the pup is not going to survive and pushes him out of the nest. The situation can be reversed if the puppy is treated and his body temperature is brought back to normal (see *Reviving a Weak Puppy*, page 445).

BODY TEMPERATURE

When a puppy is born, his body temperature is the same as his mother's. Immediately thereafter, the core temperature drops several degrees (how much depends upon the temperature of the room). Within 30 minutes, if the puppy is dry and snuggles close to his mother, his temperature begins to climb and reaches 94°F. Twenty-four hours later the core or rectal temperature is 95° to 97°F. It steadily increases until at three weeks of age the rectal temperature is 98° to 100°F. (How to take the newborn's rectal temperature is described in Appendix A.)

During the first week of life, puppies do not have the capacity to constrict the blood vessels at the surface of the skin to retain heat. A newborn is able to maintain a body temperature 10° to 12°F above his immediate surroundings only for short periods. When his mother is away for 30 minutes in a 72° room (well below the recommended level), the pup's core temperature quickly falls to 94°F or below. This gravely reduces metabolism.

Chilling is the single greatest danger to infant puppies. The temperature in the whelping box and surrounding area should be kept at 85° to 90°F for the first week. During the second week, reduce the temperature to 80°F. Then reduce the temperature gradually so that it is 70°F when the litter is six weeks old. Keep a constant check on the temperature using a thermometer placed on the floor of the whelping box (see *Preparing for Whelping* in Chapter 16).

THE IMPORTANCE OF NURSING

During the first 36 hours after whelping, mothers produce a special type of milk that is high in vitamins, minerals and protein. This is the *colostrum*, or first milk of the dam. Colostrum also contains antibodies and other immune substances (primarily IgG) that provide protection against infectious diseases. Dams vaccinated one month before breeding have antibody levels high enough to protect puppies from distemper, parvovirus and other infectious diseases for up to 16 weeks.

Newborn puppies nurse vigorously and compete for nipples. Puppies often nurse six to eight times a day, with suckling sessions lasting up to 30 minutes. Frequent nursing is essential to survival, because at this stage the energy for heat and metabolism is supplied principally through mother's milk.

Neonatal puppies have little subcutaneous fat, and reserve energy is supplied almost entirely by glycogen in the liver. The liver is the last organ to grow, while the brain is the organ that consumes the most energy, so a puppy with a brain too large in proportion to his liver rapidly runs out of energy. Accordingly, the weight of the liver at birth should be at least one and a half times the weight of the brain. It's even better if the liver is twice or three times the size of the brain. But even with a large liver–brain ratio, energy reserves are limited. The potential for low blood sugar must be offset by frequent feeding. A puppy that does not nurse frequently, for whatever reason, is headed for trouble.

THE IMPORTANCE OF WEIGHT GAIN

The weight of a puppy at birth is not influenced by the number of puppies in the litter, the sex of the puppy or the weight of the dam.

After birth, puppies should gain 1 to 1.5 grams a day for each pound of anticipated adult weight, and should double their birth weights in 10 to 12 days. The anticipated adult weight is the weight of the dam. So if the dam weighs 30 pounds, the puppies should gain 30 to 45 grams per day. (One ounce equals 28.35 grams.) A steady gain in weight is the best indicator that a puppy is doing well.

It is important to weigh each puppy at birth and 12 hours later on a scale that measures grams or ounces. Then weigh each pup daily for the first two weeks and every three days thereafter until the puppies are a month old. Failure to gain weight is a cause for immediate concern. Notify your veterinarian.

Neonatal puppies should be weighed on a scale that measures in grams or ounces.

When several puppies in the litter are not gaining at the expected rate, think of a maternal factor such as failure to produce enough milk (see *Agalactia* in Chapter 16). A nursing dam needs two to three times more nutrition than a typical adult dog. If the mother is not getting enough calories, her milk supply will be inadequate to support a large litter. How much to feed during lactation is discussed in Chapter 16.

When to Supplement

Puppies that gain weight steadily during the first seven days are in no danger. Puppies that lose some weight, but not more than 10 percent of their birth weight, for the first 48 hours of life and then begin to gain should be watched closely. Puppies that lose 10 percent or more of their birth weight in the first 48 hours and are not gaining by 72 hours are in trouble. Start supplemental feedings at once (see *Raising Puppies by Hand*, beginning on page 445).

If a puppy is 25 percent below the average weight of his littermates at birth, you can expect a high mortality unless the puppy is hand-fed. If possible, allow the pup to nurse for the first 24 hours to receive colostrum. Then place him in a homemade incubator and raise by hand. As soon as his weight approaches that of his littermates, he can be returned to the nest. Many immature puppies can be saved if supplemental feedings are started *before* they begin to fail.

DEHYDRATION

Kidney function in the newborn is 25 percent of what it will be later in life. These immature kidneys are unable to concentrate urine, and puppies therefore excrete large amounts of dilute urine regardless of whether they take in fluids. Thus, dehydration is a complicating factor whenever puppies become too weak to nurse. *This is another reason why it is important to begin supplemental feedings as soon as a puppy stops nursing or stops gaining weight.*

Signs of dehydration are lack of moisture in the mouth, a bright pink color to the tongue and mucous membranes and loss of muscle tone and weakness. When the skin is pinched, it stays up in a fold.

Neonatal diarrhea is serious cause of rapid dehydration and weight loss. When diarrhea occurs during hand feeding, it usually clears up when the strength of the formula is changed, as described in *Common Feeding Problems*, page 451. In all other cases of diarrhea, the puppies should be seen and treated by a veterinarian.

WHY PUPPIES DIE

The first two weeks of life is the period of greatest risk for the newborn pup. Unfortunately, some early neonatal deaths are due to lack of advance preparation—especially failure to provide adequate heat in the whelping quarters, failure to vaccinate the dam (which gives neonatal infections a foothold) and failure to provide an adequate diet to the dam during pregnancy. These deaths are preventable.

Maternal factors are critical to puppy survival. Novice, obese and elderly dams have higher puppy mortality rates than do experienced, well-conditioned and younger dams. The quantity of the mother's milk is also of utmost importance. Genetic influences may play a role, but in most cases milk supply is insufficient because the dam has not been fed enough calories. This is especially true for dams with large litters.

Congenital and acquired birth defects are infrequent causes of newborn deaths. Cleft palate, often accompanied by harelip, prevents effective nursing. Large navel hernias allow the abdominal organs to protrude. Heart defects can be severe enough to produce circulatory failure. Other developmental disorders that may be responsible for the occasional death include hemophilia, esophageal atresia, pyloric stenosis, anal atresia and malformations affecting the eyes and skeletal system.

The Physiologically Immature Puppy

An immature puppy is at a distinct disadvantage because of his low birth weight and lack of muscle mass and subcutaneous fat. This pup may be unable to breathe deeply, nurse effectively and maintain body warmth. His liver-brain ratio may be less than 1.5:1. His birth weight will be 25 percent below that of his littermates. Such a puppy is likely to be crowded out by his brothers and sisters and forced to nurse at the least productive nipples.

A common cause of immaturity is inadequate growth while in the uterus. The fault may be placental insufficiency, perhaps due to overcrowding or a disadvantageous placement of a placenta in the wall of the uterus. These puppies are immature because of their development rather than their age, and are at risk of developing *cardiopulmonary syndrome*.

Cardiopulmonary Syndrome

This is a shocklike state of circulatory failure that occurs in puppies under five days of age. Many affected puppies are physiologically immature. Inadequate consumption of mother's milk shortly after birth may set the stage for this problem. Thereafter, weakness and hypoglycemia lead to chilling and dehydration. There is a drop in temperature, heart and breathing rates. As the rectal temperature drops below 94°F, there is further depression of vital functions. Gradually, the crawling and righting reflexes are lost and the puppy lies on his side. Gagging and fluid in the nostrils may be noted. Later, poor circulation affects the brain, causing seizurelike spasms, accompanied by breathless periods lasting up to a minute. At this point the condition is irreversible.

A distressed puppy with cardiopulmonary syndrome. Early treatment before the seizure state is imperative.

Early treatment is imperative to avoid death (see *Reviving a Weak Puppy* in the section below). Veterinary assistance is required.

Fading Puppies

These are puppies that are vigorous at birth but fail to gain weight and gradually lose vitality and the urge to feed. For want of a better term, the condition is called the fading puppy syndrome. There is no agreement as to what causes fading puppies. Some cases may result from immaturity, others from internal birth defects, environmental stresses and maternal factors. The syndrome is reversible if the cause can be determined and steps taken to correct it, as discussed in the section that follows.

REVIVING A WEAK PUPPY

If a puppy is immature, weak, or fading, early treatment is imperative. New puppies are extremely fragile and can die quickly. Treatment involves slow warming to restore body temperature, oral fluids to correct dehydration and supplemental feedings to provide calories.

A *chilled puppy should be warmed gradually.* Rapid warming using a heating pad, for example, causes the blood vessels in the skin to dilate, increasing heat loss, expending more calories and creating a greater need for oxygen. This harms rather than helps. However, if the puppy's rectal temperature is below 90°F, rapid warming under veterinary supervision may be required as a life-saving procedure.

The best way to warm a puppy is to tuck him down next to your skin beneath a sweater or jacket, and let your own warmth seep into the puppy. If the puppy's rectal temperature is below 94°F, warming will take two to three hours.

Chilled puppies are usually *hypoglycemic* and dehydrated. Correct mild to moderate dehydration by giving a *warmed* glucose-electrolyte solution such as Pedialyte, which can be purchased at drug stores and large grocery stores. Give 1cc per ounce of body weight every hour by eyedropper or baby nurser (see *How to Give Formula*, page 449) and warm slowly until the puppy is wiggling about. If a commercial solution is not available, as a temporary expedient you can substitute a solution of one teaspoon of granulated sugar to one ounce of tap water. Severe dehydration, in which the puppy is too weak to nurse, should be treated by a veterinarian.

Never allow a cold puppy to nurse or receive formula. When chilled, the stomach and small intestines will not digest or absorb milk. The puppy will bloat and perhaps vomit.

Once the puppy is warm and wiggling about, begin supplemental feedings to restore liver glycogen and supply calories, as described below in *Raising Puppies by Hand*. If the puppy is immature, he will not be able to compete successfully with his littermates for milk, and should be placed in a homemade incubator and raised by hand.

Raising Puppies by Hand

A dam may be incapable of raising a litter because of a uterine or mammary gland infection, eclampsia or insufficient milk supply. In addition, an immature or sick puppy may need to be hand-fed for survival.

The decision to supplement is based on the puppy's general appearance and vitality, his weight at birth and his progress in comparison to his littermates. It is far better to intervene early and start hand-feeding in a borderline case, rather than to wait until a puppy is in obvious distress. In some cases it may be possible to supplement two or three times a day and let the pup remain in the nest and continue to nurse. Other pups must be raised entirely by their breeder.

Whenever possible, puppies should nurse from the mother for the first 24 to 36 hours of life. During this period they receive antibodies in the colostrum that provide temporary immunity to the common canine infectious diseases. If puppies do not receive colostrum, they should be actively immunized starting at three weeks of age.

When hand raising puppies, it is critically important to:

- Prevent chilling
- Prepare and feed the right formula
- Provide the right management

THE INCUBATOR

You can make a satisfactory incubator by dividing a cardboard box into separate compartments, one for each puppy. These compartments are important because orphaned puppies tend to suckle each other's ears, tails and genitalia. If the puppies are nursed from a bottle and not a stomach tube, this may not happen. It goes on for the first three weeks. After three weeks the puppies should be put together for socialization and to establish normal behavior patterns.

The temperature in the incubator is of critical importance, since it provides the warmth that would have been provided by the mother. Place a thermometer in the incubator to monitor the surface temperature. Keep the incubator at 85° to 90°F for the first week. During the second week, reduce it to 80°F or 85°F. Thereafter, gradually decrease the temperature to 75°F by the end of the fourth week.

The temperature in the incubator will be the same as the room temperature if there are no drafts and you insulate the floor beneath the incubator with heavy padding. If the incubator and room temperature cannot be maintained with your existing heating system, provide additional heat using infrared heat lights or electric heaters. Avoid focusing heat directly on the puppies.

Electric heating pads can be used as a heat source, but are not as safe as heating the room. Puppies can become severely dehydrated or burned by continuous exposure to heating pads. If used, they should be heavily padded and should cover only one side of the box and one half the floor. This allows the puppies to escape from the heat if they become too hot. Cover the pad with a waterproof material such as plastic or rubber.

On the floor of the incubator place a baby diaper that can be changed when it gets wet or soiled. This also provides a way to easily check the appearance of each puppy's stool, which is an excellent indicator of overfeeding.

Maintain the humidity of the room at about 55 percent to prevent dry skin and dehydration.

GENERAL CARE

Everyone who handles the puppies should wash their hands before touching them— especially if they have handled other dogs. Many diseases, including distemper, can be transmitted to puppies by someone who has recently handled an infectious dog. All feeding equipment should be thoroughly cleaned and boiled. Visitors should not be allowed in the nursery.

Keep the puppies clean with a damp cloth. Be sure to cleanse the anal area and the skin on the abdomen. You can rub a little baby oil on these areas and on the coat to prevent dry skin. Change the bedding often to prevent urine scalds. If they do appear, a light application of zinc oxide ointment will help. If infected, apply a topical antibiotic ointment such as neomycin or triple antibiotic.

For the first three weeks, gently swab the puppy's anal and genital areas after each feeding to stimulate elimination. (This is something the mother would do.) A wad of cotton or tissue soaked in warm water works well. Then dry the puppy.

HAND FEEDING

Commercial milk replacers that mirror the composition of bitch's milk are the best formulas for infant puppies. These milk replacers are available through veterinarians and many pet supply stores. They have all but replaced cow's milk, goat's milk and foster mothers.

Bitch's milk is unique in that it is high in protein and fat, low in milk sugar (lactose) and dense in calories. Cow's milk is not a suitable substitute for bitch's milk because it contains only half the number of calories per ounce and derives more calories from lactose than from protein and fat. Goat's milk, traditionally used as an animal milk substitute, does contain more calories per ounce than cow's milk, but is not ideal for puppies because it too is high in lactose and low in protein and fat. Newborn puppies do not have the intestinal enzymes to metabolize high concentrations of lactose, and feeding cow's or goat's milk often leads to diarrhea.

Artificial bitch's milk can be purchased as a premixed liquid or a powder. Powdered products are reconstituted by adding water. Refrigerate the unused formula, but don't freeze. Follow the directions of the manufacturer.

In the past, cataracts related to nutritional problems were reported in puppies fed home formulas and commercial milk replacers. These cataracts were found to have been caused by a deficiency of the amino acids phenylalanine and arginine. Commercial formulas have been fortified to eliminate this problem.

While artificial bitch's milk is the best substitute for natural milk, the following home formula can be used as a *temporary expedient* until a commercial product can be purchased:

8 ounces homogenized whole milk
3 egg yolks
1 tablespoon corn oil
1 drop liquid pediatric vitamins
Mix well and refrigerate the unused portions

This formula provides 36 to 38 calories per ounce, or 1 to 1.25 calories per milliliter of formula. This is the same caloric density as commercial bitch's milk. Feed as you would a commercial milk replacer, described in the sections that follow.

CALCULATING HOW MUCH FORMULA

Accurate record keeping is important at all times, but is absolutely essential when raising puppies by hand. Weigh them at birth on a scale that measures grams or ounces. Then weigh each puppy every eight hours for four days, daily for the next two weeks, and then every three days until they reach one month of age.

The best way to determine how much formula each puppy needs is to weigh the puppy and use a table of caloric requirements. During the first three weeks of life, puppies should receive 60 to 70 calories per pound of body weight per day. All commercial milk replacer formulas provide 1 to 1.3 calories (kcals) per milliliter (mL). Since a liter is 1,000 mL, a milk replacer with a labeled caloric value of 1,000 kcals per liter provides 1 kcal per mL. One with a labeled caloric value of 1,300 kcals per liter provides 1.3 kcals per mL. Daily requirements according to weight and age are given in the accompanying table. Divide the total daily requirement by the number of feedings per day to get the amount to give per feeding. This calculation must be made each day after the morning weighing.

	Total Daily Calorie Requirements for New Puppies	
Age in Weeks	Calories or mL Per Pound Weight Per Day (using milk replacer that provides 1 kcal per mL)	Feedings
1	60	6
2	70	4
3	80	4
4	90	3

Here's an example of how to use the table: A one-week old puppy weighs half a pound at the morning weighing. He will require 30 calories that day (that is, one half of 60 calories per pound). He requires six feedings a day, so divide that

30 calories by six and find that he needs five mL per feeding. If, as expected, the puppy's weight doubles in 10 days, he will weigh about one pound and will require 70 mL per day, or 18 mL at each of four feedings.

Note that this chart assumes the caloric density of the milk replacer is 1 kcal per mL. If the milk replacer you use has a different density, divide the number in the middle column (i.e., 60, 70, 80, or 90) by that density to determine the number of mL needed per pound weight per day. For example, if your milk replacer is 1.3 kcals per mL, divide the number in the middle column by 1.3. Then proceed as above.

If the puppy is unable to take in the required number of milliliters per feeding, reduce the volume and increase the number of feedings to meet the daily requirements.

As long as the pup does not cry excessively, feels firm, gains weight and has a light brown stool several times a day, you can be almost certain the diet is meeting his nutritional needs. Continue to increase the amount you are feeding according to the table. At three to four weeks, begin to introduce semi-solid food (see *Weaning*, page 458).

HOW TO GIVE FORMULA

Puppies can be fed using a baby nursing bottle or stomach tube. An eyedropper can be used in an emergency. Use it as described for the baby bottle. *Always be sure to feed formula at room temperature.*

Keep in mind that all hand-fed puppies need to have their anal and genital areas massaged with a wad of cotton soaked in warm water after each feeding to prevent constipation and stimulate the elimination reflexes.

The Baby Bottle

Using a bottle has the advantage of satisfying the suckling urge, but it requires a puppy that is strong enough to suck. When using a small baby bottle or a commercial puppy nurser with a soft nipple, you may need to enlarge the hole in the nipple so that the milk drips out slowly when the bottle is turned over. Otherwise, the puppy may tire after a few minutes and stop nursing. However, if the hole is too large, the milk will run out too fast and make the puppy choke.

The correct position for bottle feeding is to *place the puppy in an upright position as if standing on a flat surface, holding him under the stomach and chest.* Do not cradle him like a human baby, because the formula will run into his windpipe. Open the puppy's mouth with the tip of your finger, insert the nipple and hold the bottle at a 45-degree angle to prevent the puppy from swallowing air. Keep a slight pull on the bottle to encourage vigorous sucking.

The feeding usually takes five minutes or longer. Afterward, burp the puppy by resting him on your shoulder and gently rubbing or patting the back. Then swab the anal and genital areas with a piece of cotton soaked in warm water to stimulate voiding and defecation.

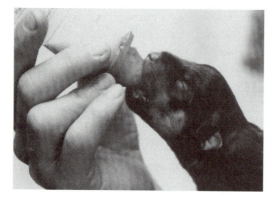

This is the correct position for bottle feeding. Do not cradle the pup on his back like a human baby.

Tube Feeding

The advantages of tube feeding are that it takes about two minutes to complete each feeding, and little air is swallowed. Tube feeding also ensures that a proper amount of formula is administered to each puppy. And *tube feeding is the only satisfactory way to feed immature or sick puppies that are too weak to nurse*. Puppies fed by tube must be kept in separate incubator compartments to avoid the suckling damage caused by littermates.

Tube feeding is not difficult and can be mastered in a few minutes. It requires a soft rubber catheter tube size 5 to 10 French, depending on the size of the puppy. A puppy weighing less than 10 ounces requires a size 5. You'll also need a 10- or 20-mL plastic or glass syringe. These items can be bought at a drug store.

A puppy's stomach is even with his last rib. Measure the tube from the mouth to the last rib and mark the tube with a piece of tape. Draw the formula into the syringe, taking care to expel all air, and warm it to body temperature by immersing the syringe in hot water.

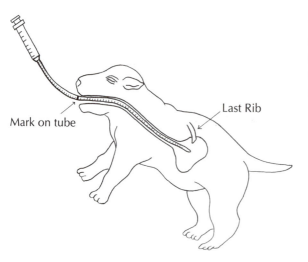

Mark on tube

Last Rib

Tube feeding is the only satisfactory way to give formula to a puppy too weak to nurse. (Rose Floyd)

Arouse the puppy and place him on his chest in a *horizontal* position. Moisten the tip of the tube with formula and allow the puppy to suckle it briefly. Then pass the tube slowly over the puppy's tongue and into the throat. With steady pressure the puppy will swallow the tube. Pass it to the level of the mark you made on the tube with tape.

Slowly inject a small amount of water (1 to 2 mL) into the tube. If the puppy coughs or gasps, the tip of the tube is in the lungs. This is not as serious a problem as if formula were injected, because water is more easily absorbed. Withdraw and reposition the tube.

When the tube is in the correct position, attach the syringe to the tube and *slowly* inject the formula into the puppy's stomach over a two-minute period. All feedings, particularly the first feeding, should be injected gradually so as not to distend the stomach. If the formula is injected too rapidly, it will be regurgitated and may cause aspiration pneumonia. This is most likely to happen during the first tube feeding.

When all the formula has been injected, remove the tube and raise the puppy into a vertical position and allow a burp. Swab the anal and genital areas with a piece of cotton soaked in warm water after each feeding to stimulate voiding and defecation.

At about 14 days of age, the windpipe of many puppies becomes large enough to easily accommodate the feeding tube. Change to a larger tube (size 8 or 10 French), or by now the puppy may be strong enough to suckle from a bottle.

COMMON FEEDING PROBLEMS

The two common feeding problems are overfeeding and underfeeding. Overfeeding causes diarrhea. An underfed pup will fail to gain weight. Both of these can be avoided by monitoring the weight of the puppy and computing the correct amount of formula to give at each feeding. Steady weight gain and a normal stool (firm and yellow to light brown) are good indications that you are feeding the right amount.

Overfeeding

Experience has shown that breeders are more likely to overfeed than underfeed a puppy. The best way to tell whether a puppy is being overfed is to monitor his stools. If the puppy is fed four times a day, you can expect four to five stools, or about one light brown stool after each feeding.

The first sign of overfeeding is a loose stool. A loose yellow stool indicates a mild degree of overfeeding. Reduce the strength of the formula by diluting it one-third with water. As the stools become firm, gradually restore the formula to its full strength.

With *moderate* overfeeding, there is more rapid movement of food through the intestinal tract, indicated by a greenish stool. The green color is due to unabsorbed bile. Dilute the strength of the formula by one-half. Mix one part water or Pedialyte to one part formula. Gradually return the formula to full strength as the stools become yellow and firm.

Unchecked overfeeding leads to very rapid transit and depletion of digestive enzymes and electrolytes. This causes a grayish diarrhea. Eventually, when there is little or no digestion of formula due to rapid transit, the stool looks like curdled milk. At this point the puppy is getting no nutrition and is rapidly dehydrating. This puppy will need to be rehydrated by giving a balanced electrolyte solution subcutaneously or hourly by stomach tube.

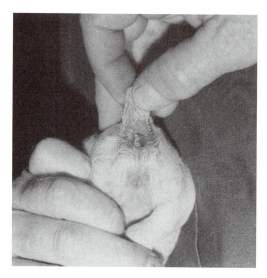

The wet, inflamed anal area of a puppy with diarrhea due to overfeeding.

Any diarrhea that does not respond to diluting the formula—or where the stools are gray or white—is serious and may be caused by neonatal infection. Call your veterinarian without delay. This requires professional attention.

Underfeeding

Puppies that are being underfed cry continuously, appear listless and apathetic, attempt to suckle littermates, gain little or no weight from one feeding to the next and begin to chill. Puppies dehydrate quickly when they're not getting enough formula. Review your feeding protocol. Check the temperature of the incubator.

Puppy Diseases

NEONATAL ISOERYTHROLYSIS

This is a rare but often fatal hemolytic anemia of the newborn that begins shortly after puppies ingest *colostrum* containing antibodies that destroy their red blood cells. These antibodies are manufactured by the dam when fetal cells of a different blood type cross the placenta and sensitize her immune system. The antibodies produced are transmitted to the puppies during the first few hours of nursing.

Symptoms of varying severity appear within hours or days. Severely affected puppies become weak, jaundiced and pass dark red urine containing hemoglobin. Death can occur in 24 hours.

Treatment: As soon as you suspect hemolytic anemia, stop all nursing and notify your veterinarian. The puppies may require blood transfusions from a compatible donor to restore their red cells. Puppies from subsequent litters should not be allowed to receive colostrum from the dam.

UMBILICAL (NAVEL) INFECTION

A common predisposing factor in navel infection is severing the umbilical cord too close to the abdominal wall. This leaves no stump to wither up and separate cleanly. Other possible causes are a dam with dental disease who transmits bacteria when she severs the umbilical cord, and an unclean whelping box contaminated by urine and stools. An infected navel looks red and swollen and may drain pus or form an abscess.

There is a direct communication between the umbilical cord and the liver, which makes even a low-grade umbilical infection potentially dangerous. Untreated, puppy septicemia is likely.

Treatment: At the first indication of navel infection, seek veterinary attention for antibiotic treatment. If one puppy has an umbilical infection, it may also be present in other puppies in the litter.

Iodine applied to the navel stump at birth as a preventive measure reduces the likelihood of umbilical infection.

PUPPY SEPTICEMIA

Bloodborne infections in young puppies are caused by bacteria that gain entrance via the respiratory and gastrointestinal tracts. They occur in puppies 5 to 12 weeks of age. At this age maternal antibodies are in decline and immunity acquired through vaccinations is not as strong as it will be later. This creates a window of vulnerability.

Very important contributing factors include overcrowding, chilling, poor nutrition, unsanitary whelping quarters, a heavy burden of intestinal parasites and coexistent viral infections. In a healthy environment, bacterial exposure usually produces only a mild, self-limiting illness. But when environmental stresses are added, the death rate is high.

Signs of respiratory involvement include fever, cough, nasal discharge and rapid, noisy breathing. When the gastrointestinal tract is involved, signs include loss of appetite, vomiting, diarrhea, weakness, dehydration and weight loss.

Treatment: Notify your veterinarian if a puppy shows any of the signs just described. Shock and dehydration are treated with antibiotics and intravenous fluids. Respiratory and GI tract infections are treated as described for *Pneumonia* (Chapter 10) and *Acute Infectious Enteritis* (Chapter 9).

HERPESVIRUS OF PUPPIES

Canine herpesvirus causes a fatal illness in puppies one to two weeks of age. It usually does not causes illness in puppies older than three weeks of age. The reason is that the body temperature of puppies younger than 3 weeeks of age is below 98°F—temperatures at which the virus replicates.

Herpesvirus is acquired by the mother during breeding and takes up residence in her vagina. Puppies acquire the virus while in utero, during passage through the birth canal or by direct contact with their dams and infected littermates.

This is an insidious disease. The dam is healthy and the puppies nurse in a normal manner until shortly before death. The illness begins with abrupt cessation of nursing, followed by abdominal distention, chilling, lack of coordination and a yellow-green diarrhea. Puppies are in agony and cry out pitifully. Death usually occurs in 24 hours.

Treatment: There is no specific treatment, but survival is possible. Unaffected littermates should be placed in a homemade incubator in a room with an ambient temperature of 100°F (see *The Incubator*, page 446). Since the virus does not multiply well at temperatures above 98°F, this may prevent it from reproducing and causing infection.

Puppies that recover may develop irreversible neurologic symptoms, including lack of coordination, dizziness and blindness. There is no available vaccine. Infected dams develop immunity and subsequent litters are rarely affected.

FLAT (SWIMMER) PUPPIES

Puppies begin to stand at 14 days and have a steady gait by three weeks of age. If this does not happen, the puppy may be a swimmer. This disease is caused by a weakness of the adductor muscles that pull the legs together. The hind legs usually are more severely affected.

Swimmers move by making swimming motions. They resemble turtles with their legs sticking out to the sides, and are flat-chested from lying on their stomachs.

The disease is more likely to occur in overweight and heavy-boned puppies. It may have a congenital basis. One theory proposes that puppies are infected by a viral or fungal disease in utero that results in a muscular dystrophy of the adductor muscles.

Treatment: Slippery floors aggravate the problem. Keep swimmers on indoor-outdoor carpeting or some other nonslippery surface that provides good traction.

Assist a swimmer puppy to stand and walk several times a day. Encourage him to sleep on his side, rather than splayed flat out. A hobble made from tape, placed from elbow to elbow or hock to hock, forces the pup to sleep on his side. It also keeps the legs beneath him when he stands.

In most cases the condition is self-correcting as the adductor muscles develop and strengthen.

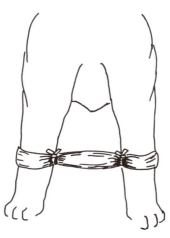

Hobbling helps a swimmer keep his feet beneath him. (Rose Floyd)

PYLORIC STENOSIS

Congenital pyloric stenosis is caused by a thickening of the ring of muscle at the outlet of the stomach, resulting in a partial or complete obstruction of the gastric outlet. The cause is unknown. An increased incidence occurs in *brachycephalic* breeds such as Boxers and Boston Terriers.

Symptoms begin at weaning time or shortly thereafter, when pups begin to eat solid food. The characteristic sign of pyloric stenosis is vomiting partially digested food several hours after eating. Typically, the vomitus does not contain green bile. The vomited meal may be ingested, only to be vomited again later.

The diagnosis is made by an upper gastrointestinal X-ray examination. The presence of barium in the stomach 12 to 24 hours after ingestion indicates an obstructed stomach. *Gastroscopy* may be recommended.

Treatment: Pyloric stenosis is treated effectively with an operation that divides the enlarged muscular ring between the stomach and the duodenum. Some cases recover without surgery, but dietary management is essential. The choice of treatment depends on a number of factors that must be determined by your veterinarian, but most cases require surgery.

An acquired form of pyloric stenosis, called *hypertrophic gastropathy*, occurs in middle-aged dogs (see Chapter 9, *Chronic Gastritis*).

SKIN INFECTIONS OF THE NEWBORN

Scabs, blisters and purulent crusts can develop on the skin of newborn puppies 4 to 10 days of age. These sores sometimes contain pus. They usually appear on the abdomen and are caused by poor sanitation in the whelping box.

Treatment: Keep the nest clean of food, stools and urine. Cleanse scabs with a dilute solution (1:10) of hydrogen peroxide or wash with a dilute antiseptic solution such as Betadine or chlorhexidine (see *Common Drugs for Home Veterinary Use* in Chapter 20). Then apply an antibiotic ointment such as triple antibiotic or neomycin.

CLEFT PALATE

Cleft palate is a birth defect caused by incomplete fusion of the two sides of the palate. This results in a passageway between the oral and nasal cavities that enables food and liquids to pass between them. Newborn puppies have a discharge from both nostrils and may find it impossible to create enough suction to nurse. Survival then depends on tube feeding.

Cleft palate occurs sporadically in all breeds, but is most common in Bulldogs, Boston Terriers, Beagles, Miniature Schnauzers, Pekingese and Cocker Spaniels. In these breeds the defect has a hereditary basis. Affected dogs should not be used for breeding.

Harelip is the result of incomplete development of the upper lip. It can occur independently or along with cleft palate. The problem is mainly cosmetic.

Cleft palate and harelip can be corrected by plastic surgery. This usually is done at three months of age.

HYPOGLYCEMIA (LOW BLOOD SUGAR)

Hypoglycemia is a syndrome that occurs primarily in toy breeds between 6 and 12 weeks of age. A hypoglycemic attack is often precipitated by stress.

The typical signs are listlessness, depression, staggering gait, muscular weakness and tremors—especially of the face. Puppies with a severe drop in blood sugar develop seizures or become stuperous and go into a coma. Death can follow. The sequence is symptoms just described is not always seen. For example, some puppies exhibit only weakness or a wobbly gait. Occasionally a puppy that seemed just fine is found in coma.

Episodes of hypoglycemia often occur without warning—for example, when a puppy is stressed by shipping. Other common causes of acute hypoglycemia are missing a meal, chilling, becoming exhausted from too much play or having an upset stomach. These events place an added strain on the energy reserves of the liver.

Hypoglycemia can occur in adult hunting dogs as a consequence of sustained exercise and depletion of liver glycogen. It is important to feed these dogs before hunting and to increase the protein content of their diets. Hypoglycemia in diabetic dogs is caused by *insulin overdose* (see Chapter 9, *Diabetes Mellitus*). Unexplained hypoglycemia that occurs in older dogs is likely to be caused by an insulin-secreting tumor of the pancreas.

Prolonged or repeated hypoglycemic attacks in Toy breed puppies can cause brain damage. Puppies with frequent attacks should undergo veterinary testing to rule out an underlying problem such as liver shunt, infection, or an enzyme or hormone deficiency.

Treatment: The treatment of an acute attack is directed toward restoring the blood sugar. Begin immediately. If the puppy is awake and able to swallow, give corn syrup or sugar water by syringe (see Chapter 20, *How to Give Medications*), or rub corn syrup or glucose paste on the gums. You should see improvement in 30 minutes. If not, call your veterinarian.

If the pup is unconscious, do not give an oral solution because it will be inhaled. Rub corn syrup or glucose paste on the gums and proceed at once to your veterinarian. This puppy will require an intravenous dextrose solution and may need to be treated for brain swelling.

Oral glucose paste is sold at pharmacies. If you know your dog is subject to hypoglycemic attacks, keep this product on hand.

Prevention: Susceptible puppies should be fed at least four times a day. It is important to feed a high-carbohydrate, high-protein, high-fat diet. *It is essential that the diet be high quality.* Your veterinarian can recommend an appropriate premium food.

Food supplements and table scraps should not exceed 5 to 10 percent of the total daily ration. Owners of toy puppies should take precautions to see that they do not become excessively tired or chilled. Many (but not all) puppies outgrow this problem.

HERNIA

A hernia is a protrusion of fat and/or bowel through an opening in the abdominal wall that would normally close during development. The protrusion produces a bulge. The two common sites for hernia are the groin and navel. A hernia in the groin is called an inguinal hernia, and one in the navel area is called an umbilical hernia.

If the bulge can be pushed back into the abdomen, the hernia is *reducible*. If not, it is *incarcerated*. An incarcerated hernia becomes *strangulated* when the blood supply to the contents of the hernia sac is pinched off. An incarcerated hernia often becomes strangulated over time. Any hard or painful swelling at the navel or in the groin could be an incarcerated hernia and will require immediate veterinary attention.

Hernias have a hereditary basis, because there is a genetic predisposition for delayed closure of the abdominal ring. Occasionally, a navel hernia may develop when the umbilical cord is cut too close to the abdominal wall.

Inguinal hernias are more common in female dogs. A bulge in the groin may not be seen until after the bitch has been bred or becomes very old, in which case a pregnant or diseased uterus may be incarcerated in the hernia. These hernias should be repaired. Small inguinal hernias in male puppies can be watched closely, as many will close spontaneously. If they do not, ask to have them repaired.

Umbilical hernias occur frequently in puppies at about two weeks of age. They usually get smaller and disappear by six months of age. Binding the abdominal wall with straps does not increase the chance of closure.

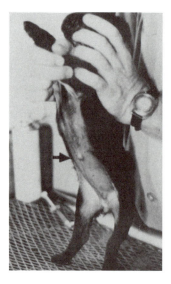

Small umbilical hernias usually disappear by six months of age.

If you can push a finger through the umbilical ring, the hernia should be repaired. The operation is not difficult and the pup can go home the same day. In females, repair of an umbilical hernia can often be delayed until the time of spaying.

Weaning

The right time to wean depends upon several factors, including the size of the litter, the condition of the dam, the quantity of mother's milk and the inclinations of the breeder. If a dam with a small litter is left to her own devices, she might continue to nurse her puppies for 10 weeks or longer.

Weaning should be a gradual process. For larger breeds, begin at about three weeks of age. For Toy breeds, begin at about four weeks. Weaning should not be completed before six to eight weeks of age. Early weaning and separation from the mother and littermates may result in adjustment problems later in life.

To stimulate the pups' appetites for solid food, remove the dam two hours before each feeding. After the meal, let her return to nurse. She should remain with the litter at night.

Choose a commercial food formulated to meet the needs of growing puppies. A number of good products are available. Read the label to be sure the product is recommended for puppies three to four weeks of age and older. Many people prefer to use dry kibble, but canned products are equally satisfactory. Vitamin-mineral supplements are not necessary or desirable when your are feeding a nutritionally balanced puppy growth food.

HOW TO FEED

To feed *dry food*, mix one part kibble to three parts water to make a gruel. Warm the food to room temperature and feed in a low-rimmed saucer or pie pan. Start by dipping your fingers into the mixture and letting the puppies lick it off. Offer this gruel three or four times a day.

When the puppies are eating the gruel well, *gradually* reduce the water content over a few weeks until they are eating the mixture dry. This usually occurs by five to seven weeks of age.

At this time there is less demand on the dam's milk supply. Decrease her food intake if you have not already begun to do so. This initiates the process of drying up her milk.

Puppies who eat too much gruel are apt to get diarrhea. Temporarily reduce the number of feedings and continue with nursing.

To feed *canned food*, begin by mixing two parts canned food with one part water. When the puppies are eating this mixture well, reduce the water content and follow the same general procedures described for feeding dry food.

Puppies need a lot of water and dehydrate quickly if they don't get enough fluids. Remember that before weaning, the pups' water requirements were being supplied entirely by the dam's milk. Accordingly, as milk feedings are reduced, *it is vital to keep a bowl of clean fresh water available at all times*.

To promote socialization and avoid behavior problems, feed puppies together until they are at least six weeks old. Allow the puppies to eat as much as they want in 20 minutes and then pick up the dish. Puppies should be fed at least three times a day from weaning to six months of age.

If it becomes necessary to dry up the dam's milk, withhold all food and water for 24 hours. The next day, feed her one-quarter of the normal amount. The third day feed one-half the normal amount, and the fourth day feed three-quarters of the normal amount. Thereafter, feed an adult maintenance food as described in Chapter 9, *Feeding and Nutrition*.

Feeding Growing Puppies

You can determine the daily caloric requirements for growing puppies by consulting the table below. Compare the daily caloric needs with the number of calories per ounce of commercial food (this information is on the product label) to determine the number of ounces of that food to give each puppy per day. Divide by the number of feedings (three or four) to determine how many ounces to feed at each meal.

Bear in mind, however, that these requirements are approximations based on the average dog. Your dog's needs will vary according to his activity level and temperament. The amount fed should be adjusted to maintain optimal weight and condition.

Body Weight		Daily kcals Required	
Kilograms	Pounds	Weaning to 3 months	3 to 6 months
1	2.2	268	214
3	6.6	649	520
5	11.0	915	732
7	15.4	1,167	934
9	19.8	1,394	1,115
11	24.3	1,670	1,331
13	28.7	1,929	1,543
15	33.1	2,179	1,743
17	37.5	2,415	1,932
19	41.9	2,640	2,112
21	46.3	2,856	2,285
23	50.7	3,062	2,450
25	55.1		2,618
27	59.5		2,785
29	63.8		2,945
33	72.8		3,250
37	81.6		3,551

Daily Caloric Requirements to Maintain Average Weight Gain in Young Puppies

(Modified from *Veterinary Pediatrics*, 2nd Edition, Johnny D. Hoskins, 1995.)

The Importance of Early Socialization

The first 12 weeks of life are extremely important and determine, to a great extent, a puppy's personality and sociability. Recent studies show that puppies go through a series of developmental stages. The successful negotiation of each stage is essential to avoiding future problems such as timidity, fear-biting, phobias and dominance aggression.

Separating puppies from their mothers and littermates before six weeks of age has been found to have adverse effects on a puppy's weight and physical condition. During the period between three and eight weeks of age, puppies are receptive to and greatly influenced by interactions with their dams, littermates and other dogs on the premises. These interactions enable the puppy to develop self-awareness and adopt appropriate dog behavior.

Successful interactions are those that build confidence, are nonstressful and do not frighten the puppy. The ability to get along with dogs later in life is due, in part, to a smooth transition through this three-to-eight-week stage. Thus, puppies should remain with their dams and littermates until they are eight to 10 weeks of age and are fully weaned and eating puppy food.

Between five and seven weeks of age, puppies become receptive to forming relationships with people. During this stage puppies learn the dominant role of human beings and also learn that people are nonthreatening and provide food, pleasure and rewards.

At eight to nine weeks, puppies develop strong preferences for urinating and defecating on certain types of surfaces—carpets, floors, grass, dirt and so on. House training can begin at this age.

At 10 to 12 weeks and again at 16 to 20 weeks, puppies are curious and do well exploring novel environments. This is a good time to begin car rides, obedience classes and trips to the park.

In summary, it is critical that breeders expose puppies to other dogs starting at three weeks of age. Handling puppies younger than five weeks of age is not detrimental, as long as it is not extremely stressful and does not induce fear. After five weeks, puppies should be picked up, petted and handled in a pleasurable manner with increasing frequency.

Acquiring a New Puppy

SELECTING A BREED

If you are planning to show and breed your puppy when he or she grows up, read *Breeding Purebred Dogs* in Chapter 15. If you want a pet or family companion, give some thought to the type of dog that best suits your lifestyle. Dogs come in all sizes, shapes and mixtures, and all are equally loveable. Some dogs require more exercise, more grooming or more training. Some are too large for apartment living or too small for ranch life. Some breeds are known for their outgoing nature and love of children. Others have strong guarding and territorial instincts. These are just some of the attributes that make one breed of dog a better choice for a specific owner than another. Mixed breeds generally have the characteristics of the breeds that are predominant in the mixture.

A large selection of books about specific breeds is available at most public libraries. *The Complete Dog Book* (an official publication of the American Kennel

Club) is an excellent reference and contains facts and information on all breeds of dog. It is available in bookstores, from the publisher Howell Book House, or from the AKC.

A huge amount of information on dogs, breeds and breed clubs, is available through the Internet. Many breeders and breed clubs maintain Web pages and provide photographs and information on their breed and their breeding programs. Keep in mind that information on the Internet is not regulated. Use it as a good reference, but confirm it from other sources.

SELECTING A BREEDER

When you know what breed you want, the next step is finding a reputable breeder. The AKC will provide, on request, the names and addresses of the current secretaries of approximately 500 member dog clubs. This information is also available on the AKC's Website (see Appendix C). You can call or write the secretary of the club you are interested in to obtain written information and a list of breeders who are members of the club. The AKC also operates a hotline that puts people in contact with breeders in their local areas. The number is (900) 407-PUPS.

After you locate several breeders who have the breed of puppy you are looking for, write or call each one and explain whether you are looking for a family companion and pet, if you plan to show and/or breed, and if you prefer a male or a female. A sincere inquiry, including information about yourself, is much more likely to elicit the type of response you are looking for than a hastily scribbled note. Be prepared for the breeder to ask questions about you and your family. A responsible breeder is concerned about the future welfare of puppies he or she places.

It is a good policy to insist on buying the puppy pending a veterinary examination (at your expense), with a 72-hour guarantee to return the puppy if a health problem is found. Conscientious breeders who are proud of their puppies and willing to stand behind them will not object to this request.

If you are interested in an older puppy or an adult dog, you may want to consider adopting a dog from the local animal shelter. Each year, animal shelters in the United States receive millions of wonderful mixed-breed and purebred dogs with one thing in common: They all need a good home.

AKC REGISTRATION

If your puppy is eligible for registration with the AKC, you should receive a registration application from the breeder, with the breeder's part already filled in. This is called the *blue slip*. Complete your part of the blue slip and send it to the AKC with the required fee.

The AKC will send you a registration certificate, which is white with an orange or purple border. An orange border means that the dog has a *Limited Registration*. With a Limited Registration, the dog's offspring, if any, are not eligible for registration with the AKC. The Limited Registration designation is made by the puppy's breeder. A pet quality puppy, for example, may be given a Limited Registration to prevent indiscriminate breeding and to protect the reputation of the kennel. The breeder can always change the designation to a *full registration* (purple border) at a later date if the puppy proves to be of breeding quality.

Be sure to obtain a completed blue slip at the time of purchase. *Do not* accept a promise that the necessary paperwork will be sent along later. It may be that the litter has not been (or cannot be) registered. If the breeder is not able to produce the dog's registration papers, consider going elsewhere for a puppy.

CHOOSING A HEALTHY PUPPY

The best time to acquire a puppy is at 8 to 12 weeks of age. At this age a puppy should be well socialized, will have received the first series of immunizations and should be weaned and eating solid food. The breeder can usually make a good guess about whether a puppy is of show or breeding quality. But keep in mind that picking a future champion at eight weeks of age is a problem, even for breeders with considerable experience.

Most puppies 8 to 12 weeks old tolerate the stresses of being shipped by air. For toy and small breeds it is best to rely on the experience of the breeder when considering this option.

If possible, visit the kennel and make your own selection. Be prepared when, on the appointed day, you find yourself standing before a litter of bouncing puppies and find that all appear to be equally lovable. Most puppies look healthy at first glance, but a closer inspection may make some puppies more desirable than others. Take your time and go over each puppy from head to tail before making the final decision.

Begin by examining the head. The nose should be cool and moist. Nasal discharge or frequent sneezing is a sign of poor health. Short-nosed breeds such as Pugs and Pekingese often have nostrils that collapse when the dog breathes in. This is undesirable.

Check the puppy for a correct bite. The correct bite for most breeds is a *scissors bite*, in which the upper incisors just slightly overlap the lower ones. An *even bite*, in which the incisors meet edge to edge, is equally acceptable. If the scissors bite is exaggerated so that the head of a match can be inserted between the upper and lower incisors, the bite is *overshot* and probably will not correct itself spontaneously. In the *undershot* bite the lower incisors overlap the uppers. This is characteristic and even required in some short-nosed breeds, such as the Bulldog. If you are uncertain about the required bite, check the breed standard, which can be found in *The Complete Dog Book* mentioned in *Selecting a Breed*.

The gums should be pink and healthy looking. Pale gums suggest anemia, possibly caused by intestinal parasites.

Feel for a soft spot on the dome of the skull. If present, the *fontanel* is open. This is not desirable. In toy breeds an open fontanel can be associated with *hydrocephalus*.

The eyes should be clear and bright. If you see tear stains on the muzzle, look for eyelids that roll in or out, extra eyelashes or conjunctivitis. The pupils should be dark and have no visible lines or white spots that may indicate congenital cataracts or retained fetal membranes. The haw (third eyelid) may be visible. This should not be taken as a sign of disease unless it is swollen and inflamed.

The ears should stand correctly for the breed. The tips should be healthy and well furred. Crusty tips with bare spots suggest a skin disease such as sarcoptic mange. The ear canals should be clean and sweet-smelling. A buildup of wax with a rancid odor may be caused by ear mites. Head-shaking and tenderness about the ears indicate an ear canal infection.

Feel the chest with the palm of your hand to see if the heart seems especially vibrant. This could be a clue to a congenital heart defect. The puppy should breathe in and out without effort. A flat chest, especially when accompanied by trouble inhaling, indicates an airway obstruction. It is seen most commonly in short-nosed breeds such as Pugs, Boston Terriers and Pekingese.

The skin of the abdomen should be clean and healthy looking. A bulge at the navel is caused by an umbilical hernia. This can correct itself spontaneously, but may require surgical repair.

The skin and hair around the anus should be clean and healthy looking. Skin irritation, redness, hair loss or adherent stool suggests the possibility of worms, chronic diarrhea or malabsorption.

A healthy coat is bright and shiny and has the correct color and markings for the breed. Excess scratching and areas of inflamed skin suggest fleas, mites or other skin parasites. Moth-eaten areas of hair loss are typical of mange and ringworm.

In *male puppies*, push the foreskin of the penis back to confirm that it slides easily. Adhesions and strictures of the foreskin require veterinary attention. Both testicles should be present in the scrotum. If one or both are absent, they may come down before six months of age. However, if the puppy is intended for showing and breeding, don't take a chance, since a dog with one or two undescended testicles cannot be shown and should not be bred.

In *female puppies*, examine the vulva. Look for pasted down hair around the vulva or vaginal discharge, a sign of juvenile vaginitis. This is a common problem. It usually resolves spontaneously after the first heat cycle.

Next, examine the puppy for soundness and correct structure. The legs should be straight and well formed. Structural faults include legs that bow in or out, weak pasterns (the area between the wrist and the foot), flat feet with spread toes and feet that toe in at the rear. Two inherited bone and joint diseases that may be present in puppies younger than four months of age (but usually not discernable on puppy selection exams) are canine *hip dysplasia* and *patella luxation*. Certification of the puppy's sire and dam by the OFA or GDC is highly desirable in breeds with a high incidence of these diseases (see *Inherited Orthopedic Diseases*, Chapter 13).

The puppy's gait should be free and smooth. A limp or faltering gait may simply be the result of a sprain or a hurt pad, but hip dysplasia and patella luxation should be considered and ruled out.

CONSIDERING DISPOSITION

Young puppies should be alert, playful and full of vitality. Personalities vary with breed type, but a sweet disposition is essential to all. An unfriendly puppy certainly has no place as a family companion, especially with children. The unfriendly puppy may struggle and bite to get loose, or growl when picked up or petted. This puppy will require considerable discipline and training.

The author with his daughter, Sarah, and her Great Pyrenees puppy, Angel.

A puppy that shrinks when spoken to or runs away and hides is shy. The puppy may possibly overcome this later, but taking a chance is hardly worthwhile. This puppy will not be easily socialized.

The ideal puppy for a family pet holds his tail high, follows you about, accepts petting, struggles when picked up but then relaxes and licks your hand.

As good health and good disposition so often go hand in hand, it is perhaps wise, in making the final selection, to pick the individual that appears to be really bursting with vitality and self-confidence.

After you have made your purchase, you will want and should receive future advice. Any guarantees concerning the puppy must be discussed and agreed upon *before* the check is signed. Be sure to ask for and receive the puppy's AKC blue slip, pedigree, health certificate, current diet sheet and immunization record.

Socializing Your New Puppy

During the first few months of life, a puppy acquires the personality traits that make up his adult character. These traits are established through interactions with other animals and people. Positive interactions lead to a well-adjusted puppy. A pup with little or no exposure to people and dogs during the first three months of life adjusts poorly as an adult—despite attempts to compensate for this at a later date. For more information, see *The Importance of Early Socialization*, page 460.

Socialize your puppy to the fullest extent possible. Take him with you in the car and go for walks where you will see other people and dogs. This allows the pup to get used to the noise and distractions of public life and meet and play with dogs that are gentle, friendly and well socialized.

If you have no plans to show or breed, it is a good idea to have the puppy spayed or neutered (see *Birth Control* in Chapter 15). Spaying and neutering has numerous health benefits and may make a pet less inclined to bite. The operations are usually done at five to six months of age, but can be done on puppies as early as eight weeks of age. Discuss this with your veterinarian.

Training Your Puppy

Start obedience training as soon as possible. The important exercises are *come*, *sit*, *stay* and *down*, and walking on the leash. It is much easier to establish a proper teacher-pupil relationship when a puppy is young and hasn't developed bad habits. Obedience classes will train you to train the puppy, so unless you already have dog training experience, it is important to attend classes. Classes also provide the opportunity for the puppy to socialize with other dogs. Puppies as young as eight weeks can be enrolled in an obedience class, as long as they are current on their vaccinations.

The two basic principals of obedience training are:

1. *Once you begin an exercise, see it through to the end.* If you allow a puppy to have his own way, he is very likely to interpret your leniency as a sign that he really doesn't need to do what he's told.

2. *Always reward a puppy with praise and petting when correct behavior is shown.* Dogs instinctively want to please. Approval builds self-confidence and reinforces the point of the exercise.

HOUSE TRAINING

The basic procedure for house training a puppy is similar to potty training a child, except that puppies learn more quickly. House training can be started as soon as the puppy comes home.

Puppies develop voluntary control over bladder and bowel functions beginning at three weeks of age. They acquire a strong preference for a surface on which to eliminate by eight to nine weeks of age, and they have an instinctive desire to keep their living area clean. You can take advantage of all these things. Confine an unsupervised puppy in a small area such as a utility room. Pups usually eliminate shortly after eating and when waking up from a nap, so choose these times, as well as the last thing at night and the first thing in the morning, to take the puppy outside—preferably to the same location. The surface can be gravel, dirt, grass or concrete. It is important to allow the puppy plenty of time to eliminate. Dogs need to sniff and smell to trigger the elimination urge. If a puppy doesn't go, many times it's because he wasn't given enough time. As soon as he does go, praise him lavishly.

If you work during the day, you can train the puppy to use newspapers. Confine as before and paper an area several feet square. Use several thicknesses. Remove the soiled papers on top and add new ones to the bottom. The middle layer will retain some odor and remind the pup of where to go. Later, when the puppy can control the urge to go for longer periods, you can develop a routine for going outside.

If the puppy makes mistakes in the house (and he will), you can startle him with a loud "no!" *but only if you catch him in the act*. Then pick the puppy up and take him outside. Otherwise, ignore the mistake. *Never rub a puppy's nose in the mess or punish him in any way for making a mistake*. As with toddlers, eliminating is normal. It is only a "mistake" because of the location. This concept takes time to sink in.

WALKING ON A LEASH

Your puppy should be taught to walk on a loose leash and have good manners. Start with a soft nylon or leather collar. Leave the collar on for short periods. When the puppy is no longer bothered by it, leave it on permanently. Attach a leash that can be dragged behind. Once this is accepted, pick up the leash and lead the puppy with occasional tugs interspersed with lots of pats and praise. Never leave a dog unsupervised with a leash on; the leash can get caught on something and injure the dog.

Train the puppy to walk on your left side, to move out smartly and stay abreast—neither lunging ahead nor lagging behind. As the exercise progresses, exert a little more force with each tug. If possible, complete the leash training exercise in an obedience class.

Choke chains should be avoided and never left in place as a permanent collar. A dog wearing a choke collar could get his paw caught between the collar and his neck and choke to death, or the collar could become snagged on a fence. Choke collars can also damage the throat. If a puppy is not responsive to a leather or nylon collar, there are other options available that may even be better than collars, such as halters or head collars (Gentle Leader and Promise Collar are two examples). Head collars, in particular, are more effective than choke collars and far more humane. Discuss these options with your veterinarian or an experienced obedience trainer.

COMING WHEN CALLED

Coming when called is basically an extension of leash training. Let your puppy out to the end of a 15- or 20-foot rope or check cord. Squat down, clap your hands and call his name. If he fails to move toward you, give a tug and shorten the lead. Don't fight the puppy on the lead. If he acts rebellious, stop the exercise. Eventually he will come to you all the way. Respond by giving lavish praise and a choice tidbit. Repeat the exercise but don't overdo it. Coming should be fun—not a burden. Six times a session, three or four sessions a week, is plenty. Once the puppy has mastered the exercise, continue without the lead.

Never call the puppy to come to you for reprimand. Dogs are smart, and your pup will quickly learn that coming when called results in something unpleasant.

Correcting Misbehavior

The best way to correct misbehavior is with the tone of your voice. Puppies are tuned in to the sounds made by their mothers, and instinctively interpret a sharp sound or loud "no!" as a warning to stop what they are doing.

Correction is effective *only when the puppy is caught in the act.* If a pup chews up a valuable item while you are out and is reprimanded when you come home several hours later, the pup sees no connection between the destructive act and the reprimand. Obviously, there is not point in scolding the puppy after the fact.

If you do catch your pup doing something wrong, show your displeasure with a loud "no!" This gains the pup's immediate attention while you substitute a chew toy for your shoe or direct his attention to a more constructive activity.

Remember that destructive activity is age-appropriate in puppies. That means unless there is a behavior problem such as separation anxiety, you can expect destructive behavior to improve as the puppy matures. It also means you must provide your puppy with appropriate toys that he is allowed to destroy.

A common mistake is to show anger (even though it may be justified). Anger equals loss of control, and usually does not teach the puppy about the cause of the anger. This creates insecurity in your pup and weakens the bond between you and your pet.

Correction should never involve physical punishment, such as hitting the puppy with an open hand or swatting him with a rolled-up newspaper. This makes a dog shy and distrustful. Fearful dogs avoid people, even their masters, and may bite when cornered.

One very effective way to deal with some kinds of misbehavior is to disregard it. Dogs often engage in annoying activity in order to get their owner's attention. They find, for example, that it is easy to attract attention by jumping up on people or running away with a new shoe. Any interaction, even scolding the dog or pushing him down, becomes part of the game. Ignore the dog, as difficult as this may be, even if it means getting up and going outside. This removes the dog's incentive to repeat the behavior.

INAPPROPRIATE CHEWING

Puppies chew to develop strong teeth and jaws. It is a good idea to provide high-impact rubber balls, Kongs or nylon chew toys as a substitute for chewing on shoes and furniture. Avoid *rawhide* toys and bones. Rawhide may be ingested and can do damage in the gastrointestinal tract.

If you catch the puppy in the act of chewing on the furniture, substitute a toy or a nylon bone. Make it clear that the toy, not the furniture, is for chewing. *If you do not catch the puppy in the act, ignore the behavior.* Various commercial spray-on products are available that leave an unpleasant scent to discourage chewing. These products work well when applied as directed.

EXCESSIVE BARKING

A puppy not accustomed to being left alone may demand to be let out of his enclosure and express this by barking, whining or howling. The barking may occur when the puppy is first put into the enclosure and continues throughout the entire period of confinement. If the barking is ignored, the puppy usually finds little reason to continue and accepts the routine. If he is let out, the barking is reinforced and the problem will take longer to correct.

Barking can also be an attention-getting device for dogs that are ignored unless they make noise. If the dog gets the attention he wants (even a reprimand, because negative attention is still attention), the behavior is reinforced. Going to the dog to quiet him down, feeding him, petting and praising him, giving him a toy or letting him into the house, are ways of unintentionally rewarding the misbehavior. Instead, reward your dog's good behavior. Give him lots of praise, play and attention when he is quiet and well behaved.

Barking in defense of territory is part of a dog's basic nature. Occasionally this can escalate to excessive levels. The dog barks at the slightest sound, or barks constantly for no apparent reason. Chaining up a dog encourages barking and is an open invitation to a bad disposition. It is far better to confine your dog in a fenced yard or a spacious enclosure that allows opportunity for exercise and play. Barking in the house may stop if the dog is confined to a room without windows where he can't see or hear what's going on outside, and thus does not feel the need to defend the house from "outside interlopers."

Chronic or neurotic barking may be a sign of boredom or lack of attention. Take your dog for daily trips to the park. Regular walks on a leash provide mental and physical stimulation and allow for social interaction: That is, the opportunity for you and the dog to patrol the dog's territory together.

Anti-bark collars are available that disrupt the barking sequence by emitting an electric impulse or an aversive odor, usually citronella oil. These devices are humane, and in most cases effective.

Humane bark collars emit an unpleasant odor when the dog barks.

There is also surgery in which part or all of the vocal cord apparatus is removed. This operation does not completely eliminate vocalization. The dog sounds hoarse, and some ability to bark often returns in time. In addition, de-barking operations can increase the risk of airway complications at a later date, including laryngeal *stenosis*.

Chronic disruptive barking should be investigated by a professional trainer to determine its cause. An effective treatment program is then based on the dog's motivation for barking, how disruptive the barking has become, and how urgently it must be stopped.

SEPARATION ANXIETY

Separation anxiety is a common behavior problem. Dogs are pack animals, so the stress of being left alone even for short periods can be overwhelming for some. These dogs chew up the sofa and urinate or defecate on the rug. They may also bark excessively, salivate and tear down curtains and blinds.

Behavioral treatment involves getting the dog used to being alone. Owners have to practice leaving home for progressively more minutes each day so the dog learns that his family will come back. The FDA has also approved an antidepressant called Clomicalm (clomipramine) to treat anxiety in dogs. When used along with behavior therapy, the drug has shown some success. It is given daily. Mild side effects include vomiting and diarrhea.

AGGRESSION

A puppy must learn to be gentle and friendly with people, particularly children. Puppies naturally mouth and bite littermates and other puppies. As a puppy grows older, he seems to realize that his bite can cause pain and usually develops a softer mouth. But playing roughly with a puppy (for example, encouraging him to growl or maul a gloved hand) can override his natural instinct to bite down softly. A young puppy playing with people may become overexcited and accidentally nip or scratch. This can be difficult to correct as the puppy grows older.

Children sometimes grab, pull, or otherwise frighten or hurt puppies, which can result in a child being bitten or knocked down. This type of interaction between children and puppies should be prevented. Children must be taught that a puppy is not a toy and should be treated with respect. They should also be taught not to bother a puppy when he is eating or sleeping.

A truly aggressive act by a puppy toward a person is serious. In an adult dog, it is downright dangerous. Threatening behavior includes growling, bristling, snapping, snarling, laying back the ears, standing stiff-legged and running toward a person in a menacing manner. Actual aggression includes biting, attacking and mauling. A threat should be taken as seriously as an actual bite, since a dog capable of a threat is probably capable of an attack.

Many people excuse aggressive behavior because they believe the dog was provoked or in some way justified (which may be true). Nonetheless, because of the potential consequences of dog attacks, any form of aggression should raise a red flag. More than 4 million Americans are bitten each year by dogs, nearly a quarter of these require medical attention and 20 Americans die each year from dog attacks. *Infants and toddlers are the most frequent victims, and the attacker is most often the family pet.*

Some people acquire dogs to guard their home and family. A well-trained guardian will bark at intruders without becoming a menace. However, dogs trained to bite usually attack the wrong person, most often a child. According to the Humane Society of the United States, of the nearly 300 people who have died in dog attacks in recent years, not one was a household intruder.

Do not attempt to discipline an aggressive dog through punishment or physical domination. You may actually provoke an attack. Isolate the dog and discuss the problem with your veterinarian or a professional dog trainer. The Humane Society advises that a dog involved in an unprovoked attack that results is serious injury should be humanely put down.

TUMORS AND CANCERS

A tumor is any sort of lump, bump, growth or swelling, such as an abscess. Tumors that are true growths are called *neoplasms*. Tumors can be divided into two broad categories: benign and malignant. *Benign tumors* grow slowly, don't invade or destroy neighboring tissue, and don't spread to other parts of the body. They are cured by surgical removal, providing that all the tumor can be removed. *Malignant tumors* are the same as cancers, and are also called carcinomas, sarcomas and lymphomas, depending on the tissue where they originated.

Cancers invade neighboring tissue and continue to grow in an unrestricted fashion. At some point, malignant cells part from the primary tumor and enter the lymphatic system or the circulatory system, and establish new colonies in other areas. This process is called metastasizing.

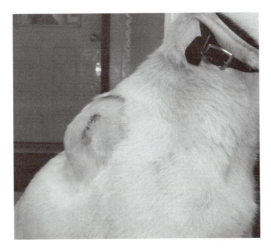

A biopsy identified this tumor on the back as a hemangiosarcoma, which arises from cells that make up the lining of small blood vessels.

What Causes Cancer?

Cancer is a condition in which rapid cell division and tissue growth occur at the expense of the host organ. Most cells in the body die and are replaced many times during the course of a dog's life. Cell reduplication follows an orderly pattern controlled by genes. When things go smoothly, each duplicated cell is an exact clone of its ancestor and assumes the same role.

Anything that disrupts the genes that govern cell duplication, however, results in the production of mutant cells. Mutant cells often reproduce at an extraordinary rate and form large masses that crowd out normal cells. Such a mass is called a cancer. Furthermore, cancerous cells do not function as normal cells and thus do not provide needed services. If the cancer grows unchecked, it eventually replaces much of the organ while also metastasizing to other parts of the body. In time, it causes the death of the dog.

Some cancer-producing genes are inherent in the breed or genetic makeup of the dog. Bernese Mountain Dogs, for example, have a high incidence of cancers affecting all body systems. Approximately one in four Bernese Mountain Dogs will develop cancer; two of the cancer types seen in this breed—histiocytosis and mastocytoma—are known to be inherited as polygenic traits.

Recently, a number of genes have been identified as causing breast, colon and other cancers in people and some animals. The reason that all individuals with these genes do not develop cancer is that there are other specific genes that suppress the cancer genes. To complicate matters, there are still other genes that inhibit the suppressors. All these genes are turned on and off by external factors, such as diet, stress and environment. Thus, cancer is a largely unpredictable phenomenon involving a complex interaction of genetics and the environment.

Carcinogens are environmental influences known to increase the likelihood of cancer in direct proportion to the length and intensity of exposure. Carcinogens gain access to tissue cells, cause alterations in genes and chromosomes, and disrupt the system of checks and balances that controls orderly growth. Examples of carcinogens known to increase the risk of cancer in humans are ultraviolet rays (which can cause skin cancers); X-rays (thyroid cancers); nuclear radiation (leukemia); various chemicals (aniline dyes cause bladder cancer); cigarettes and coal tars (lung, bladder, skin and many other cancers); viruses (sarcoma in AIDS patients); and internal parasites (bladder cancers).

Injuries are sometimes implicated as causing cancers, but there is seldom a connection. Trauma causes hematomas, bruises and contusions, but does not cause abnormal cell growth. However, an injured site is usually examined closely, and small preexisting tumors are sometimes discovered this way.

Some benign tumors, such as warts and papillomas, are clearly due to a virus. Other benign tumors simply grow for unknown reasons.

Treating Tumors and Cancers

The effectiveness of any form of treatment depends upon early diagnosis. In general, small cancers have a higher rate of cure than large cancers. This is true for all types of cancer.

Surgical removal of a cancer that has not spread is the best treatment possible. To prevent recurrence, a surrounding margin of normal tissue should also be removed. *An initial approach that removes the tumor with an adequate margin of normal tissue may be the most important factor in controlling cancer.* When a cancer recurs locally because of incomplete excision, the opportunity for cure is often lost.

A cancer that spreads only to regional lymph nodes may still be cured if all the involved nodes can be removed along with the primary tumor. Even when a cancer is widespread, removing a bleeding or infected mass can provide relief and improve the quality of life.

Electrocautery and *cryosurgery* are two techniques by which tumors on the surface of the body can be removed. Electrocautery means burning off the tumor using electricity; cryosurgery involves freezing the tumor to remove it. These methods provide an alternative to surgical removal and are suitable for benign tumors such as papillomas.

Radiation therapy is used primarily for local tumors that have not metastasized. Many canine tumors are sensitive to X-rays. They include mast cell tumors, transmissible venereal tumors, squamous cell carcinomas, cancers of the nasal cavity and soft tissue sarcomas. A potential disadvantage of radiation therapy is that it requires special equipment and must be done at a medical center.

Chemotherapy is used to prevent and control the metastatic spread of cancer cells. However, most canine cancers are only moderately sensitive to chemotherapy. It can cure only one type of cancer in dogs: transmissible venereal tumors. When used as the only form of treatment, chemotherapy usually does not extend survival; lymphosarcoma and leukemia are exceptions. Chemotherapy drugs, even when tightly controlled, have major side effects.

Immunotherapy using interferon, monoclonal antibodies and other agents that stimulate the immune system is receiving renewed interest and has the potential to become an important treatment option. Immunotherapy has been used successfully to extend survival time in dogs with late-stage lymphosarcomas and mast cell tumors. Prednisone has also been used successfully in combating these cancers.

A combination of the treatment methods (for example, surgical excision followed by radiation or chemotherapy) is often more effective than surgery alone. This is true for osteosarcoma. Only those treatments known to be effective against a particular cancer should be considered for combination therapy.

Cancer in Dogs

The majority of cancers in dogs are detected by physical examination. About half are visible as growths or sores on or beneath the skin. Perianal tumors, testicular tumors, mammary gland tumors, lymph gland tumors and cancers in the mouth can be detected by inspection and palpation. Bone tumors can be recognized by a swollen limb or the appearance of a swelling that involves the bone.

Internal cancers are most common in the spleen, liver and gastrointestinal tract. Cancers in these areas often become advanced before they are even suspected. Usually the first signs are weight loss, a palpable mass in the abdomen, vomiting, diarrhea, constipation or gastrointestinal bleeding.

Lung cancer is rare in dogs. The lungs, however, are a frequent site for metastases. The same is true of the liver.

The majority of cancers occur in middle-aged and older dogs. Because companion animals are living longer and enjoying a higher quality of life, it is likely that cancers will be diagnosed with increasing frequency. *A physical exam will detect most cancers.* Routine veterinary visits thus provide the opportunity to detect cancer at an early stage. This has significant implications for the life and health of your pet. As a rule, healthy dogs seven years of age and older should have a physical examination at least once a year. If their health is questionable, they should be seen more often. If any signs develop (see *Danger Signs in the Geriatric Dog* in Chapter 19), they should be seen at once.

The signs and symptoms of common tumors affecting the internal organs are discussed in the chapters dealing with these organs.

Common Surface Tumors

Skin tumors are common in dogs. It is often difficult to determine whether a skin tumor is benign or malignant by appearance alone. *The only conclusive way to make a diagnosis is by biopsy,* a procedure in which tissue or cells are removed and examined under a microscope by a veterinary pathologist.

For small tumors it is best to remove the growth and present the entire specimen to the pathologist. For tumors larger than an inch across, it may be advisable to obtain a tissue sample by *fine needle aspiration.* In this procedure, a needle connected to a syringe is inserted into the tumor and cells are obtained by pulling back on the plunger. Alternatively, a cutting needle can be used to obtain a core sample. An open biopsy, in which an incision is made, is preferred for suspected sarcomas and tumors that present diagnostic problems for the pathologist.

Additional information on the size of the tumor and the extent of local involvement may be important in planning treatment. Ultrasonography, available in many veterinary clinics, provides diagnostic information not obtainable through conventional X-rays. *CT scans* and *MRI* are used to diagnose internal cancers and determine the extent of local involvement. They are available at veterinary medical centers.

SKIN PAPILLOMAS

Skin papillomas are benign wartlike growths that occur on the skin of the body, on the foot pads and beneath the nails. They are caused by the canine oral papilloma virus and tend to occur in older dogs. They do not need to be removed unless they are causing a problem because of their location on the body.

HEMATOMAS

A hematoma is a blood clot beneath the skin, caused by a blow or contusion. Most hematomas clear up spontaneously. Large ones may need to be drained. Ear flap hematomas require special attention (see *Swollen Ear Flap* in Chapter 6).

Calcifying hematomas are hard masses that resemble bone. They tend to occur at fracture sites, and may be found as a bump on the skull of tall dogs that strike their heads on the underside of the dining room table. Calcifying hematomas do not have to be removed but may have to be biopsied if there is a question of bone tumor. They are difficult to treat and often recur.

EPIDERMAL INCLUSION CYSTS (WENS, SEBACEOUS CYSTS)

Epidermal inclusion cysts, also called wens or sebaceous cysts, are common surface tumors found anywhere on the body. Kerry Blue Terriers, Schnauzers and Spaniels are most often affected. Epidermal inclusion cysts begin when dry secretions block hair follicles, causing an accumulation of hair and sebum (a cheesy material), and the subsequent formation of a cyst.

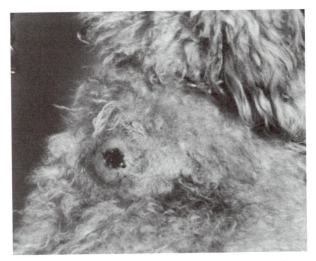

An abscessed epidermal inclusion (sebaceous) cyst. These cysts are frequently mistaken for tumors.

These cysts produce a dome-shaped swelling up to an inch or more in size beneath the skin. They can become infected and may need to be surgically drained. This sometimes leads to a cure.

Treatment: Surgical excision is the treatment of choice, although it is not always required.

LIPOMAS

A lipoma is a benign growth made up of mature fat cells interlaced with fibrous connective tissue. Lipomas are common in overweight dogs, especially females. A lipoma can be recognized by its oblong or round appearance and smooth, soft, fatlike consistency. Lipomas grow slowly and may get to be several inches in diameter. They are not painful. Rarely, what appears to be a lipoma is a malignant variant called a *liposarcoma.*

This large tumor beneath the skin of the abdomen proved to be a lipoma.

Treatment: Surgical removal is necessary if the lipoma is interfering with the dog's mobility, is growing rapidly or is cosmetically bothersome. The tumor should be biopsied if there is any question about the diagnosis.

HISTIOCYTOMAS

Histiocytomas are rapidly growing tumors found in dogs one to three years of age. They occur anywhere on the body. These benign tumors are dome-shaped, raised, hairless surface growths that are not painful. Because of their appearance, they are often called button tumors.

A raised, hairless, button-shaped growth typical of histiocytoma.

Treatment: Most histiocytomas disappear spontaneously within one to two months. Those that persist should be removed for diagnosis.

Histiocytosis

This is a rare malignant cancer in which *histiocytes* (large cells found in normal connective tissue) are widely dispersed throughout the subcutaneous tissue and internal organs, occasionally forming nodules. The typical signs are lethargy, weight loss and enlargement of the liver, spleen and lymph nodes.

The disease tends to affect male dogs of certain breeds at three to eight years of age. In Bernese Mountain Dogs, the disease is inherited as a polygenic trait, and accounts for 25 percent of all tumors in that breed.

Treatment: Histiocytosis may respond to chemotherapy.

SEBACEOUS ADENOMAS

These are common benign tumors found more often in older dogs, particularly Boston Terriers and Cocker Spaniels. The average age of dogs with sebaceous adenomas is 9 to 10 years. Sebaceous adenomas arise from oil-producing skin glands. They tend to occur on the eyelids and limbs. They may be single or multiple, usually are less than an inch across, and appear as smooth, lobulated growths on a narrow base or stem. The surface of the tumor is hairless and occasionally is ulcerated.

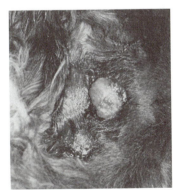

A sebaceous gland adenoma on the body of a Cocker Spaniel.

Occasionally, a sebaceous adenoma becomes malignant (becoming a sebaceous adenocarcinoma). Suspect malignancy if the tumor is larger than one inch, has an ulcerated surface and is growing rapidly.

Treatment: Small tumors do not need to be removed unless they are causing a problem. Large adenomas should be removed.

BASAL CELL TUMORS

This is a common tumor usually found on the head and neck in dogs over seven years of age. It appears as a firm, solitary nodule with distinct borders that sets it apart from the surrounding skin. The tumor may have been present for months or years. Cocker Spaniels appear to be at increased risk.

A small percent of basal cell tumors are malignant (becoming basal cell carcinomas).

Treatment: Basal cell tumors should be removed by wide surgical excision.

MASTOCYTOMAS (MAST CELL TUMORS)

Mast cell tumors are common, accounting for 10 to 20 percent of skin tumors in dogs. About half of them are malignant. *Brachycephalic* breeds such as Boxers, Boston Terriers and Bulldogs have a higher incidence. However, mast cell tumors can occur in all dogs. In Bernese Mountain Dogs, mast cell tumors are especially common and are inherited as a polygenic trait.

The mean age for dogs to develop mast cell tumors is nine years. Both sexes are equally affected. Multiple tumors are present in 10 percent of cases. Look for these tumors on the skin of the trunk and perineum, lower abdomen, foreskin of the penis and hind legs.

Mast cell tumors vary greatly in appearance. The typical tumor is a *multinodular* growth that appears reddish, hairless and ulcerated. It is impossible to tell by appearance whether the tumor is benign or malignant. Some growths may be present for months or years, then suddenly enlarge and metastasize to the regional lymph nodes, liver or spleen. Others grow rapidly right from the start.

Mast cell tumors release histamine and other substances that cause stomach and duodenal ulcers. In fact, up to 80 percent of dogs with mast cell tumors may be suffering from ulcers. Dogs with intestinal symptoms should be evaluated for ulcer disease and treated accordingly (see *Stomach and Duodenal Ulcers* in Chapter 9).

Treatment: The World Health Organization has established a system for staging mast cell tumors based on the size of the tumor, the number present, the degree of local involvement and the presence or absence of metastases. Early-stage (favorable) tumors are treated by complete local excision with a margin of normal tissue. Larger tumors that cannot be removed with adequate tissue margins are treated with surgery plus cortisone (prednisone) and/or radiation therapy. Chemotherapy and/or immunotherapy have been of benefit in treating late-stage disease.

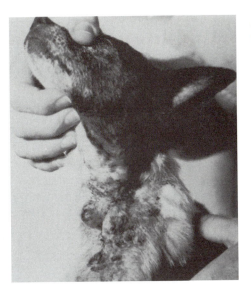

A mast cell tumor on the neck of a terrier.

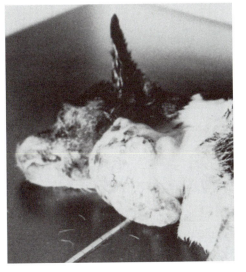

The same tumor one month later, showing rapid progression.

SQUAMOUS CELL CARCINOMAS

These tumors are induced by exposure to the ultraviolet radiation in sunlight, and occur on lightly pigmented areas of the body including the underside of the belly, trunk, scrotum, nail beds, nose and lips.

One variety of squamous carcinoma appears as a hard, flat, grayish-looking ulcer that does not heal. Another appears as a firm red patch, and still another as a cauliflower-like growth. There may be hair loss around the tumor because of constant licking.

Treatment: Squamous carcinomas invade locally and metastasize at a late stage to the regional lymph nodes and lungs. Complete surgical removal is the treatment of choice. When this cannot be accomplished due to widespread involvement, radiation therapy can be used.

MELANOMAS

Melanomas arise from melanin-producing cells in the skin. They are more common in Scottish Terriers, Boston Terriers and Cocker Spaniels. These brown or black nodules are found on darkly pigmented areas of skin, particularly on the eyelids. They also occur on the lips, in the mouth, on the trunk and limbs, and in the nail beds. Melanomas on the skin are usually benign; those in the mouth are highly malignant. About 50 percent of nail bed melanomas are malignant and metastasize. Metastases occur in the regional lymph nodes, lungs and liver.

A large pigmented growth on the leg, typical of melanoma.

Treatment: The melanoma must be removed surgically, along with a margin of normal tissue. Recurrence is common and difficult to treat. The outlook is extremely poor for melanomas in the mouth.

Soft Tissue Sarcomas

Sarcomas are malignant tumors that arise from various sources, including connective tissue, fat, blood vessels, nerve sheaths and muscle cells. Collectively they account for about 15 percent of all cancers in dogs. There is a genetic disposition among German Shepherd Dogs, Boxers, Saint Bernards, Basset Hounds, Great Danes and Golden Retrievers.

Sarcomas occur on the surface of the body and within organs. They tend to grow slowly and metastasize only when present for some time. Metastases usually involve the lungs and liver. Some sarcomas are well-defined and appear to be encapsulated; others infiltrate the surrounding tissue and have no distinct margins. Sarcomas within body cavities often grow to a large size before being discovered. Soft tissue sarcoma is diagnosed using X-rays, ultrasonography, CT scan and tissue biopsy.

The most common sarcomas found in dogs are:

- **Hemangiopericytoma,** arising from cells surrounding small arteries
- **Fibrosarcoma,** arising from fibrous connective tissue
- **Hemangiosarcoma,** arising from cells that make up the lining of small blood vessels
- **Schwannoma,** a tumor of nerve sheaths
- **Osteosarcoma,** a tumor of bones, discussed below
- **Lymphoma,** arising in lymph nodes and in organs that contain lymphoid tissue such as the spleen, liver and bone marrow, discussed below

Treatment: The World Health Organization has established a staging system for canine soft tissue sarcomas similar to that described for mast cell tumors. Depending on the type of sarcoma and the extent of local involvement, treatment may involve surgical excision with a margin of normal tissue, radiation therapy, hyperthermia (the use of electromagnetic radiation or ultrasound to heat the tumor) and chemotherapy. A specific treatment plan often uses a combination of therapies. The prognosis depends on the stage of the tumor at the time of treatment.

LYMPHOMA (LYMPHOSARCOMA)

Lymphoma, also called lymphosarcoma, is a type of cancer that arises (often simultaneously) in lymph nodes and in organs that contain lymphoid tissue such as the spleen, liver and bone marrow. The disease affects middle-aged and older dogs. It should be suspected when enlarged lymph nodes are found in the groin, armpit, neck or chest. Affected dogs appear lethargic, eat poorly and lose weight. The liver and spleen are often enlarged.

Chest involvement results in fluid in the chest cavity (*pleural effusion*) and severe shortness of breath. Skin involvement produces itchy patches or nodules on the surface of the skin that mimic other skin diseases. Intestinal involvement causes vomiting and diarrhea.

A complete blood count may show anemia and immature white blood cells. The serum calcium is elevated in 20 percent of dogs with lymphoma. Blood and liver function tests are usually abnormal. A bone marrow biopsy is helpful in determining if the disease is widespread.

Chest and abdominal X-rays and ultrasonography are particularly valuable in identifying enlarged lymph nodes, organs and masses. A diagnosis can also be made by *fine needle aspiration* of an enlarged lymph node. In questionable cases, the entire lymph node should be removed for more complete evaluation.

Treatment: Lymphoma localized to a single lymph node may be cured by surgical removal of the involved node. However, in most dogs the disease is widespread and a cure is unlikely. Chemotherapy using several agents offers the best chance of remission, which may last a year or longer.

Bone Tumors

Bone tumors can be either malignant or benign. Osteosarcoma and chondrosarcoma are the two most common malignant bone tumors. Osteomas and osteochondromas are the most common benign types.

MALIGNANT BONE TUMORS

Osteosarcoma

By far the most common malignant bone cancer in dogs is osteosarcoma. This cancer affects dogs of all ages, with a median age of eight years. It occurs with equal frequency in males and females. Giant breeds such as the Saint Bernard, Newfoundland, Great Dane and Great Pyrenees are 60 times more likely to develop an osteosarcoma than are dogs less than 25 pounds. Large breeds such as the Irish Setter and Boxer are eight times more likely to develop osteosarcoma. Toy breeds are rarely, if ever, affected.

Osteosarcoma occurs most often in the bones of the front legs, followed in order of frequency by the hind legs, the flat bones of the ribs and the mandible. Often the first sign is a limp in a mature dog that has no history of injury. Usually this receives little attention until swelling of the leg or a bone mass is observed. Pressure over the tumor causes pain. Bone X-rays can strongly suggest the disease, but a definitive diagnosis depends on biopsy of the tumor. Osteosarcoma is an aggressive cancer that spreads early to the lungs.

Chondrosarcoma

This is the second most common malignant bone tumor in dogs. The average age of onset is six years. This tumor tends to involve the ribs, nasal bones and pelvis. It presents as a large, hard, painless swelling in an area containing cartilage. This tumor also metastasizes to the lungs, but is less aggressive than osteosarcoma.

Treatment of Malignant Bone Tumor: Malignant tumors such as osteosarcomas and chondrosarcomas should be treated aggressively. Because these tumors metastasize to the lungs, it is important to obtain a chest X-ray before recommending surgery. The dog should have a complete physical examination, including a blood count, and a fine needle aspiration biopsy of any enlarged lymph nodes.

Partial or complete amputation is the only effective treatment for osteosarcomas of the limbs. Most dogs are able to get around well on three legs. Although amputation rarely cures the cancer, it does relieve pain and improves the quality of life. The amputation should be performed at least one joint above the involved bone.

Chemotherapy in addition to amputation increases the survival time for osteosarcoma, but not the cure rate. Radiation therapy may be considered if the cancer is metastatic or far advanced, but is also not a cure. Osteosarcoma of the mandible is treated with radiation therapy, to which it is moderately responsive.

Complete surgical removal of chondrosarcomas affords relief, but should not be considered curative.

BENIGN BONE TUMORS

Osteomas are raised tumors composed of dense but otherwise normal bone. They occur about the skull and face. *Osteochondromas*, also called *multiple cartilaginous exostoses*, are bone tumors that arise in young dogs from areas where cartilage grows prior to calcification. Osteochondromas may be single or multiple and are found on the ribs, vertebrae, pelvis and extremities. There is a hereditary basis to osteochondromas.

Treatment: A bone biopsy should be performed to determine the type of bone tumor, unless the appearance on X-ray is conclusive. Benign tumors can be removed by local excision. The surgery is needed when the growth impinges on structures such as nerves and tendons, producing pain or causing inactivity. Surgical removal may also be indicated for the sake of appearance.

Reproductive Tract Tumors

TUMORS OF THE TESTICLES

Testicular tumors are common in male dogs. Most affected dogs are over six years of age, with a median age of 10. The majority of tumors occur in *undescended testicles*—located in the inguinal canal or abdominal cavity. In fact, tumors develop in up to 50 percent of undescended testicles. A swelling or firm mass in the inguinal canal in a dog with an undescended testicle is characteristic of a testicular tumor.

Tumors in descended testicles are rare. The affected testicle is often larger and firmer than its neighbor and has an irregular, nodular surface. At times the testicle is normal size but feels hard.

The three common testicular tumors in dogs are the *Sertoli cell tumor*, the *interstitial (Leydig) cell tumor* and the *seminoma*. A small percentage of Sertoli cell tumors and seminomas are malignant.

Some Sertoli cell tumors produce estrogen, which can result in feminization of the male with enlargement of the mammary glands, a pendulous foreskin and bilateral symmetric hair loss. A serious complication of high estrogen levels is bone marrow suppression.

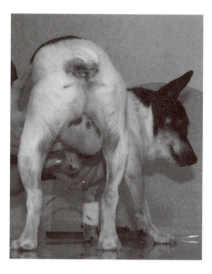

A tumor of the right testicle, causing asymmetric scrotal enlargement.

Ultrasonography is particularly useful in locating undescended testicles and in determining whether a scrotal mass is a tumor, abscess, testicular torsion or scrotal hernia. Fine needle aspiration biopsy provides information on the cell type of the tumor.

Treatment: Neutering is the treatment of choice. This is curative in nearly all cases, even when the tumor is malignant. For scrotal tumors, the normal testicle can be left if future fertility is desired. If one or both testicles is undescended, both testicles should be removed, since the condition is heritable and the dog should not be bred. Signs of feminization in Sertoli cell tumors may disappear after neutering—but this is not always the case.

Prevention: Tumors of the testicle can be prevented by neutering dogs early in life. It is particularly important to neuter all dogs with undescended testicles.

TRANSMISSIBLE VENEREAL TUMORS

An unusual neoplasm called transmissible venereal tumor occurs in both males and females. Tumor cells are transplanted from one dog to another, primarily during sexual contact, but also through licking, biting and scratching. Transmissible venereal tumors tend to occur in free-roaming dogs, particularly those living in urban areas. They appear within seven days of contact exposure.

Transmissible venereal tumors are solitary or multiple tumors that usually appear as cauliflower-like growths or as nodules on a stalk. The growths may be multinodular and/or ulcerated.

In females, transmissible venereal tumors develop in the vagina and on the vulva. In males, they occur on the penis. Other locations in both sexes include the skin of the perineum, face, mouth, nasal cavity and limbs. Transmissible venereal tumors are considered low-grade cancers. They do have the potential to metastasize, although this is rare.

Treatment: Chemotherapy is the recommended treatment. The drug of choice is vincristine, given weekly for three to six weeks. Radiation therapy is also highly effective; most dogs are cured after a single dose. Surgery is not considered an effective treatment because it is associated with a high rate of local recurrence. Dogs and bitches not intended for breeding should be neutered or spayed.

VAGINAL TUMORS

The vaginal and vulvar area is the most common site for tumors of the female genital tract. These tumors tend to occur in older, sexually intact females, at an average age of 10 years. Benign tumors include leiomyomas, lipomas and transmissible venereal tumors. They are often found on a narrow base or a long stalk.

Malignant tumors in this area are rare. They include leiomyosarcomas, squamous cell carcinomas and mast cell tumors. Malignant tumors grow locally, infiltrate surrounding tissue and become quite large. They rarely metastasize.

Signs include vaginal discharge or bleeding, a mass protruding through the vulvar lips, frequent urination and excessive licking at the vulva. Large vaginal tumors can cause swelling and deformity of the perineum, block the birth canal and cause problems in whelping. Note that a mass protruding through the vulva of a bitch in heat is most likely to be due to *vaginal hyperplasia* (see Chapter 15).

Treatment: Surgical removal with a margin of normal tissue is the treatment of choice. Recurrence may follow removal.

TUMORS OF THE OVARIES

Ovarian tumors are uncommon. Most cause no symptoms and are found incidentally during a spay operation. Occasionally, a tumor becomes large enough to produce a visible or palpable swelling in the abdomen.

Papillary adenoma is a benign tumor that may arise simultaneously in both ovaries. A malignant variety, called papillary adenocarcinoma, is the most common ovarian cancer in bitches. These tumors spread throughout the abdominal cavity and are associated with *ascites*.

Granulosa cell tumors can also become quite large. Some secrete estrogen, producing signs of hyperestrogenism with abnormal heat cycles, enlargement of the vulva, and a greasy skin and coat.

Other tumors of the ovaries also occur. Ovarian cysts, which are not true tumors, are discussed in Chapter 15 (see *Abnormal Estrous Cycles*).

Abdominal *ultrasonography* is particularly helpful in determining the size, structure and location of ovarian tumors. Finding ascites and masses in the abdominal cavity suggests malignancy.

Treatment: Removal of the ovaries by hysterectomy (spaying) cures benign tumors. The cure rate for malignant tumors is about 50 percent. The addition of chemotherapy for metastatic tumors may extend the time the dog is in remission.

MAMMARY GLAND (BREAST) TUMORS

The mammary glands in female dogs vary in number and can be determined by counting the nipples. The typical bitch has 10 mammary glands, five on each side of the midline, beginning on the chest and extending to the groin. The largest glands are located near the groin.

Mammary gland tumors are the most common tumors in dogs. In fact, among unspayed females the risk of a mammary tumor is 26 percent. This is three times the risk of breast tumors in women. Most mammary gland tumors occur in bitches over six years of age (the average age is 10). Forty-five percent are cancerous and 55 percent are benign. An increased incidence occurs in sporting breeds, Poodles, Boston Terriers and Dachshunds. Multiple tumors are common. If a bitch has one tumor, she is three times more likely to have or develop a second tumor.

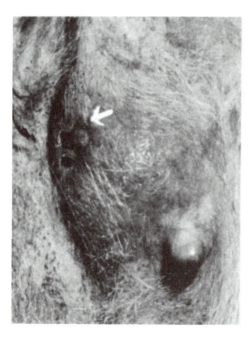

A bitch with breast cancer. Note the skin ulceration.

The principal sign is a painless lump or mass. Most lumps occur in the larger glands closest to the groin. A mass may be large or small, with boundaries that are distinct or indefinite. Some lumps are freely moveable, while others adhere to the overlying skin or underlying muscle. Occasionally, the mass ulcerates the skin and bleeds.

Inflammatory cancer is a rapidly progressive neoplasm that spreads throughout the chain of mammary glands and into surrounding skin and fat. Death usually comes in a matter of weeks. Inflammatory cancer may be difficult to distinguish from *acute septic mastitis*, which is discussed in Chapter 16.

Malignant tumors spread widely, primarily to the pelvic lymph nodes and lungs. Before embarking on treatment, a chest X-ray should be taken to rule out lung metastases, present in 30 percent of cancers. Ultrasonography is useful in determining whether the pelvic lymph nodes are involved. Biopsy of the tumor may not be necessary if surgical removal is contemplated. Inflammatory cancer, however, must be biopsied, because there is little to be gained in attempting aggressive treatment in these tumors.

Treatment: Removing the lump with adequate margins of normal tissue is the treatment of choice for all mammary tumors, whether benign or malignant. How much tissue will be removed depends on the size and location of the tumor. Removing a small tumor with a rim of normal tissue is called a lumpectomy. A simple mastectomy is the removal of the entire mammary gland. A complete unilateral mastectomy is the removal of all five mammary glands on one side of the body. The inguinal lymph nodes are often included in a unilateral mastectomy. The specimen is then submitted to a pathologist for a tissue diagnosis to determine the prognosis.

The success rate of surgery depends on the biological potential and the size of the tumor. Benign tumors are cured. Bitches with small malignant tumors less than an inch across have favorable cure rates. Those with large, aggressive tumors are more likely to have metastatic disease and a poor prognosis.

The addition of chemotherapy, immunotherapy and complete hysterectomy does not improve cure rates, although chemotherapy may offer some relief in bitches with advanced cancers not amenable to surgery.

Prevention: Spaying a female before the first heat cycle reduces her risk of breast cancer to less than 1 percent. If she is spayed after one heat period, her risk is still only 8 percent.

It is important to examine the mammary glands of unspayed bitches every month, starting at six years of age. If you feel a suspicious lump or swelling, take the dog to your veterinarian at once. Experience shows that many owners procrastinate for several months in hopes that a lump will go away. Thus, the opportunity to cure many mammary cancers is lost.

Leukemia

Leukemia is a cancer involving the blood elements in the bone marrow, including the lymphocytes, monocytes, platelets, eosinophils, basophils and erythrocytes. All of these cells can give rise to cell-specific leukemias. For example, *lymphoid leukemia* is a malignant transformation of the lymphocytes, or white blood cells. Leukemia is further subdivided into acute and chronic stages. Both stages are relatively rare in dogs.

Leukemia generally occurs in middle-aged dogs. Signs are nonspecific and include fever, loss of appetite, weight loss and sometimes anemia with pale mucous membranes. Usually the disease is discovered when blood tests are drawn to diagnose these symptoms. Leukemic cells may or may not be found circulating in the blood. A bone marrow biopsy confirms the diagnosis.

Treatment: Leukemia is treated with anti-cancer drugs. Chemotherapy does not cure leukemia, but may put the disease into remission for several months or longer. Chronic leukemia has a better prognosis than acute leukemia.

GERIATRICS

The average dog now lives about 13 years, and it is not uncommon in veterinary practice to see and care for dogs over 20 years of age. The maximum life span of dogs has been estimated to be 27 years. Large dogs have shorter lifespans than smaller dogs. Saint Bernards, German Shepherd Dogs, Great Danes and other giant breeds are considered senior at six to nine years of age and old at 10 to 12. Medium-size dogs are seniors at 9 to 10 years of age and old at 12 to 14. Toy breeds are considered senior at 9 to 13 years of age and old at 14 to 16 years. Being a purebred or mixed breed does not influence the aging process.

A table showing the comparative age of dogs and humans is found in Appendix B. However, the numbers are estimates only. All dogs do not age at the same rate. A dog's biological age depends on his genetic inheritance, nutrition, state of health and sum of lifetime stresses.

My old dog by the hearth. (Liisa Carlson)

Of greatest importance is the care the dog has received throughout his life. Well-cared-for pets suffer fewer infirmities as they grow older. But when sickness, illness or injury is neglected, the aging process is accelerated.

The Geriatric Checkup

The care of the older dog is directed at preventing premature aging, minimizing physical and emotional stresses, and meeting the special needs of the elderly. A dog older than seven years that is in good health should have a complete veterinary examination at least once a year. For giant breeds, the age for annual exams is five. If the health of the dog is questionable, he should be seen by a veterinarian more often. If symptoms appear, he should be seen at once.

The annual geriatric checkup should include a physical examination, complete blood count, blood chemistries, urinalysis and parasite examination. Liver and kidney function tests, chest X-ray and electrocardiogram may be needed if specific signs and symptoms appear. Routine dental care, including scaling the teeth, may be needed more frequently than once a year.

Danger Signs in the Geriatric Dog

If you see any of the following abnormal signs, take your dog to the veterinarian for further investigation.

- Loss of appetite or weight.
- Cough, rapid labored breathing.
- Weakness or exercise intolerance.
- Increased thirst and/or frequency of urination.
- Change in bowel function with constipation or diarrhea.
- Bloody or purulent discharge from a body opening.
- An increase in temperature, pulse or breathing rate.
- A growth or lump anywhere on the body.

Behavior Changes

Older dogs are more sedentary, less energetic, less curious and more restricted in their scope of activity. They adjust slowly to changes in diet, activity and the daily routine. They are less tolerant to extremes of heat and cold. They tend to sleep a lot and may be forgetful. When disturbed, they are cranky and irritable.

Most of these behavior changes are the result of physical ailments (such as diminished hearing and smell, arthritic stiffness and muscular weakness) that restrict a dog's activity and his ability to participate in family life. Arthritic changes in the dog's joints are often accompanied by pain and irritability, which can lead to aggressive encounters with family members and visitors.

Encourage your dog to participate more actively by finding a warm resting spot near the center of family activity. Take the dog outside twice a day for a comfortable walk in the neighborhood. Activities that provide human companionship will be deeply appreciated and will give the dog a sense of being valued and loved.

Old dogs don't tolerate boarding and hospitalization well. The older dog away from home often will not eat, and will become overanxious or withdrawn, bark excessively and sleep poorly. If possible, care for them at home under the guidance of your veterinarian. When leaving town, ask a friend to drop by once or twice a day to look in on the dog and attend to his needs. Dog-sitting services are available in most communities. The National Association of Professional Pet Sitters is an organization that maintains standards through a code of ethics, certification and attendance at national conferences. To obtain information on this organization and members living in your area, see Appendix C.

COGNITIVE DYSFUNCTION SYNDROME

This condition, once called the senile or old dog syndrome, is a newly recognized disease, somewhat similar to Alzheimer's disease in people. In cognitive dysfunction syndrome, the brain undergoes a series of changes that result in a decline in the mental faculties associated with thinking, recognition, memory and learned behavior. Fifty percent of dogs over age 10 will exhibit one or more symptoms of cognitive dysfunction syndrome. Cognitive dysfunction is a progressive disease with increasing signs of senile behavior that can lead owners to consider putting the dog to sleep (euthanasia).

Disorientation is one of the principal symptoms of cognitive dysfunction syndrome. The dog appears lost in the house or yard, gets stuck in corners or under or behind furniture, has difficulty finding the door (stands at the hinge side or goes to the wrong door), doesn't recognize familiar people and fails to respond to verbal cues or his name.

Activity and sleep patterns are disturbed. The dog sleeps more in a 24-hour period, but sleeps less during the night. There is a decrease in purposeful activity and an increase in aimless wandering and pacing. Dogs with cognitive dysfunction may also exhibit compulsive behaviors with circling, tremors, stiffness and weakness.

Housetraining is another area that suffers. The dog may urinate and/or defecate indoors, sometimes even in the view of his owners, and may signal less often to go outside.

Interactions with family members become much less intense. The dog seeks less attention, often walks away when being petted, shows less enthusiasm on greeting and may no longer greet his owner once the dog is aware that he or she has arrived.

Some of these symptoms may be due to age-related physical changes and not to cognitive dysfunction. A medical condition such as cancer, infection, organ failure or drug side effects could be the sole cause of the behavioral changes or could be aggravating the problem. Thus, medical problems must be tested for and eliminated before senile symptoms are attributed to cognitive dysfunction syndrome.

Research on the aging canine brain reveals a number of pathogenic processes that could account for many of the symptoms of cognitive dysfunction syndrome. A protein called B-amyloid is deposited in the white and gray matter of the brain and forms plaques that result in cell death and brain shrinkage. Alterations in various neurotransmitter chemicals, including serotonin, norepinephrine and dopamine, have been described. Oxygen levels in the brains of senile dogs are decreased.

There is no specific test for cognitive dysfunction syndrome. The number of symptoms the dog exhibits and the severity of the senile behavior are important considerations in making the diagnosis. An MRI may show some degree of brain shrinkage, but the test is not likely to be done unless a brain tumor is suspected.

Awareness of the diagnosis makes it easier to understand the dog's behavior. A drug called Anipryl (selegiline), used by humans to treat Parkinson's disease, has been found to dramatically improve symptoms and the quality of life for many dogs with cognitive dysfunction syndrome. The drug is given once daily as a pill. Because medical treatment is now available, it is even more important to seek veterinary consultation for behavior changes in elderly dogs.

Physical Changes

The life cycle of the dog can be divided into three stages: puppyhood, adulthood and old age. Puppyhood and old age are relatively short when compared to the length of adulthood. After puberty a dog's physique changes very little until quite close to the end of his life.

Periodic physical examinations may reveal an age-related condition that can be improved by modifying the dog's care or daily routine. *Although aging is inevitable and irreversible, some of the infirmities attributed to old age may, in fact, be due to disease, and therefore preventable or at least treatable.*

MUSCULOSKELETAL PROBLEMS

Signs of aging include loss of muscle tone and strength, especially in the legs. The abdomen may sag, the back may sway and the elbows may turn out. The muscles may begin to shake when the dog physically exerts himself.

Most older dogs suffer to some extent from osteoarthritis, more accurately called degenerative joint disease. Stiffness in the joints is made worse by drafts and by sleeping on cold, damp tile or cement. Make a comfortable bed for the dog indoors on a well-padded surface. Toy dogs may need to be covered at night.

There is nothing more beneficial to an older dog than regular exercise. Exercise improves muscle tone and strength, keeps the joints supple, helps prevent weight gain and promotes a youthful attitude. However, an older dog should not be forced to exercise beyond his comfort level. If the dog has been sedentary and out of condition, gradually begin and add more exercise as his conditioning improves.

The unwillingness to exercise in a dog with arthritis is related, in part, to muscle soreness. Although there is no way to prevent arthritis, analgesics such as Rimadyl (carprofen) can relieve muscle soreness and enable the dog to enjoy daily exercise. Etodolac is another newly approved canine analgesic that may prove just as effective.

Neutraceuticals that protect joint cartilage, such as polysulfated glycosaminoglycan and chondroitin sulfate, are available through your veterinarian and from health food stores. For more information on the treatment of *degenerative joint disease*, see Chapter 13.

COAT AND SKIN PROBLEMS

Skin tumors and coat problems are common in elderly dogs. The coat mats easily and the skin becomes dry and scaly because oil-producing skin glands don't work as well. Symmetrical loss of coat is an indication of an endocrine disease such as *Cushing's syndrome* (see Chapter 9). Stiff old dogs may have trouble keeping their anal and genital areas clean, and may need some help. The toenails may need to be trimmed more often, as they are less likely to be worn down by activity.

Comb or brush elderly dogs three or four times a week. Regularly examining the hair and skin this way may reveal tumors, parasites or other skin diseases that require prompt veterinary attention. Old dogs also enjoy the attention and companionship which accompanies these grooming sessions.

Care should be taken to prevent an old dog from becoming chilled. After a walk in the rain, the dog should be towel-dried and kept indoors.

THE SENSES

As dogs grow older they gradually lose their hearing, but this may not become apparent until after 10 years of age. A dog with impaired hearing compensates by relying more on his other senses. (Techniques to test your dog's hearing are described in *Deafness* in Chapter 6.) Senile deafness has no treatment. However, hearing problems could be exacerbated by a wax blockage in the ear canal or some other problem, such as hypothyroidism or an ear tumor, all of which can be treated. A veterinary examination is the best way to determine the proper course of action.

Loss of the senses of smell and taste may result in a decreased interest in food, with attendant problems in maintaining a healthy weight.

Loss of eyesight is difficult to assess in the dog. Senile cataracts appear as an aging disease, usually in dogs six to eight years of age. Loss of vision may be caused by *retinal diseases*, *glaucoma* and *uveitis*. These diseases are discussed in Chapter 5.

MOUTH, TEETH AND GUMS

Periodontal disease is a gradual process that begins in early adulthood. If it goes unchecked, it culminates in advanced gum disease and tooth decay in the older

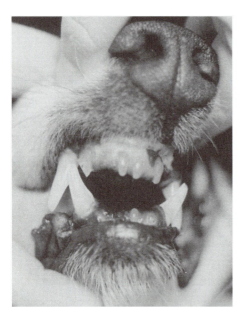

Lost and infected teeth cause old dogs to eat poorly and lose weight. Dental disease is preventable by routine dental care throughout the dog's life.

dog. But this need not happen. *Periodontal disease is preventable by routine dental care*, as described in *Taking Care of Your Dog's Teeth* in Chapter 8.

Dogs with infected gums and teeth experience mouth pain, eat poorly and lose weight. Dental treatment relieves suffering and improves health and nutrition. Elderly dogs may need more frequent dental care, including scaling the teeth at least twice a year. If your dog has lost teeth and is unable to chew dry kibble, switch to a semi-moist or canned food.

Functional Changes

Alterations in eating and drinking patterns, voiding habits and bowel functions occur frequently in older dogs. Such changes are important clues to health problems.

INCREASED THIRST AND FREQUENT URINATION

These are signs of *kidney failure*. Aging alone is not a cause of kidney failure, but kidney diseases tend to be slowly progressive, so symptoms often appear later in life. The dog urinates more frequently because the kidneys have lost the ability to concentrate wastes. These dogs are thirsty and drink larger amounts of water to compensate. Note that increased thirst and urination also occur with *diabetes mellitus* and *Cushing's syndrome*, two diseases that tend to occur in middle-aged and older dogs.

A dog with failing kidneys may be unable to keep from wetting in the house, especially at night. Take the dog out several times a day and just before bedtime. Be sure to keep fresh water available at all times. *Do not reduce water intake in an attempt to control the incontinence.* This may push the dog into acute kidney failure. *Kidney failure* and *urinary incontinence* are discussed in Chapter 14.

HOUSE SOILING

Some cases of house soiling are due to musculoskeletal problems that restrict activity. Dogs with difficulty getting about may be unwilling to proceed to the area designated for elimination. They can be helped by adding ramps and area rugs, particularly over slick surfaces.

A common cause of house soiling is hormone-responsive incontinence, seen most often in middle-aged and older spayed females, and less commonly in older neutered males. It is caused by a deficiency of estrogen in females and testosterone in males. Both these hormones are important in maintaining the muscle tone of the urethral sphincter. Hormone-responsive incontinence is much like bed wetting. The dog urinates normally but wets when relaxed or asleep. Treatment is discussed in *Urinary Incontinence* (see Chapter 14). Inappropriate defecation may also be due to loss of sphincter control.

House soiling may also be due to failing memory and a decline in learned behavior associated with *cognitive dysfunction syndrome*. Treatment with Anipryl may help to restore a normal elimination pattern.

In all cases of house soiling it is important to clean the soiled areas to prevent odors that might attract the dog to return to the area. *Do not punish the dog.* Most likely, the dog is unable to help himself. Scolding and punishment only produces fear and anxiety, which makes the problem worse.

CONSTIPATION

This is a common problem in geriatric dogs. Older dogs tend to drink less water and this produces hard dry stools that are difficult to pass. Other contributing factors are lack of exercise, improper diet, reduced bowel activity, weakness of the muscles of the abdominal wall and prostate problems. An *enlarged prostate* can narrow the rectal canal and cause straining to defecate.

Older dogs with reduced bowel activity can be helped by soaking the kibble with equal parts of water and letting the mixture stand for 20 minutes.

Nearly all older dogs can benefit from adding fiber to the diet. The best way to accomplish this is to choose a high-fiber food. Dog foods advertised as "for seniors" usually contain more fiber. Compare the analysis on the labels of various products. High-fiber diets are also available through your veterinarian. For information on preventing constipation, see *Constipation* in Chapter 9.

DIARRHEA

Elderly dogs with chronic diarrhea exhibit weakness, weight loss, and may develop kidney failure due to chronic dehydration. Diarrhea that persists for more than two or three days is abnormal. It can be a sign of kidney or liver disease, pancreatic disease, malabsorption syndrome, parasites (especially whipworms) or cancer. Veterinary examination is warranted.

ABNORMAL DISCHARGES

Abnormal discharges are those containing pus or blood. They may have an offensive odor. Discharges from the eyes, ears, nose, mouth, penis and vagina suggest infection. In the elderly dog, cancer is a consideration. If you see any such discharges, take your dog to the veterinarian.

Weight Changes

Weight loss is a serious problem in the elderly dog. Some cases are caused by kidney disease; others by cancers, periodontal disease, loss of the senses of smell and taste, and apathy associated with inactivity and lack of attention. Weigh your dog once a month. A drop in weight is a reason for a veterinary checkup.

Excessive weight gain is an important but largely preventable problem. Being obese is a complicating factor in heart and respiratory disease. Overweight dogs are less likely to exercise and maintain health and fitness. It is important to correct this problem, as discussed below in *Diet and Nutrition*.

A pendulous, pot-belly abdomen may appear to be a weight problem, but is more likely due to *Cushing's syndrome* or *ascites*, an accumulation of fluid in the abdomen as the result of heart or liver failure. See your veterinarian.

Temperature, Pulse and Respiration

Fever indicates inflammation. In the older dog the usual sites are the lungs and urinary tract.

A rapid heart rate is a sign of anemia, infection or heart disease. Anemia is suggested by paleness of the gums and tongue. Possible causes include liver disease, kidney failure, immune-mediated hemolytic anemia and cancer.

A rapid breathing rate (more than 30 breaths per minute at rest) suggests respiratory disease or congestive heart failure. A chronic cough suggests bronchitis, airway disease or cancer. Coughing at night in an elderly small dog suggests chronic valvular heart disease.

Diet and Nutrition

Preventing obesity is the single most important consideration in prolonging the life of the older dog. Geriatric dogs are less active and require 30 percent fewer calories than younger dogs. Thus, all senior dogs should be on a reduced-calorie diet as discussed below. In general, an elderly dog that is neither too fat nor too thin needs only 25 to 30 kcals per pound of body weight per day to meet his caloric needs. If the dog's diet is not lower in calories, feeding the adult maintenance amount may result in weight gain. However, you do not need to switch your dog to a senior food if he is doing well on his current adult maintenance diet (see *Feeding and Nutrition* in Chapter 9)—you may simply need to feed a little less.

Senior foods usually are more expensive per pound than maintenance foods. A senior food often contains less protein per daily feeding, but healthy geriatric dogs do not need to be on a protein-restricted diet. In fact, they may actually benefit from a higher protein source in order to maximize protein stores. To ensure that the protein is of the highest quality, look for the statement that the food has met AAFCO standards *through animal feeding tests.*

Dogs with chronic kidney or liver failure are exceptions. They lose the ability to fully metabolize protein and should be given a low-protein diet as described in the treatment of *Kidney Failure* in Chapter 14.

CALORIE-CONTROLLED FEEDING

Canned dog foods supply about 500 calories in a pound of food; moist or "chunky" dog food, about 1,300 calories; dry kibble, about 1,600 calories. The quantity of food given to the geriatric dog should be controlled to provide a daily intake of 25 to 30 calories daily per pound of body weight. The feeding instructions on the package should be taken as guidelines only; they often do not take into account the 30 percent reduction in calories required by many geriatric dogs.

The best way to determine the amount to feed is to weigh the dog and compute his caloric requirements, then determine how much to feed based on the calorie information on the package. Adjust the portions up or down depending on the dog's activity level and whether he is looking trim. Senior foods have fewer calories, so if you use one of these, the amount may not have to be reduced.

Dogs that lose weight on a calorie-adjusted feeding program may have a medical problem and should be seen by a veterinarian.

Overweight dogs should be placed on a weight-loss diet. Before doing so, consult your veterinarian to be sure there are no medical reasons for the obesity, and that it is safe to cut back the number of calories. Your veterinarian will provide you with diet instructions.

Older dogs should lose weight gradually—no more than 1.5 percent of their initial body weight per week. It is important not to feed table scraps and snacks between meals, as the additional calories unbalance the diet.

When feeding geriatric dogs, it is a good idea to divide the daily ration into two equal parts. Feed the first half in the morning and the second half in the evening. Older dogs are less tolerant of changes in diet, and even of changes in drinking water. When changes are necessary, make them gradually (see *Switching Diets*, Chapter 9).

VITAMINS AND MINERALS

Geriatric dogs may have increased mineral and vitamin requirements. B vitamins are lost in the urine of elderly dogs with reduced kidney function. The intestinal tract's ability to absorb vitamins also decreases as the individual ages. Fortunately, high-quality commercial dog foods contain enough vitamins and minerals to meet the needs of elderly individuals. If you are feeding one of these foods, vitamin supplements should not be necessary.

Antioxidants are substances given to fight free-radicals, which are the result of oxidation processes that occur in normal and damaged tissue. According to a popular theory of aging, the accumulation of free-radicals accelerates the aging process and leads to degenerative diseases such as osteoarthritis. Although specific proof is lacking, many veterinarians believe antioxidants have benefit in older dogs.

The antioxidants used most often are vitamin E, vitamin C and selenium. If desired, you can safely supplement your dog using an antioxidant product prescribed by your veterinarian.

SPECIAL DIETS

Prescription diets, such as those from Purina and Hills Pet Products, may be required for dogs with heart disease, kidney disease, intestinal disease or obesity. They are available through your veterinarian.

Bringing in a New Puppy

Adding a puppy to the household can be a rejuvenating experience for the elderly dog. When handled properly, most old dogs delight in the companionship. Through renewed interest and added exercise, they seem to recapture their youth.

Prevent jealousy by giving attention to the old dog first. Always affirm the older dog's senior privileges.

Putting Your Dog to Sleep (Euthanasia)

The time may come when you are faced with the prospect of having to put your pet to sleep. This is a difficult decision to make—both for you and for your veterinarian. Many old and infirm dogs can be made quite comfortable with just a little more thoughtfulness and tender loving care than the average healthy dog needs. Old dogs can still enjoy months or years of happiness in the company of loved ones.

But when life ceases to be a joy and a pleasure, when the dog suffers from a painful and progressive condition for which there is no hope of betterment, then perhaps at this time we owe the dog the final kindness of helping him to die easily and painlessly. This is accomplished by an intravenous injection of an anesthetic agent in sufficient amount to cause immediate loss of consciousness and cardiac arrest.

DRUGS AND MEDICATIONS

Anesthetics and Anesthesia

Anesthetics are drugs used to block the sensation of pain. They are divided into two categories: local and general.

Local anesthetics are used to numb the surface of the body. They are injected into tissue and around regional nerves. They may also be applied topically to mucous membranes. Local anesthetics such as xylocaine have the fewest risks and side effects, but are not suitable for major surgery.

General anesthetics render the dog unconscious. They can be given by injection or inhalation. Light anesthesia sedates or relaxes the dog and may be suitable for short procedures such as removing porcupine quills. Inhaled gasses, such as Isoflurane, are administered through a tube placed in the windpipe.

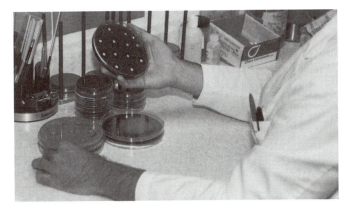

This is an antibiotic sensitivity test. Discs containing antibiotics on an agar plate show which antibiotics inhibit the growth of the cultured bacteria.

The dose of an anesthetic is computed according to the weight of the dog. Certain breeds have an increased sensitivity to barbiturates and other anesthetics, and that must also be taken into account. Toy breeds and breeds with a low percentage of body fat, particularly Greyhounds and Border Collies, require less anesthetic per pound of body weight. This is one reason why anesthetics should be given by someone who is trained to determine the degree of sedation the drugs produce.

Combinations of anesthetics are often given to lessen the potential toxicity of each.

Anesthetics are removed from the bloodstream by the lungs, liver and kidneys. Impaired function of these organs can cause dose-related complications. If your dog has a history of lung, liver, kidney or heart disease, the risk from anesthesia and surgery is increased.

A major risk of general anesthesia is having the dog vomit when going to sleep or waking up. The vomitus refluxes into the windpipe and produces asphyxiation. This can be avoided by keeping the stomach empty for 12 hours before scheduled surgery. If you know your dog is going to have an operation the next day, *do not give him anything to eat or drink after 6pm the night before*. This means picking up the water dish and keeping the dog away from the toilet bowl and other sources of water.

Analgesics

Analgesics are drugs used to relieve pain. There are many classes of pain killers. Demerol, morphine, codeine and other narcotics are subject to federal regulation and cannot be purchased without a prescription.

Buffered or enteric coated aspirin (acetylsalicylic acid) is an over-the-counter analgesic that is safe for home veterinary care in the recommended dosage for dogs. (Aspirin has a very low margin of safety and should not be used for cats.) Buffered or enteric coated aspirin is much safer than regular aspirin because it is less likely to cause stomach and duodenal ulcers.

Aspirin remains effective as a short-term analgesic for the control of pain associated with musculoskeletal injuries. It is no longer recommended for long-term control of osteoarthritis, because of its destructive effects on joint cartilage. There are better analgesics available that do not have this disadvantage.

Note that individual dogs metabolize aspirin at very different rates. This inconsistency can lead to an unexpected accumulation of dangerous breakdown products in the animal's body. As few as two regular-strength aspirin tablets can produce severe organ damage in some medium-sized (30 pound) dogs. Follow the exact dosage given in the table on page 512 to avoid this complication.

In the treatment of arthritis and other inflammations, a new *NSAID* drug called Rimadyl (carprofen) has been tested extensively in dogs. It is less upsetting to the stomach than buffered aspirin and appears to be more effective for long-term treatment. Etodolac is another newly approved canine analgesic that may prove equally effective. These drugs are available by prescription through your veterinarian.

Naproxen and ibuprofen (Motrin) are powerful analgesics, but both have a high incidence of gastrointestinal side effects. This makes them unsuitable for long-term administration. Ibuprofen, in particular, is not recommended for use in dogs. Many other NSAIDs that can be purchased over-the-counter have unpredictable absorption rates and low margins of safety. *None of these should be used without veterinary approval.*

Note that all nonsteroidal anti-inflammatory drugs (colectively known as NSAIDs), irritate the stomach and are capable of causing *stomach and duodenal ulcers* (see Chapter 9). Your veterinarian may prescribe a gastric mucosal protectant such as misoprostol (Cytotec) or sucralfate (Carafate) to prevent this complication. Remember, never use more than one NSAID (including aspirin) at the same time.

Acetaminophen (Tylenol) is an analgesic that is not an *NSAID*. It is used primarily for its fever-reducing properties. Fever should be treated in dogs only when it is high enough to produce injury by itself (that is, when it exceeds 104° to 105°F). Like aspirin, two regular-strength Tylenol tablets can cause severe toxicity in a medium-sized dog. The correct dosage is given in the table on page 512.

Phenylbutazone (Butazolidin) is an analgesic widely used in horses. In dogs it appears to have harmful effects on joint cartilage. Its other main drawback is that it can cause bone marrow suppression, especially when given in high doses for long periods. It is no longer recommended now that safer analgesics are available.

Flunixin meglumine (Banamine) is a potent analgesic that is also useful in fighting the toxins produced by bacteria. This makes it useful in treating septic shock. Gastrointestinal toxicity limits its use in dogs.

When pain relievers are used for treating sprains and acute injuries of muscles, tendons and joints, the dog should be confined or restricted from exercising. Pain relief may cause the dog to overuse the limb, which can delay recovery.

Antibiotics

Antibiotics are used to fight bacteria and fungus in and on the body. Bacteria are classified according to their ability to cause disease. Pathogenic bacteria are capable of producing a particular illness or infection. Nonpathogenic bacteria live on or within the host but do not cause illness under normal conditions. These bacteria are called normal flora. Some actually produce substances necessary to the well-being of the host. For example, bacteria in the bowel synthesize vitamin K (necessary for blood clotting).

Antibiotics fall into two categories: Bacteriostatic and fungistatic drugs inhibit the growth of microorganisms but don't kill them; bactericidal and fungicidal drugs destroy the microorganisms outright.

WHY ANTIBIOTICS FAIL

Antibiotics may not always be effective, for a number of reasons.

Inadequate Wound Care. Antibiotics enter the bloodstream and are carried to the source of the infection. Abscesses, wounds containing devitalized tissue and wounds with foreign bodies (dirt or splinters, for example) are resistant areas. Under such circumstances, antibiotics can't get into the wound. Accordingly, it is essential to drain abscesses, clean dirty wounds and remove foreign bodies.

Inappropriate Selection. An antibiotic chosen to treat an infection must be effective against the specific bacteria that is infecting the body. The best way to determine susceptibility is to sample the organism, grow it on a culture plate and identify it by the way its colony appears and by microscopic characteristics.

Antibiotic discs are then applied to the culture plate to see which discs inhibit the growth of colonies. The results are graded according to whether the bacteria is sensitive, indifferent or insensitive to the effects of the antibiotic.

Laboratory findings, however, do not always coincide with results in the patient. Nonetheless, sensitivity testing is the best way of selecting the most effective antibiotic.

Route of Administration. An important medical decision is choosing the best route for administration. With severe infections, antibiotics are given intravenously or by intramuscular injection. Some oral antibiotics should be given on an empty stomach; others with a meal. Incomplete absorption is one cause of inadequate levels of antibiotic in the blood.

Dose and Frequency of Administration. The dose is computed by weighing the dog, then dividing the total daily dose into equal parts and giving them at prescribed intervals. Other factors that must be accounted for when computing the daily dose are the severity of the infection, the age of the dog, his overall health and stamina, and whether the dog is taking another antibiotic. When the total dose is too low or the antibiotic is not given often enough, the drug may not be effective.

Resistant Strains. Antibiotics can destroy the normal flora in the body, which crowds out pathogens. This allows harmful bacteria to multiply and cause disease. Furthermore, strains of bacteria may develop that are resistant to antibiotics and thus cannot be effectively controlled. This is particularly likely to occur when antibiotics are used:

- For too short a time
- In too low a dosage
- When the antibiotic is not bactericidal

Microorganisms resistant to one antibiotic are usually resistant to other antibiotics of the same class. The development of antibiotic-resistant bacteria is one of the main reasons why antibiotics should be used exactly as prescribed and only in situations in which they will clearly benefit the dog.

ANTIBIOTICS AND STEROIDS

Steroids are often combined with antibiotics, particularly in topical preparations for the eye and ear, and on the skin. Corticosteroids have anti-inflammatory effects. By reducing swelling, redness and tenderness, they often give the impression the dog is getting better when he actually is not.

Steroids have one other side effect that is undesirable: They depress the normal immune response. This can impair the dog's ability to fight the infection. Antibiotic preparations containing steroids should be used under veterinary guidance. This is particularly true for eye preparations.

Drug Complications

TOXICITY

All drugs are poisons, capable of causing greater harm than good. There is a margin of safety between a therapeutic dose and a toxic dose. A safe drug has a wide margin of safety. Toxicity is caused by overdose, impaired elimination, giving the drug for too long a time or using a drug with a narrow margin of safety.

If a dog has advanced liver or kidney disease, drugs are not detoxified and excreted. The dosage of any drug must therefore be reduced accordingly. Young pups require a lower dose per pound of body weight than do adult dogs, because puppies' kidneys are immature.

Drug toxicity can affect one or more systems. Signs are difficult to recognize in dogs, and can be far advanced before they come to the owner's attention. The signs of drug toxicity include:

- **Ears.** Damage to the otic nerves leads to ringing in the ears, hearing loss and deafness. The hearing loss can be permanent.
- **Liver.** Jaundice and liver failure.
- **Kidneys.** Nitrogen retention, uremia and kidney failure.
- **Bone marrow.** Depresses the production of red blood cells, white blood cells and platelets, resulting in anemia, impaired immunity and spontaneous bleeding.

ALLERGIC REACTIONS

Antibiotics cause more allergic reactions in dogs than any other group of drugs. A *dog that has had any type of allergic drug reaction should not be given that drug again.*

Signs of a mild allergic reaction are hives, rash, itching and scratching, and watering eyes. Hives is characterized by the sudden appearance of raised, circular areas in which the hair sticks out in patches. Hives generally appear within 30 minutes of exposure and disappear within 24 hours. Other allergic reactions are discussed in *Allergies* in Chapter 4.

Anaphylactic shock is an uncommon, severe allergic reaction usually caused by exposure to foreign proteins such as penicillin or a vaccine. The signs are vomiting, diarrhea, weakness, *stridor*, difficulty breathing, collapse and sometimes death. *Anaphylactic shock* is a medical emergency and is discussed in Chapter 1, page 35.

How to Give Medications

Don't give your dog any medication until you have spoken to your veterinarian to make sure it is the right medicine for the circumstances. You should also receive instructions on how to give the drug and the correct dosage for your dog.

PILLS, CAPSULES AND TABLETS

To give a pill, slip a thumb into the space behind the canine tooth and press upward on the roof of the mouth. As the mouth begins to open, press down on the lower jaw with the opposite thumb.

Insert the pill well to the back of the tongue in the middle of the mouth. If you place the pill too far forward or to the side of the tongue, the dog will spit it out. Close the dog's mouth and massage or rub his throat until he swallows. If the dog licks his nose, the pill has been swallowed.

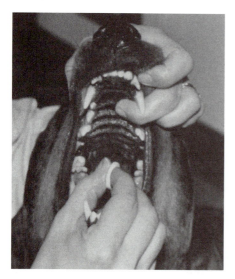

The correct way to give a pill—in the middle and well at the back of the tongue. (J. Clawson)

Do not break the pill up into a powder. Powders have an unpleasant taste that dogs don't accept well. Furthermore, some pills have a protective coating that is important for the delayed release of the medication.

LIQUIDS

Liquid medicines, including electrolytes and water solutions, are administered into the cheek pouch between the molars and the cheek. A medicine bottle, eyedropper or plastic syringe can be used to dispense the liquid.

Pinch the lips together as shown in the photo below. Insert the end of the dispenser into the cheek pouch and seal the lips with your fingers. Tilt the chin upward and slowly dispense the liquid. The dog will swallow automatically.

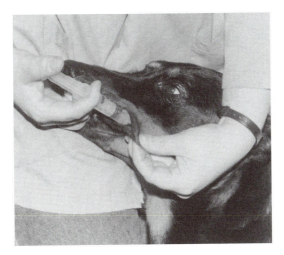

Liquids are administered into the cheek pouch using a plastic syringe or a medicine bottle. (J. Clawson)

INJECTIONS

Injecting a foreign substance into the body always carries with it the danger of causing an acute allergic or anaphylactic reaction as described in Chapter 1 (see *Anaphylactic Shock* on page 35). Treating anaphylactic shock requires immediate intravenous adrenaline and oxygen. This is one reason why it is best to have your veterinarian give injections.

If it becomes necessary to give injections at home (for example, if the dog is diabetic), have the procedure demonstrated by your veterinarian. Some injections are given under the skin (subcutaneous) and others into the muscle (intramuscular). Directions that come with the product will indicate the correct route.

The injection itself usually is not painful, although intramuscular injections may hurt somewhat as the medicine is injected. Dogs should be restrained as described in Chapter 1 under *Handling and Restraint*. Having an assistant is helpful.

Begin by drawing the medicine up into the syringe. Then point the needle toward the ceiling and press the plunger to expel all air from the syringe and needle. Select the injection site and cleanse the skin with cotton soaked in alcohol.

Subcutaneous Injections

These are given under the skin on the back of the neck or the shoulder. Here the skin is loose and easily forms a fold when pinched. Grasp a fold of skin to form a ridge. Firmly push the point of the needle through the skin into the subcutaneous fat at an angle somewhat parallel to the surface of the body.

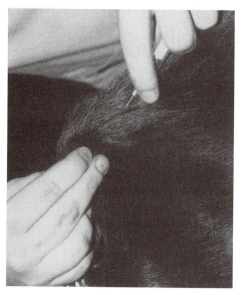

Subcutaneous injections are given beneath the skin on the back of the neck or shoulder.

Before giving the injection, pull back a bit on the plunger and look for blood. If blood appears, the medicine might be injected into a vein or artery. Withdraw the syringe and start again. Once you see no blood, push in the plunger. Withdraw the needle and rub the skin for a few seconds to disperse the medicine.

Intramuscular Injections

These are given into the muscle at the back of the thighs, halfway between the hip and the knee. Use a 3/4-inch-long needle. Note the location of the bone and plan to place the injection into muscle well away from the bone. Injections into bones, nerves and joints can be avoided by giving the shots in the location described.

Intramuscular injections are given into the back of the thigh muscle away from the bone.

Insert the needle rapidly through the skin to minimize pain. Withdraw the plunger and check for blood before giving the injection. Inject the medication slowly over five to seven seconds.

As a precaution, do not administer a drug by injection to a dog that has had any sort of past history of an allergic reaction (such as hives) to that drug.

ENEMAS

Enemas are discussed in *Fecal Impactions* in Chapter 9.

SUPPOSITORIES

When a dog cannot take a drug orally (for example, when he is vomiting), medications can be given by suppository. Your veterinarian may also prescribe a suppository to treat a bout of severe constipation.

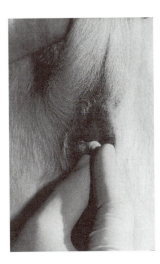

Inserting a suppository into the anal canal.
(J. Clawson)

The suppository is lubricated with petroleum jelly and slipped all the way into the rectum, where it dissolves.

Suppositories for constipation contain a mild irritant, which draws water into the rectum and stimulates a bowel movement. Dulcolax is good for this purpose, and you can buy it at any drugstore; use the pediatric size.

Do not give suppositories to dogs that are dehydrated or may have an intestinal obstruction. A dog with an *Acute Painful Abdomen,* described in Chapter 1, also should not be given a suppository.

OTHER MEDICATIONS

The proper way to medicate the eyes is discussed in Chapter 5, *How to Apply Eye Medicines.* Medicating the ears is discussed in the Chapter 6, *How to Apply Ear Medicines.*

Common Drugs for Home Veterinary Use		
Drug	Action	Dose by Weight of Dog
Aspirin (buffered; enteric coated)	Analgesic, anti-inflammatory	5 mg per pound orally every 12 hours
Benadryl (diphenhydramine)	Antihistamine	2 mg per pound orally every eight hours
Betadine solution (povidone-iodine)	Topical antiseptic	Dilute to 0.2 percent (2 mL to 2 quarts tap water)
Charcoal compressed activated charcoal	Binds stomach poisons	1 5 gm tablet per 10 pounds; keep at least 30 tablets available
Chlorhexidine solution (Nolvasan and others)	Topical antiseptic	Dilute to 0.05 percent (25 mL to 2 quarts tap water)
Dramamine (dimenhydrinate)	Motion sickness	2 to 4 mg per pound orally every eight hours
Hydrogen peroxide (3%)	Induce vomiting	1 teaspoon per 10 pounds orally; may repeat every 15 to 30 minutes (3 times only)
Kaopectate	For persistent diarrhea	1/2 to 1 mL per pound (or 1 to 2 teaspoons per 10 pounds) orally every 4 hours

Drug	Action	Dose by Weight of Dog
Milk of Magnesia (magnesium hydroxide)	Antacid, laxative	2 to 5 mL per pound orally every 4 to 6 hours (antacid); or 7 to 25 mL per pound orally once only (laxative)
Mineral oil	Lubricant, laxative	10 to 50 mL per dog; add to food
Pepto-Bismol (bismuth subsalicylate)	For diarrhea	0.5 to 1.5 mL per pound orally every 12 hours
Robitussin	Expectorant	1 teaspoon per 20 pounds orally every 4 hours, as needed
Robitussin DM or **Benylin Expectorant** (dextromethorphan)	Cough suppressant	0.5 to 1 mg per pound (or 1 teaspoon per 20 pounds) orally every 6 hours
Tylenol (acetaminophen)	Fever reducer, analgesic	7 mg per pound (or 1/2 of a 325-mg tablet per 25 pounds) orally every 8 hours

Note: 1 teaspoon is 5 mL; 1 tablespoon is 15 mL.

APPENDIX A

NORMAL PHYSIOLOGICAL DATA

Normal Temperature

Adult Dog: 100° to 102.5°F
Average is 101.3°F
Newborn Puppy: 94° to 97°F at birth
100°F at four weeks old

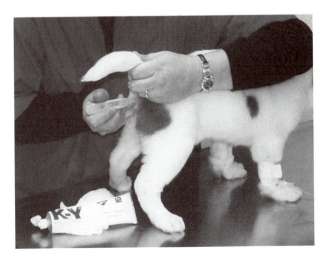

Taking a dog's rectal temperature with a digital thermometer.

HOW TO TAKE YOUR DOG'S TEMPERATURE

The only effective way to take your dog's temperature is to use a rectal thermometer. Bulb and digital rectal thermometers are equally acceptable, but the digital thermometer is more convenient and records the temperature faster.

If using a bulb thermometer, shake it down until the bulb registers 96°F (35.5°C). Lubricate the bulb with petroleum or K-Y jelly. Raise the dog's tail holding it firmly to keep him from sitting down; using a twisting motion, gently insert the bulb into the anal canal one to three inches, depending on the size of the dog.

Note: For newborn puppies, use a pediatric thermometer and insert the tip of the thermometer only as far as necessary to completely cover the bulb or tip.

Hold the thermometer in place for three minutes. Then remove it, wipe it clean and read the temperature by the height of the silver column of mercury on the thermometer scale. Clean the thermometer with alcohol to prevent the transfer of diseases.

If using a digital thermometer, insert it the same way and follow the manufacturer's directions.

Should the thermometer break off—this usually happens because the dog sits down—do not attempt to find and extract the broken end. Notify your veterinarian immediately.

Normal Heart Rate

Adult dog: 60 to 160 beats per minute
Toy breeds: Up to 180 beats per minute
Newborn puppy: 160 to 200 beats per minute at birth; 220 beats per minute at two weeks of age

To learn how to take your dog's pulse, see *Pulse* in Chapter 11.

Normal Respiratory Rate

Adult dog: Average is 24 breaths per minute at rest; range is 10 to 30 breaths per minute.
Newborn puppy: 15 to 35 breaths per minute up to two weeks of age

Gestation

Averages 63 days from the *day of ovulation*. The normal range is 56 to 66 days.

APPENDIX B

COMPARATIVE AGE OF DOGS TO HUMANS

An old rule of thumb is that one dog year is equivalent to seven human years, but this is not always accurate. Dogs age at different rates than humans. Some dog years are equivalent to more than seven years and some to less. For example, it takes puppies about a year to grow into their adult bodies while it takes children a lot longer. Thus the first year of a dog's life is perhaps equivalent to about 15 years of a child's.

Dogs also vary in how quickly they age. In general, small breeds live longer than large ones—occasionally twice as long. The chart below indicates average figures for all breeds of dogs.

Age of Dog, in Years	Age of Human, in Years
1	15
2	24
3	28
4	32
5	36
6	40
7	44
8	48

continues

Age of Dog, in Years	Age of Human, in Years
9	52
10	56
11	60
12	64
13	68
14	72
15	76
16	80

Appendix C

Organizations and Addresses

American Kennel Club
5580 Centerview Drive, Suite 250
Raleigh, NC 27606-3394
(919) 233-9767
www.akc.org

American Veterinary Medical Association
Suite 100
1931 North Meacham Road
Schaumburg, IL 60173
(847) 925-8070
www.avma.org

Canine Eye Registration Foundation (CERF)
VMDB-CERF
Purdue University
1248 Lynn Hall
West Lafayette, IN 47907
(765) 494-8179
www.vet.purdue.edu/~yshen/cerf.html

Genetic Disease Control in Animals (GDC)
P.O. Box 222
Davis, CA 95617
(530) 756-6773
www.vetmed.ucdavis.edu/gdc/gdc.html

Humane Society of the United States
2100 L Street N.W.
Washington, DC 20037
(202) 452-1100
www.hsus.org

National Animal Poison Control Center
(800) 548-2423 or (900) 680-0000

National Association of Professional Pet Sitters
1030 15th Street N.W., Suite 870
Washington, DC 20005
(202) 393-3317
www.petsitters.org

Orthopedic Foundation for Animals (OFA)
2301 East Nifong Blvd,
Columbia, MO 65201
(573) 442-0418
www.offa.org

PennHip/Internatinal Canine Genetics
271 Great Valley Parkway
Malvern, PA 19355
(610) 640-1244 or (800) 248-8099

VetGen
3728 Plaza Drive, Suite No. 1
Ann Arbor, MI 48108
(800) 483-8436
www.vetgen.com

GLOSSARY

Words in italics are defined elsewhere in the Glossary.

Abortion   Death of a fetus after organ development (28 days), followed by expulsion of the products of conception.

Abscess   A collection of pus in a cavity. It may be beneath the skin, in an organ or a body space.

Accommodate   The process during which the lens of the eye changes shape to focus light on the retina.

Acidosis   A buildup of acids in the blood, resulting in a lower pH than normal.

ACTH   Adrenocorticotropic hormone, the pituitary hormone that stimulates the adrenal cortex to produce corticosteroids.

Acute   To present for a short period; often indicates the early stage of a disease when symptoms are most pronounced.

Afebrile   Without fever.

AKC   American Kennel Club.

Allergen   Any substance capable of causing an allergic reaction. Drugs, insect toxins, pollens, molds, dust mites, foods and vaccinations are common allergens in dogs.

Alopecia   Loss of hair, or failure to regrow hair, resulting in an area of thinning or baldness.

Analgesia   Pain relief.

Anomaly   Out of the ordinary; a condition that departs from the normal.

Anestrus   The fourth phase of the estrous cycle in which there is little, if any, ovarian activity. The length of this phase varies, lasting on average 130 to 150 days.

Anorectal   Anatomically, the area encompassed by the anus, anal canal and rectum.

Anorexia   Sustained loss of appetite and failure to eat.

Anthelmintic   A medication that acts to dispel or destroy parasitic intestinal worms.

Antibody   A protein substance produced by the immune system to neutralize the effects of an *antigen*.

Antigen   A substance recognized by the immune system as foreign to the body. The immune system develops antibodies that bind the antigen and prevent it from harming the animal or causing disease.

Arrhythmia   An abnormal heart rhythm. It may be inconsequential, or serious enough to cause cardiac arrest.

Ascarids   Roundworms.

Ascites   An abnormal accumulation of fluid in the *peritoneal cavity*. Congestive heart failure and liver failure are the most common causes.

Assay   Testing the *serum* to determine the relative proportion of a substance, such as the concentration of an *antigen* or *antibody*.

Assisted breathing   Artificially filling and emptying the lungs to temporarily support the respiratory system.

Atresia   Failure of a channel or passage to open in the course of fetal development.

Atrophy   Shrinkage in the size of an organ or tissue due to disuse or death of cells.

Auto-antibodies   Antibodies that a host makes against its own tissues. Auto-antibodies cause destruction of the targeted cells.

Autoimmune disease   A disease resulting from *auto-antibodies* targeting host tissue.

Autosomal   All chromosomes that are not the X and Y sex chromosomes.

Bactericidal   Capable of killing bacteria, as opposed to just inhibiting their growth.

Benign   An abnormal growth that is not a cancer.

Bezoars   Foreign bodies in the stomach composed of hair and other ingested materials that form hard concretions too large to pass out of the stomach.

Bilateral   On both sides.

Biopsy   The removal of tissue for microscopic examination and diagnosis.

Bitch   A female dog.

Bleb   A skin blister filled with *serum* or blood.

Boil   A small skin *abscess*, usually at the site of a hair follicle.

BPH   Benign prostatic hyperplasia, a noncancerous form of prostatic enlargement.

Brachycephalic   A dog with a broad skull and a short muzzle, resulting in a flat face, as in the Pug and Pekingese.

Breeder   The owner of the bitch when the dog was bred.

Brisket   The lower chest, particularly the sternum.

Bronchoscopy   A procedure in which a rigid or flexible *endoscope* is passed into the trachea and bronchi to directly visualize the interior of the respiratory tract.

Brood bitch   A female dog used for breeding.

Bulla   A large skin blister filled with clear fluid, or, in the case of the lungs, air sacs filled with air.

Calculus   Dental calculus (also called tartar) is a *plaque*like material composed of calcium salts, food particles and bacteria.

Cancer   A *tumor* on the surface of the body or within an organ that has the potential to destroy tissue and kill the animal through local growth, and/or spread to distant parts.

Canids   Foxes, wolves, coyotes and other cousins of dogs.

Capillary refill time   The time it takes for the gums to pink up after being firmly pressed with a finger—normally one second or less. A measure of the quality of the circulation.

Cardiac massage   Compression of the heart, resulting in temporary support of the circulation.

Castrate   To remove the testicles of a male dog.

Cellulitis   Infection of all layers of the skin, characterized by redness, swelling, tenderness and increased warmth.

Cerebral edema   Swelling of the brain following injury or a period of oxygen deprivation.

Chemotherapy   The use of drugs that are cellular poisons to attack and kill cancer cells, or to suppress the immune system in the treatment of auto-immune diseases.

Choke collar   A collar that tightens around the dog's neck with tension and loosens when tension is released.

Chondroprotective   Compounds that protect joint cartilage from the destructive effects of degenerative joint disease.

Chromosomes   Strands of DNA protein that contain the sequence of *genes*.

Chronic   Present for a long period. Often indicates that stage of a disease in which symptoms persist in a milder form.

CNS   Central nervous system, including the brain and spinal cord.

Colonoscopy   A procedure that uses an *endoscope* to view the interior of the colon and rectum.

Colostrum   The first milk of the dam, containing the all-important maternal antibodies that protect puppies from common diseases for the first three months of life.

Conceptus   The products resulting from the union between egg and sperm.

Condition (of the body)   A subjective term that refers to the health as shown by the coat, general appearance and musculature.

Conformation   How the various angles, shapes and parts of the dog's body conform to the breed standard. At dog shows, dogs are judged by how well they conform to the breed standards.

Congenital A condition that exists at birth, although it is not always clinically evident until later in life. Congenital conditions can either be genetically determined or acquired before or during delivery.

Corpus luteum A growth that forms in the ovary at the site of ovulation. The corpus luteum manufactures progesterone, essential to the support of pregnancy. The plural is corpora lutea.

CPK Creatine phosphokinase, an enzyme found in muscle tissue and released when there is muscle injury or disease.

CPR Cardiopulmonary resuscitation; the combination of assisted breathing and cardiac massage.

Crossbred A dog whose sire and dam are of different breeds.

Cryopreservation Freezing and storing tissue for later use.

Cryotherapy A procedure in which tissue is destroyed by freezing it with liquid nitrogen.

CT scan Computerized tomography, a diagnostic X-ray procedure that produces cross-sectional views of a body structure. CT scans may be available only at referral centers. Sometimes also called CAT scan.

Cyanosis A bluish discoloration of the gums and tongue due to inadequate oxygen in the blood.

Cytology The microscopic examination of cells to determine the cause of a disease.

Dam The mother of a puppy.

Dementia Loss of memory and reasoning power characterized by varying degrees of confusion, disorientation, apathy and stupor.

Depigmentation Loss of dark color in the skin caused by destruction of *melanin*-producing cells. Depigmented areas are shades of white.

Depigmented Loss of black pigment in areas such as the skin of the nose.

Depression A marked decrease in activity in which the dog withdraws, spends most of his time lying down, is disinterested in his surroundings and exhibits little or no interest in eating.

Dermis The sensitive connective tissue layer of the skin located below the epidermis.

Dewclaws Vestigial toes; the equivalent of a fifth digit high on the inside of each foot.

Diestrus The third stage in the *estrous cycle*, also called the *luteal phase*, begins when the female refuses to stand for mating. It lasts, on average, about 60 days and then merges with *anestrus*.

Dominant A *gene* is dominant if it alone is capable of determining the expression of a particular trait.

Duodenum The first part of the small intestine after the stomach.

Dysfunction   Abnormal performance of an organ or system.

Dysphagia   Painful and/or difficult swallowing.

Dysplastic   Developmentally malformed.

Dysuria   Painful and/or difficult urination.

Early embryonic loss   Loss of the productions of conception before 28 days' *gestation*.

ECG   Electrocardiogram; the readings from an electrocardiograph, which measures the changes in electrical currents associated with heart activity. An ECG is used to measure heart function and detect abnormalities.

Echocardiogram   A test that uses doppler ultrasound (high-frequency sound waves) to create a computerized image of structures within the heart.

Echocardiography   The procedure that uses an *echocardiogram* to diagnose heart disease.

Edema   The accumulation of fluid beneath the skin.

Edematous   Filled with *edema* fluid.

EEG   Electroencephalography; a procedure that records the electrical activity of the cerebral cortex. It is used to diagnose epilepsy, *tumors* and brain diseases.

EGD   Esophagogastroduodenoscopy; see *gastroscopy*.

Ejaculate   The total volume of *semen* emitted by the stud dog during breeding.

Electrocautery   The use of an electric probe to destroy tissue by heat.

Electrolytes   Sodium, chloride, potassium, bicarbonate, calcium, phosphorus and other minerals required for organ function.

ELISA   Enzyme-Linked Immunosorbent Assay, a serologic test used to detect antibodies to a protein, such as those associated with a bacteria or virus.

Elizabethan collar   A wide plastic collar used to keep a dog from scratching at the ears and biting at wounds and skin sores.

Embolus   A blood clot that develops at another site and travels through the vascular system to a smaller vessel, where it becomes lodged and interrupts blood flow.

Embryo   A *conceptus* younger than 28 days' *gestation*, before the stage of organ development.

Encapsulated   Surrounded by a capsule that creates a distinct boundary between two tissue planes.

Encephalitis   Inflammation and/or infection of the brain.

Endemic   Dwelling in or native to a particular population or region.

Endometrium   A layer of glandular tissue lining the cavity of the uterus.

Endoscope   An instrument that uses lights and fiber optics or a miniaturized video camera to view the interior of a body cavity.

Endoscopy   Using an *endoscope* to visualize the interior of a body cavity.

Enteritis Inflammation of the lining of the intestine, caused by bacterial, parasitic or viral infection.

Eosinophil A type of white blood cell that is often associated with diseases having an allergic component.

Epididymis The coiled tube on top of the testicle that stores the sperm.

Epithelium A layer of nonliving cells that forms the surface of the skin, mucous membranes and cornea.

Erosion An area where a body surface has been destroyed by trauma or inflammation.

Erythrocytes Red blood cells.

Estrous cycle The entire reproductive cycle, as determined from one ovulation to the next, normally occurring about every five to nine months in the sexually mature *bitch*.

Estrus Same as *heat*. The first phase of the *estrous cycle*, during which the bitch is receptive to the male; lasts on average seven to nine days.

Etiology Cause of the disease.

Euthanasia The humane process of giving an animal a fatal, painless injection to end its suffering.

Excision The surgical removal (cutting out) of a *tumor* or *lesion*.

Excoriation A deep scratch or abrasion of the skin.

Exudate A liquid discharge containing pus and bacteria.

Face The combination of eyes, nose, mouth, lips and cheeks.

FDA Food and Drug Administration; licenses the use of human and veterinary drugs.

Fertility In stud dogs, the ability to impregnate the bitch. In brood bitches, the ability to conceive and carry a litter.

Fetus A *conceptus* older than 28 days' gestation, generally after the stage of organ development.

Fibrosis The replacement of normal tissue by scar tissue.

Flatus Breaking wind; passing gas from the rectum.

Follicle A growth within the ovary that contains an egg.

Fontanel The soft spot on the top of the skull where the bones of the skull come together. It normally closes before or shortly after birth.

Fresh semen *Semen* artificially inseminated into the bitch within a few hours of collection.

FSH *Follicle* stimulating hormone; produced by the pituitary gland. It causes the ovaries to produce egg *follicles*.

Furuncle A small skin *boil*, about two to three millimeters in size.

Gastroesophageal junction The anatomical area formed by the junction of the swallowing tube and the stomach.

Gastroscopy A procedure that uses an *endoscope* to view the interior of the esophagus, stomach and duodenum. Same as *EGD*.

GDC Institute for Genetic Disease Control in Animals.

Gene The basic unit of heredity. Each gene contains the code that produces a specific protein or molecule.

Genome (canine) The map that gives the locus (chromosome and site) of all 80,000 genes that control the makeup of the dog; the complete set of hereditary factors.

Genotype The combination of genes that determine a physical characteristic.

Gestation Length of pregnancy; the period from conception to birth. It averages 63 days from the day of ovulation, with a normal range of 56 to 66 days.

GI An abbreviation for gastrointestinal.

Gn-RH Gonadotrophin-releasing hormone; triggers the release of *FSH* and *LH* from the pituitary gland.

Gonadotropins Hormones released from the pituitary gland or placenta, acting on the ovaries or testicles to cause them to manufacture and release the sex hormones.

Gram (Gm) 1/1,000 of a kilogram. About the weight of a paper clip. Once ounce equals 28.35 grams.

Grand mal A type of seizure typical of epilepsy.

Hackles Hairs on the neck and back; they are raised in fright or anger.

Handler A person who handles a dog in the show ring or at field trials.

Haw A visible third eyelid at the inner corner of the eye.

hCG Human chorionic gonadotropin, used to induce ovulation.

Head-pressing Pressing the head against the wall or furniture without apparent purpose.

Heat See *estrus*.

Hematocrit The percentage of red blood cells in whole blood.

Hematoma A collection of clotted blood beneath the skin at the site of an injury.

Hematuria The passage of blood in the urine, recognized by red-colored urine or blood clots in the urine. Microscopic hematuria is the presence of red cells on microscopic exam.

Hemolytic anemia The disease that results when red blood cells are destroyed in the dog's circulation.

Histiocyte A cell belonging to the immune system that wanders in the connective tissue and kills foreign cells, such as bacteria.

Histology The microscopic study of the structure of tissue to determine the cause of disease.

Hives   See *wheal*.

Hydrotherapy   Cold water delivered to the site of injury using a shower head or nozzle.

Hyperpigmentation   A darkening of the skin due to the deposition of *melanin* in the *dermis*. Associated with chronic inflammation of the skin.

Hypertrophy   Enlargement of an organ or tissue; an increase in size and volume.

Hypoxia   Lack of oxygen in the blood and tissues. If untreated, it results in coma and death.

Hysterectomy   *Spaying;* the removal of the uterus and ovaries. Also called ovariohysterectomy.

Iatrogenic   An unintended disease that results from a medical treatment or procedure.

Idiopathic   A disease or condition for which no cause is known.

IFA   Immunofluorescent antibody test; a serologic test used to detect antibodies to bacteria and viruses.

Ileocecal valve   A flap of *mucosa* at the junction of the small bowel and colon that acts like a valve.

IM   Abbreviation for intramuscular; an injection given into the muscle.

Immunosuppressants   Medications that suppress the immune response—a desirable effect in *autoimmune diseases*.

Intubation   Placing a breathing tube into the trachea to establish an airway for assisted breathing.

In utero   Occurring in the uterus.

Incarceration   Trapping an organ or part of an organ within a closed space.

Infarction   Death of tissue as a consequence of an interruption in the blood supply.

Infertility   Absence of *fertility*.

Infestation   The presence of parasites in numbers which may or may not be sufficient to cause an infection.

Intact   An animal that has not been spayed or neutered.

Intersex   The condition in which an animal has genital organs that have characteristics of both sexes, and/or has chromosomes containing both male and female genetic material. Intersexuality is associated with relative or absolute infertility.

Intromission   The introduction of the penis into the vagina during breeding.

Involution   The process by which the uterus empties and returns to normal size after *whelping*.

IV   Abbreration for intravenous; an injection given into a vein.

IVP   Intravenous pyelogram; an X-ray of the kidneys taken after injecting a dye into a vein.

Jaundice   A yellow discoloration in the whites of the eyes and mucous membranes of the mouth, caused by an accumulation of bile in the *serum* and tissues.

Karotype   A "picture" of all the chromosomes in a cell.

Karyotyping   Analysis of the number, size and shape of the paired chromosomes of a specific dog to determine its sex.

Killed vaccine   A vaccine made from killed virus particles. Killed vaccines are generally safe, but may not be as effective as *modified live vaccines (MLV)*.

Laparoscopy   A surgical procedure in which an endoscope and surgical instruments are inserted into the abdomen through several small incisions.

Lavage   Flushing out a wound or cavity with large amounts of irrigating solution.

Lesion   A change in the appearance of tissue caused by an injury or a specific disease.

LH   Luteinizing hormone, produced by the pituitary gland. It causes ovarian *follicles* to mature and ovulate.

Ligation   Tying off a vessel.

Lobulated   Having the appearance of several lobes or swellings.

Luteal activity   The influence of the *corpora lutea*, particularly to the effects of *progesterone*.

Luteal phase   See *diestrus*.

Luteolysis   The process that results in the regression and disappearance of the *corpora lutea*. Accompanied by a fall in *serum progesterone*.

Luxation   See *subluxation*.

Lymphadenopathy   The enlargement of one or more lymph nodes as the result of inflammation or cancer.

Macule   A spot on the skin that is a different color (such as red or whitish) but is not elevated.

Malignant   A growth that is a cancer.

Malignant tumor   A *tumor* capable of spreading throughout the body.

Megaesophagus   An enlarged esophagus that does not contract well and interferes with normal swallowing.

Melanin   Naturally occurring dark pigment.

Melena   The dark or tarry black stools associated with upper gastrointestinal bleeding (bleeding in the stomach, duodenum or small intestine).

Meniscus   A cushioning pad of cartilage interposed between two bones.

Merle   A color pattern involving a dominant gene and characterized by dark splotches against a lighter background of the same pigment (seen in Collies, Shetland Sheepdogs, Australian Cattle Dogs and some other breeds).

Metastasize   The spread of a cancer from its site of origin to another part of the body.

Milligram (mg)   1/1,000 of a gram. There are 1,000 mg in one gram.

Milliliters (mL)   1/1,000 of a liter. There are 1,000 mL in one liter.

MLV   Modified live virus vaccine; a vaccine made from live bacteria or viruses that have been treated so that they cannot cause disease.

MRI   Magnetic resonance imaging, a diagnostic procedure that uses a nuclear magnetic spectrometer to produce computerized images of body structures. Available only at referral centers.

Mucociliary blanket   The mucosal lining of the upper respiratory tract that contains cells with *cilia* capable of propelling inhaled irritants into the back of the throat.

Mucopurulent   A discharge containing *mucus* and *pus*.

Mucosa   The inner layer of *mucus*-producing cells that lines the respiratory, gastrointestinal and genitourinary tracts.

Mucus   The slippery substance that is secreted as a protective coating by cells and glands of the mucosa.

Multinodular   A growth composed of *nodules*, giving it an irregular, bumpy surface.

Multiparous   Multiple pregnancies; having been pregnant more than once.

Mutation   An alteration in a gene causing a change in some bodily function that is perpetuated in all the cells that descend from the original mutant cell.

Muzzle (of a dog)   The head in front of the eyes, including the jaws.

Myelitis   An infection of the spinal cord.

Myelogram   An X-ray study in which a contrast material is injected into the spinal canal to show whether a disc or *tumor* is impinging on the spinal cord.

Myopathy   A disease of muscle or muscle tissue.

Necrosis   The death of a cell or group of cells in contact with living tissue.

Neoplasm   Any growth on the surface of the body or within an organ; includes noncancerous and cancerous growths.

Nephron   The basic working unit of the kidney, composed of a glomerulus that filters urine and a system of tubules that concentrates the urine and reabsorbs water and *electrolytes*.

Neutering   Removing both testicles in the male; also can refer to *spaying* in females.

Nictitating membrane   The third eyelid; a membrane at the inner corner of the eye that comes out across the eye in response to eye pain and other conditions.

NSAIDs   Nonsteroidal anti-inflammatory drugs, such as buffered aspirin.

Nystagmus   A rhythmic movement of the eyeballs in which the eyes slowly wander a few degrees in one direction and then jerk back. Seen in diseases of the inner ear and brain.

Occlusion   An obstruction or closure of a passageway or vessel.

Occult   Not evident by clinical signs or laboratory tests.

OFA   Orthopedic Foundation for Animals.

Opacity   Loss of transparency of the cornea or lens.

Organisms   Living members of the animal or plant kingdom; usually refers to bacteria, viruses and other small one-celled beings.

OTC   Over-the-counter; refers to drugs.

Oviduct   The tube that carries the egg from the ovary to the uterus.

Ovulation   The process during which the egg *follicle* releases the egg into the *oviduct*.

Palliation   Treatment that affords relief but not a cure.

Palpation   Feeling, pressing on and examining the body with the hands.

Papule   A small bump on the surface of the skin, varying in size from a pinpoint to a split pea.

Parturition   Giving birth; the period covered by labor and delivery.

Pathogenic   Having the potential to cause disease.

Pathogens   Agents such as bacteria, viruses and fungi capable of causing disease in a susceptible host.

Pedigree   The written record of a dog's genealogy of three generations or more.

Perianal   The glands and skin structures surrounding the anal opening.

Perineum   The area extending from the anus to the bottom of the *vulva* in the female, and to the scrotum in the male.

Peristalsis   Rhythmic contractions that propel ingested foods and liquids from the mouth to the anus.

Peritoneal cavity   The abdominal cavity, containing organs of the intestinal, urinary and reproductive tracts.

Placentitis   Infection of the placenta, usually caused by bacteria that ascend into the uterus through the cervix.

Plaque   A soft, yellow-brown material deposited on teeth that hardens into *calculus*.

Pleural effusion   An accumulation of fluid in the chest cavity caused by right-side heart failure, infection or *tumor*.

PMN   Polymorphonuclear leukocyte; inflammatory cells that make up *pus*.

Pneumothorax   Air in the chest caused by a tear in the lung or a wound in the chest wall. The lung collapses, resulting in respiratory distress.

Polygenic traits   Heritable traits that are controlled by the effects of multiple *genes*.

Polyuria   The passage of large amounts of urine, usually recognized by more frequent voiding.

Postmaturity   The condition in which the puppies are mature and ready to be born but the *dam* does not go into labor, especially after 67 days *gestation*.

Postpartum   After giving birth; the period after *whelping* that lasts four to six weeks.

Premature puppy   A pup born alive before 56 days' *gestation*.

Prepuce   The foreskin; the sheath that surrounds the glans or head of the penis.

Primiparous   A female carrying her first litter.

Productive cough   One that brings up a quantity of phlegm. Also known as a moist cough.

Prodromal   The period in a disease just before the onset of symptoms.

Proestrus   The initial stage of the *estrous* cycle, lasting on average nine days. The first sign is a bloody discharge from the *vulva*.

Progeny   Descendents or offspring.

Progesterone   The pregnancy hormone, produced by the ovaries (*corpora lutea*).

Prognosis   A forecast based on the probable outcome of the disease.

Prolapse   The *protrusion* or falling out of a body part.

Prophylactic   A drug (usually an antibiotic) given as a preventive.

Protrusion   The condition of being thrust foreword.

Psychogenic   Having emotional or psychological factors as a basis, as opposed to a specific disease.

Pulmonary edema   The accumulation of fluid in the lungs, usually caused by congestive heart failure.

Purebred   A dog whose ancestors have been of unmixed descent since the breed was recognized.

Purulent   Puslike; a discharge containing *pus*.

Pus   A discharge that contains *serum*, inflammatory cells, and sometimes bacteria and dead tissue.

Pustule   A small bump on the surface of the skin containing *pus*.

Pylorus   The part of the stomach forming a channel between the stomach and the *duodenum*.

Pyoderma   A *purulent* skin infection including *pustules*, *boils*, *abscesses*, *cellulitis* and infected scabs.

Recessive   A *gene* that expresses a trait only when it is combined with another recessive gene.

Recombinant vaccine   A vaccine made by splicing gene-sized fragments of DNA from one organism (a virus or bacteria) and transferring them to another organism (the dog), where they stimulate the production of antibodies.

Reflux (refluxing)   A reversal in the normal direction of flow.

Regurgitation   The passive expulsion of esophageal contents without conscious effort.

Reinfestation   An *infestation* of parasites that occurs after the original crop was eliminated.

Remission   The period during which the dog remains free of symptoms.

Renal pelvis   The funnel that collects the urine excreted by the kidney. It tapers and becomes the ureter.

Resected   The surgical removal of tissue.

Resection   The removal of *malignant,* dead or unwanted tissue by surgically cutting it out.

Retrobulbar space   A space between the back of the eyeball and the bony socket, occupied by fat and blood vessels.

Sarcoma   A cancer that arises from tissue other than glandular tissue.

Scaly   Shedding flakes of skin.

Sclera   The white membrane surrounding the cornea of the eye.

Scrotum   The bag of skin and connective tissue that surrounds and supports the testicles.

Semen   The contents of the *ejaculate,* containing sperm cells, gel and the secretions of the accessory sex glands.

Senile   An age-related decline in physical and mental faculties.

Sepsis   The presence of infection, often accompanied by fever and other signs of illness, such as vomiting and diarrhea.

Septicemic   The stage of *sepsis* in which microorganisms and/or their toxins are found in the blood.

Serosanguinous   A discharge that contains *serum* and blood, generally pink or red in color.

Serum   The clear fluid component of the blood.

Sire   The father of a puppy.

Soundness   Mental and physical health when all the organs and systems are functioning as intended.

Spay   Neutering a *bitch* by removing the ovaries and uterus.

Spermatogenesis   The production of sperm by the testicles.

Spinal tap   A procedure in which a needle is inserted into the spinal canal to remove cerebrospinal fluid for laboratory analysis.

Sporadic   Isolated, occasional or infrequent.

SQ   Abbreviation for subcutaneous; an injection given beneath the skin.

Staging   A system developed to determine the *prognosis* of a cancer and its treatment.

Standard   The set of characteristics of the breed, originally set forth by the parent breed club.

Stenosis   Constriction or narrowing, especially of a channel or passage.

Stenotic   Excessively narrowed in circumference.

Stillbirth   A full-term puppy born dead.

Strangulated   The compression or pinching off of the blood supply to an abdominal organ such as a segment of bowel; leads to death of tissue.

Stridor   A high-pitched, raspy sound caused by air passing through a narrowed larynx.

Stud dog   A male dog used for breeding.

Subclinical   A stage of illness in which infection occurs without apparent signs.

Subfertility   Less than normal *fertility*.

Subluxation   A partial dislocation, in which the bone is partly out of the joint.

Superinfection   The development of a second infection on top of (or following) the first infection.

Synovial fluid analysis   A procedure in which a needle is inserted into a joint to remove fluid for chemical and microscopic examination.

Systemic   Into the system; used in reference to widespread dissemination of infection or cancer, or to the giving of a drug by the oral, intramuscular or intravenous route.

Tartar   See *calculus*.

Teratogenic   That which causes developmental malformations in the fetus.

Testosterone   The male hormone, produced by the testicles.

Thromboembolism   The process by which a blood clot forms in a vein or artery and then moves up or down in the circulatory system, where it causes further clotting.

Titer   The concentration of a measured substance in the *serum*.

Torsion   The twisting of an organ and its blood supply, resulting in insufficient blood flow and death of that organ.

Toxemia   A state of shock induced by the absorption of bacterial toxins from an infected area in the body.

Tracheobronchitis   A viral or bacterial infection of the cells lining the trachea and bronchi.

Tracheostomy   An operation in which an opening is made through the skin into the windpipe to establish a new airway.

Trans-tracheal washings   Cells obtained by flushing the trachea with saline; used to diagnose the causes of upper respiratory infections.

Tucked up   A tightening of the muscles of the abdominal wall, creating a narrow waist and a hunched-up back.

Tumor   Any growth or swelling (such as an *abscess*). A true growth is called a *neoplasm*.

Type   A set of distinguishing physical characteristics that gives the purebred dog the defined look of its breed.

Ulcer of skin   An open sore with an inflamed base, involving the outer layer of the skin and often the *dermis*.

Ultrasonography   A diagnostic procedure that uses high-frequency sound waves to map a picture of an organ or structure inside the body.

Unilateral   On one side only.

Unsound   A dog incapable of performing the functions for which it was bred.

Urethra   The tube that conveys urine from the bladder to outside the body.

Uterine inertia   Failure of the uterus to contract to start labor or to continue to contract during labor.

Vaginal cytology   A procedure in which cells are obtained from the vaginal lining and examined microscopically to determine the stage of the *estrous cycle*.

Ventricles (of the brain)   Cavities within the brain that contain cerebrospinal fluid.

Vesicle   A small skin blister filled with clear fluid.

Vulva   The labia (lips) of the vagina.

Wheal   An intensely itchy raised patch of skin with a white center and a red rim. Varies in size from that of a pinhead to several inches. Often transient.

Whelp   To give birth.

BIBLIOGRAPHY

1996 Central Veterinary Conference. Veterinary Medicine Publishing Group, 1996.

1997 Central Veterinary Conference. Veterinary Medicine Publishing Group, 1997.

1998 Central Veterinary Conference. Booth D: Nutriceuticals in Veterinary Medicine. Veterinary Medicine Publishing Group, 1998.

American Kennel Club: *The Complete Dog Book.* 19th Ed., Howell Book House, 1998.

Atkins, C.: Heartworm disease. In *Veterinary CE Advisor.* North Carolina State University, December 1998.

Birchard, S.J., Sherding, R.J.: *Saunders Manual of Small Animal Practice.* W.B. Saunders, 1994.

Bonagura, J.B., ed., Kirk, R.W., editor emeritus: *Kirk's Current Veterinary Therapy XII, Small Animal Practice.* W.B. Saunders, 1995.

Burg, F.D., Ingelfinger, J.R., Wald, E.R.: *Current Pediatric Therapy.* W.B. Saunders, 1993.

Burke, T.J.: *Small Animal Reproduction and Infertility.* Lea & Febiger, 1986.

Case, Carey, Hirakawa: *Canine and Feline Nutrition.* Mosby-Year Book, 1995.

Leo, J., Kagan, J., eds: Feeding Fido (Dog & Cat Food Tests) in *Consumer Reports* Vol. 63, No. 2. Consumer's Union, February 1998.

Dorland, W.A.: *Dorland's Illustrated Medical Dictionary,* 26th Ed., W.B. Saunders, 1981.

Ettinger, S.J., Feldman, E.C.: *Textbook of Veterinary Internal Medicine* Vols. 1 & 2. W.B. Saunders, 1995.

Fossum, T.W., Hedlund, C.S., Hulse, D.A., Carroll. G.L., Johnson, A.L., Seim III, H.B., Willard, M.D.: *Small Animal Surgery.* Mosby-Year Book, 1997.

Gfeller, R.W., Messonnier, S.P.: *Handbook of Small Animal Toxicology & Poisonings.* Mosby, 1998.

Helper, L.C.: *Magranes Canine Ophthalmology,* 4th ed. Lea & Febiger, 1989.

Hoskins, J.D.: *Veterinary Pediatrics,* 2nd Ed., W. B. Saunders, 1995.

Jones, B.D.: *Canine & Feline Gastroenterology*. W.B. Saunders, 1986.

Kanzler, K., ed. *Veterinary Pharmaceuticals & Biologicals*, 9th Ed., Veterinary Medicine Publishing Group, 1995.

Kirk, R.W., Bistner, S.I., Ford, R.B.: *Handbook of Veterinary Procedures and Emergency Treatment*, 5th Ed., W.B. Saunders Company, 1990.

Leib, M.S., Monroe, W.E.: *Practical Small Animal Internal Medicine*. W.B. Saunders, 1997.

Lorenz, M.D., Cornelius, L.M.: *Small Animal Medical Diagnosis*, 2nd Ed., J.B. Lippincott, 1993.

Lorenz, M.D., Cornelius, L.M., Ferguson, D.C.: *Small Animal Medical Therapeutics*. J.B. Lippincott, 1992.

Mammato, B.: *American Red Cross and the Humane Society of the United States Pet First Aid*. Mosby, 1997.

Morgan, R.V.: *Handbook of Small Animal Practice*, 3rd Ed., W.B. Saunders, 1994.

Murtaugh, R.J., Kaplan, P.M.: *Veterinary Emergency and Critical Care Medicine*. Mosby-Year Book, 1992.

Ogilvie, G.K., Moore, A.S.: *Managing the Veterinary Cancer Patient*. Veterinary Learning Systems, 1995.

Ocular Disorders Proven or Suspected to be Hereditary in Dogs. American College of Veterinary Ophthalmologists, 1992.

Oliver, J.E., Lorenz, M.D., Kornegay, J.N.: *Handbook of Veterinary Neurology*, 3rd Ed., W.B. Saunders, 1997.

Overall, K.L.: *Clinical Behavioral Medicine for Small Animals*. Mosby-Year Book, 1997.

Scott, D.W., Miller, W.H., Griffin, C.: *Muller & Kirk's Small Animal Dermatology*, 5th Ed., Veterinary Ophthalmology Notes, 1995.

Slatter, D.: *Textbook of Small Animal Surgery*, 2nd ed. Vols. I & II. W.B. Saunders, 1993.

Tams, T.R.: *Handbook of Small Animal Gastroenterology*. W.B. Saunders, 1996.

Tilley, L.P., Smith, F.W.K,: *The 5 Minute Veterinary Consult, Canine & Feline*. Williams & Williams, 1997.

Tilley, L.P.: *Essentials of Canine and Feline Electrocardiography*, 3rd Ed., Lea and Febiger, 1992.

Willard, M.D., Tvedten, H., Turnwald, G.H.: *Small Animal Clinical Diagnosis by Laboratory Methods*, 2nd Ed., W.B. Saunders, 1994.

THE AUTHORS

Liisa D. Carlson, D.V.M.

Dr. Liisa Carlson received her veterinary medical degree from the University of Missouri College of Veterinary Medicine and was a member of the Veterinary Honor Society Phi Zeta. In 1988, Dr. Carlson returned to Springfield, Missouri, to join her father Dr. Delbert Carlson at the Carlson Pet Hospital.

She is a member of the American Veterinary Medical Society, Southwestern Veterinary Medical Association and a founding member of the Emergency Clinics of Southwest Missouri. Dr. Carlson contributed extensively to the *Cat Owner's Home Veterinary Handbook* (1995), newly revised and expanded.

In 1994, Dr. Carlson was honored as Humanitarian of the Year by the Southwest Humane Society of Springfield.

James M. Giffin, M.D.

Dr. Jim Giffin has had lifelong experience with cats, dogs and horses. He is co-author of the award winning books *The Complete Great Pyrenees* and *Dog Owner's Home Veterinary Handbook*; *Cat Owner's Home Veterinary Handbook* (first and second editions); *Horse Owner's Home Veterinary Handbook* (first and second editions); and *Veterinary Guide to Horse Breeding* (all published by Howell Book House).

Dr. Giffin graduated from Amherst College and received his medical degree from Yale University School of Medicine. In 1969 he established a Great Pyrenees kennel and became active in breeding, showing and judging. He finished several champions, campaigned a Best-in-Show winner, and served on the Board of Directors of the Great Pyrenees Club of America.

After years of private surgery practice in Missouri and Colorado, Dr. Giffin was activated during Operation Desert Storm, serving as Chief of Surgery at military hospitals in Alabama, Korea and Texas. He now makes his home in Colorado.

Dr. Giffin is a member of the Dog Writers' Association of America.

General Index

NOTES

NOTES

NOTES

NOTES

NOTES

NOTES